DISCARDED

# Annual Coffee Statistics

## 1966

**LIBRARY OF**
**LAMAR STATE COLLEGE OF TECHNOLOGY**

**THIRTIETH ANNIVERSARY EDITION**

↑ 946177

## Pan-American Coffee Bureau

*AN INSTRUMENTALITY OF THE GOVERNMENTS OF*
BRAZIL • COLOMBIA • COSTA RICA • CUBA • DOMINICAN REPUBLIC
ECUADOR • EL SALVADOR • GUATEMALA • HAITI • HONDURAS
MEXICO • NICARAGUA • PANAMA • PERU AND VENEZUELA

AM-GSHA   LITHO IN U.S.A.

HD
9199
A1
P3
1966

It is permissible to quote or reproduce material from this publication. When doing so, it is requested that proper acknowledgment be made of the Pan-American Coffee Bureau and of any original source cited.

# Contents

|   | Page |
|---|---|
| LIST OF CHARTS | ix |
| FOREWORD | xi |
| LOOKING AHEAD | xii |
| ACTIVITIES OF THE PAN-AMERICAN COFFEE BUREAU | xv |
| INTERNATIONAL COFFEE ORGANIZATION | 1 |
|     Introduction | 1 |
|     Export Quotas for 1966-1967 and Selective System | 2 |
|     Deductions Applicable to Excess Exports | 7 |
|     Certificates of Origin and Re-Export | 8 |
|     New Markets | 8 |
|     Imports from Non-Members | 9 |
|     Diversification | 11 |
|     Production Goals and Policy on Stocks | 12 |
|     Quality Standards | 13 |
|     Promotion | 14 |
|     Extension of the Agreement | 15 |
|     Appendix A — Members of the International Coffee Organization as of June 22, 1967 | 16 |
|     Appendix B — Non-Quota Countries of Destination ("New Markets"). Referred to in Article 40 and Annex B of the International Coffee Agreement | 18 |
|     Appendix C — Resolution 114 (Grant of Waivers and Conditions) | 19 |
|     Appendix D — Resolution 131 (Amendment to Resolution 114) | 23 |
|     Appendix E — Resolution 115 (System for Selective Adjustment of Supply) | 25 |
|     Appendix F — Resolution 128 (Adjustment of Supply) | 29 |
|     Appendix G — Resolution 118 (Strengthening of Certificates of Origin System) | 31 |
|     Appendix H — Resolution 122 (Interpretation of Article 40) | 32 |
|     Appendix I — Resolution 127 (Prohibition of Imports Destined for Annex B Countries) | 34 |
|     Appendix J — Resolution 117 (Application of Article 45 to Regulate Imports by Members from Non-Member Countries) | 35 |

## CONTENTS (Cont'd)

| | Page |
|---|---|
| Appendix K — Resolution 97 (Diversification Fund) | 37 |
| Appendix L — Resolution 120 (Diversification Fund) | 38 |
| Appendix M — Resolution 110 (Establishment of a High-Level Working Group) | 39 |
| Appendix N — Resolution 119 (Annual Verification of Stocks) | 41 |
| **PRICE MOVEMENTS** | 44 |
| Introduction | 44 |
| General Movement of Prices, 1966 | 47 |
| Import Prices, 1966 | 48 |
| Review of Import Prices, 1953-66 | 49 |
| Spot Prices, 1966 | 51 |
| Review of Spot Prices, 1953-1966 | 56 |
| Retail Prices, 1966 | 57 |
| Review of Retail Prices, 1952-66 | 60 |
| Retail Prices, Vacuum Vs. Bag-Packed Regular Coffee, 1958-66 | 62 |
| Futures Market | 63 |
| **WORLD PRODUCTION** | 69 |
| Areas of World Coffee Production | 69 |
| Trend of World Exportable Production | 71 |
| Estimates of World Exportable Production | 72 |
| Brazil | 73 |
| Colombia | 75 |
| Other Western Hemisphere | 76 |
| Mexico | 76 |
| El Salvador | 77 |
| Guatemala | 77 |
| Honduras | 77 |
| Nicaragua | 77 |
| Costa Rica | 78 |
| Panama | 78 |
| Cuba | 78 |
| Dominican Republic | 78 |
| Haiti | 79 |
| Ecuador | 79 |
| Peru | 80 |
| Venezuela | 80 |
| Other Western Hemisphere | 80 |

## CONTENTS (Cont'd)

|  | Page |
|---|---|
| Africa | 81 |
| Angola | 81 |
| Ivory Coast | 81 |
| Uganda | 82 |
| Burundi | 83 |
| Rwanda | 83 |
| Madagascar | 83 |
| Ethiopia | 83 |
| Guinea | 83 |
| Tanzania | 83 |
| Central African Republic | 84 |
| Togo | 84 |
| Congo (Kinshasa) | 86 |
| Cameroon | 86 |
| Kenya | 86 |
| Asia and Oceania | 86 |
| Indonesia | 86 |
| India | 87 |
| Yemen | 88 |
| Philippines | 88 |
| Other Asia and Oceania | 88 |
| Supply and Demand | 89 |
| NEW TECHNIQUES IN COFFEE HARVESTING | 92 |
| WORLD COFFEE TRADE | 98 |
| Coffee Exports and Imports | 98 |
| Coffee Exports by Regions | 101 |
| Coffee Imports by Regions | 102 |
| Value of World Coffee Trade | 104 |
| Share of Coffee in Foreign Exchange Revenues | 106 |
| Trade Balance Between the United States and the Latin American Coffee-Producing Countries | 107 |
| BULK TRANSPORTATION — CONTAINERIZATION | 110 |
| Types of Container Ships | 110 |
| Container Services | 111 |
| Cargo Protection | 112 |
| Turn-Around Time | 112 |
| Container Pools | 114 |
| Containerization of Coffee | 114 |
| Obstacles to Expansion | 116 |

## CONTENTS (Cont'd)

| | Page |
|---|---|
| Innovations | 116 |
| Future Prospects | 117 |
| TRENDS IN THE SOLUBLE SECTOR OF THE COFFEE MARKET | 122 |
| Soluble Coffee in the United States | 122 |
| Conversion Rates, Green to Soluble Coffee | 123 |
| Alternative Estimates of Soluble Coffee Consumption in the United States | 126 |
| United States Trade in Soluble Coffee: Imports and Exports | 130 |
| Soluble Coffee in Canada | 133 |
| Soluble Coffee in Europe | 134 |
| THE UNITED STATES MARKET | 137 |
| Green Coffee Imports into the United States, Their Origins and Dollar Value | 137 |
| Imports, Exports or Reexports and Net Imports | 142 |
| Imports and Exports of Green and Processed Coffee, Roastings and Net Civilian Visible Disappearance | 142 |
| General Patterns of Distribution, Characteristics of Household Purchases and Measurement of Coffee Drinking | 145 |
| Coffee Drinking, Winter, 1967 | 151 |
| Coffee Attitudes, Winter, 1967 | 154 |
| THE CANADIAN MARKET | 159 |
| Imports and Sources | 159 |
| Net Imports of Green and Processed Coffee and Per Capita Net Imports | 161 |
| Value of Coffee Imports | 161 |
| Import Prices | 162 |
| Domestic Processing and Imports | 162 |
| Retail Prices | 164 |
| Coffee Drinking, Winter, 1966 | 165 |
| Attitudes Toward Coffee | 169 |
| EUROPEAN MARKET | 171 |
| Imports of Robustas | 173 |
| Per-Capita Imports | 174 |
| Fiscal Burdens on Coffee | 177 |
| SUMMARY | 179 |
| APPENDIX, STATISTICAL TABLES | A-3 |
| List of Tables in Appendix | A-10 |
| I.C.O. Indicator Price Charts | A-182 |
| INDEX | A-189 |

# List of Charts

| Chart | | Page |
|---|---|---|
| 1 | Comparison of Coffee Prices, 1964-66 | 45 |
| 2 | Spot-Price Percentage Differential of Selected Coffees in Relationship to "MAMS", 1953-66 | 52 |
| 3 | Spot Coffee Prices for the New York Market, 1953-66 | 53 |
| 4 | New York Coffee Futures, 1966 | 64 |
| 5 | Volume of World Production of Exportable Coffee, 1950-66 | 70 |
| 6 | Western Hemisphere Coffee Production, 1966-67 | 81 |
| 7 | African Coffee Production, 1966-67 | 82 |
| 8 | World Coffee Supply & Demand, 1950-66 | 89 |
| 9 | Principal World Coffee-Producing Regions | 91 |
| 10 | Volume of World Exports of Green Coffee, 1965-66 | 98 |
| 11 | Volume of Coffee Exports from Latin America, 1964-66 | 99 |
| 12 | Value of Coffee Exports from Latin America, 1964-66 | 101 |
| 13 | World Coffee Consumption, 1940-65 | 101 |
| 14 | Volume of World Imports of Green Coffee, 1965-66 | 103 |
| 15 | Importance of Coffee Exports to Latin American Coffee-Producing Countries, 1966 | 107 |
| 16 | U.S. Soluble Coffee Imports | 131 |
| 17 | U.S. Soluble Coffee Exports | 131 |
| 18 | United States Coffee Imports, 1964-66 | 138 |
| 19 | United States Sources of Coffee Imports, 1965-66 | 140 |
| 20 | United States Per Capita Coffee Consumption, 1956-66 | 143 |
| 21 | 1966 Net Civilian Visible Disappearance | 144 |
| 22 | Green Coffee Required for Household Purchases, 1965-66 | 145 |
| 23 | Household Expenditures for Coffee, 1965-66 | 147 |
| 24 | Percent of Drinkers Drinking Regular & Soluble Coffee, Winter, 1967 | 152 |
| 25 | Coffee Drinking By Age Groups, Winter 1967 | 153 |
| 26 | Coffee Drinking By Place of Consumption, Winter 1966-67 | 153 |
| 27 | Canada — Sources of Coffee Imports, 1953-66 | 159 |
| 28 | Canada — Per Capita Net Imports of All Coffee, 1960-66 | 161 |
| 29 | Canada — Type of Coffee Served at Home, Winter 1966-67 | 164 |
| 30 | Canada — Coffee Drinking By Place of Consumption, Winter 1965-67 | 166 |

## LIST OF CHARTS (Cont'd)

**Chart**                                                              **Page**

| | | |
|---|---|---|
| 31 | Canada — Coffee Drinking By Age Groups, Winter 1966-67 | 167 |
| 32 | Europe — Sources of Coffee Imports — 1955-66 | 171 |
| 33 | Europe — Per Capita Net Imports of Green Coffee, 1961-66 | 175 |
| 34 | I.C.O. Indicator Price, 1958-1965 | A-182 |
| 35 | I.C.O. Indicator Price, Jan.-Sept., 1966 | A-183 |
| 36 | I.C.O. Indicator Price, Columbian Mild Arabicas | A-185 |
| 37 | I.C.O. Indicator Price, Other Mild Arabicas | A-186 |
| 38 | I.C.O. Indicator Price, Unwashed Arabicas | A-187 |
| 39 | I.C.O. Indicator Price, Robustas | A-188 |

# Foreword

The Pan-American Coffee Bureau completed 30 years of continuous existence in February 1966. It was also the year for the 30th edition of this continuous series of reviews of the coffee industry prepared by the Department of Statistics and Economic Research.

During that anniversary year, the International Coffee Agreement moved in several areas towards the ultimate solution of the difficult, long-standing problems which have affected the world coffee market.

Therefore, in preparing this issue we have not only attempted to make it more complete than earlier editions but have also delayed its publication in order to cover the important developments which took place during the coffee year October 1966 - September 1967.

Commentary and treatment of the data are limited to technical aspects and no attempt is made to analyze or comment on the coffee policies of the various producing countries nor on the policies of the coffee industry or the trade in the coffee-importing countries.

In addition to the subjects traditionally covered in the *Annuals*, we have incorporated new information on experimentation with mechanical harvesting of coffee. Recent developments in bulk transportation or containerization of commodities in domestic and international trade are also discussed in a new section. Those technical innovations may represent important breakthroughs which in the future may have a significant impact on the coffee industry.

The results of additional psychological research on the coffee drinker have been included in this volume. That information will undoubtedly be valuable in providing direction to promotional efforts to augment coffee consumption.

Official data on international trade in coffee production, consumption and prices are used wherever possible. But in some instances, due to time lags in reporting or due to lack of sufficient information, it is not always possible to obtain statistics from official sources. Whenever such difficulties are encountered, estimates are made.

Data on the export-import trade in coffee generally cover green coffee. Wherever roasted or soluble coffee appear in the trade statistics, conversion is made to green-coffee equivalent by use of standard factors adopted by the International Coffee Organization. In the analysis of the United States market, further refinement of the data is possible due to availability of more comprehensive information. Therefore, all the available statistics are utilized and notations are made to that effect. Wherever the term "bag" is used, it denotes units of 60 kilos or 132.276 pounds each. It will be noted that in most instances monetary values have been converted to U.S. dollar equivalents to facilitate comparison and comprehension of the material.

A word about the Net Civilian Visible Disappearance estimates, which are being reexamined. Some revisions already have been made in the series presented in this issue. Those data are being studied further to determine whether closer agreement can be achieved between various sources of statistical information. Aspects of consumption which require further analysis are the relationship between home and out-of-home consumption, yield ratios for regular and soluble coffee in manufacturing and in home brewing and, of course, the institutional market, knowledge of which is sparse indeed.

The PACB gratefully acknowledges the cooperation of statistical offices and other agencies of governments, coffee associations and trading firms, firms specializing in information on coffee and the International Coffee Organization.

Pan-American Coffee Bureau<br>
New York City<br>
September 1967

# LOOKING AHEAD....

Over the past three decades the Pan-American Coffee Bureau has developed and published its coffee reviews and statistics as a service not only to the 15 Member countries of the Bureau, but also to the coffee world.

This service, essential to a better understanding of coffee's production, marketing, and consumption activities, is perhaps the most visible and widely recognized of the activities carried out by the Pan-American Coffee Bureau. These PACB activities directly benefit the coffees of Latin America but, of course, the cause of all coffees is advanced by the daily research, promotional and public relations operations of the Bureau.

In its 30-year career, the Pan-American Coffee Bureau has fought indefatigably to increase consumption in the United States and Canada against increasingly strong competition from other beverages. The "coffee break", today a part of the way of life in the U.S.A., was popularized by the Bureau. The Bureau has steadfastly sought to improve the quality of the coffee that reaches the consumer's lips.

On another front, the Member countries of the Pan-American Coffee Bureau, individually and together, played a leading role in the long and arduous campaign that led to the establishment of the International Coffee Agreement. This achievement, basic to the stabilization of the world coffee market, was a tremendous economic advance for developing nations of Latin America and other regions of the world.

Yet, thirty years is a youthful age and is a fitting time to look ahead, to think ahead about our "think drink," which provides a cup of satisfaction to the millions who consume it and which provides a cup of sustenance to the millions who produce it.

Looking ahead, it is clear that the Agreement is not an end in itself, but only a step forward. Already the countries of the Pan-American Coffee Bureau are thinking of the next stage, the balancing of production with world consumption.

To the developing countries of Latin America and of the world, the balancing of coffee production with consumption is vital to the economic well-being of their people.

However, production controls call for crop diversification, the growing of needed foods and fibers, industrialization, financing, technical know-how, and planning. The problems involved reach beyond individual boundaries and beyond the capabilities of any one country. But together the coffee-producing countries of the world, with the cooperation of the consumer countries, can arrive at reasonable solutions. I am hopeful that on the basis of its experience and past performance, the Pan-American Coffee Bureau can lead the way.

Looking ahead, it is also clear that the producers must find means of more effective cooperative effort with the importers, roasters and distributors of our coffees in order to stimulate consumption with the help of their Members. Here, too, I believe the Pan-American Coffee Bureau can help lead the way, through intelligent research, through vigorous promotion and public relations in developing more efficient ways to market and prepare coffees high in quality, flavor and taste.

Looking ahead, it is surely clear that the 30th anniversary marks the beginning of a new era — new challenges and horizons — for the Pan-American Coffee Bureau.

Alexandre F. Beltrão
President
Pan-American Coffee Bureau

# Activities of the Pan American Coffee Bureau

The PACB functions as a permanent, nonprofit, regional organization of the Latin American coffee-producing countries. It is governed by a Board of Directors consisting of a representative of each Member country and an Executive Committee elected by the Board. The Bureau's structure consists of a Secretariat, the Office of the Executive Director, the Department of Statistics and Economic Research, the Consumer Information Department and the Coffee Brewing Center. The Executive Director is empowered to direct all activities and functions of the Bureau under the supervision of the Executive Committee. In addition, public relations activities are conducted under contract with the World Coffee Information Center, with offices in Washington, D.C. and New York, which also coordinates the public information aspects of the different activities of the Bureau. At the present time approximately 45 persons are employed by the PACB.

In maintaining a close contact with the trade, the Executive Director reviewed during fiscal 1966-1967, the Bureau's activities in formal presentations at the annual business meetings of the three principal domestic coffee organizations of the United States and Canada: The National Coffee Association, The Pacific Coast Coffee Association and The Tea and Coffee Association of Canada. Together with the field staff of the Coffee Brewing Center, the Executive Director actively participated in the annual convention of the world's largest association of restaurateurs, the National Restaurant Association. At the International Coffee Organization's Promotion Seminar held in London in December, the Executive Director made a presentation reviewing activities of the Bureau's various departments which are carried out under its contract with the World Coffee Promotion Committee of the International Coffee Organization in the educational promotion and research segment of the World Coffee Promotion Committee's campaign in the United States and Canada.

On the annual Coffee Day celebrated during Pan-American Week in April, the Executive Director addressed diplomats and press representatives assembled in the Pan-American Union Building in Washington, D.C. on the importance of coffee as a commodity. The Coffee Brewing Center prepared and served correctly brewed coffee to hundreds of people attending the ceremonies.

*The Secretariat* — The responsibilities of the Bureau's Secretariat include contacts with Member countries, preparation and publication of documents for meetings of the Board of Directors and the Executive Committee, and the translation of all pertinent material into the official languages of the Bureau, i.e., Spanish and Portuguese. The latter includes market information and news items for the Weekly Letter and Monthly Bulletin which the Secretariat edits, publishes and distributes in those two languages to organizations and individuals in the Member countries, as well as various international organizations.

A brief description of the Bureau's activities in the areas of publicity, public relations and consumer education, together with a chronology of outstanding events in the coffee world, also are included in the Monthly Bulletin.

*Department of Statistics and Economic Research* — The collection, analysis and dissemination of statistics on all aspects of the world coffee industry, with particular emphasis on the United States-Latin America area, are among the primary functions of the Department of Statistics and Economic Research. In addition to compiling and editing *Annual Coffee Statistics,* the Department sponsors comprehensive surveys and reports on coffee-drinking habits in the United States and Canada. It also prepares the material for the Weekly Letter and the Monthly Bulletin, such as import and retail price movements, imports, roastings, inventories, household consumption and other related data and analyses.

The Department's cooperation has been frequently requested by other agencies such as the International Coffee Organization, the International Bank for Reconstruction and Development and the United Nations Food and Agriculture Organization on worldwide analysis and projections of trends in coffee.

During fiscal 1966-1967, the Department sponsored a research and promotion project which included coffee-brewing demonstrations and interviews with consumers on their coffee-drinking habits. Two other research programs conducted for the Department surveyed reactions to the International Coffee Organization's advertising campaign in the United States.

*Consumer Information Department* — It is the purpose of the Bureau's Consumer Information Department to sustain in the minds of consumers a constant awareness of coffee, its proper preparation and its versatility. The Department accomplishes this by producing and directing a steady flow of publicity releases to newspapers, magazines and radio and television media and by providing educational materials to consumers and schools. These materials are eagerly accepted and constantly requested. The publicity releases receive national coverage by the various media at no cost to the Bureau.

During fiscal 1966-1967, the Department's social studies program for elementary and junior high school classes and its home economics program for high schools achieved unprecedented acceptance. More than 2,000,000 student workbooks, teachers' guides, wall maps, picture sets, and sound and color filmstrips have been supplied upon written request.

Among the special accomplishments of the Department during the year was publicity given to two of its newest booklets in major daily newspapers, in mass circulation magazines and on public bus posters displayed in thirteen principal cities.

*The Coffee Brewing Center* — The general objective of the Bureau's Coffee Brewing Center is to conduct research and educational activities that will result in an improvement of coffee as a beverage. To that end, the Center initiates and supervises studies relating to the scientific, technical and consumer-preference aspects of coffee brewing, especially in restaurants and public eating facilities. The Center also offers an equipment-evaluation service to assist manufacturers in advancing the design of brewing devices.

In its own completely equipped laboratory, the Center conducts hundreds of soluble solids tests, grind analyses, bulk density and roast color measurements, water analyses and sediment tests.

The Coffee Brewing Center offers intensive courses of training in the latest methods and techniques developed for the preparation and evaluation of beverage coffee. These courses are available to individuals or companies. Another course in vended coffee trains personnel involved in the growing automatic merchandising industry.

Two awards sponsored by the Coffee Brewing Center have become prestige symbols in the restaurant and coffee brewing equipment industries. The first of these is the "Golden Cup" Award for proprietors who prove that they consistently serve quality coffee. The second is the Coffee Brewing Center's Seal of Approval, which is awarded to brewing equipment tested and found capable of yielding a quality cup.

Seven Coffee Brewing Center representatives, based in strategically located areas throughout the country, maintain rigorous schedules of coffee-brewing demonstrations for groups of coffee salesmen, hotel and restaurant employees, food personnel at military bases, students at colleges and vocational schools and clubwomen in conventions. The field representatives also present demonstrations on television and radio programs and assist in publicizing "Golden Cup" Awards.

While executing their individual responsibilities, all of the Bureau's departments cooperate toward the fulfillment of its general objectives, including that which is "to study and pursue means contributing to the steady increase of coffee consumption in the world."

# International Coffee Organization

*Introduction*

In 1966, the International Coffee Organization (ICO), installed in London in the Summer of 1963, entered its fourth year of operation with the beginning of coffee year 1966-1967 in October.

Between late 1965 and mid-1967, the following countries acceded to the International Coffee Agreement (ICA) negotiated at the United Nations during the Summer of 1962: Haiti, Kenya, Honduras, Jamaica and Liberia as exporters and Czechoslovakia and Italy as importers.

As of June 22, 1967, therefore, a total of 62 countries had ratified the ICA or acceded to it, thus becoming Members of the ICO: 39 exporting countries, representing 99.2 percent of 1961 world exports and 23 importing countries, representing 96.0 percent of 1961 world imports.[1]

A system of selective adjustment of quotas was introduced with the beginning of coffee year 1966-1967 to allow for the separate adjustment of four different groups of coffees.

The International Coffee Council (ICC) decided to apply limitations on imports of coffee produced in non-Member countries and to prohibit the entry of coffee originally destined to "New Market" countries.[2] A system of Coffee Export Stamps was introduced in April 1967 in order to strengthen the System of Certificates of Origin and Re-Export.

In addition to those measures aimed at stricter compliance with export quotas, progress was made with respect to the longer-term provisions of the Agreement concerning diversification, production goals, policy on stocks, quality standards and promotion.

At the Eighth Period of Sessions in September, new officers of the Council and the Executive Board were elected for coffee year 1966-1967.

Mr. Jean Wahl of France was elected Chairman of the Council to succeed Mr. Roger Joseph Mukasa of Uganda. Mr. Gunnar Kjoelstad of Norway, Mr. Ato Lemma Frehywot of Ethiopia and Mr. U.K. Ahuja of India were elected First, Second and Third Vice Chairmen.

---

[1] As shown in Annex D of the ICA. For list of Members see Appendix A of this Chapter.
[2] For list of "New Market" and non-Member countries, see Appendix B of this Chapter.

Mr. Arturo Ramón González of El Salvador was again elected Chairman of the Executive Board (a post he had held during 1964-1965) succeeding Mr. Pierre Staner of Belgium.

The Agreement provides for alternate selection of representatives of Exporting and Importing Members in the elective posts of the Council and the Board each year.

The Board consists of seven Exporting and seven Importing Members also chosen each year. For 1966-1967 the countries named to the Executive Board were:

| **Exporting Members** | **Importing Members** |
|---|---|
| Brazil | Belgium |
| Colombia | Federal Republic of Germany |
| Congo (D.R.) | France |
| Dominican Republic | New Zealand |
| Nicaragua | Norway |
| OAMCAF | United Kingdom |
| Uganda | United States |

In the World Coffee Promotion Committee (WCPC), a separate committee of the Organization within the framework of the Executive Board, Mr. Alexandre Fontana Beltrão of Brazil was elected Chairman and Mr. Arturo Ramón González of El Slavador was elected Vice Chairman.

The WCPC consists of nine Exporting Members and the countries named for 1966-1967 were Brazil, Colombia, Dominican Republic, El Salvador, Mexico, Nigeria, OAMCAF, Portugal and Tanzania.

*Export Quotas for 1966-1967 and Selective System*

Three Resolutions approved by the Council on September 6, 1966 established the initial authorized exports for this coffee year and certain conditions under which parts of such allotments were granted.

Resolution 114 granted 2,078,500 bags in waivers; 1,732,000 to fifteen countries and to the OAMCAF group and 346,500 as special entitlement to Kenya and Honduras. The 1,732,000 bags were subject to the Selective System of Resolution 115 and were granted on the basis of their making an effective contribution to the solution of the world coffee problem. Part of Resolution 114 was later amended by Resolution 131, approved on March 31, 1967.

Resolution 115 granted 1,083,500 bags prorated among all countries as special export authorizations and established the system of selective adjustment of quotas for four different Groups of coffees. This system, which replaced the former overall *Indicator Price* and overall *pro rata* adjustments established by Resolution 67, was to be applied to the portions of waivers and special authorizations and was based on the following floor and ceiling prices:

|  | (U.S. Cents per pound) | |
| --- | --- | --- |
|  | Floor | Ceiling |
| Colombian Mild Arabicas | 43.50 | 47.50 |
| Other Mild Arabicas | 40.50* | 44.50 |
| Unwashed Arabicas | 37.50 | 41.50 |
| Robustas | 30.50 | 34.00 |

*40.00 during the October-December quarter.

Adjustments downward and upward were to be made up to 2.5 percent of the total authorized exports as of October 1, 1966 (annual quotas plus waivers and special authorizations) of a group, in the event that the daily prices of that particular group remained below the floor or above the ceiling for fifteen consecutive market days.

Complete texts of Resolutions 114, 131, and 115 are shown in Appendixes C, D and E of this Chapter.

Finally, Resolution 116 established annual quotas at 43,700,000 bags (not subject to the Selective System). Together with waivers and special authorizations, the initial total authorized exports became 46,862,000 bags, as shown in the table on page 4.

The following adjustments occurred as a result of the operation of the Selective System:

1) December 26, 1966: reduction of 233,628 bags in Other Mild Arabicas, triggered by its *Indicator Price* having averaged 39.76 cents per pound during the period November 30-December 20. A full 2.5 percent reduction would have amounted to 259,532, except that waivers and special export authorizations for the first quarter could not be touched anymore. New waivers and special authorizations became 1,906,985 and 1,021,387;

2) January 23, 1967: second reduction in Other Mild Arabicas (164,319 bags) triggered by its *Indicator Price* having averaged 38.91 cents per pound during the period December 27-January 17. New waivers and special authorizations became 1,791,832 and 972,221;

## COFFEE YEAR 1966-67
## TOTAL AUTHORIZED EXPORTS AS OF OCTOBER 1, 1966

(60-kilo bags)

| EXPORTING COUNTRY | Annual Quota Res. 116 | Waivers Res. 114 | Special Export Authoriz. Res. 115 | Total |
|---|---|---|---|---|
| **Colombian Milds Arabicas** | | | | |
| Colombia | 5,645,474 | | 136,021 | 5,781,495 |
| Kenya** | 485,384 | 227,407* | 31,451 | 744,242 |
| **Sub-Total** | **6,130,858** | **227,407** | **167,472** | **6,525,737** |
| **Other Milds Arabicas** | | | | |
| Burundi | 270,005 | | 6,505 | 276,510 |
| Costa Rica | 892,189 | | 21,496 | 913,685 |
| Cuba | 187,829 | | 4,526 | 192,355 |
| Dominican Republic | 399,137 | 40,000 | 9,617 | 448,754 |
| Ecuador | 518,409 | 58,000 | 12,490 | 588,899 |
| El Salvador | 1,342,510 | 225,000 | 32,346 | 1,599,856 |
| Guatemala | 1,262,683 | 135,000 | 30,423 | 1,428,106 |
| Haiti | 394,442 | 30,000 | 9,504 | 433,946 |
| Honduras** | 267,657 | 119,093* | 17,343 | 404,093 |
| India | 338,093 | 50,000 | 8,146 | 396,239 |
| Mexico | 1,417,172 | | 34,145 | 1,451,317 |
| Nicaragua | 393,596 | 70,000 | 9,483 | 473,079 |
| Panama | 25,000 | | 588 | 25,588 |
| Peru | 544,705 | 61,000 | 13,124 | 618,829 |
| Rwanda | 199,569 | | 4,808 | 204,377 |
| Tanzania | 408,959 | 50,000 | 9,853 | 468,812 |
| Venezuela | 446,095 | | 10,748 | 456,843 |
| **Sub-Total** | **9,308,050** | **838,093** | **235,145** | **10,381,288** |
| **Unwashed Arabicas** | | | | |
| Bolivia** | 25,000 | | 566 | 25,566 |
| Brazil | 16,904,640 | | 407,298 | 17,311,938 |
| Ethiopia | 1,103,497 | 75,000 | 26,587 | 1,205,084 |
| **Sub-Total** | **18,033,137** | **75,000** | **434,451** | **18,542,588** |
| **Robustas** | | | | |
| Congo (D.R.) | 1,070,627 | | 25,796 | 1,096,423 |
| Ghana | 40,383 | 6,000 | 973 | 47,356 |
| Indonesia | 1,104,436 | | 26,610 | 1,131,046 |
| Nigeria | 41,492 | | 1,000 | 42,492 |
| OAMCAF | 4,040,326 | 414,000 | 97,347 | 4,551,673 |
| Portugal | 2,055,462 | 279,000 | 49,524 | 2,383,986 |
| Sierra Leone | 61,045 | 17,000 | 1,471 | 79,516 |
| Trinidad & Tobago | 41,322 | 25,000 | 996 | 67,318 |
| Uganda | 1,772,862 | 197,000 | 42,715 | 2,012,577 |
| **Sub-Total** | **10,227,955** | **938,000** | **246,432** | **11,412,387** |
| **Total** | **43,700,000** | **2,078,500** | **1,083,500** | **46,862,000** |

*Special export entitlement
**Pending accession

3) February 13, 1967: reduction of 120,622 bags in Colombian Mild Arabicas, triggered by its *Indicator Price* having averaged 42.59 cents per pound during the period January 18-February 7. A full 2.5 percent reduction would have amounted to 163,143. New special authorizations became 851,599, waivers remaining unchanged;

4) February 20, 1967: third reduction in Other Mild Arabicas (135,054 bags) triggered by its *Indicator Price* having averaged 38.49 cents per pound during the period January 24-February 14. This reduction would have amounted to 146,774 but Tanzania was reclassified under Colombian Mild Arabicas as of October 1, thus regaining 11,720 of waivers. New waivers and special authorizations became 1,675,106 and 833,271;

5) March 13, 1967: second reduction in Colombian Mild Arabicas (16,703 bags) triggered by its *Indicator Price* having averaged 42.10 cents per pound during the period February 14-March 7. New waivers and special authorizations became 1,665,849 and 825,825, the annual quota being now 41,700,000, as per Resolution 128;

6) March 20, 1967: fourth reduction in Other Mild Arabicas (100,126 bags) triggered by its *Indicator Price* having averaged 37.49 cents per pound during the period February 21-March 14. New waivers and special authorizations became 1,592,595 and 798,953;

7) April 27, 1967: third reduction in Colombian Mild Arabicas (152,014 bags) and fifth reduction in Other Mild Arabicas (217,908 bags) triggered by their *Indicator Prices* having averaged 41.34 and 38.37 respectively during the period April 3-21. New waivers and special authorizations became 1,610,528 and 1,447,104;

8) May 3, 1967: restoration of 1/4 of the *pro rata* reduction in the Robustas (117,021 bags) as per Resolution 128, triggered by its *Indicator Price* having averaged 34.23 during the period April 12-May 2. New special authorizations became 1,564,125, waivers remaining unchanged;

9) May 29, 1967: restoration of another 1/4 of the *pro rata* reduction in the Robustas as per Resolution 128 (117,021 bags) triggered by its *Indicator Price* having averaged 34.93 during the period May 3-23 (0.50 below the ceiling). This average, being also above the ceiling itself, triggered a parallel increase in its special authorization (285,316 bags) equivalent to 2.5 percent of its total authorized exports as of October 1, 1966;

## COFFEE YEAR 1966-1967
## TOTAL AUTHORIZED EXPORTS
## AS OF 18 JULY 1967[1]

(60-kilo bags)

| EXPORTING COUNTRY | Annual Quota | Waivers | Special Export Authorizations | Total |
|---|---|---|---|---|
| **Colombian Mild Arabicas** | | | | |
| Colombia | 5,387,100 | | 34,005 | 5,421,105 |
| Kenya | 463,170 | 227,407* | 7,862 | 698,439 |
| Tanzania | 381,528 | 12,500 | 6,588 | 400,616 |
| **Sub-Total** | **6,231,798** | **239,907** | **48,455** | **6,520,160** |
| **Other Mild Arabicas** | | | | |
| Burundi | 257,648 | | 1,819 | 259,467 |
| Costa Rica | 848,803 | | 6,013 | 854,816 |
| Cuba | 179,233 | | 1,265 | 180,498 |
| Dominican Republic | 379,841 | 10,000 | 2,690 | 392,531 |
| Ecuador | 483,771 | 89,500 | 3,494 | 576,765 |
| El Salvador | 1,244,551 | 56,250 | 17,135 | 1,317,936 |
| Guatemala | 1,191,539 | 33,750 | 8,509 | 1,233,798 |
| Haiti | 376,390 | 7,500 | 2,658 | 386,548 |
| Honduras | 255,407 | 119,093* | 4,527 | 379,027 |
| India | 322,620 | 12,500 | 19,685 | 354,805 |
| Jamaica | 25,000 | | | 25,000 |
| Mexico | 1,345,197 | | 9,551 | 1,354,748 |
| Nicaragua | 373,438 | 17,500 | 5,023 | 395,961 |
| Panama | 24,835 | | 165 | 25,000 |
| Peru | 516,998 | 15,250 | 3,671 | 535,919 |
| Rwanda | 190,435 | | 1,346 | 191,781 |
| Venezuela | 425,679 | | 3,006 | 428,685 |
| **Sub-Total** | **8,441,385** | **361,343** | **90,557** | **8,893,285** |
| **Unwashed Arabicas** | | | | |
| Bolivia** | 23,862 | | 1,138 | 25,000 |
| Brazil | 16,130,972 | | 806,237 | 16,937,209 |
| Ethiopia | 1,052,994 | 75,000 | 52,629 | 1,180,623 |
| **Sub-Total** | **17,207,828** | **75,000** | **860,004** | **18,142,832** |
| **Robustas** | | | | |
| Congo (D.R.) | 1,021,628 | | 130,384 | 1,152,012 |
| Ghana | 37,168 | 6,000 | 5,218 | 48,386 |
| Indonesia | 1,020,617 | | 134,499 | 1,155,116 |
| Liberia | 60,000 | | | 60,000 |
| Nigeria | 38,343 | | 5,053 | 43,396 |
| OAMCAF | 3,779,160 | 414,000 | 512,736 | 4,705,896 |
| Portugal | 1,961,390 | 315,000 | 266,068 | 2,542,458 |
| Sierra Leone | 49,056 | 8,500 | 8,285 | 65,841 |
| Trinidad & Tobago | 39,431 | 25,000 | 6,283 | 70,714 |
| Uganda | 1,688,744 | 197,000 | 225,751 | 2,111,495 |
| **Sub-Total** | **9,695,537** | **965,500** | **1,294,277** | **11,955,314** |
| **Total** | **41,576,548** | **1,641,750** | **2,293,293** | **45,511,591** |

*Special export entitlement
**Pending accession

[1] Annual quotas, waivers and special export authorizations as at 27 June 1967 (ED-258/67) adjusted to reflect a 2.5% reduction for Colombian Mild Arabicas as a consequence of the application of paragraph 5 of Resolution No. 115 and with readjustments in respect of Panama and Bolivia.

10) June 27, 1967: fourth reduction in Colombian Mild Arabicas and second increase in Robustas, triggered by their *Indicator Prices* having averaged 42.48 and 35.58 during the periods May 22-June 13 and May 31-June 20, respectively. Other adjustments under Resolutions 131,132, 135 and 136 resulted in the following net adjustments: Colombian Mild Arabicas: minus 20,141 bags, Other Mild Arabicas: plus 22,282 bags, Unwashed Arabicas: plus 12,895 bags and Robustas: plus 161,617 bags.

11) July 18, 1967: fifth reduction in Colombian Mild Arabicas (3,537 bags) triggered by its *Indicator Price* having averaged 42.25 during the period June 20-July 12. Other minor adjustments were made for Panama (plus 1,479 bags) and Bolivia (plus 6 bags), while 60,000 bags were also added to the quotas, due to the accession of Liberia.

In view of the need for additional measures to adjust the supply of coffee to actual market conditions, the Council approved Resolution 128 on February 20, 1967. By means of this Resolution, the annual quotas were reduced by one million bags and another one million were suspended until April 1, when they were then added to the special authorization portion granted by Resolution 115. Thus, the annual quotas were reduced from 43.7 to 41.7 million bags on February 20, but one million of that reduction was subsequently reinstated as special authorizations on April 1, becoming, therefore, subject to the Selective System.

A complete text of Resolution 128 is shown in Appendix F of this Chapter.

A comparison of total authorized exports as of July 18, 1967 (shown in the table on page 6) with the original allocations on October 1, 1966 (shown in the table on page 4) illustrate the changes.

*Deductions Applicable to Excess Exports*

In line with Resolution 123 of September 6, 1966, which required the examination of the question of excess exports, deductions found to be applicable in respect of coffee years 1963-1964, 1964-1965 and 1965-1966 amounted to 5,923,141 bags. With Resolution 132 of June 5, 1967, the Council decided to deduct 533,010 bags (to be applied to the last quarter of 1966-1967 and to all four quarters of 1967-1968) and to suspend the balance, in view of the fact that practical considerations rendered it impossible to impose the full deductions within the lifetime of the current Agreement, which terminates on September 30, 1968.

|  | (60-kilo bags) | | |
| Exporting Country | Deductions Applicable | Deductions Applied | Deductions Suspended |
| --- | --- | --- | --- |
| Dominican Republic | 228,147 | 1,029 | 227,118 |
| Ecuador | 587,587 | 54,559 | 533,028 |
| El Salvador | 184,262 | 36,517 | 147,745 |
| Ghana | 117,542 | 6,833 | 110,709 |
| Guatemala | 858,661 | 66,775 | 791,886 |
| Indonesia | 2,277,424 | 166,364 | 2,111,060 |
| Mexico | 93,816 | 35,579 | 58,237 |
| Nicaragua | 137,360 | 10,719 | 126,641 |
| Nigeria | 155,168 | 6,250 | 148,918 |
| OAMCAF | 382,342 | 76,254 | 306,088 |
| Panama | 17,344 | 2,500 | 14,844 |
| Peru | 117,279 | 13,888 | 103,391 |
| Sierra Leone | 228,410 | 9,195 | 219,215 |
| Tanzania | 432,734 | 43,568 | 389,166 |
| Uganda | 105,065 | 2.980 | 102,085 |
| **Total** | **5,923,141** | **533,010** | **5,390,131** |

*Certificates of Origin and Re-Export*

The System of Certificates of Origin and Re-Export was considerably strengthened with the introduction of the Coffee Export Stamps on April 1, 1967.

Resolution 118, approved by the Council on September 6, 1966, required the Executive Director to supply to each Exporting Member for each quarter a quantity of Export Stamps corresponding to their authorized exports for such quarter. It also required the following: 1) that Exporting Members advise the ICO by cable on April 15, 1967 and on the first and fifteenth day of each month thereafter of the amount of coffee for which stamps were used during the preceding fifteen-day period; 2) that, in issuing supplies of stamps, the Executive Director take into account adjustments in quarterly authorized exports, overshipments either reported by Members or coming to his attention, penalties or waivers and any other factors pertaining to the application of the System.

Appendix G of this Chapter transcribes the complete text of Resolution 118.

*New Markets*

Two Resolutions regarding shipments not subject to quotas were also approved by the Council.

Resolution 122 of September 6, 1966, clarified and reinforced the provisions of Article 40 of the Agreement dealing with reexports from Annex B countries and diversions of shipments while in transit to those countries. This Resolution confirmed the mandatory and automatic charging to the quotas of the Exporting Members of the quantities of coffee involved.

A latter Resolution (127) approved on January 28, 1967, prohibited the entry of coffees destined to "New Markets" and the issuance of Certificates of Re-Export or of "split" certificates covering the same type of shipments.

Resolutions 122 and 127 are transcribed in Appendixes H and I of this Chapter.

*Imports from Non-Members*

The third and final area of important measures concerned with the reinforcement of adherence to export quotas was dealt with by Resolution 117, also approved on September 6, 1966, the text of which appears in Appendix J of this Chapter. This Resolution decided to limit imports of coffee from non-Members in accordance with the provisions of Article 45 of the Agreement, as soon as practicable after October 1, 1966 but not later than January 1, 1967.

Following that Resolution, several Importing Members took the necessary steps to put it into effect. For example, in the United States the following import quotas were established for coffees entering from non-Members, effective for the twelve-month period beginning on November 15, 1966:

| Non-Member Producer | Green Pounds | 60-kilo Bags |
|---|---|---|
| Bolivia | 1,850,800 | 13,992 |
| Guinea | 1,454,200 | 10,994 |
| Honduras | 28,026,400 | 211,878 |
| Kenya | 11,765,800 | 88,949 |
| Liberia | 2,511,800 | 18,989 |
| Paraguay | 2,644,000 | 19,989 |
| Yemen | 1,850,800 | 13,992 |
| "Basket" Quota | 6,610,000 | 49,971 |
| **Total** | **56,713,800** | **428,754** |

NOTE: In addition to the 50,103,800 pounds (378,783 bags) allotted to specific countries, a "basket" quota of 6,610,000 pounds (49,971 bags) was added for all coffee not specifically identified as a product of or shipment from a non-Member country and not charged to the quotas listed above. Shipments in excess of the above quotas were also to be charged to the "basket" quota.

To illustrate the application of the above quotas, the situation as of July 19, 1967 is shown below, as reported by the U.S. Department of Commerce:

| Non-Member Producer | Import Quotas | | Charged as of July 18, 1967 | |
|---|---|---|---|---|
| | Green Pounds | 60-Kilo Bags | Green Pounds | 60-Kilo Bags |
| Bolivia | 1,850,800 | 13,992 | 1,593,246 | 12,045 |
| Guinea | 1,454,200 | 10,994 | 1,454,200 | 10,994 |
| Paraguay | 2,644,000 | 19,989 | — | — |
| Yemen | 1,850,800 | 13,992 | 464,840 | 3,514 |
| "Basket" Quota | 6,610,000 | 49,971 | 5,895,699 | 44,571 |
| **TOTAL** | **14,409,800** | **108,938** | **9,407,985** | **71,124** |

SOURCE: *"Complete Coffee Coverage"*, George Gordon Paton, 19 July 1967.

NOTE: 1) All coffee not specifically identified as a product of/or shipment from an ICO member country and not charged to the quota of one of the countries listed above is charged to an annual "basket" quota.

2) Coffee from any one of the countries listed above shall be charged to the "basket" quota after the specific quota for that country has been filled. If the "basket" quota is filled, coffee from such country will be forbidden entry.

3) Since the establishment of the original quotas on November 15, 1966, Honduras, Kenya and Liberia have acceded to the Agreement.

Other developments regarding non-Members were as follows:

1) Kenya and Honduras, each finally acceding to the Agreement in late 1966 and early 1967 respectively, received the following total export entitlements for 1966-1967: Kenya — 744,242 and Honduras — 404,093 bags. At the same time, initial basic quotas were set at 516,835 and 285,000 bags respectively, pending a report by the Executive Director to be presented to the Council by July 1, 1967 with recommendations toward the establishment of basic quotas for subsequent years.[3]

2) Resolution 130, approved by the Council on March 17, 1967, authorized Portugal to export an additional 36,000 bags for the remainder of 1966-1967 as an export entitlement to cover the extension of the Agreement to her coffee-producing provinces of Timor, São Tomé and Príncipe and Cape Verde. At the same time, it was also established that such entitlement should be subject to the Selective System of Resolution 115.

---

[3] Resolutions 112 and 113 of September 6, 1966.

3) Among coffee-producing countries, the Council, acting upon a request made by Bolivia, established in September the conditions for her accession to the Agreement.[4] Similarly, the Council also established conditions for the accession of Israel as an Importing Member.[5] Those two countries, as well as Poland, for which the Council had established conditions in March 1965 for accession as an Importing Member,[6] have not as yet acceded to the Agreement. Singapore and Cyprus,[7] net importers of coffee, have also applied for accession. No action has been taken as yet in the case of Cyprus, whereas in the case of Singapore a special study was required in view of her special position as an *entrepot* in coffee trading.[8]

*Diversification*

Further work was carried out in connection with Article 57 of the Agreement, which provides for the establishment of an International Coffee Fund aimed at bringing coffee production into reasonable balance with demand. In connection with this objective as well as the other objectives of the Agreement, developments during the year also included measures taken along the lines of basic quotas, production goals and stocks, as described in this and in the following section.

As to the Coffee Fund, developments go back to the time of the introduction of the price-quota mechanism on March 19, 1965.[9] At that time, the Council also approved Resolution 68, which established an International Coffee Fund initially aimed at financing retentions and the facilities necessary to deal with them.[10]

During the Seventh Period of Sessions in December 1965, a group of producing countries presented a proposal which was approved as Resolution 97 on December 12, 1965 (text in Appendix K of this Chapter).[11] This Resolution instructed the Executive Director to: 1) prepare a draft proposal to adapt the International Coffee Fund to the purposes of diversification; 2) seek the cooperation of other international financial institutions in the preparation of such a proposal; and 3) consult with those institutions on the possibility of their participation in administering the Diversification Fund and on the coordination of programs. It also requested the Executive Board to review the draft proposal and submit it to Members, with a view to considering it at the next Period of Sessions.

At the same time the Council also approved Resolution 98, which instructed the Executive Director to bring to the attention of the Joint Coffee Study, FAO-IBRD-

---

[4] Resolution 111 of September 6, 1966.
[5] Resolution 134 of June 8, 1967.
[6] Resolution 59 of March 11, 1967.
[7] Document EB-539/67 of July 28, 1967.
[8] Document EB-473/67, Add. 1 of May 15, 1967.
[9] Resolution 67 of March 19, 1965, as described on page 4 of *Annual Coffee Statistics*, 1964.
[10] *Annual Coffee Statistics*, 1965, page 8.
[11] Document ICC-7-83 of December 16, 1965, *Decisions and Resolutions Adopted*.

ICO,[12] the primary importance of those aspects of the study which would be related to diversification.

As a result of Resolution 97, the Executive Director presented the draft of a Coffee Diversification Fund[13] which was considered by the Council during its Eighth Period of Sessions in September, when it approved Resolution 120 (September 6, 1966) resolving to: 1) approve in principle the establishment of a Coffee Diversification and Development Fund: 2) establish a Working Group to review the draft proposal of the Executive Director, circulating a revised draft to Members for their comments; and 3) include the question of the establishment of the Fund on the agenda of the first regular session of the Council to be held after March 31, 1967. The Working Group referred to in the preceding section has been working along the scheduled directions; it is composed of representatives of Brazil, Colombia, Costa Rica and OAMCAF (Exporting Members); Federal Republic of Germany, France, United Kingdom and United States (Importing Members); the International Bank for Reconstruction and Development (World Bank), the Inter-American Development Bank, the African Development Bank, the Food and Agriculture Organization of the United Nations and the Executive Director. El Salvador, Guatemala and Uganda have also participated in the work of this Group. The text of Resolution 120 is shown in Appendix L of this Chapter.

*Production Goals and Policy on Stocks*

In Chapters XI and XII, the Agreement makes several provisions regarding the establishment of production goals and of a policy on stocks, whereby the producing members should undertake to adjust production to the amount needed for domestic consumption, exports and reserve stocks; the Council is to ascertain world coffee stocks and, on the basis of the data obtained, to establish a policy on stocks in line with the production goals recommended by the Council itself.

Also during the September Sessions the Council approved a Resolution[14] creating a High Level Working Group composed of representatives of Brazil, Colombia, Costa Rica, El Salvador, OAMCAF, Uganda and Tanzania as Exporting Members, and France, Italy, the United Kingdom and the United States as Importing Members, as well as the Executive Director. It also invited the participation of the Director of the Joint Coffee Study, FAO-IBRD-ICO.

The terms of reference for the Working Group were directed toward the gathering of all elements relevant to quotas, stocks, production goals and diversification in order to assist the Council in making decisions on such matters.

The Group is presently proceeding with its work in order to report to the Council before the end of the present coffee year, 1966-1967.

---

[12] *Annual Coffee Statistics*, 1965, page 7.
[13] Document EB-389/66 of June 16, 1966.
[14] Resolution 110 of September 6, 1966; text in Appendix M of this Chapter.

Actual verifications of stocks began in 1965, as described in page 8 of *Annual Coffee Statistics,* 1965. At that time, initial reports placed the accumulated inventories as of the end of coffee year October 1964-September 1965 at 69,087,000 bags; composed of *Mild Arabicas* — 6,798,000, *Unwashed Arabicas* — 55,224,000 and *Robustas* — 7,065,000. On December 12, 1965, Resolution 93 stated that further investigations were necessary for the formulation of a policy on stocks.

In June 1966, a report was submitted containing information on additional verifications and revised estimates of working stock requirements, taking into account the period which had to be bridged between October 1, 1965 and the new 1965-1966 crops.[15] With the additional stock checks conducted in Brazil, Colombia, Ecuador, Madagascar and Togo, the estimates of total stocks held by Exporting Members on September 30, 1965 were revised to 70,160,000 bags, of which, after allowance for the working stocks (i.e. for both domestic consumption and exports) only 60,180,000 bags should be considered as net surplus stocks. They were distributed as follows: Brazil — 50,974,000, Other Latin America — 4,001,000 and Africa-Asia — 5,205,000.

During the 8th Period of Sessions in September the Council approved Resolution 119 (text in Appendix N of this Chapter) which established an annual verification of stocks beginning with coffee year 1966-1967, in order to enable it to move further in the area of establishing production goals and a policy on stocks.

In February 1967 a first report was circulated by the Executive Board.[16] Of the 23 countries where stocks had to be checked on September 30, 1966, no verification was ordered in nine countries — Costa Rica, Dahomey, Ghana, Nigeria, Panama, Sierra Leone, Trinidad and Tobago, Uganda and Venezuela — all of which had reported the absence of a next surplus as of that date. In the other thirteen countries — Cameroon, Central African Republic, Colombia, Congo, El Salvador, Ethiopia, Guatemala, India, Ivory Coast, Kenya, Nicaragua, Tanzania and Togo — a net surplus was confirmed in nine, whereas the Central African Republic, Guatemala, Kenya and Nicaragua showed none. Comparisons between the net surplus on September 30, 1965 and the same date in 1966 show that the net surplus increased to eight countries — Cameroon, Colombia, El Salvador, Ethiopia, India, Ivory Coast, Nicaragua and Tanzania — the greatest additions having occurred in Colombia, Ivory Coast and Ethiopia, whereas the greatest decreases took place in Guatemala and the Congo, among the other five.

*Quality Standards*

As Article 59 of the Agreement makes provision for the Council to discuss recommendations as to the practicability of prescribing minimum standards for exports, the Council approved Resolution 106 on August 30, 1966 creating a Working

---

[15] Document EB-388/66 of June 10, 1966.
[16] Document EB-474/67 of February 13, 1967.

Group to study ways and means of introducing an international code of quality for coffee exports, with a scientific basis corresponding to the needs of the trade and the consumer; the Working Group was also instructed to consult with members of the trade and experts from those international and national institutions specializing in uniform quality and processing standards.

In order to enable the Working Group to proceed with its work, the Executive Board circulated a preliminary report in May 1967,[17] containing information on quality standards in use in some countries and on work related to this area which has been done by such international organizations as the Association Scientifique Internationale du Café (ASIC) and the International Organization for Standardization (ISO).

*Promotion*

The activities of the World Coffee Promotion Committee have been divided into four general categories: advertising, public relations, consumer education and research. The Promotion Fund, which finances the campaigns in several consuming countries of the world, is maintained by the Exporting Members of the Agreement, whose compulsory contributions are usually assessed proportionately to export volumes on the basis of a certain amount of U. S. currency per bag.

Promotion activities under the present long-term Agreement started in late 1965 and are about to enter their third year with the coming coffee year 1967-1968.

In 1965-1966 the WCPC conducted campaigns in nine countries — Belgium, Denmark, France, Netherlands, Norway, Spain, Sweden, United Kingdom and United States — extending them to two more in 1966-1967: Japan and Switzerland. Those campaigns are conducted through national subcommittees which are usually Promotion Committees established by the local Trade, except in the case of the United States and Canada, where it is made up jointly by the President of the National Coffee Association and representatives of the Pan-American Coffee Bureau and the Inter-African Coffee Organization. These local Promotion Committees are:

| | |
|---|---|
| Belgium | — Office Belge du Café |
| Denmark | — Dansk Kaffekomite |
| France | — Comité Francais du Café |
| Japan | — Japan Coffee Promotion Committee |
| Netherlands | — Stichting Koffiepropaganda Nederland |
| Norway | — Den Norske Komite for Kaffeoplysning |
| Spain | — Comité Español de Promoción del Café |
| Sweden | — Swedish Coffee Promotion Committee |
| Switzerland | — Swiss Coffee Promotion Committee (Procafe) |
| United Kingdom | — Coffee Promotion Council, Ltd. |
| United States | — Coffee Promotion Committee for the U.S. and Canada |

---

[17] Document EB-505/67 of May 1, 1967, *Notes on the Establishment of Quality Standards for Coffee Exports.*

The following table shows the allocations made by the WCPC and the contributions made by the local trade during the last two years:[18]

(thousands of U. S. dollars)

| Countries | 1965-1966 WCPC | Trade | Total | 1966-1967 WCPC | Trade | Total |
|---|---|---|---|---|---|---|
| Belgium | 100 | — | 100 | 253 | — | 253 |
| Denmark | 100 | 25 | 125 | 149 | 25 | 174 |
| France | 400 | 125 | 525 | 720 | — | 720 |
| Japan | — | — | — | 250 | 10 | 260 |
| Netherlands | 100 | 14 | 114 | 250 | 14 | 264 |
| Norway | 80 | 20 | 100 | 161 | 27 | 188 |
| Spain | 150 | 75 | 225 | 222 | 92 | 314 |
| Sweden | 100 | — | 100 | 98 | — | 98 |
| Switzerland | — | — | — | 91 | 98 | 189 |
| United Kingdom | 200 | 17 | 217 | 225 | 39 | 264 |
| United States | 3,582 | — | 3,582 | 4,418 | — | 4,418 |
| **TOTAL** | **4,812** | **276** | **5,088** | **6,837** | **305** | **7,142** |

NOTE: The total $12,230,000 allocated for the two years were earmarked as follows: Advertising — $9,213,000, Public Relations, Brewing Education and Special Projects — $2,269,000, Research — $661,000 and General Expenses — $87,000.

In addition to contributing directly to the WCPC campaigns, the local Promotion Committees have defrayed their own administrative expenses. In the United States, the National Coffee Association conducted its own public relations campaign during 1965-1966 in coordination with the WCPC, with a budget of $350,000. It is expected that the NCA will continue and expand its campaign for 1966-1967.

Allocations for 1967-1968 have been set at $6,875,000 plus any carry overs from the previous year; with the contributions of the local trade, the third-year campaigns should total well above $7.0 million.

*Extension of the Agreement*

As the International Coffee Agreement of 1962 remains in force until September 30, 1968, the Council, in view of the necessity of deciding on its extension, requested the Executive Board by Resolution 125 of September 6, 1966, to consider the question and report back at the next regular session.

---

[18] Document WCPC-44/67 of March 28, 1967, *Aide-Memoire Promotion Campaigns 1965-1966 and 1966-1967*.

# APPENDIX A

## MEMBERS OF THE INTERNATIONAL COFFEE ORGANIZATION

### As of June 22, 1967

### Exporting Members[1]

Brazil
Burundi
Cameroon*
Central African Republic*
Colombia
Congo (B)*
Congo (D.R.)
Costa Rica
Cuba
Dahomey*
Dominican Republic
Ecuador
El Salvador
Ethiopia
Gabon*
Ghana
Guatemala
Haiti
Honduras
India
Indonesia
Ivory Coast*
Jamaica
Kenya
Liberia
Malagasy Republic*
Mexico
Nicaragua
Nigeria
Panama
Peru
Portugal
   Including: Metropolitan Portugal, Angola, Cape Verde, São Tomé and Príncipe, Timor, Azores, Macao, Madeira, Mozambique, and Portuguese Guinea.
Rwanda
Sierra Leone
Tanzania
Togo*
Trinidad and Tobago
Uganda
Venezuela

### Importing Members[2]

Argentina
Australia
   Including: Papua and New Guinea
Austria
Belgium
Canada
Czechoslovakia
Italy
Japan
Luxembourg
Netherlands
New Zealand
   Including: Cook, Niue and Tokelau Islands

---

[1] Thirty-nine Exporting Members representing 99.2 percent of 1961 world exports.
[2] Twenty-three Importing Members representing 96.0 percent of 1961 world imports.

### Importing Members (Cont'd.)

| | |
|---|---|
| Denmark | Norway |
| Federal Republic of Germany | Spain |
| Finland | Sweden |
| France | Switzerland |
|    Including: French Guiana, French | Tunisia |
|       Polynesia, French Somaliland, | U.S.S.R. |
|       Martinique, Reunion, Comores, | United Kingdom |
|       Guadeloupe and New Caledonia. |    Including: Hong Kong |
| | United States of America |

*Organisation Africaine et Malgache du Café (OAMCAF), a group membership under the ICA.

## APPENDIX B

NON-QUOTA COUNTRIES OF DESTINATION ("NEW MARKETS") REFERRED TO IN ARTICLE 40 AND ANNEX B OF THE INTERNATIONAL COFFEE AGREEMENT

Bahrein
Botswana
Ceylon
China (Taiwan)
China (Mainland)
Hungary
Iran
Iraq
Japan*
Jordan
Korea (North)
Korea (South)
Kuwait
Lesotho
Malawi
Muscat and Oman
Oman

Philippines
Poland
Qatar
Rhodesia
Roumania
Saudi Arabia
Somalia
South Africa
South-West Africa
Sudan
Swaziland
Thailand
Union of Soviet Socialist Republics*
Viet-Nam (North)
Viet-Nam (South)
Zambia

*Member of ICA

## COFFEE-PRODUCING AREAS NOT MEMBERS OF THE INTERNATIONAL COFFEE AGREEMENT

Bolivia
British Honduras
British Pacific Islands
British West Indies
Guinea
Guyana
Malaysia
Mauritania
New Hebrides

Paraguay
Philippine Islands
Puerto Rico
Spanish Guinea
Surinam
Upper Volta
Viet-Nam
Western Samoa
Yemen

## APPENDIX C

## RESOLUTION ICC-114

(September 6, 1966)

### GRANT OF WAIVERS AND CONDITIONS

*WHEREAS:*

The Council will have to take decisions, as soon as possible, on the review of basic quotas, production goals, policy relative to stocks, production control and diversification of the coffee economy;

Measures are being adopted to obtain the basic information essential to the full comprehension of the coffee economy of each exporting Member country;

In the meanwhile it is vitally important to deal with the growing problem of mounting coffee stocks in a number of Member countries resulting from the absence of specific plans to deal with the basic problem;

In these circumstances it is necessary to give to certain Members some immediate relief in the coffee year 1966-67; and

The granting of this relief should be associated with the introduction of new measures entailing the mutual cooperation of Members in providing a foundation for the solution of these problems,

THE INTERNATIONAL COFFEE COUNCIL

*RESOLVES:*

1. To establish the principle that all waivers to be granted from hereon shall be on the basis of effective contribution to the solution of the world coffee problem.

2. Notwithstanding the provisions of the rules for the granting of waivers under Article 60, to grant the waivers listed in the Annex to this Resolution for the export of quantities additional to the quotas set for 1966-67.

3. The waivers granted by this Resolution shall be distributed equally over the four quarters of the coffee year and shall form part of the export entitlement subject to the system of selective adjustment established by Resolution No. 115.

4. The portions of the waivers granted for the first and second quarters of the coffee year may be exported without reference to the options hereinafter described in respect of the portions of the waivers relating to the third and fourth quarters of the coffee year.

5. The Members listed in the Annex to this Resolution shall be granted the portions of the waivers for the third and fourth quarters of the coffee year subject to the following options:

   (a) To establish a reserve in foreign exchange under the joint control of the Member and the Executive Director of the ICO equal to 20 percent of the foreign exchange value of the coffee granted as waivers. This reserve shall be held for utilization in the country of the Member concerned in financing schemes of diversification and development; or

   (b) To place under the joint control of the Member and the Executive Director of the ICO a quantity of exportable coffee equal to the quantity of the total waiver granted for the coffee year; or

   (c) To accept a combination of options (a) and (b) above in such a way that any percentage change in one is matched by a corresponding percentage change in the other.

6. If a Member listed in the Annex by 15 March 1967 exercises any of the foregoing options and provides evidence of having fulfilled the requirements of that option the Executive Director shall release the portions of the waiver relating to the third and fourth quarters.

7. If any Member decides not to exercise any of the options set out in paragraph 5, the portions of the waivers relating to the third and fourth quarters of the coffee year shall be cancelled and the Executive Director shall then distribute the amount of the waiver concerned *pro rata* among all exporting Members as special export authorizations within the meaning of Resolution No. 115.

8. The amounts forming the reserve in foreign exchange established in option (a) of paragraph 5 of this Resolution shall be calculated by multiplying 20 percent of the amount of the waiver granted by the mean of the price bracket for the group of coffee in question as established by Resolution No. 115.

9. If part or whole of the waiver of any Member is cancelled by application of the system of selective adjustment under Resolution No. 115 the amount to be established as a reserve under option (a) of paragraph 5 of this Resolution shall be reduced by an amount equivalent to the sum represented by 20 percent of the amount of the waiver so cancelled multiplied by the mean of the appropriate price bracket.

10. For the purposes of this Resolution when there is any reduction of the special export authorizations under the provisions of Resolution No. 115 the reductions shall be deemed to be first made from the waivers granted under this Resolution.

11. The Working Group referred to in Resolution No. 120 shall be instructed to work out in consultation with the Governments concerned not later than 28 February 1967 the administrative arrangements required to implement these proposals and the rules for their operation. In so doing the Working Group shall have particular regard to the following:

    (a) The need to integrate the purposes of this Resolution with national plans for diversification and development;

    (b) The means by which the funds in the reserve referred to in option (a) of paragraph 5 could in conjunction with the national development plans be utilized for achieving the purposes of this Resolution;

    (c) The method of utilizing funds which might otherwise be left idle in the reserve so that the Member country may secure the maximum benefit therefrom in pursuance of objectives which directly or indirectly will achieve the purpose of this Resolution.

12. The administrative arrangements and rules referred to in paragraph 11 of this Resolution shall be presented by the Working Group to the Executive Board for consideration and approval not later than 28 February 1967.

## LIST OF WAIVERS

*Other Mild Arabicas*

| | |
|---|---:|
| Dominican Republic | 40,000 |
| Ecuador | 58,000 |
| El Salvador | 225,000 |
| Guatemala | 135,000 |
| Haiti | 30,000 |
| India | 50,000 |
| Nicaragua | 70,000 |
| Peru | 61,000 |
| Tanzania | 50,000 |
| Total | 719,000 |

## LIST OF WAIVERS (Continued)

*Unwashed Arabicas*

| | |
|---|---:|
| Ethiopia | 75,000 |
| Total | 75,000 |

*Robustas*

| | |
|---|---:|
| Ghana | 6,000 |
| OAMCAF | 414,000 |
| Portugal | 279,000 |
| Sierra Leone | 17,000 |
| Trinidad and Tobago | 25,000 |
| Uganda | 197,000 |
| Total | 938,000 |
| GRAND TOTAL | 1,732,000 |

# APPENDIX D

# RESOLUTION ICC-131

## (March 31, 1967)

### AMENDMENT TO RESOLUTION NUMBER 114
### (Grant of Waivers and Conditions)

*WHEREAS:*

Practical considerations have demonstrated the desirability of amending certain provisions of Resolution No. 114 in order better to achieve the objectives thereof,

THE INTERNATIONAL COFFEE COUNCIL

*RESOLVES:*

1. That sub-paragraph (a) of paragraph 5 of Resolution No. 114 be deleted and replaced by the following:

    (a) To establish a reserve in freely-convertible currency under the joint control of the Member and the Executive Director of the International Coffee Organization equal to 20 percent of the US dollar value of the coffee covered by the portions of waivers applicable to the third and fourth quarters of the current coffee year. This reserve shall be held for utilization in the country of the Member concerned for financing schemes of diversification and development and shall be maintained in freely-convertible currency at a constant value in relation to the original US dollar equivalent."

2. That paragraphs 6, 7, 8 and 9 of the Resolution be deleted and replaced by the following:

    6. When a Member listed in the Annex exercises one of the foregoing options and provides evidence of having fulfilled the requirements of that option the Executive Director shall release the portions of the waiver relating to the third and fourth quarters."

    7. If before 1 June 1967 a Member fails to exercise, or decides not to exercise, one of the options set out in paragraph 5, the portions of the waiver of that Member relating to the third and fourth quarters of the coffee year shall be

cancelled and the Executive Director shall then distribute the amount of the waiver concerned *pro rata* among all exporting Members as special export authorizations within the meaning of Resolution No. 115. Similarly, if a Member having exercised one of the options set out in paragraph 5 fails to fulfill the requirements of that option before 1 June 1967 the foregoing provisions shall also apply."

8. The amounts forming the reserve in freely-convertible currency established in accordance with option (a) of paragraph 5 of this Resolution shall be calculated by multiplying 20 percent of the portions of the waivers relating to the third and fourth quarters by the mean of the price bracket for the group of coffee in question as established by Resolution No. 115."

9. If part of the whole of the portions of the waivers relating to the third and fourth quarters is cancelled by application of the system of selective adjustment under Resolution No. 115 the amount to be established as a reserve in accordance with option (a) of paragraph 5 of this Resolution shall be reduced by an amount equivalent to the sum represented by 20 percent of the amount of the portions of the waiver so cancelled multiplied by the mean of the appropriate price bracket."

# APPENDIX E

# RESOLUTION ICC-115

## (September 6, 1966)

## SYSTEM FOR SELECTIVE ADJUSTMENT OF SUPPLY OF COFFEE

*WHEREAS:*

Resolution No. 67 provided for adjustments of annual quotas under certain conditions established by the Council:

It is advisable, under present circumstances, to replace the provisions of Resolution No. 67 in order to make possible the more prompt adjustment of the supply of coffees within each of the various groups of coffee; and

Provisions for such selective adjustments may be made by the Council within the provisions of Article 41 of the Agreement.

THE INTERNATIONAL COFFEE COUNCIL

*RESOLVES:*

1. To allot under the provisions of Article 41 to each exporting Member, in addition to the annual export quotas fixed under the provisions of Article 30 of the Agreement, special export authorizations totalling 1,083,500 bags which shall be distributed *pro rata* to basic quotas.

2. Whenever the daily price of any group of coffee goes below its respective floor or above its respective ceiling, as defined in the following paragraph, the provisions of this Resolution shall apply to the special export authorizations of the Members comprised in the group or groups thus affected. The Executive Board is authorized to amend the composition of the groups of coffee set out in Annex 1 on receipt of appropriate evidence.

3. For the purposes of this Resolution, to establish, as set out in Annex 1, four groups of coffees and their respective *Indicator price* ranges, which shall be:

U.S. cents per lb.

|  | Floor prices | Ceiling prices |
|---|---|---|
| Colombian Milds | 43.50 | 47.50 |
| Other Milds | 40.50 | 44.50 |
| Unwashed Arabica | 37.50 | 41.50 |
| Robusta | 30.50 | 34.50 |

4. The Executive Director shall compute the daily price of each group in the manner prescribed in Annex 2.

5. If the average of the daily price of any group of coffee, taken over a period of fifteen consecutive market days, is below the floor or above the ceiling of its *Indicator price* range, the Executive Director shall, subject to the provisions of paragraphs 6, 7 and 8 below, adjust the special export authorization of each member of that group by an amount equal to two and-a-half percent of the Member's total authorized exports as at 1st October 1966. The period of fifteen market days shall commence on the first day on which the daily price is below the floor or above the ceiling of the *Indicator price* range.

6. The adjustment made under paragraph 5 above shall be upwards in the case of a price rise and downwards in the case of a price fall. The adjustment shall, in the case of an increase of special export authorizations, be applied wholly to the special export authorizations for the quarter in which the fifteen-day period ends. In the case of a reduction of special export authorizations, the adjustment shall if possible be applied to the special export authorizations for the quarter in which the fifteen-day period ends; but in cases where this is impracticable, the Executive Director may apply part or all of the adjustment to the special export authorizations for the next succeeding quarter.

7. Notwithstanding the *Indicator price* ranges established for the coffee year 1966-67 in paragraph 3 above, during the first quarter, the rules for downward adjustment established in this Resolution shall apply to the group of other Milds only if the average of the daily price of this group referred to in paragraph 5 is below the level of 40.00 US cents per lb.

8. Any adjustment made under paragraph 5 above shall take effect six days after the fifteen-day period ends, except that the Executive Board may by two-thirds distributed majority decide, within this period of six days, that no adjustment shall be made or that a different adjustment shall be made to the special export authorizations of Members of the group affected.

9. If, after an adjustment of the special export authorizations under paragraphs 5 or 8 has been effected, or after the Executive Board has decided under paragraph 8 that no adjustment shall be made, the average of the daily price of the group of coffee affected is below the floor or above the ceiling of the *Indicator price* range for a further complete period of fifteen market days, as laid down in paragraph 5, then the provisions of paragraphs 5, 6, 7 and 8 shall again apply. These provisions shall apply irrespective of the number of adjustments made in the course of the coffee year, provided that no downward adjustments under paragraphs 5, 6, 7, 8 and 9 of this Resolution shall be applied to the annual quotas fixed under the provisions of Article 30 of the Agreement.

10. To confirm the provisions of Resolution No. 87 relating to the fulfillment of contracts in the event of a downward adjustment of quotas.

11. This Resolution shall remain in force until 30 September 1967.

ANNEX 1

# COMPOSITION OF TYPES OF COFFEES BY COUNTRIES OF ORIGIN

*Colombian Mild Arabicas*

Colombia
(Kenya)*

*Unwashed Arabicas*

Bolivia*
Brazil
Ethiopia

*Other Mild Arabicas*

Burundi
Costa Rica
Cuba
Dominican Republic
Ecuador
El Salvador
Guatemala
Haiti*
Honduras
India
Mexico
Nicaragua
Panama
Peru
Rwanda
Tanzania
Venezuela

*Robustas*

Congo (D.R.)
Ghana
Indonesia
Nigeria
OAMCAF
   Cameroon
   Central African Republic
   Congo (Brazzaville)
   Dahomey
   Gabon
   Ivory Coast
   Malagasy Republic
   Togo
Portugal
Sierra Leone
Trinidad and Tobago
Uganda

---

*Pending accession

ANNEX 2

# METHOD OF CALCULATING THE DAILY PRICE OF THE FOUR TYPES OF COFFEE ON THE BASIS OF EX-DOCK NEW YORK FOR PROMPT SHIPMENT

(Paragraph 3 of the Resolution)

1. *Mild Arabicas*

    *Colombian Milds:* Each day the Executive Director shall take the price of Colombian Mams as representative of Colombian Mild Arabicas;

2. *Other Milds*

    Each day the Executive Director shall take the price of the following coffees:

    El Salvador Central Standard
    Guatemala Prime Washed
    Mexico Prime Washed

    and find the arithmetic average thereof.

    In the event that the prices of one or two of the coffees mentioned in paragraph 2 above are not quoted, the average price of the remaining two, or the price of third one will be retained as daily price.

3. *Unwashed Arabicas*

    Each day the Executive Director shall take the price of Santos 4 (New York classification, strictly soft) as representative of unwashed Arabicas.

4. *Robustas*

    The daily prices for Robustas shall be calculated by averaging the daily prices of the following types of unwashed coffees:

    Angola Ambriz 2 AA
    Ivory Coast Superior 2
    Uganda Native Standard

    In the event that quotations for one of the last two coffees are not available, the other shall carry a double weight in the calculation of the average for this type.

5. *Source of price quotations*

    All quotations referred to in this Annex shall be taken from a source to be agreed by the Executive Board.

# APPENDIX F

# RESOLUTION ICC-128

# (FEBRUARY 20, 1967)

## ADJUSTMENT OF SUPPLY OF COFFEE TO THE MARKET

*WHEREAS:*

One of the prime objectives of the International Coffee Agreement is to achieve a reasonable balance between supply and demand;

Recent price trends on the world coffee market indicate a serious, if temporary, imbalance between demand and the supply of coffee available under the provisions of Resolution No. 116;

It has been found desirable in present circumstances to supplement the provisions of Resolution No. 115 for the selective adjustment of the supply of coffee; and

Article 32 of the Agreement empowers the Council if market conditions so require to adjust annual export quotas within the procedures established by Article 35,

THE INTERNATIONAL COFFEE COUNCIL

*RESOLVES:*

1. To reduce immediately on a *pro rata* basis the annual export quotas for 1966-67 set by Resolution No. 116 from 43,700,000 to 41,700,000 bags and to apply this reduction to the quarterly quotas for the second quarter of the coffee year.

2. To increase with effect from 1 April 1967 on a *pro rata* basis the special export authorizations allotted under paragraph 1 of Resolution No. 115 by 1,000,000 bags and to apply this increase to the special export authorizations for the third quarter of the coffee year provided that such increase to the special export authorizations shall become subject to downward adjustment under the provisions of Resolution No. 115 only as a result of any fifteen market day count starting subsequent to 31 March 1967.

3. To provide that if the average of the daily price of any group of coffee (as established under Resolution No. 115), taken over a period of fifteen consecutive market days is at or above a level of 0.75 US cents per lb. below the ceiling of its *Indicator price* range, the special export authorization of each Member of that

group shall be increased by an amount equal to one fourth of the amount deducted from that Member's annual export quota pursuant to paragraph 1 above. The period of fifteen market days shall commence on the first day, after 1 April 1967, on which the daily price is at or above a level of 0.75 US cents per lb. below the ceiling of the relevant *Indicator price* range. The increase in special export authorizations shall be released by the Executive Director to each Member concerned during the quarter in which the fifteen day period ends.

4. To provide further that if subsequent to the increase provided for in paragraph 3 above, the average of the daily price of the same group of coffee, taken over a further period of fifteen consecutive market days, is at or above a level of 0.50 US cents per lb. below the ceiling of its *Indicator price* range, the special export authorization of each Member of the group shall be increased by a further amount equal to one fourth of the amount deducted from that Member's annual export quota pursuant to paragraph 1 above. The period of fifteen market days referred to in this paragraph shall commence on the first day on which the daily price is at or above a level of 0.50 US cents per lb. below the ceiling of the relevant *Indicator price* range but may not commence prior to the day following the end of the fifteen-day period referred to in paragraph 3 above. The increase in special export authorizations provided for in this paragraph shall be released by the Executive Director to each Member concerned during the quarter on which the relevant fifteen-day period ends.

5. To confirm that the provisions of Resolution No. 115 will continue to operate concurrently with the provisions of this Resolution.

6. To confirm the provisions of Resolution No. 87 relating to the fulfillment of contracts in the event of a downward adjustment of quotas.

# APPENDIX G

# RESOLUTION ICC-118

## (September 6, 1966)

## STRENGTHENING OF CERTIFICATES OF ORIGIN SYSTEM

*WHEREAS:*

Exports from some exporting Member countries have exceeded amounts authorized under the Agreement;

Article 36 of the Agreement states that exporting Members shall adopt the measures required to insure full compliance with all provisions of the Agreement relating to quotas, and authorizes the Council to request exporting Members to adopt the measures required to insure full compliance with these provisions; and

Article 58 of the Agreement provides that the Council may require Members to furnish such information as it considers necessary for its operations, and that the Members shall furnish information requested in as detailed and accurate a manner as is practicable.

THE INTERNATIONAL COFFEE COUNCIL

1. *RESOLVES:*

   1. To aid exporting Members to comply with their quota obligations under the Agreement by requiring the Executive Director to supply to such Members for each quarter, commencing 1 April 1967, a quantity of Coffee Export Stamps in an amount corresponding to their authorized exports for such quarter.

   2. To require that each Certificate of Origin issued by a producing Member to cover exports to countries other than those listed in Annex B shall have affixed to it a number of Coffee Export Stamps corresponding to the weight of coffee covered by the Certificate.

   3. To provide that Certificates of Origin issued by producing Members on and after 1 April 1967 shall be acceptable for the entry of coffee into other Member countries (other than Annex B) or for the issuing of Certificates of Re-export only for the amount of coffee corresponding to the weight of coffee indicated by the Coffee Export Stamps which are affixed to the Certificate.

   4. To instruct the Executive Director to convene a technical advisory committee representative of both exporting and importing Members to work out the detailed instructions required for implementation of the coffee export stamp system, with a view to circulation of such instructions prior to 31 December 1966.

5. To require producing Members to advise the International Coffee Organization by telegraph on 15 April 1967 and on the 1st and 15th day of each month thereafter of the amount of coffee for which stamps were used during the preceding 15 day period.

6. To establish the following special procedure for bringing the stamp system into operation with effect from 1 April 1967:

   (a) Producing Members shall apply to the International Coffee Organization for their first allotment of Coffee Export Stamps, not later than 1 March 1967. The allotment of stamps shall cover authorized exports during the third quarter of 1966-67 plus any authorized carry over of export entitlement from the first and second quarter, 1966-67. Applications for Coffee Export Stamps shall state whether the Member has made or is likely to make any over shipments or under shipments in the preceding quarters of the coffee year 1966-67.

   (b) In reviewing requests for stamps for the period beginning 1 April 1967 the Executive Director shall assume that there have not been any under shipments in cases where exporting Members:

   (1) are more than 60 days in arrears in the submission of statistics of monthly exports; or

   (2) are more than 30 days in arrears in the dispatch to the International Coffee Organization of duplicates of Certificates of Origin.

7. To instruct the Executive Director, in issuing future supplies of Coffee Export Stamps, to take into account any adjustments that may have taken place in the quarterly authorized exports; any over shipments reported by exporting Members or otherwise coming to the attention of the Executive Director; any penalties or waivers that may be in effect; and other factors that the Executive Director believes will enable him to administer the Certificate of Origin System and the Stamp System in the manner best calculated to achieve the objectives of the Agreement.

8. To authorize the Executive Director to take all necessary steps to cope with administrative problems and unforeseen practical difficulties which may arise during the first six months of operation of the System in order that the flow of coffee within the total of authorized exports shall not be impeded.

9. To appropriate the sum of US$40,000 from International Coffee Organization funds to pay for preparation of the necessary stamps and other expenses necessary to bring the Stamp System into operation during the coffee year 1966-67.

# APPENDIX H

# RESOLUTION ICC-122

## (September 6, 1966)

## INTERPRETATION OF ARTICLE 40

*WHEREAS:*

There has been a material increase during the coffee year 1965-66 in the volume of coffee exported to the countries listed in Annex B which has been re-exported or diverted to importing Member countries; and

There has been doubt cast upon the provisions of sub-paragraph (1) (f) of Article 40.

THE INTERNATIONAL COFFEE COUNCIL

*RESOLVES:*

To confirm that the provisions of the first sentence of sub-paragraph (1) (f) of Article 40 are mandatory and that coffee shipped by an exporting Member to a country listed in Annex B which is subsequently imported by any country not listed in Annex B shall be charged automatically to the quota of the exporting Member concerned regardless of whether the coffee in question is re-exported from the country listed in Annex B or is diverted therefrom while in transit.

# APPENDIX I

## RESOLUTION ICC-127

### (January 28, 1967)

## PROHIBITION OF IMPORT OF COFFEE DESTINED FOR ANNEX B COUNTRIES

*WHEREAS:*

The provisions of Resolution No. 121 have proved ineffective in preventing exports from Members destined for countries listed in Annex B of the Agreement from being introduced into importing Member countries not listed in that Annex; and

It is urgently necessary to remedy this situation,

THE INTERNATIONAL COFFEE COUNCIL

*RESOLVES:*

1. To cancel Resolution No. 121 of 6 September 1966.

2. To require all Members (other than those listed in Annex B to the International Coffee Agreement) to prohibit the entry of coffee accompanied by any Certificate showing a destination in a country listed in Annex B, or marked "New Market."

3. To require all Member countries to prohibit the issue by Certifying Agencies of a Certificate of Re-export or of 'Split' Certificate(s), against a Certificate of Origin showing a destination in a country listed in Annex B, or marked "New Market."

4. To determine that the provisions of this Resolution shall become effective fourteen (14) days after the date of notification thereof by the Executive Director.

5. To instruct the Executive Director to modify the Special Instructions on the handling of Certificates of Origin and Re-export in order to include therein the provisions of this Resolution.

# APPENDIX J

# RESOLUTION ICC-117

# (September 6, 1966)

## APPLICATION OF ARTICLE 45 (3) TO REGULATE IMPORTS OF COFFEE BY MEMBERS FROM NON-MEMBER COUNTRIES

*WHEREAS:*

Exports of coffee from non-member countries have increased since the International Coffee Agreement came into force in 1963;

The International Coffee Organization adopted a price policy under the provisions of Resolution No. 67 entailing semi-automatic adjustments of export quotas in relation to market price changes which, in coffee year 1964-65, resulted in a 4.5 percent reduction in quotas, and thus placed Members of the Agreement in a less favorable position than non-member countries;

Several countries which are not members of the International Coffee Organization have planned increases in coffee production;

There has been an increase in the clandestine movement of coffee through the medium of certain non-Member countries;

Article 48 requires the Council, in consultation with producing Members, to recommend production goals for each of such Members, thereby again placing these Members in a less favorable position than non-Member countries; and

Article 45 (3), (4) and (5) empowers the Council to impose limitations upon imports from non-Member countries under certain circumstances,

THE INTERNATIONAL COFFEE COUNCIL

*RESOLVES:*

1. To recognize that exports from non-Member countries as a group are disturbing the exports of Members within the meaning of Article 45 (3).

2. To apply the limitations of Article 45 (2), in respect of imports of coffee produced in non-Member countries as soon as practicable after 1 October 1966 but in any event not later than 1 January 1967 and as far as practicable on a quarterly basis, in accordance with procedures to be adopted by individual Members in consultation with the Executive Director; such consultation is to be completed as soon as possible and the outcome of these shall be reported to the Council at its next regular Session.

3. To reiterate the provisions of paragraph 3 of Resolution No. 94, which requires that all imports of coffee grown in a Member country, whether imported directly or via a non-Member, shall be accompanied by a valid Certificate of Origin.

4. To stipulate that the limitations of Article 45 (2) shall be applied to all imports of coffees which are not of established Member origin.

5. To stipulate that no Certificate of Re-export shall be issued in respect of any shipment of coffee produced in a non-Member country unless such coffee has been imported within the limitations of Article 45 (2) and in accordance with the procedures adopted under the provisions of paragraph 2 of this Resolution.

6. To require the Executive Director to notify Members of any withdrawals from, or accessions to, the Agreement and of the resultant changes in the limitations of annual imports within the provisions of Article 45 (2).

7. To require each Member to adjust its annual imports from non-member countries within the limitations specified in Article 45 (2), as soon as practicable after a Member country withdraws from, or a non-Member country accedes to, the Agreement.

8. That this Resolution shall expire on 30 September 1967 unless extended by the Council.

# APPENDIX K

# RESOLUTION ICC-97

# (December 12, 1965)

## DIVERSIFICATION FUND

CONSIDERING that the control of production is necessary for bringing the available supply of coffee into balance with world demand, for preventing the wastage of resources and for ensuring the continuing effectiveness of the International Coffee Agreement;

RECOGNIZING that production controls and the achievement of production goals are dependent on shifting resources from surplus coffee production to more productive uses in other fields;

BELIEVING that such diversification would be furthered by the cooperative efforts of all producing Members and should be made an integral part of the Coffee Agreement; and

HOPEFUL that international agencies will recognize the need for furthering such diversification programs as part of their support for economic development and will cooperate toward their fulfilment,

THE INTERNATIONAL COFFEE COUNCIL

RESOLVES:

1. To instruct the Executive Director to prepare a draft proposal to adapt the International Coffee Fund to the purposes of diversification and to seek the cooperation of other international financial institutions in the preparation of such a proposal. The Executive Director is also to conduct consultations with those institutions to examine the possibility of their participation in administering the Diversification Fund, in helping to identify specific projects that would fit into the country programs of diversification an in integrating such programs into its overall activities in promoting economic development.

2. To request the Executive Board to review the draft proposal and submit its recommendations to Member Governments for their active consideration well in advance of the Council's next regular session.

# APPENDIX L

# RESOLUTION ICC-120

## (September 6, 1966)

## DIVERSIFICATION FUND

*WHEREAS:*

By Resolution No. 97 and for the reasons indicated in its preamble, the Council instructed the Executive Director to prepare a draft proposal to adapt the International Coffee Fund to the purposes of diversification and

The Executive Director has submitted the draft of a Coffee Diversification Fund together with an explanatory memorandum (EB-389/66),

THE INTERNATIONAL COFFEE COUNCIL

*RESOLVES:*

1. To approve in principle the establishment of a Coffee Diversification and Development Fund as a means of helping to bring equilibrium to the world coffee economy.

2. To establish a Working Group composed of the Executive Director, representatives of Member countries appointed by the Council and invited representatives of interested international financial institutions and specialized agencies, to review the draft proposal submitted by the Executive Director, recommend such changes as it considers advisable regarding the administration and operation of the Fund, and circulate a revised draft to Members not later than 31 December 1966.

3. To request Members to present their comments on the revised draft proposal prepared by the Working Group to the Executive Board not later than 31 March 1967, so as to enable the Executive Board to submit a definitive proposal to the Council.

4. To include the question of the establishment of a Coffee Diversification Fund on the Agenda of the first regular Session of the Council to be held after 31 March 1967 with the view of bringing the Fund into operation in the coffee year 1967-68.

## APPENDIX M

## RESOLUTION ICC-110

### (September 6, 1966)

### ESTABLISHMENT OF A HIGH-LEVEL WORKING GROUP

*WHEREAS:*

The Council must take decisions, as soon as possible, in regard to the review of basic quotas, production goals, policy relative to stocks, production control and diversification of the coffee economy;

Those decisions are essential to a sound eventual revision of the International Coffee Agreement;

These decisions cannot be taken profitably unless the Council has sufficient knowledge of the several aspects of the coffee economy of exporting Members;

The required knowledge of these aspects calls for the receiving of information and for its adequate evaluation by the Secretariat and Members of the Council; and

The information available from several sources — such as waiver missions and other sources — needs to be compared and evaluated in order to provide a sound basis for co-ordinated decisions and action;


THE INTERNATIONAL COFFEE COUNCIL

*RESOLVES:*

1. To establish a high-level standing Working Group composed of four importing Members and seven exporting Members and of the Executive Director of ICO, and to invite the participation of the Director of the Tripartite Coffee Study Group.

2. To set the following terms of reference for the Working Group:

    (a) To obtain the maximum reliable information on all relevent aspects of the international market and the economies of exporting Members facing problems and necessary for the Council to take effective decisions on basic quotas, production goals, diversification and control of production, retention, stocks and waivers of annual export quotas;

    (b) To assist the Executive Director in appointing fact finding and other similar Missions, and in setting the Terms of Reference for those Missions:

    (c) To supplement such information, whenever necessary, with information from other sources;

(d) To analyse and co-ordinate all the information thus collected so as to present to the Council a comprehensive picture of the coffee economy in each exporting Member;

(e) To make specific recommendations to the Executive Board and to the Council with a view to facilitating the solution of those problems.

3. To establish that:

   (a) The seat of the Working Group will be in London;

   (b) The Members of the Working Group shall appoint high-level representatives and advisers;

   (c) The travel, wages, and *per diem* expenses of these representatives shall be covered by their respective countries;

   (d) All the Members of the Council shall co-operate with the Working Group, especially by making available information and experts or specialists for consultation or for participation in fact-finding Missions;

   (e) The wages, travel expenses, and *per diem* of such experts or specialists shall be met by the countries making them available, or, where appropriate, by the country in which the fact finding is to be carried out;

   (f) The task of the Working Group shall be completed in time to have the Council make a decision before the end of coffee year 1966-67;

   (g) Whenever it is decided to send a Mission to exporting Member countries, this shall always be done with the agreement of the government of the country to which it is proposed to send the Mission.

4. To instruct the Executive Director to invite the Working Group to convene as soon as possible, at the latest by 1 October, and to provide the necessary Secretariat facilities.

# APPENDIX N

# RESOLUTION ICC-119

# (September 6, 1966)

## ANNUAL VERIFICATION OF COFFEE STOCKS

*WHEREAS:*

It is essential to take steps which will enable the Council in future to measure periodically the progress being made towards the recommended global and individual production goals;

Article 51 of the Agreement provides for measures to ascertain world coffee stocks, taking into account origin, location, quality and condition;

Annual verification of the stock situation in each producing Member country will serve the two purposes mentioned above;

Annual verification of stocks will also contribute to the better understanding and judgement of requests for waiver under the provisions of Article 60;

Detailed knowledge of the world stock situation with regard to origin, location, quality and condition will facilitate the adoption of any corrective measures necessary to protect importing Members from a shortage of any particular type of coffee;

Resolution No. 93 recognizes the urgent need for a policy relative to coffee stocks; and

Coffee stocks in individual countries are most effectively recorded immediately prior to the beginning of each crop year,

THE INTERNATIONAL COFFEE COUNCIL

*RESOLVES:*

1. To adopt the following definitions of stocks:

    (a) Normal trading stocks: stocks traditionally on hand at any time with individual exporters and/or central marketing and regulating organizations for export purposes, and with these organizations, individual traders and roasters for domestic consumption;

    (b) Surplus stocks: stocks of exportable quality coffee on hand which are additional to normal trading stocks.

2. To establish the amount of coffee falling within the above definition of surplus stocks by means of an annual verification of the quantity and quality of stocks in

each producing Member country at the end of the quarter immediately preceding the beginning of a new crop year, as laid down in the Annex hereto for each individual country. The Executive Director is authorized to make changes in the timetable contained in the Annex to this Resolution.

3. To include in the verification all exportable coffee, included in the definition in paragraph (1) of Article 2 of the Agreement, which at the time of verification is in the hands of traders, exporters, central marketing or regulation organizations, is moving, or has moved, from the farms into local trade, either for export or for domestic consumption.

4. To authorize the Executive Director to call on the services of agencies of international repute equipped to carry out the annual stock verification in accordance with instructions given by the Executive Director.

5. To require each producing Member concerned to reimburse the cost of its respective stock verification to the International Coffee Organization.

6. To establish that the annual stock verification shall commence during the coffee year beginning 1 October 1966.

7. To instruct the Executive Director to present an annual report on the stock situation to the Council for analysis during its second regular session each coffee year.

# TIMETABLE FOR ANNUAL VERIFICATION OF COFFEE STOCKS

I. *At the end of each coffee year (30 September)*

| Western Hemisphere | Africa-Asia |
|---|---|
| Colombia | Cameroon |
| Costa Rica | Central African |
| El Salvador | Republic |
| Guatemala | Congo (D.R.) |
| Honduras | Dahomey |
| Jamaica | Ethiopia |
| Nicaragua | Ghana |
| Panama | India |
| Trinidad and Tobago | Ivory Coast |
| Venezuela | Kenya |
|  | Nigeria |
|  | Togo |
|  | Sierra Leone |
|  | Uganda |

II. *At the end of the first quarter of each coffee year (31 December)*

Western Hemisphere

Bolivia
Peru

III. *At the end of the second quarter of each coffee year (31 March)*

| Western Hemisphere | Africa-Asia |
|---|---|
| Brazil | Burundi |
| Cuba | Indonesia |
| Ecuador | Malagasy Republic |
|  | Portugal (Angola) |
|  | Rwanda |

IV. *At the end of the third quarter of each coffee year (30 June)*

| Western Hemisphere | Africa-Asia |
|---|---|
| Dominican Republic | Congo (Brazzaville) |
| Haiti | Gabon |
| Mexico | Tanzania |

# Price Movements

*Introduction*

This review of trends in the structure of coffee prices is limited to the United States market, and more specifically at the primary levels of the New York market. New York is far and away the largest coffee import center in the world, and quotations there reflect accurately prevailing conditions in the world coffee trade.

From the time the green coffee reaches the ports of importation until it is in the hands of the ultimate consumer it moves through several levels of distribution. The green coffee market is the primary sector of the coffee industry in this country. The green coffee price structure has three distinct aspects: import prices, spot prices and futures prices. After processing, the coffee moves through jobber, wholesale and retail channels. The price structure of processed coffee separates into wholesale quotations and retail prices at the grocery store level. As the commodity moves from the import level to the distribution, processing and retail channels, the price of the commodity increases to reflect the value added.

Green coffee gains commercial value in dollar terms for the first time when it is sold to an importer. The importer on his customs declaration specifies the FOB value of the coffee he has purchased for shipment to this country. Import values as published by the Department of Commerce therefore are accurate reflections of the export values of coffee entering channels of international trade from the various producing origins. Import prices by definition do not include cost of ocean freight, insurance or other incidental expenses involved in the purchase and import of the commodity.

Spot prices or quotations for green coffee represent actual values of transactions or, in the absence thereof, asking prices of sellers for lots of coffee immediately available at points of importation. Spot coffee prices generally are cited in terms of ex-dock (which includes the CIF basis plus handling charges and commissions), or ex-warehouse (in-store) basis which is calculated similarly. All spot quotations in this volume are for the New York market. That port now handles 45 to 50 percent of the total U. S. green coffee import traffic. New York spot quotations are widely cited by the world coffee trade as standards of comparison and, in fact, the ICO *Indicator Price* System in practice is based thereon.

Futures prices in New York are quoted for forward contracts for delivery over the ensuing thirteen months on the New York Coffee and Sugar Exchange. Existing contracts on the Exchange are for Brazilian coffee on the B contract and for *robusta* coffee on the R contract. Coffee from most origins also is traded in the actuals market for forward shipment; those transactions usually are for 30 to 90-day shipment. In the past year or two trader interest in *robusta* futures has shifted to The London Terminal Market where the volume of options transacted has been very heavy. The

CHART 1

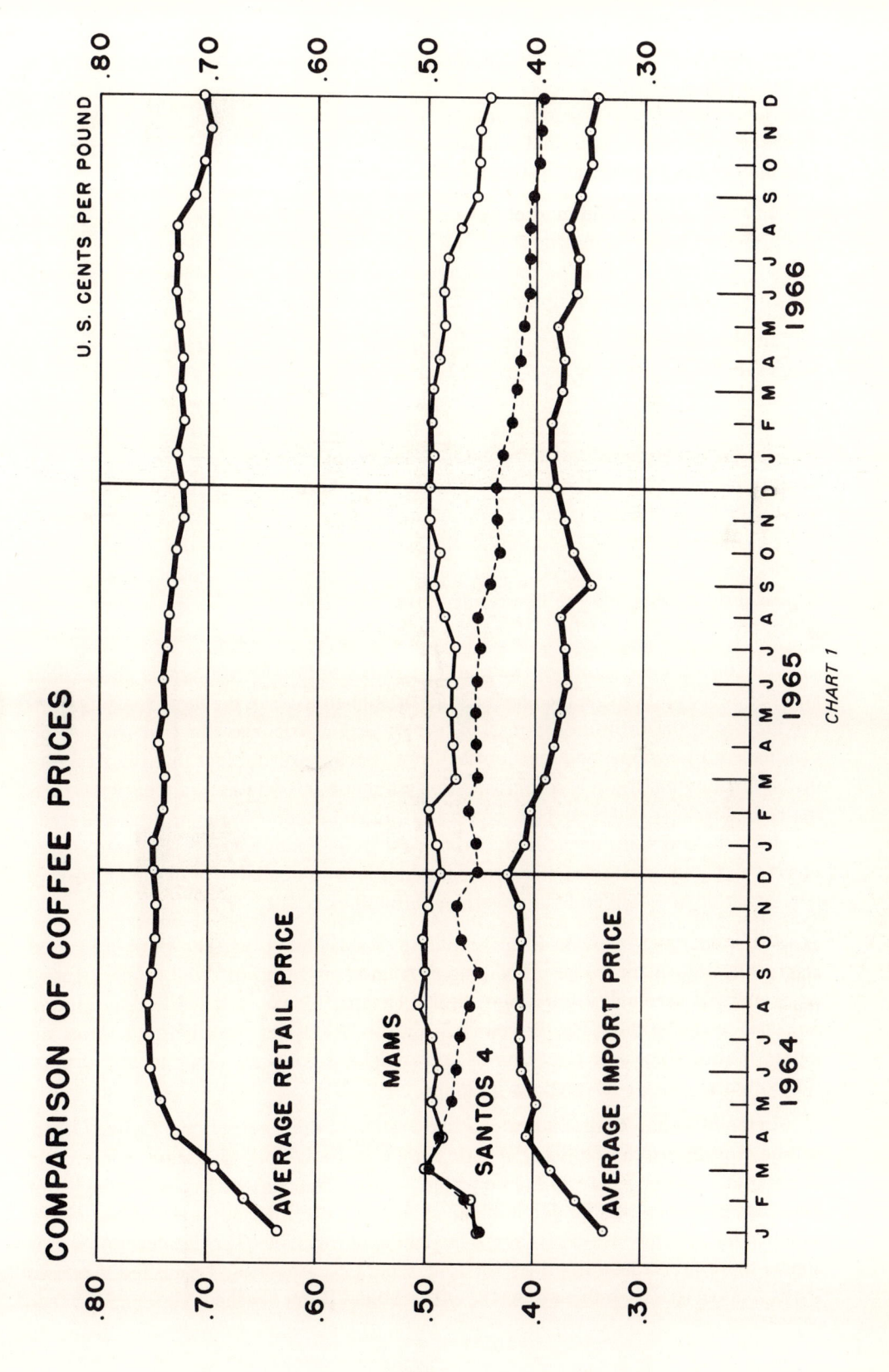

COMPARISON OF COFFEE PRICES

active market in London assures the trader of liquidity so that he can take a position in the futures market with confidence that he can liquidate commitments with facility at or near going prices. For some months now trader activity on the New York Coffee Exchange has been at a virtual standstill, thereby effectively preventing traders and speculators from operating in the futures market.

In a fast-moving fluid market buyers and sellers of actual coffee can protect their positions by "hedge operations" i.e., by taking an opposite position on the futures exchange. Gains or losses on the actual coffee then are offset by losses or gains on the corresponding futures options.

In the wholesale market processors quote to the grocery trade. The level of wholesale prices generally is set by the largest processors. Changes in wholesale quotations by one or more of the industry leaders is soon followed by widespread competitive moves in the coffee trade. Because of the rigidity inherent in the wholesale price structure it is characterized by a greater degree of stability than are green coffee quotations in the spot market. At the same time there are factors operating in the wholesale market which tend to render quotations at that distributional level of dubious analytical value. Even though the wholesale quotations of the major roasters may be static for long periods, various types of promotional discounts, special promotional tie-in sales and the like result in *real* wholesale prices to the grocery trade which are quite different from month to month.

The institutional sector of the market consists of hotels, restaurants and various types of public and private feeding facilities. Although some of the large roasting firms are factors in the institutional market, a very large proportion of that trade is accounted for by regional and local coffee firms. Because of the fact that the structure of the institutional trade is so diffused no systematic information on a national basis has been developed thereon. Data on the movement of coffee in the institutional trade are difficult to obtain, particularly from local or regional roasters. Because of the diversity of eating establishments, a sampling survey similar to consumer surveys now being done would encounter serious difficulties.

While a large proportion of the reputable establishments are known to use coffee of a grade equivalent to the premium-type blends purveyed to retail grocery customers, many lower-quality restaurants utilize cheaper blends. Wholesale prices therefore vary considerably. The Bureau of Labor Statistics publishes a series on representative wholesale prices on a delivered basis to destinations in the Eastern United States, but its coverage is limited.

In the first chapter the Indicator Price System of the International Coffee Organization was discussed. Those prices are based on New York quotations for prompt shipment i.e., shipments from source within 30 days. The construction of the Indicator Price System is reviewed in detail in the chapter on the International Coffee Organization. That system was revised at the beginning of the 1966-67 coffee year. As it now stands there are indicator prices for four separate categories: Unwashed *Arabicas* (basis Santos 4s), Colombian MAMS, Other Milds (Prime washed Mexico, El Salvador, Guatemala), and *Robustas* (Uganda, Ambriz and Ivory Coast). There is a floor and ceiling for each Indicator Group and quotas for the producing countries whose coffees are included in a particular indicator price group are adjusted according to the performance of that particular *Indicator*.

Under the system in force up to October 1, 1966 an overall indicator price was calculated which was an average of the price groups. Quotas of all producer-country members were adjusted proportionately on the basis of the performance of the overall *Indicator*.

*General Movement of Prices, 1966*

The coffee market experienced a generally declining trend throughout 1966. The persistent weakness evident in quotations for practically all groups and types of green coffee was reflected at all levels of the coffee trade. Although efforts to regulate the supply of green coffee to world markets through automatic adjustment of export quotas tied to a system of indicator prices was not altogether effective in arresting the lowering trend, partial success undoubtedly was achieved in confining the decline to an orderly and limited movement. The deterioration in coffee prices reflected in the main an excess of production over exports in the current crop year and large carryover stocks from previous harvests. A loss of about 2.6 percent was registered in the average annual unit import price of green coffee during 1966. Over most of the year roasted coffee prices to the consumer were down one to 3.5 percent over the corresponding months of 1965. Those figures serve to illustrate the fact that the easier trend in coffee prices was gradual and of relatively minor magnitude.

The softening of coffee prices during 1966 was in effect a re-emergence of the downward trend in part which was interrupted in the latter half of 1965. In the *arabica* sector of the market price developments reflected improved supply prospects. In a sense the downtrend in *arabica* quotations was a continuing reaction from the high levels attained in 1964 in the aftermath of the crop disaster in Brazil. It will be recalled that in the latter part of 1963 frost, drought and brush fires were expected to curtail the oncoming harvest in Brazil to four or five million bags of exportable coffee which compared with approximately 20 million bags picked in the preceding season. The speculative run-up in green coffee prices peaked out in early 1964. A brief period of strength in mild coffee prices in the latter part of 1965 disrupted the long-run tendency, but the undertone of the market was not buoyant as the Brazils did not follow that reaction. The latter types, of course, were under bearish pressure due to the easing of speculative and trade demand following optimistic forecasts for Brazilian output in the 1965-66 season and the fact that the exportable shortfall in the 1964-65 season apparently was being made up by withdrawals from surplus stocks. The stage was set for the softening trend evident in 1966.

The *robusta* types experienced a precipitous drop extending from early 1964 to mid-1965. The washed Uganda type for example went from 40.78 cents in March 1964 to 23.25 cents in May 1965 — a drop of 17.53 cents or 43.0 percent in fourteen months. In that interim the differential between the washed Ugandas and the Santos 4s widened from 9.07 cents in March 1964 to 22.00 cents in May 1965. That almost cataclysmic fall undoubtedly affected all sectors of the market and, in fact, only the crop disaster in Brazil prevented *arabica* prices from following a similar pattern. In mid-1965 the *robusta* market reversed itself abruptly. A case in point, the washed Ugandas recouped 11.00 cents in a period of three months — a gain of 42.2 percent from the trough of the previously lowering trend. Thereafter an irregular but easier trend set in in the *robusta* sector of the market and it was not until the latter half of 1966 that *robusta* quotations appeared to stabilize somewhat. The latter phase was in contrast to the weakness evident in the *arabica* sector.

*Import Prices, 1966*

Import prices here refer to the monthly average unit import price for all green coffee entering the United States. The averages are calculated on the basis of quantities of green coffee and their FOB values as declared by importers or agents. Quantity and value figures, collected and tabulated by the U.S. Department of Commerce, are aggregated for each month and represent a wide variety of coffees, ranging from those of high quality and relatively high prices to those of low quality and relatively low prices.

From a high of 42.49 cents per pound in December 1964, average monthly import prices of all green coffee entering the United States declined gradually, reflecting increased production of green coffee and lower consumer demand in the United States, to a level of 34.85 cents per pound in September 1965. In the final quarter of 1965 both green and packaged stocks of coffee reached rather low levels and renewed roaster interest brought slightly higher prices culminating in an average of 38.42 cents per pound in February 1966. From that point through the end of the year prices moved downward, closing at a lowpoint of 34.44 cents per pound for December. Two principal factors are implicit in the declining average — weakening of the price structure and the changing import mix, the proportion of lower-priced growths gaining relatively to the higher-priced growths.

The average annual price for all green coffee imported into the United States during 1966 was 2.6 percent lower than the corresponding figure for 1965. Similar year-to-year comparisons over the past thirteen years show declines in all instances but one; an increase of 31 percent for 1964 compared with 1963. On a per-bag basis the average price for 1966 was $48.37; the corresponding figure for 1965 was $49.68; it was $52.43 in 1964; and $40.05 in 1963. During 1966 average monthly import prices of green coffee brought into the United States declined from $50.74 per bag in January to $45.56 in December, a decline of $5.18 or 10.2 percent. During the corresponding months of 1965 a decrease of $3.69 or 6.8 percent was sustained, while in each of the two previous years, 1964 and 1963, an increase was shown. In each year from 1957 through 1962 there was an increase in the average monthly import price for December compared with January. Figures in the table below give monthly averages on a per-bag and per-pound basis for 1965 and 1966.

## UNITED STATES: AVERAGE MONTHLY IMPORT PRICES OF GREEN COFFEE, 1965-1966

|  | 1966 Per Bag ($) | 1966 Per Pound (¢) | 1965 Per Bag ($) | 1965 Per Pound (¢) | 1966 Compared with 1965 (Dollars per Bag) | (Cents per Lb.) | (Percent Change) |
|---|---|---|---|---|---|---|---|
| January | 50.74 | 38.36 | 53.90 | 40.75 | −3.16 | −2.39 | −5.9 |
| February | 50.82 | 38.42 | 53.16 | 40.19 | −2.34 | −1.77 | −4.4 |
| March | 49.55 | 37.46 | 51.50 | 38.93 | −1.95 | −1.47 | −3.8 |
| April | 49.38 | 37.33 | 50.46 | 38.15 | −1.08 | −0.82 | −2.1 |
| May | 50.13 | 37.90 | 49.70 | 37.57 | +0.43 | +0.33 | +0.9 |
| June | 47.70 | 36.06 | 48.97 | 37.02 | −1.27 | −0.96 | −2.6 |
| July | 47.49 | 35.90 | 49.17 | 37.17 | −1.68 | −1.27 | −3.4 |
| August | 48.69 | 36.81 | 49.71 | 37.58 | −1.02 | −0.77 | −2.0 |
| September | 47.45 | 35.87 | 46.10 | 34.85 | +1.35 | +1.02 | +2.9 |
| October | 46.07 | 34.83 | 48.19 | 36.43 | −2.12 | −1.60 | −4.4 |
| November | 46.19 | 34.92 | 49.35 | 37.31 | −3.16 | −2.39 | −6.4 |
| December | 45.56 | 34.44 | 50.21 | 37.96 | −4.65 | −3.52 | −9.3 |
| **Annual Average** | **48.37** | **36.57** | **49.68** | **37.56** | **−1.31** | **−0.99** | **−2.6** |

SOURCE: *U. S. Department of Commerce.*

*Review of Import Prices, 1953-66*

A broader perspective of import prices can be obtained by examining them over a longer period of time. Table CP-16 in the Appendix shows, for the United States in the years 1953 through 1966, average monthly and annual import prices per pound of green coffee. A highpoint of 78.64 cents was recorded in July 1954 and a lowpoint of 27.70 cents in November 1962. The decrease between those two points was 50.94 cents or about 65 percent. On an annual basis the greatest year-to-year declines were recorded between 1954 and 1955, 13.50 cents or 21 percent, and between 1957 and 1958, 5.93 cents or 19 percent. The only year-to-year increases in the 14-year period occurred between 1953 and 1954, 12.98 cents or 24.6 percent, and between 1963 and 1964, 9.35 cents or 30.9 percent. The remaining year-to-year differences were less than two cents each and ranged from one to six percent. The annual average for 1966 compared with that of 1953 shows a decline of 16.13 cents per pound or some 31 percent, which on the average was roughly 2.3 percent per year.

An examination of the monthly average import prices over the 1953-66 period indicates that there were two periods of general increase, July 1953 through July 1954 and November 1963 through December 1964. In both of those periods rapidly rising prices resulted directly from extensive frost damage to coffee trees in Brazil with consequent shortages or fear of shortages of green coffee. Both periods of upswing also lasted roughly the same number of months — thirteen or fourteen. The interim period, August 1954 through October 1963, was one of general decline, as has been the period subsequent to December 1964. If a 10-year cycle does in fact exist, it must be dependent on the weather. At this writing we have no evidence of an approximate

10-year severe frost cycle in Brazil. If a trend can be said to exist, it is downward interrupted only by severe weather conditions. Such a trend has resulted from the tendency for the supply of green coffee to remain sufficiently ahead of demand to depress import prices. It already has been noted in this book that the International Coffee Organization is engaged in a program to contain the downward trend of prices by encouraging producing countries to restrict their production of coffee and by stimulating consuming countries to increase their consumption of the product. Should the efforts of the ICO fail to achieve their intended purposes, the long-range trend of excessive supplies of green coffee with consequent downward pressure on prices interrupted by sporadic outbreaks of adverse weather and consequent 13-14 month periods of rising prices would appear to be the expected future pattern.

Since the production of coffee is seasonal in character and since the demand for coffee also shows seasonal change, it would be expected that the import price of coffee would show seasonal change. To some extent the production and consumption seasonals are offsetting. Coffee from Brazil is harvested largely from May through September with the heaviest import of new-crop coffee beginning in July. Other Latin American growths have their greatest impact in the November-March period, although Colombians are generally available throughout the year. African coffees are harvested mainly from August through December. Coffee consumption is inversely related to temperature, the heaviest demand occurring in the winter months.

An analysis of the 1953-1966 period shows a mild seasonal pattern in the import prices of green coffee brought into the United States. The pattern indicates a high in July and a low in December and is, thus, more related to production than to demand. Figures for each month are given in the table below.

### UNITED STATES: SEASONAL FACTORS FOR IMPORT PRICES OF GREEN COFFEE, BASED ON YEARS 1953-1966

| Month | Factor |
|---|---|
| January | 1.002 |
| February | 1.003 |
| March | 0.994 |
| April | 1.005 |
| May | 1.011 |
| June | 1.014 |
| July | 1.025 |
| August | 1.022 |
| September | 1.004 |
| October | 0.974 |
| November | 0.970 |
| December | 0.976 |

NOTE: The factors total 12.000, thus an average month would be equal to 1.000. Each monthly factor may be read as a ratio to one, e.g., July = $\frac{1.025}{1.000}$ or July prices are 2.5 percent higher than those of an average month.

SOURCE: Department of Statistics and Economic Research, PACB.

*Spot Prices, 1966*

The Department of Statistics and Economic Research of the Pan-American Coffee Bureau conducts a weekly spot-price survey of a sample of traders in the New York market, and price quotations are thus obtained for the principal growths and types of coffee trades. The survey is conducted each Thursday, or if Thursday is a holiday, on the closest business day thereto; consequently, the prices obtained reflect prices for that day only.

Data collected from the sample are averaged on a monthly and on an annual basis. The averages thus calculated are shown, together with yearly highs and lows, in Appendix Table CP-1. Not all growths are traded each week; when a particular growth is not quoted in weekly surveys, it, of course, does not appear in the monthly averages, and if the number of monthly means is insufficient an annual average is not calculated. It should be noted that the averages are those of the quotations collected; they cannot be weighted since there is no way of knowing the volume of coffee that is offered or that may change hands at any given price. Nevertheless, the quotations obtained are considered to reflect closely the prices at which the various types and grades of coffee are transacted in the periods specified.

As an aid in the comparison of spot prices for 1966 with respect to 1965, certain key figures from both years were selected and are shown in the following table.

A comparison of annual averages shows that all of the selected *arabica* growths were lower on the average in 1966 than they were in 1965, while the two *robusta* growths selected were higher. Among the *arabicas* Brazils showed the largest decline in terms of the annual average, but experienced the smallest decline of all growths in a comparison of the average for January 1966 with that of December of the same year. In comparing the average annual spot price for 1966 with the corresponding figure for the preceding year, Colombian MAMS showed the smallest decline of all *arabica* growths.

Spot prices of the Brazil growths increased during 1964 in reaction to reports of lower production of coffee in that country during crop year 1964-65. However, prices showed signs of easing in December of 1964 as it became apparent that shortages would not occur. For the first eight months of 1965 spot prices of Brazils hovered near their levels of December 1964. For example, at the end of 1964 the monthly average spot price of Santos 4s was 45.18 cents per pound; the corresponding figure for August 1965 was 45.23 cents per pound. They moved downward during the latter months of 1965 reaching 43.45 cents per pound in December. That decline apparently came in reaction to bullish forecasts of the 1965-66 crop in Brazil that indicated ample supplies. Moreover, Brazil's ICO quota allocation seemed to offer sufficient product from surplus stocks to meet demand in the months immediately ahead.

The monthly average spot price of Santos 4s for December of the current year was 8.8 percent lower than the January figure. The corresponding comparison for 1965 showed a decrease of 4.1 percent, while for 1964 and 1963 there were increases of 0.8 percent and 11 percent respectively.

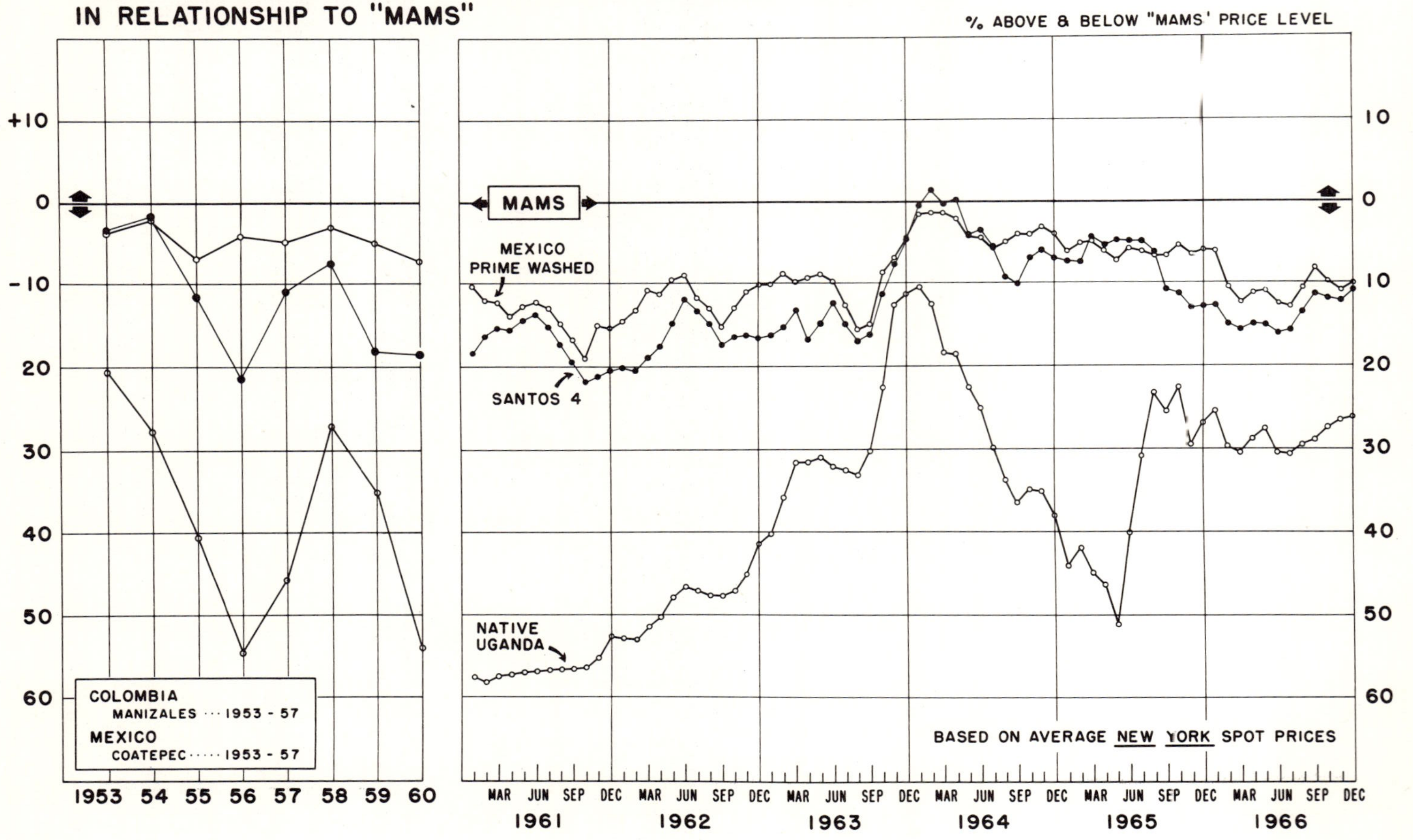

CHART 2

SPOT-PRICE PERCENTAGE DIFFERENTIAL OF SELECTED COFFEES IN RELATIONSHIP TO "MAMS"

SPOT COFFEE PRICES FOR THE NEW YORK MARKET

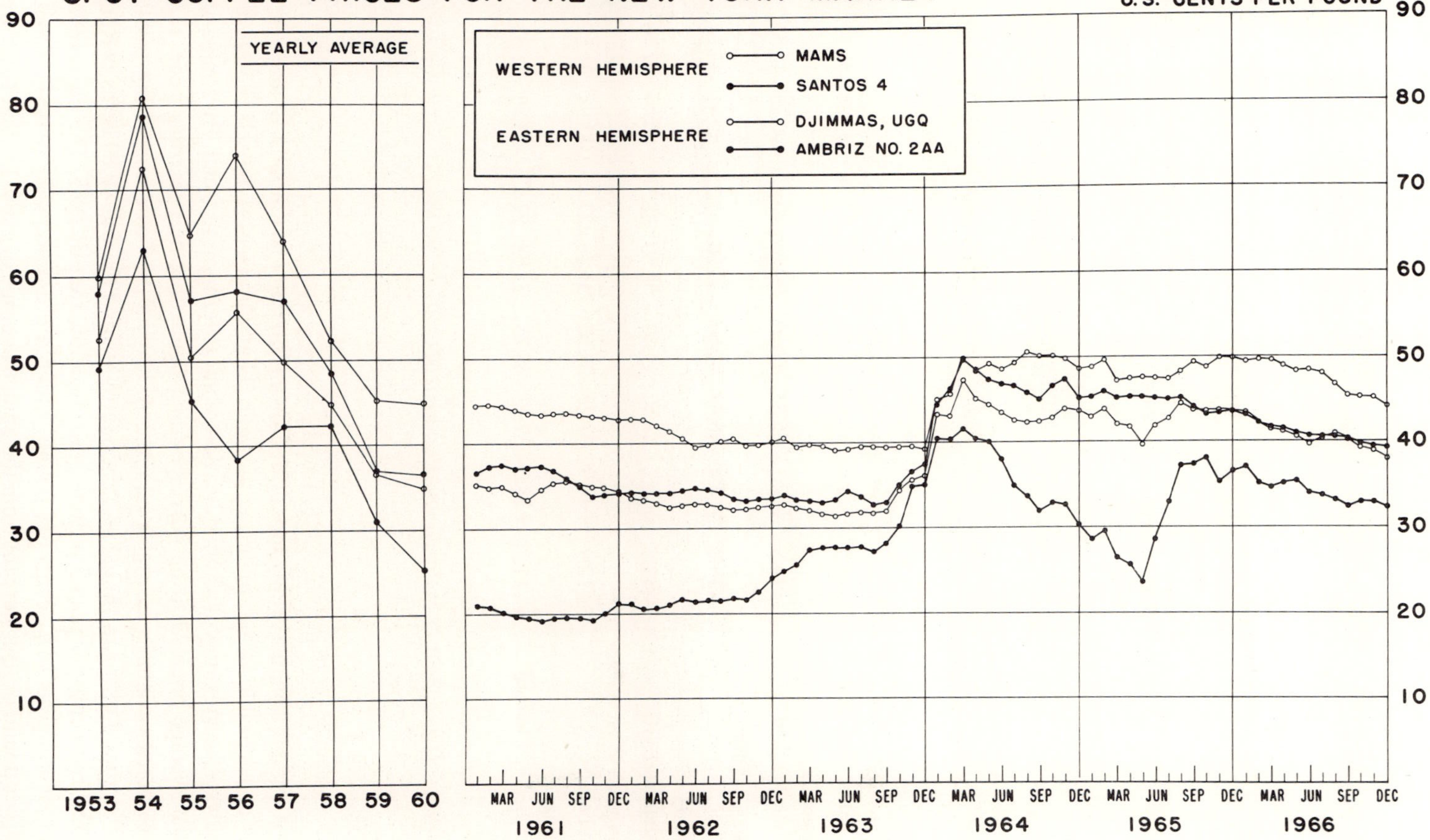

CHART 3

## NEW YORK MARKET: COMPARISON OF AVERAGE MONTHLY SPOT PRICES FOR SELECTED GROWTHS BETWEEN JANUARY AND DECEMBER AND THEIR ANNUAL HIGHS, LOWS AND AVERAGES, 1966 AND 1965

|  | Relative Change (percent) Jan. vs. Dec. 1966 | Jan. vs. Dec. 1965 | Highs 1966 | 1965 | Lows 1966 | 1965 | Annual Averages 1966 | 1965 | 1966 Compared with 1965 (percent change) |
|---|---|---|---|---|---|---|---|---|---|
| **Brazil** Santos 4 | −8.8 | −4.1 | 43.50 | 46.13 | 39.25 | 43.00 | 40.83 | 44.71 | −8.7 |
| **Colombia** MAMS | −10.7 | +2.1 | 49.88 | 50.63 | 44.00 | 46.75 | 47.43 | 48.49 | −2.2 |
| **El Salvador** Central Standard | −14.5 | +2.2 | 46.88 | 47.50 | 39.50 | 43.00 | 42.54 | 45.55 | −6.4 |
| **Guatemala** Prime Washed | −14.5 | +2.1 | 46.88 | 47.50 | 39.25 | 43.13 | 42.25 | 45.51 | −7.2 |
| **Mexico** Prime Washed | −14.3 | +2.4 | 46.88 | 47.50 | 39.50 | 43.25 | 42.41 | 45.54 | −6.9 |
| **Ethiopia** Djimmas UGQ | −12.5 | +1.2 | 43.50 | 44.50 | 37.50 | 38.50 | 40.44 | 42.76 | −5.4 |
| **Portuguese West Africa** Ambriz No. 2 AA | −12.9 | +27.9 | 37.25 | 38.50 | 31.75 | 22.75 | 33.98 | 31.59 | +7.6 |
| **Uganda** Washed & Cleaned | −11.7 | +28.7 | 37.13 | 38.25 | 31.88 | 22.13 | 33.88 | 31.33 | +8.1 |

SOURCE: *Department of Statistics and Economic Research, PACB.*

A comparison of average spot prices for the first and last months of any year may mask considerable variation during the year. That comparison in itself therefore may not always be meaningful as an indication of short-term price trend. By comparing an annual average price with the corresponding figure for the preceding year, random and seasonal variability is largely eliminated, leaving the basic underlying trend and cycle factors. The mean annual price of Santos 4s for 1966 was 40.83 cents per pound, roughly four cents per pound or nine percent below that of 1965. The corresponding mean for 1965 was 44.71 cents per pound, which represented a decrease of about two cents per pound or four percent from the annual average of 1964. In 1964 there was an increase of 12.5 cents per pound or 37 percent over 1963.

The average price of Santos 4s for each month of 1966 was slightly lower than in the preceding month — a decline of roughly 0.3 cents per pound per month. However, the price of that growth was relatively steady in comparison with earlier years. One indication of variability is given by the range, or the difference between annual high and low prices. For 1966 the range of prices for Santos 4s was 4.25 cents per pound. In view of the generally downward trend, as indicated by a difference of 3.80 cents per pound between the monthly averages of January and December, the magnitude of the maximum range was not large. By comparison the ranges for 1964 and 1963 were 9.37 cents and 6.25 cents respectively. However, it was only 3.13 cents in 1965 and 1.75 cents in 1962. A high value for the range is frequently indicative of marked price fluctuations during the year.

Throughout the year 1966 generally good supplies of the Mild growths pressed against a gently easing demand situation. As a consequence, spot quotations sought lower levels. The decline followed five months, August through December 1965, of increases with most growths reaching a highpoint in December; the earlier months of 1965 had been characterized by a downward trend. On balance, the average prices of the Mild growths in December 1966 were some 11 to 15 percent below their monthly averages in January of that year. In the previous year a similar comparison showed modest increases of one or two percent, while in 1964 the increases reached six to eight percent.

The average annual prices of Mild coffees for 1966 decreased with respect to those of the preceding year by 2.2 to 7.2 percent. A similar comparison between 1965 and 1964 showed increases of 0.6 to 3.5 percent. Between 1964 and 1963 increases of 23 to 27 percent occurred, while for 1963 compared with 1962 decreases of four to six percent were noted. For 1962 compared with 1961 the decreases were of the order of 4 to 6-1/2 percent.

The range of the Colombian MAMS was 5.88 cents per pound for the year under review; for 1965 it was 3.88 cents and it reached 8.63 cents in 1964. By contrast it was only 2.25 cents in 1963. In 1966 the range of the Other Milds was, for the most part, just over seven cents per pound — larger than the range of approximately four and one-third cents in 1965, but under the 8.25 cents of 1964.

During the year under review prices of African *robustas* moved irregularly downward, with December averages roughly twelve percent below their January averages. The volatility of the *robusta* growths is demonstrated by noting that January-December comparisons for 1965 show increases of about 28 percent, compared with decreases of 25 percent in 1964 and increases of 40 percent or more in 1963. Annual average prices of African *robustas* for 1966 were some eight percent above those of the preceding years in spite of the January-December declines in the later year. Annual average prices for 1965 were about 13 percent below their levels of 1964; prices of African *arabicas*, as exemplified by Ethiopian Djimmas, followed the pattern of their counterparts in the Western Hemisphere during 1966. Their average monthly price for December was 12.5 percent below their January mean. Similar comparisons for 1965 and 1964 showed increases of 1.2 percent and 1.0 percent respectively. The 1966 annual average price of Djimmas was 5.4 percent below that of 1965, while the latter figure was 3.4 percent above that of 1964.

The range of prices for African *robustas* in 1966 was some six cents; that was far less than the 16 cents per pound of 1965. For African *arabicas* it was four cents per pound; that was less than the six cents per pound range of 1965 and roughly of the same order as in the past few years.

*Review of Spot Prices, 1953-1966*

The average annual spot prices of types and growths of coffee traded on the New York market over a longer term will be found in Appendix Table CP-17. Shown there are the prices of selected types and growths for the period 1953-66. Starting the examination with 1953 seems appropriate, since it was in the following year that spot prices reached all-time high levels, following the frost in Brazil in the summer of 1953 and the consequent severe damage to a large portion of the coffee trees in that country. Reflecting the prospective reduction of world coffee availabilities, prices of all coffees rose in the latter part of 1953 and in the first months of 1954.

A distinction between the general movement of spot prices of *arabicas* and *robustas* is apparent. The prices of both Western and Eastern Hemisphere *arabicas* declined sharply during 1955; they rose again in 1956 (the price of Santos 4s only slightly) and then showed fairly sharp declines in subsequent years until 1959. With adjustments of offerings to approximate effective demand under international coffee agreements from 1959 through most of 1963, the prices of the *arabicas* showed a relative degree of stability but a continuing downward tendency; and it was not until the last few months of 1963, following reports of extensive damage to trees in Brazil, that the trend was reversed. A rising trend continued for some of the *arabicas* during most of 1964, but it tapered off and declined slightly during the last quarter. During 1965 prices of the *arabicas* eased downward in an orderly fashion. The same downward trend continued through 1966, but at an accelerated rate.

The *robustas* demonstrated a somewhat different trend. Following a precipitous decline in 1955 from their 1954 levels, their prices again dropped in 1956 (while those for *arabicas* increased). *Robusta* prices recovered somewhat in 1957 and again in 1958 (when the *arabica* prices declined). From 1959 through 1961 the prices of *robustas* showed annual decreases (while those of the *arabicas* were relatively stable). In 1962, however, the *robusta* prices rose over their 1961 levels as production declined while the market continued firm. The rise continued throughout 1963, but leveled off early in 1964, and thereafter the *robusta* prices generally declined. The softer trend continued through May of 1965, but the direction was reversed at that point and quotations climbed back to mid-1964 levels, reaching a highpoint in October of 1965. Since then and through 1966, the *robustas* have moved irregularly downward.

In 1966 the average prices of Ambriz No. 2AA and Uganda Native Standard were still below their 1954 levels (the recent-year highpoint) by 85.5 and 72.2 percent, respectively. Santos 4s, MAMS, Mexican Prime Washed and Djimmas UGQ were lower by 92.8, 68.7, 82.1, and 79.2 percent, respectively. The decline in the spot prices of the *robustas* is somewhat more significant than at first appears, since they dropped from considerably lower price bases in 1954 than did the *arabicas*.

A further analysis appears in the table below. The purpose is to note changes in the relative positions of prices of the major growths for selected years between 1954 and 1966. That is accomplished by comparing the annual average prices of selected growths with Colombian MAMS in each of the years shown. While the relative positions in 1964 approximated those in 1954, they changed in 1965 with all of the growths shown losing ground with respect to MAMS. The 1965 positions remained in effect with only modest changes in 1966.

**NEW YORK MARKET: INDICES OF AVERAGE ANNUAL SPOT PRICES OF SELECTED GROWTHS COMPARED WITH MAMS, 1954-1966**

(Basis MAMS)

|  | 1954 | 1957 | 1960 | 1963 | 1966 | 1966 Compared with 1954 (percentage points) |
|---|---|---|---|---|---|---|
| MAMS | 100 | 100 | 100 | 100 | 100 | — |
| Santos 4 | 98 | 89 | 82 | 86 | 86 | −12 |
| Mexican Prime Washed | 98 | 95 | 93 | 90 | 89 | − 9 |
| Djimmas UGQ | 90 | 78 | 78 | 83 | 85 | − 5 |
| Ambriz No. 2 AA | 79 | 63 | 56 | 73 | 72 | − 7 |
| Uganda Washed & Cleaned | 72 | 54 | 46 | 71 | 71 | − 1 |

SOURCE: *Department of Statistics and Economic Research, PACB.*

*Retail Prices, 1966*

Import and spot prices tend to move closely together. Listed wholesale prices follow the same general direction but with considerable time-lag in their response to changes in raw product costs. Retail prices follow the lead of green coffee prices but lag behind them and show less variation. The lag is to be expected in view of the processing, packaging and distribution time required before the processed coffee is placed on sale to the consumer. As in the case of many agricultural products, coffee prices tend to be less volatile and to demonstrate less variability as the product moves closer to the ultimate consumer. In recent years much of the volatility that in earlier times was characteristic of green coffee prices has been reduced as a result of the operation of the international coffee agreements.

Two series of retail coffee prices for the United States are available to the Pan-American Coffee Bureau. The Bureau of Labor Statistics (BLS) publishes average monthly prices for vacuum- and for bag-packs, which series are continuous from January 1956 (See Table CP-14, Appendix). In the absence of statistical weights for each type of pack, which would require a special study and special arrangements which the BLS has not undertaken, that agency does not have a combined average-price series for the two packs of regular coffee. It also publishes a price series for soluble coffee, started in September 1961.

The other retail price series are those prepared for the Pan-American Coffee Bureau by Market Research Corporation of America (MRCA), which series have been calculated from weekly panel reports received from a nationwide sample of 7,500 households. These households are selected so as to be representative of all households in the country. The average prices obtained from MRCA have the principal advantage that a combined average price can be calculated for the two packs of regular coffee (See Table CP-15, Appendix).

A comparison of the mean monthly prices of regular coffee at retail (MRCA) in 1964, 1965 and 1966, of green coffee in the spot market and of green coffee at the time of import (MAMS and Santos 4s) is shown in Chart 1. The change in direction of price movement and the lag in retail prices noted earlier are clearly shown.

During 1966 the average monthly retail price of regular coffee (MRCA) decreased by 2.4 cents per pound or 3.3 percent for December compared with January; that decrease was identical to the 3.3 percent noted in 1965. In the two years preceding 1965 increases of 17.8 percent and 1.5 percent were recorded. Declines of 3.7, 3.4 and 3.0 percent occurred in the same span in 1962, 1961 and 1960, respectively.

Much of the overall decline that occurred between January and December of 1966 took place in the last four months with a lowpoint of 69.8 cents per pound being registered in November. Prices in the earlier months remained at a fairly constant plateau with a highpoint of 72.9 cents per pound in June. Since retail prices lag behind import prices and since import prices rose during the last quarter of 1965, it is not surprising that higher prices resulted in the first eight months of 1966 as compared with levels prevailing toward the end of 1965. The average annual price of regular coffee at retail for 1966 was 71.9 cents per pound, 1.7 cents or 2.3 percent below that of the preceding year. The mean annual and monthly figures for 1965 and 1966 are shown, together with absolute and relative comparisons in the table below.

## UNITED STATES: AVERAGE MONTHLY RETAIL PRICES OF REGULAR COFFEE, VACUUM- AND BAG-PACKED, 1965-1966

(U.S. cents per pound)

|  | 1966 | 1965 | 1966 Compared with 1965 Cents | Percent |
|---|---|---|---|---|
| January | 72.8 | 74.8 | −2.0 | −2.7 |
| February | 72.2 | 74.1 | −1.9 | −2.6 |
| March | 72.4 | 73.9 | −1.5 | −2.0 |
| April | 72.3 | 74.4 | −2.1 | −2.8 |
| May | 72.5 | 74.0 | −1.5 | −2.0 |
| June | 72.9 | 74.1 | −1.2 | −1.6 |
| July | 72.8 | 73.7 | −0.9 | −1.2 |
| August | 72.8 | 73.5 | −0.7 | −1.0 |
| September | 71.7 | 73.2 | −1.5 | −2.0 |
| October | 70.3 | 72.8 | −2.5 | −3.4 |
| November | 69.8 | 72.2 | −2.4 | −3.3 |
| December | 70.4 | 72.3 | −1.9 | −2.6 |
| **Annual Average** | **71.9** | **73.6** | **−1.7** | **−2.3** |

SOURCE: Market Research Corporation of America.

The average retail price of a two-ounce equivalent unit of soluble coffee in December 1966 was 1.7 cents or 6.0 percent higher than it was in January of the same year. A similar comparison for 1965 showed a decrease of 4.1 cents or 12.5 percent, although in the two preceding years there were increases of 11.9 and 0.7 percent. Declines of 4.0, 4.4 and 2.7 percent occurred over that 12-month span in 1962, 1961 and 1960, respectively.

From a 1966 average monthly lowpoint of 28.2 cents per two-ounce unit in January, the monthly averages rose to a highpoint of 30.0 cents in July and in August. Average prices eased to 29.4 cents over the September-November period, rising slightly to 29.9 cents in December. Thus, average monthly prices during the March-December months of 1966 were quite constant varying within a narrow range of one cent. For 1966 the mean annual price of soluble coffee was 29.4 cents per two-ounce equivalent unit, which was only slightly lower − 0.3 cents or one percent − than the 29.7-cent average for 1966. The figure for 1965 compared with that for 1964 showed a decrease of 3.3 cents or 11.1 percent. A similar comparison between 1964 and 1963 disclosed an increase of 4.4 cents or 15.4 percent; for 1963 compared with 1962 the decrease was 0.5 cents or 1.7 percent; and for 1962 compared with 1961 the decrease was 1.5 cents or 4.9 percent.

## UNITED STATES: AVERAGE MONTHLY RETAIL PRICES OF SOLUBLE COFFEE, 1965-1966

(U.S. cents per two-ounce equivalent unit)

|  | 1966 | 1965 | 1966 Compared with 1965 Cents | Percent |
|---|---|---|---|---|
| January | 28.2 | 32.9 | −4.7 | −14.3 |
| February | 28.4 | 32.7 | −4.3 | −13.1 |
| March | 29.0 | 30.0 | −1.0 | − 3.3 |
| April | 29.6 | 28.9 | +0.7 | + 2.4 |
| May | 29.6 | 28.5 | +1.1 | + 3.9 |
| June | 29.9 | 28.8 | +1.1 | + 3.8 |
| July | 30.0 | 29.0 | +1.0 | + 3.4 |
| August | 30.0 | 29.1 | +0.9 | + 3.1 |
| September | 29.4 | 29.2 | +0.2 | + 0.7 |
| October | 29.4 | 29.3 | +0.1 | + 0.3 |
| November | 29.4 | 29.5 | +0.1 | − 0.3 |
| December | 29.9 | 28.8 | +1.1 | + 3.8 |
| **Annual Average** | **29.4** | **29.7** | **−0.3** | **− 1.0** |

SOURCE: *Market Research Corporation of America.*

*Review of Retail Prices, 1952-66*

The discussion in this section is based on Appendix Table CP-15. That table contains average monthly prices paid by consumers in the United States for packaged coffee, regular and soluble, at retail in the period 1952-66. The figures in that table represent actual prices paid as opposed to list prices, in other words, deals and special promotions are incorporated in the computations. The data were gathered from the Market Research Corporation of America's National Consumer Panel. Although historical series on import and spot prices contained in this volume begin with the year 1953, one earlier year, 1952, has been added to the retail price series since that is the first year for which MRCA data are available to the Bureau.

It will be seen that the prices of both regular and soluble coffee reached their respective highest and lowest points concurrently. In July 1954 regular coffee at retail reached $1.175 per pound, whereas in November and December 1962 and again in October 1963 the average price was 60.1 cents per pound, which was 57.4 cents or 48.9 percent lower. Soluble coffee also registered its monthly high of 65.5 cents per two-ounce equivalent unit in July 1954, whereas in July 1962 and in November 1963 it was at its lowest level, 28.1 cents per two-ounce equivalent unit — 37.4 cents or 57.1 percent lower than the peak figure.

The average annual retail price of regular coffee declined from 84.5 cents per pound in 1952 to 71.9 cents per pound in 1966, a drop of 12.6 cents or 14.9 percent. In the same period the price of soluble coffee declined from 51.0 cents per two-ounce equivalent unit in 1952 to 29.4 cents per unit in 1966, a decrease of 21.6 cents or 43.4 percent.

An examination of the average monthly retail price of regular coffee for the 1952-66 period was undertaken to determine whether a trend, cycle, or seasonal was evident. With respect to trend and cycle the comments made earlier in this chapter regarding import prices would apply. That is, trend and cycle, if they can be said to exist, are related to heavy damaging frosts in Brazil. Seasonal factors for retail prices follow the pattern for import prices quite closely, although within a narrower range. Like import prices, the mild seasonal shown is more related to supply than to demand. Seasonal factors for the retail prices of regular coffee for the 1952-66 period are given in the table below.

**UNITED STATES: SEASONAL FACTORS FOR THE RETAIL PRICE OF REGULAR COFFEE, BASED ON YEARS 1952-1966**

| Month | Factor |
|---|---|
| January | 1.001 |
| February | 0.995 |
| March | 1.000 |
| April | 1.005 |
| May | 1.007 |
| June | 1.010 |
| July | 1.012 |
| August | 1.010 |
| September | 1.000 |
| October | 0.988 |
| November | 0.987 |
| December | 0.985 |

NOTE: The factors total 12.000, thus an average month would be equal to 1.000. Each monthly factor may be read as a ratio to one, e.g., July = $\frac{1.012}{1.000}$ or July prices are 1.2 percent higher than those of an average month.

SOURCE: Department of Statistics and Economic Research, PACB.

It was noted earlier that changes in average retail prices of regular coffee lag behind changes in average import prices. The lag accounts in part for changes in the spread between the prices of green coffee and the prices at retail. Other factors, such as increases or decreases in the costs of processing, packaging and distribution, changes in the types and sources of coffee imported, and fluctuations in supply and demand also influence the spread. An illustration of the spread — the difference between the average annual retail prices of regular coffee and the average annual import prices of green coffee — in the period 1953-66 is shown in the table below.

**UNITED STATES: COMPARISON OF ANNUAL AVERAGE RETAIL AND IMPORT PRICES, 1953-1966**

(U.S. cents per pound)

|  | Retail (regular) | Import (green) | Spread Between Retail and Import |
|---|---|---|---|
| 1953 | 86.9 | 52.7 | 34.2 |
| 1954 | 105.6 | 65.7 | 39.9 |
| 1955 | 90.1 | 52.2 | 37.9 |
| 1956 | 93.7 | 51.2 | 42.5 |
| 1957 | 92.2 | 49.8 | 42.4 |
| 1958 | 82.1 | 43.9 | 38.2 |
| 1959 | 68.8 | 35.6 | 33.2 |
| 1960 | 66.2 | 34.3 | 31.9 |
| 1961 | 63.8 | 32.4 | 31.4 |
| 1962 | 61.7 | 30.4 | 31.3 |
| 1963 | 60.8 | 30.3 | 30.5 |
| 1964 | 72.5 | 39.6 | 32.9 |
| 1965 | 73.6 | 37.6 | 36.0 |
| 1966 | 71.9 | 36.6 | 35.3 |

SOURCE: *Department of Statistics and Economic Research, PACB, from retail price data supplied by Market Research Corporation of America and import price data published by the U.S. Department of Commerce.*

*Retail Prices, Vacuum- Vs. Bag-Packed Regular Coffee, 1958-66*

The table below shows average prices for vacuum-packed cans and bags of regular coffee in March, June, September, and December of each year from 1958 through 1966. For each year the four monthly figures were weighted by their respective quantities in order to provide an annual average.

**UNITED STATES: AVERAGE RETAIL PRICES OF REGULAR COFFEE, VACUUM-PACKED AND BAG-PACKED, SELECTED MONTHS, 1958-1966**

(U. S. cents per pound)

|  | 1958 | 1959 | 1960 | 1961 | 1962 | 1963 | 1964 | 1965 | 1966 |
|---|---|---|---|---|---|---|---|---|---|
| **Vacuum-Packed** | | | | | | | | | |
| March | 87.1 | 73.7 | 68.8 | 65.2 | 63.0 | 61.4 | 70.4 | 74.4 | 72.9 |
| June | 86.0 | N.A. | 68.9 | 65.1 | 63.4 | 62.1 | 75.6 | 74.3 | 73.4 |
| September | 82.4 | 70.4 | N.A. | 65.0 | 63.5 | 62.0 | 75.7 | 73.5 | 71.5 |
| December | 79.8 | 69.2 | N.A. | 63.5 | 61.2 | 62.7 | 75.3 | 72.6 | 70.5 |
| **Annual Average** | **83.8** | **N.A.** | **N.A.** | **64.7** | **62.7** | **62.1** | **74.3** | **73.7** | **72.0** |
| | | | | | | | | | |
| **Bag-Packed** | | | | | | | | | |
| March | 80.0 | 65.0 | 61.5 | 60.1 | 58.8 | 57.7 | 65.7 | 72.2 | 69.8 |
| June | 77.8 | N.A. | 61.6 | 60.4 | 59.0 | 57.6 | 73.1 | 73.4 | 70.5 |
| September | 73.3 | 60.3 | N.A. | 60.0 | 58.3 | 57.6 | 72.4 | 71.7 | 69.8 |
| December | 69.0 | 60.7 | N.A. | 58.9 | 56.9 | 58.6 | 72.4 | 71.2 | 70.0 |
| **Annual Average** | **75.0** | **N.A.** | **N.A.** | **59.8** | **58.2** | **57.9** | **70.9** | **71.2** | **70.0** |

*N.A.: Not available*

SOURCE: Market Research Corporation of America.
NOTE:   Annual averages have been estimated from the four months data available for each year.

*Futures Market*

Trader interest in the coffee futures options on the New York Coffee and Sugar Exchange in 1966 continued to wane, and turnover for the twelve-month period totaled 801,000 bags (3,204 lots) hardly more than one-fifth the volume traded in the preceding year. In the more active trading sessions in 1965 a total of 3,780,750,000 bags (15,123 lots) changed hands.

In comparison with the activity in 1964 when 8,220,750 bags (32,903 lots) were traded, the current year's total amounted to less than one tenth that of the former year. In the most active session in 1966 on March 25, only 62 lots were sold. Trading volume reached the peak of 164 lots in February. In contrast, turnover in July amounted to only two lots and in September four lots changed hands.

In the course of the year open interest in the coffee contracts declined from 517 lots to 234 lots — no more than ordinarily would be expected to be outstanding in one particular option in more active times in the past. Deliveries of actual coffee on the futures options amounted to 34,000 bags (136 lots). That quantity was less than one half the recorded total for 1965 which came to 77,500 bags (310 lots).

# NEW YORK COFFEE FUTURES
## HIGH, LOW & MONTHLY AVERAGE

NEAREST "B" OPTION

CENTS PER POUND

SALES

LOTS OF 250 BAGS

—1966—

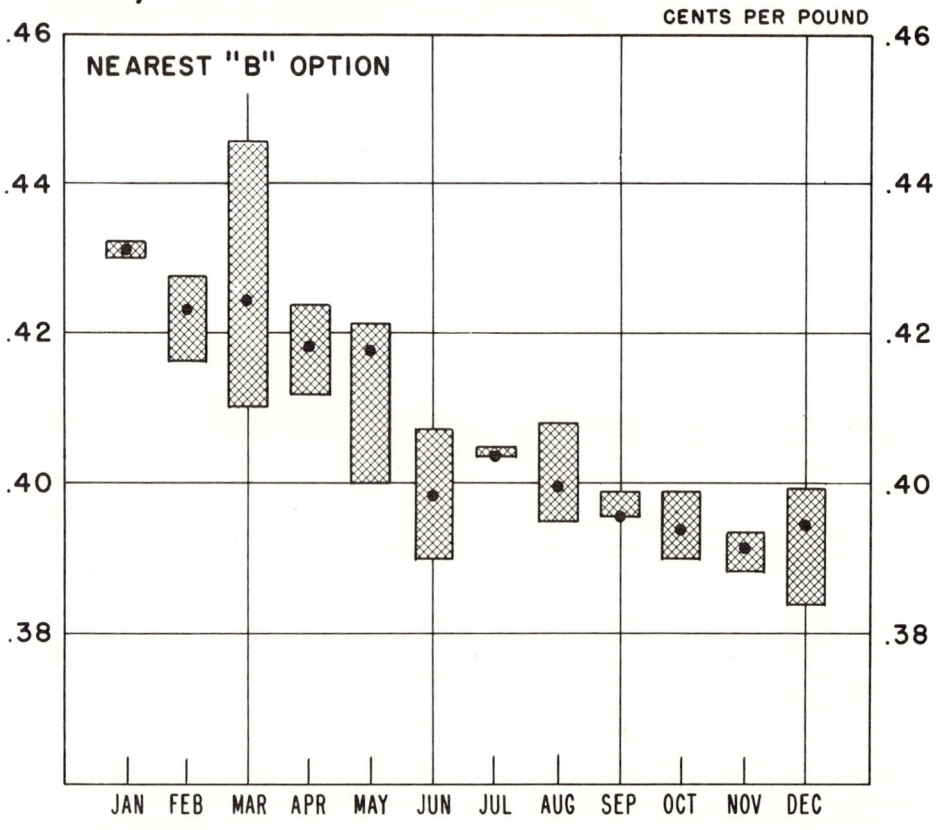

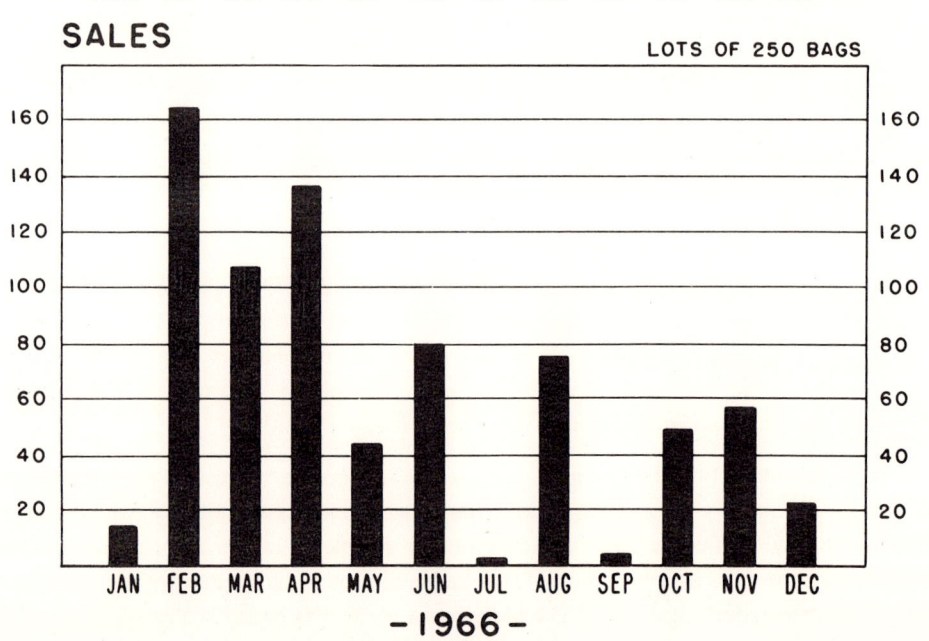

CHART 4

Futures prices trended downward following fairly closely the course of spot prices. The nearby "B" option for example was quoted in January at an average of 43.10 cents. That was the highpoint of the year. The gradual downtrend through the ensuing months brought that average to a lowpoint of 39.16 cents in November. From that trough there was a slight recovery to 39.46 cents in December.

## FUTURE SALES

| Contracts | 1966 Bags | 1966 Lots | 1965 Bags | 1965 Lots |
|---|---|---|---|---|
| Contract B* | 738,750 | 2,955 | 3,751,250 | 15,005 |
| Contract C** | — | — | 8,500 | 34 |
| Contract R*** | 62,250 | 249 | 21,000 | 84 |
| **Total** | **801,000** | **3,204** | **3,780,750** | **15,123** |

## DELIVERIES

| Contracts | 1966 Bags | 1966 Lots | 1965 Bags | 1965 Lots |
|---|---|---|---|---|
| Contract B* | 33,250 | 133 | 76,500 | 306 |
| Contract C** | — | — | — | — |
| Contract R*** | 750 | 3 | 1,000 | 4 |
| **Total** | **34,000** | **136** | **77,500** | **310** |

*N.B.: One lot = 250 bags.*

SOURCE: *New York Coffee and Sugar Exchange*

  *Basis Brazils
 **Basis coffees of Colombia, Mexico, El Salvador and Guatemala
***Basis Robustas

The prolonged slowdown in futures trading has caused a gradual reduction in the open position and at the same time spreads between futures options on the Exchange have become narrower. Ordinarily, in the futures market the more distant options tend to sell at discounts from the nearby position. As the time interval for delivery of the option lengthens various factors such as risks of the marketplace, financing costs, trends in demand, crop forecasts, supply prospects, and other imponderables are discounted. The magnitudes of those spreads mirror the consensus of the coffee trade concerning the outlook for the market over the time interval represented by the futures options. Contracts on the New York Coffee and Sugar Exchange are sold for delivery up to 12 and 13 months from the date of sale. The maximum discount for a futures delivery 12 or 13 months hence declined from a level around nine cents per pound to less than two cents per pound at the end of 1966.

### NEW YORK COFFEE AND SUGAR EXCHANGE
### MONTHLY AVERAGES OF THE NEARBY "B" OPTION
(cents per pound)

|   |   | Monthly Average | High | Low | Lots Traded |
|---|---|---|---|---|---|
| Jan. — 1965 | Mar. — 1965 | 44.58 | 45.50 | 43.20 | 632 |
| Feb. | Mar. | 45.47 | 45.95 | 44.60 | 309 |
| Mar. | Mar. | 45.70 | 49.00 | 43.75 | 247 |
| Apr. | May | 44.69 | 45.50 | 43.50 | 251 |
| May | May | 46.70 | 49.95 | 44.45 | 222 |
| June | July | 45.43 | 46.30 | 44.80 | 365 |
| July | July | 45.62 | 46.50 | 44.25 | 114 |
| Aug. | Sept. | 44.68 | 45.55 | 43.20 | 283 |
| Sept. | Sept. | 44.00 | 45.15 | 42.90 | 130 |
| Oct. | Dec. | 42.90 | 43.50 | 42.40 | 225 |
| Nov. | Dec. | 43.60 | 43.95 | 43.00 | 283 |
| Dec. | Dec. — 1965 | 43.53 | 43.90 | 43.01 | 131 |
| Jan. — 1966 | Mar. — 1966 | 43.10 | 43.20 | 43.00 | 14 |
| Feb. | Mar. | 42.32 | 42.75 | 41.60 | 164 |
| Mar. | Mar. | 42.45 | 44.53 | 41.00 | 107 |
| Apr. | May | 41.81 | 42.35 | 41.16 | 137 |
| May | May | 41.78 | 42.10 | 40.00 | 44 |
| June | July | 39.87 | 40.71 | 39.00 | 80 |
| July | July | 40.40 | 40.50 | 40.50 | 2 |
| Aug. | Sept. | 39.98 | 40.80 | 39.50 | 75 |
| Sept. | Sept. | 39.56 | 39.90 | 39.75 | 4 |
| Oct. | Dec. | 39.39 | 39.90 | 39.00 | 49 |
| Nov. | Dec. | 39.16 | 39.35 | 38.82 | 57 |
| Dec. | Dec. — 1966 | 39.46 | 39.95 | 38.40 | 22 |

The widespread disinterest among traders and speculators which has caused the attrition in coffee futures trading, has been ascribed by commentators in the trade in part to operation of the International Coffee Agreement. In the past several years that accord, through seasonal redistribution of trade, has been an important influence in working to eliminate or at least minimize the volatile short-term fluctuations that historically had characterized the coffee market. Another factor cited in certain quarters was the fact that some major producing nations lately have resorted to direct

## NEW YORK COFFEE AND SUGAR EXCHANGE
## AVERAGE DISCOUNTS IN THE B CONTRACT, 1965-1966

(in U. S. cents per pound)

|  | 1965 |  |  |  |  |  |  |  |  |  |  |  | 1966 |  |  |  |  |  |  |  |  |  |  |  |
|---|---|---|---|---|---|---|---|---|---|---|---|---|---|---|---|---|---|---|---|---|---|---|---|---|---|
| Option | Jan. | Feb. | Mar. | Apr. | May | June | July | Aug. | Sept. | Oct. | Nov. | Dec. | Jan. | Feb. | Mar. | Apr. | May | June | July | Aug. | Sept. | Oct. | Nov. | Dec. |
| May | -1.03 | -1.03 | -2.49 | — | | | | | | | | | | | | | | | | | | | | |
| July | -2.56 | -2.05 | -4.69 | -2.99 | -4.13 | — | | | | | | | | | | | | | | | | | | |
| September | -4.00 | -3.35 | -6.46 | -5.29 | -7.44 | -2.33 | -1.93 | — | | | | | | | | | | | | | | | | |
| December | -4.74 | -4.20 | -7.35 | -6.26 | -8.45 | -4.47 | -3.98 | -1.96 | -1.35 | — | | | | | | | | | | | | | | |
| March 1966 | — | — | -8.04 | -7.00 | -9.23 | -5.55 | -5.42 | -3.18 | -2.51 | -1.65 | -1.03 | -0.43 | -0.05 | — | | | | | | | | | | |
| May | — | — | — | — | -9.64 | -6.47 | -6.46 | -4.01 | -2.93 | -2.16 | -1.56 | -1.09 | -0.74 | -0.87 | -1.30 | — | | | | | | | | |
| July | — | — | — | — | — | -6.95 | -4.51 | -3.26 | -2.49 | -2.03 | -1.67 | -1.27 | -1.67 | -2.61 | -1.26 | -0.76 | — | | | | | | | |
| September | — | — | — | — | — | — | — | -3.52 | -2.86 | -2.55 | -2.14 | -1.78 | -2.28 | -3.49 | -2.40 | -1.54 | -0.10 | -0.25 | — | | | | | |
| December | — | — | — | — | — | — | — | — | — | -2.64 | -2.29 | -2.66 | -4.31 | -3.31 | -2.59 | -1.10 | -1.05 | -0.48 | -0.53 | — | | | | |
| March 1967 | — | — | — | — | — | — | — | — | — | — | — | — | -5.04 | -4.12 | -3.50 | -2.10 | -1.78 | -1.39 | -1.47 | -1.13 | -0.76 | -0.68 | | |
| May | — | — | — | — | — | — | — | — | — | — | — | — | — | — | -3.97 | -2.39 | -2.16 | -1.77 | -2.09 | -1.60 | -1.20 | -1.02 | | |
| July | — | — | — | — | — | — | — | — | — | — | — | — | — | — | — | -2.52 | -2.17 | -2.68 | -2.09 | -1.66 | -1.28 | | | |
| September | — | — | — | — | — | — | — | — | — | — | — | — | — | — | — | — | — | — | — | -2.30 | -2.24 | -1.67 | | |

selling through official entities. Coffee exports from those sources thereby are taken out of the traditional channels of trade. The quantity of coffee available for free trading is reduced and there is less necessity for hedging operations in the futures market by local importers, dealers and roasters who formerly had dealt as free agents in the coffees affected.

Another important factor of no mean consequence which has diverted traders' attention from the New York futures market is the highly-successful operation of the *robusta* futures market in London. The ease of modern long-distance communication enables traders and speculators in New York to operate on the London Terminal Market with the same facility with which they can transact business on the New York Exchange. The heavy daily turnover on the London Terminal Market enables traders to operate thereon with complete assurance that they can either take positions in coffee futures or liquidate their holdings of options quickly at or near prevailing levels. Astute traders quite possibly can engage in limited hedging operations utilizing the *robusta* futures, because the extreme short-run volatility of coffee prices has been absent from the price structure of the commodity over most of the period in which the International Coffee Agreements have been operative. That semblance of relative stability has resulted in very slow changes in the differentials between growths and types in the spot market. Coffee men who specialized in *arabicas* therefore can operate in the *robusta* futures market to a certain extent to hedge their positions in actual coffee.

Some observers in the trade have commented on the fact that the futures options as presently constituted have too narrow a base in relation to the structure of the green-coffee market. The quality standards set for coffee deliverable on contracts on the Exchange are too restrictive. The basis for trading on the Exchange therefore is limited to a relatively small proportion of the green coffee traded in the actual market. In some quarters of the coffee trade, mention is made of the contract traded on the New York Cocoa Exchange which permits the tender of all grades and growths within the limits of certain minimum specifications. An all-inclusive coffee contract such as one in use for cocoa, on which all types and growths of coffee permitted entry into this country by the Food and Drug Administration, would be deliverable at specified discounts from a standard growth (e.g. Colombian MAMS) and might hold appeal for a much broader cross section of coffee traders and commodity speculators. Certainly, such a trading medium with its broad coverage of the local commerce in coffee would provide better opportunities for hedging by buyers and sellers. In any event, there is need to generate interest among outside speculators as well as in the coffee trade in order to form a broadly based large volume futures market. Once assured of sufficient liquidity, traders and speculators can be encouraged to participate in the coffee futures market.

# World Production

Crop developments in the various producing countries and regions described in this section are based on data published by the Foreign Agricultural Service (FAS) of the United States Department of Agriculture (USDA). Information on the world coffee crop published by that agency constitute the only comprehensive world-wide appraisal available on a current and periodic basis. Those exhaustive crop estimates have been published over a period of many years and therefore comprise not only an overall evaluation of world coffee output but also statistical series of long standing. Four crop estimates are issued each year in June, September, December and March.

Two separate yet complementary sets of estimates are set forth in the FAS bulletins; those are for total production and for exportable production. Differences derived therefrom constitute the FAS estimates of domestic consumption in each producing country.

It is a well-known fact that crop estimates as a rule, even in highly developed economies, vary widely from one source to another. Moreover, those estimates often differ greatly at various points during the growing season.

In the past several years the International Coffee Organization has made a major effort to assemble and tabulate detailed statistics on the coffee industry in the producing countries. Data processing facilities were set up at the headquarters of the ICO in London to compile systematically past and current data submitted by the member countries. However, much work needs to be done in the producing areas to modernize reporting procedures, set up administrative apparatus and to train requisite technical and professional personnel. Until the reporting systems are organized and begin to function smoothly, gaps in the statistical information obtained by the ICO are inevitable. For these reasons the FAS data probably will remain the only complete and consistent estimates of the world coffee crop in the immediate future.

*Areas of World Coffee Production*

The three major species of coffee are found in the tropical belt between the Tropic of Cancer and the Tropic of Capricorn. Coffee trees can yield beans when cultivated at altitudes from sea level up to 6,000 feet, but the highest-quality beans are grown on mountainous slopes 4,500 to 6,000 feet above sea level. The *arabica* species, which accounts for about 70 percent of the coffee taken by the importing nations of the world, accounts for all the Western Hemisphere outturn with the exception of part of the crop in Trinidad and Tobago. In the Eastern Hemisphere the East African highland region (except Uganda) and the Arabian peninsula produce mainly *arabicas*. A substantial proportion of the Indian crop is also *arabica*. *Robustas*

**VOLUME OF WORLD PRODUCTION OF EXPORTABLE COFFEE**

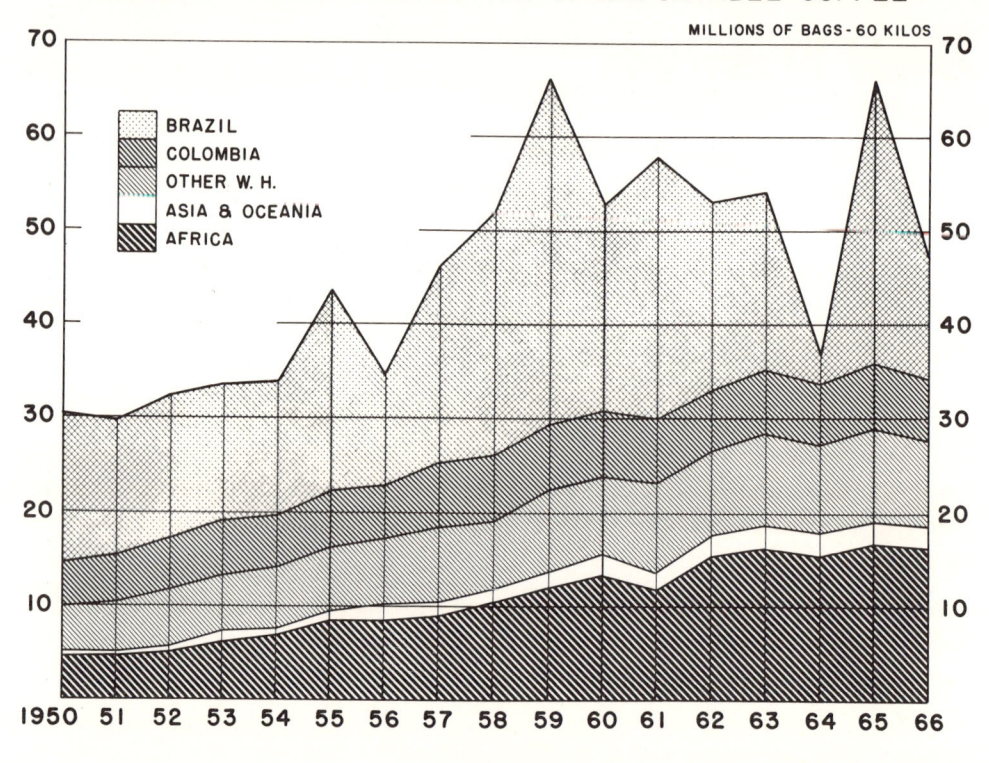

[Chart 5: Area chart showing millions of bags (60 kilos) from 1950 to 1966, with categories: Brazil, Colombia, Other W. H., Asia & Oceania, Africa]

CHART 5

are the main variety of coffee cultivated in Indonesia, the islands of Oceania, Madagascar, and West Africa.

Optimum temperatures for coffee cultivation range about the average annual temperature of 65° to 75°F. (18° to 24°C.), but deviations outside this range may be tolerated to some extent. Thus *arabica* is somewhat more resistant to lower temperatures, while *liberica* and *robusta* species are capable of withstanding greater heat, provided sunlight is adequately diffused. Rainfall is essential in coffee cultivation and ideally should total 70 to 80 inches annually. The plant may survive prolonged dry spells (generally not exceeding three months) provided humidity is present in the atmosphere. Although coffee cultivation requires adequate sunlight, shade is also needed to cool the soil around the plants. To secure shade for at least part of the day, hillsides are preferred as sites for cultivation.

Soils of a powdery consistency or clay-like composition are considered ideal and constitute the most favorable environment for plant cultivation. For this reason gently rising slopes covered by volcanic debris are often sought as locales for coffee plantations. Characteristic soils are generally of brown, chocolate or red color. High potash content and sufficient humus cover are necessary to insure healthy growth, although soils low in phosphates may be utilized as secondary sites. Chart 5 shows the major coffee producing regions in the world.

*Trend of World Exportable Production*

The aggregate volume of green coffee produced for export in the 1966-67 coffee year is expected to reach 47.3 million bags. That figure represents 75.4 percent of estimated total output. The Eastern Hemisphere is expected to account for 39.3 percent of total world exportable coffee. African growers probably will account for 16.1 million bags or approximately 34.2 percent, while producers in Asia and Oceania are expected to supply 2.4 million bags or 5.1 percent of the current harvest.

The contraction in the world exportable outturn this season reflects for the most part a relatively small crop of 13.0 million bags in Brazil. This pronounced decline in Brazilian outturn may be attributed to the combined effects of a number of factors. Under normal circumstances a downward adjustment in the export crop would be anticipated since 1966-67 might be considered to be an "off-year". Another factor of considerable importance is the current and cumulative effect of Brazil's ambitious tree eradication program. Adverse weather and pestilential conditions affecting output in Brazil's major coffee-growing states also may have contributed to the reduced size of the current year's export crop.

Lower exportable outturn has characterized other Latin-American harvests. This season Costa Rica, El Salvador, Nicaragua and Panama are expected to register small gains. Member entities of the Pan-American Coffee Bureau will contribute approximately 28.7 million bags to the world exportable total. That represents a decline of 38.9 percent from the level attained in the preceding season. Except for the extremely small exportable output registered in 1964-65 which in the main reflected the crop disaster in Brazil, the current harvest is the poorest since 1956-57.

Outturn during a ten-year span ending in 1966-1967 exhibited an erratic pattern. Examination of the crop pattern over the past ten years reveals alternating peaks and troughs. Variations in output are, of course, strongly influenced by the fortunes of the Brazilian crop. As the largest producer by far, its harvests largely determine the level of output of the region as a whole. Modern agricultural technology gradually is assuming importance as a mitigating factor reducing the volatility of the production cycles. But technology cannot entirely compensate for the vicissitudes of natural phephenomena, especially in the tropics.

Eastern Hemisphere production will fall somewhat short of the record crop registered in the preceding harvest, but it will be the third largest outturn for growers in that area since 1950. Production in that hemisphere is placed at 18.6 million bags, a 2.8 percent contraction from the 1965-66 highpoint. It is estimated that the Eastern Hemisphere will account for 39.3 percent of total new-crop export availabilities.

In the seven-year span 1960-1966 the Western Hemisphere contributed 67.1 percent of the aggregate exportable coffee crop, while Eastern Hemisphere production comprised 32.9 percent of the world total. Similarly in the preceding seven-year interval (1953-1959) a breakdown of world exportable coffee production by region puts the Western Hemisphere contribution at 74.1 percent, and the Eastern Hemisphere's share at 25.9 percent. Thus Eastern Hemisphere exportable outturn has increased its percentage of total world exportable production while the Western Hemisphere has experienced a concomitant loss.

Producers in Africa will have 16.1 million bags for export from the current crop: — that figure represents a decline of approximately 600,000 bags or 3.6 percent from the all-time high recorded last year. Production in Asia and Oceania is expected to show an almost imperceptible increase to 2.4 million bags.

*Estimates of World Exportable Production*

The fourth estimate of the U.S. Department of Agriculture is published each year in March. During nine-months' lapse of time between the issuance of the first and fourth estimates considerable adjustments are made as conditions change and as the new information is received. The fourth estimate is still not considered definitive and is revised over subsequent periods as more refined data are made available.

**ESTIMATES OF WORLD EXPORTABLE PRODUCTION OF GREEN COFFEE, 1966-67**

(thousands of 60-kilo bags)

|  | First Estimate | Second Estimate | Third Estimate | Fourth Estimate |
|---|---|---|---|---|
| Brazil | 20,600 | 22,000 | 13,600 | 13,000 |
| Colombia | 6,660 | 7,800 | 6,560 | 6,560 |
| Other Western Hemisphere | 10,049 | 14,253 | 9,677 | 9,115 |
| Africa | 16,320 | 16,884 | 16,406 | 16,151 |
| Asia and Oceania | 2,337 | 4,247 | 2,437 | 2,437 |
| **Total** | **55,966** | **65,184** | **48,680** | **47,263** |

SOURCE: *FAS, World Agricultural Production and Trade, June, September and December, 1965 and March 1966.*

As can be seen from the above table, the range between the first and fourth estimates for the current year, 56.0 and 47.3 million bags is quite substantial. This variance is largely due to failure of Brazil's exportable crop to fulfill early optimistic reports. Differentials between the high estimate and the low figure were even more disparate. Most of the early overstatement was confined to Western Hemisphere producers. Estimates of exportable production in the Eastern Hemisphere ranged between 21.1 million and 18.6 million bags.

*Brazil*

Recent trade reports indicate a rather substantial decline in Brazil's exportable production. In contrast to the 1965-66 outturn of 30.2 million bags, the current crop year will yield 13.0 million bags for the export trade. That decrease of 54 percent from the level of the previous year may be attributed to severe climatic and pestilential conditions particularly in the important coffee-growing state of Paraná, the possibility of this being an "off-year" after a heavy crop last season, and the cumulative effects of Brazil's program of tree eradication.

Four states — Paraná, São Paulo, Minas Gerais and Espirito Santo — together produce 97 percent of Brazil's coffee. The internal composition of regional growers has undergone recent change. In the crop year 1950-51, for example, production in São Paulo exceeded the combined output of Minas Gerais and Paraná. Since 1958-59, however, production in Paraná has climbed rapidly making it the largest producer while in the most recent years output in Minas Gerais has fallen to a poor third, behind Paraná and São Paulo. In 1965-66 these two states accounted for more than 87 percent of the nation's exportable coffee output.

Geographically Paraná is the most southerly of Brazil's large coffee-growing states and lies mostly below the Tropic of Capricorn, generally termed the southern boundary of world coffee cultivation. As a consequence, Paraná is subject to cold spells and frost emanating from the Southern Hemisphere's temperate zone, as well as from intrusions of antarctic air masses. As is evident from the following table, any extreme variation in year-to-year production in Parana and São Paulo because of their predominance is clearly reflected in Brazilian aggregate output. Recently the Paraná crop has frequently been affected by severe winter frost, summer drought and insect damage. The hardiness and recuperative powers of these coffee trees are demonstrated by Paraná's record in bringing forth from 40 to 60 percent of Brazil's export outturn since 1959-60, despite those natural setbacks.

Activities of the Executive Group for the Rationalization of Coffee Production (GERCA) have been directed toward the eradication of marginal trees that are poor producers and the substitution of other agricultural crops on the land thus freed for more general cultivation. Brazil has supported this movement since 1962 when the original plan was proposed. The avowed purpose of the diversification plan has been the eventual elimination of two billion trees representing a potential annual harvest of more than twelve million bags.

## BRAZIL: PRODUCTION OF GREEN COFFEE BY STATE

(Thousands of 60-Kilo bags)
1950-1966

| Crop Year | Paraná Bags | Paraná Percent | São Paulo Bags | São Paulo Percent | Minas Gerais Bags | Minas Gerais Percent | Espirito Santo Bags | Espirito Santo Percent | Rio de Janeiro Bags | Rio de Janeiro Percent | Other Bags | Other Percent | Total Bags |
|---|---|---|---|---|---|---|---|---|---|---|---|---|---|
| 1950-51 | 4,026 | 24.0 | 8,118 | 48.5 | 2,751 | 16.4 | 1,388 | 8.3 | 210 | 1.2 | 261 | 1.6 | 16,754 |
| 1951-52 | 2,843 | 18.9 | 6,261 | 41.7 | 3,374 | 22.5 | 2,040 | 13.6 | 324 | 2.1 | 179 | 1.2 | 15,021 |
| 1952-53 | 5,048 | 31.4 | 7,185 | 44.6 | 1,843 | 11.4 | 1,530 | 9.5 | 208 | 1.3 | 286 | 1.8 | 16,100 |
| 1953-54 | 3,198 | 21.1 | 6,162 | 40.7 | 3,372 | 22.3 | 1,828 | 12.1 | 235 | 1.6 | 353 | 2.3 | 15,148 |
| 1954-55 | 1,337 | 9.2 | 7,333 | 50.5 | 3,172 | 21.9 | 1,848 | 12.7 | 287 | 2.0 | 535 | 3.7 | 14,512 |
| 1955-56 | 6,306 | 28.6 | 9,268 | 42.0 | 3,743 | 17.0 | 2,048 | 9.3 | 231 | 1.0 | 468 | 2.1 | 22,064 |
| 1956-57 | 2,178 | 17.4 | 6,019 | 48.0 | 1,930 | 15.4 | 1,561 | 12.4 | 160 | 1.3 | 687 | 5.5 | 12,535 |
| 1957-58 | 4,731 | 21.9 | 9,538 | 44.1 | 3,696 | 17.1 | 2,505 | 11.6 | 157 | 0.7 | 999 | 4.6 | 21,628 |
| 1958-59 | 8,590 | 32.0 | 10,697 | 39.9 | 4,236 | 15.8 | 2,572 | 9.6 | 247 | 0.9 | 464 | 1.8 | 26,806 |
| 1959-60 | 20,691 | 46.9 | 15,620 | 35.4 | 4,501 | 10.2 | 1,914 | 4.3 | 361 | 0.8 | 1,043 | 2.4 | 44,130 |
| 1960-61 | 14,320 | 48.0 | 8,242 | 27.6 | 3,475 | 11.6 | 3,102 | 10.4 | 238 | 0.8 | 471 | 1.6 | 29,848 |
| 1961-62 | 17,942 | 50.0 | 11,558 | 32.2 | 3,600 | 10.0 | 1,796 | 5.0 | 287 | 0.8 | 677 | 2.0 | 35,860 |
| 1962-63 | 18,032 | 62.8 | 4,999 | 17.4 | 2,488 | 8.7 | 2,405 | 8.4 | 281 | 1.0 | 498 | 1.7 | 28,703 |
| 1963-64 | 9,157 | 39.5 | 9,579 | 41.4 | 2,165 | 9.4 | 1,576 | 6.8 | 167 | 0.7 | 509 | 2.2 | 23,153 |
| 1964-65 | 7,146 | 39.5 | 6,821 | 37.8 | 1,799 | 10.0 | 1,698 | 9.4 | 142 | 0.8 | 457 | 2.5 | 18,063 |
| 1965-66 | 21,046 | 55.9 | 11,798 | 31.3 | 2,835 | 7.5 | 1,406 | 3.7 | 93 | 0.3 | 494 | 1.3 | 37,672 |
| 1966-67* | 7,780 | 44.2 | 5,113 | 29.1 | 2,716 | 15.4 | 1,493 | 8.5 | 109 | 0.6 | 385 | 2.2 | 17,596 |

SOURCE: *Anuario Estatístico 1965, Departamento Economico, Instituto Brasileiro do Café*

\* 1966-67 figures obtained from *Comunicado 34/67, Instituto Brasileiro do Café*

Major emphasis is placed on tree destruction in regions subject to recurrent drought and frost. Eradication of such marginal trees, observers feel, will result in a more stable and higher-quality crop yield. Between 1962 and the end of 1965 it is estimated that slightly more than 716 million coffee trees have been eliminated. Farmers have been indemnified 11 to 22 cents for each tree taken out of cultivation. The disbursement procedure transfers one-third of the monies to the planter when the trees are leveled, and one-third when the land has been cultivated and seeded with an alternate crop, with the final payment coming no more than two months later. Farmers are encouraged by government price supports to plant sunflowers, rice, maize, soybeans, peanuts and castor beans. It is anticipated that the new plantings will be utilized mainly for domestic consumption and hopefully, for exports as well. The provision of incentives to small-holders offers marginal producers an opportunity to earn more from new cultivation than was possible in inefficient modes of coffee production.

One informed commentator, reporting favorably on the effort of the government to encourage conversion to diversified agriculture, stated:

> To spur the trend, the Brizilian government left unchanged its minimum guaranteed price for coffee, despite the smaller crop, and, in addition, raised its quality standards for coffee that will qualify for price supports.
>
> To be sure, the program is expensive. A minimum of the equivalent of $70 million has been earmarked for the first year of the enlarged program, which started last July. The money comes from revenue retained by the Brazilian government from coffee exports.
>
> To expand storage space, Brazil is spending about $10 million for new warehouses which will have a capacity of 15 million bags. Brazil is modernizing all its warehouses to better maintain quality and to adapt them to other products as the coffee surplus dwindles.[1]

Another important development which has taken place in Brazil is the progress made by the local soluble coffee industry. In 1966 exports of the fledgling soluble coffee industry totaled 198,843 60-kilo bags of green equivalent valued at slightly more than $9.5 million. Of this amount, 191,400 bags valued at $9.1 million entered the United States.

*Colombia*

The fourth and most recent estimate prepared by the FAS of total coffee production for the marketing year 1966-67 indicates that 7.8 million bags should be produced, of which approximately 6.6 million bags will be sent into export com-

---

[1] Walter V. Woodworth, "Coffee Men See Output Curbs as Solution to World Surfeit, Brazilian Plan as Model," *Wall Street Journal*, January 31, 1967

merce. This "off-year" figure is only slightly less than the exportable yield from the preceding harvest. In the past decade the level of Colombia's exportable output has ranged between 6.0 and 8.0 million bags averaging about 11 percent of total world output. In the current year Colombia is expected to account for 13.9 percent of world exportable production.

The National Federation of Coffee Growers has continued to devise new methods leading to improvements in Colombia's agricultural economy.[2] Long-range planning has proceeded with a view toward introducing a measure of crop diversification. Incentives have been introduced whereby farmers are encouraged to uproot poor yielding coffee trees in areas unsuited to their cultivation, and to substitute selected crops more amenable to local soil and climatic conditions. Colombia also has been foremost among those nations interested in research and development of storage facilities for bulk coffee. Some of the most modern storage units are to be found in the vicinity of Bello where sixty concrete and steel silos 165 feet high, with a capacity equivalent to 600,000 bags are expected to become operational in mid-1967.

## OTHER WESTERN HEMISPHERE

The remaining Western Hemisphere countries are expected to produce an exportable crop of 9.1 million bags in 1966-67. That represents a decrease of approximately 900,000 bags or 9.0 percent from the record outturn of 10.0 million bags produced in the preceding year. Despite this recent downtrend, these countries have continued to increase their share of world exportable production since 1959-60; their share reached 19.2 percent in the current year compared with 15.7 percent in the previous year and 25.5 percent in 1964-65.

### Mexico

In most recent years the exportable coffee crop in Mexico has fluctuated about the 1.5 million bag level. For several years Mexico's export crop has varied from a low of 1.25 million bags recorded in 1962-63 to a high of 1.9 million bags produced in 1963-64. The relatively stable production pattern is testimony to the success the Mexican coffee economy has achieved in dampening the volatility of the two-year production cycle.

The Mexican Coffee Institute has devoted much attention to promotional efforts effectively designed to increase domestic consumption of coffee beverage. At this writing Mexicans consume coffee at the rate of 1.25 million bags annually, a threefold increase in the past decade.

---

[2] Cf *Annual Coffee Statistics*, 1965, pp. 36-7.

In terms of agricultural exports coffee generally ranks second in value to cotton and accounts for roughly one-fifth of the value of total exports. In recent years Mexico has achieved rapid expansion in the industrial sector and, therefore the dependence on coffee export revenue to some degree has lessened. Mexican exportable outturn accounts for 3.2 percent of total world production.

*El Salvador*

Recent FAS estimates place El Salvador's current-year exportable crop at 1.8 million bags — an increase of approximately 100,000 bags or 5.9 percent over the preceding year's production level. This increase as an "off-year" reflects not only the effect of adverse weather on last year's harvest, but also the improvement in production practices which lessen the effects of the biennial production cycle.

The current exportable crop outturn is approximately 8.7 percent below the record outturn in 1964-65, and represents 3.7 percent of total world exportable coffee output.

*Guatemala*

Exportable production is expected to reach 1.5 million bags according to recent FAS estimates. That represents a decline of 16.7 percent from last year's record exportable outturn. In recent years Guatemala has introduced measures designed to lessen dependence on coffee exports by encouraging plantings of other crops. Current production probably has been influenced by damage wrought by the leaf miner which according to USDA reports last year, had defoliated as much as 90 percent of coffee trees at elevations 2,500 feet and below. The National Coffee Association of Guatemala has recognized the need to enlist entomologists and other scientific personnel in an attempt to eradicate the leaf miner in that country. The exportable crop in Guatemala is an estimated 3.1 percent of the world total.

*Honduras*

In 1966-67 the exportable coffee crop declined by 9.3 percent relative to the preceding year. At 340,000 bags Honduras will account for approximately 0.7 percent of the world total.

*Nicaragua*

Production for export is expected to reach 490,000 bags. This represents a 10.1 percent increase over the preceding year's crop. An important factor in that expansion has been the construction of a network of roads which facilitates the movement of coffee from the interior growing areas with a concomitant decrease in local marketing costs. Nicaragua is expected to contribute 1.0 percent to total world exportable output.

*Costa Rica*

Continued recovery from the low exportable yield of 600,000 bags in 1964-65 is indicated. The most recent estimate places Costa Rica's production at slightly more than 1.0 million bags or 13.9 percent higher than output in the preceding year. Costa Rica's coffee economy has achieved a healthy recovery from natural disasters which reduced the country's coffee crop in recent years. Insect damage which heretofore has played a major role in contributing to diminished export yield apparently has been contained. The estimated production figure for 1966-67 allocates to Costa Rica 2.2 percent of world production for the current season.

*Panama*

The current-year's export crop is expected to attain a level of 25,000 bags, roughly equal to previous recorded production highs. Panama is regarded as having a small but highly-efficient coffee agriculture.

*Cuba*

Domestic coffee production is considered adequate for internal consumption. Reports have been received of efforts to revitalize Cuba's lagging coffee economy. This country has not had any recent production available for export.

*Dominican Republic*

Exportable outturn in the Dominican Republic in 1966-67, an "off-year" in the production cycle, is expected to reach 395,000 bags. That represents a decrease of 60,000 bags or 13.1 percent from the previous year's output. Current production will account for 0.8 percent of total world production. An ICO Working Group has commented on the organization of that country's coffee economy:

> In the Dominican Republic there have been various official controls over coffee matters but they were all abolished by Decree No. 6743 of 6 June 1961 or by other laws. The first control was created by Law No. 324 of 10 September 1934 which declared that the control of the cultivation, production, milling and sale of coffee in all national territory was a matter of public concern. Decree No. 238 of 12 September 1942 established the principle that any person or company exporting coffee should first obtain an export license from the Coffee Defence Committee. The last of these controls was established by Decree No. 4699 of 6 April 1959 and provided for the control of purchase, sale, handling and distribution of coffee produced in the Dominican Republic; the Decree also fixed the price.
>
> Government departments and their functions: Law No. 5586 of 27 July 1961 created the General Administration of Coffee and Cocoa dependent upon the State Secretariat of Agriculture and its aims, powers and management were fixed. At present, and as a consequence of reorganization, it is called the Coffee and Cocoa Department.
>
> This Department has no say in the internal marketing of coffee except with regard to the control of roasting in order to prevent the adulteration of coffee for domestic consumption.

In external marketing, it is responsible for controlling sales prices and establishes minimum prices in line with those for Santos 4 contract ex-New York with the corresponding differentials for each type of Dominican coffee.

The Department is also required to check the quality of coffee exported and follow the set of regulations No. 7107 of 18 September 1961.

Other forms of internal organization: since 1965 there has existed the Federation of Provincial Coffee Associations embracing the main producers in the country. It must however be pointed out that this Association is still in the process of organization.

The Co-operative Credit and Development Institute promotes coffee co-operatives throughout the land and the Dominican Institute of Agrarian Services — a private organization — helps co-operatives, particularly with regard to marketing.

The Banco Agrícola maintains a close relationship with producers as it gives credit and technical assistance to its clients.

The Dominican Agrarian Institute is also connected with the coffee-growers because coffee is cultivated on its settlements and with the assistance of experts from the Institute.

Internal marketing policy: in the Dominican Republic coffee is marketed under a completely free system from the moment the harvested coffee enters the domestic market for processing and export.

This is because the sources of finance available to the country have been used for crops which the Government is interested in stimulating and which are mainly those in short supply.[3]

## Haiti

The quantity of coffee available for export during 1966-67 is expected to reach 325,000 bags, a decrease of approximately 80,000 bags or 19.8 percent from the preceding year.

## Ecuador

After two consecutive years of peak exportable production generated by favorable climatic conditions, excellent yields from new plantations and attractive incentive prices to producers, Ecuador's exportable production has tapered off to 640,000 bags. This represents a 100,000 bag drop from the approximate 750,000 bag level of the past two crop years when heavy crop yields were attributed to a vigorous reflowering of coffee trees previously damaged by prolonged drought. After a period of extremely low yield, or semi-dormancy, the affected trees, aided by heavy and well-timed precipitation characteristically achieved heavy yields. This situation is expected to be modified only slightly when presently high-yielding trees return to normal, while others still in the process of regeneration. Ecuador will account for 1.3 percent of total world production.

---

[3] Mission Report on Dominican Republic, Mission Report No. 4, 5 April 1967: ICO, London.

*Peru*

Recent FAS estimates place the magnitude of Peru's exportable outturn at 680,000 bags. This country's exportable crop has stabilized since 1964-65, following a period of steady expansion. In recent years higher prices paid to producers and easier credit terms have encouraged small growers to increase both yields and acreage. Offsetting this production increase somewhat has been a rise in domestic consumption of coffee beverage. Per capita coffee consumption has been estimated to have been increasing at a rate of five percent annually. In the current year Peru's share of the world market is expected to reach 1.4 percent.

*Venezuela*

The quantity of coffee available for export during 1966-67 is expected to decline slightly. The most recent estimate of 275,000 bags falls short of the previous outturn by 5.2 percent. Of late this country has made efforts to restrict acreage devoted to coffee cultivation, but improved crop yields, technical assistance to growers and easier credit extended to producers have acted to stabilize the exportable harvest around the 300,000 bag level.

## OTHERS (WESTERN HEMISPHERE)

The remaining coffee-producing countries in the Western Hemisphere are expected to produce 160,000 bags for export during the current year. Figures supplied by the FAS for some of those countries are given below.

### EXPORTABLE PRODUCTION
(60-kilo bags)

|  | 1963-64 | 1964-65 | 1965-66 | 1966-67 |
|---|---|---|---|---|
| Trinidad and Tobago | 68,000 | 72,000 | 40,000 | 45,000 |
| Puerto Rico | 45,000 | 25,000 | 25,000 | 25,000 |
| Paraguay | 45,000 | 40,000 | 60,000 | 30,000 |
| Bolivia | 20,000 | 20,000 | 30,000 | 35,000 |
| Jamaica | 16,000 | 16,000 | 11,000 | 6,000 |
| Surinam | 8,000 | 8,000 | 8,000 | 5,000 |
| Guyana | 4,000 | N.A. | N.A. | N.A. |
| Others | 44,000 | 27,000 | 14,000 | 14,000 |
| **Total Other Western Hemisphere** | 250,000 | 207,000 | 188,000 | 160,000 |

*N.A.: Not available*

**WESTERN HEMISPHERE COFFEE PRODUCTION...1966-67**

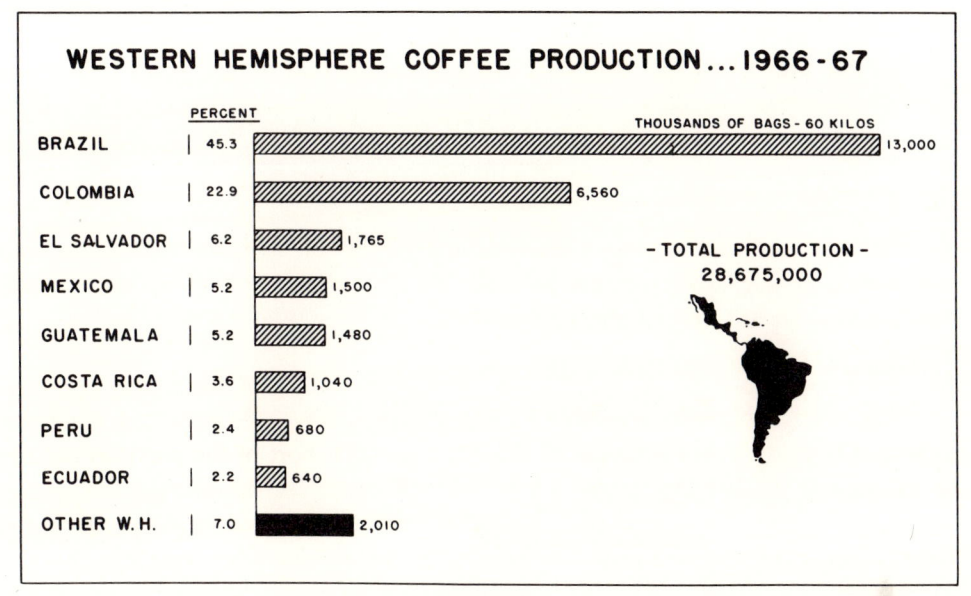

| | PERCENT | THOUSANDS OF BAGS - 60 KILOS |
|---|---|---|
| BRAZIL | 45.3 | 13,000 |
| COLOMBIA | 22.9 | 6,560 |
| EL SALVADOR | 6.2 | 1,765 |
| MEXICO | 5.2 | 1,500 |
| GUATEMALA | 5.2 | 1,480 |
| COSTA RICA | 3.6 | 1,040 |
| PERU | 2.4 | 680 |
| ECUADOR | 2.2 | 640 |
| OTHER W.H. | 7.0 | 2,010 |

– TOTAL PRODUCTION –
28,675,000

CHART 6

## AFRICA

The 1965-66 exportable estimate for Africa has been revised slightly downward by the FAS and now stands at 16,724,000 bags. The current crop, now estimated at 16,161,000 bags, will fall short of that amount by 3.4 percent. In view of the expected reduction in total exportable coffee for the world, Africa is expected to increase its share from 25.3 percent in 1965-66 to 34.2 percent in 1966-67.

### Angola

Angola is expected to be the leading volume producer of exportable coffee on the African continent in crop year 1966-67. Current outturn of 3,440,000 bags approaches dimensions of a new record output for this area. On the basis of the latest estimates Angola will contribute 7.2 percent of the world total. The Angolan product consists mainly of *robustas*.

### Ivory Coast

Recent FAS estimates indicate a 36.8 percent decline in exportable output from outturn in the preceding year. That represents an absolute decline of 1,665,000 bags from the record level of 4,500,000 bags attained the previous year. The Ivory Coast is one of the major coffee producers in Africa currently ranking as the second leading coffee exporter on that Continent, and as the fourth-ranking world producer. In crop year 1966-67 the Ivory Coast's exportable harvest will represent 6.0 percent of world total.

## AFRICAN COFFEE PRODUCTION... 1966-67

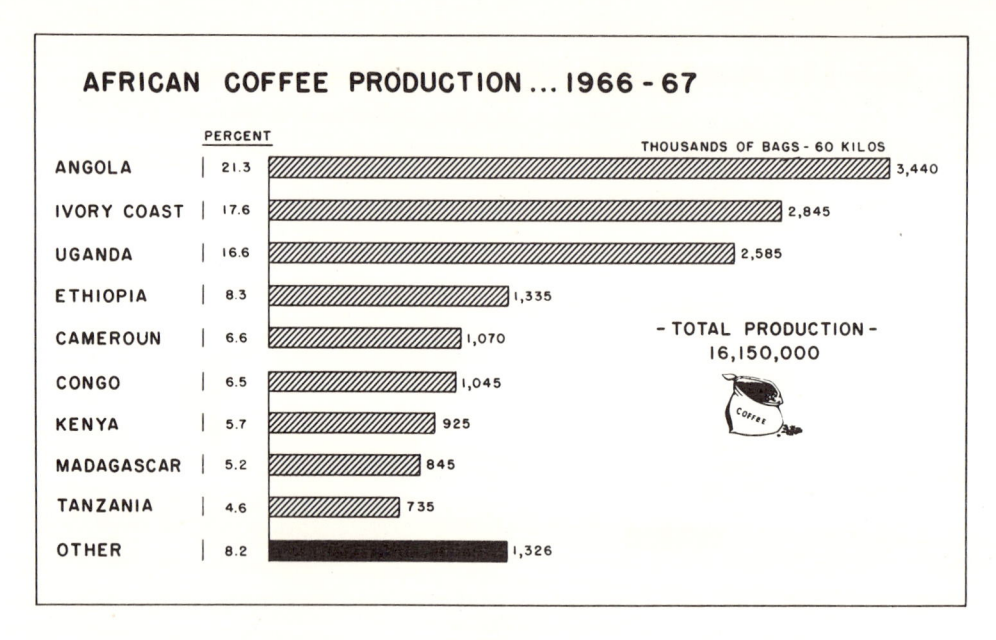

| Country | Percent | Thousands of Bags - 60 Kilos |
|---|---|---|
| ANGOLA | 21.3 | 3,440 |
| IVORY COAST | 17.6 | 2,845 |
| UGANDA | 16.6 | 2,585 |
| ETHIOPIA | 8.3 | 1,335 |
| CAMEROUN | 6.6 | 1,070 |
| CONGO | 6.5 | 1,045 |
| KENYA | 5.7 | 925 |
| MADAGASCAR | 5.2 | 845 |
| TANZANIA | 4.6 | 735 |
| OTHER | 8.2 | 1,326 |

- TOTAL PRODUCTION - 16,150,000

CHART 7

D. G. Williams[4] of the FAS describes diversification of the Ivory Coast's agricultural economy:

> Diversification of the Ivory Coast's agriculture, a major objective of the nation's current development plan, is moving steadily forward, and the outlook is for continued progress in the years ahead.
>
> Largest crops continue to be coffee and cocoa, with the Ivory Coast ranking third and fourth, respectively, in world production of these commodities.
>
> The diversification program, however, is de-emphasizing coffee, in which there is a world surplus, and emphasizing crops for which future marketing prospects are more favorable. These include oil palms, coconuts, rubber, cotton, and such already-important exports as bananas, pineapples, and tropical wood.
>
> At the same time, the country is attempting to increase rice production with the goal of eliminating imports and eventually exporting. This priority given to rice is important in view of threatening world food shortages. If goals are achieved, the Ivory Coast should be supplying its rice needs by the time world shortages reach critical stages. Additionally, self-sufficiency in rice will free normal foreign-exchange expenditures for imported rice, making more funds available for development.

### Uganda

Production is expected to reach 2,585,000 bags, which volume roughly approximates the most recent FAS estimates of the 1965-66 exportable harvest. Uganda main-

---
[4]Dudley G. Williams, "Ivory Coast Working to Diversify Its Agriculture," *Foreign Agriculture,* January 16, 1967, pp. 8-9.

tains its rank as the third leading African producer while contributing 6.0 percent of current total world production. Uganda is actively exploring the feasibility of widespread agricultural diversification. In an effort to reduce dependency on a single agricultural commodity that country is planning support programs designed to encourage substitute crops on land previously devoted to coffee cultivation. Uganda coffee production consists mainly of *robustas*.

*Burundi*

Production for export in Burundi will reach 220,000 bags in the current year. This represents a decline of 15,000 bags or 6.4 percent from the preceding year. In recent years governmental encouragement has enabled growers to raise total exportable production to over the 200,000 bag level. Burundi coffee is of the *arabica* variety.

*Rwanda*

Exportable production in Rwanda is expected to reach 145,000 bags, which approximates revised FAS estimates of this country's exportable harvest in the previous year. Rwanda also is primarily an *arabica* producer.

*Madagascar*

FAS reports indicate an increase in exportable production in Madagascar. Latest estimates place the current exportable crop at 845,000 bags — an increase of 120,000 bags or 16.6 percent over the previous season. That country now is producing in excess of 80 percent of the proposed long-term annual production goal (set for the 1973-1974 season) of 1,165,000 bags. There are approximately one-half million acres planted in coffee, almost all of which are devoted to the *robusta* variety.

*Ethiopia*

An exportable crop of 1,335,000 bags is predicted for Ethiopia during coffee year 1966-67. That quantity is 7.2 percent greater than the previous crop and approximately 2.8 percent of the world total. Government assistance for construction of highway and harbor facilities has allowed for freer access to areas hitherto deemed uneconomical for coffee marketing. Large tracts of coffee acreage previously left unharvested now are being tended by coffee farmers. That country is the largest consumer of coffee among African coffee producers and its usage is reported to be increasing. In Ethiopia coffee is appreciated as a basic food item as well as a beverage. Ethiopia is the original producer of *arabicas*.

*Guinea*

Exportable production of green coffee is expected to reach 135,000 bags in 1966-67, equivalent to the exportable total last year.

*Tanzania*

Recent FAS estimates indicate that this country will produce 735,000 bags in 1966-67, a decrease of 50,000 bags or 6.5 percent compared with the preceding year. Production in this country consists of both generic types, *arabicas* and *robustas*.

*Central African Republic*

The current exportable crop is expected to reach 195,000 bags; that quantity is about the same as the revised FAS estimate for the preceding crop year. Coffee grown in this country is of the *robusta* type.

*Togo*

Production for export is expected to reach 195,000 bags in the current year. This represents a decrease of 25,000 bags or almost 11.4 percent from the preceding year. Government programs have encouraged pest control and motivated growers to use more efficient methods of crop cultivation. The resultant effect should be toward improving future harvest yield. Coffee and cocoa variously alternate as Togo's main export commodities. An International Coffee Organization Mission visiting that country in April 1967 reported extensively on Togo's coffee economy:

> Developments in agricultural practices: a characteristic of the coffee stands is the very high tree density which is 1,600 per hectare [5] and even higher in the case of plantings outside the control of the extension services. Coffee is grown under natural shade, often too heavy. The high density and heavy shade act as a deterrent to high yields. This unfavorable environment coupled with low husbandry standards has contributed to the very pronounced two-year coffee cycles in Togo.
>
> Due to the lack of accurate figures on acreage, it is difficult to analyze yield figures. It is generally estimated that average yields vary from 150 kilos in the marginal (maritime) zone to 300-400 kilos in the "Plateau Zone". The overall average for 1965-66 — an "on" year — was about 340 kilos per hectare while in 1966-67 — an "off" year — it is expected to be only approximately 150 kilos per hectare (see table 7). Average production over the last 4 years (including two "off" and two "on" years) was 12,000 tons as against 9,600 tons for the 1958-62 average. Two-year averages indicate, however, that since 1963-64, a peak year, production has been declining.

|  | Two-Year Averages (thousand tons) |
|---|---|
| 1958-60 | 8.3 |
| 1959-61 | 7.2 |
| 1960-62 | 10.8 |
| 1961-63 | 9.3 |
| 1962-64 | 12.8 |
| 1963-65 | 13.5 |
| 1964-66 | 11.0 |
| 1965-67 | 9.5 |

---

[5] Approximately 1,000 in most other countries.

The declining trend can be attributed not so much to the aging of trees (which are generally less than 15 years old) but to the fact that most of the trees which have been planted between 1956 and 1960 are now at the end of their first bearing cycle and require regeneration. The Government is fully aware of the urgent need to rejuvenate these plantations and has taken steps in that direction. The Mission, which visited the main coffee growing areas around Atakpame and Palime, fully shares the views of the local coffee experts that yields will increase again as soon as rejuvenation has been carried out.

According to the Authorities, the present low level of husbandry is due to lack of financial means and falling coffee prices. The Mission is of the opinion that lack of proper extension facilities has been one other major cause for decreasing productivity.

No fertilizers are applied to coffee as yet, although the Government plans to encourage their application in small doses only when regeneration is carried out. Indeed, given the present husbandry techniques, or lack thereof, fertilizers have little effect during the production cycle. No coffee research work has been carried out until now. The Government has, however, recently concluded an agreement

### DISTRIBUTION OF WORLD EXPORTABLE PRODUCTION, 1966-1967

| Rank | Country | Exportable Production (thousands of 60-kilo bags) | Percent of World Total |
|---|---|---|---|
| 1 | Brazil | 13,000 | 27.5 |
| 2 | Colombia | 6,560 | 13.9 |
| 3 | Angola | 3,440 | 7.3 |
| 4 | Ivory Coast | 2,845 | 6.0 |
| 5 | Uganda | 2,585 | 5.5 |
| 6 | El Salvador | 1,765 | 3.7 |
| 7 | Indonesia | 1,640 | 3.5 |
| 8 | Mexico | 1,500 | 3.2 |
| 9 | Guatemala | 1,480 | 3.1 |
| 10 | Ethiopia | 1,335 | 2.8 |
| 11 | Cameroun | 1,070 | 2.3 |
| 12 | Congo | 1,045 | 2.2 |
| 13 | Costa Rica | 1,040 | 2.2 |
| 14 | Kenya | 925 | 2.0 |
| 15 | Malagasy Republic | 845 | 1.8 |
| 16 | Tanzania | 735 | 1.6 |
| 17 | Peru | 680 | 1.4 |
| 18 | Ecuador | 640 | 1.4 |
| 19 | India | 585 | 1.2 |
| 20 | Nicaragua | 490 | 1.0 |
|  | Others | 3,058 | 6.4 |
|  | **Total** | **47,263** | **100.0** |

SOURCE: FAS.

with the IFCC[6] which will start applied research programmes in the very near future. The Research Centre will be located at Tove near Palime. Research will mainly be concerned with improvement of husbandry techniques, more adequate insect and pest control and observation on new genetic material received from the IFCC-Cameroon.

*Congo (Kinshasa)*

Production of exportable coffee will expand to 1,045,000 bags in the current marketing year. That represents an increase of 95,000 bags or ten percent from the level of 1965-66. Production in the Congo represents 2.2 percent of world total. *Robustas* account for the major share of the crop, but a substantial volume of *arabicas* is produced in the eastern province of Kivu.

*Cameroun*

Recent FAS estimates indicate production of exportable coffee totaled 1,070,000 bags, an increase of 100,000 bags or 10.3 percent over output recorded in the preceding year. More than 80 percent of exportable coffee grown in this country is of the *robusta* variety. That country's share of total world market is expected to reach 2.2 percent.

*Kenya*

Exportable production is expected to rise by 70,000 bags or 8.1 percent to reach 925,000 bags in 1966-67. In the past few years growers have successfully eradicated the "coffee berry disease" and the country's exportable coffee production has shown sizeable increase. Kenya has set up a program designed to restrict coffee production. It is estimated that one million, or 20 percent of the coffee plants in Kenya nurseries are designated as surplus. Coffee production in Kenya is entirely of the *arabica* type.

## ASIA AND OCEANIA

The quantity of exportable green coffee produced in Asia and Oceania during 1966-67 is expected to attain a near-record level of 2,437,000 bags or 2.0 percent increase compared with the preceding year. In the current year the coffee growing nations of Asia and Oceania are expected to produce 5.1 percent of the world's exportable coffee.

*Indonesia*

The quantity of green coffee produced in Indonesia for the export trade during 1966-67 is estimated at 1.64 million bags, about equal to the preceding year's outturn. That quantity represents approximately 3.5 percent of the world's exportable coffee, and consists primarily of *robustas*.

---

[6] Institut Français du Café et du Cacao.

An ICO Mission to that country commented:[7]

> According to the latest estimates smallholder acreage increased by about 55,000 hectares between 1962 and 1965, an annual growth of about 7 percent. Estate acreage, on the contrary, has declined by 3,800 hectares or almost 10 percent. Robusta is produced on more than 90 percent of coffee acreage. Some high quality Arabica is produced in Java and Bali. Coffee is often interplanted with pepper, cloves, maize, etc. on smallholdings and forms only part of farm revenue. The Government has been promoting the development of co-operatives. In 1962 over 52,000 societies were in operation with over 9 million members, 2,747 being "producer" co-operatives with 263,000 members.
>
> The general use of fertilizers is increasing steadily. Expansion is, however, limited by availability. Imports of fertilizers rose from 228,000 tons in 1962 to 376,000 tons in 1965. They have since declined to the 200,000 ton level. Nitrogenous fertilizers are now being locally produced at Palembang, the annual output of 100,000 tons being all locally consumed. Heavy subsidies (up to 90 percent) existed for fertilizers until October 1966 when all were withdrawn. Fertilizers are applied mainly to food crops. Traditionally estate plantations were heavily fertilized but at present prices the practice has been suspended or reduced. No detailed figures are available of the use of fertilizers on coffee estates and smallholdings.

*India*

At current levels estimates of the 1966-67 exportable crop range to 585,000 bags. That figure represents a 17.0 percent gain over total outturn last year, and 1.2 percent of world exportable output. The Government has been actively promoting the cultivation of coffee. Coffee culture is now a major agricultural industry in South India, centered mainly in the states of Mysore, Madras and Kerala. India produces both *arabicas* and *robustas*. In a report issued March 30, 1967 an ICO Mission has reported:[8]

> The declared policy of the Indian authorities is to increase coffee production in order to meet their future internal requirements, and improve export earnings derived from coffee.
>
> They are confident of achieving the production goal of 1,416,700 bags (85,000 tons) fixed for the end of the 4th Development Plan (1970-71) primarily by encouraging productivity and only secondarily by expanding acreage. Measures to encourage productivity include:
>
> (a) an internal price policy aimed at guaranteeing a fair return to growers;
>
> (b) Credit facilities: these are available for large and small growers from various sources (e.g. the Coffee Development Fund, private banks and the Agricultural Refinance Corporations) and the authorities, who have the matter under constant review, are prepared to take steps to improve cheap credit facilities still further;

---
[7] Mission Report on Indonesia, Mission Report No. 1, 30 March 1967: ICO, London.
[8] Mission Report on India, Mission Report No. 1, 30 March 1967, ICO., London.

(c) Technical assistance: this is available for the numerous small coffee farmers; the Extension Team under the Research Department is now fully staffed.

Achievement of the production target will depend largely on the success of these incentives since production at the end of the 3rd Development Plan at 63,000 tons was lagging behind the fixed objective of 75,000 tons.

Diversification: In the view of the Authorities this is a problem which does not apply to India because (i) coffee represents only 0.001 of land under cultivation, (ii) it is grown only in mountain areas where substitute crops cannot be produced with the same profitability, and (iii) India's agriculture is already most highly diversified.

On the contrary, they consider the real problem is the aging of the trees. A plan for facilitating the replanting of the remaining 40 percent of old low productive Arabica trees is now under consideration at Central Government level.

*Yemen*

Exportable production of 50,000 bags is estimated in Yemen during the crop year 1966-67. This represents a decline of slightly more than 23 percent from the harvest last year. Yemeni coffee is of the *arabica* variety.

*Philippines*

Historically rather small quantities of coffee were imported by that counry to supplement domestic production. In the past several years the coffee crop has attained a level of 500,000-600,000 bags — sufficient to meet the demands of the Philippine market. Both *arabicas* and *robustas* are cultivated in that country.

OTHERS (ASIA AND OCEANIA)

Estimates of exportable production for several other areas of Asia and Oceania are listed below:

**Exportable Production**
(60-kilo bags)

|  | 1961-62 | 1962-63 | 1963-64 | 1964-65 | 1965-66 | 1966-67 |
|---|---|---|---|---|---|---|
| New Caledonia | 30,000 | 30,000 | 30,000 | 30,000 | 30,000 | 30,000 |
| New Hebrides | 4,000 | N.A. | N.A. | N.A. | N.A. | N.A. |
| Papua and New Guinea | 65,000 | 70,000 | 75,000 | 80,000 | 80,000 | 80,000 |
| Portuguese Timor | 30,000 | 30,000 | 30,000 | 30,000 | 33,000 | 33,000 |

N.A.: Not available

SOURCE: FAS

*Supply and Demand*

Over the past decade the world coffee industry has been confronted with a chronic condition of ever-widening imbalance between coffee production and accumulated stocks and consumer demand. Coffee production now is running approximately 20 percent ahead of demand. Consumption in the importing countries of the world presently shows a modest growth rate of 2.5 to 3.0 percent annually.

In the decade up to 1957 worldwide inventories of coffee were maintained at comparatively moderate or even low levels. World production varied about the 40-million bag level during most of that decade while world consumption, comprising net exports from producing nations plus their own domestic disappearance, was not far behind. Uncommitted production or carryover reached its lowest ebb in the marketing periods 1949-50 to 1953-54, when an average of about 6.4 million bags per year was held over each year. Beginning in 1954-55 the condition of imbalance began to assume serious proportions, as the new postwar plantings in Latin America and in certain African countries began to bear fruit. In the interim to 1966-67 carryover grew to 87.2 million bags — more than a thirteen-fold accumulation in twelve to thirteen years.

The following table illustrates the dramatic growth of the world coffee surplus in recent years.

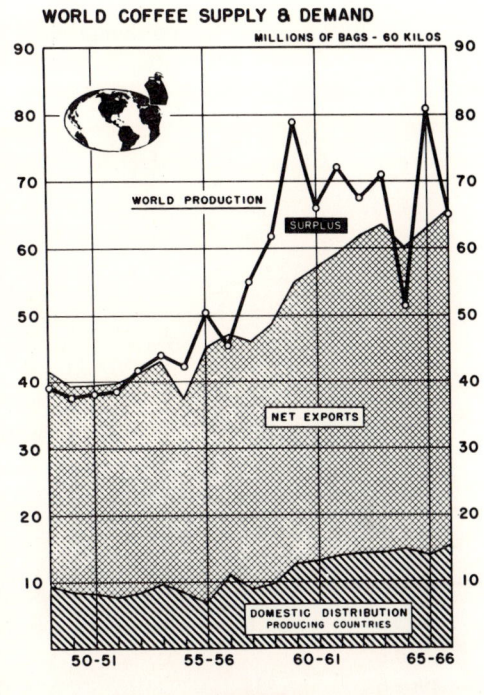

CHART 8

## Estimated World Supply And Distribution Of Green Coffee

(in thousands of bags of 60 kilos)

| Marketing Year | Beginning Carry-over | Production | Total Supply | Net Exports | Domestic 1/ Distribution | Ending Carry-over |
|---|---|---|---|---|---|---|
| 1946-47 | 16,390 | 35,308 | 51,698 | 27,158 | 7,490 | 17,050 |
| 1947-48 | 17,050 | 34,618 | 51,668 | 30,848 | 8,292 | 12,528 |
| 1948-49 | 12,528 | 39,095 | 51,623 | 32,266 | 9,330 | 10,027 |
| 1949-50 | 10,027 | 37,615 | 47,642 | 31,205 | 8,304 | 8,133 |
| 1950-51 | 8,133 | 38,164 | 46,297 | 31,593 | 8,163 | 6,541 |
| 1951-52 | 6,541 | 38,530 | 45,071 | 32,152 | 7,646 | 5,273 |
| 1952-53 | 5,273 | 41,513 | 46,786 | 32,939 | 8,236 | 5,611 |
| 1953-54 | 5,611 | 43,996 | 49,607 | 33,458 | 9,656 | 6,493 |
| 1954-55 | 6,493 | 42,188 | 48,681 | 29,219 | 8,266 | 11,196 |
| 1955-56 | 11,196 | 50,348 | 61,544 | 38,296 | 6,731 | 16,517 |
| 1956-57 | 16,517 | 45,420 | 61,937 | 36,203 | 10,778 | 14,956 |
| 1957-58 | 14,956 | 55,009 | 69,965 | 37,340 | 8,779 | 23,846 |
| 1958-59 | 23,846 | 61,665 | 85,511 | 38,977 | 9,664 | 36,870 |
| 1959-60 | 36,870 | 78,919 | 115,789 | 42,351 | 12,498 | 60,940 |
| 1960-61 | 60,940 | 65,768 | 126,708 | 44,220 | 12,954 | 2/ 66,534 |
| 1961-62 | 66,534 | 72,043 | 138,577 | 45,361 | 13,768 | 3/ 72,448 |
| 1962-63 | 72,448 | 67,387 | 139,835 | 47,909 | 13,971 | 4/ 70,655 |
| 1963-64 | 70,655 | 70,990 | 141,645 | 49,214 | 14,089 | 78,342 |
| 1964-65 | 78,342 | 51,272 | 129,614 | 45,400 | 14,671 | 69,543 |
| 1965-66 | 69,543 | 80,878 | 150,421 | 49,000 | 13,971 | 87,450 |
| 1966-67 | 87,450 | 65,184 | 152,634 | 50,000 | 15,430 | 87,204 |

SOURCE: Foreign Agricultural Service, USDA.

NOTE: In recent years some of the carry-over stocks were not of exportable quality. 1/ Domestic distribution in producing countries. 2/ Stocks reduced by 3 million bags which were allocated for industrial use in Brazil. 3/ Stocks reduced by 7 million bags which were destroyed in Brazil in mid-1961. 4/ Stocks reduced by 7.3 million bags due to revision in IBC stocks.

## CHART 9
## PRINCIPAL WORLD COFFEE PRODUCING REGIONS

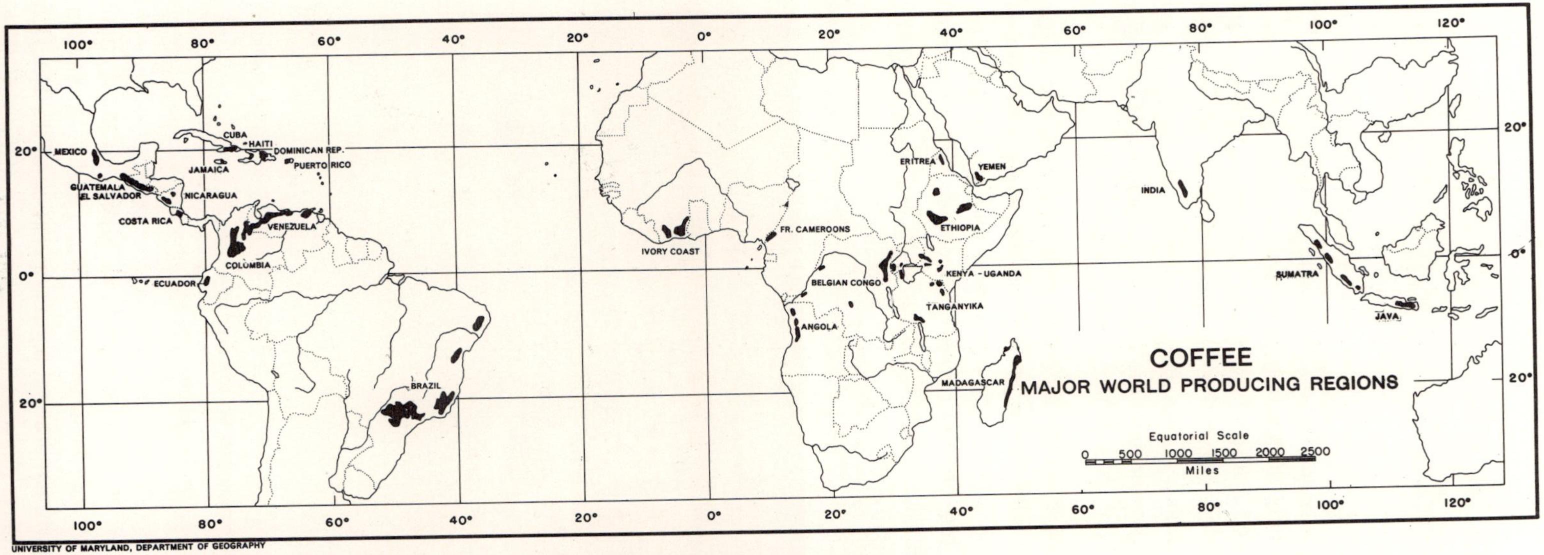

Coffee is generally cultivated in regions between the Tropic of Capricorn and the Tropic of Cancer.

# New Techniques In Coffee Harvesting

An almost classic economic exercise, capital substitution for labor, promises to revitalize Hawaii's fading coffee agriculture. Expansion of the industrial and service sectors of the economy and the resultant heavy demand for labor have drawn manpower into the developing urban areas and away from agriculture. Coffee culture as traditionally practiced in the world is labor intensive; indeed in many underdeveloped nations the seeding, harvesting and local finishing of coffee represents a welcome opportunity for many hundreds of thousands of people to earn money income. For more and more farmers the high wage levels prevailing in Hawaii's economy render it prohibitive to continue coffee cultivation.

In a parallel to experience on the mainland rising wages in the industrial sector are attracting the available labor force, so that the island's agricultural sector finds itself hard-pressed to retain workers for cultivation and harvesting. The Hawaiian coffee industry therefore has become vitally concerned with experimentation on mechanized harvesting methods currently in progress at the University of Hawaii Agricultural Experiment Station.

*(photo courtesy of U.S. Dept. of Agriculture)*
The mechanical shaker mounted on the rear of a jeep.

Agricultural engineers G. E. Monroe and A. L. Myers, of the Agricultural Research Service of the U.S.D.A. and Professors J. K. Wang and F. A. Shellenberger of the Hawaii Agricultural Experiment Station, a joint operation of the U.S.D.A. and the University of Hawaii, have been engaged in development of harvesting equipment which, when perfected, will vibrate coffee cherries off the trees and convey them into containers without harming either the berries or the tree.[1]   The economic implications are such that in the event that this experimental system is proven successful, it could increase production of Hawaii's third largest export crop (next to pineapples and sugar), while halving the cost and labor required for production.

Investigation in the current year has centered about more intensive research into the separation process between cherry and stem. When vibration is applied above a critical removal-force-to-weight ratio, a coffee cherry will go through a definite number of cycles before becoming separated from its stem. This phenomenon is similar to the fatigue effect commonly observed in the stressing of metals. The research group has been able to establish a relationship between successive displacements and energy absorption per cycle. Total energy necessary for detachment differs for mature and immature cherries; therefore it becomes necessary to choose a proper vibration amplitude in order to achieve high selectivity. Dr. Wang has commented on the effect of vibration on different plant materials:

*(photo courtesy of U.S. Dept. of Agriculture)*
Closeup of shaker and laterally moving catching frame in process of agitating a coffee tree.

---

[1] *Annual Coffee Statistics* 1965, p.41

Studies in vibration show that when plant material with high internal damping is forced to vibrate, the applied frequency will remain unchanged throughout the system, while at points away from the point of application, the internal damping will cause the amplitude to be reduced.

Thus, depending on the size and the structure of the tree, the applied amplitude must be increased in order to obtain the desired effective amplitude on branches.

Laboratory and field tests indicate that a frequency range of between 1,500 cpm to 2,500 cpm and an applied amplitude of 3/4" to 1-1/2" will achieve a selectivity of between 70 percent to 85 percent. The choice of frequency and amplitude is dependent on the size of the tree and, to a certain extent, the ratio of mature and immature cherries on the tree.

*(photo courtesy of U.S. Dept. of Agriculture)*

Catching frame capable of harvesting two trees at one jeep position when proper in-row planting has been observed.

High quality in coffee has been achieved by carefully picking the mature cherries from the tree. In order to maintain high quality in mechanical harvesting, equipment is needed to separate the mature and immature cherries.

Research on the mechanical separation of mature and immature cherries is currently underway. However, the research has not reached the stage where results can be quoted with confidence.[2]

Further progress has been reported on development of a "mass harvest system". As reported in the previous publication[3] a mechanical shaker was mounted on the

---
[2] Dr. Wang, letter, March, 1967.
[3] Cf. *Annual Coffee Statistics*, 1965, pp. 41-43

*(photo courtesy of U.S. Dept. of Agriculture)*

Closeup of circular shaker and umbrella-like catching device.

*(photo courtesy of U.S. Dept. of Agriculture)*

Circular shaker and umbrella device — in harvest operation.

*(photo courtesy of U.S. Dept. of Agriculture)*

Portable electric-powered device capable of harvesting a single lateral at a time.

*(photo courtesy of U.S. Dept. of Agriculture)*

Closeup of mobile harvester and brush segment capable of sweeping or pulling ripe coffee from the branch or lateral.

rear of a jeep and integrated with a laterally moving umbrella-like collecting frame. The umbrella-collecting frame has been integrated with a new shaker device that agitates the coffee tree in a circular motion. This movement removes coffee more uniformly than the linear-type shaker, but with the present clamp arrangement causes more bark damage than the translational approach. The circular shaker has a 3/4-inch stroke and operates at 2,500 cycles per minute. In the present "state of the art" mass harvest systems are limited only to a small percentage of Hawaii's coffee orchards, given the existing terrain and current pruning practices.

Two types of hand-held harvesters are in initial stages of testing at the Agricultural Experiment Station. Broadly conceived as an attempt to circumvent difficulties in operative maneuverability obtaining with the mass-harvest system the portable device promises advantages in low start-up cost and excellent field adaptability. A prototype hand-held harvester is a balanced shaker with 1 3/8" stroke and frequency rate of 1,400 rpm. Sometimes two or three attachments are required to remove most of the coffee. This shaker appears to be less selective than mass-harvest shakers due to its longer stroke and slower cycling rate. Although prototypes were hydraulically powered it is anticipated in future models that an electric motor can be substituted.

Another prototype portable harvester consists of two rotating brushes "that tend to sweep or pull the ripe coffee from the branch or lateral". Presently this device is driven by a small electric motor. Both "hand-held" harvest implements were field-tested on a limited scale in the past season; on the basis of that experience the engineers are expected over the near term to incorporate a considerable amount of redesign into the equipment. Although both machines indicate promise, the researchers feel it is premature at this time to draw definitive conclusions or to make recommendations.

# World Coffee Trade

*Coffee Exports and Imports*

The coffee-producing countries of the world exported approximately 50.3 million bags of green coffee in 1966. At the same time imports of green coffee into the consuming nations totaled 49.9 million bags. Those figures are cumulated on a gross basis, reexports not being taken into account. A net export balance of 396,000 bags is indicated by the aforementioned figures. Aggregate world exports gained 5.4 million bags or 11.9 percent over the 1965 total. At the same time world imports rose by 2.7 million bags or 5.8 percent.

Reexports probably fell somewhat short of the one million bag level. Utilizing the estimate for annual reexports of 700,000 bags cited by a committee of experts at the United Nations Coffee Conference, 1962 as a rough approximation, a lower net world import figure of, say, 49.2 million bags may be derived. The volume of reexports may very well have expanded somewhat in the intervening years, as the general level of international trade in coffee has expanded. The likelihood therefore is that, on a net basis, imports were short about 1.2 million bags or so of the indicated export volume.

Data for 1964 and 1965 showed total world import volume substantially in excess of world exports for those years. That situation has been reversed in the current year. The foregoing calculation showed an import deficit.

**VOLUME OF WORLD EXPORTS OF GREEN COFFEE**

■ 1966
▨ 1965

THOUSANDS OF BAGS - 60 KILOS

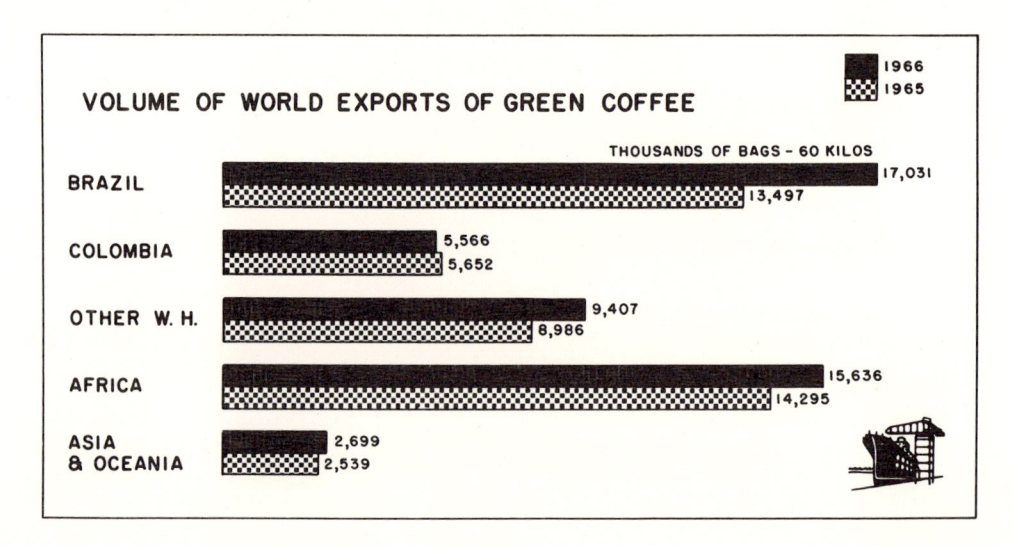

| | 1966 | 1965 |
|---|---|---|
| BRAZIL | 17,031 | 13,497 |
| COLOMBIA | 5,566 | 5,652 |
| OTHER W. H. | 9,407 | 8,986 |
| AFRICA | 15,636 | 14,295 |
| ASIA & OCEANIA | 2,699 | 2,539 |

CHART 10

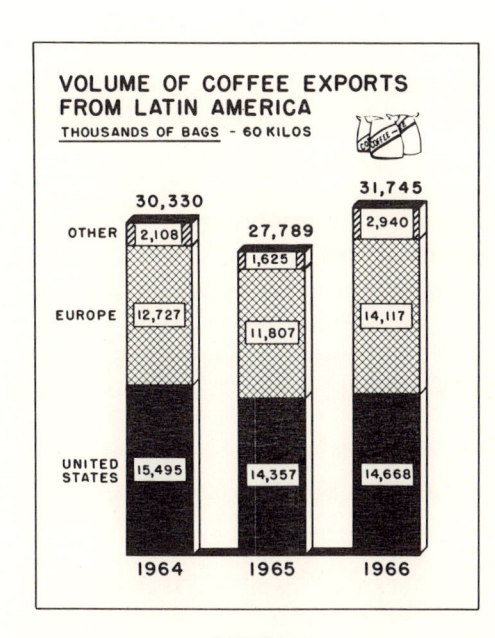

**VOLUME OF COFFEE EXPORTS FROM LATIN AMERICA**
THOUSANDS OF BAGS - 60 KILOS

| | 1964 | 1965 | 1966 |
|---|---|---|---|
| OTHER | 2,108 | 1,625 | 2,940 |
| EUROPE | 12,727 | 11,807 | 14,117 |
| UNITED STATES | 15,495 | 14,357 | 14,668 |
| Total | 30,330 | 27,789 | 31,745 |

CHART 11

Observers in the coffee trade generally attribute the large import surpluses shown by data of the past two years to the fact that a number of substantial shipments of green coffee from several of the exporting countries went unrecorded. They therefore conclude that aggregate exports in actuality approximated aggregate imports more closely than is indicated by the statistics. Further modification and improvement of the system of Certificates of Origin and Re-Export of the International Coffee Organization and the new export stamp requirement apparently have curtailed in large part the clandestine traffic in green coffee. Export data for the current year therefore can be considered to be a more accurate measure of the movement of green coffee in international trade.

### WORLD: INDICES OF ANNUAL VOLUME OF EXPORTS AND IMPORTS OF GREEN COFFEE BY COUNTRIES OR REGIONS
### 1957-1966
### (1957 = 100)

#### EXPORTS

| EXPORTS FROM | 1957 | 1958 | 1959 | 1960 | 1961 | 1962 | 1963 | 1964 | 1965 | 1966 |
|---|---|---|---|---|---|---|---|---|---|---|
| West Hem. | 100.0 | 100.9 | 121.0 | 117.4 | 117.1 | 122.0 | 132.4 | 117.3 | 107.8 | 110.0 |
| Africa | 100.0 | 110.2 | 120.3 | 137.5 | 147.8 | 167.9 | 165.2 | 183.4 | 185.6 | 203.0 |
| Asia & Oceania | 100.0 | 105.5 | 99.7 | 87.7 | 139.2 | 112.9 | 123.4 | 148.9 | 123.2 | 205.4 |
| World Total | 100.0 | 103.1 | 120.1 | 120.7 | 124.6 | 131.7 | 139.2 | 133.0 | 128.0 | 143.3 |

#### IMPORTS

| IMPORTS INTO | 1957 | 1958 | 1959 | 1960 | 1961 | 1962 | 1963 | 1964 | 1965 | 1966 |
|---|---|---|---|---|---|---|---|---|---|---|
| United States | 100.0 | 96.7 | 111.6 | 105.9 | 107.7 | 117.7 | 114.6 | 109.8 | 102.3 | 105.9 |
| Canada | 100.0 | 107.1 | 121.4 | 119.0 | 133.9 | 147.1 | 154.1 | 149.3 | 150.5 | 139.2 |
| Other W. Hem. | 100.0 | 110.5 | 68.2 | 81.8 | 97.0 | 80.9 | 80.2 | 80.9 | 89.6 | 114.7 |
| Europe | 100.0 | 105.0 | 119.9 | 131.5 | 137.6 | 143.5 | 154.5 | 165.0 | 167.0 | 177.2 |
| Africa | 100.0 | 99.9 | 104.7 | 112.2 | 104.3 | 106.2 | 118.8 | 118.6 | 83.5 | 95.9 |
| Asia & Oceania | 100.0 | 99.1 | 120.5 | 159.0 | 160.3 | 192.0 | 219.9 | 288.6 | 321.0 | 417.3 |
| World Total | 100.0 | 100.3 | 113.8 | 115.6 | 119.2 | 127.3 | 130.2 | 131.9 | 128.1 | 135.5 |

Differences invariably occur between export and import data. That can be explained in part by the time lag between the date of departure of the coffee from origin and arrival at a distant import center. Other factors to be taken into account are losses in transit and errors in record keeping which inevitably must be dealt with in the con-

### WORLD: EXPORTS AND IMPORTS OF GREEN COFFEE BY COUNTRIES OR REGIONS, 1957-1966

(thousands of 60-Kilo bags)

#### EXPORTS

| EXPORTS FROM | 1957 | 1958 | 1959 | 1960 | 1961 | 1962 | 1963 | 1964 | 1965 | 1966 |
|---|---|---|---|---|---|---|---|---|---|---|
| Western Hem. | 26,109 | 26,355 | 31,591 | 30,639 | 30,562 | 31,843 | 34,560 | 30,635 | 28,135 | 32,004 |
| Africa | 7,702 | 8,490 | 9,267 | 10,594 | 11,387 | 12,928 | 12,724 | 14,129 | 14,295 | 15,636 |
| Asia & Oceania | 1,314 | 1,386 | 1,310 | 1,153 | 1,829 | 1,484 | 1,622 | 1,957 | 2,539 | 2,699 |
| World Total | 35,125 | 36,231 | 42,168 | 42,386 | 43,778 | 46,255 | 48,906 | 46,721 | 44,969 | 50,339 |

#### IMPORTS

| IMPORTS INTO | 1957 | 1958 | 1959 | 1960 | 1961 | 1962 | 1963 | 1964 | 1965 | 1966 |
|---|---|---|---|---|---|---|---|---|---|---|
| United States | 20,858 | 20,169 | 23,270 | 22,091 | 22,464 | 24,549 | 23,893 | 22,892 | 21,347 | 22,092 |
| Canada | 836 | 895 | 1,015 | 995 | 1,119 | 1,230 | 1,288 | 1,248 | 1,258 | 1,164 |
| Other West. Hem. | 742 | 820 | 506 | 607 | 720 | 600 | 595 | 600 | 665 | 851 |
| Europe | 12,938 | 13,590 | 15,513 | 17,018 | 17,807 | 18,563 | 19,994 | 21,347 | 21,604 | 22,925 |
| Africa | 1,021 | 1,020 | 1,069 | 1,146 | 1,065 | 1,084 | 1,213 | 1,211 | 853 | 979 |
| Asia & Oceania | 463 | 459 | 558 | 736 | 742 | 889 | 1,018 | 1,336 | 1,486 | 1,932 |
| World Total | 36,858 | 36,953 | 41,931 | 42,593 | 43,917 | 46,915 | 48,001 | 48,633 | 47,213 | 49,943 |

#### DIFFERENCE BETWEEN IMPORTS AND EXPORTS

| | 1957 | 1958 | 1959 | 1960 | 1961 | 1962 | 1963 | 1964 | 1965 | 1966 |
|---|---|---|---|---|---|---|---|---|---|---|
| World Total | +1,733 | +722 | −237 | +207 | +139 | +660 | −905 | +1,912 | +2,244 | −396 |

SOURCE: PACB, Department of Statistics and Economic Research, based on official data and estimates.

N.B.:(+) = *Import excess*
(−) = *Import deficit*

duct of international trade. In the accompanying table, world exports and imports of green coffee are set forth by countries or regions. It will be seen on examination of the variations between the export and import data from year to year that the gap usually amounts to a small and at times a fractional percentage of total world trade in coffee. The very sharp widening of the differences from 1963 to 1964 and again from 1965 to 1966 are indicated clearly therein.

## Coffee Exports by Regions

The Western Hemisphere producing countries registered an increase of 13.8 percent in the volume of green coffee shipments — to 32.0 million bags in 1966. That figure represents an increase of 3.9 million bags from the 1965 total of 28.1 million bags. Meanwhile the producers of the Eastern Hemisphere showed a relatively smaller increase of 8.9 percent over their 1965 performance to attain a level of 18.3 million bags. That figure represents an expansion of 1.5 million bags over the preceding year's export total of 16.8 million bags.

Total export volume in 1966 represented an expansion over the past decade of 15.2 million bags, or 43.3 percent, from a level of 35.1 million bags. In that period the proportion of world supply originating in the Western Hemisphere declined from 74.3 percent to 63.6 percent. The 1957-66 interim witnessed expansion of offerings on the world market from the Eastern Hemisphere by 9.3 million bags or 103.4 percent from a base of 9.0 million bags.

Shown in accompanying tables are changes in the relative distribution of the coffee trade by regions, changes since 1957 for each of the regions, and trends of exports and imports in terms of index numbers.

Most African coffee producers have figured in the expansion on that Continent. However the bulk of the growth in Africa's share of the world total is accounted for by several of the largest robusta-producing countries. The most notable cases in that category are Angola, Ivory Coast and Uganda.

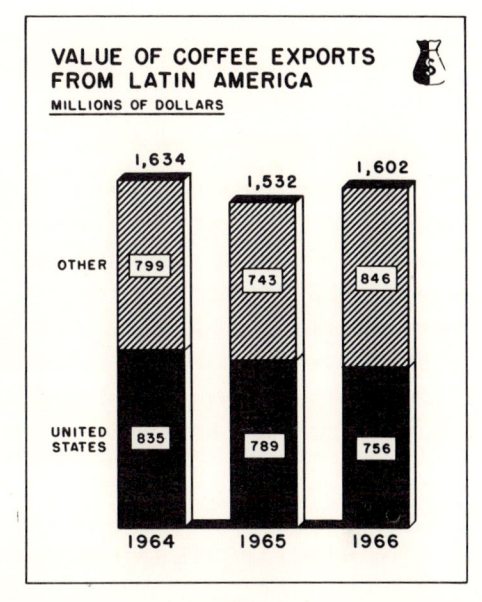

CHART 12

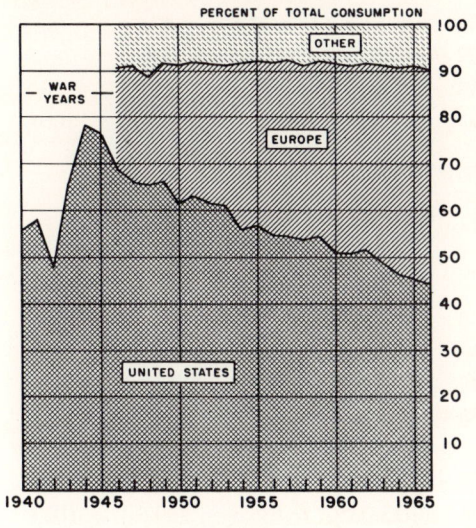

CHART 13

101

*Coffee Imports by Regions*

The consuming countries of the Western Hemisphere took 24.1 million bags in 1966, as compared with 23.3 million bags in the preceding year, an improvement of 3.6 percent. Over the past decade that region raised its annual offtake of green coffee by 1.7 million bags or 7.4 percent.

The coffee-importing countries of the Americas accounted for 48.2 percent of world demand in the current year as compared with 49.3 percent in 1965. The seeming paradox of a declining share of the world market in a period of expanding imports is explained by the fact that other importing areas of the world also are expanding their consumption of coffee and at a faster rate than is evident in the Western Hemisphere. As compared with the present shares of the world market, a decade ago the United States absorbed about three-fifths of the world coffee trade, while Europe's share amounted to a little more than one third.

**WORLD: EXPORTS AND IMPORTS OF GREEN COFFEE BY COUNTRIES OR REGIONS, 1957 and 1966**

(thousands of 60-kilo bags)

**EXPORTS**

|  | 1966 | 1957 | Increase or Decrease 1966 Over 1957 Volume | Percent | Percent of Total 1966 | 1957 |
|---|---|---|---|---|---|---|
| Western Hemisphere | 32,004 | 26,109 | + 5,895 | + 22.6 | 63.6 | 74.3 |
| Africa | 15,636 | 7,702 | + 7,934 | + 103.0 | 31.1 | 21.9 |
| Asia & Oceania | 2,699 | 1,314 | + 1,385 | + 105.4 | 5.3 | 3.8 |
| Total Exports | 50,339 | 35,125 | +15,214 | + 43.3 | 100.0 | 100.0 |

**IMPORTS**

|  | 1966 | 1957 | Increase or Decrease 1966 Over 1957 Volume | Percent | Percent of Total 1966 | 1957 |
|---|---|---|---|---|---|---|
| United States | 22,092 | 20,858 | + 1,234 | + 5.9 | 44.2 | 56.6 |
| Canada | 1,164 | 836 | + 328 | + 39.2 | 2.3 | 2.3 |
| Other West. Hem. | 851 | 742 | + 109 | + 14.7 | 1.7 | 2.0 |
| Europe | 22,925 | 12,938 | + 9,987 | + 77.2 | 45.9 | 35.1 |
| Africa | 979 | 1,021 | − -42 | − 4.1 | 2.0 | 2.8 |
| Asia & Oceania | 1,932 | 463 | + 1,469 | +317.3 | 3.9 | 1.2 |
| Total Imports | 49,943 | 36,858 | +13,085 | + 35.5 | 100.0 | 100.0 |

*SOURCE: PACB estimates.*

## WORLD: PERCENTAGE DISTRIBUTION OF ANNUAL EXPORTS AND IMPORTS OF GREEN COFFEE BY COUNTRIES OR REGIONS 1957-1966

### EXPORTS

| EXPORTS FROM | 1957 | 1958 | 1959 | 1960 | 1961 | 1962 | 1963 | 1964 | 1965 | 1966 |
|---|---|---|---|---|---|---|---|---|---|---|
| Western Hemisphere | 74.3 | 72.8 | 74.9 | 72.3 | 69.8 | 68.8 | 70.7 | 65.6 | 62.6 | 63.6 |
| Africa | 21.9 | 23.4 | 22.0 | 25.0 | 26.0 | 28.0 | 26.0 | 30.2 | 31.8 | 31.1 |
| Asia & Oceania | 3.8 | 3.8 | 3.1 | 2.7 | 4.2 | 3.2 | 3.3 | 4.2 | 5.6 | 5.3 |
| World Total | 100.0 | 100.0 | 100.0 | 100.0 | 100.0 | 100.0 | 100.0 | 100.0 | 100.0 | 100.0 |

### IMPORTS

| IMPORTS INTO | 1957 | 1958 | 1959 | 1960 | 1961 | 1962 | 1963 | 1964 | 1965 | 1966 |
|---|---|---|---|---|---|---|---|---|---|---|
| United States | 56.6 | 54.6 | 55.5 | 51.9 | 51.2 | 52.3 | 49.8 | 47.1 | 45.2 | 44.2 |
| Canada | 2.3 | 2.4 | 2.4 | 2.3 | 2.6 | 2.6 | 2.7 | 2.6 | 2.7 | 2.3 |
| Other West. Hem. | 2.0 | 2.2 | 1.2 | 1.4 | 1.6 | 1.3 | 1.2 | 1.2 | 1.4 | 1.7 |
| Europe | 35.1 | 36.8 | 37.0 | 40.0 | 40.5 | 39.6 | 41.7 | 43.9 | 45.8 | 45.9 |
| Africa | 2.8 | 2.8 | 2.6 | 2.7 | 2.4 | 2.3 | 2.5 | 2.5 | 1.8 | 2.0 |
| Asia & Oceania | 1.2 | 1.2 | 1.3 | 1.7 | 1.7 | 1.9 | 2.1 | 2.7 | 3.1 | 3.9 |
| World Total | 100.0 | 100.0 | 100.0 | 100.0 | 100.0 | 100.0 | 100.0 | 100.0 | 100.0 | 100.0 |

SOURCE: Department of Statistics and Economic Research, PACB.

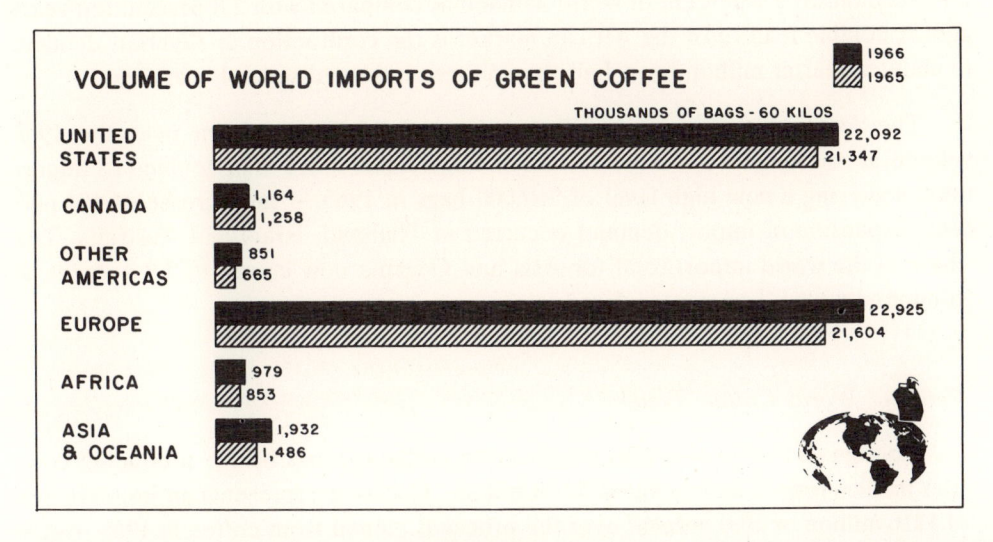

### VOLUME OF WORLD IMPORTS OF GREEN COFFEE
THOUSANDS OF BAGS - 60 KILOS

| | 1966 | 1965 |
|---|---|---|
| UNITED STATES | 22,092 | 21,347 |
| CANADA | 1,164 | 1,258 |
| OTHER AMERICAS | 851 | 665 |
| EUROPE | 22,925 | 21,604 |
| AFRICA | 979 | 853 |
| ASIA & OCEANIA | 1,932 | 1,486 |

CHART 14

The United States accounted for the largest single increase in import volume this year. The recent improvement reversed a declining import trend that began in 1963. That country's import growth amounted to 745,000 bags or 3.5 percent over the total for the preceding year. In contrast to developments in the United States market, Canadian demand for green coffee eased slightly by 44,000 bags or 7.5 percent in the current year.

Other consumer nations in the Western Hemisphere increased their offtake of green coffee. Shipments into Argentina rose 168,000 bags to 673,000 bags, an improvement of one-third from the volume recorded in 1965. Uruguay and Chile also raised their import totals this year.

Demand for coffee for European consumption now takes 45.9 percent of the world total as compared with 35.1 percent a decade ago. European coffee imports have grown by ten million bags, or more than 75 percent, in the past decade, whereas the U. S. market has expanded only 5.9 percent. Dynamic consumer interest in this beverage has caused Continental demand for coffee to exceed the volume taken by the United States for the second consecutive year. At current relative rates of growth the European coffee market will continue to enlarge its role as the leading consuming area. Demand was buoyant in all areas of Europe in 1966. The six countries of the EEC took 110,000 bags more than in 1965 — an improvement of 0.9 percent. Other West European markets took 943,000 bags or 13.3 percent more than in the preceding year. The Soviet Bloc increased its offtake by 268,000 bags or 15.1 percent. The Continent in the aggregate absorbed 1.3 million bags more this year — an expansion of 3.1 percent.

The consuming countries of Africa took more coffee in 1966, registering an increase of 14.8 percent to a level of 1.0 million bags. Outlets for green coffee in Africa now account for 2.0 percent of world demand as compared with 2.8 percent ten years ago. A notable feature of the African market is the contraction in Algerian demand to about a quarter million bags, half the volume consumed several years ago.

The Asian markets augmented their imports by 30.0 percent over the 1965 volume, accounting for a total of 1.9 million bags. Japan more than doubled its import total, achieving a new high level of 769,000 bags in 1965 — an increase of 101 percent. Expansion of import demand occurred in Thailand, Israel and Australia. The share of the world import total for Asia and Oceania now comes to 3.9 percent, as compared with 1.3 percent a decade ago.

*Value of World Coffee Trade*

Foreign exchange revenues earned from coffee exports by the producing countries in 1966 rose to an estimated $2.38 billion. That sum represents an improvement of $216 million or 10.0 percent over the proceeds gained from coffee in 1965. Aggregate world exports of all goods and services in 1966 are valued at $181.3 billion —

9.5 percent above the level attained in 1965. Although world coffee exports grew at a slightly better rate than did overall international commerce, that commodity's share did not change from the 1965 figure as it accounted for 1.3 percent of the aggregate value of world trade.

Expanding economic activity and rising standards of living in the industrialized countries, and in the developing countries as well, have generated demand for a larger volume of goods and services and a much broader variety of commodities and goods. That multi-faceted expansion in trade in recent years has outpaced the relatively slow growth in world import demand for coffee. The share of coffee in total world trade therefore has been experiencing gradual attrition. A decade ago, coffee exports comprised 2.6 percent of total international commerce — about double its present share.

The contraction in the proportion of coffee in total trade is only partially explained by the relatively rapid growth of world trade in general. The long-run decline in coffee prices, which began in the latter part of the 1950 s, has contributed to the deterioration in the relative trade position of coffee. Numerous other commodity markets, of course, have experienced falling prices over prolonged periods. On the other hand, industrial goods and services have tended to be stable or have tended to rise in cost over the years.

Western Hemisphere producers earned approximately $1.6 billion from exports of coffee. This was the largest regional share, amounting to 67.6 percent of the total value of world coffee trade. That region's importance as a coffee supplier has been lessening; in 1965 their proportion of the world total was 71.3 percent and a decade ago they supplied 81.1 percent of the world market. It is interesting to note that the Western Hemisphere's share of the *volume* of world coffee exports was 63.6 percent whereas in 1965 their share was 62.6 percent. The explanation for those changing relationships i.e., a smaller share of world coffee revenues contrasted with a concomitant improvement in terms of their volume share, lies in the fact that prices of Eastern Hemisphere coffees, particularly the *robusta* types, were buoyant in a period when *arabica* prices were generally easing. Of course, in absolute terms the Latin American producers scored a revenue gain in the current year.

Among the major producing countries of the Western Hemisphere, Brazil increased its coffee export earnings in 1966 by 9.5 percent while coffee revenues for Colombia were down 1.5 percent. Those two countries together gained about $1.1 billion from coffee sales in 1966 — about six percent over the 1965 figure. Other Western Hemisphere producers showing increases were Guatemala, with a gain of 19 percent over 1965, Costa Rica and Mexico. Others in that region either maintained their export revenues or experienced a falling-off in exchange earnings.

Coffee exports from Africa, Asia and Oceania were valued at $779 million. That figure represents a substantial gain from the total value of $621 million registered in 1965. Exporters from the Eastern Hemisphere experienced vigorous demand for their coffees and the rising volume of exports was accompanied by a concurrent uptrend in world prices of *robusta* types which constitute by far the largest component of Eastern Hemisphere coffees. The major *robusta* producers were the chief beneficiaries of the favorable market situation in which the Eastern Hemisphere exporters found themselves. Angola and Uganda had gains of five and 30 percent respectively. Kenya, an *arabica* producer, also experienced a sharp expansion in export earnings of about 36 percent.

The Western Hemisphere producers took 67.7 percent of world coffee sales in the current year. The share of world coffee revenues taken by Africa, Asia and Oceania in 1966 came to 32.3 percent. That proportion compares with their market share a decade ago of 18.9 percent. Rapid development of *robusta* production in the postwar period accounts largely for the gains made by that regional aggregation of coffee producers.

Brazil accounted for 32.5 percent of the total value of world coffee trade in 1966. Colombia's share was 14.2 percent, while El Salvador, Guatemala and Mexico together took 11.5 percent. The five largest Western Hemisphere producers together earned approximately three fifths of the world's coffee sales. The four major African producers, Ivory Coast, Uganda, Angola and Ethiopia together earned 17.6 percent of total coffee revenues in the current year. Nine major producing nations therefore supplied three-quarters of the world market. In 1960 the Western Hemisphere group of five countries had a larger share of coffee earnings — 66.3 percent, while the four major African countries as a group had 10.9 percent of the world total. (See Appendix Table Rev. 5)

*Share of Coffee in Foreign Exchange Revenues*

The overall share of coffee in foreign exchange earnings of all producing countries came to 13.6 percent in 1966. The Latin America countries earned 19.0 percent of their exchange receipts from coffee. For the African producers the degree of dependence on coffee was somewhat higher at 20.7 percent. Coffee does not rank as high in importance in Asia and Oceania, its share of foreign revenues amounting to only 1.5 percent.

In the Western Hemisphere, Brazil, Colombia, El Salvador, Guatemala, Costa Rica and Haiti each earned more than 40 percent of their foreign exchange earnings from coffee sales abroad. Their reliance on coffee export revenues ranged from 67.0 to 42.1 percent. On the African Continent five countries, Uganda, Angola, Ethiopia, Rwanda and Burundi depended on coffee for one-half to four-fifths of their earnings abroad. Another group of five countries Kenya, Ivory Coast, Madagascar, Togo, and the Central African Republic gained in the neighborhood of one-third of their exchange receipts from coffee. (See Appendix Table Rev. 4)

```
IMPORTANCE OF COFFEE EXPORTS
TO LATIN AMERICAN COFFEE-PRODUCING COUNTRIES...1966

COLOMBIA        67.0%
HAITI           54.3
EL SALVADOR     47.2
GUATEMALA       45.9
BRAZIL          44.7
COSTA RICA      42.1
ECUADOR         16.9
NICARAGUA       16.1
DOMINICAN REP.  15.3
HONDURAS        13.9
MEXICO          6.7
PERU            3.8
PANAMA          2.5
VENEZUELA       0.6

TOTAL           19.0%

VALUE OF COFFEE EXPORTS
AS PERCENT OF TOTAL EXPORTS
```

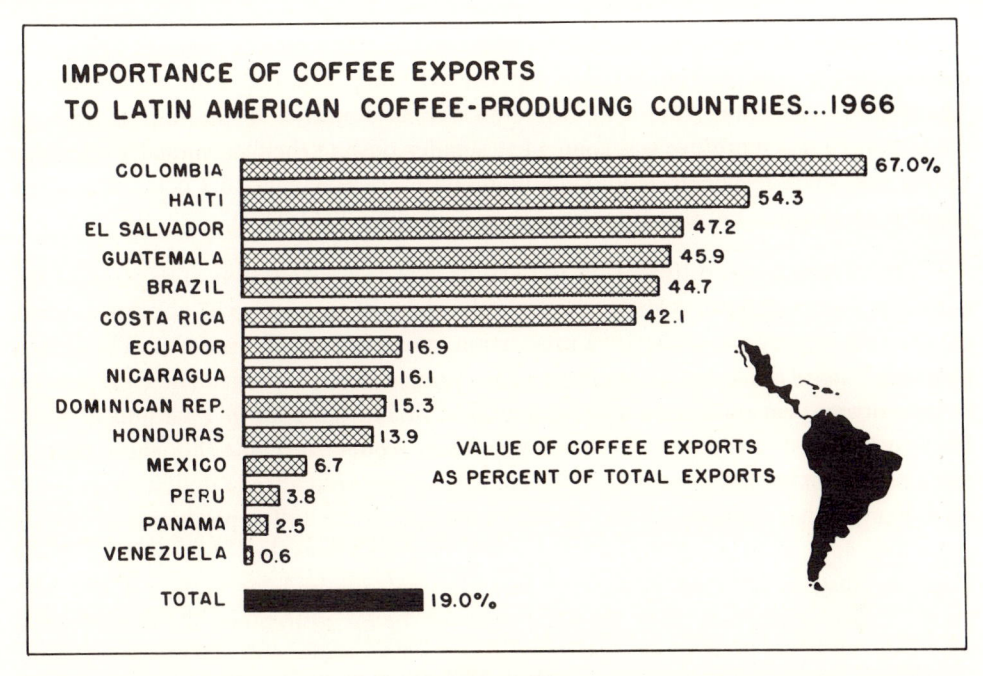

CHART 15

*Trade Balance Between the United States and the Latin American Coffee-Producing Countries*

United States imports from the fifteen major coffee-producing countries of Latin America in 1966 amounted to $3.5 billion. That figure represents an improvement of $224 million or 6.8 percent over the value of shipments received from those fifteen countries in 1965. At the same time, exports to the Latin American coffee countries totaled $3.6 billion as compared with a corresponding export figure of $3.2 billion in 1965. The balance of trade for the United States was favorable this year with exports surpassing imports by $68 million. That situation contrasts with conditions a year earlier when the balance of trade for the U. S. was unfavorable — imports exceeding exports by $92 million. The converse of that situation, of course, is that the coffee countries found themselves in a better trade position vis-à-vis the United States.

The level of export-import trade with the Latin American coffee countries this year reached record levels. Imports into the U. S. from the majority of those coffee countries increased. That was especially true in the case of the larger trading partners. Shipments to practically all the coffee countries in the Latin American area were higher this year.

There was the customary heavy trade surplus with Mexico amounting this year to $426 million. On the other hand, the usual trade deficit was registered in commerce with Venezuela, mainly due to heavy purchases of Venezuelan petroleum. Trade balances with other coffee countries on either side of the ledger were of relatively small magnitudes.

Although imports from the coffee countries of Latin America expanded by a substantial margin, overall imports into the United States climbed even more rapidly. The share of the Latin American coffee-producing countries in the import trade of the United States therefore was somewhat smaller despite their expanded shipments. In fact that share has been steadily declining and now stands at 13.7 percent as compared with 18.6 percent five years ago. (See Appendix Table T-1).

The situation was different on the export side. The expansion in exports to the coffee countries of Latin America brought the share of that group of countries in the export total slightly above the 1965 proportion and it is now 11.9 percent. The fifteen countries' share of United States exports has remained fairly stable. Their proportion in the current year compares with percentages of 12.2 percent in 1964 and in 1962. Data for the last five years which are set out in Appendix Table T-1 show that on three occasions in that interim the United States registered a trade deficit — at times quite heavy. That situation of course was beneficial to the coffee-producing countries since they sold more goods and services to the United States than they bought. Their trade surpluses could then be used to buy material required for economic development, for strenghthening their financial reserves, or for retirement of external debt.

The Western Hemisphere countries in 1966 shipped coffee valued at $0.76 billion to the United States. In that year, United States exports to the coffee-producing countries of this hemisphere amounted to $3.56 billion. Coffee, therefore, paid for 21.3 percent of that region's purchases of goods and services from the United States.

### UNITED STATES EXPORTS TO AND IMPORTS FROM THE 15 COFFEE-PRODUCING COUNTRIES OF LATIN AMERICA

(millions of dollars)

| Year | Exports | Percent of Total Exports | Imports | Percent of Total Imports |
|------|---------|--------------------------|---------|--------------------------|
| 1966 | 3,555.7 | 11.9 | 3,487.9 | 13.7 |
| 1965 | 3,172.6 | 11.7 | 3,264.3 | 15.3 |
| 1964 | 3,199.6 | 12.2 | 3,141.9 | 16.8 |
| 1963 | 2,766.9 | 12.0 | 3,048.0 | 17.8 |
| 1962 | 2,609.6 | 12.2 | 3,046.8 | 18.6 |
| 1961 | 2,601.0 | 12.4 | 2,845.6 | 19.4 |
| 1960 | 2,837.5 | 15.0 | 2,198.6 | 21.8 |
| 1959 | 2,039.6 | 17.3 | 3,183.9 | 21.2 |
| 1958 | 2,403.5 | 19.6 | 3,232.2 | 25.2 |
| 1957 | 3,868.5 | 18.8 | 3,405.1 | 26.4 |

SOURCE: *U.S. Department of Commerce.*

Coffee is the most important agricultural commodity in the import list of the United States. In fact, it traditionally has been the second major commodity import exceeded in value only by petroleum. In 1966 green coffee imports into the United States were valued at $1.07 billion, whereas the total value of all goods and services imported was $25.4 billion. The share of coffee in the import trade of the United States therefore was 4.21 percent. In 1965 coffee accounted for 4.96 percent of total U. S. imports. A decade ago, the share of coffee in the U. S. import trade was 10.60 percent.

# Bulk Transportation - Containerization

Economic expansion throughout the two postwar decades has been swift. Production of both finished goods and raw materials has been steadily growing and, so also has the volume of world trade. In order to meet the growing requirements of international trade, broader and more efficient transportation services are needed.

The past decade has witnessed the development of a new concept in movement of freight — containerization. That term describes the use of bulk containers of large scale ranging in size to the dimensions of a truck trailer or railroad boxcar. The large-capacity units can accomodate numerous smaller boxes, crates or bags, thereby reducing sharply every aspect of labor, space, accounting and risk involved in the distribution process. The bulk container provides the most efficient means of moving goods from seller to buyer as inexpensively and as quickly as possible, with maximum safety and minimum additional packaging — in short, the purpose of the container is to provide smoother service between warehouses of the producer and those of the consumer.

A bulk container is an enclosed, reusable, non-disposable, weather-tight shipping conveyance, which has been fitted with at least one door. It can be handled and transported by existing carrier-owned equipment, both on land and sea. Containers vary in size. Non-standard units range between 140 and 400 cubic ft.

Other types are known as van-containers, which are standardized and can be transported on carrier equipment; those are built according to specifications of the International Standards Organization. Almost all van-containers are demountable and capable of being handled as an independent unit. Their advantage lies in the fact that they can be mounted and fastened in or on marine, rail or highway carrier conveyances and thus become fixed components of the carrying conveyance during transit.

*Types of Container Ships*

As bulk containers first came into use most vessels accomodating containerized cargo were modified general cargo ship types or regular freighters with one or more holds fitted with vertical cells. Recently constructed vessels have been fitted with vertical guides within their holds so that they can provide regular containerized service. Those holds are designed for standardized containers. Containers are stacked therein one atop the other to maximize utilization of space.

A new type of specially designed vessel is the all-containership or full containership which has vertical cells built in throughout its holds for van-containers. Additional containers can be carried on the open decks which are designed with that purpose in mind. Containers placed on open decks can be double the size of the standard units which fit within the cells. Those vessels are equipped to load cargo only in van-containers.

A variation of the all-containership is the trailership or roll-on/roll-off ship. Those vessels carry container-vans which have their own wheels and which can be put on the vessels directly from trains or trucks without requiring an intermediate loading-unloading procedure. At the port of destination those vans can move directly off the trailership thereby eliminating the interval of waiting for the arrival of the inland conveyance which ordinarily would take on the van-containers.

Recent technical developments have made it possible for some general cargo freighters to be equipped with foldaway container stowage systems. Such systems permit the vessel in the event of sufficient demand for service to carry up to 130 containers under deck.

Once unloaded from the vessel, containers (except those which have rolled off directly from trailerships) must be lifted from the carrying vessel onto the next carrying conveyance — either rail or motor. By rail or highway, the containers generally are carried from unloading point to final destination "piggyback" either on a railroad flatcar or on a chassis or bogey.

*Container Services*

Cargo lines carry about 20 percent of the volume of ocean freight. Several container services are offered by these regularly scheduled steamship lines. The various operations offer different advantages. The most complete service is the one providing transport from "house-to-house," that is, from the shipper's facility to the warehouse or factory of his overseas customer. The shipment is containerized on the shipper's premises and then moved overland by rail or motor to the steamship line's pier for loading on board vessel. Upon arrival at an overseas port, the container is removed from the vessel to pier to overland carrier and finally delivered to the ultimate consignee's premises for unloading of the cargo. The cargo is thus physically handled only twice — upon loading by shipper and unloading by recipient.

A less complete service is that of "house-to-pier." As with the first described method, cargo is loaded into containers on the shipper's premises, moved overland and then by sea to the vessel's arrival berth at port. There it is available to the consignee. At that point the container is removed to pier, the cargo within it is unloaded on the pier whereupon the consignee takes delivery.

"Pier-to-house" movements are initially containerized at the pier of the ocean carrier. Upon arrival at port of destination, the container is removed from the vessel either onto pier or directly to an inland carrier. It then is delivered without further unloading of cargo to the recipient's factory or warehouse where the cargo is taken out of the container.

The last of the common methods of container service is that of "pier-to-pier." Cargo is containerized at the loading pier and placed aboard a vessel. Removal from the container takes place after its placement on dock.

In its present state of development containerized shipment may not be the ideal method for every type of manufactured item or raw commodity. But in recent years technical innovation in container design and adoption of larger standardized units by segments of the transportation industry have made possible application to a broader range of cargoes. In certain instances, containerization offers advantages; that is especially true in the case of high unit-value items that lend themselves to container packing.

*Cargo Protection*

Once cargo is packed and loaded into containers, no further handling or packing is required. Packaging requirements for merchandise carried in containers are less rigorous than for items carried on a break-bulk basis because of reduced physical handling and loading. Important savings in freight can be effected through reduced packaging. Rates, which are based on weight and measurement of only the commodities shipped, fall with reduction in weight or cubic displacement achieved through elimination of some of the packaging of the goods within the container. Labeling of the packages need not be as all encompassing when containerized shipment is made, since all the packages are held within one space until final unloading.

Pilferage is virtually eliminated in containerized shipments. Even the most professional thievery is often foiled by container usage. Besides this protection, cargo, if properly packed within the container, acquires further protection from the ravages of weather, as well as of ocean transit.

Because of the relatively large size of the containers, they can be manipulated only by mechanical devices. Those machines can be operated with little manpower. The containers are handled fewer times and rarely by inexperienced personnel. Damage in unloading therefore is held to a minimum.

Insurance premiums for containerized cargo often are lower than coverage for conventional shipments. When cargo moves from "house-to-house" with no unloading at any point en route, better protection from damage and pilferage quite obviously is provided as compared with cargo handled possibly four or five times per movement by traditional methods. When cargo is unloaded at the consignee's facility, the out-turn normally is undamaged and conforms to the bill of lading. Claims for undelivered packages accordingly are rarely possible. That factor favorably influences insurance premiums. An interesting development in the marine insurance field and a portent for the future is an announcement by a large insurance company connected with a steamship line involved in South American traffic offering reduced premium all-risk insurance for shipments forwarded in their containers on a "house-to-house" basis, provided these are carried on vessels which are equipped with the necessary and acceptable container-handling facilities.

*Turn-Around Time*

Time in transit is substantially reduced by use of containers. Ocean steamers carrying containerized freight are detained in port for shorter periods because of the ease in loading and unloading their cargo. Bulk containers eliminate numerous loading and unloading operations so that considerable economy of time and labor is made possible. As mentioned heretofore containers are less prone to damage, pilferage, weather, exposure and the like. Warehousing costs quite possibly would be much lower. Faster and more reliable delivery would obviate the need for inventories as large as those required where conventional shipments are the chief means of transport. There are important implications here for financial operations. Lower capital costs to carry lighter inventories and faster turnover of stocks mean sharply lower unit money charges.

J. E. M. Beale of the British Board of Trade comments at length on the subject of containers in ocean transport: [1]

> Some 20% of the tonnage of international seaborne trade, and a far higher proportion of its value, is carried by cargo liner services. These ships may well spend 60% of their time in port. The length of time they spend in port is critical to their profitability, and therefore to the cost of transporting goods in them. This period has a cumulative effect, which becomes more pronounced as the proportion of time in port increases. If time spent in port could be reduced from 60% to say 20% of the ship's time, the freight rate could be cut by something of the order of 25% to 30% without affecting the shipowner's profit.
>
> In the great majority of ports a great deal of time is either wasted, for example during weekends and at nighttime, when there is no shift work, or alternatively consumed in work like opening and closing hatches, rigging or shipping derricks, rest breaks and the like. Studies on the route between the United Kingdom and one Commonwealth member showed that something like 70% of the time spent in its ports was idle time when no work was done, and for nearly half the working time either no actual loading or unloading was being done or work was only in progress at one or two hatches. This is true in greater or less measure of many other ports throughout the world.
>
> This means that the shipowner has a valuable asset that finds itself lying idle, in effect, for something like 80% of its time in port, and therefore for half its active life. During this time virtually all costs incurred by the ship except fuel costs are still having to be borne by the owner in one way or another. Moreover, because of the high costs of dock labour in developed areas, the cash costs of cargo handling amount to some 25 to 30% of the total cost of sea transport in cargo liners. It therefore seems that in total something like 75% of the total cost of sea transport is incurred in port. This means that the port is the first place in which the shipowner should look for greater efficiency in the use of his valuable capital asset. There must be greater speed in cargo handling, and unit transport is one way of ensuring this . . . .
>
> The greatest advantages of these services are the likelihood of far greater speed of transit and the prospect of a faster turn-round. The Matson Line have been able to unload a specially-designed ship of 6,500 tons in 850 man-hours by comparison with 11,000 required for a conventional ship of the same tonnage. This gave simultaneously a 90% reduction in stevedoring man-hours and an 80% reduction in the

---

[1] "Containers in International Transport," *International Trade Forum.* GATT, Geneva, March 1967, p.22

ships' turn-around time. It has been estimated that the potential yearly throughput per yard of quayside should rise from 200 tons of general cargo to 1,100 tons of containerized cargo. Another advantage is that the total of various port charges should in the long run be less (although labour problems may make this difficult to achieve).

Some lines may find it to their advantage to offer freight concessions on containerized cargo in order to encourage shippers to utilize containers particularly on a "house-to house" basis. More of their vessels then can be converted to all-container cargo and the turn-around time can be drastically reduced. Steamship companies no doubt are reexamining their tariff schedules relating to containerized cargo and are planning revisions or modifications thereof as they gain more experience in that mode of shipping.

In respect of turn-around time, it has been noted in shipping circles that in order to secure the maximum benefits of containerization it is necessary to use all-container vessels. Vessels partially equipped to accommodate containers may be held up in any event to discharge or take on conventional cargo so that the time economies obtained in container handling are dissipated while the vessel is involved in other cargo operations.

*Container Pools*

Usually the primary factor to be considered in making shipments is that of freight cost. Many carriers offer reduced rates to encourage the use of containers. Smaller shipments from two or more firms may be moved together in container lots. Smaller shippers thereby can gain the sizeable benefits of reduced container rates.

Ocean freight forwarders in the principal ports are becoming increasingly active in forming container cargo consolidation pools as a service to small shippers. Industry reports have it that the shipping companies themselves are initiating similar container cargo services for the convenience of smaller firms. The feasibility of such operations has been greatly enhanced by the rapid expansion of containerized cargo movement in international commerce.

*Containerization of Coffee*

Some use of containerization already has been made in the coffee trade. All shipments of green coffee from Buenaventura, Colombia, on Grace Line vessels to New York are made in this manner. That movement is encouraged by the steamship line, if for no other reason than that the containers otherwise would be making the northbound voyage empty. There is no difference in the freight rate assessed for coffee moved in containers or coffee moved in the conventional manner. The containers used are designed to contain full "chop" lots. Most of the loading at Buenaventura is effected at the Customs warehouse; unloading upon arrival in New York is handled at Port Newark or at the consignee's warehouse.

Another steamship line active in traffic from the Latin American area occasionally has handled shipments of soluble coffee in containers. The cargo is packed in polyethylene bags within the container. Freight rates vary depending upon whether movement is "house-to-house," "pier-to-house," etc. The rate structure is quite complicated and the line apparently is still working to establish definitive tariffs. That line has not shipped green coffee in containers. A third line serving Latin American routes has not had call for containerized coffee shipments, and they apparently are not encouraging such movement. Since that line's vessels arriving in New York are usually nearly empty, coffee shipments are carried under most favorable conventional stowage ('tween decks). That line does have small containers available which sometimes are used for cargoes that are easily broken or stolen, but it is not felt that this situation is applicable to the coffee trade.

The Brazil-U. S. coffee traffic to date has not witnessed wide application of containerization. Few vessels in that trade are suitable for large container movement. Moreover, at Brazilian ports and many other coffee ports in South America as well as in other producing areas there are no facilities for handling container shipments. In most localities adequate vessels and containers are not now available. Terminal and transport facilities in the various ports presently are not adequate or suitable, and the special equipment for handling containers has not been acquired nor will it be in the immediately foreseeable future. From a management point of view, most of those ports would have to coordinate land and sea transport to a much greater degree in order to fully derive the benefits of containerization. A sudden switch-over to containerized transport would be exorbitantly expensive and require tremendous outlays for construction of facilities and for specialized equipment. Those ports are not in position to make such large financial commitments.

The heavy capital investment factor necessary precludes any expectation that containerization soon will assume the importance in the coffee trade that it now has attained in the heavy North Atlantic cargo movement. United States and European coffee-import centers having highly-developed facilities cannot make use of their equipment for the coffee trade, so long as their counterparts in the producing countries dispatch the commodity by the standard method.

There are some unfavorable considerations in the use of bulk containers which may to some extent offset their advantages and which may deter certain segments of the coffee trade from making widespread use of such units. If humidity control is poor in the cargo space "sweating" may occur resulting in damage to the coffee cargo. Another danger is seepage or contamination if the container is improperly sealed.

Coffee is traded on the basis of samples. At points of importation each lot is weighed and sampled upon discharge from the vessel. When coffee is transported in the usual manner in bags it is very easy to obtain a representative sample as the sampler tries different bags randomly through each lot. In the case of containerized cargo it may be quite difficult to obtain a representative sample of the lot or lots which have been containerized. Personnel attending to sampling may not always find it practical to reach all parts of the container, and will secure samples only from the most accessible parts of the lot of coffee held therein.

Bulk containers offer substantial advantages of scale to roasters or importers who handle large quantities. However, for those consignees who may want to trade the coffee in small parcels the bulk container could present a considerable disadvantage because of the fact that they may have to be unloaded in one operation.

An interesting shipment arrived late in 1966 in Chicago. A lot of eighty thousand pounds of green Kona coffee was sent by rail to Hilo on the island of Oahu in two 24-foot aluminum cargo containers, eight feet wide and eight and one-half feet high. Provided by the Matson Line, those units were barged from Hilo to Honolulu and loaded on board the SS HAWAIIAN for the voyage to San Francisco, from whence transshipment was made to Chicago via three railways. That shipment was the first Hawaii-mainland containerized through consignment of coffee.

*Obstacles to Expansion*

Considerations which may not necessarily be classified as disadvantages but which nevertheless may weigh heavily in decision-making concerning acquisition or use of containers are a) the initial cost factor — substantial capital investment may be involved depending on the capacity and complexity of the unit; b) loss of space — the usable cubic capacity on board a container ship is considerably less than in the case of a conventional cargo ship. The containers themselves occupy both weight and bulk which may be only partially offset by more efficient packing of the cargo inside the containers themselves. Moreover it is more than likely that a good proportion of the containers will not be fully loaded so that much of the economies made possible by use of containers would be negated. In that connection industry sources state that the maximum net utilized capacity in the aggregate containerized trade might be less than three-fourths of the average capacity utilization in conventional cargo vessels.

*Innovations*

Van-containers designed for shipment of agricultural products are being perfected. In one developmental type, equipment is installed for maintenance of different temperatures in each section of the van-container to enable it to carry a variety of refrigerated cargo. New concepts in transport refrigeration and engineering now make it possible to overcome problems that have prevented efficient van transport of mixed freight requiring varied temperatures. Placing the refrigerated unit on the removable chassis rather than within the van increases the multi-purpose van-container's flexibility and allows it to hold more non-refrigerated cargo when the chassis is used for the latter purpose. A removable wheeled chassis, furthermore, converts the van into a more compact unit for transport by whichever conveyance is used. Reduction in transport weight and added versatility can eventually reduce shipping costs of agricultural products to the ultimate consumer.

A second innovation inspired by containerization is that of automatic warehouses. Some are already in operation. It is thought that design of warehouses around container delivery, storage and display will eventually become more important. Various savings in loading time and handling expenses, and increases in capacity of warehouses are the expected advantages.

*Future Prospects*

An indication of the expectation of further need for containerized shipment facilities may be had from the recent plans of American Export-Isbrandtsen Lines. Early in 1967 that line disclosed details of a 550-acre containership terminal on New York's Staten Island capable of handling 14,000,000 tons of general cargo annually. Eventually that project would have two miles of bulkhead docking and facilities for marshaling and transshipping the 20-foot and 40-foot containers that are expected to carry the bulk of general cargo in the near future. Proponents of the plan believe they can eventually reduce the cost of cargo handling in New York from $10.00-$20.00 down to $1.00 per ton.

According to forecasts of German freight forwarders, 30 percent of all general cargo shipped across the North Atlantic will be containerized by the end of 1967. A Maryland Port Authority staff report estimates that 80 percent of North Atlantic range import-export trade with the United Kingdom, Western Europe and Scandinavia may be carried in containers by 1970 and about 25 percent of trade with other ports of the world as well. The Japanese shipping industry may by 1977 attain 70 percent containerization.

Some observers believe that 95 percent of all general cargo eventually could be transported in containers. That expectation has validity for the North Atlantic traffic. Ports on both sides are highly developed, have wealthy and extensive hinterlands and can afford much more readily the expense necessary for providing adequate facilities for handling container shipments. Close cooperation is possible between the steamship lines and the highly-developed transport facilities on land in these areas to assure utilization of the containers to maximum capacity.

Diamond Head, Honolulu

(photo courtesy of Matson Lines)

The *Raphael Semms* laden with demountable container-trailers — ship's capacity 226 containers

(photo courtesy of Sea-Land Service Inc.)

35 foot-long Sea-Land trailers demountable from truck chassis are fitted precisely into the vessel's shaft-like, steel holds. Temperature-controlled trailers are carried above deck.

*(photo courtesy of Sea-Land Service Inc.)*

*(photo courtesy of Sea-Land Service Inc.)*

Gantry loading operation — container-trailers transferred ship board in a simple continuous movement.

# Trends In The Soluble Sector Of The Coffee Market

*Soluble Coffee in the United States*

Since 1954 when the United States Department of Commerce began its series of measurements of green coffee utilized in the production of soluble, or instant, coffee[1], the industry has experienced an early expansionary stage characterized by dramatic growth followed by moderating rates of increase and, subsequent to a highpoint in 1962, a period of decline. Thus, to date, the soluble coffee industry has followed the traditional "product cycle" in classic fashion through stages of introduction, early adoption, wide-spread adoption, maturity, and decline. It is not clear at this juncture whether production of soluble coffee in the United States will continue to ease downward, stabilize at some lower level or increase as a result of potential breakthroughs in taste and aroma technology. Since 1962 an average of approximately 17 percent of all bags of green coffee roasted have gone into soluble coffee compared with roughly 18 percent in the 1960-62 period.

It is not to be inferred that the decline in soluble coffee production is due solely to decreasing consumption. Actually lower rates of consumption have been evident since 1962, but two other factors have exerted a dampening influence: improved technology that has enabled manufacturers to extract a greater percentage of end product from green beans and decreasing exports of soluble coffee from the United States (the U. S. became a net importer in 1966 for the first time). All three of these factors will be discussed in greater length in later sections of this chapter.

The year under review marks the fourth consecutive year in which green coffee roastings, the basic input required in soluble coffee manufacture, declined. In 1966 aggregate green coffee roastings for both regular and soluble coffee came to 21,300,000 bags, down 380,000 bags or 1.8 percent from last year. The amount of green coffee utilized in producing the soluble product was 3,522,000 bags in 1966, down 254,000 bags or 6.7 percent from 1965. The greater rate of decrease in roastings of green coffee for soluble than in total roastings brought the percentage of the first quantity related to the second to 16.5 in the later year compared with 17.4 in the earlier. The current year marked the third consecutive period in which both regular and soluble coffee decreased concurrently.

Several years ago demand from the burgeoning vending machine industry was considered to be a major additional outlet for soluble coffee sales. But recent innovations in vending machine technology have encouraged fabricators of those machines to place emphasis on units which can brew small amounts or even individual cups of

---

[1] The terms, soluble coffee and instant coffee will be used interchangeably in this chapter.

freshly-brewed regular coffee. That product is so much superior to the instant coffee brewed by earlier models that the fresh-brew regular coffee machines account for practically all the growth in use of beverage-vending units, and at the same time they are displacing the older machines as well. Soluble coffee usage therefore can be expected to revert in the main to its former pattern, relying primarily on household purchase volume.

Production of soluble coffee has declined in each year since 1962. At the same time the number of bags of green coffee utilized in the production of the soluble product as a proportion of total bags of green coffee roasted has decreased from 18 percent in 1962 to 16.5 percent in 1966. The table below gives details of changes in total roastings of green coffee, green coffee roastings for soluble use and the relationships between the two measures for 1954 through 1966.

**UNITED STATES: ROASTINGS OF GREEN COFFEE, 1954-1966**

(thousands of bags of 60 kilos or 132.276 pounds each)

| Year | Total Bags of Green Coffee Roasted (1) | Number of Bags Going Into Regular Coffee (2) | Number of Bags Going Into Soluble Coffee (3) | Percent (3) of (1) (4) | Percent Change in Roastings for Soluble Coffee (5) |
|---|---|---|---|---|---|
| 1954 | 17,601 | 15,549 | 2,052 | 11.7 | — |
| 1955 | 18,813 | 16,490 | 2,323 | 12.3 | +13.2 |
| 1956 | 20,263 | 17,123 | 3,140 | 15.5 | +35.2 |
| 1957 | 20,321 | 16,985 | 3,336 | 16.4 | + 6.2 |
| 1958 | 20,937 | 17,445 | 3,492 | 16.7 | + 4.7 |
| 1959 | 21,698 | 17,954 | 3,744 | 17.3 | + 7.2 |
| 1960 | 21,895 | 17,896 | 3,999 | 18.3 | + 6.8 |
| 1961 | 22,294 | 18,284 | 4,010 | 18.0 | + 0.3 |
| 1962 | 22,677 | 18,595 | 4,082 | 18.0 | + 1.8 |
| 1963 | 22,815 | 18,881 | 3,934 | 17.2 | − 3.6 |
| 1964 | 22,374 | 18,582 | 3,792 | 16.9 | − 3.6 |
| 1965 | 21,680 | 17,904 | 3,776 | 17.4 | − 0.4 |
| 1966 | 21,300 | 17,778 | 3,522 | 16.5 | − 6.7 |

SOURCE: *U.S. Department of Commerce, Bureau of the Census, Green Coffee Inventories and Roastings, 1966 (Fourth Quarter),* release of February 16, 1967.

NOTE: Before 1957 roastings by, or sales to, the military services were excluded. Roastings for sale to the military services, included since 1957, represent about two percent of the total.

*Conversion Rates, Green to Soluble Coffee*

In order to analyze the consumption of soluble coffee in greater depth, it is necessary to determine equivalency ratios for green and soluble coffee. Since soluble coffee is a derivative product of green coffee, an input-output ratio will give the exact relationship between the raw commodity and the final product. Information on either item then can readily be converted into the equivalent of its counterpart for purposes of comparison or analysis.

A factor known as the *extraction rate* has been determined to perform the desired conversions. The *extraction rate* may be defined as the percentage of yield of soluble coffee from a unit of green coffee. For example, in 1966 the rate was 37 percent, i.e., 100 pounds of green coffee would yield 37 pounds of soluble coffee on the average in that year.

Continuing refinements in soluble coffee processing technology have increased the extraction rate over the past decade or two. In 1951 and 1952 the rate was only 27.8 percent, while in 1965 and 1966 the rate was 37.0 percent. Values for the intervening years are given in the table below.

**UNITED STATES: EXTRACTION RATES, SOLUBLE COFFEE OUTPUT AS A PERCENTAGE OF GREEN COFFEE INPUT, 1951-1966.**

| Years | Percent |
| --- | --- |
| 1951-52 | 27.8 |
| 1953-54 | 29.0 |
| 1955-56 | 30.0 |
| 1957-58 | 31.0 |
| 1959-60 | 32.0 |
| 1961 | 33.3 |
| 1962 | 34.0 |
| 1963 | 35.0 |
| 1964 | 36.0 |
| 1965-66 | 37.0 |

SOURCE: *Department of Statistics and Economic Research, PACB.*

Soluble coffee manufacturers understandably are reluctant to disclose details of their operations. Data on yield ratios therefore are sparse indeed. The Department of Research has constructed estimates based on informal trade surveys. Thus, the figures in the table above indicate only rough averages for the industry for a given year; the extraction rates for individual roasters may vary widely from these averages.

The extraction rates shown in the preceding table have been used, where appropriate, in all tables relating to the United States.

Since no comparable figures have been computed for other countries, the International Coffee Organization has adopted an "official" extraction rate of 33.3 percent in dealing with international transactions in soluble coffee. Where the ICO rate has been used in the tables of this book, that fact has been noted in the footnotes.

## UNITED STATES: NET AVAILABILITIES OF SOLUBLE COFFEE, 1954-1966
(thousands of bags of green-coffee equivalent)

| Year | Number of Bags Roasted for Soluble Coffee (1) | Net Exports of Soluble Coffee (2) | Net Availabilities of Soluble Coffee (3) | Percentage Change in Net Availabilities (4) |
|------|---|---|---|---|
| 1954 | 2,052 | 19 | 2,033 | — |
| 1955 | 2,323 | 35 | 2,288 | +12.5 |
| 1956 | 3,140 | 43 | 3,097 | +35.4 |
| 1957 | 3,336 | 37 | 3,299 | + 6.5 |
| 1958 | 3,492 | 21 | 3,471 | + 5.2 |
| 1959 | 3,744 | 41 | 3,703 | + 6.7 |
| 1960 | 3,999 | 51 | 3,948 | + 6.6 |
| 1961 | 4,010 | 139 | 3,871 | + 2.0 |
| 1962 | 4,082 | 200 | 3,882 | + 0.3 |
| 1963 | 3,934 | 178 | 3,756 | − 3.2 |
| 1964 | 3,792 | 202 | 3,590 | − 4.4 |
| 1965 | 3,776 | 189 | 3,587 | − 0.1 |
| 1966 | 3,522 | (58)* | 3,580 | − 0.2 |

SOURCE: U. S. Department of Commerce
*Net Imports

## UNITED STATES: NET AVAILABILITIES OF SOLUBLE COFFEE, 1954-1966
(thousands of pounds of soluble coffee)

| Year | Domestic Production of Soluble Coffee (1) | Net Exports of Soluble Coffee (2) | Net Availabilities of Soluble Coffee (3) | Percentage Change in Net Availabilities (4) |
|------|---|---|---|---|
| 1954 | 78,715 | 728 | 77,987 | — |
| 1955 | 92,183 | 1,381 | 90,802 | +16.4 |
| 1956 | 124,604 | 1,962 | 122,912 | +35.4 |
| 1957 | 136,795 | 1,498 | 135,297 | +10.1 |
| 1958 | 143,191 | 843 | 142,348 | + 5.2 |
| 1959 | 158,477 | 1,721 | 156,756 | +10.1 |
| 1960 | 169,271 | 2,169 | 167,102 | + 6.6 |
| 1961 | 176,809 | 6,117 | 170,692 | + 2.1 |
| 1962 | 183,583 | 8,995 | 174,588 | + 2.3 |
| 1963 | 182,131 | 8,241 | 173,890 | − 0.4 |
| 1964 | 180,572 | 9,619 | 170,953 | − 1.7 |
| 1965 | 184,805 | 9,250 | 175,555 | + 2.7 |
| 1966 | 172,374 | (2,839)* | 175,213 | − 0.2 |

SOURCE: U.S. Department of Commerce
*Net Imports

*Alternative Estimates of Soluble Coffee Consumption in the United States*

In analyzing the consumption of soluble coffee, production measured in bags of green coffee should be considered only a broad indicator. That measure must be further refined by adjustment for net exports of soluble coffee. Details of that adjustment are shown in the two tables on the preceding page. The first table estimates the net availabilities of soluble coffee in terms of green coffee, while the second table estimates it in terms of the finished product.

Figures in the second of the above tables indicate a slight loss of 0.2 percent in estimated availabilities of soluble coffee for 1966 from the volume estimated for 1965. From 1954 through 1959 availabilities of the soluble product more than doubled. During that period annual increases varied from 5.2 to 35.4 percent as the product gained favor with consumers. During the 1960-1962 interim, year-to-year gains ranged from 2.1 to 6.6 percent — significantly smaller increases than in the earlier period. Moreover, the percentage gain from the beginning to the end of the 1960-1962 period was only 4.5 percent compared with 15.9 percent for the previous period. For 1963 and subsequent years the product has experienced declines in year-to-year comparisons in all years but one, 1965. However, that one year of increase, due entirely to an in-

**UNITED STATES: RATE OF SOLUBLE COFFEE DRINKING, 1953-1967**

| Year | Soluble Coffee | Percent of Cups of All Coffee |
|---|---|---|
| | (cups per person per day) | |
| 1953 | .26 | 10.1 |
| 1954 | .30 | 11.5 |
| 1955 | .37 | 13.9 |
| 1956 | .46 | 17.2 |
| 1957 | .50 | 17.7 |
| 1958 | .65 | 19.2 |
| 1959 | .60 | 20.4 |
| 1960 | .56 | 20.2 |
| 1961 | .64 | 21.5 |
| 1962 | .67 | 21.5 |
| 1963 | .65 | 21.6 |
| 1964 | .61 | 21.0 |
| 1965 | .58 | 20.8 |
| 1966 | .63 | 22.0 |
| 1967 | .65 | 22.9 |

SOURCE: *Psychological Corporation, 1953-56;*
*Corby Research Service, 1957-64;*
*Professional Research Associates, 1965-67.*

creased extraction rate, was enough to bring the end of the 1963-1966 period 0.8 percent above the beginning.

Net availabilities of soluble coffee for 1966 surpassed 175 million pounds, 124 percent more than the 78 million bags recorded in 1954. However, on the basis of green coffee required to produce those quantities of soluble coffee, the increase was only 76 percent — a clear indication of the increased extraction rate.

Conversion of powdered soluble into its end-beverage form suggests another measure of soluble coffee consumption. That gauge, derived from the annual winter coffee-drinking surveys conducted for the Bureau by a private research organization, is presented in the preceding table. This schedule demonstrates the daily per capita cup consumption of soluble coffee and the proportion that it represents of total cup consumption of coffee.

The figures in the table above indicate that soluble consumption as measured cups per person per day has increased for the second consecutive year. While the rate of drinking for all coffee has been higher in the last two years, soluble consumption has shown a greater gain than that of regular. Thus, in terms of the proportion of all cups of coffee consumed soluble now stands at a record highpoint of almost 23 percent. For 1966 the rate of soluble consumption was .65 cup per person per day, up

**UNITED STATES: HOUSEHOLD PURCHASES OF SOLUBLE COFFEE, 1951-1966**

| Year | Equivalent 2-ounce Units (millions) | Percent Change |
|---|---|---|
| 1951 | 227 | — |
| 1952 | 286 | +126.0 |
| 1953 | 383 | + 33.9 |
| 1954 | 555 | + 44.9 |
| 1955 | 651 | + 17.3 |
| 1956 | 770 | + 18.3 |
| 1957 | 930 | + 20.8 |
| 1958 | 988 | + 6.2 |
| 1959 | 1,044 | + 5.7 |
| 1960 | 1,098 | + 5.2 |
| 1961 | 1,172 | + 6.6 |
| 1962 | 1,211 | + 3.3 |
| 1963 | 1,181 | − 2.5 |
| 1964 | 1,159 | − 1.9 |
| 1965 | 1,154 | − 0.4 |
| 1966 | 1,122 | − 2.8 |

SOURCE: *Market Research Corporation of America.*

slightly from the .63 cup mark established in 1965 and just under the peak of .67 cup recorded in 1962. The effect of recent increases in cup consumption has been, of course, to stimulate production of the soluble product, but these gains have been greatly offset by the higher extraction rates.

Market Research Corporation of America (MRCA) surveys weekly a national panel of households that is selected to be representative of the composition of the population. It has been providing the Bureau with information concerning all aspects of household coffee purchases since 1951. MRCA reported that consumer sales of soluble coffee in the current year decreased by 2.8 percent from the level recorded in 1965. That reflects the relative sluggishness of this sector in recent years. Purchases of soluble coffee for household consumption in 1966 amounted to 1,122 million equivalent two-ounce units. Such purchases, together with their annual percentage changes for the period 1951-66, are shown in the preceding table.

The conversion of soluble and regular coffee purchases into green-coffee equivalent permits the comparison of the relative importance of each type of coffee in terms of the raw product. In 1966 soluble coffee represented 19.9 percent of all household purchases — the same proportion as in 1965. That figure reached its highest level of 21.0 percent in 1962. Figures for other years are shown in the table below.

### UNITED STATES: PROPORTION OF SOLUBLE COFFEE IN TOTAL COFFEE PURCHASES BY HOUSEHOLDS, 1951-1966

| Year | Percent of Total Green Coffee Required |
|---|---|
| 1951 | 5.5 |
| 1952 | 6.5 |
| 1953 | 8.2 |
| 1954 | 12.7 |
| 1955 | 13.6 |
| 1956 | 16.0 |
| 1957 | 18.4 |
| 1958 | 19.3 |
| 1959 | 19.9 |
| 1960 | 20.6 |
| 1961 | 20.7 |
| 1962 | 21.0 |
| 1963 | 20.4 |
| 1964 | 20.1 |
| 1965 | 19.9 |
| 1966 | 19.9 |

SOURCE: Market Research Corporation of America

Another method of determining the relative importance of soluble coffee in households is to estimate the total number of cups consumed by them and then compute the number and proportion prepared from the soluble product. These calculations done by the Department of Statistics and Economic Research are based on field studies made to determine cup-yield rates in homes for regular and soluble coffee and, in the years before such studies were made, on data on cup-drinking rates, household consumption and other pertinent information. With the Data on household purchases of coffee supplied to the Bureau regularly by MRCA, together with cup-yield and cup-drinking rates, it is possible to arrive at close approximations of the total cup consumption by households and the proportion of it which is soluble coffee. (See table below.)

In summarizing the recent trend of soluble coffee consumption in the United States, it is apparent that consumers have increased their daily cup consumption in the last two years by an almost insignificant amount. However, they have probably obtained a greater number of cups of beverage per unit of soluble product since household sales have eased downward in spite of the slightly increased rate of per capita drinking and a larger aggregate population — in short, more cups from fewer units.

**UNITED STATES: PROPORTION OF SOLUBLE COFFEE IN TOTAL CUPS OF COFFEE CONSUMED BY HOUSEHOLDS, 1951-1966**

| Year | Percent |
|------|---------|
| 1951 | 7.2 |
| 1952 | 8.4 |
| 1953 | 11.1 |
| 1954 | 16.5 |
| 1955 | 17.6 |
| 1956 | 19.8 |
| 1957 | 22.4 |
| 1958 | 23.5 |
| 1959 | 24.4 |
| 1960 | 25.3 |
| 1961 | 26.2 |
| 1962 | 26.8 |
| 1963 | 26.6 |
| 1964 | 26.8 |
| 1965 | 27.4 |
| 1966 | 27.2 |

SOURCES: *MRCA and Department of Statistics and Economic Research, PACB.*

There is some evidence that an additional factor contributing to this divergence is a small increase in soluble coffee consumption outside of the home. However, the influence of the non-home sector is believed to be quite small since it is estimated that 79 percent of all soluble coffee is consumed in the home and, as it was noted earlier, the increase for that sector was quite small. One possible conclusion that merits consideration is that housewives have been reducing the amount of soluble coffee that they use to make a cup of beverage.

*United States Trade in Soluble Coffee:*
*Imports and Exports*

During 1966, 10,552,788 pounds of soluble coffee were imported into the United States. That amount was almost four times the quantity imported in 1965 and represented the largest volume of soluble coffee ever imported in a year. Brazil supplied almost six million pounds or 56.8 percent of the total and displaced Nicaragua as the principal source of supply. The increase for Brazil was 20-fold over the quantity that country exported to the United States in 1965.

Guatemala maintained its position as the second largest supplier. That country contributed 13.3 percent of the total — about the same as last year — even though it increased shipments by almost 300 percent. Mexico was in third position with a little over one million pounds or 9.6 percent of the total. That country was the largest supplier to the U. S. in 1964 but contributed only 8,047 pounds to the import total last year. In fourth and fifth positions respectively, were Nicaragua with 8.2 percent of total soluble imports and El Salvador with 7.3 percent. Two European countries, France with three percent and Switzerland with 1.3 percent, followed. A number of

**UNITED STATES: IMPORTS OF SOLUBLE COFFEE, QUANTITY AND VALUE, BY COUNTRY OF ORIGIN, 1966.**

| Countries | Pounds of Soluble Coffee | Equivalent* 60-Kilo Bags Green | Total Import Value ($ U.S.) | Average Import Price Per Pound ($ U.S.) |
|---|---|---|---|---|
| Brazil | 5,996,349 | 135,996 | 6,471,142 | 1.08 |
| Guatemala | 1,404,738 | 31,859 | 1,231,245 | 0.88 |
| Mexico | 1,011,349 | 22,937 | 723,820 | 0.72 |
| Nicaragua | 863,637 | 19,587 | 1,134,808 | 1.31 |
| El Salvador | 769,143 | 17,444 | 749,541 | 0.97 |
| France | 320,544 | 7,270 | 507,503 | 1.58 |
| Switzerland | 132,277 | 3,000 | 66,850 | 0.51 |
| Others | 54,751 | 1,242 | 64,917 | 1.19 |
| **Total Imports** | **10,552,788** | **239,335** | **10,949,826** | **1.04** |

SOURCE: U. S. Department of Commerce.
*Conversion rate = 33.3 percent; the standard factor in international trade adopted by the ICO.

## U.S. SOLUBLE COFFEE IMPORTS

| | PERCENT* | THOUSANDS OF POUNDS |
|---|---|---|
| BRAZIL | 56.8 | 5,996 |
| | 9.7 | 276 |
| | 0.6 | 33 |
| GUATEMALA | 13.3 | 1,405 |
| | 13.0 | 370 |
| | 12.3 | 652 |
| NICARAGUA | 8.2 | 864 |
| | 65.4 | 1,858 |
| | 30.0 | 1,588 |
| OTHER W.H. | 16.9 | 1,786 |
| | 11.7 | 331 |
| | 57.0 | 3,011 |
| OTHER | 4.8 | 502 |
| | 0.2 | 4 |
| | 0.1 | 6 |

TOTAL
1966 10,553
1965 2,839
1964 5,290

*PERCENT OF ANNUAL IMPORTS

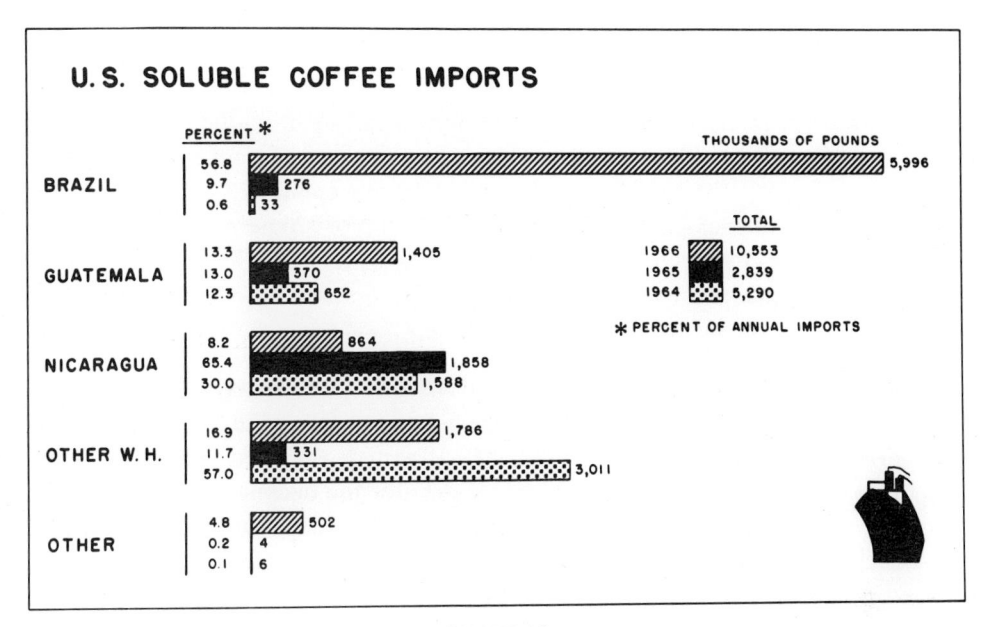

CHART 16

## U.S. SOLUBLE COFFEE EXPORTS

| | PERCENT* | THOUSANDS OF POUNDS |
|---|---|---|
| JAPAN | 25.0 | 1,899 |
| | 59.0 | 7,192 |
| | 48.1 | 7,227 |
| CANADA | 28.9 | 2,193 |
| | 15.8 | 1,910 |
| | 17.9 | 2,685 |
| UNITED KINGDOM | 22.2 | 1,688 |
| | 7.6 | 925 |
| | 18.9 | 2,790 |
| AUSTRALIA | 3.2 | 243 |
| | 2.7 | 326 |
| | 4.5 | 669 |
| OTHERS | 20.7 | 1,574 |
| | 14.5 | 1,759 |
| | 10.3 | 1,500 |

TOTAL
1966 7,597
1965 12,112
1964 14,884

*PERCENT OF TOTAL EXPORTS

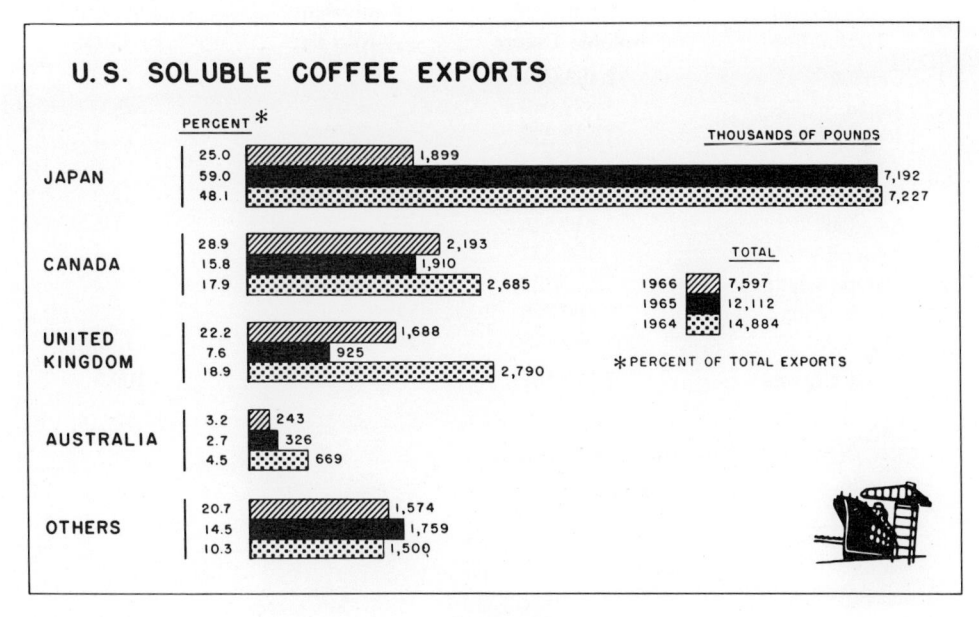

CHART 17

countries shipped small amounts accounting as a group for only one-half of one percent of the total.

The dramatic increase in soluble coffee imports in 1966 from the level of the preceding year was reflected in a very large though not commensurate rise in aggregate import value. In 1965 the total value of soluble imports came to $3,414,641. In comparison importers in 1966 paid $10,949,826, an increase of 320 percent. Average price per pound fell from the 1965 level of $1.20 to $1.04 in 1966, the lowest unit value on record. The amounts received from each supplying country together with other related information appear in the preceding table.

Exports of soluble coffee from the United States in 1966 totaled 7,597,137 pounds, a decline of 37.3 percent from the 12,112,459 pounds registered in 1965 and a decline of 49 percent from the record level of 14,884,421 pounds achieved in 1964. A sizeable drop in demand from Japan was the major reason for the decline. The average price of soluble coffee exports was $1.64 per pound in 1966 compared with $1.94 in 1965. The principal destinations of soluble coffee exports from the United States are summarized in the table that follows.

**UNITED STATES: EXPORTS OF SOLUBLE COFFEE, 1966.**

| Country of Destination | Pounds of Soluble Coffee | Equivalent* 60-Kilo Bags | Percent of Total |
|---|---|---|---|
| Canada | 2,193,069 | 49,739 | 28.9 |
| Japan | 1,899,049 | 43,070 | 25.0 |
| United Kingdom | 1,688,238 | 38,289 | 22.2 |
| Australia | 243,646 | 5,526 | 3.2 |
| Mexico | 150,849 | 3,421 | 2.0 |
| Sweden | 110,546 | 2,507 | 1.5 |
| Finland | 108,837 | 2,468 | 1.4 |
| Nampo Islands | 102,832 | 2,332 | 1.3 |
| Netherlands | 100,096 | 2,270 | 1.3 |
| Other | 999,975 | 22,680 | 13.2 |
| **Total Exports** | **7,597,137** | **172,302** | **100.0** |

SOURCE: U.S. Department of Commerce.
*See footnote to preceding table.

Exports of soluble coffee in 1966 were down to the lowest level since 1960, and the United States became a net importer of the soluble product for the first time. In terms of net imports the United States in 1966 absorbed 2,955,651 pounds. Exports, imports and the import deficit or surplus in pounds of soluble coffee in the period 1956-1966 are set forth in the table below.

## UNITED STATES: IMPORTS AND EXPORTS OF SOLUBLE COFFEE, 1956-1966.

(Soluble Pounds)

| Year | Imports | Exports | Net Exports |
|------|---------|---------|-------------|
| 1956 | 1,375,033 | 3,066,586 | 1,691,553 |
| 1957 | 3,309,117 | 4,806,914 | 1,497,797 |
| 1958 | 3,635,913 | 4,479,323 | 843,410 |
| 1959 | 4,616,403 | 6,337,127 | 1,720,724 |
| 1960 | 4,626,742 | 6,796,057 | 2,169,315 |
| 1961 | 3,425,347 | 9,542,225 | 6,116,878 |
| 1962 | 4,020,769 | 12,979,879 | 8,959,110 |
| 1963 | 6,258,617 | 14,492,199 | 8,233,582 |
| 1964 | 5,289,696 | 14,884,421 | 9,594,725 |
| 1965 | 2,838,803 | 12,112,459 | 9,273,656 |
| 1966 | 10,552,788 | 7,597,137 | (2,955,651)* |

SOURCE: U.S. Department of Commerce.

*Net Imports

### Soluble Coffee in Canada

The production of soluble coffee in Canada rose to 20,362,000 pounds in 1966, a gain of almost 11 percent over the 18,967,000 pounds produced in 1965. In retrospect the 1965 output appears to be an exception to the steady annual increases of earlier years which had caused domestic production to quadruple in the period since 1956. The contraction in output last year could well have been caused by liquidation of finished inventories, so that the 1966 performance indicates a return to more normal operations in the industry. As domestic production has expanded to meet consumer demand, imports have become less important in fulfilling domestic requirements.

Imports of soluble coffee into Canada amounted to 2,600,861 pounds in 1966, a decline of 12 percent from the 2,145,573 pounds imported in 1965 and almost 60 percent below the record high established in 1960. The United States again was the principal supplier of soluble coffee imports into Canada, accounting for 84 percent of the total. In 1965 the United States share was 97 percent. That decline in the U.S. import share apparently was compensated largely by the increase in the proportion for Brazil which expanded to 12 percent of the total in the most recent year. The remaining four percent was distributed among several countries, primarily the United Kingdom and Mexico.

Although Canada remained a net importer of soluble coffee in 1966, that country continued to export large quantities of the product. In the year under review, Canada exported 1,134,689 pounds of soluble coffee of which 90 percent was shipped to the

United Kingdom, six percent to Australia, two percent to West Germany, and the remaining two percent to various countries.

An estimate of per capita supply of soluble coffee in Canada for 1966 can be obtained by taking production, adding net imports and dividing by the number of persons. The procedure is shown in the table below.

**Canada: Per Capita Availabilities of Soluble Coffee, 1966**

(in pounds of soluble coffee)

| | |
|---|---:|
| Production | 20,362,000 |
| Plus: Imports | 2,600,861 |
| Gross Availabilities | 22,962,861 |
| Less: Exports | 1,134,689 |
| Net Availabilities | 21,828,172 |
| Population | (19,960,000) |
| Per Capita Availabilities | 1.09 |

SOURCE: *Dominion Bureau of Statistics.*

*Soluble Coffee in Europe*

The figures in the table below give the estimated percentages of total coffee consumption represented by soluble for the principal coffee-consuming nations of Western Europe.

M. François Le Chevalier, President of Jacques Louis-Delamare et Cie., has commented as follows on the soluble coffee scene in Europe during 1966.[2]

> Up to now in the United States the freeze dried soluble seems to have remained under the regime of development control. On the other hand, in Western Europe the freeze-dried soluble has been dropped on the market somewhat like a bull in a China shop. After a timid start in Northern Germany at the beginning of 1965, it was rapidly launched in many European Countries, preceded by or accompanied with successive vague publicity . . . .
>
> According to last report, there are presently five plants fully processing soluble coffee through the freeze drying methods in Western Europe. Half a dozen more plants are reported to be under construction. Besides, a few freeze-drying dairies are processing coffee concentrated liquids to turn them into crystals . . . between vegetables and fruits . . . .

---

[2] François Le Chevalier, *Coffee Report* No. 279, January-February 1967, Jacques Louis–Delamare & Cie., S.A. Le Havre, France.

The welcome of consumers to "freeze-dried" solubles is said to have been, almost everywhere, "better than expected", although the 50-gram tin is commonly offered in Continental Europe at a premium of US $ 0.20 to 0.25 above good average quality spray-dried instant coffees (in U.K. the premium is reduced to US dollar 0.10 or 0.15: in this Country, solubles have always been sold much cheaper than elsewhere) . . . .

It is the first time since many years that a quality coffee, sold at substantial premium, is reported to have enjoyed a favourable welcome in several European Countries; the fact itself is noticeable. However, it is also to be noticed that, spray dried or freeze dried, the soluble has not yet shaken the traditional reluctance of Norwegian, Finnish and Italian consumers against all forms of instant coffee. . . .

It is too early to say whether the freeze-dried soluble is promised to a bright career. But, one thing is sure: during the first two years of the freeze-dried life in Europe, the soluble coffee family has registered substantial progress . . . .

A per-country calculation reveals that the proportion of soluble coffees in the total coffee consumption of Western Europe has now reached about 12.5 percent in cup terms, against about 9 percent in 1962 . . . .

No doubt that the progress of soluble coffee consumption in Europe may be due also to other factors than the introduction of crystallized coffee. The soluble coffee has gained also in Greece and Spain where the freeze-dried process has not yet been introduced. However, the promotional campaigns which have accompanied the launching of crystallized coffee, the incentive effects of these campaigns on the commercial policy of traditional soluble factories and also the improvement of all soluble qualities, have created a favourable climate and shaken the apathy of consumers . . . .

Another factor has facilitated the promotion of soluble coffee in Europe: most coffee advertised labels and grocery store organizations are now selling and promoting their own soluble coffee. There are presently about 35 soluble coffee plants in Europe, plus six or seven under construction. When they do not process their soluble coffee in their own plants, European roasters can now get their supplies from plants working on a toll basis . . . .

The evolution in this respect is to be noticed: while the European soluble coffee industry was increasing its turnover, sales of soluble coffee coming from overseas have lost ground. This is mainly due to preference custom tariffs inside the E.E.C., to the cost of ocean freight and to the exigencies of most European roasters, each of them willing to have their own soluble blend . . . .

Soluble coffee has now become a product of current sale in the smallest European grocery shops. Last consumption reports reveal that soluble coffee consumers are presently belonging to all categories of the population, with a larger proportion among young generations . . . .

## PERCENTAGE OF TOTAL COFFEE CONSUMPTION REPRESENTED BY SOLUBLE

| Country | 1962 | 1963 | 1964 | 1965 | 1966 |
|---|---|---|---|---|---|
| United Kingdom | 75 | 75 | 77.5 | 75 | 72 |
| Switzerland | 18 | 19/20 | 20 | 25 | 30 |
| Netherlands | 14 | 14 | 13 | 15 | N.A. |
| France | 11 | 11.3* | 11.7 | 12.5 | N.A. |
| Greece | 10 | N.A. | 15 | N.A. | N.A. |
| Spain | 7 | 9 | N.A. | N.A. | 16 |
| Germany (F.R.) | 7 | 8.5 | 11 | 11 | 11.5 |
| Austria | 5 | N.A. | N.A. | N.A. | N.A. |
| Belgium | 5 | 5 | 5 | 7 | N.A. |
| Denmark | 5 | 5 | 5 | 5 | N.A. |
| Portugal | 2 | N.A. | N.A. | N.A. | N.A. |
| Italy | 1 | 1.5 | 1 | 1 | N.A. |
| Finland | 1 | 1 | 3 | 0.75 | N.A. |
| Norway | 1 | 1 | 1 | 1 | N.A. |
| Sweden | 1 | 1 | 2 | 1 | N.A. |
| **Western Europe** | **9** | **N.A.** | **N.A.** | **N.A.** | **12.5** |

SOURCE: Jacques Louis-Delamare & Cie. S.A., Le Havre

*REVISED

N.A.:— Not Available.

# The United States Market

*Green-Coffee*[1] *Imports into the United States, Their Origins and Dollar Value*

During 1966 the United States imported 22,055,292 bags of green coffee and a small amount of roasted coffee — 4,826,354 pounds — which amount is equivalent to 36,487 bags of green coffee. Together they totaled 22,091,779 bags which was 744,996 or 3.5 percent more than the 21,346,783 bags imported during 1965. It was the first year-to-year increase following three consecutive annual declines. Current-year imports are roughly equivalent to the volume registered in 1960. Yearly increases followed in subsequent years bringing the 1962 total to 24,548,939 bags — a record high point. The 1966 figure is 2,457,160 bags or 10 percent below that highpoint. However, it is well to note that the quantity for 1962 was inflated by inventory accumulation of some 1.1 million bags, largely as a result of the acceleration of imports during the latter months of 1962 in anticipation of a waterfront strike in the Atlantic and Gulf ports. Further inventory accumulation occurred in 1963 and there was only partial liquidation of those heavy stocks in 1964. But during 1965 there was a net drawdown of roughly 1.2 million bags from inventories, and stocks remained at a constant level of some 3.14 million bags in 1966. However, changes in inventory suggest only a partial reason for the 1962-1966 decline — at the heart of the matter is an underlying trend of attrition in per capita consumption of green coffee.

Green-coffee imports into the United States represented 44.2 percent of world imports in 1966 compared with shares of 45.0, 47.0, 49.8, and 52.1 percent respectively in 1965, 1964, 1963, and 1962. The preceding figures indicate a continuing deterioration in the relative position of the United States as a coffee importer compared with the other importing nations of the world. The position of the United States has clearly declined from the post World War II years, 1946-52, when its share of world imports was roughly 66 percent; and it is presently below its prewar level of some 49 percent.

The import figures shown above do not include soluble-coffee imports or coffee received from Hawaii and Puerto Rico. Total coffee imports into the United States, including net supplies from Hawaii [2] and Puerto Rico and imports of soluble coffee, were 22,330,000 bags in 1966 compared with 21,512,000 bags in 1965 and 23,072,000 bags in 1964.

---

[1] It has been the custom of the Department of Statistics and Economic Research, Pan-American Coffee Bureau to include a small quantity of roasted-coffee imports with green-coffee imports into the United States. Thus, reference to green-coffee imports in this chapter will include a small amount (roughly 1.5 to 2.5 percent) of roasted coffee — unless otherwise noted.

[2] The coffee received in Continental United States from Hawaii is, of course, an internal transfer and not an import. United States import data therefore do not show entries of coffee into Hawaii, but that state could have received some coffee from the mainland.

The countries of the Western Hemisphere continued to be the principal source of green-coffee imports into the United States; however, the proportion originating in those countries in the import total continued to decline during the year under review. In 1966 imports into the United States from Western Hemisphere countries came to 14,512,845 bags — an increase of 115,427 bags or 0.8 percent from the 14,397,418 bags in 1965 — but they made up only 65.7 percent of total imports into the United States. The corresponding percentages for 1965, 1964, 1963, and 1962 were 67.0, 71.2, 76.6, and 77.9 respectively. Much of the increase in imports from Western Hemisphere countries was accounted for by the increase in imports from Brazil. An abnormally low volume of only 5,744,024 bags were imported from that country in 1965. In 1966 that figure rose by almost one million bags or more than 17 percent to 6,730,398 bags. In the earlier year Brazil supplied 26.9 percent of total green-coffee imports into the United States, — in the later year 30.5 percent. In 1964 Brazil's share was 31.5 percent; it was 38.8 percent in 1963 and 37.0 percent in 1962.

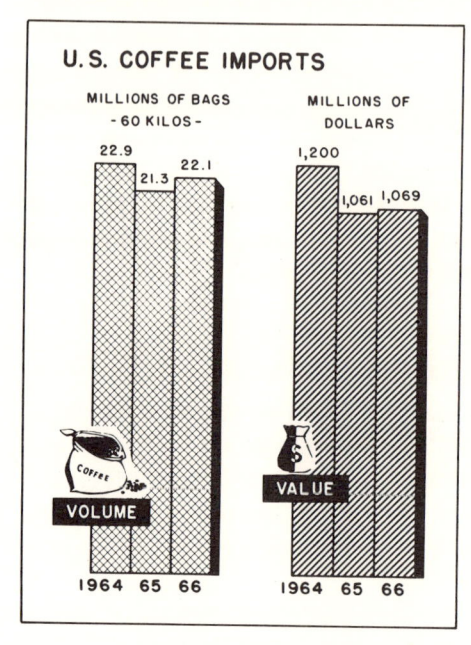

CHART 18

The only other Latin American country registering a major gain in exports to the United States during 1966 was Guatemala. In the past two years that country has made a remarkable recovery in regaining its earlier position in the United States market. In 1963 Guatemala was the third largest Western Hemisphere supplier of green coffee to the United States. In that year imports to the United States from that country were 1,079,816 bags or 4.9 of the total imports. In the following year a severe infestation of leaf miner brought Guatemalan coffee production to a low level, causing a reduction in imports into the United States from that source to 788,843 bags or 3.6 percent of the total. A fifteen-percent increase brought its 1965 figure to 903,830 bags and another increase of 23 percent brought its 1966 volume to 1,110,122 bags or five percent of the total. For the years 1964 and 1965 Guatemala slipped to the position of fourth largest Western Hemisphere supplier of coffee to the United States. In 1966 it regained its previous position of third.

Colombia remained the second most important source of coffee imports into the United States among all supplying countries of the world. However, its volume decreased from its 1965 level by 18.3 percent to 2,716,078 bags and its share became 12.3 percent. In 1965 the volume of imports from Colombia decreased by 10.5 per-

138

cent which reduced its share to 15.6 percent compared with 16.2 percent in 1964, 16.6 percent in 1963 and 17.7 percent in 1962. Decreases of more than 100,000 bags in 1966 among other Latin American producing countries were also sustained by Mexico, El Salvador and Nicaragua.

During 1966 the coffee-producing countries of Africa increased their volume of green-coffee imports into the United States and also their share of the total. The coffee-growing countries of Africa accounted for 6,455,305 bags as against 6,162,875 bags in 1965, their gain being 292,430 bags or 4.7 percent. Last year the corresponding gain over 1964 was more modest, 91,807 bags or 1.5 percent. In 1963 the increase was more than a million bags or almost 20 percent. Their share in the total rose from 26.6 percent in 1964 to 28.9 percent in 1965 and 29.2 percent in 1966. Cameroun, Liberia, Sierra Leone, Tanganyika, and Uganda each increased their respective quantities in the import total of the United States by more than 100,000 bags during 1966, while Congo (D.R.), Ethiopia and Madagascar each experienced decreases in excess of the same amount. Of particular interest was a 520,925 bag or 276.8 percent increase in imports from Liberia and a 366,156 bag or 31.6 percent decrease in imports from Ethiopia. The increase in the volume for Sierra Leone represented a gain of 550.6 percent while that of Cameroun was an increase of 125.4 percent. Although the increase for Nigeria was only 11,132 bags, that represented a gain of 116.1 percent.

The increase in imports of green coffee into the United States from Africa has been in evidence for some years. The proportion of coffee imported into the United States from African producers in the period 1951-1966 is shown in the table below.

| Year | Percent | Year | Percent |
| --- | --- | --- | --- |
| 1951 | 4.8 | 1959 | 13.0 |
| 1952 | 6.1 | 1960 | 17.2 |
| 1953 | 7.0 | 1961 | 20.4 |
| 1954 | 9.0 | 1962 | 20.8 |
| 1955 | 11.4 | 1963 | 21.4 |
| 1956 | 11.8 | 1964 | 26.6 |
| 1957 | 14.9 | 1965 | 28.9 |
| 1958 | 14.7 | 1966 | 29.2 |

SOURCE: Department of Statistics and Economic Research, PACB based on data from the U.S. Department of Commerce.

Imports from Asia and Oceania rose significantly in 1966 over the preceding year. The increase was 337,833 bags or 43.1 percent, attributable for the most part to imports from Indonesia which increased by 331,058 bags or 51.5 percent. Imports from Asia and Oceania represented 5.1 percent of all green coffee imported into the

**UNITED STATES SOURCES OF COFFEE IMPORTS**

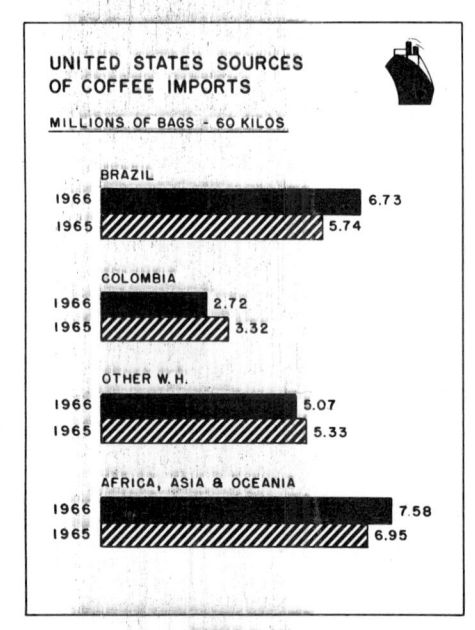

MILLIONS OF BAGS - 60 KILOS

BRAZIL
1966: 6.73
1965: 5.74

COLOMBIA
1966: 2.72
1965: 3.32

OTHER W.H.
1966: 5.07
1965: 5.33

AFRICA, ASIA & OCEANIA
1966: 7.58
1965: 6.95

CHART 19

United States during 1966. The corresponding figure for the preceding year was 3.7 percent; in 1964 it was 2.2 percent.

The aggregate value of green-coffee imports into the United States in 1966 was $1,068,580,000, which was $8,049,000 or 0.8 percent more than in the preceding year. In 1966 the average price per bag of green coffee was $48.37; while it was $49.68 in 1965, $52.43 in 1964, $40.05 in 1963, and $40.27 in 1962. The following tables show the aggregate volume and value of green-coffee imports and related details for the years 1954-1966.

While the volume of green-coffee imports into the United States during 1966 increased by 3.5 percent over the preceding year, the value of those imports increased by only 0.8 percent. The total value came to $1,068,580,000 — $8,049,000 over the

**UNITED STATES: AGGREGATE VOLUME OF GREEN-COFFEE IMPORTS, 1954-1966**

| Year | Volume (in thousands of bags) | Percentage Change From Preceding Year | Import Volume Index (1954 = 100) |
|---|---|---|---|
| 1954 | 17,092 | — | 100.0 |
| 1955 | 19,651 | +15.0 | 115.0 |
| 1956 | 21,252 | + 8.1 | 124.3 |
| 1957 | 20,858 | − 1.9 | 122.0 |
| 1958 | 20,168 | − 3.3 | 118.0 |
| 1959 | 23,270 | +15.4 | 136.1 |
| 1960 | 22,091 | − 5.1 | 129.2 |
| 1961 | 22,464 | + 1.7 | 131.4 |
| 1962 | 24,549 | + 9.3 | 143.6 |
| 1963 | 23,893 | − 2.7 | 139.8 |
| 1964 | 22,892 | − 4.2 | 133.9 |
| 1965 | 21,347 | − 6.8 | 124.9 |
| 1966 | 22,092 | + 3.5 | 129.3 |

SOURCE: *Department of Statistics and Economic Research, PACB based on basic data from the U.S. Department of Commerce.*

**UNITED STATES: AGGREGATE VALUE OF GREEN-COFFEE**
**1954-1966**

| Year | Value (in Thousands of U.S. Dollars) | Percentage Change From Preceding Year | Import Value Index (1954 = 100) |
|---|---|---|---|
| 1954 | 1,485,688 | — | 100.0 |
| 1955 | 1,356,538 | − 8.7 | 91.3 |
| 1956 | 1,438,961 | + 6.1 | 96.9 |
| 1957 | 1,375,456 | − 4.4 | 92.6 |
| 1958 | 1,170,687 | −14.9 | 78.8 |
| 1959 | 1,097,215 | − 6.3 | 73.9 |
| 1960 | 1,002,654 | − 8.6 | 67.5 |
| 1961 | 964,017 | − 3.9 | 65.0 |
| 1962 | 988,965 | + 2.6 | 66.6 |
| 1963 | 956,875 | − 3.2 | 64.4 |
| 1964 | 1,200,281 | +25.4 | 80.8 |
| 1965 | 1,060,531 | −11.6 | 71.4 |
| 1966 | 1,068,580 | + 0.8 | 71.9 |

SOURCE: *Department of Statistics and Economic Research, PACB based on basic data from the U.S. Department of Commerce.*

1965 figure. The highest value in recent years occurred in 1964 and amounted to $1,200,281,000; that was the largest aggregate subsequent to 1957. A high point of $1,485,688,000 was achieved in 1954.

In 1966 the Western Hemisphere countries received $756,098,000 from the United States for their green coffee compared with $793,108,000 in 1965. The difference represents a decrease of $37,010,000 or 4.7 percent. Dollar earnings for Brazil were higher by some $24 million or eight percent while those for Colombia were about $36 million or 18 percent less. Together, those two countries earned more than two-fifths of all United States expenditures on green coffee. They earned about the same share in 1965. Guatemala became the third largest recipient of United States payments for green coffee as a consequence of an increase of 16 percent, while Mexico was a close fourth despite a twelve percent decrease. The only other country in the Western Hemisphere earning more than $30 million from exports to the United States during 1966 was El Salvador.

While the coffee-producing countries of Africa increased their shipments of green coffee to the United States in 1966 by 4.7 percent, those shipments brought 13.4 percent more revenue. Uganda and Portuguese Africa each earned more in United States coffee trade than any other African country — about $50 million each. Large amounts, more than $30 million each, also were received by Ethiopia and Ivory Coast, with Liberia raising its total to $29.5 million — up almost $23 million from last year.

The African countries received 26.1 percent of total United States expenditures on green coffee in 1966 compared with 23.3 percent in 1965. The Western Hemisphere countries not only supplied a smaller proportion of green coffee requirements of the United States, but their share of total expenditures for coffee by that country dropped from 74.8 to 70.8 percent. Asia and Oceania received 3.1 percent in 1966 and 1.9 percent in 1965.

Although its percentage of total coffee imports declined to a level of 43.2 in 1966 from 45.4 in 1965 and from 50.0 in 1962, New York continued to be the principal customs district for the entry of coffee into the United States. New Orleans, Houston and San Francisco with 18.1, 14.2 and 11.7 percent, ranked respectively, in importance in 1966. By coastal zones 45.4 percent of the total was received in Atlantic ports, 38.7 percent in Gulf ports and 15.1 percent in Pacific ports during 1966 (the remaining 0.8 percent was not classified by port of entry).

*Imports, Exports or Re-Exports and Net Imports*

The Continental United States receives small amounts of green coffee from Hawaii and Puerto Rico as well as quantities of roasted and soluble coffee from several countries. A relatively small portion of the coffee imported into the United States is exported or reexported in green, roasted or soluble form. The movements of all coffee into and out of Continental United States are shown in the table below.

**UNITED STATES: COFFEE IMPORTS, EXPORTS, RE-EXPORTS AND TOTAL NEW SUPPLY**
**1966 and 1965**

(thousands of 60-kilo bags of green coffee or its equivalent)

|  | 1966 | 1965 |
|---|---|---|
| **Imports** | | |
| Green | 22,056 | 21,291 |
| Roasted | 36 | 56 |
| **Total Green and Roasted** | 22,092 | 21,347 |
| Soluble Imports | +215 | + 58 |
| **Total Imports** | 22,307 | 21,405 |
| **Exports and Reexports** | | |
| Green (Reexports) | 437 | 477 |
| Roasted (Exports) | 59 | 49 |
| Soluble (Exports) | 157 | 247 |
| **Total Exports or Reexports** | 653 | 773 |
| **Net Imports** | 21,654 | 20,632 |
| Net Supply From Hawaii and Puerto Rico | + 23 | +107 |
| **Total New Supply** | 21,677 | 20,739 |

N.B.:  *Ratio of green coffee to soluble = 2.70:1.00*
       *Ratio of green coffee to roasted = 1.19:1.00*

The figures in the table above indicate that net new supply, in green-coffee equivalent, totaled 21,677,000 bags in 1966 compared with 20,739,000 bags in 1965, an increase of 4.5 percent. Total value of all imports (not including Hawaii and Puerto Rico) in 1966 was $1,068,820,000 compared with $1,063,946,000 in 1965 and $1,212,178,000 in 1964. After deducting the value of exports and reexports, the result is net imports valued at $1,028,367,000, $1,006,862,000 and $1,144,390,000, respectively, in each of those three years.

*Imports and Exports of Green and Processed Coffee, Roastings and Net Civilian Visible Disappearance*

In this section we account, as far as possible, for the distribution of total coffee imports during 1966 into the domestic channels of distributions, to the Armed Forces and to foreign destinations. This distribution is shown in the next table, which is similar to those in the six previous *Annuals*. It will be noted that certain amounts of both green and roasted coffee cannot be accounted for. They amount to less than two percent of all coffee entering channels of distribution and may be attributed, at least in part, to the use of different statistical series in working out the demonstration.

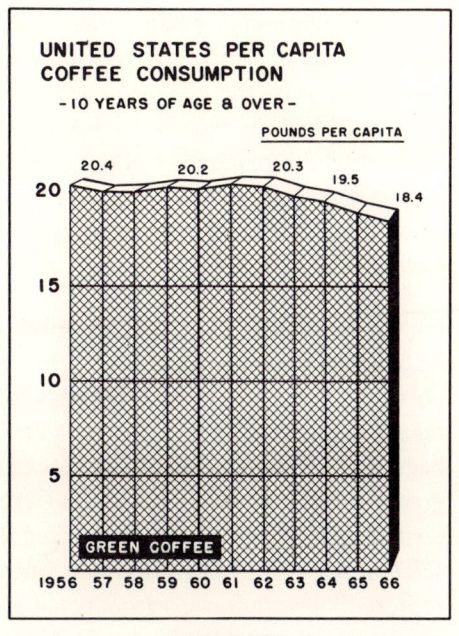

UNITED STATES PER CAPITA COFFEE CONSUMPTION
— 10 YEARS OF AGE & OVER —
POUNDS PER CAPITA

CHART 20

(thousands of 60-kilo bags or the equivalent thereof)

Green-Coffee Imports and Exports and Domestic Roastings

| | |
|---|---|
| Green-coffee imports (including net supplies from Hawaii and Puerto Rico) | 22,079 |
| Plus withdrawals from green-coffee inventories | + 2 |
| Green-coffee imports plus withdrawals from green inventories | 22,081 |
| Less shipment of green-coffee abroad | − 437 |
| Net green-coffee imports less shipment of green-coffee abroad | 21,644 |
| Total green-coffee roasted | 21,300 |
| Green-coffee available but otherwise unaccounted for | + 344 |

Domestic Roastings, Imports and Exports of Processed Coffee, Sales to the Armed Forces and Net Civilian Visible Disappearance

| | |
|---|---|
| Total green-coffee roasted | 21,300 |
| Imports of soluble coffee | + 215 |
| Total roastings plus imports of soluble coffee | 21,515 |
| Imports of roasted coffee | + 36 |
| Total roastings plus imports of soluble and roasted coffee | 21,551 |

| | |
|---|---:|
| Less exports of soluble and roasted coffee | − 216 |
| Domestic and foreign processed coffee minus exports of same | 21,335 |
| Less sales of processed coffee to the Armed Forces | − 440 |
| Civilian availabilities of processed coffee | 20,895 |
| Estimated net withdrawals from wholesale and retail inventories | + 130 |
| Total availabilities of processed coffee for civilian consumption | 21,025 |
| Less Net Civilian Visible Disappearance | 21,369 |
| Coffee consumed but otherwise unaccounted for | − 344 |

Consumption of green coffee or its equivalent in the United States, as measured by Net Civilian Visible Disappearance (NCVD), defined as all coffee processed for consumption by the civilian population, decreased to 21,369,000 bags in 1966 from 21,650,000 bags in 1965 or by 1.3 percent. At the same time imports of all coffee increased by 3.8 percent — while exports, reexports and consumption by the Armed Forces remained quite constant. The apparent discrepancy is explained by the augmented imports in 1965 by more than one million bags drawn from the heavy inventories of green coffee that existed at the close of 1964.

During 1966 the total imports of 22,330,000 bags were reduced by exports and reexports of 653,000 bags, offtake by the Armed Forces of 440,000 bags, and net withdrawals from stocks of green coffee of 2,000 bags. However, civilian availabilities were increased by 130,000 bags of green-coffee equivalent, representing withdrawals from retail and wholesale inventories. Thus, 21,369,000 bags of green coffee and green-coffee equivalent found their way into eating places, places of work, households, institutions, and manufacturing establishments. That quantity is assumed to represent consumption, although not all coffee arriving at ultimate destinations is consumed within the same calendar year in which it arrived.

1966 NET CIVILIAN VISIBLE DISAPPEARANCE
PERCENT OF TOTAL

OTHER 2.8
AT WORK 15.2
HOME PURCHASES 67.5
AT EATING PLACES 14.5

2.83 BILLION POUNDS OF GREEN COFFEE

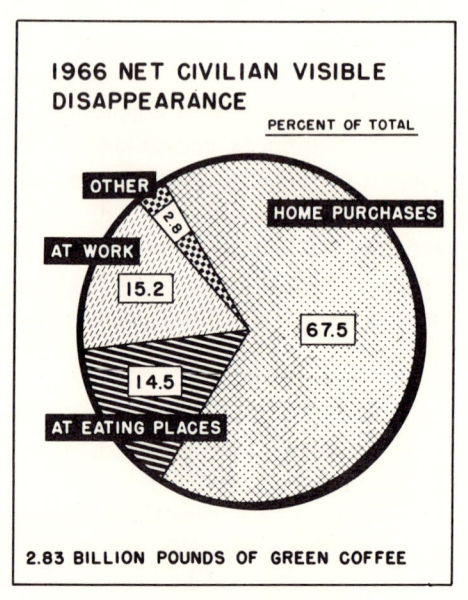

CHART 21

At the same time that NCVD in 1966 decreased slightly, the population of the United States increased by roughly one percent. The divergent trends in population and NCVD brought per capita consumption down to 14.6 pounds. That represented the fourth consecutive year-to-year decline, two percent below the 1965 figure of 14.9 pounds and eight percent less than the 1962 level of 15.9 pounds. For the civilian population 10 years of age and over, the per capita consumption figures were 20.3 pounds in 1962, 18.9 pounds in 1965, and 18.4 pounds in 1966.

*General Patterns of Distribution, Characteristics of Household Purchases and Measurement of Coffee Drinking*

NCVD of 21,369,000 bags in 1966 is equivalent to 2,827 million green pounds. By means of data supplied by Market Research Corporation of America (MRCA), together with the results of other consumer reports on coffee consumption, estimates can be made of the distribution of coffee to the various consuming sectors of the economy.

### UNITED STATES: ESTIMATED DISTRIBUTION OF GREEN COFFEE BY PLACE OF CONSUMPTION, 1966 and 1965
(millions of pounds)

|  | 1966 Pounds | Percent | 1965* Pounds | Percent |
|---|---|---|---|---|
| Households | 1,908 | 67.5 | 1,953 | 68.2 |
| Eating Places | 409 | 14.5 | 421 | 14.7 |
| At Work | 431 | 15.2 | 415 | 14.5 |
| Institutions | 56 | 2.0 | 53 | 1.9 |
| Others** | 23 | 0.8 | 22 | 0.7 |
| TOTAL | 2,827 | 100.0 | 2,864 | 100.0 |

*Revised.
**Manufacturers of flavors and extracts.

Total coffee consumption, expressed in pounds of green-coffee equivalent, decreased by 37 million pounds in 1966 in comparison with the preceding year. The decline was most evident in households and in eating places; those locations experienced decreases of 2.3 percent and 2.9 percent, respectively. The at-work sector showed a gain of almost four percent, while use by both institutions and manufacturers of flavors and extracts remained at about the same level.

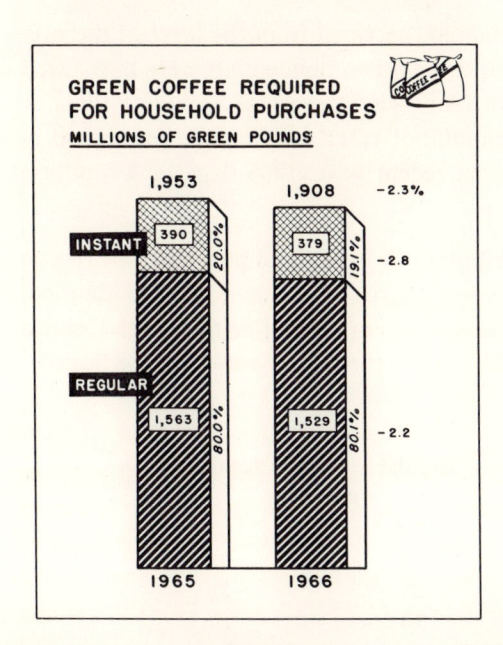

CHART 22

The value of all coffee purchased by both ultimate and industrial consumers during the year under review was below the comparable value for the preceding year. The lower aggregate value was due both to the smaller quantity consumed and to lower average prices. The estimated value for 1966 is $1,820 million as against $1,908 million in 1965 (revised).

For 1966 the value of all household purchases of coffee was $1,252 million and that of non-household purchases was $568 million. Regular coffee accounted for $922 million or 73.6 percent, while soluble coffee was credited with $330 million or 26.4 percent. Expenditures for regular coffee by the non-household sector in 1966 were estimated to be $482 million; for soluble coffee the figure was $86 million. Of the total value of all household and non-household expenditures for coffee, regular coffee accounted for $1,404 million and soluble coffee for $416 million.

The salient features of the household sector of the coffee market during 1966, according to data collected for the Bureau by MRCA, are summarized below.

(1) Aggregate household purchases of regular coffee in 1966 declined with respect to their level in the preceding year. In the year under review they were 1,285 million pounds, 29 million pounds or 2.2 percent less than the amount purchased in the preceding year. It was the fifth consecutive year-to-year decline in household purchases of regular coffee. The figure for 1966 is 133 million pounds or 9.4 percent below the recent-year highpoint of 1,418 million pounds established in 1961. Since that year the coffee industry in the United States has lost some 30 million pounds of regular coffee each year in sales to households.

(2) Purchases of soluble coffee by households declined from the level of the preceding year. In 1966, 1,122 million equivalent two-ounce units were purchased compared with 1,154 million units in 1965 — a decrease of 32 million units or 2.8 percent. Compared with the highpoint of 1,211 million units purchased in 1962, the quantity bought in the most recent year, 1966, lags by 89 million units or 7.3 percent.

(3) The following table shows the distribution of household purchases by region for 1966. For soluble coffee the regional shares of the market were identical to those in the preceding year. In the case of regular coffee the North Central States lost two percentage points, one each to the Northeast and to the South.

|  | Regular | Soluble |
|---|---|---|
|  | (percent) |  |
| Northeast | 26 | 32 |
| North Central | 30 | 27 |
| South | 26 | 31 |
| West | 18 | 10 |
| **USA** | **100** | **100** |

(4) A seasonal distribution of household purchases of coffee appears below. As in the case of the regional distributions above, the figures for 1966 were practically the same as those for 1965. Slight relative gains in the last quarter of 1966 in the soluble sector made the patterns for both soluble and regular identical.

*Chart I*

|  | Regular | Soluble |
|---|---|---|
|  | (percent) | |
| January-March | 27 | 27 |
| April-June | 24 | 24 |
| July-September | 23 | 23 |
| October-December | 26 | 26 |
| **1966** | **100** | **100** |

(5) In terms of green-coffee equivalent, average household purchases amounted to 32.8 pounds in 1966. That quantity represented a decline of 1.3 pounds from the 34.1 pounds (revised) recorded for 1965. The decline in this measurement has been significant in recent years. For example, in 1958 the average U.S. household bought regular and instant coffee equivalent to 40.8 pounds of green coffee. In other words it would have required 40.8 pounds of green coffee to produce the instant and regular coffee purchased on the average by each household in that year. The corresponding figure for 1966 was eight pounds or almost one-fifth less. Nor was 1958 a record year — averages of slightly over 43 pounds were calculated for 1952 and 1953.

(6) The average coffee bill per household in 1966 was $21.49; that figure represents a decrease of $1.39 from the 1965 level. It was the second consecutive year-to-year decrease following a rather sharp increase of $2.77 for 1964 over 1963. Prior to that there had been consistent year-to year decreases since 1956 when the average household spent some $35.00 on coffee. The decrease from 1956 to the present is due both to decreasing per-household purchases and lower prices. The decline appears somewhat less severe when the decreasing average size of households is taken into consideration.

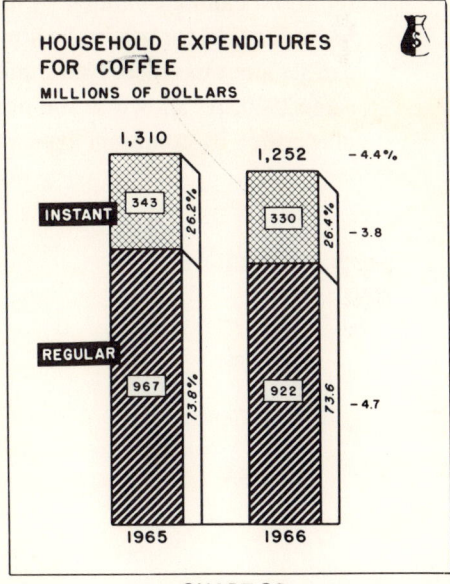

HOUSEHOLD EXPENDITURES FOR COFFEE
MILLIONS OF DOLLARS

1965: 1,310 total — INSTANT 343 (26.2%), REGULAR 967 (73.8%)
1966: 1,252 total — INSTANT 330 (26.4%), REGULAR 922 (73.6%)
-4.4% total; -3.8 instant; -4.7 regular

CHART 23

(7) The average retail price per pound of regular coffee (can and bag packs combined) in 1966 was 71.9 cents or 1.7 cents less than the average price in

1965. The 1965 level, 73.6 cents per pound, was the highest since 1958 when the figure was 82.1 cents per pound. From that highpoint the price moved downward reaching a low of 60.8 cents per pound in 1963. The most recent annual average is some ten cents per pound under the 1958 high and is about eleven cents over the 1963 low.

(8) The annual average price per two-ounce equivalent unit of soluble coffee was 29.4 cents in 1966, just under the 29.7 cents registered in 1965. The 1965 mark followed a recent-year highpoint of 33 cents per unit in the preceding year. In 1958 the figure was 40.6 cents per unit; it was followed by successive declines until a lowpoint of 28.6 cents per unit occurred in 1963. The 1966 figure is roughly eleven cents per unit below that of 1958 and is 3.6 cents per unit over that of 1963. In contrast to regular coffee for which the current annual average price is roughly midway between the 1958-63 range, the corresponding figure for soluble coffee is much closer to the low of 1963 than to the high of 1958. Observers in the trade have asserted that the producers of soluble coffee have been able to maintain relatively low prices by increasing the extraction rate (green to soluble) and by utilizing less expensive growths of green coffee.

(9) The trend toward the purchase of regular coffee in vacuum-packed cans continued in 1966 with 84 percent of all such coffee purchased for household use in that type of container and 16 percent in bags. A better perspective of the trend can be obtained by noting that in 1960 70 percent of all regular coffee purchased for use in the home was packaged in cans. Thus the share of the can segment has increased some 2.5 percentage points per year on the average since 1960. As shown in the next table based on 1966 data, purchases of regular coffee by container type vary considerably by region.

|  | Canned | Bagged |
|---|---|---|
|  | (percent) |  |
| Northeast | 80 | 20 |
| South | 69 | 31 |
| North Central | 89 | 11 |
| West | 98 | 2 |
| USA | 84 | 16 |

(10) For a number of years a trend toward the purchase of regular coffee in larger-size containers has been evident. However, only slight changes were recorded

for 1966 compared with 1965. It now appears that the trend just noted has eased and that each of the three most popular size containers has established a relatively stable share of the total market. At the present time it appears that roughly one-half of all coffee at retail will be in one-pound containers with two-pound containers holding on to just under one-third of the total volume and three-pound containers accounting for the remainder of, perhaps, 18 percent. The share of other container sizes, one-half pound for example, is relatively insignificant. It should be noted that, in the tables that follow, the figures represent percentage distributions of the total volume of coffee by size of units and not percentage distributions based on a count of discrete units. It should also be noted that the figures in the tables below are estimates based on the months of March, June, September, and December in each year.

### ALL REGULAR COFFEE
(percent)

|       | 1956 | 1960 | 1961 | 1962 | 1963 | 1964 | 1965 | 1966 |
|-------|------|------|------|------|------|------|------|------|
| 1 lb. | 76   | 64   | 59   | 57   | 55   | 53   | 51   | 51   |
| 2 lb. | 14   | 26   | 31   | 32   | 30   | 32   | 32   | 31   |
| 3 lb. | 8    | 9    | 9    | 10   | 15   | 15   | 17   | 18   |
| Other | 2    | 1    | 1    | 1    | *    | *    | *    | *    |

\* Less than one-half of one percent.

### VACUUM-PACKED COFFEE
(percent)

|       | 1956 | 1960 | 1961 | 1962 | 1963 | 1964 | 1965 | 1966 |
|-------|------|------|------|------|------|------|------|------|
| 1 lb. | 81   | 66   | 60   | 58   | 54   | 51   | 48   | 49   |
| 2 lb. | 18   | 33   | 39   | 40   | 37   | 38   | 38   | 36   |
| 3 lb. | 1    | 1    | 1    | 2    | 9    | 11   | 14   | 15   |
| Other | *    | *    | *    | *    | *    | *    | *    | *    |

\*Less than one-half of one percent.

### BAGGED-PACKED COFFEE
(percent)

|       | 1956 | 1960 | 1961 | 1962 | 1963 | 1964 | 1965 | 1966 |
|-------|------|------|------|------|------|------|------|------|
| 1 lb. | 59   | 60   | 57   | 54   | 56   | 60   | 59   | 60   |
| 2 lb. | 9    | 9    | 9    | 9    | 8    | 8    | 8    | 7    |
| 3 lb. | 19   | 30   | 33   | 36   | 35   | 32   | 33   | 33   |
| Other | 3    | 1    | 1    | 1    | 1    | *    | *    | *    |

\*Less than one-half of one percent.

(11) A similar trend was shown in the habits of soluble coffee purchasers, with the larger than 10-ounce unit becoming increasingly popular. The following figures are by percentage.

| Size of Jar (ounces) | 1959 | 1960 | 1961 | 1962 | 1963 | 1964 | 1965 | 1966 |
|---|---|---|---|---|---|---|---|---|
| 2 | 12 | 9 | 8 | 7 | 8 | 7 | 6 | 6 |
| 4 | 8 | 7 | 2 | 1 | 1 | * | * | * |
| 5 | 5 | 3 | 11 | 11 | 11 | 11 | 9 | 10 |
| 6 | 70 | 49 | 44 | 38 | 29 | 29 | 27 | 23 |
| 8 | 3 | 6 | 2 | 2 | 4 | 4 | 5 | 6 |
| 10 | 2 | 23 | 31 | 37 | 43 | 42 | 40 | 34 |
| Over 10 | * | 2 | 1 | 2 | 2 | 4 | 8 | 15 |
| Other | * | 1 | 1 | 2 | 2 | 3 | 5 | 6 |

(12) Purchases of regular and soluble coffee for household use by type of store are shown in the table that follows.

|  | Regular 1964 | Regular 1965 | Regular 1966 | Soluble 1964 | Soluble 1965 | Soluble 1966 |
|---|---|---|---|---|---|---|
|  | (percent) |  |  | (percent) |  |  |
| Chain Stores | 53 | 53 | 53 | 53 | 53 | 54 |
| Other Grocery | 42 | 42 | 42 | 42 | 42 | 42 |
| Other Outlets | 5 | 5 | 5 | 5 | 5 | 4 |

(13) The table below shows the percentages of households buying regular coffee only, both regular and soluble, and soluble only in each quarter of 1966.

|  | Regular Only | Soluble Only | Both Regular and Soluble | Total* |
|---|---|---|---|---|
| January-March | 46 | 24 | 28 | 98 |
| April-June | 46 | 24 | 24 | 94 |
| July-September | 46 | 23 | 24 | 93 |
| October-December | 45 | 23 | 27 | 95 |

*Totals do not add to 100 percent because a varying proportion of households do not purchase any coffee in any given quarter of the year.

(14) Purchases of adulterated coffee (coffee mixed with chicory or other adulterants), accounted for approximately two percent of all regular-coffee purchases in 1966 compared with 2.3 percent in 1965 and 2.4 percent in 1964. Perhaps the decline in the relative share of adulterated coffee can be attributed to the increasing spread between the price of regular and adulterated coffee. The annual average price of adulterated coffee was estimated to be 73.3 cents per pound in 1966, while the corresponding figure for regular coffee was 71.9. It is interesting to note that regular coffee commanded a premium of 0.6 cent per pound in the first quarter, but that adulterated coffee was 1.4 cents per pound over the price of the regular type in the second quarter, 1.5 cents more in the third, and 2.8 cents greater in the fourth. Coffee mixed with other substances is sold primarily in the Southern States. Most of the loss in the consumption of adulterated coffee occurred in the South Atlantic States (West Virginia, Maryland, Delaware, and the states to the south that border on the Atlantic Ocean). The percentage of such coffee in all retail coffee purchases in that region has been above 10 percent for a number of years. But from a recent highpoint of 13.5 percent in the fourth quarter of 1964, each successive quarter has shown a decline with the fourth quarter of 1966 showing a percentage of only 6.6. The East South Central states (Kentucky, Tennessee, Mississippi, and Alabama) are currently at a percentage of about 5.7 — not very far from the norm for that region, while the figure for the West South Central states (Oklahoma, Arkansas, Texas and Louisiana) is roughly 4.6 percent.

*Coffee Drinking, Winter of 1967*

In the early months of 1967, the seventeenth annual coffee-drinking survey was conducted for the Bureau by a private research organization. As in previous surveys the nationwide probability sample consisted of approximately 6,000 persons 10 years of age and older selected so as to be representative of the civilian population of the United States with the exception of two groups: the farm and non-farm population living in open country outside towns or villages and persons in hospitals and other institutions (those persons comprise only a negligible fraction of the total population). The surveys are conducted in January and February of each year; the respondent is asked by an interviewer to recall the beverages and the quantities of each drunk on the day preceding the interview. The principal findings of the 1967 survey, with some references to those made previously are as follows:

(1) Persons 10 years of age and older consumed an average of 2.84 cups of coffee beverage per day during the winter months of 1967. That figure showed no significant change from the 2.86 cups reported in the 1966 study. The stability over 1966-1967 may indicate that the small increase, .07 cup, for 1966 over 1965 has been largely maintained and that the period of decline, 1962-1965, has been arrested. In each of the years, 1963, 1964 and 1965, .11 cup was lost in comparison with each preceding

year. On balance, the decline from the 1962 highpoint of 3.12 cups per person per day to the most recent figure is .28 cup or nine percent. The rate of consumption per coffee drinker in 1967 was 3.97 cups compared with 4.04 cups in 1966 and 4.17 cups in 1962. The current figure did not fall as low as the 3.90 cup level reached in 1965.

Over the long run, per capita drinking of cups of coffee, with one exception, showed an unbroken record of year-to-year increases since 1951, when the series was inaugurated, to 1962, the year of the record highpoint. From 2.38 cups per person per day in that first year, a peak of 3.12 cups was attained in 1962. That represented a gain of .74 cup or .31 percent. The current level of 2.84 cups represents a gain of .46 cup or 16 percent over 1951. The bumper crop of post-war babies now is reaching an age level that traditionally is associated with higher rates of coffee consumption. Thus, the coffee industry in the United States may be about to enjoy a rise in overall per capita consumption provided that young adults continue to accept coffee as the most desired adult beverage.

CHART 24

(2) Further evidence of the mitigating effect of large numbers of young people, who drink relatively small quantities of coffee and who dilute the overall rate of consumption, is found in the proportion who drank coffee on the day preceding the interview. In 1967 that figure was 71.4 percent, up from the 70.9 percent reported in 1966 and the first increase in several years. That figure had been contracting as greater numbers of young persons — those 10 to 19 years old — entered the coffee-drinking age groups of the population.

(3) There has been little change in the relative amounts of coffee consumed at various times of the day: 40 percent at breakfast, 27 percent at other meals and the remaining 33 percent at other periods of the day. However, over the long run coffee drinking at meals other than breakfast has been losing ground to between-meal drinking.

(4) Eighty percent of all cups of coffee is consumed in the home, eleven percent in work locations and nine percent in eating places.

(5) Persons in the West have regained first position in per capita consumption of coffee beverage after lagging behind those in the Midwest for the past two years. Rates of consumption in the four general regions of the United States — West, Midwest, South, and East — are, respectively, 3.19, 3.18, 2.63, and 2.39 cups per person per day.

(6) Persons in the 40-49 age group presently drink coffee at a higher rate than those in any other, averaging 4.48 cups per day. Those 30-39 years old consume coffee at a rate of 3.99 cups person per day and rank in second place, followed in order by those 50-59 and 25-29. Although an increased rate of drinking was shown by the 10-14 group, a decline for those 15-19 brought the two groups taken together, somewhat below the rate for last year.

(7) In 1967 the non-white segment of the population drank an average of 1.60 cups of coffee per day. That was .16 cup or 11 percent greater than the 1.44 cups recorded for that group in 1964, 1965 and 1966. Since non-whites have traditionally consumed far fewer cups on a per capita basis than whites, an increase by that population segment would lend strong impetus to the overall coffee-drinking rate.

The rate of consumption for the white population was 3.00 cups per person per day in 1967, compared with 3.05 cups in 1966, 2.96 cups in 1965, 3.08 cups in 1964 and 3.15 cups in 1963.

(8) Eighty-two percent of those who work indoors reported that coffee was available to them during their workbreaks. The corresponding figures for 1966, 1965 and 1964 were 76, 74 and 74 percent; in both 1963 and 1962 the figure was 77 percent. Forty-eight percent of all employed persons drank coffee at their breaks in the current year, the same percentage as in 1966. The rate of coffee consumption at work of those employed persons was 1.14 cups per day in the current year; the corresponding figure was 1.05 cups in 1966.

**COFFEE DRINKING ...BY AGE GROUPS** — WINTER 1967

CUPS PER PERSON PER DAY

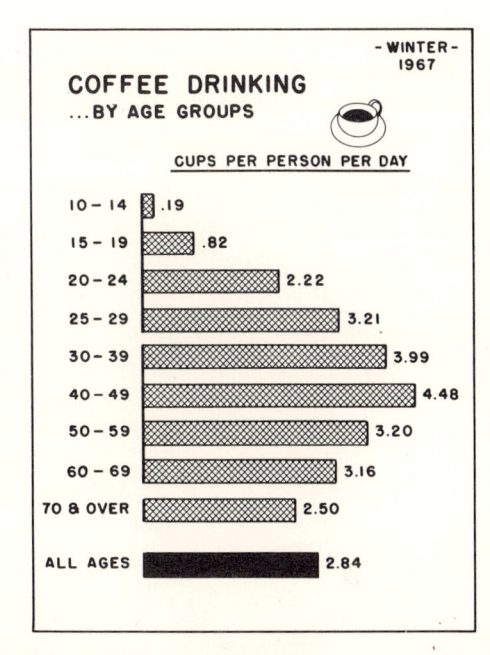

| Age | Cups |
|---|---|
| 10–14 | .19 |
| 15–19 | .82 |
| 20–24 | 2.22 |
| 25–29 | 3.21 |
| 30–39 | 3.99 |
| 40–49 | 4.48 |
| 50–59 | 3.20 |
| 60–69 | 3.16 |
| 70 & OVER | 2.50 |
| ALL AGES | 2.84 |

CHART 25

**COFFEE DRINKING ...BY PLACE OF CONSUMPTION** — WINTER

CUPS PER PERSON PER DAY

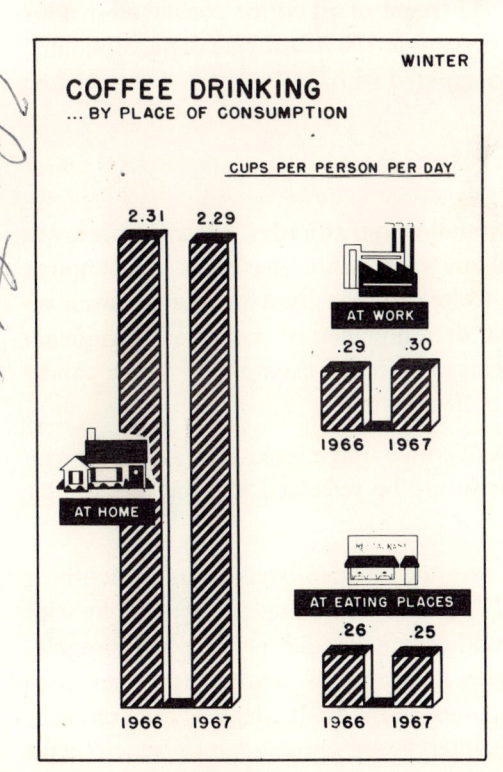

AT HOME: 2.31 (1966), 2.29 (1967)
AT WORK: .29 (1966), .30 (1967)
AT EATING PLACES: .26 (1966), .25 (1967)

CHART 26

(9) Among persons working indoors 52 percent stated in the most recent survey that vending machines were accessible for their work-break refreshment needs. In 1966 the figure was 51 percent. Of all vending machines to which indoor workers had access in 1967, 28 percent offered coffee.

(10) While the usual price of a cup of coffee away from home continues to be ten cents, there has been a significant increase in the relative number of cups of coffee that cost more than that sum and a significant decrease in the relative number of cups of coffee that cost less than ten cents. A distribution of prices paid for a cup of coffee at eating places and at places of employment in recent years is shown below.

**(percentage of all cups purchased)**

|  | At Eating Places ||| At Places of Employment |||
| --- | --- | --- | --- | --- | --- | --- |
|  | 1965 | 1966 | 1967 | 1965 | 1966 | 1967 |
| Under 10¢ | 4 | 3 | 2 | 16 | 12 | 14 |
| 10¢ | 77 | 72 | 68 | 74 | 73 | 75 |
| Over 10¢ | 19 | 25 | 30 | 10 | 15 | 11 |

(11) Decaffeinated coffee accounted for 5.5 percent of all coffee consumed in 1967 compared with 4.5 percent in 1966 and 3.7 percent in 1965. Drinkers of decaffeinated coffee averaged 2.54 cups per day in 1967 compared with 2.84 cups in 1966 and 2.83 cups in 1965.

*Coffee Attitudes, Winter, 1967*

For the second consecutive year information on attitudes toward coffee was obtained as part of the continuing annual study on winter beverage consumption patterns conducted for the Pan-American Coffee Bureau by a private research organization. Since attitudes are important determinants of behavior, significant clues toward understanding behavioral aspects of coffee consumption may be gained by study and analysis of attitudes toward coffee.

A favorable disposition toward coffee and coffee usage, especially among younger persons in the population, may in the future be reflected in rising per capita consumption.

All persons interviewed were asked to rate sixteen statements concerning coffee on a seven-point scale. A rating of "1" indicates complete agreement with the statement, while a rating of "7", on the other hand, registers complete disagreement. The central position "4" demonstrates neutrality — neither agreement nor disagreement — and the other intervening points on the scale, degrees of agreement or disagreement. Thus, "2" shows that the interviewee agreed "pretty much" with the statement and "3", agreed "somewhat". Ratings of "6" and "5" carry corresponding connotations of disagreement.

Attitudes toward coffee drinking can be categorized roughly into six basic factors:[3] taste and aroma, sociability, occasion orientation, refreshment, health, and adult image. The results of the most recent attitude study will be summarized with respect to those dimensions.

(1) *Taste and Aroma:* It is evident that a decided majority liked the *aroma* and *taste* of coffee. Eighty-four percent of all respondents agreed that coffee has a wonderful *aroma* and 74 percent liked the *taste*. *Taste and aroma* provided the areas of greatest agreement; the fact should be noted that a large number of persons drink coffee because they enjoy its pleasurable effects on their senses of smell and taste. It is difficult to reconcile that liking for coffee with the undersirable procedures reported in general by housewives in the preparation of coffee.[4] The Coffee Brewing Center of the Pan-American Coffee Bureau has found that brewing practices in many out-of-home locations also leave much to be desired. *Taste and aroma* are at their best only when coffee is properly prepared. The converse also is true. Poor preparation or an unsatisfactory blend can reduce *taste and aroma* to a low level and, consequently, inhibit coffee drinking.

The enjoyment of coffee *taste and aroma* undoubtedly was an important factor leading three out of five respondents to agree that coffee is *one of the good things in life.*

(2) *Sociability:* The term sociability indicates the degree to which coffee drinking is associated with other persons. While none of the statements in this year's attitude survey directly elicited further information in that connection, it was determined in last year's study that about two-thirds of respondents found coffee "sociable" and more than half found it "fashionable".

In an earlier motivational study[5] it was learned that coffee had a warm and friendly image. Respondents noted that, while coffee was frequently drunk in the company of others, it brought feelings of companionship when consumed while the drinker was alone.

(3) *Occasion Orientation:* Some products are related to special occasions only and thus their consumption tends to be limited to those occasions. Coffee is fortunate in possessing a broad occasion orientation. Seventy percent of those interviewed agreed that coffee is suitable for all occasions. More than one-half thought that coffee goes better with work than does any other beverage and, at the same time, two-thirds felt that a cup of coffee provided a good reason to take a break from work.

---

[3] A different set of dimensions obtained by factor analysis was discussed in the Bureau's publication, *Coffee Drinking in the United States, Winter 1966*, p. 38-43.

[4] On several occasions the Bureau has conducted surveys of coffee brewing practices in the home. The results of the last survey were reported in *Coffee Drinking in the United States, Winter 1965.*

[5] The results of that study were summarized in 1955 in a Bureau publication entitled, *New Horizons for Coffee Promotion.*

(4) *Refreshment:* Coffee has an invigorating, refreshing image; it is a drink for active people. Seventy-three percent agreed that coffee is a good drink for people on the go; 69 percent felt that coffee gives a lift; 69 percent agreed that coffee is one of the best things to help one get started in the morning; and 65 percent found coffee a refreshing drink.

(5) *Health:* About half the respondents regarded coffee as being low in calories; forty-three percent agreed completely and another 17 percent agreed less strongly. Almost one-third were neutral on this point.

More than two out of five persons found that coffee agreed with them completely; yet 13 percent felt that coffee completely disagreed with them. Does coffee prevent one from getting a good night's sleep? There was stronger feeling that it does not, than that it does. A sizeable proportion, 43 percent hold either neutral or lukewarm attitudes.

Although 26 percent of the respondents rejected the idea that they often would like to refuse coffee that is offered, 19 percent admitted they would. That could be an indication of a feeling by many persons that too much coffee may be harmful, or simply that some persons, heavy drinkers in particular, are overexposed to the beverage and tire of it.

More persons regarded coffee as not harmful to health than as harmful; 26 percent expressed neutrality and another 33 percent did not have strong opinions on this point. Thus, almost 60 percent held either neutral or mild attitudes.

(6) *Adult Image:* Coffee generally is regarded as an adult beverage. About half of the respondents in last year's survey regarded coffee as more for older people than for young and most of the remainder was neutral.

In the current survey, interviewers were asked to express agreement or disagreement with the notion that teenagers should be discouraged from drinking coffee. Twenty-one percent agrred completely, while 17 percent disagreed. However, over one-half of those interviewed expressed either neutral feelings or were not strongly committed on this point.

The first four dimensions noted above — taste and aroma, sociability, broad occasion orientation, and refreshment — comprise a rough summary of the attitudinal factors underlying coffee drinking. They represent the primary dynamic forces that motivate individuals to reach for a cup of coffee. The last two dimensions — health and adult image — form the two major attitudinal constraints to coffee consumption.

Psychologically, an individual decision to drink coffee represents a triumph of the first four motivational factors over the last two. But since both positive and negative influences impinge on the individual, the coffee consumer at times may drink with mixed emotions — he enjoys a refreshing cup of coffee, but feels that perhaps he should limit his consumption or perhaps stop drinking the beverage entirely.

**UNITED STATES: ATTITUDES TOWARD COFFEE DRINKING, 1967**
(percentage of persons 10 years of age and older)

|  | Agree | Neither Agree nor Disagree | Disagree |
|---|---|---|---|
| **(1) Taste and Aroma** | | | |
| Coffee has a wonderful aroma or odor | 84 | 9 | 7 |
| Coffee has a taste I like | 74 | 10 | 16 |
| Coffee is one of the good things in life | 59 | 21 | 20 |
| **(2) Sociability** | | | |
| (No related statements in current survey) | | | |
| **(3) Occasion Orientation** | | | |
| Coffee is a drink for all occasions | 70 | 11 | 19 |
| A cup of coffee provides a good reason to take a break from work | 66 | 18 | 16 |
| Coffee goes better with work than any other drink | 53 | 19 | 28 |
| **(4) Source of Refreshment** | | | |
| Coffee is a good drink for people on the go | 73 | 17 | 10 |
| Coffee gives one a lift, peps one up | 69 | 16 | 15 |
| Coffee is one of the best things to help one get started in the morning | 69 | 13 | 18 |
| Coffee is a refreshing drink | 65 | 15 | 20 |
| **(5) Health** | | | |
| Coffee is low in calories | 60 | 32 | 8 |
| Coffee doesn't agree with me | 25 | 16 | 59 |
| Coffee keeps me from getting a good night's sleep | 33 | 21 | 46 |
| I often would like to refuse coffee that is offered me | 37 | 18 | 45 |
| Coffee is harmful or bad for one's health | 34 | 26 | 40 |
| **(6) Adult Image** | | | |
| Teenagers should be discouraged from drinking coffee | 40 | 25 | 35 |

SOURCE: *A Report on Coffee Drinking in the United States, Winter of 1967*, prepared for the Department of Statistics and Economic Research, Pan-American Coffee Bureau by Professional Research Associates.

Inquiries on psychological factors affecting coffee consumption recently undertaken by the Department of Statistics and Economic Research constitute an initial effort to obtain information on, and direct attention toward the more profound aspects of the difficult marketing problems of an industry beset with declining per capita consumption of its product.

More intensive study of consumer attitudes toward coffee must be undertaken by the industry in order to develop a sound body of knowledge on which to base programming of educational and promotional efforts to encourage coffee drinking. Development of favorable attitudes especially among the younger age groups is of critical importance in influencing their beverage consumption behavior.

A summary of the results of the attitude study are shown in the preceding table.

# The Canadian Market

*Imports and Sources*

Canadian imports of green coffee in 1966 fell off slightly to 1,163,601 bags. The contraction in imports amounted to 94,047 bags or 7.5 percent. Green coffee imports into Canada had been consistently above the 1.2 million bag level since 1962. The latest annual import total represents an attrition of 123,936 bags or 9.6 percent from the record level of 1,287,538 bags registered in 1963.

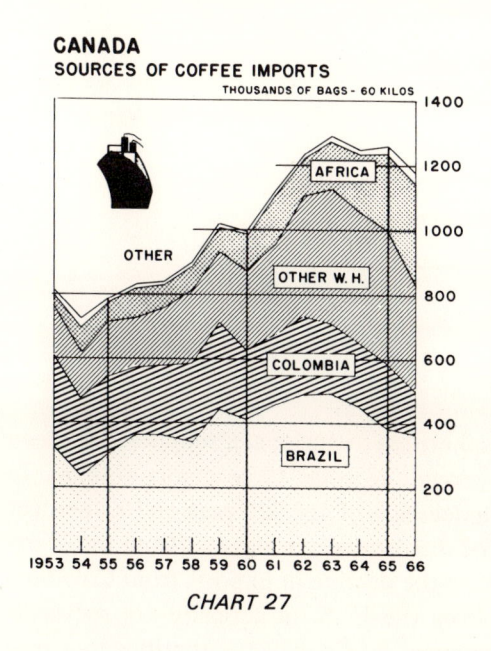

**CANADA**
**SOURCES OF COFFEE IMPORTS**
THOUSANDS OF BAGS - 60 KILOS

CHART 27

Soluble coffee imports in terms of green equivalent for 1966 totaled 53,088 bags as compared with 45,801 bags in 1965 — an increase of 15.9 percent. Practically all the soluble coffee imported into Canada originates in the United States. In the past five years import demand for the soluble product had been steadily declining. The highest level of demand for soluble coffee of foreign origin was recorded in 1960 when 128,122 bags of green-coffee equivalent were taken. A dramatic drop of 25.9 percent in import volume was registered between 1960 and 1961. That change and the pattern of the import trade reflected the fact that new plant capacity was being put on stream.

Foreign trade in soluble coffee in the case of Canada is not a one-way street. Due to geographic considerations the coffee distribution areas of the coffee-roasting companies straddle the international boundary line. It therefore is economically feasible for certain of the Canadian distributors to sell in U. S. markets and, conversely, some Canadian marketing areas are better served by U. S. distributors. The net Canadian import demand for soluble coffee therefore is smaller than the import statistics would tend to indicate. Net imports of soluble coffee into Canada in the past three years averaged 19,227 bags of green-coffee equivalent.

Economic reasons cited heretofore for the Canadian soluble coffee market in the preceding paragraphs also hold true in the case of roasted coffee. Roasted coffee imports in 1966 came to 31,272 bags of green-coffee equivalent — most of which came from the U. S. In 1965, 23,770 bags were imported and, in fact, in the past five years roasted coffee imports have averaged 22,505 bags of green-coffee equivalent.

## CANADA: IMPORTS, EXPORTS AND PER CAPITA NET IMPORTS 1965-66*
(in terms of green coffee equivalent)

|  | 1966 60-kilo Bags | 1966 Pounds | 1965 60-kilo Bags | 1965 Pounds |
|---|---|---|---|---|
| Green Coffee Imports | 1,163,602 | 153,916,486 | 1,257,648 | 166,356,647 |
| Roasted Coffee Imports | 31,272 | 4,136,535 | 23,770 | 3,144,201 |
| Soluble Coffee Imports | 53,088 | 7,022,268 | 45,801 | 6,058,373 |
| **Total Imports** | **1,247,962** | **165,075,289** | **1,327,219** | **175,559,220** |
| Less: Exports | 21,525 | 2,847,241 | 33,810 | 4,472,252 |
| Net Imports | 1,226,437 | 162,228,048 | 1,293,409 | 171,086,969 |
| Population | (19,960,000) |  | (19,571,000) |  |
| Net Lbs. Per Person |  | 8.13 |  | 8.74 |

*See Appendix Table C-20 for previous years' data.
SOURCE: Dominion Bureau of Statistics.
  NOTE: A small quantity of coffee substitutes is included in the soluble import and export figures.


The countries of the Western Hemisphere were the main suppliers of green coffee into Canada accounting for 71.6 percent of total 1966 import volume. In quantity this amounted to 835,797 bags — a decrease of 162,921 bags or 16.3 percent from the 998,718 bag total of 1965. Much of the decrease in imports from the Western Hemisphere countries can be attributed to the decline in imports from Colombia and the United States. Canadian imports from the U. S. in actuality are reexports from the latter country which cannot be assigned by Canadian authorities to a true country of origin. Only 307,009 bags were imported from these two countries in 1966; compared with 1965 that figure represented a drop of 102,392 bags or 25.0 percent. Brazil, once again, was the single largest source representing 31.2 percent of total green-coffee imports into Canada. Brazil's relative share was up slightly from 1965, but volume was down by 21,120 bags or 5.5 percent.

During 1966 the coffee-producing countries of Africa increased their volume of green-coffee imports into Canada and also their relative share of the total. These countries accounted for 305,034 bags in 1966 as against 237,816 bags in 1965, their gain being 67,218 bags or 28.3 percent. Their share in the import trade rose from 19.0 percent in 1965 to 26.2 percent in 1966. The main source of green coffee from this group during 1966 was Uganda which sent to Canada 100,753 bags, compared with 92,469 bags in the preceding year.

*Net Imports of Green and Processed Coffee and Per Capita Net Imports*

As mentioned heretofore, in addition to green coffee, Canada also imports minor quantities of soluble and roasted coffee. Subtracting exports and re-exports of coffee from gross imports leaves a net import figure which includes all the new coffee supply available for consumption during a given year.

In 1966 net imports totaled 1,226,437 bags of green equivalent as compared with 1,293,409 bags during the preceding year. The decline in net imports was 66,972 bags or 5.2 percent. During 1966 an increase in population of about two percent was registered. This increase coupled with the drop in net import volume caused the per capita import figure to drop seven percent from 8.74 green pounds per person in 1965 to 8.13 pounds per person in 1966. Appendix Table C-20 gives comparable data from 1950.

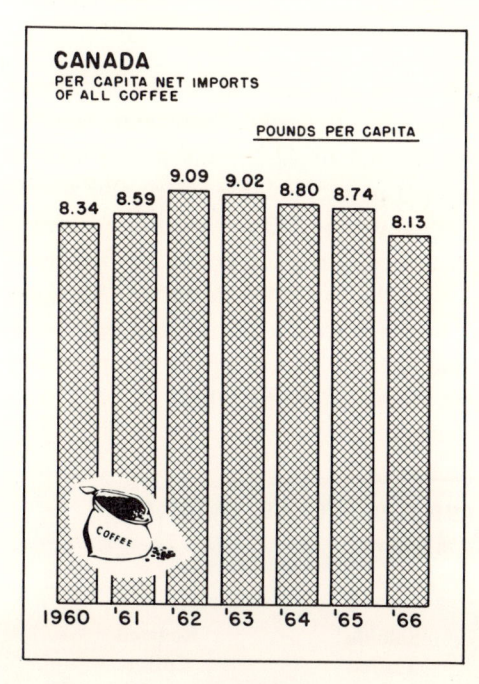

CHART 28

*Value of Coffee Imports*

Coffee imports declined in 1966 in value as well as volume. The decline was more than 8 percent from the 1965 level; total value of coffee imports in 1966 was $72,315,000 in contrast with $78,615,986 in 1965. Green coffee, as always, was the chief component of total coffee imports — 89.7 percent, followed by soluble with 6.0 percent, and roasted coffee accounted for the balance. In monetary

**CANADA: VALUE OF COFFEE IMPORTS, 1961-1966**

(in Canadian dollars)

| Year | Green Coffee | Soluble Coffee | Roasted Coffee | Total | Percent Change from 1961 |
|---|---|---|---|---|---|
| 1961 | 52,184,193 | 5,417,848 | 1,339,965 | 58,942,006 | — |
| 1962 | 55,655,056 | 4,790,109 | 1,439,303 | 61,884,468 | + 5.0 |
| 1963 | 58,907,185 | 4,597,059 | 1,650,830 | 65,155,074 | +10.5 |
| 1964 | 74,953,236 | 5,708,311 | 1,861,744 | 82,533,291 | +40.0 |
| 1965 | 72,128,860 | 4,208,995 | 2,278,131 | 78,615,986 | +33.4 |
| 1966 | 64,877,000 | 4,533,000 | 2,905,000 | 72,315,000 | +22.7 |

SOURCE: Dominion Bureau of Statistics

terms, these three types were valued at $64,877,000, $4,533,000 and $2,905,000 respectively. The above table lists data for Canada's outlays for coffee imports during the past six years.

*Import Prices*

The annual average import price of green coffee continued in the decline begun in 1965, following the brief 1963-1964 hiatus in the long-run downtrend. In 1966 the annual average import price of green coffee fell to 42.2 cents per pound; in 1965 the comparable price had been 43.4 cents per pound. Soluble coffee also shared in the price decline in 1966; the average for 1966 was $1.743 per pound, compared with $1.962 in 1965. The annual average import price of roasted coffee in 1966 stood at $.836 per pound. This price also was lower than that recorded in 1965 — $.862 per pound, but the price of roasted coffee had shown a steady rise in five years, culminating in a record high in 1965. The annual average import prices per pound of the three types of coffee discussed are shown in the following table.

**CANADA: AVERAGE IMPORT PRICE PER POUND, 1961-1966**

(in Canadian dollars)

| Year | Green Coffee | Soluble Coffee | Roasted Coffee |
|---|---|---|---|
| 1961 | 0.353 | 1.609 | 0.670 |
| 1962 | 0.342 | 1.650 | 0.732 |
| 1963 | 0.346 | 1.680 | 0.739 |
| 1964 | 0.455 | 2.182 | 0.851 |
| 1965 | 0.434 | 1.962 | 0.862 |
| 1966 | 0.422 | 1.743 | 0.836 |

SOURCE: *Dominion Bureau of Statistics; calculation made by the Department of Statistics and Economic Research, PACB.*

*Domestic Processing and Imports*

In terms of green-coffee equivalent, processing of coffee in Canada totaled 1,314,756 bags in 1966 up from the revised 1965 total of 1,289,625 bags — an indicated rise of nearly two percent. Production of soluble coffee in 1966 nearly reached the levels of the 1964 peak, and reversed the downtrend recorded in 1965 for that sector of the coffee industry. The rise was approximately 4.3 percent over the 1965 level.

## CANADA: VOLUME OF COFFEE PROCESSED DOMESTICALLY, 1961-1966

| Year | Regular | Soluble* | Total | Percent Increase over 1961 | Percent Regular of Total | Percent Soluble of Total |
|---|---|---|---|---|---|---|
| | (60-kilo bags of green equivalent) | | | | | |
| 1961 | 831,851 | 307,301 | 1,139,152 | — | 73.0 | 27.0 |
| 1962 | 858,368 | 386,689 | 1,245,057 | + 9.3 | 68.9 | 31.1 |
| 1963 | 873,552 | 405,511 | 1,279,063 | +12.3 | 68.3 | 31.7 |
| 1964 | 867,193 | 416,844 | 1,284,037 | +12.7 | 67.5 | 32.5 |
| 1965 | 891,002 | 398,623 | 1,289,625 | +13.2 | 69.1 | 30.9 |
| 1966 | 899,130 | 415,626 | 1,314,756 | +15.4 | 68.4 | 31.6 |

SOURCE: Dominion Bureau of Statistics. Conversion to green-coffee equivalent made by Department of Statistics and Economic Research, PACB.

* Extraction rates (soluble from green) are applied as follows; 1961: 33.3%, 1962: 34.0%, 1963: 35.0%, 1964: 36.0%, 1965-1966: 37.0%.


## CANADA: DOMESTIC PRODUCTION OF ROASTED COFFEE AND ROASTED-COFFEE IMPORTS, 1961-1966

(in pounds of finished product)

| Year | Domestic Production | Foreign Product | Total | Foreign Product as percent of Total |
|---|---|---|---|---|
| 1961 | 92,465,430 | 1,914,521 | 94,379,951 | 2.0 |
| 1962 | 95,413,023 | 1,966,993 | 97,380,016 | 2.0 |
| 1963 | 97,101,000 | 2,235,052 | 99,336,052 | 2.2 |
| 1964 | 96,394,000 | 2,187,845 | 98,581,845 | 2.2 |
| 1965 | 99,040,000 | 2,642,200 | 101,682,200 | 2.6 |
| 1966 | 99,944,000 | 3,476,074 | 103,420,074 | 2.2 |

SOURCE: Dominion Bureau of Statistics


The regular coffee sector expanded as well, to produce a total of 99,944,000 pounds of roasted coffee in 1966; that was almost one percent above the revised 1965 production of 99,040,000 pounds. On the basis of green-coffee equivalent, roastings for soluble coffee rose from 30.9 percent of the total in 1965 to 31.6 percent of total domestic production in 1966.

Imports of soluble coffee into Canada in 1966 reversed the trend apparent since 1961 of diminishing importance for imports. For the first time since 1961, the year-to-year import trend was upward. The gain over 1965 was better than 21 percent, or an additional 455,288 pounds. The share of imports rose somewhat in 1966 to 11.3 percent of the domestic soluble market in contrast to 10.2 percent of the 1965 market. Imports of roasted coffee were up 833,874 pounds over the 1965 total for an increase of 31.6 percent. These imports represented 2.2 percent of the home market. The relationship between the volume of coffee processed in Canada and the volume of processed coffee from abroad is shown on the preceding page and below.

### CANADA: NET NEW SUPPLY OF SOLUBLE COFFEE 1961-1966
(in pounds of finished product)

| Year | Domestic Production | Imports | Exports | Net New Supply | Percent Change from 1961 |
|------|---------------------|---------|---------|----------------|--------------------------|
| 1961 | 13,549,502 | 3,367,550 | 1,509,516 | 15,407,536 | — |
| 1962 | 17,397,853 | 2,903,896 | 1,877,755 | 18,423,994 | +19.6 |
| 1963 | 18,755,000 | 2,736,632 | 3,764,488 | 17,727,144 | +15.1 |
| 1964 | 19,834,000 | 2,615,768 | 2,082,740 | 20,367,028 | +32.2 |
| 1965 | 18,967,000 | 2,145,573 | 1,655,075 | 19,457,498 | +26.3 |
| 1966 | 20,362,000 | 2,600,861 | 1,037,910 | 21,924,951 | +42.3 |

SOURCE: Dominion Bureau of Statistics.

NOTE: A small quantity of substitutes is included in the export figures as there is no way of excluding it.

*Retail Prices*

The trends in annual average retail prices of regular and soluble coffee continued in their 1965 directions. Regular coffee rose again over the previous year to 93.0 cents per pound from 92.4 cents, while on the other hand, soluble coffee declined in the same period from 113.8 cents per 6-ounce jar to 112.3 cents. On a percentage basis the rise for regular coffee was a slight 0.7 percent and for soluble coffee the decline was 1.3 percent. Retail price series for regular and soluble coffee are set forth in the following table.

**CANADA**
TYPE OF COFFEE SERVED AT HOME

REGULAR 24%
SOLUBLE 46%
BOTH 30%

— WINTER —
1966-67

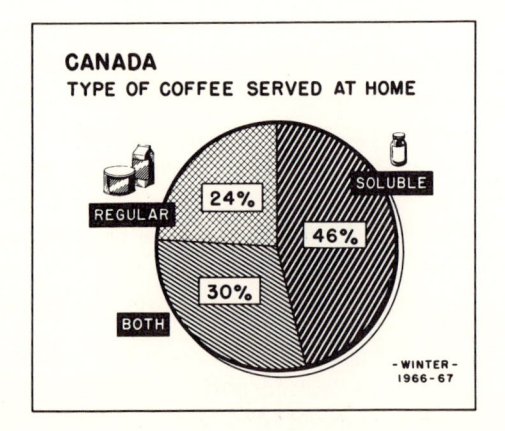

CHART 29

## CANADA: RETAIL COFFEE PRICES, 1961-1966

(in Canadian cents per unit)

| Year | Regular (per pound of medium quality package) | Soluble (per 6 oz. jar) |
|------|------|------|
| 1961 | 74.0 | 100.7 |
| 1962 | 75.6 | 102.3 |
| 1963 | 74.7 | 100.7 |
| 1964 | 90.0 | 117.1 |
| 1965 | 92.4 | 113.8 |
| 1966 | 93.0 | 112.3 |

SOURCE: *Dominion Bureau of Statistics*

*Coffee Drinking, Winter 1966*

A fourth survey of coffee drinking was conducted in Canada in 1966. A probability sample of 4000 persons representative of the civilian, non-institutionalized population 10 years of age and over was interviewed in the course of the study, as in the three earlier surveys conducted. This project was designed so as to maintain general comparability between it and similar surveys conducted in the United States. Consumer bases of comparison therefore have been established to make it possible to analyze similarities and differences between the coffee-drinking habits of the two neighboring North American countries. The major findings of the 1966 survey in Canada with some reference to the United States market are discussed below.

(1) In the Winter of 1966, Canadians ten years of age and older consumed an average of 2.02 cups of coffee per person per day. In the 1965 season consumption was 2.18 cups of coffee daily per person, while for the two earlier surveys it was 1.94 cups per days in winter 1961 and 1.91 in the 1959 period. The decline in 1966 was 7.3 percent from the 1965 figure, though there was a gain of .11 cup, or 5.1 percent, for the eight-year period since the first of this series of surveys was undertaken. The current average for the United States is 2.86 cups daily per person — .84 cup or more than 41 percent greater than Canadian daily per capita consumption. The net gain for the United States over the previous year was 2.5 percent in contrast with the Canadian decline of 7.3 percent during the same period. Up to 1965 the uptrend in per capita consumption in Canada contrasted with developments in the United States where in the past several years there actually was a decline followed by apparent stabilization at a lower level. The current decrease raises the question whether a stabilizing tendency also has set in there.

(2) Of the representative sample of 4000 persons surveyed in Canada, 66 percent disclosed that they drank coffee during the day prior to the interview. That percentage contrasts with the 67.3 percent of coffee drinkers of the preceding survey. The percentage of coffee drinkers in Canada has remained quite constant. In the United States the current survey shows 70.9 percent of persons ten years and over drinking coffee. In the past few years there has been a noticeable decline in the United States in the relative number of those interviewed who reported drinking coffee.

(3) In the table below the relative amounts of coffee consumed at various times of the day in Canada and in the United States are shown, according to results of the latest survey for each country.

(4) Ninety-two percent of all those interviewed who had drunk coffee during the day prior to the interview had drunk the beverage at home, 19 percent had had their coffee at work, and 8 percent at eating places; the previous survey had indicated respective percentages of 93, 21 and 8.

(5) British Columbians maintained their position as the heaviest coffee drinkers in Canada. Their average rate in 1966 was 2.78 cups per day per person, down from 3.01 cups per day in winter 1965. Previous surveys have shown that the rate of drinking falls off steadily as one travels eastward through Canada. Per capita consumption for the Prairie Provinces stands at 2.61, for Ontario at 2.14, for Quebec at 1.61, and for the Atlantic Provinces at 1.11. In the prior survey, the respective figures were 2.86, 2.31, 1.71 and 1.16.

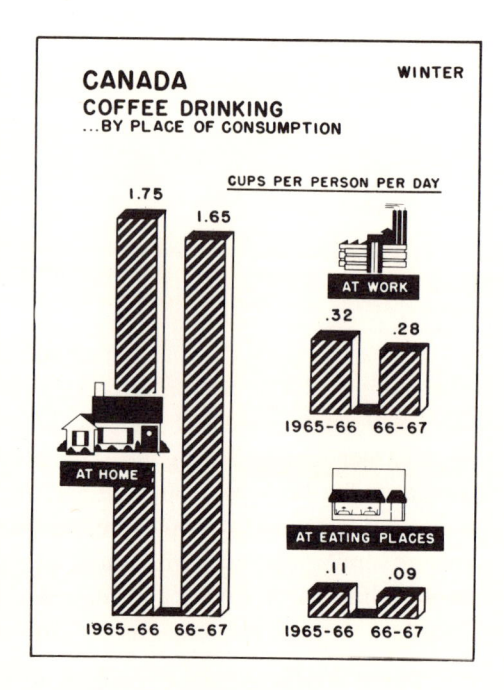

CHART 30

(percentage of cups consumed)

|  | Canada | United States |
|---|---|---|
| At Breakfast | 35.6 | 39.5 |
| At Other Meals | 24.8 | 28.7 |
| Between Meals | 39.6 | 31.8 |

(6) Per capita consumption of all coffee in Canada averaged 2.02 cups daily. The 30 to 39 age group average was the highest rate among all age categories — 3.03 cups per day (down from 3.07 cups in the previous survey). This group also rated highest in all of the prior surveys. In the United States as well, the 30-39 group ranked highest in per capita consumption. The 1966 United States survey placed that group's consumption at 4.21 cups per day. In Canada the next highest group of drinkers was in the 40-49 year age category at 2.66 cups; that class was followed by the 20-29 year group at 2.46 cups. The cups per day for the remaining age groups are: 65 and over, 1.55; 15-19 years, 0.89; and 10-14 years, 0.25 cup.

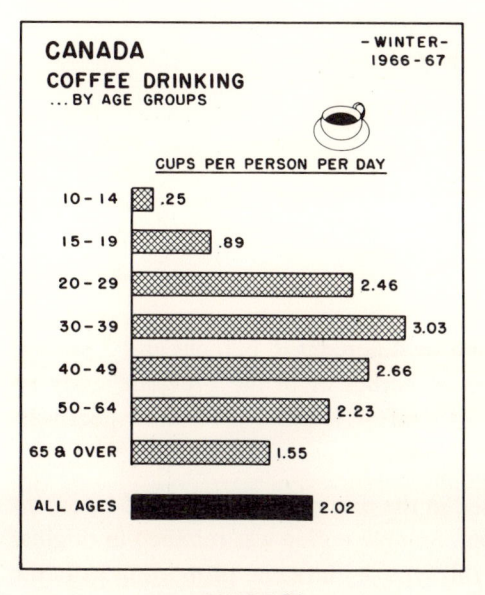

**CANADA COFFEE DRINKING ... BY AGE GROUPS — WINTER 1966-67**

CUPS PER PERSON PER DAY

| Age | Cups |
|---|---|
| 10-14 | .25 |
| 15-19 | .89 |
| 20-29 | 2.46 |
| 30-39 | 3.03 |
| 40-49 | 2.66 |
| 50-64 | 2.23 |
| 65 & OVER | 1.55 |
| ALL AGES | 2.02 |

CHART 31

(7) A very high proportion of indoor workers indicated that coffee was available to them during their work-breaks — 87 percent (91 percent in the last survey), while in the United States the corresponding figure is 77 percent. After coffee, the most widely available beverage was soft drinks (76 percent), tea (62 percent), milk (50 percent) and hot chocolate or cocoa (37 percent). All of these percentages were down from the 1965 figures. Thirteen percent of inside workers could get some other beverage besides the types mentioned, but five percent had no beverage of any sort available.

(8) Among persons working indoors the percentage who reported having access to vending machines dispensing beverages declined from 52 percent in 1965 to 46 percent for the latest survey. Soft drinks again were most frequently available (to 43 percent) and coffee followed in second place (18 percent). Both, however, were down in availability (1965 figures were 49 percent and 25 percent respectively).

(9) A breakdown of prices paid for a cup of coffee at eating places and at places of employment in each of the four surveys is shown on the following page. The modal price has remained at 10 cents throughout the years covered by the surveys, but the underlying trend toward higher prices is evident.

(10) Responses of users of regular coffee to the query on what type of grind usually was purchased indicated that 50 percent bought an all-purpose or regular grind (51 percent in 1965), and 32 percent purchased percolator grind (29 percent in 1965).

**PRICE PER CUP AT EATING PLACES**

(percentage of cups purchased)

|  | 1959 | 1961 | 1965 | 1966 |
|---|---|---|---|---|
| Under 10¢ | 5 | 5 | 1 | 1 |
| 10¢ | 94 | 92 | 84 | 69 |
| Over 10¢ | 1 | 3 | 15 | 30 |

**PRICE PER CUP AT PLACES OF EMPLOYMENT**

(percentage of cups purchased)

|  | 1959 | 1961 | 1965 | 1966 |
|---|---|---|---|---|
| Under 10¢ | 24 | 22 | 16 | 20 |
| 10¢ | 75 | 76 | 72 | 64 |
| Over 10¢ | 1 | 2 | 12 | 16 |

Both fine grind and drip grind were each used by 4 percent (8 percent and 5 percent respectively in 1965). The same percentages of homes as in the previous study reported using store-ground coffee and home-ground — 9 and 2 percent respectively.

(11) In the home regular coffee was retained in the original container by 54 percent of the families (up from 33 percent in 1965-66). Soluble coffee was retained in original containers by 95 percent of homes that use this type — the same proportion as in the prior survey. Based on a 1965 survey, the corresponding figures for United States households were 54 percent and 97 percent respectively.

(12) Forty-four percent of those consuming regular coffee at home reported that percolators were used while 27 percent made use of automatic devices. Ten percent reported use of a drip pot; 14 percent used a glass coffee maker; and approximately 6 percent drank boiled coffee.

The *coffee-measure* is the most commonly used device in Canadian households (50 percent). The tablespoon ranked next in usage as a measuring device (26 percent); the teaspoon (14 percent); marks on the basket of the drip percolator (4 percent), and other means, largely guessing (6 percent).

(13) Respondents who indicated that they were coffee drinkers were asked what additives, creaming or sweetening agents were used. The results for each of the four surveys are indicated below. The trend toward black coffee in the United States is not paralleled in Canada.

(percentage of coffee drinkers)

|  | 1959 | 1961 | 1965 | 1966 |
|---|---|---|---|---|
| Use Creaming Agent | 85 | 83 | 84 | 86 |
| Use Sweetening Agent | 75 | 72 | 75 | 75 |
| Use Neither | 9 | 9 | 10 | 10 |

*Attitudes Toward Coffee*

Persons interviewed in this survey were shown 23 sets of phrases in order to determine their attitudes toward coffee. Each set consisted of two phrases, each phrase the opposite of the other, *e.g.*, Expensive/Inexpensive. The respondent was asked to record his choice between every pair on the basis of a five-point scale. Using the example above, a rating of "1" would indicate "very" expensive and a score of "5" would mean "very" inexpensive. A rating of "3" would indicate that the respondent felt that coffee fell midway between expensive and inexpensive, while "2" or "4" would show "somewhat" feelings toward expensive or inexpensive, respectively.

In order to reduce complexity, the 23 sets of bi-polar phrases regarding coffee can be grouped, arbitrarily, into eight basic dimensions: *taste and aroma, sociability, occasion orientation, refreshment, health, adult image, expensiveness* and *gender image*. The results of this second study of attitudes toward coffee in Canada will be summarized with respect to those dimensions. Scores have been indicated to show divergence from neutrality and to facilitate comparisons.

(1) *Taste and Aroma:* Pleasant aroma and likeable taste received high ratings. Those attributes of coffee were most highly regarded in Ontario and British Columbia, least in the Atlantic Provinces. Young persons, those 10-19, were much less enthusiastic about the *taste and aroma* of coffee than were their elders. Occasional drinkers of the beverage rated those qualities less than did heavy users.

(2) *Sociability:* Coffee is generally regarded by Canadians as a sociable drink as shown by a high average score. Those interviewed liked to serve coffee to their friends, although young persons and women who were not homemakers did not agree with the majority. Also, the sociability of coffee and the desire to serve it to friends is somewhat less in evidence in Eastern than in Western Canada.

(3) *Occasion Orientation:* Coffee has a broad *occasion orientation* as indicated by an excellent rating for being good anytime, anywhere as opposed to being for special occasions. There was more preference for beverage after meals rather than with meals and it was highly regarded as being good for a break from work or study.

(4) *Refreshment:* Coffee is generally regarded as a refreshing drink. However, French-speaking persons from Quebec did not rate it as enthusiastically as did other Canadians.

(5) *Health:* Persons interviewed felt that coffee may be somewhat habit-forming, but they also found it to be relaxing. Coffee apparently keeps French-speaking Canadians awake, but other Canadians in general are not so affected. In any event, there was a more pronounced tendency among those interviewed to often want to accept coffee that is offered to them rather than to refuse it.

(6) *Adult Image:* Most persons interviewed felt that coffee is more popular among older people than among younger people. That feeling, however, tended to be inversely related to the age of the respondent.

(7) *Expensiveness:* Results of the interviews showed that coffee in Canada is regarded as more expensive than inexpensive, especially among the French-speaking sector.

(8) *Gender Image:* Apparently coffee appeals to both women and men. By comparison, tea was regarded by those interviewed as being somewhat more of a woman's drink, especially by British Columbians.

# The European Market

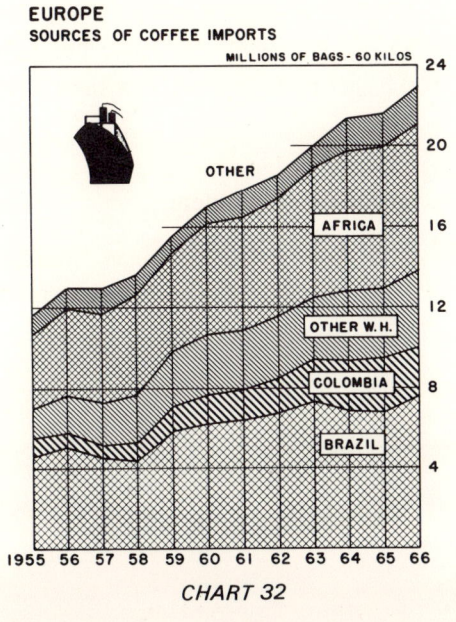

**EUROPE**
**SOURCES OF COFFEE IMPORTS**

CHART 32

The long-term uptrend in demand for green coffee in Europe again was in evidence in 1966. European imports of green coffee now have shown steady improvement for nine consecutive years. Aggregate shipments entering European ports came to 22.9 million bags; that figure represents an increase of 6.1 percent over the 1965 record level of 21.6 million bags and compares with offtake of 13.0 million bags in 1956.

The resurgence of demand for coffee on the Continent represents, in a sense, a return to a normal market situation after liquidation of heavy inventories. Liquidation of coffee stocks in Europe in 1965 has been estimated to have involved a drawdown of about one million bags. The accumulation of inventories in European import centers occurred in late 1963 and in the early part of 1964 in the aftermath of disastrous weather conditions in Brazil which damaged a major portion of that country's exportable crop in the 1964-65 season. Subsequent absorption of those excess holdings by the European trade required an extended time period.

Nearly all Western European countries raised their import totals in 1966. Germany, the leading importer on the Continent now taking 4.7 million bags, registered a small improvement of 66,000 bags or 1.4 percent this year. France, currently the second largest Continental consumer, took 177,000 bags or 4.9 percent more than in 1965. Italy, third-ranking market in Europe, registered an increase of 52,000 bags (2.6 percent).

Exceptions to that buoyant trend among the more important consuming countries were Belgium-Luxembourg and Switzerland; the former registered an import decline of 224,000 bags or 19.8 percent and shipments recorded by the latter destination were lower by 65,000 bags or 8.8 percent. The wide fluctuation in the import statistics of the Belgium-Luxembourg Economic Union probably represents the changing fortunes of dealers engaged in transshipments and a concomitant change in inventory policy of the Belgian coffee trade.

The Scandinavian countries which lead the world in per-capita consumption of coffee all registered significant expansion in green coffee imports. Norway's performance this year in that respect was best in that area, the recorded improvement being 94,000 bags or 19.5 percent over 1965; Finland followed with an increase of 13.2 percent or 89,000 bags; Sweden and Denmark registered expansion of 82,000 bags (5.4 percent) and 61,000 bags (7.4 percent) respectively. Among other major importers the United Kingdom registered a sharp recovery of 387,000 bags or 39.8 percent, thereby surpassing by a small margin the record level of 1964. Spain continued its rapid growth by augmenting import volume by 12 percent or 101,000 bags. The Low Countries raised their import total by only 40,000 bags or 2.9 percent over their 1966 level.

| Year | Volume (million bags) | Percent Change |
|---|---|---|
| 1931 | 12.7 | — |
| 1946 | 5.2 | — |
| 1947 | 6.8 | +30.8 |
| 1948 | 7.3 | + 7.4 |
| 1949 | 7.7 | + 5.5 |
| 1950 | 8.4 | + 9.1 |
| 1951 | 8.6 | + 2.4 |
| 1952 | 9.7 | +12.8 |
| 1953 | 10.2 | + 5.2 |
| 1954 | 10.5 | + 2.9 |
| 1955 | 11.5 | + 9.5 |
| 1956 | 13.0 | +13.0 |
| 1957 | 12.8 | − 1.5 |
| 1958 | 13.8 | + 7.8 |
| 1959 | 15.5 | +12.3 |
| 1960 | 17.0 | + 9.9 |
| 1961 | 17.8 | + 4.7 |
| 1962 | 18.5 | + 3.9 |
| 1963 | 20.0 | + 6.7 |
| 1964 | 21.3 | + 6.5 |
| 1965 | 21.6 | + 1.4 |
| 1966 | 22.9 | + 6.1 |

SOURCE: *Official statistics and trade publications.*

Eastern Europe this year took an estimated two-million bags. That is a new high level for that region and represents an expansion in demand of 268,000 bags or 15.1 percent from the 1965 level. Poland and Hungary made notable gains and accounted for practically all the additional import volume in 1966.

All producing areas participated in the increase in European coffee imports in 1966. Therefore the relative shares of the market were held quite constant. Latin America maintained its position as the major supplier to the Continent, shipping 60 percent of the coffee taken this year — the same proportion as in 1965. The African producers' share of the market also was unchanged at 32 percent. The Asian producers raised their share from six to seven percent. The regional composition of Europe's coffee imports has changed very little in the past five or six years.

*Imports of Robustus*

The volume of *robusta* coffee shipments into European consuming centers continued to expand in 1966. Aggregate *robusta* volume attained a level of 7.1 million bags as compared with 6.8 million bags last year. The gain amounted to 294,710 bags or 4.4 percent. Despite the improvement in import volume the *robusta* share of the European coffee market declined slightly to 30.9 percent; in 1965 the *robusta* share of the market was 31.3 percent.

Major factors in the somewhat less favorable position of the *robustas* in the European import picture were the decreases registered in *robusta* shipments into France and the United Kingdom. Those two countries are the principal consumers of that variety taking 2.7 million bags and 1.0 million bags respectively. In France the *robusta* share went down from 75.4 percent in 1965 to 70.8 percent of the total in the current year; in the United Kingdom *robustas* took 71.9 percent of the total imports as compared with 73.2 percent of the total in 1965.

Other important *robusta* markets in Europe also witnessed losses in the *robusta* share. In the Netherlands, *robustas* diminished in importance from 42.2 percent to 41.6 percent this year; in Switzerland the relative position of *robustas* dropped from 42.7 percent in 1965 to 30.3 percent this year; in Italy also the position of *robustas* declined from 34.6 percent in 1965 to 31.9 percent.

**EUROPE: ROBUSTA IMPORTS**

| Year | Bags | Percent of Total |
|------|------|------------------|
| 1961 | 5,548,000 | 31.1 |
| 1962 | 5,132,000 | 27.9 |
| 1963 | 6,050,000 | 30.2 |
| 1964 | 6,626,000 | 30.9 |
| 1965 | 6,764,290 | 31.3 |
| 1966 | 7,059,000 | 30.9 |

SOURCE: *Jacques Louis-Delamare et Cie, Le Havre, 1961-1966; PACB 1965.*

The *robusta* variety registered a dramatic gain of 48 percent in the Spanish market — its volume rising by 351,000 bags. *Robustas* accounted for 38.5 percent of imports into Spain — up from 29.2 percent in 1965. Belgium-Luxembourg took 10.9 percent more *robustas* in the current year. However, a more vigorous concurrent expansion in *arabica* volume caused the *robusta* share to drop from 34.5 percent in 1965 to 23.6 percent this year.

In the high-consumption areas of Northern Europe which are predominantly *arabica* markets, some attrition was noted in the relative share of the *robustas*.

**EUROPE: ROBUSTA IMPORT SHARES**

|  | Bags | Percent |
|---|---|---|
| France | 2,685,000 | 70.8 |
| United Kingdom | 977,000 | 71.9 |
| Italy | 657,000 | 31.9 |
| Netherlands | 589,000 | 41.6 |
| Germany (F.R.) | 445,000 | 9.5 |
| Spain | 351,000 | 38.5 |
| Belgium-Luxembourg | 312,000 | 34.5 |
| Switzerland | 203,000 | 30.2 |
| Denmark | 130,000 | 14.7 |
| Sweden | 49,000 | 3.0 |
| Norway | 26,000 | 4.5 |
| Finland | 23,000 | 3.0 |
| Others | 612,000 | 19.0 |
| **Total** | **7,059,000** | **30.9** |

SOURCE: Jacques Louis-Delamare et Cie.

*Per Capita Imports*

Expansion of arrivals of green coffee in European-consuming centers outpaced population growth, so that overall per capita off take of coffee improved. The European per-capita figure had been static at 4.03 pounds in the past two years. In 1966 that measure of coffee consumption moved up to 4.5 pounds.

The Swedish people maintained their position as the leading coffee consumers in the world. Per capita offtake of green coffee in 1966 climbed to a new record high of 27.4 pounds — an improvement of 1.2 pounds over the record level of 26.2 pounds registered in 1965. Other countries in the Scandinavian region also increased their per capita coffee consumption. That was in contrast to the situation of apparent stability in 1965 when, in that region, only Denmark registered an increase and that of minor consequence. Denmark continues to follow Sweden as the second country in the world in terms of per capita coffee consumption, with a current rate of 24.5 pounds as compared with 22.9 pounds in 1965. Norway and Finland also are high on the list of per capita consumers; current rates per head in those countries are 20.3 pounds and 21.9 pounds respectively. The fact that the heaviest coffee-consuming countries are concentrated in the northern regions tends to support the notion generally held by the coffee trade that coffee consumption is a function of climatic conditions. In the United States, for example, the trend of coffee consumption shows an inverse pattern in relation to the level of average temperatures. That consumption curve usually has its trough in midsummer and its peak in midwinter.

**EUROPE**
PER CAPITA NET IMPORTS OF GREEN COFFEE
POUNDS PER CAPITA

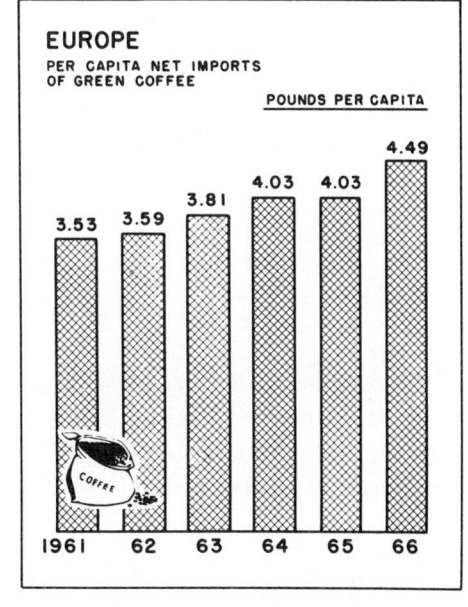

| 1961 | 62 | 63 | 64 | 65 | 66 |
|------|------|------|------|------|------|
| 3.53 | 3.59 | 3.81 | 4.03 | 4.03 | 4.49 |

CHART 33

The level of the standard of living which in general is relatively high throughout the Scandinavian region has an important influence on coffee consumption. Personal incomes in Sweden are the second highest in the world after the United States. Taxation on coffee also is relatively low in those countries. The table below shows the impressive coffee-drinking rates in those four northern countries.

|  | 1963 | 1964 | 1965 | 1966 |
|---|---|---|---|---|
|  |  | (green pounds per capita) |  |  |
| Sweden | 25.1 | 26.3 | 26.2 | 27.4 |
| Denmark | 24.9 | 22.6 | 22.9 | 24.5 |
| Finland | 20.2 | 22.9 | 19.3 | 21.9 |
| Norway | 20.2 | 19.8 | 17.1 | 20.3 |

Implicit in the short series presented therein is the possibility that per capita rates may fluctuate in future along a plateau — which for each country may be approximately in the range shown. Sweden is the only country to register a steady year-to-year uptrend. Denmark's excellent recovery this year has not brought per-head coffee drinking back to the 1963 level. The rate for Finland has not recouped the loss from the 1964 level that occurred last year. The consumption pattern in Norway has regained the 1963 level after two years of sharp decline.

Six countries form another per capita grouping well below the Scandinavian region.

|  | 1963 | 1964 | 1965 | 1966 |
|---|---|---|---|---|
|  |  | (green pounds per capita) |  |  |
| Netherlands | 12.9 | 15.2 | 14.8 | 15.1 |
| Switzerland | 13.1 | 13.9 | 16.3 | 14.8 |
| Belgium-Luxembourg | 12.8 | 14.7 | 15.2 | 12.1 |
| Germany (F.R.) | 9.4 | 9.8 | 10.7 | 10.7 |
| France | 10.0 | 10.5 | 9.8 | 10.1 |

The Netherlands has almost regained its 1964 record. Swiss coffee drinking has fallen off sharply from last year's rate. Belgian consumption has retrogressed five years or more. The German market has levelled off for the first time in the postwar period and France now barely exceeds it 1963 per-capita level.

The Common Market with a combined population of 183 million in 1966 averaged 9.3 pounds per capita. Italy is the sole low coffee-consumption area in that market, but that country is making steady progress. The official data for that country do not reveal the true level of coffee consumption because of the fact that clandestine traffic in coffee is sizeable. That situation arises from the fact that coffee is taxed very heavily in Italy. The combined fiscal burden from port of entry to the ultimate consumer has been estimated at close to 100 percent of the original value of the green coffee.

Some of the "New Markets" of Eastern Europe have raised their imports of coffee this year. Although as a group those countries imported two-million bags in 1966, they represent a vast potential for the coffee producers, as their per-capita consumption is very low.

### EUROPE: Green Coffee Stocks in Selected Countries*

|  | 1966 | 1965 | 1964 | Change Bags | 1964 to 1966 Percent |
|---|---|---|---|---|---|
| Italy** | 507,091 | 424,789 | 603,168 | − 96,077 | − 15.9 |
| Germany (F.R.) | 493,497 | 407,678 | 617,722 | − 124,225 | − 20.1 |
| France | 231,417 | 211,767 | 437,350 | − 205,933 | − 47.1 |
| Sweden | 222,483 | 199,567 | 212,583 | + 9,900 | + 4.6 |
| Netherlands | 296,863*** | 164,729 | 402,337 | − 105,474 | − 26.2 |
| Belgium | 196,750 | 156,883 | 267,933 | − 71,183 | − 26.6 |
| **Total** | **1,948,101** | **1,565,413** | **2,541,093** | **− 592,992** | **− 23.3** |

SOURCE: Café Vert.

(*) *Port stocks at end of year.*
(**) *Includes consignments at Trieste.*
(***) *May 31.*

*Fiscal Burdens on Coffee*

Taxation remains a major roadblock in the path of expansion of coffee consumption in a number of European countries. In the year under review there were no changes of significance in European tariffs on coffee imports.

Among the six countries of the Common Market, which together account for more than a quarter of European coffee imports, changes in tariff regulations in 1966 were noted in Germany and Italy. In France the maximum common external tariff of the EEC which is 9.6 percent *ad valorem* remains in effect. In the Low Countries, which for most of the postwar period had entered coffee duty-free, there now is a five percent *ad valorem* tariff on coffee. In the Belgium-Luxembourg Economic Union which also had entered coffee duty-free in prior years, there now is a two percent *ad valorem* tariff.

The Italian external duty is 0.01 percent of the import value on non-decaffeinated green coffee and 0.15 cents per pound on the decaffeinated form. In that country the relatively low import duty on coffee is only a small part of the story. Coffee is subject to numerous imposts beginning at the port of entry. Then there are the various government consumption taxes and additional transaction or turnover taxes imposed by municipalities and other localities. The end result is that the fiscal burden on coffee in Italy is about equal to the value of the green coffee itself. Taxation in that country, therefore, exercises a strong depressant influence on coffee consumption.

In Germany which now is the leading coffee market on the Continent in terms of aggregate volume, a complex tax schedule levies a 4.6 percent impost on non-decaffeinated coffee from origins accorded General/MFN/Greece status. Federal and state taxes on coffee in Germany are perhaps an even more important factor than the import duty because of the fact that they are quite high. In 1966 an estimated $250 million was derived by the Federal Government from coffee taxation. Since that tax is such an important source of revenue for the Federal Government, the coffee trade has found it extremely difficult to cope with the problem of taxation. The Government at the same time has found it no less easy to sustain its position vis-a-vis the coffee tax. That tax has at times become a significant political issue, with consumer interest being allied with the coffee trade in efforts to eliminate or at least reduce the incidence of taxation on this commodity.

There are only two major importing countries that enter green coffee duty-free; they are Austria and Norway. The United Kingdom levies a nominal duty of 1.2 cents per pound; coffee from Commonwealth sources enters duty-free. Sweden, where the per-capita rate of coffee drinking is the highest in the world, also has a nominal duty on coffee of 1.8 cents per pound, while elsewhere in the Scandinavian region, Denmark and Finland levy duties of 12.3 and 17.7 cents per pound respectively. Switzerland's tariff is 5.7 cents per pound. In Spain the temporary reduction in the green coffee tariff to one percent *ad valorem* remains in effect. Country details relating to duties on coffee imports are contained in Appendix Table M-1.

# Summary

1) Five years have elapsed since the signing of the International Coffee Agreement at the United Nations headquarters in New York. Membership in the International Coffee Organization has grown to 39 exporting and 23 importing countries. About 99 percent of the world coffee exports are now covered by quota provisions under the Agreement.

Significant progress was made in respect of adjustment of supply to market conditions, as well as of other provisions of the Agreement concerned with long-term measures aimed at a reasonable balance between production and demand.

A Selective System allowing for the independent movement of four different Groups of coffees was introduced to replace the former overall *Indicator Price* System.

Great improvements were achieved in control measures aimed at stricter compliance with quotas; Export Stamps were introduced to strengthen the System of Certificates of Origin and Re-Export and controls over "New Market" shipments were tightened further.

The Eighth Period of Sessions of the International Coffee Council in September produced, among the many descisions adopted, a group of eight important Resolutions concerned with the questions of waivers, adjustment of supply, controls of exports and reexports, production goals, stocks and diversification. Those Resolutions were complemented by three others approved in early 1967 (Resolutions 114, 115, 118, 122, 117, 120, 110, 119, 131, 128 and 127, all shown in the Appendixes of the Chapter on the ICO).

The World Coffee Promotion Committee continued its activities into a second year, extending its coffee promotion campaigns from nine to eleven consuming countries, at the tune of about $7.0 million.

2) During the year under review coffee prices in general were characterized by an orderly easing to slightly lower levels. The softening of prices in 1966 appeared to be a continuation of the downward trend that emerged in 1964 and that has dominated the price structure into 1967, with the exception of small increases in spot prices in the latter part of 1965. The lower price trend reflects in the main the continuing problem of excessive stocks of green coffee.

The average price per pound of green coffee imported into the United States during 1966 was 36.57 cents, about one cent or 2.6 percent below the 1965 average of 37.56 cents. While monthly averages during 1966 indicate a generally declining price trend, the major break occurred in June. The average price for that month was almost two cents per pound below that of May. The average import price for the first five months of 1966 was roughly 38.00 cents per pound, while the corresponding price for the last seven months was about 35.5 cents per pound, an indication of the May-June gradient. A comparison of December with January shows a loss of almost four cents per pound or about 10 percent.

On balance, spot prices were somewhat lower at the end of 1966 than they were at the beginning. Brazils were about nine percent lower on the basis of a January-December comparison; the other *arabicas* and the *robustas* were from 11 to over 14 percent lower. The somewhat smaller relative declines for Brazils helped to compensate for the small losses sustained by that growth in a similar comparison in 1965, while other growths showed increases. On the basis of annual averages the *arabicas* were lower in 1966 than they were in the previous year, while the *robustas* were higher. The former growths were lower by two percent for MAMS to nine percent for Brazils and the latter growths were higher by some eight percent.

The MRCA average price of regular coffee at retail, including both vacuum and bag packs, was 71.9 cents per pound in 1966, a decrease of 1.7 cents or 2.3 percent from the 1965 average of 73.6 cents per pound. For soluble coffee the annual average price for 1966 was 29.4 cents per two ounce equivalent unit, 0.3 cent or one percent less than the 1965 average of 29.7 cents per pound. Monthly average prices of regular coffee remained at a fairly constant level for the January-August period and lost several cents in the last four months. The corresponding values for soluble coffee inched upward in the January-August period and then eased off slightly in the remaining four months. In January the price for regular coffee was 72.8 cents per pound, while it was 70.4 cents in December — 2.4 cents or 3.3 percent lower. The vacuum-pack coffees had an average price of 72.9 cents per pound in March and 70.5 cents in December; the price for the year was estimated to be 72.0 cents per pound based on data for the last month in each calendar quarter. Bag-pack coffees averaged 69.8 cents per pound in March, 70.0 cents in December and 70.0 cents for the year. As a consequence of a greater decrease in the average annual retail price of regular coffee than in the average annual import price of green coffee, the spread between them narrowed a bit to 35.3 cents — a decrease of 1.9 percent from the 1965 value of 36 cents. The average monthly price of soluble coffee increased from 28.2 cents per two ounce equivalent unit in January to 29.9 cents in December — a gain of 1.7 cents or six percent.

Trading interest on the New York Coffee and Sugar Exchange diminished to a practical standstill in the latter months of 1966. There were many days when no trading occurred. During 1966 a total of 2,955 "B" lots (738,750 bags) were traded compared with 15,005 "B" lots (3,751,250 bags) in 1965. In the *robusta* contract 249 "R" lots (62,250 bags) changed hands as compared with 84 "R" lots (21,000 bags) a year earlier. Most of the interest in coffee-futures trading has shifted to the London Terminal Market, where traders have been exceedingly active.

(3) Exportable production in crop year 1966-67 is estimated in the aggregate by the FAS at 47.3 million bags. That figure is 28.5 percent less than the revised 1965-66

estimate of 66.1 million bags. The primary factor in that decline was the 18.3 million bag short fall in the countries of the Western Hemisphere. Most of the short fall can be attributed to lower output in Brazil as the ambitious coffee-tree eradication program in that country appeared to be effectively curtailing supply. Moreover, the current year in Brazil was expected to be an "off-year" following an exceptionally large harvest in 1965-66. It also was reported that growing conditions were not favorable in Brazil's major coffee-growing states.

Total exportable production in the African countries was expected to be some 600,000 bags lower for the current crop year, compared with the preceding year, while the corresponding figure for Asia and Oceania was 35,000 bags higher.

It is estimated by the United States Department of Agriculture (U.S.D.A.) that about 87.4 million bags of green coffee would remain as total world surplus stock at the end of 1965-66. The Agency predicts that 65.2 million bags are expected to be produced in the current year.[1] Of that total, the U.S.D.A. assumes that 50.0 million bags will be exported and 15.4 million bags will be utilized in the producing countries. Should those estimates be borne out, 87.2 million bags of green coffee would be carried over into the 1967-68 season.

(4) World exports of coffee rose by 11.9 percent to a new high of 50.3 million bags. The new total was 5.4 million bags greater than total shipments in the preceding year. World imports expanded by 5.8 percent to a new record level of 49.9 million bags. The new figure represents an improvement of 2.7 million bags over 1965. Total exports in the current year therefore exceeded imports on a gross basis by 396,000 bags. That difference can be partially explained by time-lag losses in transit and errors in record keeping in the countries of origin and in the countries of destination.

The coffee-producing countries of the world gained an estimated $2.4 billion in foreign exchange in 1966 from coffee exports. That valuation is ten percent higher than the estimated exchange earning from coffee in 1965. Exchange receipts from shipments of coffee in 1966 represented 1.3 percent of total world trade which presently is calculated at $181.3 billion. In the preceding year total world trade was put at $165.5 billion and exchange earnings from coffee represented 1.3 percent of that value total. The Latin American coffee-producing countries this year earned $1.6 billion from shipments of that commodity whereas in 1965 their coffee shipments were valued at $1.5 billion.

Six countries in Latin America derive more than one third of their foreign-exchange revenues from coffee. The extent of their dependence on coffee export revenue ranged from 42.1 to 67.0 percent of total foreign exchange receipts.

---

[1] Note that this is total production, not exportable production.

Aggregate United States imports of goods and services from the fifteen Latin American coffee-producing countries in 1966 came to $3.5 billion while U. S. exports to those countries had an overall valuation of $3.6 billion. The U. S. therefore had a favorable balance of trade of $67.8 million with those coffee countries. The U. S. accounts showed trade surpluses with six of those coffee countries, but the U. S. had deficits in trade relations with nine countries in that group, the largest of which by far was Venezuela. The latter country ships a heavy volume of petroleum to the U. S., the value of which exceeds substantially the shipments of U. S. goods to that country. The fifteen coffee-growing countries of Latin America received 11.9 percent of total U. S. export shipments in 1966. In that year, shipments from those countries of coffee and other commodities accounted for 13.7 percent of total U. S. imports. In recent years, the fifteen countries' share of the U. S. export/import trade has diminished somewhat. In 1966, total U. S. exports to those fifteen countries amounted to $3.56 billion, whereas total U. S. coffee imports from that group came to $0.75 billion. For that group of countries coffee amounted to 21 percent of their purchases in the United States.

(5) The quantity of green coffee processed into soluble declined for the fourth consecutive year and was at the lowest level in eight years. During 1966 soluble coffee manufacturers utilized some 3.5 million bags or 16.5 percent of all green coffee roasted in the United States. That was seven percent less than the 3.8 million bags utilized in 1965, when their share was 17.4 percent.

However, the total quantity of soluble product available for consumption remained at almost the same level as in the preceding year. There were two reasons for this: first, the United States, for the first time became a net importer of coffee in soluble form and, second, soluble coffee producers continued to become increasingly efficient in transforming green beans into soluble product and consequently continued to require fewer green beans to produce the same amount of end product.

At the retail level households bought about three percent less soluble coffee in 1966 than they did in the preceding year. At the same time the number of cups of soluble beverage remained roughly the same as in 1965. While out-of-home consumption might account for part of this divergence, it is more likely that housewives used slightly less soluble coffee in preparing their beverage.

Soluble coffee imports into the United States in 1966 were 10,552,788 pounds or almost four times the volume registered in the preceding year. The total value of those imports was $10,949,826 or $1.04 per pound, the lowest unit value on record. Imports of soluble coffee from Brazil, which had been only 0.3 million pounds in 1965, rose to six million pounds in 1966 and that country became the largest supplier with 57 percent of the total. Exports of soluble coffee from the United States during 1966 reached only 7,597,137 pounds, a decline of 37 percent from the 12,-112,459 pounds recorded in 1965. Thus, the United States became, for the first time, a net importer of soluble coffee.

(6) Total imports of all types of coffee into the United States during 1966 amounted to 22,330,000 bags compared with 21,512,000 bags in 1965 — an increase of 3.8 percent and the first year-to-year increase since 1962. In the final weeks of 1962 heavy imports reflected anticipation of an impending port strike. Those usually heavy imports were inflated further by inventory accumulation in 1963 as the industry sought to insure itself against the eventuality of a severe shortage of high-grade Brazilian coffee because of damage to plantations in that country by frost and drought. Only partial liquidation of the abnormally high stocks was effected in 1964. In 1965, however, an appreciable reduction in green-coffee inventories and also of stocks of finished goods took place. With inventories back to a more normal level, it was possible for net imports in 1966 to more closely approximate demand.

The coffee-producing countries of the Western Hemisphere maintained their predominant position as suppliers to the United States market. Their share in that market nevertheless continues to diminish. Imports from those countries came to 14,512,845 bags in 1966, an increase of 0.8 percent from the 1965 total of 14,397,418 bags. But their proportion of the market in the more recent year was 65.7 percent as compared with 77.9 percent in 1962. A larger volume of Brazilian shipments to this country in 1966 was the major factor in the increase of the Western Hemisphere group. African Suppliers increased their volume to the United States market to 6,455,305 bags, a gain of 4.7 percent over last year. The Africans share of the U.S. market expanded to 29.2 percent as compared with 28.9 percent in 1965.

Net Civilian Visible Disappearance (NCVD) decreased to 21,369,000 bags in 1966 — down 1.3 percent from the 1965 level. While NCVD declined slightly, the United States population grew by roughly one percent. Per-capita consumption, therefore, fell to 14.6 pounds in 1966 from 14.9 pounds in 1965. Aggregate coffee consumption in terms of green-coffee equivalent decreased by 37 million pounds from the level of the preceding year. In 1966 the main incidence of the declining consumption occurred at home where purchases were lower by 45 million pounds and in eating places where 12 million fewer pounds were taken. Improvement in demand for coffee in the at-work sector partially offset that decrease, as did smaller increases in both the institutional and flavors and extracts sectors. The average household spent $21.49 in 1966 for coffee as compared with an average expenditure of $22.88 in 1965. There was continued preference among household purchasers of regular coffee for cans rather than for bags; that also was true for larger-size packs of both regular and soluble coffee.

In the Winter of 1967 average daily coffee consumption for persons 10 years of age and over was 2.84 cups. That figure represents practically no change over 1966 when the average stood at 2.86 cups. In comparison with the 1962 consumption peak of 3.12 cups per person per day, the current rate of coffee drinking is .28 cup or nine percent lower. The overall coffee-drinking rates for 1966 and 1967 indicate that the downtrend in coffee drinking during the 1963-1965 period may well have been halted.

(7) Gross imports of coffee in all forms into Canada during 1966 were placed at

1,247,962 bags of green-coffee equivalent. That was 79,257 bags or six percent less than the 1,327,219 bags — a record high point attained in 1965. Per capita net imports declined from 8.74 pounds in the earlier year to 8.13 pounds in the later year as imports decreased and population increased. The coffee-growing countries of the Western Hemisphere continued to be the major suppliers of green coffee to Canada, but their share of total imports declined. In the year under review their share was 71.6 percent compared with 79.4 percent in 1965 and 84.8 percent in 1964. The value of all coffee entering Canada in 1966 was $72.3 million, eight percent under the total value for 1965 and 12 percent below the 1964 highpoint.

During the Winter of 1966, Canadians ten years of age and older consumed an average of 2.02 cups of coffee per person per day compared with 2.18 cups in the Winter of 1965.

(8) European demand for coffee rose to a new record level in 1966. Aggregate imports of green coffee came to 22.9 million bags, about 6.5 percent over the previous high established in 1965. Resurgent demand for coffee this year reflected in the main liquidation of heavy inventories in the principle-consuming centers. Although the volume of *robusta* imports expanded somewhat, the share of the market taken by that variety declined slightly. The improvement in import volume exceeded the rate of population growth so that on an overall basis per capita coffee consumption moved upward and now stands at 4.5 pounds. Sweden established what probably is a world's record of 27.4 pounds per capita. Fiscal policy continues to be a major hindrance to the growth of coffee consumption in Europe. Although there were some changes in the tariff and tax structure on the Continent no significant reduction in imposts on coffee were noted.

# Appendix
STATISTICAL TABLES

# Appendix Tables

    **Page**

## PRODUCTION

| | | | |
|---|---|---|---|
| PQ | 3. | World: Exportable Production of Green Coffee, 1957-58 Through 1966-67 | A-10 — A-11 |
| PQ | 4. | World: Exportable Production of Green Coffee by ICO Membership, 1957-58 Through 1966-67 | A-12 — A-13 |

## EXPORTS

| | | | |
|---|---|---|---|
| EQ | 1. | World: Exports of Green Coffee, 1965-66 | A-9 |
| EQ | 2. | World: Exports of Green Coffee, 1947-66 | A-14 — A-15 |
| REV | 4. | World: Relative Importance of Coffee in Value of Total Trade, 1966 | A-75 |
| REV | 5. | World: Value of Coffee Exports by Countries, 1960-1966 | A-76 — A-77 |
| REV | 6. | World: Share of Coffee in Foreign Exchange Revenues, 1960-1966 | A-78 — A-79 |
| EQ | 5. | World: Exports of Green Coffee by ICO Membership, 1947-66 | A-24 — A-25 |
| EQ | 21. | Angola: Exports of Green Coffee, 1965-66 | A-56 |
| EQ | 21A. | Angola: Exports of Green Coffee, 1960-65 | A-57 |
| EQ | 6. | Brazil: Exports of Green Coffee, 1965-66 | A-26 — A-27 |
| EQ | 6A. | Brazil: Exports of Green Coffee, 1960-65 | A-28 — A-29 |
| EQ | 7. | Colombia: Exports of Green Coffee, 1965-66 | A-30 |
| EQ | 7A. | Colombia: Exports of Green Coffee, 1960-65 | A-31 |
| EQ | 26A. | Congo (Kinshasa): Exports of Green Coffee, 1960-65 | A-68 |
| EQ | 12. | Costa Rica: Exports of Green Coffee, 1965-66 | A-40 |
| EQ | 12A. | Costa Rica: Exports of Green Coffee, 1960-65 | A-41 |
| EQ | 19A. | Cuba: Exports of Green Coffee, 1960-65 | A-74 |
| EQ | 13. | Dominican Republic: Exports of Green Coffee, 1965-66 | A-42 |
| EQ | 13A. | Dominican Republic: Exports of Green Coffee, 1960-65 | A-43 |
| EQ | 17. | Ecuador: Exports of Green Coffee, 1965-66 | A-50 |
| EQ | 17A. | Ecuador: Exports of Green Coffee, 1960-65 | A-51 |
| EQ | 8. | El Salvador: Exports of Green Coffee, 1965-66 | A-32 |

# APPENDIX TABLES (cont'd)

|   |   |   | Page |
|---|---|---|---|
| EQ | 8A. | El Salvador: Exports of Green Coffee, 1960-65 | A-33 |
| EQ | 28A. | Ethiopia: Exports of Green Coffee, 1960-65 | A-69 |
| EQ | 9. | Guatemala: Exports of Green Coffee, 1965-66 | A-34 |
| EQ | 9A. | Guatemala: Exports of Green Coffee, 1960-65 | A-35 |
| EQ | 15. | Haiti: Exports of Green Coffee, 1965-66 | A-46 |
| EQ | 15A. | Haiti: Exports of Green Coffee, 1960-65 | A-47 |
| EQ | 14. | Honduras: Exports of Green Coffee, 1965-66 | A-44 |
| EQ | 14A. | Honduras: Exports of Green Coffee, 1960-65 | A-45 |
| EQ | 29. | India: Exports of Green Coffee, 1965-66 | A-70 |
| EQ | 29A. | India: Exports of Green Coffee, 1960-65 | A-71 |
| EQ | 25. | Ivory Coast: Exports of Green Coffee, 1965-66 | A-66 |
| EQ | 25A. | Ivory Coast: Exports of Green Coffee, 1960-65 | A-67 |
| EQ | 22. | Kenya: Exports of Green Coffee, 1965-66 | A-58 |
| EQ | 22A. | Kenya: Exports of Green Coffee, 1960-65 | A-59 |
| EQ | 3. | Latin America: Exports of Green Coffee, 1965-66 | A-16 — A-17 |
| EQ | 3A. | Latin America: Exports of Green Coffee, 1955-65 | A-18 — A-21 |
| EQ | 4. | Latin America: Volume of Green Coffee Exports to Principal Markets, 1965-66 | A-22 — A-23 |
| EV | 2. | Latin America: Value of Green Coffee Exports, 1965-66 | A-82 |
| EQ | 10. | Mexico: Exports of Green Coffee, 1965-66 | A-36 |
| EQ | 10A. | Mexico: Exports of Green Coffee, 1960-65 | A-37 |
| EQ | 16. | Nicaragua: Exports of Green Coffee, 1965-66 | A-48 |
| EQ | 16A. | Nicaragua: Exports of Green Coffee, 1960-65 | A-49 |
| EQ | 30. | "OAMCAF" Countries: Exports of Green Coffee, 1966 | A-72 — A-73 |
| EQ | 20. | Panama: Exports of Green Coffee, 1965-66 | A-54 |
| EQ | 20A. | Panama: Exports of Green Coffee, 1960-65 | A-55 |
| EQ | 18. | Peru: Exports of Green Coffee, 1965-66 | A-52 |

## APPENDIX TABLES (cont'd)

                                                                                   **Page**

| | | | |
|---|---|---|---|
| EQ | 18A. | Peru: Exports of Green Coffee, 1960-65 | A-53 |
| EQ | 23. | Tanzania: Exports of Green Coffee, 1965-66 | A-60 |
| EQ | 23A. | Tanzania: Exports of Green Coffee, 1960-65 | A-61 |
| EQ | 24. | Uganda: Exports of Green Coffee, 1965-66 | A-62 — A-63 |
| EQ | 24A. | Uganda: Exports of Green Coffee, 1960-65 | A-64 — A-65 |
| EQ | 11. | Venezuela: Exports of Green Coffee, 1965-66 | A-38 |
| EQ | 11A. | Venezuela: Exports of Green Coffee, 1960-65 | A-39 |

**IMPORTS** - (Green Coffee)

| | | | |
|---|---|---|---|
| IQ | 1. | World: Imports of Green Coffee, 1965-66 | A-83 |
| IQ | 2. | World: Imports of Green Coffee, 1947-66 | A-84 — A-85 |
| IQ | 3. | World: Imports of Green Coffee by Country or Region and by Generic Type, 1953-66 | A-86 |
| IQ | 3a. | World: Imports of Green Coffee by Country or Region and by Generic Type, 1953-66 | A-87 |
| IQ | 3b. | World: Imports of Green Coffee by Country or Region and by Generic Type, 1953-66 | A-88 |
| IQ | 6. | United States: Origin and Volume of Imports of Coffee, 1966, by Customs Districts | A-94 — A-95 |
| IV | 7. | United States: Origin and Value of Imports of Coffee, 1966 by Customs Districts | A-96 — A-97 |
| IQ | 8. | United States: Volume of Imports of Coffee by Month, 1966 | A-98 — A-99 |
| IV | 9. | United States: Value of Imports of Coffee by Month, 1966 | A-100 — A-101 |
| IQ | 11. | United States: Volume of Coffee Imports by Country of Origin, 1953-66 | A-106 — A-109 |
| IQ | 10. | United States: Imports of Coffee, Coffee Year (October 1 to September 30) 1962-63 to 1965-66 | A-102 — A-103 |
| IQV | 10. | United States: Statistical Summary of Imports of Coffee, 1966 | A-93 |
| IQV | 3. | United States: Volume and Value of Imports of Coffee, 1965-66 | A-90 — A-91 |
| IQ | 4. | United States: Volume of Imports of Coffee, 1965-66 by Coastal Zones and Customs Districts | A-89 |

## APPENDIX TABLES (cont'd)

                                                                                     **Page**

| | | | |
|---|---|---|---|
| IV | 5. | United States: Value of Imports of Coffee, 1965-66 by Coastal Zones and Customs Districts | A-92 |
| IQ | 15. | Europe: Imports of Green Coffee, 1966 | A-114 — A-115 |
| IQ | 16. | Europe: Imports of Green Coffee, 1955-66 | A-116 — A-117 |
| IQV | 11. | Canada: Volume and Value of Green-Coffee Imports, 1965-66 | A-104 — A-105 |
| IQ | 12. | Canada: Volume of Green-Coffee Imports, 1953-66 | A-112 — A-113 |

**SOLUBLE COFFEE**

| | | | |
|---|---|---|---|
| IS | 1. | United States: Imports of Soluble Coffee, 1956-66 | A-166 |
| IS | 5. | United States: Imports of Soluble Coffee, 1966 | A-168 |
| IS | 7. | United States: Imports of Soluble Coffee, 1965 | A-170 |
| ISV | 1. | United States: Value of Soluble Coffee Imports, 1956-66 | A-167 |
| ISV | 5. | United States: Value of Soluble Coffee Imports, 1966 | A-169 |
| ISV | 7. | United States: Value of Soluble Coffee Imports, 1965 | A-171 |
| ISV | 10. | United States: Average Import Price of Soluble Coffee, 1956-66 | A-172 |
| ES | 1. | United States: Exports of Soluble Coffee, 1956-66 | A-154 — A-155 |
| ES | 5. | United States: Exports of Soluble Coffee, 1966 | A-158 — A-159 |
| ES | 7. | United States: Exports of Soluble Coffee, 1965 | A-162 — A-163 |
| ESV | 1. | United States: Value of Soluble Coffee Exports, 1956-66 | A-156 — A-157 |
| ESV | 5. | United States: Value of Soluble Coffee Exports, 1966 | A-160 — A-161 |
| ESV | 7. | United States: Value of Soluble Coffee Exports, 1965 | A-164 — A-165 |
| ESV | 10. | United States: Average Export Price of Soluble Coffee, 1956-66 | A-173 |

**CONSUMPTION**

| | | | |
|---|---|---|---|
| C | 5. | United States: Consumption of Coffee, Net Civilian Visible Disappearance, 1965-66 | A-120 |

# APPENDIX TABLES (cont'd)

**Page**

| | | | |
|---|---|---|---|
| C | 6. | United States: Net Civilian Visible Disappearance, 1957-66 | A-118 — A-119 |
| C | 7. | United States: Trends of Coffee-Drinking, Winters of 1960-67, by Place of Consumption and Period of Day | A-122 |
| C | 8. | United States: Review of Coffee Consumption, 1950-67 | A-123 |
| C | 15. | United States: Per Capita Consumption (Based on Net Civilian Visible Disappearance) 1946-66 | A-121 |
| C | 20. | Canada: Net Imports of Coffee, 1950-66 | A-124 — A-125 |
| C | 25. | World: Per Capita Imports of Green Coffee in Principal Countries, 1956-66 | A-126 |

## PRICES

| | | | |
|---|---|---|---|
| IV | 11. | United States: Average Unit Value of Green Coffee Imports, 1947-66 | A-110 — A-111 |
| CP | 16. | United States: Average Monthly Import Prices of Green Coffee, 1953-66 | A-145 |
| CP | 19. | United States: Average Import Prices of Green Coffee by Country of Origin, 1953-66 | A-152 — A-153 |
| CP | 17. | United States: Average Annual Spot Prices of Selected Growths and Types of Coffees in the New York Market, 1953-66 | A-127 |
| CP | 1. | United States: Spot Coffee Prices for the New York Market, 1966 | A-128 — A-129 |
| CP | 2. | United States: Spot Coffee Prices for the New York Market, 1947-66 | A-130 — A-131 |
| CP | 3. | United States: Spot Coffee Price Differentials (Basis MAMS) 1953-66 | A-132 — A-141 |
| CP | 9. | United States: Average Monthly Wholesale Prices of Coffee, 1954-66 | A-142 |
| CP | 14. | United States: Average Monthly Retail Prices of Coffee, 1939-66 | A-143 |
| CP | 15. | United States: Average Monthly Prices Paid by Consumers for Regular and Instant Coffee, 1952-66 | A-144 |

## APPENDIX TABLES (cont'd)

|  |  |  | Page |
|---|---|---|---|
| CP | 18A. | International Coffee Organization: Daily Indicator Price, March-December, 1965 | A-146 — A-147 |
| CP | 18B. | International Coffee Organization: Daily Indicator Price, January-December, 1966 | A-148 — A-149 |
| CP | 18C. | International Coffee Organization: Daily Indicator Price, January-April, 1967 | A-150 |
| CP | 18D. | International Coffee Organization: Unofficial Composite Average Indicator Prices, October 1966-March 1967 | A-151 |

**TRADE**

| T | 1. | United States: Balance of Trade with 15 Latin American Coffee-Producing Countries, 1962-66 | A-80 — A-81 |
|---|---|---|---|
| M | 1. | World: Customs Duties and Internal Taxes on Coffee in Selected Countries and Per Capita Coffee Consumption, 1966 | A-174 — A-175 |
| M | 6. | World: Ocean Freight Rates for Coffee | A-176 — A-177 |

**QUOTAS**

| ICO | 2. | International Coffee Organization: Effective Quotas, 1963-64 | A-178 |
|---|---|---|---|
| ICO | 3. | International Coffee Organization: Effective Quotas, 1964-65 | A-179 |
| ICO | 4. | International Coffee Organization: Effective Quotas, 1965-66 | A-180 |
| ICO | 5. | International Coffee Organization: Effective Quotas, 1966-67 | A-181 |

## EQ-1. WORLD: EXPORTS OF GREEN COFFEE, 1965-1966

(Thousands of bags of 60 kilograms or 132.276 pounds each)

| COUNTRIES OF ORIGIN | 1966+ | 1965* | Percentage of Total 1966 | Percentage of Total 1965 | Increase or Decrease 1966 over 1965 VOLUME | Increase or Decrease 1966 over 1965 PERCENT |
|---|---|---|---|---|---|---|
| **WESTERN HEMISPHERE** | | | | | | |
| Pan-American Coffee Bureau | | | | | | |
| Brazil | 17,031 | 13,497 | 33.8 | 30.0 | +3,534 | + 26.2 |
| Colombia | 5,566 | 5,652 | 11.1 | 12.6 | − 86 | − 1.5 |
| Guatemala | 1,864 | 1,511 | 3.7 | 3.4 | + 353 | + 23.3 |
| El Salvador | 1,619 | 1,655 | 3.2 | 3.7 | − 36 | − 2.2 |
| Mexico | 1,536 | 1,327 | 3.1 | 2.9 | + 209 | + 15.8 |
| Costa Rica | 901 | 794 | 1.8 | 1.8 | + 107 | + 13.5 |
| Ecuador | 728 | 764 | 1.4 | 1.7 | − 36 | − 4.7 |
| Peru | 586 | 548 | 1.2 | 1.2 | + 38 | + 7.1 |
| Dominican Republic | 418 | 404 | 0.8 | 0.9 | + 14 | + 3.3 |
| Nicaragua | 422 | 508 | 0.8 | 1.1 | − 86 | − 17.0 |
| Honduras | 376 | 407 | 0.8 | 0.9 | − 31 | − 7.7 |
| Haiti | 350 | 399 | 0.7 | 0.9 | − 49 | − 12.2 |
| Venezuela | 303 | 299 | 0.6 | 0.7 | + 4 | + 1.4 |
| Panama | 45 | 24 | 0.1 | — | + 21 | + 88.6 |
| Cuba | — | — | — | — | — | — |
| Total Pan-American Coffee Bureau | 31,745 | 27,789 | 63.1 | 61.8 | +3,956 | + 14.2 |
| **OTHER WESTERN HEMISPHERE (1)** | 259 | 346 | 0.5 | 0.8 | − 87 | − 25.1 |
| **TOTAL WESTERN HEMISPHERE** | 32,004 | 28,135 | 63.6 | 62.6 | +3,869 | + 13.8 |
| **AFRICA** | | | | | | |
| Uganda | 2,976 | 2,488 | 5.9 | 5.5 | + 488 | + 19.6 |
| Kenya | 907 | 630 | 1.8 | 1.4 | + 277 | + 43.9 |
| Tanzania | 849 | 474 | 1.7 | 1.1 | + 375 | + 79.2 |
| Ivory Coast | 3,013 | 3,099 | 6.0 | 6.9 | − 86 | − 2.8 |
| Angola | 2,633 | 2,715 | 5.2 | 6.0 | − 82 | − 3.0 |
| Ethiopia | 1,012 | 1,360 | 2.0 | 3.0 | − 348 | − 25.6 |
| Cameroun | 1,211 | 893 | 2.4 | 2.0 | + 318 | + 35.6 |
| Madagascar | 761 | 834 | 1.5 | 1.9 | − 73 | − 8.8 |
| Congo (Kinshasa) | 560 | 588 | 1.1 | 1.3 | − 28 | − 4.8 |
| Burundi | 246 | 227 | 0.5 | 0.5 | + 19 | + 8.4 |
| Rwanda | 143 | 165 | 0.3 | 0.4 | − 22 | − 13.3 |
| Togo | 231 | 194 | 0.5 | 0.4 | + 37 | + 19.1 |
| Central African Republic | 190 | 127 | 0.4 | 0.3 | + 63 | + 49.6 |
| Guinea | 207 | 180 | 0.4 | 0.4 | + 27 | + 15.0 |
| Spanish Africa | 120 | 120 | 0.2 | 0.3 | — | — |
| Various (2) | 577 | 201 | 1.2 | 0.4 | + 376 | +187.1 |
| **TOTAL AFRICA** | 15,636 | 14,295 | 31.1 | 31.8 | +1,341 | + 9.4 |
| **ASIA & OCEANIA** | | | | | | |
| Indonesia | 1,786 | 1,803 | 3.5 | 4.0 | − 17 | − 0.9 |
| India | 417 | 412 | 0.8 | 0.9 | + 5 | + 1.2 |
| Yemen | 95 | 91 | 0.2 | 0.2 | + 4 | + 4.4 |
| Various (3) | 401 | 233 | 0.8 | 0.5 | + 168 | + 72.1 |
| **TOTAL ASIA & OCEANIA** | 2,699 | 2,539 | 5.3 | 5.6 | + 160 | + 6.3 |
| **TOTAL EXPORTS** | 50,339 | 44,969 | 100.0 | 100.0 | +5,370 | + 11.9 |

Source: Central offices and official trade entities of exporting countries.
(+) Preliminary.
(*) Revised.
(1) Includes: Bolivia, Guadeloupe, Guyana, Hawaii, Jamaica, Paraguay, Trinidad & Tobago, Surinam and Puerto Rico.
(2) Includes: Cape Verde, Congo (Brazzaville), Dahomey, Gabon, Ghana, Liberia, Nigeria, São Thome and Principe, Senegal and Sierra Leone.
(3) Includes: Comores Islands, New Caledonia, New Guinea, New Hebrides, Singapore, South Viet Nam and Timor.

## PQ-3. WORLD: EXPORTABLE
### 1957-58
(Thousands of bags of 60)

| PRODUCING COUNTRIES | 1957-58 | 1958-59 | 1959-60 | 1960-61 |
|---|---|---|---|---|
| **WESTERN HEMISPHERE** | | | | |
| **PAN-AMERICAN COFFEE BUREAU** | | | | |
| Brazil | 20,800 | 26,000 | 37,000 | 22,000 |
| Colombia | 7,000 | 6,900 | 7,000 | 7,000 |
| Guatemala | 1,225 | 1,200 | 1,400 | 1,300 |
| Mexico | 1,540 | 1,200 | 1,550 | 1,450 |
| El Salvador | 1,280 | 1,375 | 1,475 | 1,350 |
| Peru | 250 | 300 | 375 | 415 |
| Costa Rica | 725 | 815 | 800 | 1,050 |
| Ecuador | 465 | 350 | 475 | 500 |
| Venezuela | 475 | 600 | 410 | 425 |
| Nicaragua | 335 | 320 | 325 | 443 |
| Dominican Republic | 525 | 300 | 460 | 375 |
| Honduras | 265 | 280 | 300 | 225 |
| Haiti | 550 | 300 | 500 | 275 |
| Panama■ | — | 23 | 25 | 20 |
| Cuba | 250 | 60 | 200 | 100 |
| **TOTAL P.A.C.B.** | 35,685 | 40,023 | 52,295 | 36,928 |
| OTHER WESTERN HEMISPHERE▲ | 220 | 230 | 409 | 177 |
| **TOTAL WESTERN HEMISPHERE** | 35,905 | 40,253 | 52,704 | 37,105 |
| **AFRICA** | | | | |
| Angola | 1,275 | 1,440 | 1,775 | 2,700 |
| Ivory Coast | 1,800 | 2,430 | 2,530 | 3,150 |
| Uganda | 1,365 | 1,500 | 1,920 | 1,895 |
| Ethiopia | 850 | 850 | 905 | 960 |
| Congo (D.R.) | 1,200 | 1,490 | 1,365 | 850 |
| Cameroun | 415 | 440 | 545 | 660 |
| Madagascar | 825 | 750 | 750 | 840 |
| Kenya | 390 | 380 | 428 | 545 |
| Tanzania | 375 | 385 | 420 | 485 |
| Burundi †† | — | — | — | — |
| Guinea ● | — | 175 | 180 | 190 |
| Rwanda †† | — | — | — | — |
| Togo | 80 | 178 | 138 | 148 |
| Central African Republic | — | 90 | 95 | 120 |
| Rwanda-Burundi* | — | — | 590 | 390 |
| Various ‡ | 310 | 296 | 355 | 406 |
| **TOTAL AFRICA** | 8,885 | 10,404 | 11,996 | 13,339 |
| **ASIA & OCEANIA** | | | | |
| Indonesia | 1,100 | 975 | 1,300 | 1,600 |
| India | 213 | 240 | 275 | 550 |
| Yemen | 80 | 65 | 80 | 80 |
| Various° | 47 | 64 | 66 | 140 |
| **TOTAL ASIA & OCEANIA** | 1,440 | 1,344 | 1,721 | 2,370 |
| **WORLD TOTAL** | 46,230 | 52,001 | 66,421 | 52,814 |

Source: U. S. Department of Agriculture.

- (●) Revised.
- (†) Fourth Estimate, March 1967, FAS, Foreign Crops and Markets.
- (■) Prior to 1958-59 included in Various under Other Western Hemisphere.
- (▲) Includes: Jamaica, Trinidad & Tobago, Surinam, Guadaloupe, Puerto Rico, Hawaii, Bolivia, British Guiana and Paraguay.

# PRODUCTION OF GREEN COFFEE
Through 1966-67
kilograms or 132.276 pounds each)

| 1961-62 | 1962-63 | 1963-64● | 1964-65● | 1965-66● | 1966-67† |
|---|---|---|---|---|---|
| 28,000 | 20,000 | 21,200 | 3,000 | 30,200 | 13,000 |
| 6,800 | 6,500 | 7,200 | 6,500 | 7,000 | 6,560 |
| 1,500 | 1,700 | 1,580 | 1,420 | 1,835 | 1,480 |
| 1,500 | 1,250 | 1,855 | 1,550 | 1,800 | 1,500 |
| 1,800 | 1,540 | 1,885 | 1,935 | 1,670 | 1,765 |
| 570 | 605 | 630 | 680 | 680 | 680 |
| 1,025 | 930 | 980 | 700 | 895 | 1,040 |
| 650 | 630 | 525 | 750 | 745 | 640 |
| 310 | 370 | 395 | 275 | 290 | 275 |
| 395 | 460 | 405 | 525 | 445 | 490 |
| 450 | 420 | 540 | 520 | 455 | 395 |
| 290 | 335 | 320 | 370 | 375 | 340 |
| 525 | 425 | 365 | 385 | 405 | 325 |
| 40 | 19 | 26 | 20 | 15 | 25 |
| 200 | 50 | — | — | — | — |
| 44,055 | 35,234 | 37,906 | 18,630 | 46,810 | 28,515 |
| 173 | 248 | 200 | 196 | 188 | 160 |
| 44,228 | 35,482 | 38,106 | 18,826 | 46,998 | 28,675 |
| 2,750 | 3,050 | 2,750 | 3,045 | 2,740 | 3,440 |
| 1,600 | 3,300 | 4,300 | 3,325 | 4,500 | 2,845 |
| 1,933 | 2,930 | 2,885 | 2,440 | 2,585 | 2,585 |
| 1,100 | 1,150 | 1,250 | 1,300 | 1,245 | 1,335 |
| 850 | 1,050 | 1,050 | 900 | 950 | 1,045 |
| 820 | 805 | 775 | 840 | 970 | 1,070 |
| 700 | 900 | 735 | 950 | 725 | 845 |
| 505 | 615 | 720 | 640 | 855 | 925 |
| 390 | 455 | 530 | 560 | 785 | 735 |
| — | 105 | 245 | 195 | 235 | 220 |
| 220 | 200 | 160 | 135 | 145 | 135 |
| — | 80 | 140 | 170 | 150 | 145 |
| 170 | 175 | 225 | 195 | 220 | 195 |
| 140 | 100 | 205 | 145 | 195 | 195 |
| 390 | — | — | — | — | — |
| 284 | 367 | 396 | 398 | 424 | 436 |
| 11,852 | 15,282 | 16,366 | 15,238 | 16,724 | 16,151 |
| 1,650 | 2,080 | 1,600 | 1,850 | 1,650 | 1,640 |
| 315 | 365 | 620 | 460 | 540 | 585 |
| 80 | 72 | 70 | 80 | 65 | 50 |
| 150 | 135 | 139 | 147 | 147 | 162 |
| 2,195 | 2,652 | 2,429 | 2,537 | 2,402 | 2,437 |
| 58,275 | 53,416 | 56,901 | 36,601 | 66,124 | 47,263 |

(††) Prior to 1962-63 included in Rwanda-Urundi.
(♦) Prior to 1958-59 included in French Africa.
(*) Prior to 1959-60 included in Republic of Congo.
(‡) Includes: Liberia, Cape Verde, Ghana, Sierra Leone, São Tomé and Principe, Spanish Guinea, Nigeria, Dahomey, Gabon, Republic of Congo and Comores Islands.
(o) Includes: Timor, New Caledonia and New Hebrides.

**PQ-4. WORLD: EXPORTABLE**
By ICO
1957-58

(Thousands of bags of 60 kilograms or 132.276 pounds each)

| ICO MEMBERS | 1957-58 | 1958-59 | 1959-60 | 1960-61 |
|---|---|---|---|---|
| **PAN-AMERICAN COFFEE BUREAU** | | | | |
| Brazil | 20,800 | 26,000 | 37,000 | 22,000 |
| Colombia | 7,000 | 6,900 | 7,000 | 7,000 |
| Costa Rica | 725 | 815 | 800 | 1,050 |
| Cuba | 250 | 60 | 200 | 100 |
| Dominican Republic | 525 | 300 | 460 | 375 |
| Ecuador | 465 | 350 | 475 | 500 |
| El Salvador | 1,280 | 1,375 | 1,475 | 1,350 |
| Guatemala | 1,225 | 1,200 | 1,400 | 1,300 |
| Haiti | 550 | 300 | 500 | 275 |
| Honduras | 265 | 280 | 300 | 225 |
| Mexico | 1,540 | 1,200 | 1,550 | 1,450 |
| Nicaragua | 335 | 320 | 325 | 443 |
| Panama º | — | 23 | 25 | 20 |
| Peru | 250 | 300 | 375 | 415 |
| Venezuela | 475 | 600 | 410 | 425 |
| **TOTAL P. A. C. B.** | **35,685** | **40,023** | **52,295** | **36,928** |
| **IACO** | | | | |
| Burundi** | — | — | 365 | 390 |
| Congo (D.R.) | 1,200 | 1,490 | 1,365 | 850 |
| Ethiopia | 850 | 850 | 905 | 960 |
| Ghana | 9 | 12 | 30 | 33 |
| Kenya | 390 | 380 | 428 | 545 |
| Nigeria | 40 | 57 | 75 | 100 |
| Portugal | 1,275 | 1,440 | 1,775 | 2,700 |
| Rwanda** | — | — | — | — |
| Sierra Leone | 70 | 73 | 75 | 75 |
| Tanzania | 375 | 385 | 420 | 485 |
| Uganda | 1,365 | 1,500 | 1,920 | 1,895 |
| OAMCAF | (3,120) | (3,888) | (4,098) | (4,983) |
|   Cameroun | 415 | 440 | 545 | 660 |
|   Central African Republic | — | 90 | 95 | 120 |
|   Congo (Brazzaville) | — | — | 10 | 10 |
|   Dahomey | — | — | 20 | 40 |
|   Gabon | — | — | 10 | 15 |
|   Ivory Coast | 1,800 | 2,430 | 2,530 | 3,150 |
|   Madagascar | 825 | 750 | 750 | 840 |
|   Togo | 80 | 178 | 138 | 148 |
| **TOTAL IACO** | **8,694** | **10,075** | **11,456** | **13,016** |
| **OTHER MEMBERS** | | | | |
| India | 213 | 240 | 275 | 550 |
| Indonesia | 1,100 | 975 | 1,300 | 1,600 |
| Trinidad & Tobago | 40 | 40 | 40 | 45 |
| **TOTAL OTHER MEMBERS** | **1,353** | **1,255** | **1,615** | **2,195** |
| **TOTAL ICO** | **45,732** | **51,353** | **65,366** | **52,139** |
| Non-Members | | | | |
| Bolivia | 20 | 15 | 20 | 16 |
| Guinea† † | — | 175 | 180 | 190 |
| Philippine Republic | — | — | — | — |
| Yemen | 80 | 65 | 80 | 80 |
| Various | 398 | 393 | 775 | 389 |
| **TOTAL NON-MEMBERS** | **498** | **648** | **1,055** | **675** |
| **WORLD TOTAL** | **46,230** | **52,001** | **66,421** | **52,814** |

Source:   U. S. Department of Agriculture.
(*)     Revised.
(†)     Fourth Estimate, March 1967. FAS, Foreign Crops and Markets.

# PRODUCTION OF GREEN COFFEE
Membership
Through 1966-1967

| 1961-62 | 1962-63 | 1963-64* | 1964-65* | 1965-66* | 1966-67 † |
|---|---|---|---|---|---|
| 28,000 | 20,000 | 21,200 | 3,000 | 30,200 | 13,000 |
| 6,800 | 6,500 | 7,200 | 6,500 | 7,000 | 6,560 |
| 1,025 | 930 | 980 | 700 | 895 | 1,040 |
| 200 | 50 | — | — | — | — |
| 450 | 420 | 540 | 520 | 455 | 395 |
| 650 | 630 | 525 | 750 | 745 | 640 |
| 1,800 | 1,540 | 1,885 | 1,935 | 1,670 | 1,765 |
| 1,500 | 1,700 | 1,580 | 1,420 | 1,835 | 1,480 |
| 525 | 425 | 365 | 385 | 405 | 325 |
| 290 | 335 | 320 | 370 | 375 | 340 |
| 1,500 | 1,250 | 1,855 | 1,550 | 1,800 | 1,500 |
| 395 | 460 | 405 | 525 | 445 | 490 |
| 40 | 19 | 26 | 20 | 15 | 25 |
| 570 | 605 | 630 | 680 | 680 | 680 |
| 310 | 370 | 395 | 275 | 290 | 275 |
| 44,055 | 35,234 | 37,906 | 18,630 | 46,810 | 28,515 |
| | | | | | |
| 390 | 105 | 245 | 195 | 235 | 220 |
| 850 | 1,050 | 1,050 | 900 | 950 | 1,045 |
| 1,100 | 1,150 | 1,250 | 1,300 | 1,245 | 1,335 |
| 38 | 43 | 48 | 48 | 58 | 68 |
| 505 | 615 | 720 | 640 | 855 | 925 |
| 18 | 18 | 33 | 33 | 32 | 34 |
| 2,750 | 3,050 | 2,750 | 3,045 | 2,740 | 3,440 |
| — | 80 | 140 | 170 | 150 | 145 |
| 75 | 65 | 80 | 90 | 110 | 110 |
| 390 | 455 | 530 | 560 | 785 | 735 |
| 1,933 | 2,930 | 2,885 | 2,440 | 2,585 | 2,585 |
| (3,497) | (5,350) | (6,300) | (5,516) | (6,660) | (5,200) |
| 820 | 805 | 775 | 840 | 970 | 1,070 |
| 140 | 100 | 205 | 145 | 195 | 195 |
| 10 | 11 | 14 | 14 | 14 | 14 |
| 40 | 40 | 28 | 28 | 23 | 23 |
| 17 | 19 | 18 | 19 | 13 | 13 |
| 1,600 | 3,300 | 4,300 | 3,325 | 4,500 | 2,845 |
| 700 | 900 | 735 | 950 | 725 | 845 |
| 170 | 175 | 225 | 195 | 220 | 195 |
| 11,546 | 14,911 | 16,031 | 14,937 | 16,405 | 15,842 |
| | | | | | |
| 315 | 365 | 620 | 460 | 540 | 585 |
| 1,650 | 2,080 | 1,600 | 1,850 | 1,650 | 1,640 |
| 35 | 53 | 68 | 65 | 40 | 45 |
| 2,000 | 2,498 | 2,288 | 2,375 | 2,230 | 2,270 |
| | | | | | |
| 57,601 | 52,643 | 56,225 | 35,942 | 65,445 | 46,627 |
| | | | | | |
| 20 | 20 | 20 | 20 | 30 | 35 |
| 220 | 200 | 160 | 135 | 145 | 135 |
| — | — | — | — | — | — |
| 80 | 72 | 70 | 80 | 65 | 50 |
| 354 | 481 | 426 | 424 | 439 | 416 |
| 674 | 773 | 676 | 659 | 679 | 636 |
| | | | | | |
| 58,275 | 53,416 | 56,901 | 36,601 | 66,124 | 47,263 |

  (o)  Prior to 1958-59 included in Various under Other Western Hemisphere.
  (**)  Prior to 1962-63 included in Rwanda-Urundi.
  (††)  Prior to 1958-59 included in French Africa.

## EQ-2. WORLD: EXPORTS OF
(thousands of bags of 60

| COUNTRIES OF ORIGIN | 1947 | 1948 | 1949 | 1950 | 1951 | 1952 | 1953 | 1954 |
|---|---|---|---|---|---|---|---|---|
| **WESTERN HEMISPHERE** | | | | | | | | |
| Pan-American Coffee Bureau | | | | | | | | |
| Brazil | 14,688 | 17,492 | 19,368 | 14,835 | 16,358 | 15,821 | 15,562 | 10,918 |
| Colombia | 5,339 | 5,588 | 5,410 | 4,472 | 4,794 | 5,032 | 6,632 | 5,754 |
| Mexico | 548 | 524 | 817 | 767 | 865 | 870 | 1,267 | 1,112 |
| El Salvador | 1,127 | 976 | 1,260 | 1,107 | 1,059 | 1,098 | 1,149 | 996 |
| Guatemala | 889 | 806 | 919 | 919 | 848 | 1,007 | 1,159 | 885 |
| Costa Rica | 327 | 379 | 268 | 312 | 309 | 333 | 465 | 365 |
| Peru | 14 | 15 | 15 | 14 | 37 | 43 | 78 | 76 |
| Dominican Republic | 197 | 224 | 287 | 223 | 290 | 442 | 374 | 400 |
| Nicaragua | 167 | 241 | 114 | 350 | 268 | 303 | 312 | 285 |
| Ecuador | 161 | 231 | 175 | 335 | 273 | 340 | 311 | 351 |
| Haiti | 373 | 381 | 553 | 390 | 417 | 541 | 372 | 517 |
| Venezuela | 508 | 596 | 367 | 309 | 308 | 498 | 733 | 431 |
| Honduras | 32 | 54 | 103 | 113 | 137 | 138 | 187 | 154 |
| Panama | — | — | — | — | — | 2 | 4 | — |
| Cuba | — | — | — | — | — | — | — | — |
| **TOTAL P.A.C.B.** | 24,370 | 27,507 | 29,656 | 24,146 | 25,963 | 26,468 | 28,605 | 22,244 |
| OTHER WESTERN HEMISPHERE | 127 | 95 | 72 | 45 | 52 | 66 | 86 | 93 |
| **TOTAL WESTERN HEMISPHERE** | 24,497 | 27,602 | 29,728 | 24,191 | 26,015 | 26,534 | 28,691 | 22,337 |
| **AFRICA** | | | | | | | | |
| Uganda | 356 | 640 | 473 | 573 | 771 | 707 | 597 | 614 |
| Kenya | 179 | 242 | 146 | 170 | 168 | 291 | 251 | 191 |
| Tanzania | 234 | 190 | 205 | 258 | 276 | 319 | 250 | 325 |
| Ivory Coast | 734 | 938 | 1,062 | 962 | 1,321 | 1,250 | 940 | 1,585 |
| Portugal | 745 | 903 | 773 | 616 | 1,074 | 794 | 1,193 | 737 |
| Ethiopia | 297 | 297 | 353 | 399 | 458 | 424 | 467 | 527 |
| Cameroun | 135 | 121 | 138 | 128 | N.A. | N.A. | N.A. | 11 |
| Madagascar | 489 | 332 | 427 | 551 | 509 | 697 | 604 | 691 |
| Congo (Kinshasa) | 619 | 509 | 524 | 554 | 590 | 515 | 566 | 573 |
| Rwanda-Burundi | * | * | * | * | * | * | c * | * |
| Togo | 41 | 28 | 34 | 20 | + | + | + | 70 |
| Central African Republic | 99 | 40 | 45 | 78 | + | + | + | 82 |
| Guinea | + | + | + | + | + | + | + | + |
| Spanish Africa | 98 | 116 | 87 | 110 | 94 | 102 | 92 | 105 |
| Various | 119 | 134 | 96 | 139 | 10 | 13 | 20 | 69 |
| **TOTAL AFRICA** | 4,145 | 4,490 | 4,363 | 4,558 | 5,271 | 5,112 | 4,980 | 5,580 |
| **ASIA & OCEANIA** | | | | | | | | |
| Indonesia | — | 90 | 88 | 228 | 402 | 313 | 548 | 637 |
| India | 38 | 27 | 15 | 15 | 14 | 40 | 15 | 96 |
| Yemen | ° | ° | ° | ° | ° | ° | 73 | 75 |
| Various | 150 | 112 | 123 | 142 | 140 | 145 | 150 | 66 |
| **TOTAL ASIA & OCEANIA** | 188 | 229 | 226 | 385 | 556 | 498 | 786 | 874 |
| **TOTAL EXPORTS** | 28,830 | 32,321 | 34,317 | 29,134 | 31,842 | 32,144 | 34,457 | 28,794 |

Source: Central statistical offices and official trade entities of exporting countries. See note to table EQ-1.
(*) Included in Congo (Kinshasa).
(+) Included in Various Africa.
(°) Included in Various Asia & Oceania.

**GREEN COFFEE 1947-1966**
kilograms or 132.276 pounds each)

| 1955 | 1956 | 1957 | 1958 | 1959 | 1960 | 1961 | 1962 | 1963 | 1964 | 1965 | 1966 |
|---|---|---|---|---|---|---|---|---|---|---|---|
| 13,696 | 16,805 | 14,319 | 12,894 | 17,723 | 16,819 | 16,971 | 16,377 | 19,514 | 14,948 | 13,497 | 17,031 |
| 5,867 | 5,070 | 4,824 | 5,441 | 6,413 | 5,938 | 5,651 | 6,561 | 6,134 | 6,412 | 5,652 | 5,566 |
| 1,367 | 1,260 | 1,448 | 1,312 | 1,240 | 1,384 | 1,483 | 1,458 | 1,199 | 1,772 | 1,327 | 1,536 |
| 1,185 | 1,132 | 1,270 | 1,399 | 1,345 | 1,178 | 1,431 | 1,478 | 1,586 | 1,755 | 1,655 | 1,619 |
| 982 | 1,026 | 1,038 | 1,205 | 1,385 | 1,329 | 1,255 | 1,552 | 1,667 | 1,446 | 1,511 | 1,864 |
| 463 | 393 | 468 | 771 | 712 | 766 | 835 | 902 | 929 | 841 | 794 | 901 |
| 114 | 118 | 185 | 275 | 331 | 440 | 567 | 624 | 668 | 696 | 548 | 586 |
| 409 | 440 | 361 | 429 | 362 | 481 | 335 | 487 | 457 | 573 | 404 | 418 |
| 379 | 282 | 367 | 382 | 273 | 361 | 349 | 338 | 467 | 430 | 508 | 422 |
| 384 | 408 | 470 | 503 | 397 | 522 | 381 | 551 | 499 | 417 | 764 | 728 |
| 355 | 459 | 315 | 547 | 364 | 394 | 348 | 514 | 390 | 380 | 399 | 350 |
| 497 | 387 | 460 | 585 | 473 | 408 | 406 | 319 | 390 | 327 | 299 | 303 |
| 149 | 195 | 174 | 189 | 255 | 258 | 210 | 266 | 334 | 309 | 407 | 376 |
| 11 | — | — | 9 | 16 | 21 | 5 | 27 | 8 | 25 | 24 | 45 |
| 75 | 347 | 190 | 121 | 52 | 90 | 85 | 139 | — | — | — | — |
| 25,933 | 28,322 | 25,889 | 26,062 | 31,341 | 30,389 | 30,312 | 31,593 | 34,242 | 30,331 | 27,789 | 31,745 |
| 105 | 162 | 220 | 293 | 250 | 250 | 250 | 250 | 318 | 304 | 346 | 259 |
| 26,038 | 28,484 | 26,109 | 26,355 | 31,591 | 30,639 | 30,562 | 31,843 | 34,560 | 30,635 | 28,135 | 32,004 |
| 1,274 | 1,806 | 1,420 | 1,337 | 1,536 | 1,949 | 1,806 | 2,314 | 2,438 | 2,354 | 2,488 | 2,976 |
| 304 | 504 | 374 | 437 | 405 | 477 | 536 | 492 | 580 | 703 | 630 | 907 |
| 296 | 381 | 297 | 356 | 316 | 420 | 438 | 426 | 425 | 554 | 474 | 849 |
| 1,583 | 2,242 | 1,687 | 1,875 | 1,745 | 2,707 | 2,618 | 2,670 | 2,867 | 3,259 | 3,099 | 3,013 |
| 964 | 1,398 | 1,267 | 1,317 | 1,483 | 1,454 | 1,976 | 2,620 | 2,397 | 2,309 | 2,715 | 2,633 |
| 702 | 496 | 845 | 639 | 754 | 849 | 950 | 1,023 | 1,080 | 1,234 | 1,360 | 1,012 |
| 7 | 28 | 11 | 12 | 54 | 510 | 591 | 635 | 516 | 868 | 893 | 1,211 |
| 791 | 875 | 805 | 797 | 632 | 670 | 651 | 934 | 740 | 633 | 834 | 761 |
| 728 | 867 | 613 | 1,156 | 1,523 | 878 | 555 | 600 | 773 | 624 | 588 | 560 |
| * | * | * | * | * | * | 389 | 383 | 173 | 451 | 392 | 389 |
| 64 | 107 | 102 | 76 | 193 | 61 | 171 | 192 | 104 | 273 | 194 | 231 |
| 57 | 98 | 74 | 88 | 102 | 99 | 121 | 130 | 97 | 208 | 127 | 190 |
| + | + | + | 171 | 239 | 240 | 253 | 199 | 175 | 63 | 180 | 207 |
| 95 | 85 | 102 | 104 | 85 | 80 | 132 | 110 | 110 | 123 | 120 | 120 |
| 71 | 104 | 105 | 125 | 200 | 200 | 200 | 200 | 249 | 473 | 201 | 577 |
| 6,936 | 8,991 | 7,702 | 8,490 | 9,267 | 10,594 | 11,387 | 12,928 | 12,724 | 14,129 | 14,295 | 15,636 |
| 386 | 958 | 850 | 900 | 850 | 687 | 1,091 | 961 | 980 | 1,016 | 1,803 | 1,786 |
| 60 | 127 | 224 | 248 | 240 | 272 | 533 | 331 | 374 | 526 | 412 | 417 |
| 78 | 88 | 90 | 88 | 70 | 69 | 80 | 67 | 104 | 100 | 91 | 95 |
| 55 | 49 | 150 | 150 | 150 | 125 | 125 | 125 | 164 | 315 | 233 | 401 |
| 579 | 1,222 | 1,314 | 1,386 | 1,310 | 1,153 | 1,829 | 1,484 | 1,622 | 1,957 | 2,539 | 2,699 |
| 33,553 | 38,697 | 35,125 | 36,231 | 42,168 | 42,386 | 43,778 | 46,255 | 48,906 | 46,721 | 44,969 | 50,339 |

A-15

## EQ-3. LATIN AMERICA: EXPORTS OF GREEN COFFEE, 1965-1966
(Bags of 60 kilograms or 132.276 pounds each)

| COUNTRIES OF DESTINATION | 1966* | 1965 | Percent of Total 1966 | Percent of Total 1965 | Increase or Decrease 1966 over 1965 VOLUME | PERCENT |
|---|---|---|---|---|---|---|
| UNITED STATES | 14,687,749 | 14,356,527 | 46.3 | 51.7 | + 331,222 | + 2.3 |
| CANADA | 408,917 | 465,855 | 1.3 | 1.7 | − 56,938 | − 12.2 |
| OTHER AMERICAS | | | | | | |
| Argentina | 657,394 | 505,125 | 2.1 | 1.8 | + 152,269 | + 30.1 |
| Chile | 153,704 | 150,654 | 0.5 | 0.5 | + 3,050 | + 2.0 |
| Uruguay | 12,902 | 7,772 | — | — | + 5,130 | + 66.0 |
| British Honduras | 554 | 575 | — | — | − 21 | − 3.7 |
| Netherlands West Indies | 479 | 517 | — | — | − 38 | − 7.4 |
| Guatemala | 469 | 155 | — | — | + 314 | + 202.6 |
| Surinam | 427 | 5 | — | — | + 422 | + (o) |
| Nicaragua | — | 1,063 | — | — | − 1,063 | − --- |
| Various (1) | 590 | 505 | — | — | + 85 | + 16.8 |
| TOTAL OTHER AMERICAS | 826,519 | 666,371 | 2.6 | 2.3 | + 160,148 | + 24.0 |
| EUROPE | | | | | | |
| Germany (F.R.) | 3,389,164 | 3,186,232 | 10.7 | 11.5 | + 202,932 | + 6.4 |
| Italy | 1,653,433 | 808,553 | 5.2 | 2.9 | + 844,880 | + 104.5 |
| Sweden | 1,404,258 | 1,362,464 | 4.4 | 4.9 | + 41,794 | + 3.1 |
| Netherlands | 1,269,621 | 1,145,395 | 4.0 | 4.1 | + 124,226 | + 10.8 |
| France | 818,025 | 682,822 | 2.6 | 2.5 | + 135,203 | + 19.8 |
| Denmark | 762,415 | 684,927 | 2.4 | 2.5 | + 77,488 | + 11.3 |
| Belgium − Luxembourg | 712,744 | 733,831 | 2.3 | 2.6 | − 21,087 | − 2.9 |
| Finland | 708,467 | 488,413 | 2.2 | 1.8 | + 220,054 | + 45.1 |
| Spain | 653,057 | 464,188 | 2.1 | 1.7 | + 188,869 | + 40.7 |
| Norway | 489,286 | 384,454 | 1.5 | 1.4 | + 104,832 | + 27.3 |
| Germany (D.R.) | 407,511 | 348,603 | 1.3 | 1.3 | + 58,908 | + 16.9 |
| Yugoslavia | 387,909 | 243,818 | 1.2 | 0.9 | + 144,091 | + 59.1 |
| U.S.S.R. | 310,827 | 261,661 | 1.0 | 0.9 | + 49,166 | + 18.8 |
| Hungary | 204,922 | 109,569 | 0.6 | 0.4 | + 95,353 | + 87.0 |
| Poland | 168,613 | 174,963 | 0.5 | 0.6 | − 6,350 | − 3.6 |
| United Kingdom | 158,516 | 100,556 | 0.5 | 0.4 | + 57,960 | + 57.6 |
| Greece | 151,655 | 138,265 | 0.5 | 0.5 | + 13,390 | + 9.7 |
| Czechoslovakia | 142,041 | 137,168 | 0.5 | 0.5 | + 4,873 | + 3.6 |
| Rumania | 95,255 | 12,664 | 0.3 | — | + 82,591 | + 652.2 |
| Switzerland | 86,990 | 122,560 | 0.3 | 0.4 | − 35,570 | − 29.0 |
| Bulgaria | 74,487 | 98,379 | 0.2 | 0.4 | − 23,892 | − 24.3 |
| Iceland | 37,232 | 32,550 | 0.1 | 0.1 | + 4,682 | + 14.4 |
| Austria | 20,452 | 23,341 | 0.1 | 0.1 | − 2,889 | − 12.4 |
| Cyprus | 8,854 | 1,800 | — | — | + 7,054 | + 391.9 |
| Turkey | 82 | 58,218 | — | 0.2 | − 58,136 | − 99.9 |
| Various (2) | 1,261 | 1,425 | — | — | − 164 | − 11.5 |
| TOTAL EUROPE | 14,117,077 | 11,806,819 | 44.5 | 42.6 | +2,310,258 | + 19.6 |

A-16

EQ-3. LATIN AMERICA: EXPORTS OF GREEN COFFEE, 1965-1966 (Continued)

| COUNTRIES OF DESTINATION | 1966* | 1965 + | Percent of Total 1966 | Percent of Total 1965 | Increase or Decrease 1966 over 1965 VOLUME | PERCENT |
|---|---|---|---|---|---|---|
| **AFRICA** | | | | | | |
| South Africa | 145,819 | 127,030 | 0.5 | 0.5 | + 18,789 | + 14.8 |
| Sudan | 72,634 | 7,603 | 0.2 | — | + 65,031 | +855.3 |
| Algeria | 54,164 | — | 0.2 | — | + 54,164 | + --- |
| United Arab Republic | 16,320 | 11,000 | 0.1 | — | + 5,320 | + 48.4 |
| Tunisia | 10,000 | 10,000 | — | — | — | — |
| Morocco | 1,891 | — | — | — | + 1,891 | + --- |
| Various (3) | 2,122 | 1,021 | — | — | + 1,101 | +107.8 |
| TOTAL AFRICA | 302,950 | 156,654 | 1.0 | 0.5 | +146,296 | + 93.4 |
| **ASIA & OCEANIA** | | | | | | |
| Lebanon | 612,999 | 58,834 | 1.9 | 0.2 | +554,165 | +941.9 |
| Japan | 305,902 | 137,872 | 1.0 | 0.5 | +168,030 | +121.9 |
| Hong Kong | 300,000 | 45,000 | 0.9 | 0.2 | +255,000 | +566.7 |
| Jordan | 59,839 | 55,285 | 0.2 | 0.2 | + 4,554 | + 8.2 |
| Kuwait | 52,167 | 467 | 0.2 | — | + 51,700 | (o) |
| Syria | 34,787 | 15,388 | 0.1 | 0.1 | + 19,399 | +126.1 |
| Malaysia | 9,775 | 5,750 | — | — | + 4,025 | + 70.0 |
| Saudi Arabia | 8,821 | 802 | — | — | + 8,019 | +999.9 |
| Israel | 7,021 | 3,428 | — | — | + 3,593 | +104.8 |
| Australia | 5,584 | 6,109 | — | — | − 525 | − 8.6 |
| New Zealand | 2,803 | 2,052 | — | — | + 751 | + 36.6 |
| Iran | 1,150 | — | — | — | + 1,150 | + --- |
| Philippine Republic | — | 1,883 | — | — | − 1,883 | − --- |
| Ceylon | — | 3,507 | — | — | − 3,507 | − --- |
| Various (4) | 1,050 | 587 | — | — | + 463 | + 78.9 |
| TOTAL ASIA & OCEANIA | 1,401,898 | 336,964 | 4.3 | 1.2 | +1,064,934 | +316.0 |
| **OTHERS** | 2 | — | — | — | + 2 | + --- |
| **TOTAL EXPORTS** | 31,745,112 | 27,789,190 | 100.0 | 100.0 | +3,955,922 | + 14.2 |

Source: Central statistical offices and official trade entities of exporting countries.
(*) Estimated.
(†) Revised.
(1) Includes: Bolivia, Costa Rica, Ecuador, Honduras, Panama, Paraguay, Peru and Puerto Rico.
(2) Includes: Andorra, Eire, Gibraltar, Malta, Monaco and Portugal.
(3) Includes: Libya, Mozambique, Nigeria and Southern Rhodesia.
(4) Includes: Bahrein, China, Formosa, North Africa and Southern Rhodesia.

A-17

## EQ-3A. LATIN AMERICA: EXPORTS OF
(Bags of 60 kilograms)

| COUNTRIES OF DESTINATION | 1955 | 1956 | 1957 | 1958 | 1959 |
|---|---|---|---|---|---|
| UNITED STATES | 17,285,763 | 18,664,238 | 17,219,978 | 16,666,561 | 19,514,201 |
| CANADA | 326,177 | 440,285 | 388,637 | 332,432 | 476,238 |
| **OTHER AMERICAS** | | | | | |
| Argentina | 489,134 | 458,886 | 587,458 | 690,114 | 244,715 |
| Chile | 131,776 | 72,363 | 87,381 | 79,210 | 107,997 |
| Uruguay | 67,939 | 54,634 | 41,079 | 52,486 | 79,676 |
| Colombia | 2,875 | — | — | — | — |
| Netherlands West Indies | 2,851 | 1,127 | 486 | 497 | 612 |
| Puerto Rico | 2,429 | 18 | — | — | — |
| Panama | 815 | 4,428 | 6,133 | 350 | 1,167 |
| Dominican Republic | — | 845 | — | — | — |
| Honduras | — | — | — | 3,472 | — |
| Paraguay | — | — | — | 1,167 | 8,246 |
| Guatemala | 212 | — | — | 915 | 140 |
| Bolivia | 575 | — | — | 583 | 584 |
| El Salvador | 99 | 390 | 68 | 330 | 14,532 |
| Cuba | — | — | — | 491 | 114 |
| Mexico | — | — | — | — | — |
| Nicaragua | — | — | — | — | — |
| British Honduras | — | — | — | — | — |
| Various (1) | 18 | 32 | — | 70 | 224 |
| **TOTAL OTHER AMERICAS** | 698,723 | 592,723 | 722,605 | 829,685 | 458,007 |
| **EUROPE** | | | | | |
| Germany (F.R.) | 1,824,972 | 2,103,906 | 2,127,513 | 2,497,620 | 3,051,175 |
| France | 859,111 | 859,695 | 667,706 | 616,165 | 718,177 |
| Sweden | 844,128 | 968,284 | 888,230 | 989,155 | 1,108,318 |
| Italy | 724,748 | 739,597 | 596,113 | 662,370 | 1,123,391 |
| Netherlands | 620,213 | 833,189 | 554,993 | 513,031 | 809,856 |
| Finland | 496,264 | 619,454 | 487,160 | 432,674 | 565,016 |
| Belgium — Luxembourg | 489,433 | 588,591 | 439,086 | 499,192 | 758,888 |
| Denmark | 404,058 | 443,873 | 465,475 | 481,288 | 572,614 |
| Norway | 321,162 | 305,002 | 344,393 | 341,086 | 346,787 |
| Spain | 192,940 | 116,132 | 120,090 | 156,887 | 198,309 |
| United Kingdom | 118,770 | 182,819 | 154,724 | 132,814 | 204,636 |
| Greece | 87,717 | 87,799 | 89,362 | 106,620 | 73,710 |
| Czechoslovakia | 73,768 | 119,884 | 70,349 | 64,213 | 157,535 |
| Austria | 61,098 | 58,087 | 28,372 | 25,744 | 35,081 |
| Yugoslavia | 59,171 | 136,411 | 60,304 | 38,835 | 63,376 |
| Switzerland | 34,844 | 49,496 | 49,851 | 86,849 | 149,152 |
| Turkey | 26,749 | 26,663 | 8,335 | 4 | 28,110 |
| Iceland | 25,680 | 18,920 | 20,754 | 22,655 | 25,472 |
| Poland | 18,077 | 21,415 | 28,742 | 50,996 | 127,546 |
| Hungary | 15,998 | 44,965 | 31,716 | 19,203 | 91,927 |
| Gibraltar | 13,158 | 13,086 | 12,900 | 18,450 | 19,825 |
| Russia | 10,384 | 5,017 | — | 29,584 | 69,161 |
| Malta | 6,224 | 1,970 | 920 | 2,472 | 3,181 |
| Trieste | 3,262 | 17,486 | 5,882 | 1,937 | 462 |
| Germany (D.R.) | — | — | — | 21,624 | 106,881 |
| Cyprus | 7,602 | 14,028 | 9,318 | 12,953 | 13,453 |
| Albania | — | — | — | 2,166 | 2,500 |
| Rumania | — | — | — | 2,033 | — |
| Bulgaria | — | — | — | 166 | 250 |
| Portugal | — | 3 | — | — | 700 |
| Various (2) | 190 | 100 | 146 | 220 | 214 |
| **TOTAL EUROPE** | 7,339,721 | 8,375,872 | 7,262,434 | 7,829,006 | 10,425,703 |

**GREEN COFFEE, 1955-1965**

or 132.276 pounds each)

| 1960 | 1961 | 1962 | 1963 | 1964 | 1965* |
|---|---|---|---|---|---|
| 18,166,067 | 17,339,913 | 17,554,865 | 17,676,300 | 15,495,205 | 14,285,631 |
| 447,258 | 487,660 | 522,498 | 577,261 | 479,993 | 474,505 |
| 466,455 | 418,066 | 400,437 | 435,041 | 482,118 | 505,125 |
| 88,755 | 107,442 | 147,354 | 110,476 | 101,389 | 150,654 |
| 19,250 | 31,798 | 24,547 | 25,050 | 16,775 | 7,772 |
| — | — | — | — | — | — |
| 720 | 716 | 238 | 892 | 359 | 517 |
| — | — | — | 102 | — | 1 |
| — | — | 11 | 8 | 6,107 | 72 |
| — | — | — | — | — | — |
| — | 117 | — | 240 | 298 | 219 |
| 8,106 | 4 | 8 | 4 | 4 | 4 |
| 358 | — | — | 197 | 54 | 155 |
| — | 3 | 6 | 5 | 14 | 7 |
| 21,958 | 14,679 | 12 | — | — | — |
| — | — | — | 71,089 | 12,244 | — |
| — | 1,726 | — | 583 | — | — |
| — | — | 18,856 | 151 | — | 1,063 |
| — | — | — | 93 | 177 | 575 |
| 1 | 12 | 1,716 | 1,141 | 121 | 207 |
| 605,603 | 574,563 | 593,185 | 645,072 | 619,660 | 666,371 |
| 3,035,375 | 2,875,359 | 3,342,888 | 3,352,639 | 3,430,794 | 3,191,959 |
| 736,065 | 722,712 | 718,234 | 823,114 | 600,316 | 687,698 |
| 1,156,975 | 1,256,567 | 1,399,683 | 1,370,201 | 1,292,414 | 1,361,297 |
| 1,096,849 | 1,246,665 | 948,356 | 1,587,333 | 1,343,962 | 823,074 |
| 693,105 | 1,015,003 | 1,405,887 | 2,133,905 | 1,243,319 | 1,139,831 |
| 452,403 | 550,966 | 543,423 | 656,917 | 666,657 | 488,413 |
| 700,208 | 681,929 | 756,102 | 907,953 | 804,650 | 735,650 |
| 594,870 | 599,612 | 666,260 | 736,215 | 654,848 | 686,069 |
| 447,462 | 421,006 | 414,917 | 470,914 | 414,931 | 384,453 |
| 271,800 | 332,704 | 335,170 | 426,339 | 444,780 | 465,625 |
| 275,039 | 286,334 | 296,309 | 274,129 | 220,176 | 101,464 |
| 76,081 | 93,635 | 98,596 | 139,146 | 112,998 | 138,265 |
| 84,160 | 175,105 | 53,876 | 104,174 | 116,276 | 137,168 |
| 63,274 | 40,948 | 43,371 | 43,774 | 32,226 | 26,018 |
| 143,717 | 87,988 | 74,372 | 177,638 | 214,362 | 243,818 |
| 130,952 | 210,303 | 378,763 | 361,797 | 119,204 | 112,200 |
| 7,268 | 32,201 | 21,074 | 3,834 | 36,791 | 58,218 |
| 24,300 | 25,575 | 28,670 | 31,930 | 25,700 | 32,550 |
| 63,825 | 71,793 | 31,477 | 134,746 | 92,098 | 175,713 |
| 38,566 | 27,665 | 57,191 | 68,758 | 107,973 | 110,506 |
| 20,229 | 13,723 | 19,425 | 18,821 | 7,868 | 290 |
| 253,333 | 333,333 | 366,665 | 216,666 | 291,703 | 261,661 |
| 375 | 1,230 | 688 | 1,073 | 1,239 | 604 |
| 242 | 2,168 | 230 | 1,764 | — | — |
| 270,630 | 225,925 | 249,642 | 327,079 | 342,064 | 348,603 |
| 13,932 | 12,693 | 4,133 | 18,893 | 12,250 | 1,800 |
| 2,452 | — | 4,833 | 1,668 | — | — |
| 11,863 | 3,833 | 14,839 | 19,309 | 33,754 | 12,664 |
| 51,794 | 1,915 | 35,752 | 28,849 | 63,505 | 96,504 |
| — | — | 90 | 1,046 | 46 | — |
| 872 | 521 | 458 | 500 | 324 | 531 |
| 10,718,016 | 11,349,411 | 12,311,374 | 14,441,124 | 12,727,228 | 11,822,646 |

A-19

## EQ-3A. LATIN AMERICA: EXPORTS

(Bags of 60 kilograms or

| COUNTRIES OF DESTINATION | 1955 | 1956 | 1957 | 1958 | 1959 |
|---|---|---|---|---|---|
| **AFRICA** | | | | | |
| South Africa | 46,428 | 52,289 | 56,305 | 57,219 | 74,779 |
| Morocco | 43,073 | 29,148 | 38,139 | 69,684 | 42,321 |
| United Arab Republic | 16,497 | 6,806 | 55,988 | 95,059 | 63,355 |
| Tunisia | 14,432 | 14,170 | 10,000 | 9,460 | 19,136 |
| Tangier | 6,858 | 11,406 | 9,250 | 15,316 | 31,625 |
| Canary Islands | 5,001 | — | 14,490 | 1,690 | — |
| Algeria | 3,139 | 500 | 6,611 | 29,738 | 61,454 |
| Somalia | 1,225 | — | — | — | — |
| Mozambique | 360 | 653 | 935 | 754 | 1,139 |
| Sudan | — | — | — | — | — |
| Various (3) | 335 | 441 | 405 | 76 | 214 |
| **TOTAL AFRICA** | 137,348 | 115,413 | 192,123 | 278,996 | 294,023 |
| **ASIA & OCEANIA** | | | | | |
| Syria | 46,058 | 49,638 | — | — | — |
| Japan | 36,706 | 36,091 | 38,704 | 56,525 | 79,953 |
| Philippine Republic | 21,959 | 19,596 | 19,935 | 20,053 | 21,709 |
| Lebanon | 21,743 | 9,029 | 24,196 | 36,226 | 47,887 |
| Australia | 3,661 | 5,735 | 4,422 | 755 | 5,370 |
| Jordan | 3,331 | 12,571 | 12,343 | 10,922 | 7,321 |
| Israel | 1 | — | 395 | 17 | 9,596 |
| New Zealand | — | — | 67 | 445 | 894 |
| Hong Kong | — | 3 | — | — | 33 |
| China | — | — | — | — | — |
| Saudi Arabia | — | — | — | — | 70 |
| Iran | — | 32 | — | — | — |
| Formosa | — | — | — | — | — |
| Trucial Oman | — | — | — | — | — |
| Malaysia | — | — | — | — | — |
| Various (4) | — | 47 | — | 350 | 133 |
| **TOTAL ASIA & OCEANIA** | 133,459 | 132,742 | 100,062 | 125,293 | 172,966 |
| **OTHERS (5)** | 18 | 10 | 3,496 | 7 | 6 |
| **TOTAL EXPORTS** | 25,921,209 | 28,321,283 | 25,889,335 | 26,061,980 | 31,341,144 |

Source: Central statistical offices and official trade entities of exporting countries.
(1) Includes: Bahamas, Barbados, British West, Costa Rica, Ecuador, Guatemala, Malvina Island, Surinam, Peru.
(2) Includes: Andorra, Ireland and Monaco.
(3) Includes: Ivory Coast, Libya, Rhodesia, Southwest Africa and destination unknown.
(4) Includes: Bahrein Island, Ceylon, Far East, Hawaii, Iraq, Korea, Kuwait, Muscat & Oman, Other Arabia and Thailand.
(5) Destination Unknown.
(*) Preliminary.

## OF GREEN COFFEE, 1955-1965 (Continued)

132.276 pounds each)

| 1960 | 1961 | 1962 | 1963 | 1964 | 1965* |
|---|---|---|---|---|---|
| 70,229 | 72,074 | 70,912 | 68,812 | 67,348 | 127,030 |
| 21,418 | 17,227 | 3,952 | 5,012 | 7,499 | — |
| 55,857 | 37,868 | 1 | 36,900 | 33,825 | 11,000 |
| 6,817 | 8,127 | 14,789 | 34,999 | 5,000 | 10,000 |
| 13,265 | — | — | 292 | — | — |
| — | — | — | — | — | — |
| 10,020 | 15,925 | 2,445 | 87,000 | 235,004 | — |
| — | — | — | — | — | — |
| 1,128 | 530 | 923 | 735 | 406 | 591 |
| — | — | — | 122,000 | — | 7,603 |
| 540 | 370 | 461 | 283 | 260 | 430 |
| 179,274 | 152,121 | 93,483 | 356,033 | 349,342 | 156,654 |
| 4,738 | 5,200 | 19,685 | 63,696 | 10,122 | 15,388 |
| 94,912 | 104,537 | 159,097 | 318,846 | 123,955 | 142,702 |
| 12,369 | 2,497 | 5,394 | — | 3,103 | 9,383 |
| 68,190 | 125,863 | 191,543 | 50,920 | 273,686 | 58,834 |
| 12,445 | 13,652 | 13,595 | 14,388 | 9,037 | 6,109 |
| 6,813 | 4,495 | 950 | 20,425 | 5,450 | 55,284 |
| 28,638 | 26,551 | 11,432 | 8,938 | 1,694 | 3,428 |
| 1,545 | 3,124 | 1,514 | 1,596 | 1,082 | 2,052 |
| 40,000 | 120,000 | 50,000 | 48,827 | 230,002 | 45,000 |
| 1,783 | 233 | 234 | 117 | 233 | 350 |
| 917 | 420 | — | 20,000 | — | — |
| 100 | — | 18 | 10 | 10 | — |
| — | — | 7,000 | — | — | 115 |
| — | — | — | 2,300 | 400 | — |
| — | — | — | — | — | 5,750 |
| — | — | 665 | 3,057 | 517 | 2,311 |
| 272,450 | 406,572 | 461,127 | 553,120 | 659,291 | 346,706 |
| 18 | 869 | 56,282 | 2,205 | — | — |
| 30,388,686 | 30,311,109 | 31,592,814 | 34,251,115 | 30,330,719 | 27,752,513 |

A-21

## EQ-4. LATIN AMERICA: VOLUME OF GREEN 1965-

(Bags of 60 kilograms

### UNITED STATES

| COUNTRIES OF ORIGIN | 1966 | 1965 | Increase or Decrease 1966 over 1965 VOLUME | PERCENT |
|---|---|---|---|---|
| **PAN-AMERICAN COFFEE BUREAU** | | | | |
| Brazil | 6,958,784 | 6,027,587 | + 931,197 | + 15.4 |
| Colombia | 2,713,342 | 3,048,905 | − 335,563 | − 11.0 |
| Guatemala | 1,047,942 | 846,787 | + 201,155 | + 23.8 |
| El Salvador | 662,566 | 738,703 | − 76,137 | − 10.3 |
| Mexico | 1,083,922 | 1,133,596 | − 49,674 | − 4.4 |
| Costa Rica | 245,001 | 316,975 | − 71,974 | − 22.7 |
| Ecuador | 422,052 | 513,337 | − 91,285 | − 17.8 |
| Peru | 452,719 | 433,180 | + 19,539 | + 4.5 |
| Dominican Republic | 325,418 | 358,715 | − 33,297 | − 9.3 |
| Nicaragua | 157,152 | 285,748 | − 128,596 | − 45.0 |
| Honduras | 244,694 | 285,525 | − 40,831 | − 14.3 |
| Haiti | 85,825 | 110,086 | − 24,261 | − 22.0 |
| Venezuela | 264,035 | 245,991 | + 18,044 | + 7.3 |
| Panama | 24,297 | 11,392 | + 12,905 | +113.3 |
| Cuba | — | — | — | — |
| **TOTAL PAN-AMERICAN COFFEE BUREAU** | 14,687,749 | 14,356,527 | +331,222 | + 2.3 |
| **SUMMARY BY PRINCIPAL SOURCES** | | | | |
| Brazil | 6,958,784 | 6,027,587 | + 931,197 | + 15.4 |
| Colombia | 2,713,342 | 3,048,905 | − 335,563 | − 11.0 |
| Fedecame | 5,015,623 | 5,280,035 | − 264,412 | − 5.0 |
| **TOTAL PAN-AMERICAN COFFEE BUREAU** | 14,687,749 | 14,356,527 | +331,222 | + 2.3 |

Source: Statistical offices and official trade entities of exporting countries.

(*) See Table EQ-1 for totals.

**COFFEE EXPORTS TO PRINCIPAL MARKETS,***
**1966**

or 132.276 pounds each)

| | EUROPE | | | | | OTHERS | | |
|---|---|---|---|---|---|---|---|---|
| | | Increase or Decrease 1966 over 1965 | | | | | Increase or Decrease 1966 over 1965 | |
| 1966 | 1965 | VOLUME | PERCENT | 1966 | 1965 | VOLUME | PERCENT |
| 7,901,908 | 6,345,219 | + 1,556,689 | + 24.5 | 2,170,077 | 1,124,484 | + 1,045,593 | + 93.0 |
| 2,568,917 | 2,399,986 | + 168,931 | + 7.0 | 283,355 | 202,653 | + 80,702 | + 39.8 |
| 609,434 | 486,550 | + 122,884 | + 25.3 | 206,551 | 177,937 | + 28,614 | + 16.1 |
| 916,755 | 872,532 | + 44,223 | + 5.1 | 39,881 | 43,948 | − 4,067 | − 9.3 |
| 355,998 | 159,627 | + 196,371 | + 123.0 | 96,569 | 33,815 | + 62,754 | + 185.6 |
| 629,732 | 462,855 | + 166,877 | + 36.1 | 25,865 | 13,431 | + 12,434 | + 92.6 |
| 221,788 | 243,007 | − 21,219 | − 8.7 | 84,216 | 7,751 | + 76,465 | + 986.5 |
| 108,819 | 100,584 | + 8,235 | + 8.2 | 24,915 | 13,871 | + 11,044 | + 79.6 |
| 87,174 | 41,859 | + 45,315 | + 108.3 | 5,046 | 3,732 | + 1,314 | + 35.2 |
| 263,320 | 219,815 | + 43,505 | + 19.8 | 1,142 | 2,629 | − 1,487 | − 56.6 |
| 130,977 | 121,983 | + 8,994 | + 7.4 | 351 | − | + 351 | + --- |
| 262,544 | 288,047 | − 25,503 | − 8.9 | 1,865 | 600 | + 1,265 | + 210.8 |
| 38,790 | 52,171 | − 13,381 | − 25.6 | 453 | 992 | − 539 | − 54.3 |
| 20,921 | 12,584 | + 8,337 | + 66.3 | − | 1 | − 1 | − --- |
| − | − | − | − | − | − | − | − |
| 14,117,077 | 11,806,819 | +2,310,258 | + 19.6 | 2,940,286 | 1,625,844 | +1,314,442 | + 80.8 |
| | | | | | | | |
| 7,901,908 | 6,345,219 | + 1,556,689 | + 24.5 | 2,170,077 | 1,124,484 | +1,045,593 | + 93.0 |
| 2,568,917 | 2,399,986 | + 168,931 | + 7.0 | 283,355 | 202,653 | + 80,702 | + 39.8 |
| 3,646,252 | 3,061,614 | + 584,638 | + 19.1 | 486,854 | 298,707 | + 188,147 | + 63.0 |
| 14,117,077 | 11,806,819 | +2,310,258 | + 19.6 | 2,940,286 | 1,625,844 | +1,314,442 | + 80.8 |

## EQ-5. WORLD: EXPORTS OF GREEN
(thousands of bags of 60)

| ICO MEMBERS | 1947 | 1948 | 1949 | 1950 | 1951 | 1952 | 1953 | 1954 |
|---|---|---|---|---|---|---|---|---|
| **Pan-American Coffee Bureau** | | | | | | | | |
| Brazil | 14,688 | 17,492 | 19,368 | 14,835 | 16,358 | 15,821 | 15,562 | 10,918 |
| Colombia | 5,339 | 5,588 | 5,410 | 4,472 | 4,794 | 5,032 | 6,632 | 5,754 |
| Costa Rica | 327 | 379 | 268 | 312 | 309 | 333 | 465 | 365 |
| Cuba | — | — | — | — | — | — | — | — |
| Dominican Republic | 197 | 224 | 287 | 223 | 290 | 442 | 374 | 400 |
| Ecuador | 161 | 231 | 175 | 335 | 273 | 340 | 311 | 351 |
| El Salvador | 1,127 | 976 | 1,260 | 1,107 | 1,059 | 1,098 | 1,149 | 996 |
| Guatemala | 889 | 806 | 919 | 919 | 848 | 1,007 | 1,159 | 885 |
| Haiti | 373 | 381 | 553 | 390 | 417 | 541 | 372 | 517 |
| Honduras | 32 | 54 | 103 | 113 | 137 | 138 | 187 | 154 |
| Mexico | 548 | 524 | 817 | 767 | 865 | 870 | 1,267 | 1,112 |
| Nicaragua | 167 | 241 | 114 | 350 | 268 | 303 | 312 | 285 |
| Panama | — | — | — | — | — | 2 | 4 | — |
| Peru | 14 | 15 | 15 | 14 | 37 | 43 | 78 | 76 |
| Venezuela | 508 | 596 | 367 | 309 | 308 | 498 | 733 | 431 |
| **TOTAL P.A.C.B.** | 24,370 | 27,507 | 29,656 | 24,146 | 25,983 | 26,468 | 28,605 | 22,244 |
| **AFRICA** | | | | | | | | |
| Burundi | + | + | + | + | + | + | + | + |
| Congo (Kinshasa) | 619 | 509 | 524 | 554 | 590 | 515 | 566 | 573 |
| Ethiopia | 297 | 297 | 353 | 399 | 458 | 424 | 467 | 527 |
| Ghana | ° | ° | ° | ° | ° | ° | ° | ° |
| Kenya | 179 | 242 | 146 | 170 | 168 | 291 | 251 | 191 |
| Nigeria | ° | ° | ° | ° | ° | ° | ° | ° |
| Portugal | 745 | 903 | 773 | 616 | 1,074 | 794 | 1,193 | 737 |
| Rwanda | + | + | + | + | + | + | + | + |
| Sierra Leone | 6 | 6 | 4 | 6 | ° | ° | ° | ° |
| Tanzania | 234 | 190 | 205 | 258 | 276 | 319 | 250 | 325 |
| Uganda | 356 | 640 | 473 | 573 | 771 | 707 | 597 | 614 |
| (OAMCAF) | | | | | | | | |
| Cameroun | 135 | 121 | 138 | 128 | ° | ° | ° | 11 |
| Central African Republic | 99 | 40 | 45 | 78 | ° | ° | ° | 82 |
| Congo (Brazzaville) | ° | ° | ° | ° | ° | ° | ° | ° |
| Dahomey | ° | ° | ° | ° | ° | ° | ° | ° |
| Gabon | ° | ° | ° | ° | ° | ° | ° | ° |
| Ivory Coast | 734 | 938 | 1,062 | 962 | 1,321 | 1,250 | 940 | 1,585 |
| Madagascar | 489 | 332 | 427 | 551 | 509 | 697 | 604 | 691 |
| Togo | 41 | 28 | 34 | 20 | ° | ° | ° | 70 |
| **TOTAL AFRICA** | 3,934 | 4,246 | 4,184 | 4,315 | 5,167 | 4,997 | 4,868 | 5,406 |
| **OTHER MEMBERS** | | | | | | | | |
| India | 38 | 27 | 15 | 15 | 14 | 40 | 15 | 96 |
| Indonesia | — | 90 | 88 | 228 | 402 | 313 | 548 | 637 |
| Jamaica | ° | ° | ° | ° | ° | ° | ° | ° |
| Trinidad & Tobago | 27 | ° | ° | ° | ° | ° | 18 | 30 |
| **TOTAL OTHER MEMBERS** | 65 | 117 | 103 | 243 | 416 | 353 | 581 | 763 |
| **TOTAL ICO** | 28,369 | 31,870 | 33,943 | 28,704 | 31,546 | 31,818 | 34,054 | 28,413 |
| **NON-MEMBERS** | | | | | | | | |
| Bolivia | ° | ° | ° | ° | ° | ° | ° | ° |
| Guinea | — | — | — | — | — | — | — | — |
| Philippine Republic | — | — | — | — | — | ° | 73 | 75 |
| Yemen | ° | ° | ° | ° | ° | ° | ° | ° |
| Various | 461 | 451 | 374 | 430 | 296 | 326 | 330 | 236 |
| **TOTAL NON-MEMBERS** | 461 | 451 | 374 | 430 | 296 | 326 | 403 | 311 |
| **WORLD TOTAL** | 28,830 | 32,321 | 34,317 | 29,134 | 31,842 | 32,144 | 34,457 | 28,724 |

Source: Central statistical offices and official trade entities of exporting countries.
(*) Included in Congo (D.R.).
(+) Included in Burundi.
(°) Included in Various.

**COFFEE BY ICO MEMBERSHIP, 1947-1966**
kilograms or 132.276 pounds each)

| 1955 | 1956 | 1957 | 1958 | 1959 | 1960 | 1961 | 1962 | 1963 | 1964 | 1965 | 1966 |
|---|---|---|---|---|---|---|---|---|---|---|---|
| 13,696 | 16,805 | 14,319 | 12,894 | 17,723 | 16,819 | 16,971 | 16,377 | 19,514 | 14,948 | 13,497 | 17,031 |
| 5,867 | 5,070 | 4,824 | 5,441 | 6,413 | 5,938 | 5,651 | 6,561 | 6,134 | 6,412 | 5,652 | 5,566 |
| 463 | 393 | 468 | 771 | 712 | 766 | 835 | 902 | 929 | 841 | 794 | 901 |
| 75 | 347 | 190 | 121 | 52 | 90 | 85 | 139 | — | — | — | — |
| 409 | 440 | 361 | 429 | 362 | 481 | 335 | 487 | 457 | 573 | 404 | 418 |
| 384 | 408 | 470 | 503 | 397 | 522 | 381 | 551 | 499 | 417 | 764 | 728 |
| 1,185 | 1,132 | 1,270 | 1,399 | 1,345 | 1,178 | 1,431 | 1,478 | 1,586 | 1,755 | 1,655 | 1,619 |
| 982 | 1,026 | 1,038 | 1,205 | 1,385 | 1,329 | 1,255 | 1,552 | 1,667 | 1,446 | 1,511 | 1,864 |
| 355 | 459 | 315 | 547 | 364 | 394 | 348 | 514 | 390 | 380 | 399 | 350 |
| 149 | 195 | 174 | 189 | 255 | 258 | 210 | 266 | 334 | 309 | 407 | 376 |
| 1,367 | 1,260 | 1,448 | 1,312 | 1,240 | 1,384 | 1,483 | 1,458 | 1,199 | 1,772 | 1,327 | 1,536 |
| 379 | 282 | 367 | 382 | 273 | 361 | 349 | 338 | 467 | 430 | 508 | 422 |
| 11 | — | — | 9 | 16 | 21 | 5 | 27 | 8 | 25 | 24 | 45 |
| 114 | 118 | 185 | 275 | 331 | 440 | 567 | 624 | 668 | 696 | 548 | 586 |
| 497 | 387 | 460 | 585 | 473 | 408 | 406 | 319 | 390 | 327 | 299 | 303 |
| 25,933 | 28,322 | 25,889 | 26,062 | 31,341 | 30,389 | 30,312 | 31,593 | 34,242 | 30,331 | 27,789 | 31,745 |
| + | + | + | + | + | + | 389 | 383 | 173 | 305 | 227 | 246 |
| 728 | 867 | 613 | 1,156 | 1,523 | 878 | 555 | 600 | 773 | 624 | 588 | 560 |
| 702 | 496 | 845 | 639 | 754 | 849 | 950 | 1,023 | 1,080 | 1,234 | 1,360 | 1,012 |
| ° | 12 | 3 | 8 | 34 | 40 | 28 | 64 | 44 | 111 | 33 | 97 |
| 304 | 504 | 374 | 437 | 405 | 477 | 536 | 492 | 580 | 703 | 630 | 907 |
| ° | ° | 25 | 40 | 55 | 79 | 10 | 13 | 26 | 69 | 12 | 120 |
| 964 | 1,398 | 1,267 | 1,317 | 1,483 | 1,454 | 1,976 | 2,620 | 2,397 | 2,309 | 2,715 | 2,633 |
| + | + | + | + | + | + | * | * | * | 146 | 165 | 143 |
| ° | ° | 63 | 57 | 84 | 86 | 85 | 41 | 32 | 100 | 64 | 171 |
| 296 | 381 | 297 | 356 | 316 | 420 | 438 | 426 | 425 | 554 | 474 | 849 |
| 1,274 | 1,806 | 1,420 | 1,337 | 1,536 | 1,949 | 1,806 | 2,314 | 2,438 | 2,354 | 2,488 | 2,976 |
| 7 | 28 | 11 | 12 | 54 | 510 | 591 | 635 | 516 | 868 | 893 | 1,211 |
| 57 | 98 | 74 | 88 | 102 | 99 | 121 | 130 | 97 | 208 | 127 | 190 |
| ° | ° | ° | ° | ° | ° | 11 | 18 | 11 | 12 | 8 | 19 |
| 16 | 22 | 17 | 8 | 20 | 14 | 35 | 29 | 17 | 46 | 14 | 13 |
| ° | ° | ° | 3 | 2 | 4 | 8 | 10 | 11 | 18 | 12 | 16 |
| 1,583 | 2,242 | 1,687 | 1,875 | 1,745 | 2,707 | 2,618 | 2,670 | 2,867 | 3,259 | 3,099 | 3,013 |
| 791 | 875 | 805 | 797 | 632 | 670 | 615 | 934 | 740 | 633 | 834 | 761 |
| 64 | 107 | 102 | 76 | 193 | 61 | 171 | 192 | 104 | 273 | 194 | 231 |
| 6,786 | 8,836 | 7,603 | 8,206 | 8,938 | 10,297 | 10,943 | 12,594 | 12,331 | 13,826 | 13,937 | 15,168 |
| 60 | 127 | 224 | 248 | 240 | 272 | 533 | 331 | 374 | 526 | 412 | 417 |
| 386 | 958 | 850 | 900 | 850 | 687 | 1,091 | 961 | 980 | 1,016 | 1,803 | 1,786 |
| ° | ° | ° | ° | ° | ° | ° | ° | ° | 15 | 10 | 8 |
| 30 | 21 | 30 | 32 | 42 | 30 | 38 | 28 | 58 | 64 | 59 | 40 |
| 476 | 1,106 | 1,104 | 1,180 | 1,132 | 989 | 1,662 | 1,320 | 1,412 | 1,621 | 2,284 | 2,251 |
| 33,195 | 38,264 | 34,596 | 35,448 | 41,411 | 41,675 | 42,917 | 45,507 | 47,985 | 45,778 | 44,010 | 49,164 |
| ° | ° | ° | ° | ° | ° | ° | ° | ° | 28 | 20 | 72 |
| — | — | — | 171 | 239 | 240 | 253 | 199 | 175 | 63 | 180 | 207 |
| — | — | — | — | — | — | — | — | — | — | — | — |
| 78 | 88 | 90 | 88 | 70 | 69 | 80 | 67 | 104 | 100 | 91 | 95 |
| 280 | 345 | 439 | 524 | 448 | 402 | 475 | 483 | 642 | 752 | 668 | 801 |
| 358 | 433 | 529 | 783 | 757 | 711 | 808 | 749 | 921 | 943 | 959 | 1,175 |
| 33,553 | 38,697 | 35,125 | 36,231 | 42,168 | 42,386 | 43,725 | 46,256 | 48,906 | 46,721 | 44,969 | 50,339 |

## EQ-6. BRAZIL: EXPORTS OF GREEN COFFEE,* 1965-1966
(Bags of 60 kilograms or 132.276 pounds each)

| COUNTRIES OF DESTINATION | 1966 | 1965 | Percent of Total 1966 | Percent of Total 1965 | Increase or Decrease 1966 over 1965 VOLUME | PERCENT |
|---|---|---|---|---|---|---|
| UNITED STATES | 6,958,784 | 6,027,587 | 40.9 | 44.7 | + 931,197 | + 15.4 |
| CANADA | 258,013 | 262,884 | 1.5 | 1.9 | − 4,871 | − 1.9 |
| OTHER AMERICAS | | | | | | |
| Argentina | 560,736 | 466,529 | 3.3 | 3.5 | + 94,207 | + 20.2 |
| Chile | 144,448 | 144,382 | 0.8 | 1.1 | + 66 | + 0.05 |
| Uruguay | 10,985 | 6,764 | 0.1 | 0.1 | + 4,221 | + 62.4 |
| Paraguay | 33 | 4 | --- | --- | + 29 | +725.0 |
| Peru | --- | 11 | --- | --- | --- | --- |
| Surinam | --- | 5 | --- | --- | --- | --- |
| Bolivia | --- | 3 | --- | --- | --- | --- |
| Ecuador | --- | 2 | --- | --- | --- | --- |
| TOTAL OTHER AMERICAS | 716,202 | 617,700 | 4.2 | 4.7 | + 98,502 | + 15.9 |
| EUROPE | | | | | | |
| Italy | 1,391,627 | 567,955 | 8.2 | 4.2 | + 823,672 | +145.0 |
| Sweden | 1,009,294 | 960,160 | 5.9 | 7.1 | + 49,134 | + 5.1 |
| Denmark | 679,440 | 610,194 | 4.0 | 4.5 | + 69,246 | + 11.3 |
| Germany (F.R.) | 663,918 | 705,085 | 3.9 | 5.2 | − 41,167 | − 5.8 |
| Netherlands | 594,063 | 478,853 | 3.5 | 3.5 | + 115,210 | + 24.1 |
| France | 569,366 | 487,550 | 3.3 | 3.6 | + 81,816 | + 16.8 |
| Norway | 424,868 | 334,710 | 2.5 | 2.5 | + 90,158 | + 26.9 |
| Finland | 391,473 | 285,770 | 2.3 | 2.1 | + 105,703 | + 37.0 |
| Yugoslavia | 379,742 | 209,899 | 2.2 | 1.6 | + 169,843 | + 80.9 |
| Belgium—Luxembourg | 354,408 | 343,755 | 2.1 | 2.5 | + 10,653 | + 3.1 |
| Germany (D.R.) | 285,511 | 269,945 | 1.7 | 2.0 | + 15,566 | + 5.8 |
| U.S.S.R. | 277,495 | 249,994 | 1.6 | 1.9 | + 27,501 | + 11.0 |
| Spain | 174,508 | 118,736 | 1.0 | 0.9 | + 55,772 | + 47.0 |
| Greece | 151,597 | 138,265 | 0.9 | 1.0 | + 13,332 | + 9.6 |
| Czechoslovakia | 109,393 | 98,221 | 0.6 | 0.7 | + 11,172 | + 11.4 |
| Hungary | 106,216 | 94,988 | 0.6 | 0.7 | + 11,228 | + 11.8 |
| United Kingdom | 90,636 | 49,504 | 0.5 | 0.4 | + 41,132 | + 83.1 |
| Bulgaria | 70,987 | 96,504 | 0.4 | 0.7 | − 25,517 | − 26.4 |
| Rumania | 46,832 | 12,664 | 0.3 | 0.1 | + 34,168 | +269.8 |
| Poland | 43,875 | 89,296 | 0.3 | 0.7 | − 45,421 | − 50.9 |
| Iceland | 37,232 | 32,550 | 0.2 | 0.2 | + 4,682 | + 14.4 |

A-26

E2-6. BRAZIL: EXPORTS OF GREEN COFFEE,* 1965-1966 (Continued)

| COUNTRIES OF DESTINATION | 1966 | 1965 | Percent of Total 1966 | Percent of Total 1965 | Increase or Decrease 1966 over 1965 VOLUME | PERCENT |
|---|---|---|---|---|---|---|
| EUROPE (Continued) | | | | | | |
| Switzerland | 24,630 | 33,899 | 0.1 | 0.3 | − 9,269 | − 27.3 |
| Austria | 15,259 | 15,883 | 0.1 | 0.1 | − 624 | − 3.9 |
| Cyprus | 8,652 | 1,800 | 0.1 | — | + 6,852 | +380.7 |
| Malta | 478 | 604 | — | — | − 126 | − 20.9 |
| Eire | 180 | 50 | — | — | + 130 | +260.0 |
| Andorra | 167 | 167 | — | — | — | --- |
| Portugal | 61 | — | — | — | + 61 | --- |
| Turkey | — | 58,218 | — | 0.4 | − 58,218 | --- |
| TOTAL EUROPE | 7,901,908 | 6,345,219 | 46.3 | 46.9 | +1,556,689 | + 24.5 |
| AFRICA | | | | | | |
| Algeria | 54,164 | 52,998 | 0.3 | 0.4 | + 1,166 | + 2.2 |
| South Africa | 52,128 | — | 0.3 | — | + 52,128 | --- |
| Sudan | 46,759 | — | 0.3 | — | + 46,759 | --- |
| United Arab Republic | 16,320 | 11,000 | 0.1 | 0.1 | + 5,320 | + 48.4 |
| Tunisia | 10,000 | 10,000 | 0.1 | 0.1 | — | --- |
| Morocco | 1,891 | — | — | — | + 1,891 | --- |
| Mozambique | 711 | 591 | — | — | + 120 | + 20.3 |
| Nigeria | 666 | — | — | — | + 666 | --- |
| Libya | 550 | 63 | — | — | + 487 | +773.0 |
| Southern Rhodesia | 145 | 285 | — | — | − 140 | − 49.1 |
| TOTAL AFRICA | 183,334 | 74,937 | 1.1 | 0.6 | + 108,397 | +144.7 |
| ASIA & OCEANIA | | | | | | |
| Lebanon | 606,454 | 52,808 | 3.6 | 0.4 | + 553,646 | + (o) |
| Hong Kong | 300,000 | 45,000 | 1.8 | 0.3 | + 255,000 | +566.7 |
| Japan | 65,748 | 53,045 | 0.4 | 0.4 | + 12,703 | + 23.9 |
| Syria | 31,570 | 12,000 | 0.2 | 0.1 | + 19,570 | +163.1 |
| Australia | 4,235 | 3,056 | — | — | + 1,179 | + 38.6 |
| Israel | 3,933 | 650 | — | — | + 3,283 | +505.1 |
| New Zealand | 588 | 521 | — | — | + 67 | + 12.9 |
| Philippine Republic | — | 1,883 | — | — | − 1,883 | --- |
| TOTAL ASIA & OCEANIA | 1,012,528 | 168,963 | 6.0 | 1.2 | + 843,565 | +499.3 |
| TOTAL EXPORTS | 17,030,769 | 13,497,290 | 100.0 | 100.0 | +3,533,479 | + 26.2 |

Source: Instituto Brasileiro do Café.
(o) Increase over 1,000 percent.
(*) Includes green equivalent of soluble coffee 198,649 bags (14,901); green equivalent of roasted coffee 194 bags (8); green coffee exports totaled 16,831,926 (13,482,381).

## EQ-6A. BRAZIL: EXPORTS OF GREEN COFFEE, 1960-1965

(Bags of 60 kilograms or 132.276 pounds each)

| COUNTRIES OF DESTINATION | 1960 | 1961 | 1962 | 1963 | 1964 | 1965 |
|---|---|---|---|---|---|---|
| UNITED STATES | 9,380,806 | 8,592,090 | 8,157,863 | 8,717,186 | 6,348,939 | 6,027,587 |
| CANADA | 293,554 | 320,348 | 336,885 | 356,958 | 278,750 | 262,884 |
| **OTHER AMERICAS** | | | | | | |
| Argentina | 464,030 | 412,598 | 388,310 | 428,454 | 447,721 | 466,529 |
| Chile | 78,369 | 105,479 | 141,462 | 104,525 | 95,169 | 144,382 |
| Uruguay | 19,250 | 29,756 | 24,197 | 25,044 | 16,775 | 6,764 |
| Paraguay | 8,000 | 4 | 41 | 4 | 4 | 4 |
| Netherlands West Indies | 345 | 65 | 190 | — | — | — |
| Trinidad & Tobago | — | 4 | — | — | — | — |
| Bolivia | — | 3 | 54 | 3 | 3 | 3 |
| Peru | — | 3 | 6 | 23 | 3 | 11 |
| Ecuador | — | 2 | 4 | 2 | 2 | 2 |
| Surinam | — | 1 | 2 | 1 | 1 | 5 |
| Cuba | — | — | — | 71,089 | 12,244 | — |
| Barbados | — | — | — | — | 25 | — |
| TOTAL OTHER AMERICAS | 569,994 | 547,915 | 554,266 | 629,145 | 571,947 | 617,700 |
| **EUROPE** | | | | | | |
| Sweden | 867,871 | 955,034 | 978,158 | 1,023,036 | 944,114 | 960,160 |
| Germany (F.R.) | 801,473 | 735,546 | 799,158 | 889,323 | 564,951 | 705,085 |
| Italy | 719,369 | 859,895 | 589,635 | 1,268,481 | 1,077,532 | 567,955 |
| France | 577,130 | 526,009 | 539,666 | 638,933 | 422,574 | 487,550 |
| Denmark | 530,310 | 538,581 | 594,503 | 663,721 | 575,746 | 610,194 |
| Norway | 411,041 | 391,439 | 364,113 | 421,065 | 340,921 | 334,710 |
| Finland | 398,251 | 451,263 | 397,449 | 489,406 | 418,155 | 285,770 |
| Belgium—Luxembourg | 358,758 | 410,911 | 435,429 | 571,961 | 398,258 | 343,755 |
| Netherlands | 279,998 | 669,659 | 874,651 | 1,502,103 | 547,096 | 478,853 |
| U.S.S.R. | 250,000 | 333,333 | 366,676 | 216,666 | 291,703 | 249,994 |
| Germany (D.R.) | 247,463 | 209,274 | 179,660 | 291,109 | 261,732 | 269,945 |
| United Kingdom | 162,064 | 185,579 | 207,902 | 198,862 | 111,682 | 49,504 |
| Yugoslavia | 138,752 | 66,188 | 23,932 | 137,655 | 172,688 | 209,899 |
| Spain | 127,763 | 219,012 | 118,519 | 117,181 | 116,178 | 118,736 |
| Greece | 74,379 | 92,223 | 98,596 | 138,274 | 108,795 | 138,265 |
| Austria | 55,667 | 36,704 | 38,397 | 38,482 | 22,047 | 15,883 |
| Poland | 51,729 | 71,660 | 23,474 | 98,779 | 51,683 | 89,296 |
| Switzerland | 48,185 | 87,858 | 140,870 | 175,075 | 49,588 | 33,899 |
| Czechoslovakia | 40,731 | 119,880 | 26,842 | 64,751 | 108,159 | 98,221 |
| Iceland | 24,300 | 25,575 | 28,670 | 31,930 | 25,700 | 32,550 |
| Hungary | 20,151 | 24,331 | 25,662 | 57,026 | 99,390 | 94,988 |
| Gibraltar | 20,114 | 13,723 | 19,425 | 16,300 | 7,750 | — |
| Cypress | 13,932 | 12,693 | 4,133 | 18,893 | 12,250 | 1,800 |
| Rumania | 11,383 | — | 10,192 | 9,583 | 33,754 | 12,664 |
| Turkey | 7,268 | 32,201 | 21,074 | 3,834 | 36,791 | 58,218 |
| Albania | 2,452 | — | — | — | — | — |
| Malta | 375 | 1,230 | 638 | 1,073 | 1,239 | 604 |
| Andorra | 239 | 165 | 199 | 200 | 66 | 167 |
| Ireland | 170 | 270 | — | — | — | 50 |
| Bulgaria | — | — | 33,317 | 28,849 | 63,505 | 96,504 |
| Portugal | — | — | 90 | 1,046 | 46 | — |
| TOTAL EUROPE | 6,241,318 | 7,070,236 | 6,941,030 | 9,113,597 | 6,864,093 | 6,345,219 |

### EQ-6A.  BRAZIL: EXPORTS OF GREEN COFFEE, 1960-1965 Continued)

(Bags of 60 kilograms or 132.276 pounds each)

| COUNTRIES OF DESTINATION | 1960 | 1961 | 1962 | 1963 | 1964 | 1965 |
| --- | --- | --- | --- | --- | --- | --- |
| **AFRICA** | | | | | | |
| South Africa (Rep.) | 68,197 | 70,446 | 65,318 | 67,242 | 64,905 | 52,998 |
| Morocco | 34,566 | 15,874 | 106 | 2,500 | 33,825 | — |
| United Arab Republic | 21,725 | 8,011 | — | 36,900 | 6,953 | 11,000 |
| Algeria | 10,020 | 8,835 | 2,121 | 87,000 | 235,004 | — |
| Tunisia | 6,817 | 8,127 | 14,789 | 34,999 | 5,000 | 10,000 |
| Mozambique | 1,128 | 530 | 923 | 735 | 406 | 591 |
| Southern Rhodesia | 415 | 307 | 345 | 220 | 260 | 285 |
| Ivory Coast | 125 | — | 84 | — | — | — |
| Libya | — | 63 | 32 | 63 | — | 63 |
| Sudan | — | — | — | 122,000 | — | — |
| **TOTAL AFRICA** | 142,993 | 112,193 | 83,718 | 351,659 | 346,353 | 74,937 |
| **ASIA & OCEANIA** | | | | | | |
| Lebanon | 61,931 | 124,023 | 188,043 | 47,976 | 268,737 | 52,808 |
| Japan | 42,740 | 40,308 | 35,080 | 130,567 | 29,813 | 53,045 |
| Hong Kong | 40,000 | 120,000 | 50,000 | 48,827 | 230,000 | 45,000 |
| Israel | 28,152 | 25,676 | 10,962 | 8,292 | 14 | 650 |
| Australia | 7,400 | 8,014 | 8,329 | 8,240 | 1,890 | 3,056 |
| Jordan | 6,813 | 4,495 | 950 | 20,425 | 2,000 | — |
| China | 1,666 | — | — | — | — | — |
| Philippine Republic | 1,163 | 70 | — | — | 783 | 1,883 |
| New Zealand | 353 | 2,573 | 51 | 505 | 209 | 521 |
| Iran | 100 | — | 18 | 10 | 10 | — |
| Syria | — | 2,624 | 9,469 | 55,949 | 3,954 | 12,000 |
| Kuwait | — | — | 200 | — | 400 | — |
| Trucial Oman | — | — | — | 2,300 | 400 | — |
| Saudi Arabia | — | — | — | 20,000 | — | — |
| Other Arabia | — | — | — | 1,000 | — | — |
| Muscat & Oman | — | — | — | 900 | — | — |
| Bahrein | — | — | — | 800 | — | — |
| Thailand | — | — | — | 100 | — | — |
| **TOTAL ASIA & OCEANIA** | 190,318 | 327,783 | 303,102 | 345,891 | 538,210 | 168,963 |
| **TOTAL EXPORTS** | 16,818,983 | 16,970,565 | 16,376,864 | 19,514,436 | 14,948,292 | 13,497,290 |

Source:  Instituto Brasileiro do Café.

## EQ-7. COLOMBIA: EXPORTS OF GREEN COFFEE, 1965-1966

(Bags of 60 kilograms or 132.276 pounds each)

| COUNTRIES OF DESTINATION | 1966 | 1965 | Percentage of Total 1966 | 1965 | Increase or Decrease 1966 over 1965 VOLUME | PERCENT |
|---|---|---|---|---|---|---|
| UNITED STATES | 2,713,342 | 3,048,905 | 48.8 | 53.9 | − 335,563 | − 11.0 |
| CANADA | 78,177 | 117,642 | 1.4 | 2.1 | − 39,465 | − 33.5 |
| OTHER AMERICAS | | | | | | |
| Argentina | 95,561 | 36,421 | 1.7 | 0.6 | + 59,140 | +162.4 |
| Chile | 3,524 | 3,236 | 0.1 | 0.1 | + 288 | + 8.9 |
| Panama | 147 | 72 | — | — | + 75 | +104.2 |
| Bolivia | 14 | 4 | — | — | + 10 | +250.0 |
| Peru | — | 1 | — | — | − 1 | --- |
| TOTAL OTHER AMERICAS | 99,246 | 39,734 | 1.8 | 0.7 | + 59,512 | +149.8 |
| EUROPE | | | | | | |
| Germany (F.R.) | 910,991 | 807,981 | 16.4 | 14.3 | +103,010 | + 12.7 |
| Spain | 333,572 | 300,201 | 6.0 | 5.3 | + 33,371 | + 11.1 |
| Sweden | 269,566 | 302,120 | 4.8 | 5.4 | − 32,554 | − 10.8 |
| Finland | 206,062 | 154,286 | 3.7 | 2.7 | + 51,776 | + 33.6 |
| Netherlands | 196,834 | 242,782 | 3.5 | 4.3 | − 45,948 | − 18.9 |
| Germany (D.R.) | 121,750 | 78,658 | 2.2 | 1.4 | + 43,092 | + 54.8 |
| Belgium | 97,714 | 141,822 | 1.8 | 2.5 | − 44,108 | − 31.1 |
| Poland | 84,165 | 50,417 | 1.5 | 0.9 | + 33,748 | + 66.9 |
| United Kingdom | 51,431 | 39,634 | 0.9 | 0.7 | + 11,797 | + 29.8 |
| Denmark | 53,350 | 44,664 | 1.0 | 0.8 | + 8,686 | + 19.4 |
| Italy | 48,426 | 50,472 | 0.9 | 0.9 | − 2,046 | − 4.1 |
| Norway | 42,394 | 29,100 | 0.7 | 0.5 | + 13,294 | + 45.7 |
| Hungary | 38,081 | 14,581 | 0.7 | 0.3 | + 23,500 | +161.2 |
| U.S.S.R. | 33,332 | 11,667 | 0.6 | 0.2 | + 21,665 | +185.7 |
| France | 30,244 | 36,143 | 0.5 | 0.6 | − 5,899 | − 16.3 |
| Czechoslovakia | 19,740 | 25,437 | 0.4 | 0.5 | − 5,697 | − 22.4 |
| Switzerland | 19,138 | 35,489 | 0.3 | 0.6 | − 16,351 | − 46.1 |
| Yugoslavia | 8,167 | 33,919 | 0.1 | 0.6 | − 25,752 | − 75.9 |
| Bulgaria | 3,500 | — | 0.1 | — | + 3,500 | --- |
| Austria | 320 | 496 | — | — | − 176 | − 35.5 |
| Turkey | 82 | — | — | — | + 82 | --- |
| Greece | 58 | — | — | — | + 58 | --- |
| Eire | — | 117 | — | — | − 117 | --- |
| TOTAL EUROPE | 2,568,917 | 2,399,986 | 46.1 | 42.5 | +168,931 | + 7.0 |
| OTHERS | | | | | | |
| Japan | 100,061 | 38,137 | 1.8 | 0.7 | + 61,924 | +162.4 |
| Israel | 2,659 | 2,777 | 0.1 | 0.1 | − 118 | − 4.2 |
| South Africa | 1,254 | 1,371 | — | — | − 117 | − 8.5 |
| New Zealand | 1,142 | 1,011 | — | — | + 131 | + 13.0 |
| Australia | 641 | 1,252 | — | — | − 611 | − 48.8 |
| China | 116 | 350 | — | — | − 234 | − 66.9 |
| Syria | 59 | 175 | — | — | − 116 | − 66.3 |
| South Korea | — | 122 | — | — | − 122 | --- |
| Libya | — | 82 | — | — | − 82 | --- |
| TOTAL OTHERS | 105,932 | 45,277 | 1.9 | 0.8 | + 60,655 | +134.0 |
| TOTAL EXPORTS | 5,565,614 | 5,651,544 | 100.0 | 100.0 | − 85,930 | − 1.5 |

Source: Federación Nacional de Cafeteros.

## EQ-7A. COLOMBIA: EXPORTS OF GREEN COFFEE 1960-1965
(Bags of 60 kilograms or 132,276 pounds each)

| COUNTRIES OF DESTINATION | 1960 | 1961 | 1962 | 1963 | 1964 | 1965 |
|---|---|---|---|---|---|---|
| UNITED STATES | 4,349,699 | 3,949,177 | 4,327,729 | 3,816,511 | 3,729,109 | 3,048,905 |
| CANADA | 108,966 | 116,759 | 126,334 | 147,710 | 128,325 | 117,642 |
| **OTHER AMERICAS** | | | | | | |
| Chile | 9,641 | 560 | 5,005 | 3,851 | 3,634 | 3,236 |
| Argentina | 1,862 | 3,219 | 12,127 | 6,184 | 32,696 | 36,421 |
| Mexico | – | 1,726 | – | – | – | – |
| Uruguay | – | 123 | – | 6 | – | – |
| Costa Rica | – | 1 | – | – | – | – |
| Peru | – | 1 | – | 1 | – | 1 |
| Panama | – | – | 11 | 8 | 90 | 72 |
| Bolivia | – | – | – | 2 | 11 | 4 |
| Guatemala | – | – | – | 50 | – | – |
| TOTAL OTHER AMERICAS | 11,503 | 5,630 | 17,143 | 10,102 | 36,431 | 39,734 |
| **EUROPE** | | | | | | |
| Germany (F.R.) | 595,482 | 673,357 | 807,934 | 780,130 | 885,081 | 807,981 |
| Sweden | 178,880 | 176,862 | 240,724 | 227,778 | 277,471 | 302,120 |
| Netherlands | 152,356 | 66,544 | 164,549 | 176,625 | 276,159 | 242,782 |
| United Kingdom | 89,836 | 83,561 | 53,264 | 52,446 | 101,850 | 39,634 |
| Belgium | 61,672 | 50,083 | 67,340 | 77,074 | 147,840 | 141,822 |
| Finland | 51,794 | 89,311 | 109,824 | 104,205 | 146,487 | 154,286 |
| Bulgaria | 51,392 | – | – | – | – | – |
| Czechoslovakia | 38,967 | 37,567 | 20,994 | 37,053 | 5,617 | 25,437 |
| Spain | 33,325 | 100,188 | 204,866 | 250,394 | 235,065 | 300,201 |
| Italy | 29,643 | 90,391 | 65,479 | 64,980 | 74,618 | 50,472 |
| Denmark | 26,472 | 25,025 | 32,235 | 32,581 | 37,146 | 44,664 |
| Germany (D.R.) | 23,167 | – | 31,516 | 35,970 | 80,045 | 78,658 |
| Norway | 17,907 | 17,701 | 25,442 | 29,021 | 50,528 | 29,100 |
| France | 17,598 | 28,132 | 26,103 | 37,134 | 54,227 | 36,143 |
| Hungary | 15,084 | 3,334 | 11,666 | 11,582 | 8,583 | 14,581 |
| Poland | 12,096 | – | – | 28,686 | 34,582 | 50,417 |
| Switzerland | 7,700 | 52,019 | 113,435 | 104,125 | 23,108 | 35,489 |
| Yugoslavia | 4,965 | 21,800 | 50,440 | 33,376 | 33,334 | 33,919 |
| U.S.S.R. | 3,333 | – | – | – | – | 11,667 |
| Austria | 574 | 518 | 204 | 513 | 1,108 | 496 |
| Rumania | – | 1,666 | – | 3,333 | – | – |
| Andorra | – | – | – | 16 | – | – |
| Ireland | – | – | – | – | – | – 117 |
| TOTAL EUROPE | 1,412,243 | 1,518,059 | 2,026,015 | 2,087,022 | 2,472,849 | 2,399,986 |
| **OTHERS** | | | | | | |
| Japan | 42,695 | 54,149 | 55,094 | 65,977 | 35,592 | 38,137 |
| Lebanon | 4,885 | – | 117 | – | 58 | – |
| Australia | 4,307 | 5,076 | 4,472 | 4,221 | 5,523 | 1,252 |
| South Africa | 1,890 | 1,493 | 2,345 | 1,341 | 1,837 | 1,371 |
| Philippine Republic | 500 | – | – | – | – | – |
| Syria | 467 | – | 282 | – | – | 175 |
| New Zealand | 352 | 216 | 1,176 | 532 | 503 | 1,011 |
| China | 117 | 233 | 234 | 117 | 233 | 350 |
| Morocco | 117 | – | 50 | – | – | – |
| Israel | – | – | 233 | 140 | 1,680 | 2,777 |
| Far East | – | – | 208 | – | – | – |
| Kuwait | – | – | – | – | 117 | – |
| Korea | – | – | – | – | – | 122 |
| Libya | – | – | – | – | – | 82 |
| TOTAL OTHERS | 55,330 | 61,167 | 64,211 | 72,328 | 45,543 | 45,277 |
| TOTAL EXPORTS | 5,937,741 | 5,650,792 | 6,561,432 | 6,133,673 | 6,412,257 | 5,651,544 |

Source: Federación Nacional de Cafeteros de Colombia.

## EQ-8. EL SALVADOR: EXPORTS OF GREEN COFFEE,* 1965-1966
(Bags of 60 kilograms or 132.276 pounds each)

| COUNTRIES OF DESTINATION | 1966 | 1965 | Percent of Total 1966 | Percent of Total 1965 | Increase or Decrease 1966 over 1965 VOLUME | Increase or Decrease 1966 over 1965 PERCENT |
|---|---|---|---|---|---|---|
| UNITED STATES | 662,566 | 738,703 | 40.9 | 44.6 | − 76,137 | − 10.3 |
| CANADA | 23,619 | 27,502 | 1.5 | 1.7 | − 3,883 | − 14.1 |
| OTHER AMERICAS | | | | | | |
| British Honduras | 209 | 156 | --- | --- | + 53 | + 34.0 |
| Costa Rica | 189 | 93 | --- | --- | + 96 | + 103.2 |
| Honduras | 187 | 216 | --- | --- | − 29 | − 13.4 |
| Guatemala | 67 | 144 | --- | --- | − 77 | − 53.5 |
| Peru | 5 | 7 | --- | --- | − 2 | − 28.6 |
| TOTAL OTHER AMERICAS | 657 | 616 | --- | --- | + 41 | + 6.7 |
| EUROPE | | | | | | |
| Germany (F.R.) | 790,759 | 710,783 | 48.8 | 43.0 | + 79,976 | + 11.3 |
| Netherlands | 62,405 | 55,639 | 3.9 | 3.4 | + 6,766 | + 12.2 |
| Belgium | 13,509 | 28,722 | 0.8 | 1.7 | − 15,213 | − 53.0 |
| Switzerland | 11,128 | 8,271 | 0.7 | 0.5 | + 2,857 | + 34.5 |
| Finland | 10,925 | 8,625 | 0.7 | 0.5 | + 2,300 | + 26.7 |
| Sweden | 7,612 | 15,294 | 0.5 | 0.9 | − 7,682 | − 50.2 |
| Spain | 6,950 | 4,601 | 0.4 | 0.3 | + 2,349 | + 51.1 |
| Norway | 6,864 | 4,375 | 0.4 | 0.3 | + 2,489 | + 56.9 |
| Italy | 3,834 | 3,513 | 0.2 | 0.2 | + 321 | + 9.1 |
| Czechoslovakia | 2,500 | 2,168 | 0.2 | 0.1 | + 332 | + 15.3 |
| Austria | 202 | 1,727 | --- | 0.1 | − 1,525 | − 88.3 |
| France | 67 | 58 | --- | --- | + 9 | + 15.5 |
| Poland | --- | 28,750 | --- | 1.7 | − 28,750 | --- |
| United Kingdom | --- | 6 | --- | --- | − 6 | --- |
| TOTAL EUROPE | 916,755 | 872,532 | 56.6 | 52.7 | + 44,223 | + 5.1 |
| OTHERS | | | | | | |
| Japan | 15,283 | 15,703 | 1.0 | 1.0 | − 420 | − 2.7 |
| South Korea | 320 | --- | --- | --- | + 320 | --- |
| Formosa | --- | 115 | --- | --- | − 115 | --- |
| Australia | --- | 12 | --- | --- | − 12 | --- |
| TOTAL OTHERS | 15,603 | 15,830 | 1.0 | 1.0 | − 227 | − 1.4 |
| SHIP STORE | 2 | --- | --- | --- | + 2 | --- |
| TOTAL EXPORTS | 1,619,202 | 1,655,183 | 100.0 | 100.0 | − 35,981 | − 2.2 |

Source: Departamento Nacional del Café.

(*) Includes green equivalent of soluble coffee 20,703 bags (10,651); green coffee exports totaled 1,598,499 bags (1,644,532).

A-32

## EQ-8A. EL SALVADOR: EXPORTS OF GREEN COFFEE, 1960-1965
(Bags of 60 kilograms or 132.276 pounds each)

| COUNTRIES OF DESTINATION | 1960 | 1961 | 1962 | 1963 | 1964 | 1965 |
|---|---|---|---|---|---|---|
| **UNITED STATES** | 371,424 | 666,893 | 670,242 | 670,516 | 688,379 | 738,703 |
| **CANADA** | 4,542 | 12,026 | 13,024 | 12,794 | 26,191 | 27,502 |
| **OTHER AMERICAS** | | | | | | |
|   Chile | 230 | — | — | — | — | — |
|   Puerto Rico | — | — | — | 1 | — | — |
|   Nicaragua | — | — | 18,856 | — | — | — |
|   Peru | — | — | 12 | — | — | 7 |
|   Honduras | — | — | — | 240 | 298 | 216 |
|   British Honduras | — | — | — | 93 | 141 | 156 |
|   Guatemala | — | — | — | 147 | 7 | 144 |
|   Costa Rica | — | — | — | — | 14 | 93 |
|   Panama | — | — | — | — | 2,942 | — |
| **TOTAL OTHER AMERICAS** | 230 | — | 18,868 | 481 | 3,402 | 616 |
| **EUROPE** | | | | | | |
|   Germany (F.R.) | 657,651 | 641,687 | 657,099 | 645,268 | 845,740 | 710,783 |
|   Netherlands | 51,136 | 45,818 | 40,327 | 59,741 | 47,288 | 55,639 |
|   Sweden | 29,659 | 16,784 | 34,471 | 31,107 | 20,067 | 15,294 |
|   Belgium | 17,657 | 19,176 | 16,655 | 23,503 | 30,650 | 28,722 |
|   Italy | 13,442 | 7,866 | 6,586 | 5,253 | 4,785 | 3,513 |
|   Switzerland | 8,658 | 14,775 | 5,023 | 9,564 | 12,824 | 8,271 |
|   Spain | 8,334 | 5 | 3,412 | — | 5,004 | 4,601 |
|   Norway | 5,348 | 2,432 | 5,945 | 4,899 | 7,474 | 4,375 |
|   United Kingdom | 1,955 | — | 805 | — | 120 | 6 |
|   Finland | 1,035 | 1,524 | 3,622 | 4,485 | 21,603 | 8,625 |
|   Bulgaria | 402 | — | — | — | — | — |
|   Austria | 293 | 236 | 609 | 402 | 4,740 | 1,727 |
|   France | 230 | — | 173 | 230 | 231 | 58 |
|   Poland | — | — | — | — | — | 28,750 |
|   Czechoslovakia | — | — | — | — | — | 2,168 |
| **TOTAL EUROPE** | 795,800 | 750,303 | 774,727 | 784,452 | 1,000,526 | 872,532 |
| **OTHERS** | | | | | | |
|   Philippine Republic | 5,888 | 1,208 | — | — | — | — |
|   Japan | 276 | 95 | 1,341 | 116,642 | 35,719 | 15,703 |
|   Australia | — | — | — | 690 | 837 | 12 |
|   Formosa | — | — | — | — | — | 115 |
|   Various | 18 | — | — | — | — | — |
| **TOTAL OTHERS** | 6,182 | 1,303 | 1,341 | 117,332 | 36,556 | 15,830 |
| **TOTAL EXPORTS** | 1,178,178 | 1,430,525 | 1,478,202 | 1,585,575 | 1,755,054 | 1,655,183 |

Source: Departamento Nacional del Café.

## EQ-9. GUATEMALA: EXPORTS OF GREEN COFFEE,* 1965-1966
(Bags of 60 kilograms or 132.276 pounds each)

| COUNTRIES OF DESTINATION | 1966 | 1965 | Percent of Total 1966 | Percent of Total 1965 | Increase or Decrease 1966 over 1965 VOLUME | PERCENT |
|---|---|---|---|---|---|---|
| UNITED STATES | 1,047,942 | 846,787 | 56.2 | 56.0 | + 201,155 | + 23.8 |
| CANADA | 9,830 | 8,746 | 0.5 | 0.6 | + 1,084 | + 12.4 |
| OTHER AMERICAS | | | | | | |
| British Honduras | 345 | 419 | — | — | — 74 | — 17.7 |
| Honduras | — | 3 | — | — | — 3 | — — — |
| Puerto Rico | — | 1 | — | — | — 1 | — — — |
| TOTAL OTHER AMERICAS | 345 | 423 | — | — | — 78 | — 18.4 |
| EUROPE | | | | | | |
| Germany (F.R.) | 357,438 | 284,484 | 19.2 | 18.8 | + 72,954 | + 25.6 |
| Netherlands | 83,272 | 78,044 | 4.5 | 5.2 | + 5,228 | + 6.7 |
| Finland | 47,017 | 18,758 | 2.5 | 1.2 | + 28,259 | + 150.7 |
| Belgium | 33,700 | 31,235 | 1.8 | 2.1 | + 2,465 | + 7.9 |
| Sweden | 21,883 | 13,165 | 1.2 | 0.9 | + 8,718 | + 66.2 |
| Spain | 16,946 | 16,667 | 0.9 | 1.1 | + 279 | + 1.7 |
| Switzerland | 13,508 | 13,066 | 0.7 | 0.9 | + 442 | + 3.4 |
| Italy | 11,656 | 8,181 | 0.6 | 0.5 | + 3,475 | + 42.5 |
| Norway | 10,131 | 11,911 | 0.5 | 0.8 | − 1,780 | − 14.9 |
| Denmark | 5,063 | 5,188 | 0.3 | 0.4 | − 125 | − 2.4 |
| France | 4,564 | 1,928 | 0.2 | 0.1 | + 2,636 | + 136.7 |
| United Kingdom | 2,714 | 1,892 | 0.1 | 0.1 | + 822 | + 43.4 |
| Austria | 1,484 | 1,978 | 0.1 | 0.1 | + 494 | + 25.0 |
| Eire | 58 | 52 | — | — | + 6 | + 11.5 |
| Monaco | — | 1 | — | — | − 1 | — — — |
| TOTAL EUROPE | 609,434 | 486,550 | 32.8 | 32.2 | + 122,884 | + 25.3 |
| OTHERS | | | | | | |
| Jordan | 57,989 | 53,302 | 3.1 | 3.5 | + 4,687 | + 8.8 |
| South Africa | 39,897 | 72,140 | 2.1 | 4.8 | − 32,243 | − 44.7 |
| Kuwait | 28,592 | — | 1.5 | — | + 28,592 | — — — |
| Sudan | 25,875 | 7,603 | 1.4 | 0.5 | + 18,272 | + 240.3 |
| Japan | 23,619 | 25,296 | 1.3 | 1.7 | − 1,677 | − 6.6 |
| Malaysia | 9,775 | 5,750 | 0.5 | 0.4 | + 4,025 | + 70.0 |
| Saudi Arabia | 8,821 | 802 | 0.5 | 0.1 | + 8,019 | + 999.9 |
| Iran | 1,150 | — | 0.1 | — | + 1,150 | — — — |
| Bahrein | 254 | — | — | — | + 254 | — — — |
| New Zealand | 230 | 322 | — | — | − 92 | − 28.6 |
| Formosa | 174 | — | — | — | + 174 | — — — |
| Ceylon | — | 3,507 | — | 0.2 | − 3,507 | — — — |
| Australia | — | 46 | — | — | − 46 | — — — |
| TOTAL OTHERS | 196,376 | 168,768 | 10.5 | 11.2 | + 27,608 | + 16.4 |
| TOTAL EXPORTS | 1,863,927 | 1,511,274 | 100.0 | 100.0 | + 352,653 | + 23.3 |

Source: Asociación Nacional del Café.

(*) Includes green equivalent of soluble coffee 44,935 bags (9,554); green coffee exports totaled 1,818,992 bags (1,501,720).

## EQ-9A. GUATEMALA: EXPORTS OF GREEN COFFEE, 1960-1965

(Bags of 60 kilograms or 132.276 pounds each)

| COUNTRIES OF DESTINATION | 1960 | 1961 | 1962 | 1963 | 1964 | 1965 |
|---|---|---|---|---|---|---|
| UNITED STATES | 825,014 | 791,895 | 745,972 | 1,107,607 | 890,585 | 846,787 |
| CANADA | 4,054 | 5,882 | 8,061 | 6,855 | 3,506 | 8,746 |
| **OTHER AMERICAS** | | | | | | |
| Jamaica | — | — | — | — | 47 | — |
| British Honduras | — | — | — | — | 36 | 419 |
| Honduras | — | — | — | — | — | 3 |
| Puerto Rico | — | — | — | — | — | 1 |
| TOTAL OTHER AMERICAS | — | — | — | — | 83 | 423 |
| **EUROPE** | | | | | | |
| Germany (F.R.) | 311,913 | 264,434 | 430,088 | 307,899 | 319,097 | 284,484 |
| Netherlands | 61,998 | 62,400 | 106,342 | 107,278 | 108,818 | 78,044 |
| Sweden | 41,495 | 60,542 | 51,943 | 22,253 | 12,524 | 13,165 |
| Belgium | 33,734 | 27,857 | 47,145 | 44,661 | 38,490 | 31,235 |
| Italy | 18,769 | 9,923 | 27,903 | 14,104 | 8,211 | 8,181 |
| Spain | 9,672 | 8,336 | 4,167 | 4,361 | 2,117 | 16,667 |
| Switzerland | 5,688 | 1,925 | 18,725 | 11,593 | 11,696 | 13,066 |
| Denmark | 3,644 | 3,282 | 4,793 | 4,862 | 5,277 | 5,188 |
| Norway | 3,077 | 2,886 | 8,856 | 5,482 | 7,173 | 11,911 |
| United Kingdom | 2,599 | 1,303 | 9,476 | 8,561 | 734 | 1,892 |
| Austria | 1,633 | 1,643 | 2,283 | 2,496 | 3,439 | 1,978 |
| France | 1,073 | 1,923 | 1,379 | 1,617 | 2,855 | 1,928 |
| Finland | 690 | 4,821 | 11,039 | 12,034 | 23,341 | 18,758 |
| Gibraltar | 115 | — | — | — | — | — |
| Ireland | — | 52 | 144 | 167 | 172 | 52 |
| Bulgaria | — | — | 2,435 | — | — | — |
| Rumania | — | — | 1,455 | — | — | — |
| Monaco | — | — | — | — | — | 1 |
| TOTAL EUROPE | 496,100 | 451,327 | 728,173 | 547,368 | 543,944 | 486,550 |
| **OTHERS** | | | | | | |
| Japan | 3,993 | 6,168 | 59,673 | 5,109 | 4,092 | 25,296 |
| Australia | 52 | 14 | — | 30 | 59 | 46 |
| South Africa | 57 | — | 3,011 | — | 370 | 72,140 |
| New Zealand | — | 98 | — | — | 115 | 322 |
| Formosa | — | — | 7,000 | — | — | — |
| Syria | — | — | — | 57 | — | — |
| Jordan | — | — | — | — | 3,450 | 53,302 |
| Sudan | — | — | — | — | — | 7,603 |
| Malaysia | — | — | — | — | — | 5,750 |
| Ceylon | — | — | — | — | — | 3,507 |
| Saudi Arabia | — | — | — | — | — | 802 |
| TOTAL OTHERS | 4,102 | 6,280 | 69,684 | 5,196 | 8,086 | 168,768 |
| **TOTAL EXPORTS** | 1,329,270 | 1,255,384 | 1,551,890 | 1,667,026 | 1,446,204 | 1,511,274 |

Source: Asociación Nacional del Café.

## EQ-10. MEXICO: EXPORTS OF GREEN COFFEE,* 1965-1966

(Bags of 60 kilograms or 132.276 pounds each)

| COUNTRIES OF DESTINATION | 1966 | 1965 | Percent of Total 1966 | Percent of Total 1965 | Increase or Decrease 1966 over 1965 VOLUME | Increase or Decrease 1966 over 1965 PERCENT |
|---|---|---|---|---|---|---|
| UNITED STATES | 1,083,922 | 1,133,596 | 70.5 | 85.4 | − 49,674 | − 4.4 |
| CANADA | 12,193 | 29,379 | 0.8 | 2.2 | − 17,186 | − 58.5 |
| OTHER AMERICAS | | | | | | |
| Chile | — | 345 | — | — | − 345 | − --- |
| EUROPE | | | | | | |
| Spain | 99,571 | 2,875 | 6.5 | 0.2 | + 96,696 | + (o) |
| Germany (F.R.) | 97,240 | 105,472 | 6.3 | 8.0 | − 8,232 | − 7.8 |
| Rumania | 48,423 | — | 3.2 | — | + 48,423 | + --- |
| Hungary | 34,500 | — | 2.3 | — | + 34,500 | + --- |
| Poland | 21,850 | 5,000 | 1.4 | 0.4 | + 16,850 | +337.0 |
| Netherlands | 17,055 | 13,229 | 1.1 | 1.1 | + 3,826 | + 28.9 |
| Belgium | 15,371 | 21,254 | 1.0 | 1.6 | − 5,883 | − 27.7 |
| Italy | 6,818 | 4,233 | 0.4 | 0.3 | + 2,585 | + 61.1 |
| Czechoslovakia | 5,335 | — | 0.4 | — | + 5,335 | + --- |
| France | 5,169 | 5,075 | 0.3 | 0.4 | + 94 | + 1.9 |
| United Kingdom | 2,472 | 288 | 0.2 | — | + 2,184 | +758.3 |
| Denmark | 1,153 | 1,382 | 0.1 | 0.1 | − 229 | − 16.6 |
| Finland | 575 | 431 | — | — | + 144 | + 33.4 |
| Norway | 409 | — | — | — | + 409 | + --- |
| Sweden | 57 | 315 | — | — | − 258 | − 81.9 |
| Switzerland | — | 73 | — | — | − 73 | − --- |
| **TOTAL EUROPE** | 355,998 | 159,627 | 23.2 | 12.1 | +196,371 | +123.0 |
| OTHERS | | | | | | |
| Japan | 84,169 | 3,224 | 5.5 | 0.3 | + 80,945 | + (o) |
| Australia | 150 | 867 | — | — | − 717 | − 82.7 |
| New Zealand | 57 | — | — | — | + 57 | + --- |
| **TOTAL OTHERS** | 84,376 | 4,091 | 5.5 | 0.3 | + 80,285 | + (o) |
| **TOTAL EXPORTS** | 1,536,489 | 1,327,038 | 100.0 | 100.0 | +209,451 | + 15.8 |

Source: Instituto Mexicano del Café.

(o) Increase over 1,000 percent.

(*) Includes green equivalent of soluble coffee 23,202 bags (182); green equivalent of roasted coffee 59,559 bags (49,515); green coffee exports totaled 1,453,728 bags (1,277,341).

## EQ-10A  MEXICO: EXPORTS OF GREEN COFFEE 1960-1965
(Bags of 60 kilograms or 132.276 pounds each)

| COUNTRIES OF DESTINATION | 1960 | 1961 | 1962 | 1963 | 1964 | 1965 |
|---|---|---|---|---|---|---|
| UNITED STATES | 1,127,712 | 1,333,923 | 1,304,451 | 934,914 | 1,487,870 | 1,133,596 |
| CANADA | 16,349 | 16,476 | 16,679 | 24,865 | 15,219 | 29,379 |
| **OTHER AMERICAS** | | | | | | |
| Guatemala | 358 | — | — | — | — | — |
| Honduras | — | 117 | — | — | — | — |
| Bahama Islands | — | — | — | 575 | — | — |
| Argentina | — | — | — | 403 | 1,322 | — |
| Chile | — | — | — | 115 | 230 | 345 |
| TOTAL OTHER AMERICAS | 358 | 117 | — | 1,093 | 1,552 | 345 |
| **EUROPE** | | | | | | |
| Germany (F.R.) | 141,168 | 89,311 | 64,259 | 115,852 | 113,658 | 105,472 |
| Spain | 42,342 | 55 | 3,868 | 46,185 | 66,257 | 2,875 |
| Switzerland | 29,699 | 24,833 | 52,744 | 35,397 | 3,583 | 73 |
| Netherlands | 9,533 | 8,701 | 4,779 | 7,483 | 9,331 | 13,229 |
| Belgium — Luxembourg | 8,001 | 2,916 | 2,170 | 9,041 | 22,388 | 21,254 |
| Sweden | 4,807 | 1,400 | 1,265 | 517 | 3,450 | 315 |
| United Kingdom | 1,267 | 230 | 1,265 | 259 | 115 | 288 |
| Czechoslovakia | 1,184 | — | — | 937 | 1,667 | — |
| Italy | 906 | 2,127 | 519 | 3,623 | 4,503 | 4,233 |
| France | 362 | 1,423 | 731 | 1,638 | 5,305 | 5,075 |
| Norway | 58 | — | — | 261 | 522 | — |
| Denmark | — | 922 | 1,311 | 2,937 | 2,759 | 1,382 |
| Finland | — | — | 766 | 540 | 1,955 | 431 |
| Ireland | — | — | 57 | — | — | — |
| Yugoslavia | — | — | — | 6,607 | 8,333 | — |
| Poland | — | — | — | 6,682 | 5,833 | 5,000 |
| TOTAL EUROPE | 239,327 | 131,918 | 133,734 | 237,959 | 249,659 | 159,627 |
| **OTHERS** | | | | | | |
| Japan | 93 | 350 | 2,587 | 172 | 18,195 | 3,224 |
| Israel | 2 | — | — | 2 | — | — |
| Australia | — | — | — | 74 | 69 | 867 |
| TOTAL OTHERS | 95 | 350 | 2,587 | 248 | 18,264 | 4,091 |
| TOTAL EXPORTS | 1,383,841 | 1,482,784 | 1,457,451 | 1,199,079 | 1,772,564 | 1,327,038 |

Source:  Instituto Mexicano del Café.

## EQ-11. VENEZUELA: EXPORTS OF GREEN COFFEE, 1965-1966

(Bags of 60 kilograms or 132.276 pounds each)

| COUNTRIES OF DESTINATION | 1966 | 1965 | Percent of Total 1966 | Percent of Total 1965 | Increase or Decrease 1966 over 1965 VOLUME | Increase or Decrease 1966 over 1965 PERCENT |
|---|---|---|---|---|---|---|
| **UNITED STATES** | 264,035 | 245,991 | 87.1 | 82.2 | + 18,044 | + 7.3 |
| **CANADA** | 26 | 494 | — | 0.2 | − 468 | − 94.7 |
| **OTHER AMERICAS** | | | | | | |
| Surinam | 427 | 498 | 0.1 | 0.2 | − 71 | − 14.3 |
| **EUROPE** | | | | | | |
| France | 10,166 | 16,222 | 3.4 | 5.4 | − 6,056 | − 37.3 |
| Germany (F.R.) | 8,816 | 8,933 | 2.9 | 3.0 | − 117 | − 1.3 |
| Denmark | 5,593 | 6,971 | 1.8 | 2.3 | − 1,378 | − 19.8 |
| Belgium | 5,187 | 3,746 | 1.7 | 1.3 | + 1,441 | + 38.5 |
| Netherlands | 5,182 | 3,041 | 1.7 | 1.0 | + 2,141 | + 70.4 |
| Czechoslovakia | 2,334 | 10,634 | 0.8 | 3.6 | − 8,300 | − 78.1 |
| Italy | 1,362 | 2,227 | 0.4 | 0.7 | − 865 | − 38.8 |
| Spain | 150 | 144 | 0.1 | — | + 6 | + 4.2 |
| Austria | — | 150 | — | 0.1 | − 150 | − --- |
| Switzerland | — | 101 | — | — | − 101 | − --- |
| Finland | — | 1 | — | — | − 1 | − --- |
| United Kingdom | — | 1 | — | — | − 1 | − --- |
| **TOTAL EUROPE** | 38,790 | 52,171 | 12.8 | 17.4 | − 13,381 | − 25.6 |
| **TOTAL EXPORTS** | 303,278 | 299,154 | 100.0 | 100.0 | + 4,124 | + 1.4 |

Source:  Ministerio de Agricultura y Cría, Dirección de Economía y Estadística Agropecuaria.

## EQ-11A. VENEZUELA: EXPORTS OF GREEN COFFEE, 1960-1965
(Bags of 60 kilograms or 132.276 pounds each)

| COUNTRIES OF DESTINATION | 1960 | 1961 | 1962 | 1963 | 1964 | 1965 |
|---|---|---|---|---|---|---|
| UNITED STATES | 358,612 | 351,204 | 257,119 | 315,566 | 261,833 | 245,991 |
| CANADA | — | 750 | 1,285 | 989 | 1,000 | 494 |
| **OTHER AMERICAS** | | | | | | |
| Netherlands West Indies | 61 | 92 | — | 356 | 359 | 498 |
| British West Indies | — | — | 5 | 5 | — | — |
| TOTAL OTHER AMERICAS | 61 | 92 | 5 | 361 | 359 | 498 |
| **EUROPE** | | | | | | |
| Germany (F.R.) | 16,914 | 20,981 | 24,973 | 17,843 | 14,155 | 8,933 |
| Denmark | 16,116 | 13,803 | 14,303 | 12,814 | 12,396 | 6,971 |
| France | 8,691 | 7,804 | 9,455 | 22,654 | 22,587 | 16,222 |
| Belgium | 4,706 | 3,975 | 6,891 | 6,743 | 6,695 | 3,746 |
| Netherlands | 1,700 | 2,562 | 1,024 | 10,480 | 5,285 | 3,041 |
| Italy | 704 | 3,532 | 2,078 | 969 | 1,205 | 2,227 |
| Sweden | — | 892 | 1,000 | 174 | — | — |
| Norway | — | 100 | — | — | — | — |
| Spain | — | 2 | — | 124 | 116 | 144 |
| Switzerland | — | — | 500 | 21 | — | 101 |
| Finland | — | — | 125 | 500 | 1 | 1 |
| United Kingdom | — | — | 2 | — | — | 1 |
| Czechoslovakia | — | — | — | 550 | 833 | 10,634 |
| Austria | — | — | — | 267 | 200 | 150 |
| TOTAL EUROPE | 48,831 | 53,651 | 60,351 | 73,139 | 63,473 | 52,171 |
| **OTHERS** | | | | | | |
| Saudi Arabia | 250 | — | — | — | — | — |
| Japan | 3 | — | 4 | — | — | — |
| Morocco | — | 39 | — | — | — | — |
| Syria | — | — | 104 | — | — | — |
| Australia | — | — | 85 | — | 200 | — |
| United Arab Republic | — | — | 1 | — | — | — |
| Hong Kong | — | — | — | — | 2 | — |
| TOTAL OTHERS | 253 | 39 | 194 | — | 202 | — |
| TOTAL EXPORTS | 407,757 | 405,736 | 318,954 | 390,055 | 326,867 | 299,154 |

Source: Ministerio de Agricultura y Cría, Dirección de Economía y Estadística Agropecuaria.

EQ-12. COSTA RICA: EXPORTS OF GREEN COFFEE, 1965-1966
(Bags of 60 kilograms or 132.276 pounds each)

| COUNTRIES OF DESTINATION | 1966 | 1965 | Percentage of Total 1966 | Percentage of Total 1965 | Increase or Decrease 1966 over 1965 VOLUME | Increase or Decrease 1966 over 1965 PERCENT |
|---|---|---|---|---|---|---|
| UNITED STATES | 245,001 | 316,975 | 27.2 | 40.0 | − 71,974 | − 22.7 |
| CANADA | 16,362 | 12,262 | 1.8 | 1.5 | + 4,100 | + 33.4 |
| OTHER AMERICAS | | | | | | |
| Nicaragua | — | 19 | — | — | − 19 | --- |
| EUROPE | | | | | | |
| Germany (F.R.) | 251,286 | 207,490 | 27.9 | 26.2 | + 43,796 | + 21.1 |
| Netherlands | 117,434 | 107,011 | 13.0 | 13.5 | + 10,423 | + 9.7 |
| Sweden | 77,836 | 47,465 | 8.7 | 6.0 | + 30,371 | + 64.0 |
| Belgium | 55,877 | 38,134 | 6.2 | 4.8 | + 17,743 | + 46.5 |
| Finland | 35,866 | 10,349 | 4.0 | 1.3 | + 25,517 | + 246.6 |
| Italy | 28,236 | 15,466 | 3.1 | 2.0 | + 12,770 | + 82.6 |
| France | 27,863 | 14,596 | 3.1 | 1.8 | + 13,267 | + 90.9 |
| Poland | 9,122 | — | 1.0 | — | + 9,122 | --- |
| Spain | 6,600 | 6,685 | 0.7 | 0.8 | − 85 | − 1.3 |
| Switzerland | 5,846 | 3,829 | 0.7 | 0.5 | + 2,017 | + 52.7 |
| United Kingdom | 5,278 | 5,378 | 0.6 | 0.7 | − 100 | − 1.9 |
| Denmark | 4,287 | 4,104 | 0.5 | 0.5 | + 183 | + 4.5 |
| Czechoslovakia | 2,739 | 708 | 0.3 | 0.1 | + 2,031 | + 286.9 |
| Austria | 1,088 | 1,267 | 0.1 | 0.2 | − 179 | − 14.1 |
| Eire | 317 | 144 | — | — | + 173 | + 120.1 |
| Norway | 57 | 229 | — | — | − 172 | − 75.1 |
| TOTAL EUROPE | 629,732 | 462,855 | 69.9 | 58.4 | +166,877 | + 36.1 |
| OTHERS | | | | | | |
| Japan | 7,465 | 207 | 0.8 | — | + 7,258 | + (o) |
| New Zealand | 557 | 198 | 0.1 | — | + 359 | + 181.3 |
| South Africa | 544 | 115 | 0.1 | — | + 429 | + 373.0 |
| Australia | 508 | 344 | 0.1 | 0.1 | + 164 | + 47.7 |
| Israel | 429 | — | — | — | + 429 | --- |
| Lebanon | — | 286 | — | — | − 286 | --- |
| TOTAL OTHERS | 9,503 | 1,150 | 1.1 | 0.1 | + 8,353 | + 726.3 |
| TOTAL EXPORTS | 900,598 | 793,261 | 100.0 | 100.0 | +107,337 | + 13.5 |

Source: Oficina del Café.
(o) Increase over 1,000 percent.

### EQ-12A. COSTA RICA: EXPORTS OF GREEN COFFEE, 1960-1965
(Bags of 60 kilograms or 132.276 pounds each)

| COUNTRIES OF DESTINATION | 1960 | 1961 | 1962 | 1963 | 1964 | 1965 |
|---|---|---|---|---|---|---|
| UNITED STATES | 273,692 | 361,281 | 351,036 | 318,450 | 272,156 | 316,975 |
| CANADA | 8,695 | 7,450 | 10,459 | 12,291 | 10,331 | 12,262 |
| **OTHER AMERICAS** | | | | | | |
| Chile | 34 | — | 96 | — | — | — |
| Nicaragua | — | — | — | 151 | — | 19 |
| TOTAL OTHER AMERICAS | 34 | — | 96 | 151 | — | 19 |
| **EUROPE** | | | | | | |
| Germany (F.R.) | 316,487 | 290,363 | 335,846 | 316,230 | 321,410 | 207,490 |
| Belgium | 48,547 | 32,556 | 30,346 | 43,515 | 31,120 | 38,134 |
| Netherlands | 44,495 | 61,188 | 82,967 | 111,967 | 103,909 | 107,011 |
| Italy | 25,203 | 30,364 | 26,809 | 30,662 | 20,238 | 15,466 |
| Switzerland | 14,875 | 8,263 | 5,109 | 9,403 | 11,210 | 3,829 |
| Sweden | 13,377 | 19,660 | 28,271 | 46,853 | 21,736 | 47,465 |
| United Kingdom | 9,618 | 7,268 | 8,606 | 7,997 | 3,884 | 5,378 |
| France | 4,356 | 6,018 | 7,417 | 11,519 | 12,436 | 14,596 |
| Austria | 2,076 | 115 | 918 | 539 | 356 | 1,267 |
| Czechoslovakia | 1,089 | — | — | — | — | 708 |
| Finland | 633 | 1,265 | 8,050 | 13,355 | 18,138 | 10,349 |
| Ireland | 463 | 34 | 29 | 117 | 86 | 144 |
| Denmark | 299 | 2,956 | 3,520 | 2,557 | 4,586 | 4,104 |
| Spain | — | 4,986 | — | — | 6,204 | 6,685 |
| Poland | — | 133 | — | 599 | — | — |
| Norway | — | 115 | 1,000 | 426 | 1,766 | 229 |
| Greece | — | — | — | 81 | — | — |
| Germany (D.R.) | — | — | — | — | 287 | — |
| TOTAL EUROPE | 481,518 | 465,284 | 538,888 | 595,820 | 557,366 | 462,855 |
| **OTHERS** | | | | | | |
| Japan | 864 | 461 | 1,061 | — | 544 | 207 |
| Australia | 359 | 429 | 458 | 568 | 109 | 344 |
| New Zealand | 246 | 237 | 117 | 441 | 255 | 198 |
| Israel | 172 | — | — | — | — | — |
| South Africa | 85 | 135 | 238 | 229 | 57 | 115 |
| Syria | — | — | — | 592 | — | — |
| Lebanon | — | — | — | — | — | 286 |
| TOTAL OTHERS | 1,726 | 1,262 | 1,874 | 1,830 | 965 | 1,150 |
| TOTAL EXPORTS | 765,665 | 835,277 | 902,353 | 928,542 | 840,818 | 793,261 |

Source: Oficina del Café.

## EQ-13. DOMINICAN REPUBLIC: EXPORTS OF GREEN COFFEE, 1965-1966

(Bags of 60 kilograms or 132.276 pounds each)

| COUNTRIES OF DESTINATION | 1966 | 1965* | Percentage of Total 1966 | 1965 | Increase or Decrease 1966 over 1965 VOLUME | PERCENT |
|---|---|---|---|---|---|---|
| UNITED STATES | 325,418 | 358,715 | 77.9 | 88.7 | − 33,297 | − 9.3 |
| CANADA | 3,125 | 1,875 | 0.7 | 0.5 | + 1,250 | + 66.7 |
| OTHER AMERICAS | | | | | | |
|   Netherlands West Indies | 46 | − | − | − | + 46 | + --- |
| EUROPE | | | | | | |
|   Italy | 26,761 | 8,104 | 6.4 | 2.0 | + 18,657 | + 230.2 |
|   France | 24,568 | 2,207 | 5.9 | 0.5 | + 22,361 | + (o) |
|   Netherlands | 16,980 | 7,640 | 4.1 | 1.9 | + 9,340 | + 122.3 |
|   Belgium | 5,590 | 2,408 | 1.3 | 0.6 | + 3,182 | + 132.1 |
|   Spain | 5,000 | 5,000 | 1.2 | 1.2 | − | − |
|   Hungary | 3,125 | − | 0.7 | − | + 3,125 | + --- |
|   United Kingdom | 1,938 | 1,375 | 0.5 | 0.3 | + 563 | + 40.9 |
|   Denmark | 1,700 | 625 | 0.4 | 0.2 | + 1,075 | + 172.0 |
|   Finland | 750 | − | 0.2 | − | + 750 | + --- |
|   Switzerland | 512 | 12,500 | 0.1 | 3.1 | − 11,988 | − 95.9 |
|   Germany (F.R.) | 250 | 125 | 0.1 | − | + 125 | + 100.0 |
|   Bulgaria | − | 1,875 | − | 0.5 | − 1,875 | − --- |
| TOTAL EUROPE | 87,174 | 41,859 | 20.9 | 10.3 | + 45,315 | + 108.3 |
| OTHERS | | | | | | |
|   Japan | 1,875 | 1,857 | 0.5 | 0.5 | + 18 | + 1.0 |
| TOTAL EXPORTS | 417,638 | 404,306 | 100.0 | 100.0 | + 13,332 | + 3.3 |

Source: Secretaría de Estado de Agricultura, Dirección General del Café y del Cacao.

(*) Revised.

(o) Increase over 1,000 percent.

## EQ-13A. DOMINICAN REPUBLIC: EXPORTS OF GREEN COFFEE, 1960-1965
(Bags of 60 kilograms or 132.276 pounds each)

| COUNTRIES OF DESTINATION | 1960 | 1961 | 1962 | 1963 | 1964 | 1965 |
|---|---|---|---|---|---|---|
| **UNITED STATES** | 413,412 | 281,537 | 416,614 | 397,938 | 517,191 | 295,860 |
| **CANADA** | 6,250 | 4,181 | 379 | 1,266 | 7,644 | 10,525 |
| **OTHER AMERICAS** | | | | | | |
| Netherlands West Indies | — | — | 48 | 165 | — | — |
| Puerto Rico | — | — | — | 101 | — | — |
| French West Indies | — | — | — | 124 | — | — |
| Others | — | — | 1,267 | — | — | — |
| TOTAL OTHER AMERICAS | — | — | 1,315 | 390 | — | — |
| **EUROPE** | | | | | | |
| Italy | 39,697 | 33,528 | 40,989 | 30,473 | 25,748 | 22,458 |
| Belgium | 9,140 | 6,459 | 6,384 | 5,586 | 5,558 | 5,393 |
| Netherlands | 6,287 | 5,301 | 8,331 | 7,997 | 4,980 | 1,817 |
| Germany (F.R.) | 2,376 | 602 | 1,336 | 506 | 885 | 389 |
| France | 1,005 | 2,087 | 11,005 | 7,079 | 7,224 | 7,083 |
| Austria | 787 | — | — | 253 | — | 2,677 |
| Sweden | 688 | — | — | — | — | — |
| Denmark | 500 | 634 | — | 3,635 | 2,475 | 2,379 |
| United Kingdom | 350 | 570 | 887 | 1,330 | 497 | 2,283 |
| Norway | 62 | — | — | — | — | — |
| Spain | — | — | 128 | — | — | 6,437 |
| Gibraltar | — | — | — | 254 | 118 | — |
| Switzerland | — | — | — | — | — | 2,290 |
| Hungary | — | — | — | — | — | 937 |
| Poland | — | — | — | — | — | 750 |
| TOTAL EUROPE | 60,892 | 49,181 | 69,060 | 57,113 | 47,485 | 54,893 |
| **OTHERS** | | | | | | |
| Morocco | — | — | — | 292 | 296 | — |
| South Africa | — | — | — | — | 63 | — |
| Philippine Republic | — | — | — | — | — | 7,500 |
| Japan | — | — | — | — | — | 6,687 |
| TOTAL OTHERS | — | — | — | 292 | 359 | 14,187 |
| **TOTAL EXPORTS** | 480,554 | 334,899 | 487,368 | 456,999 | 572,679 | 375,465 |

Source: Secretaria de Estado de Agricultura, Dirección General del Café y del Cacao.

pg. A-44—

## EQ-14. HONDURAS: EXPORTS OF GREEN COFFEE, 1965-1966
(Bags of 60 kilograms or 132.276 pounds each)

| COUNTRIES OF DESTINATION | 1966 | 1965* | Percentage of Total 1966 | Percentage of Total 1965 | Increase or Decrease 1966 over 1965 VOLUME | PERCENT |
|---|---|---|---|---|---|---|
| UNITED STATES | 244,694 | 285,525 | 65.1 | 70.1 | −40,831 | − 14.3 |
| CANADA | 351 | — | 0.1 | — | + 351 | + — |
| EUROPE | | | | | | |
| Germany (F.R.) | 81,443 | 84,225 | 21.7 | 20.7 | − 2,782 | − 3.3 |
| Netherlands | 18,573 | 10,827 | 4.9 | 2.6 | + 7,746 | + 71.5 |
| France | 13,215 | 1,457 | 3.5 | 0.4 | +11,758 | +807.0 |
| Italy | 5,375 | 4,243 | 1.4 | 1.0 | + 1,132 | + 26.7 |
| Finland | 4,888 | 6,900 | 1.3 | 1.7 | − 2,012 | − 29.2 |
| Switzerland | 4,859 | 8,351 | 1.3 | 2.0 | − 3,492 | − 41.8 |
| Belgium | 1,466 | 3,910 | 0.4 | 1.0 | − 2,444 | − 62.5 |
| Sweden | 402 | — | 0.1 | — | + 402 | + — |
| Spain | 354 | — | 0.1 | — | + 354 | + — |
| United Kingdom | 287 | 230 | 0.1 | 0.1 | + 57 | + 24.8 |
| Austria | 115 | 1,840 | — | 0.4 | − 1,725 | − 93.8 |
| TOTAL EUROPE | 130,977 | 121,983 | 34.8 | 29.9 | + 8,994 | + 7.4 |
| TOTAL EXPORTS | 376,022 | 407,508 | 100.0 | 100.0 | −31,486 | − 7.7 |

Source: Banco Nacional de Fomento.

(*) Revised.

A-44

EQ-14A.  HONDURAS:  EXPORTS OF GREEN COFFEE, 1960-1965
(Bags of 60 kilograms or 132.276 pounds each)

| COUNTRIES OF DESTINATION | 1960 | 1961 | 1962 | 1963 | 1964 | 1965 |
|---|---|---|---|---|---|---|
| UNITED STATES | 148,994 | 133,472 | 150,129 | 217,527 | 197,698 | 285,525 |
| CANADA | — | 525 | 1,393 | 1,898 | — | — |
| OTHER AMERICAS | | | | | | |
| El Salvador | 21,958 | 14,679 | 12 | — | — | — |
| British West Indies | — | — | — | — | — | — |
| TOTAL OTHER AMERICAS | 21,959 | 14,679 | 12 | — | — | — |
| EUROPE | | | | | | |
| Germany (F.R.) | 37,982 | 21,036 | 49,917 | 84,206 | 74,199 | 84,225 |
| Italy | 26,947 | 14,539 | 18,462 | 16,402 | 10,522 | 4,243 |
| Switzerland | 12,175 | 14,043 | 29,191 | 1,553 | 754 | 8,351 |
| United Kingdom | 3,128 | 5,398 | 3,939 | — | — | 230 |
| Netherlands | 2,762 | 2,988 | 7,698 | 12,125 | 9,424 | 10,827 |
| Belgium | 2,322 | 232 | — | — | 5,232 | 3,910 |
| Denmark | 1,314 | 1,258 | — | — | — | — |
| Norway | 399 | 142 | 47 | — | 402 | — |
| Trieste | 242 | — | — | — | — | — |
| Sweden | — | 350 | — | — | — | 1,457 |
| France | — | — | 350 | — | — | 1,840 |
| Austria | — | — | 105 | — | — | — |
| Spain | — | — | — | 83 | — | — |
| Finland | — | — | — | — | 10,350 | 6,900 |
| Greece | — | — | — | — | 230 | — |
| TOTAL EUROPE | 87,271 | 59,986 | 109,709 | 114,369 | 111,113 | 121,983 |
| OTHERS | | | | | | |
| Syria | — | — | 351 | — | — | — |
| Others | — | 869 | 4,616 | 489 | — | — |
| TOTAL OTHERS | — | 869 | 4,967 | 489 | — | — |
| TOTAL EXPORTS | 258,224 | 209,531 | 266,210 | 334,283 | 308,811 | 407,508 |

Source:  Direccion General de Estadistica; Oficina del Café; Banco Nacional de Fomento.

A-45

EQ-15.  HAITI:  EXPORTS OF GREEN COFFEE, 1965-1966

(Bags of 60 kilograms or 132.276 pounds each)

| COUNTRIES OF DESTINATION | 1966 | 1965 | Percentage of Total 1966 | Percentage of Total 1965 | Increase or Decrease 1966 over 1965 VOLUME | Increase or Decrease 1966 over 1965 PERCENT |
|---|---|---|---|---|---|---|
| UNITED STATES | 85,825 | 110,086 | 24.5 | 27.6 | − 24,261 | − 22.0 |
| EUROPE | | | | | | |
| Belgium | 84,056 | 84,620 | 24.0 | 21.2 | − 564 | − 0.7 |
| Italy | 62,704 | 82,497 | 17.9 | 20.7 | − 19,793 | − 24.0 |
| France | 50,411 | 52,843 | 14.4 | 13.3 | − 2,432 | − 4.6 |
| Netherlands | 41,903 | 42,436 | 12.0 | 10.6 | − 533 | − 1.3 |
| Denmark | 11,685 | 11,684 | 3.3 | 2.9 | + 1 | − |
| Norway | 4,260 | 3,782 | 1.2 | 1.0 | + 478 | + 12.6 |
| Switzerland | 4,150 | 3,380 | 1.2 | 0.8 | + 770 | + 22.8 |
| Germany (F.R.) | 2,100 | 2,925 | 0.6 | 0.7 | − 825 | − 28.2 |
| Sweden | 1,250 | 2,230 | 0.4 | 0.6 | − 980 | − 43.9 |
| Finland | 25 | 50 | − | − | − 25 | − 50.0 |
| Poland | − | 1,500 | − | 0.4 | − 1,500 | --- |
| Spain | − | 100 | − | − | − 100 | --- |
| TOTAL EUROPE | 262,544 | 288,047 | 75.0 | 72.2 | − 25,503 | − 8.9 |
| OTHERS | | | | | | |
| Syria | 1,699 | 600 | 0.5 | 0.2 | + 1,099 | + 183.2 |
| Jordan | 161 | − | − | − | + 161 | --- |
| Japan | 5 | − | − | − | + 5 | --- |
| TOTAL OTHERS | 1,865 | 600 | 0.5 | 0.2 | + 1,265 | + 210.8 |
| TOTAL EXPORTS | 350,234 | 398,733 | 100.0 | 100.0 | − 48,499 | − 12.2 |

Source:  Office National Du Café.

## EQ-15A. HAITI: EXPORTS OF GREEN COFFEE, 1960-1965
(Bags of 60 kilograms or 132.276 pounds each)

| COUNTRIES OF DESTINATION | 1960 | 1961 | 1962 | 1963 | 1964 | 1965 |
|---|---|---|---|---|---|---|
| UNITED STATES | 60,450 | 85,365 | 139,224 | 112,893 | 114,446 | 110,086 |
| OTHER AMERICAS | — | — | — | — | 25 | — |
| **EUROPE** | | | | | | |
| Italy | 122,252 | 85,478 | 121,547 | 82,643 | 61,547 | 82,497 |
| Belgium | 114,761 | 77,038 | 111,596 | 94,081 | 92,164 | 84,620 |
| France | 38,512 | 40,060 | 65,344 | 35,022 | 36,665 | 52,843 |
| Netherlands | 18,565 | 30,177 | 38,474 | 34,909 | 41,582 | 42,436 |
| Denmark | 16,210 | 13,151 | 15,128 | 12,136 | 14,306 | 11,684 |
| Norway | 8,908 | 5,814 | 6,805 | 6,450 | 5,275 | 3,782 |
| Sweden | 3,893 | 2,373 | 1,828 | 2,175 | 2,595 | 2,230 |
| Switzerland | 2,700 | 2,655 | 5,805 | 3,525 | 4,350 | 3,380 |
| Germany (F.R.) | 2,200 | 2,545 | 1,525 | 715 | 2,700 | 2,925 |
| Austria | 975 | 1,100 | 550 | 300 | 250 | — |
| Czechoslovakia | 850 | — | — | 550 | — | — |
| Finland | — | 275 | 50 | — | — | 50 |
| United Kingdom | — | 200 | — | — | — | — |
| Spain | — | — | — | — | 250 | 100 |
| Poland | — | — | — | — | — | 1,500 |
| **TOTAL EUROPE** | 329,826 | 260,866 | 368,652 | 272,506 | 261,684 | 288,047 |
| **OTHERS** | | | | | | |
| Syria | 3,980 | 1,888 | 5,843 | 4,450 | 3,250 | 600 |
| Morocco | — | 175 | 47 | — | 250 | — |
| Japan | — | — | — | 30 | — | — |
| **TOTAL OTHERS** | 3,980 | 2,063 | 5,890 | 4,480 | 3,500 | 600 |
| **TOTAL EXPORTS** | 394,256 | 348,294 | 513,766 | 389,879 | 379,655 | 398,733 |

Source: Office National Du Café.

## EQ-16. NICARAGUA: EXPORTS OF GREEN COFFEE,* 1965-1966
(Bags of 60 kilograms or 132.276 pounds each)

| COUNTRIES OF DESTINATION | 1966 | 1965 | Percent of Total 1966 | Percent of Total 1965 | Increase or Decrease 1966 over 1965 VOLUME | PERCENT |
|---|---|---|---|---|---|---|
| UNITED STATES | 157,152 | 285,748 | 37.3 | 56.2 | − 128,596 | − 45.0 |
| CANADA | 725 | 1,725 | 0.2 | 0.3 | − 1,000 | − 58.0 |
| OTHER AMERICAS | | | | | | |
| Guatemala | 402 | 11 | 0.1 | — | + 391 | + (o) |
| Honduras | 15 | — | — | — | + 15 | + — |
| Costa Rica | — | 88 | — | — | − 88 | − — |
| TOTAL OTHER AMERICAS | 417 | 99 | 0.1 | — | + 318 | + 321.2 |
| EUROPE | | | | | | |
| Germany (F.R.) | 150,173 | 133,848 | 35.7 | 26.3 | + 16,325 | + 12.2 |
| Netherlands | 58,621 | 45,186 | 13.9 | 8.9 | + 13,435 | + 29.7 |
| Belgium | 34,832 | 26,985 | 8.3 | 5.3 | + 7,847 | + 29.1 |
| Italy | 13,997 | 11,074 | 3.3 | 2.2 | + 2,923 | + 26.4 |
| United Kingdom | 1,955 | 288 | 0.5 | 0.1 | + 1,667 | + 578.8 |
| Switzerland | 1,843 | — | 0.4 | — | + 1,843 | + — |
| France | 1,409 | 977 | 0.3 | 0.2 | + 432 | + 44.2 |
| Austria | 202 | — | — | — | + 202 | + — |
| Norway | 173 | — | — | — | + 173 | + — |
| Sweden | 115 | 1,207 | — | 0.2 | − 1,092 | − 90.5 |
| Finland | — | 250 | — | 0.1 | − 250 | − — |
| TOTAL EUROPE | 263,320 | 219,815 | 62.4 | 43.3 | + 43,505 | + 19.8 |
| OTHERS | | | | | | |
| Syria | — | 632 | — | 0.1 | − 632 | − — |
| Japan | — | 173 | — | 0.1 | − 173 | − — |
| TOTAL OTHERS | — | 805 | — | 0.2 | − 805 | − — |
| TOTAL EXPORTS | 421,614 | 508,192 | 100.0 | 100.0 | − 86,578 | − 17.0 |

Source: Instituto Nicaraguense del Café.
(o) Increase over 1,000 percent.
(*) Includes green equivalent of soluble coffee 20,561 bags (26,481); green coffee exports totaled 401,053 bags (481,711).

A-48

## EQ-16A. NICARAGUA: EXPORTS OF GREEN COFFEE, 1960-1965

(Bags of 60 kilograms or 132.276 pounds each)

| COUNTRIES OF DESTINATION | 1960 | 1961 | 1962 | 1963 | 1964 | 1965 |
|---|---|---|---|---|---|---|
| UNITED STATES | 187,554 | 208,848 | 187,966 | 278,580 | 188,357 | 285,748 |
| CANADA | 1,227 | 574 | 552 | 523 | 1,440 | 1,725 |
| OTHER AMERICAS | | | | | | |
| Chile | 114 | 115 | — | — | — | — |
| Costa Rica | — | — | — | — | 51 | 88 |
| Guatemala | — | — | — | — | — | 11 |
| TOTAL OTHER AMERICAS | 114 | 115 | — | — | 51 | 99 |
| EUROPE | | | | | | |
| Germany (F.R.) | 100,991 | 78,836 | 79,869 | 108,691 | 169,987 | 133,848 |
| Netherlands | 30,767 | 29,091 | 35,128 | 32,957 | 37,505 | 45,186 |
| Italy | 19,949 | 7,985 | 14,253 | 10,148 | 7,618 | 11,074 |
| Belgium | 15,967 | 17,515 | 13,126 | 20,713 | 20,709 | 26,985 |
| France | 2,205 | 548 | 1,125 | 517 | 863 | 977 |
| Austria | 1,144 | 574 | 72 | 172 | 86 | — |
| United Kingdom | 403 | — | 230 | 575 | 57 | 288 |
| Sweden | 389 | 1,380 | 376 | 117 | 1,786 | 1,207 |
| Trieste | — | 2,168 | 230 | 1,764 | — | — |
| Finland | — | 894 | 3,450 | 805 | 264 | 250 |
| Switzerland | — | 800 | — | 11,309 | — | — |
| TOTAL EUROPE | 171,815 | 139,791 | 147,859 | 187,768 | 238,875 | 219,815 |
| OTHERS | | | | | | |
| Japan | 282 | 86 | 812 | — | 345 | 173 |
| Syria | 92 | — | 1,182 | — | 517 | 632 |
| Lebanon | 58 | — | — | — | — | — |
| TOTAL OTHERS | 432 | 86 | 1,994 | — | 862 | 805 |
| TOTAL EXPORTS | 361,142 | 349,414 | 338,371 | 466,871 | 429,585 | 508,192 |

Source: Instituto Nicaraguense del Café.

## EQ-17. ECUADOR: EXPORTS OF GREEN COFFEE, 1965-1966

(Bags of 60 kilograms or 132.276 pounds each)

| COUNTRIES OF DESTINATION | 1966 | 1965 | Percentage of Total 1966 | Percentage of Total 1965 | Increase or Decrease 1966 over 1965 VOLUME | Increase or Decrease 1966 over 1965 PERCENT |
|---|---|---|---|---|---|---|
| UNITED STATES | 422,052 | 513,337 | 58.0 | 67.2 | − 91,285 | − 17.8 |
| CANADA | 290 | 696 | − | 0.1 | − 406 | − 58.3 |
| OTHER AMERICAS | | | | | | |
| Chile | 5,543 | 2,200 | 0.8 | 0.3 | + 3,343 | + 152.0 |
| Uruguay | 1,917 | 1,008 | 0.3 | 0.1 | + 909 | + 90.2 |
| Argentina | 1,097 | 1,624 | 0.1 | 0.2 | − 527 | − 32.5 |
| Netherlands West Indies | 433 | 19 | 0.1 | − | + 414 | + (o) |
| Nicaragua | − | 1,044 | − | 0.1 | − 1,044 | − --- |
| TOTAL OTHER AMERICAS | 8,990 | 5,895 | 1.3 | 0.7 | + 3,095 | + 52.5 |
| EUROPE | | | | | | |
| France | 71,732 | 50,915 | 9.9 | 6.7 | + 20,817 | + 40.9 |
| Germany (F.R.) | 46,065 | 94,977 | 6.3 | 12.4 | − 48,912 | − 51.5 |
| Italy | 32,778 | 31,443 | 4.5 | 4.1 | + 1,335 | + 4.2 |
| Netherlands | 24,688 | 41,083 | 3.4 | 5.4 | − 16,395 | − 39.9 |
| Hungary | 23,000 | − | 3.2 | − | + 23,000 | + --- |
| Spain | 9,406 | 9,179 | 1.3 | 1.2 | + 227 | + 2.5 |
| Sweden | 7,431 | 9,628 | 1.0 | 1.3 | − 2,197 | − 22.8 |
| Belgium | 4,845 | 1,659 | 0.7 | 0.2 | + 3,186 | + 192.0 |
| Switzerland | 1,376 | 3,601 | 0.2 | 0.5 | − 2,225 | − 61.8 |
| United Kingdom | 288 | − | − | − | + 288 | + --- |
| Denmark | 144 | − | − | − | + 144 | + --- |
| Finland | 35 | − | − | − | + 35 | + --- |
| Gibraltar | − | 290 | − | − | − 290 | − --- |
| Norway | − | 232 | − | − | − 232 | − --- |
| TOTAL EUROPE | 221,788 | 243,007 | 30.5 | 31.8 | − 21,219 | − 8.7 |
| OTHERS | | | | | | |
| South Africa | 50,600 | − | 6.9 | − | + 50,600 | + --- |
| Kuwait | 23,575 | − | 3.2 | − | + 23,575 | + --- |
| Japan | 575 | − | 0.1 | − | + 575 | + --- |
| North Africa | 186 | − | − | − | + 186 | + --- |
| Syria | − | 1,160 | − | 0.2 | − 1,160 | − --- |
| TOTAL OTHERS | 74,936 | 1,160 | 10.2 | 0.2 | + 73,776 | + (o) |
| TOTAL EXPORTS | 728,056 | 764,095 | 100.0 | 100.0 | − 36,039 | − 4.7 |

Source: Banco Central del Ecuador.

(o) Increase over 1,000 percent.

**EQ-17A. ECUADOR: EXPORTS OF GREEN COFFEE, 1960-1965**

(Bags of 60 kilograms or 132.276 pounds each)

| COUNTRIES OF DESTINATION | 1960 | 1961 | 1962 | 1963 | 1964 | 1965 |
|---|---|---|---|---|---|---|
| UNITED STATES | 319,022 | 191,402 | 373,182 | 295,798 | 232,827 | 513,337 |
| CANADA | 1,073 | 1,818 | 1,236 | 917 | 139 | 696 |
| **OTHER AMERICAS** | | | | | | |
| Chile | 332 | 1,271 | 302 | 1,139 | 1,598 | 2,200 |
| Netherlands West Indies | 314 | 559 | — | 532 | — | 19 |
| Surinam | — | — | 357 | — | — | — |
| Panama | — | — | — | — | 3,075 | — |
| Argentina | — | — | — | — | — | 1,624 |
| Nicaragua | — | — | — | — | — | 1,044 |
| Uruguay | — | — | — | — | — | 1,008 |
| TOTAL OTHER AMERICAS | 646 | 1,830 | 659 | 1,671 | 4,673 | 5,895 |
| **EUROPE** | | | | | | |
| France | 66,259 | 78,528 | 44,748 | 50,610 | 27,440 | 50,915 |
| Italy | 47,409 | 40,619 | 40,781 | 33,834 | 22,225 | 31,443 |
| Germany (F.R.) | 36,956 | 37,918 | 53,812 | 54,590 | 69,015 | 94,977 |
| Netherlands | 21,811 | 13,181 | 15,855 | 43,300 | 35,261 | 41,083 |
| Sweden | 12,368 | 5,904 | 4,902 | 1,624 | 2,668 | 9,628 |
| Belgium | 5,945 | 2,188 | 1,791 | 1,305 | 504 | 1,659 |
| United Kingdom | 1,983 | 538 | 1,926 | 116 | — | — |
| Greece | 1,702 | 1,412 | — | 522 | 3,973 | — |
| Switzerland | 805 | 348 | 464 | 232 | 464 | 3,601 |
| Norway | 575 | 377 | 609 | 835 | 696 | 232 |
| Denmark | 5 | — | 290 | 682 | 157 | — |
| Spain | — | 120 | 210 | 7,817 | 13,589 | 9,179 |
| Finland | — | 58 | 232 | 697 | — | — |
| Czechoslovakia | — | — | 842 | — | — | — |
| Ireland | — | — | 29 | — | — | — |
| Gibraltar | — | — | — | 2,267 | — | 290 |
| TOTAL EUROPE | 195,818 | 181,191 | 166,491 | 198,431 | 175,992 | 243,007 |
| **OTHERS** | | | | | | |
| Philippine Republic | 4,818 | 1,160 | 5,394 | — | 2,320 | — |
| Saudi Arabia | 667 | 420 | — | — | — | — |
| Algeria | — | 2,215 | 324 | — | — | — |
| Morocco | — | 886 | 3,749 | 1,758 | — | — |
| Israel | — | — | — | 504 | — | — |
| Syria | — | — | — | — | 1,454 | 1,160 |
| TOTAL OTHERS | 5,485 | 4,681 | 9,467 | 2,262 | 3,774 | 1,160 |
| TOTAL EXPORTS | 522,044 | 380,922 | 551,035 | 499,079 | 417,405 | 764,095 |

Source: Banco Central del Ecuador.

## EQ-18. PERU: EXPORTS OF GREEN COFFEE, 1965-1966
(Bags of 60 kilograms or 132.276 pounds each)

| COUNTRIES OF DESTINATION | 1966 | 1965 | Percentage of Total 1966 | Percentage of Total 1965 | Increase or Decrease 1966 over 1965 VOLUME | Increase or Decrease 1966 over 1965 PERCENT |
|---|---|---|---|---|---|---|
| UNITED STATES | 452,719 | 433,180 | 77.2 | 79.1 | + 19,539 | + 4.5 |
| CANADA | 6,206 | 2,650 | 1.1 | 0.5 | + 3,556 | + 134.2 |
| OTHER AMERICAS | | | | | | |
| Chile | 189 | 491 | --- | 0.1 | -- 302 | -- 61.5 |
| Argentina | -- | 551 | --- | 0.1 | -- 551 | --- |
| TOTAL OTHER AMERICAS | 189 | 1,042 | --- | 0.2 | -- 853 | -- 81.9 |
| EUROPE | | | | | | |
| Netherlands | 32,611 | 19,624 | 5.6 | 3.6 | + 12,987 | + 66.2 |
| Italy | 19,859 | 19,044 | 3.4 | 3.5 | + 815 | + 4.3 |
| Germany (F.R.) | 13,898 | 27,421 | 2.4 | 5.0 | -- 13,523 | -- 49.3 |
| Poland | 9,601 | -- | 1.6 | -- | + 9,601 | --- |
| France | 9,251 | 12,851 | 1.6 | 2.3 | -- 3,600 | -- 28.0 |
| Sweden | 8,812 | 10,880 | 1.5 | 2.0 | -- 2,068 | -- 19.0 |
| Finland | 6,937 | 2,993 | 1.2 | 0.5 | + 3,944 | + 131.8 |
| Belgium | 6,189 | 5,581 | 1.1 | 1.0 | + 608 | + 10.9 |
| United Kingdom | 1,517 | 1,960 | 0.3 | 0.4 | -- 443 | -- 22.6 |
| Austria | 115 | -- | -- | -- | + 115 | --- |
| Norway | 29 | 115 | -- | -- | -- 86 | -- 74.8 |
| Denmark | -- | 115 | -- | -- | -- 115 | --- |
| TOTAL EUROPE | 108,819 | 100,584 | 18.7 | 18.3 | + 8,235 | + 8.2 |
| OTHERS | | | | | | |
| Japan | 7,102 | 230 | 1.2 | -- | + 6,872 | + (o) |
| Lebanon | 6,545 | 5,740 | 1.1 | 1.0 | + 805 | + 14.0 |
| Jordan | 1,689 | 1,983 | 0.3 | 0.4 | -- 294 | -- 14.8 |
| Syria | 1,459 | 821 | 0.2 | 0.2 | + 638 | + 77.7 |
| South Africa | 1,396 | 406 | 0.2 | 0.1 | + 990 | + 243.8 |
| New Zealand | 229 | -- | -- | -- | + 229 | --- |
| Australia | 50 | 532 | -- | 0.1 | -- 482 | -- 90.6 |
| Libya | 50 | -- | -- | -- | + 50 | --- |
| Kuwait | -- | 467 | -- | 0.1 | -- 467 | --- |
| TOTAL OTHERS | 18,520 | 10,179 | 3.0 | 1.9 | + 8,341 | + 81.9 |
| TOTAL EXPORTS | 586,453 | 547,635 | 100.0 | 100.0 | + 38,818 | + 7.1 |

Source: Comité Cafetalero del Perú.
(o) Increase over 1,000 percent.

## EQ-18A. PERU: EXPORTS OF GREEN COFFEE, 1960-1965
(Bags of 60 kilograms or 132.276 pounds each)

| COUNTRIES OF DESTINATION | 1960 | 1961 | 1962 | 1963 | 1964 | 1965 |
|---|---|---|---|---|---|---|
| UNITED STATES | 331,943 | 390,125 | 467,932 | 492,814 | 563,957 | 433,180 |
| CANADA | 2,542 | 871 | 6,211 | 10,195 | 7,448 | 2,650 |
| **OTHER AMERICAS** | | | | | | |
| Argentina | 563 | 2,249 | — | — | 379 | 551 |
| Chile | 35 | 17 | 489 | 846 | 758 | 491 |
| Uruguay | — | 1,919 | 350 | — | — | — |
| Mexico | — | — | — | 583 | — | — |
| Malvina Islands | — | — | — | 223 | — | — |
| Others | — | — | 63 | 187 | — | — |
| TOTAL OTHER AMERICAS | 598 | 4,185 | 902 | 1,839 | 1,137 | 1,042 |
| **EUROPE** | | | | | | |
| Italy | 32,559 | 49,039 | 34,304 | 25,762 | 25,210 | 19,044 |
| Belgium | 18,998 | 31,023 | 16,462 | 9,770 | 5,042 | 5,581 |
| France | 18,644 | 30,180 | 10,738 | 16,166 | 7,909 | 12,851 |
| Netherlands | 11,572 | 15,096 | 19,510 | 24,464 | 16,528 | 19,624 |
| Germany (F.R.) | 10,506 | 15,966 | 22,364 | 26,367 | 27,059 | 27,421 |
| Sweden | 3,548 | 15,386 | 15,756 | 14,567 | 6,003 | 10,880 |
| United Kingdom | 1,836 | 1,687 | 8,007 | 3,846 | 1,237 | 1,960 |
| Austria | 125 | 58 | 233 | 350 | — | — |
| Norway | 87 | — | 2,100 | 2,475 | 174 | 115 |
| Finland | — | 1,555 | 8,816 | 30,852 | 26,363 | 2,993 |
| Switzerland | — | — | 178 | — | 1,627 | — |
| Denmark | — | — | 177 | 290 | — | 115 |
| Malta | — | — | 50 | — | — | — |
| Greece | — | — | — | 269 | — | — |
| Spain | — | — | — | 219 | — | — |
| Yugoslavia | — | — | — | — | 7 | — |
| TOTAL EUROPE | 97,875 | 159,990 | 138,695 | 155,397 | 117,159 | 100,584 |
| **OTHERS** | | | | | | |
| Japan | 3,966 | 2,920 | 3,445 | 349 | — | 230 |
| Lebanon | 1,316 | 1,840 | 3,383 | 2,944 | 4,374 | 5,740 |
| Syria | 758 | 688 | 2,454 | 2,648 | 1,119 | 821 |
| New Zealand | 594 | — | 170 | 118 | — | — |
| Australia | 327 | 119 | 251 | 565 | 350 | 532 |
| Israel | 312 | 875 | 237 | — | — | — |
| Algeria | — | 4,875 | — | — | — | — |
| Morocco | — | 253 | — | 754 | — | — |
| Philippine Republic | — | 59 | — | — | — | — |
| Kuwait | — | — | 257 | 257 | — | 467 |
| South Africa | — | — | — | — | 116 | 406 |
| Jordan | — | — | — | — | — | 1,983 |
| TOTAL OTHERS | 7,273 | 11,629 | 10,197 | 7,635 | 5,959 | 10,179 |
| TOTAL EXPORTS | 440,231 | 566,800 | 623,937 | 667,880 | 695,660 | 547,635 |

Source: Comité Cafetalero del Peru.

## EQ-20. PANAMA: EXPORTS OF GREEN COFFEE, 1965-1966

(Bags of 60 kilograms or 132.276 pounds each)

| COUNTRIES OF DESTINATION | 1966* | 1965 | Percentage of Total 1966 | Percentage of Total 1965 | Increase or Decrease 1966 over 1965 VOLUME | Increase or Decrease 1966 over 1965 PERCENT |
|---|---|---|---|---|---|---|
| UNITED STATES | 24,297 | 11,392 | 53.7 | 47.5 | + 12,905 | + 113.3 |
| EUROPE | | | | | | |
| Germany (F.R.) | 15,037 | 12,483 | 33.3 | 52.1 | + 2,554 | + 20.5 |
| Finland | 3,914 | — | 8.7 | — | + 3,914 | + --- |
| Austria | 1,869 | — | 4.1 | — | + 1,869 | + --- |
| Norway | 101 | — | 0.2 | — | + 101 | — --- |
| Italy | — | 101 | — | 0.4 | — 101 | — --- |
| TOTAL EUROPE | 20,921 | 12,584 | 46.3 | 52.5 | + 8,337 | + 66.3 |
| OTHERS | | | | | | |
| Israel | — | — | — | — | — | — --- |
| TOTAL EXPORTS | 45,218 | 23,977 | 100.0 | 100.0 | +21,241 | + 88.6 |

Source: Instituto Panameño del Café.

(*) Estimated.

**EQ-20A. PANAMA: EXPORTS OF GREEN COFFEE, 1960-1965**

(Bags of 60 kilograms or 132.276 pounds each)

| COUNTRIES OF DESTINATION | 1960 | 1961 | 1962 | 1963 | 1964 | 1965 |
|---|---|---|---|---|---|---|
| UNITED STATES | 17,733 | 2,701 | 5,406 | — | 1,858 | 11,392 |
| EUROPE | | | | | | |
| Germany (F.R.) | 3,276 | 2,777 | 14,708 | 5,020 | 22,857 | 12,483 |
| Netherlands | 125 | — | 6,252 | 859 | 153 | — |
| Belgium | — | — | 767 | — | — | — |
| Finland | — | — | — | 38 | — | — |
| Italy | — | — | — | — | — | 101 |
| TOTAL EUROPE | 3,401 | 2,777 | 21,727 | 5,917 | 23,010 | 12,584 |
| OTHERS | | | | | | |
| Israel | — | — | — | — | — | — |
| Others | — | — | — | 1,716 | — | — |
| TOTAL OTHERS | — | — | — | 1,716 | — | — |
| TOTAL EXPORTS | 21,134 | 5,478 | 27,133 | 7,633 | 24,868 | 23,977 |

Source: Instituto Panameño del Café.

A-55

EQ-21. ANGOLA: EXPORTS OF GREEN COFFEE, 1965-1966
(Bags of 60 kilograms or 132.276 pounds each)

| COUNTRIES OF DESTINATION | 1966 | 1965 | Percentage of Total 1966 | Percentage of Total 1965 | Increase or Decrease 1966 over 1965 VOLUME | Increase or Decrease 1966 over 1965 PERCENT |
|---|---|---|---|---|---|---|
| UNITED STATES | 1,281,762 | 1,319,494 | 48.7 | 48.6 | − 37,732 | − 2.9 |
| CANADA | 91,968 | 30,027 | 3.5 | 1.1 | + 61,941 | + 206.3 |
| EUROPE | | | | | | |
| Netherlands | 572,473 | 547,418 | 21.7 | 20.2 | + 25,055 | + 4.6 |
| Portugal | 224,479 | 222,152 | 8.5 | 8.2 | + 2,327 | + 1.0 |
| Germany (F.R.) | 97,415 | 75,644 | 3.7 | 2.8 | + 21,771 | + 28.8 |
| Belgium | 52,103 | 116,417 | 2.0 | 4.3 | − 64,314 | − 55.2 |
| Poland | 44,175 | 23,500 | 1.7 | 0.9 | + 20,675 | + 88.0 |
| Spain | 42,766 | 21,047 | 1.6 | 0.8 | + 21,719 | + 103.2 |
| Switzerland | 31,133 | 30,044 | 1.2 | 1.1 | + 1,089 | + 3.6 |
| United Kingdom | 25,911 | 9,474 | 1.0 | 0.3 | + 16,437 | + 173.5 |
| France | 20,443 | 243,149 | 0.8 | 9.0 | − 222,706 | − 91.6 |
| Finland | 13,693 | 12,090 | 0.5 | 0.4 | + 1,603 | + 13.3 |
| Denmark | 9,828 | 4,695 | 0.4 | 0.2 | + 5,133 | + 109.3 |
| Norway | 8,232 | 6,884 | 0.3 | 0.1 | + 1,348 | + 19.6 |
| Italy | 3,609 | 2,308 | 0.1 | 0.1 | + 1,301 | + 56.4 |
| Austria | 3,092 | 3,800 | 0.1 | 0.1 | − 708 | − 18.6 |
| Sweden | 167 | 11,037 | — | 0.4 | − 10,870 | − 98.5 |
| Greece | 75 | — | — | — | + 75 | --- |
| Hungary | — | 6,338 | — | 0.2 | − 6,338 | --- |
| TOTAL EUROPE | 1,149,594 | 1,335,997 | 43.6 | 49.2 | − 186,403 | − 14.0 |
| OTHERS | | | | | | |
| South Africa | 87,719 | 19,116 | 3.3 | 0.7 | + 68,603 | + 358.9 |
| Kuwait | 11,950 | 8,334 | 0.5 | 0.3 | + 3,616 | + 43.4 |
| Jordan | 7,272 | — | 0.3 | — | + 7,272 | --- |
| Australia | 1,251 | — | 0.1 | — | + 1,251 | --- |
| Japan | 917 | 1,900 | — | 0.1 | − 983 | − 51.7 |
| Southern Rhodesia | 450 | 91 | — | — | + 359 | + 394.5 |
| Southwest Africa | 48 | 7 | — | — | + 41 | + 585.7 |
| Guinea | — | 50 | — | — | − 50 | --- |
| TOTAL OTHERS | 109,607 | 29,498 | 4.2 | 1.1 | + 80,109 | + 271.6 |
| TOTAL EXPORTS | 2,632,931 | 2,715,016 | 100.0 | 100.0 | − 82,085 | − 3.0 |

Source: Instituto do Café de Angola.

## EQ-21A. ANGOLA: EXPORTS OF GREEN COFFEE, 1960-1965

(Bags of 60 kilograms or 132.276 pounds each)

| COUNTRIES OF DESTINATION | 1960 | 1961 | 1962 | 1963 | 1964 | 1965 |
|---|---|---|---|---|---|---|
| **UNITED STATES** | 761,466 | 1,087,105 | 1,360,852 | 1,073,412 | 1,212,369 | 1,319,494 |
| **CANADA** | 6,917 | 4,587 | 15,232 | 24,234 | 8,674 | 30,027 |
| **OTHER AMERICAS** | | | | | | |
| Chile | 1,768 | — | — | — | — | — |
| **EUROPE** | | | | | | |
| Netherlands | 311,998 | 463,616 | 511,788 | 609,745 | 502,428 | 547,418 |
| Portugal | 187,032 | 201,196 | 203,772 | 244,804 | 143,700 | 222,152 |
| Bulgaria | 43,055 | 1,751 | 84,069 | — | — | — |
| Germany (F.R.) | 27,575 | 51,170 | 79,693 | 108,818 | 81,315 | 75,644 |
| Belgium | 26,556 | 33,839 | 72,590 | 94,296 | 57,561 | 116,417 |
| Finland | 17,097 | 13,333 | 15,177 | 7,986 | 9,981 | 12,090 |
| U.S.S.R. | 11,738 | — | — | — | — | — |
| Switzerland | 11,585 | 31,564 | 25,319 | 34,740 | 32,583 | 30,044 |
| United Kingdom | 10,853 | 5,872 | 39,971 | 26,183 | 140,191 | 9,474 |
| Norway | 4,490 | 5,674 | 8,664 | 6,492 | 6,525 | 6,884 |
| France | 4,089 | 4,334 | 7,316 | — | 76,868 | 243,149 |
| Italy | 2,858 | 6,500 | 29,308 | 12,346 | 2,504 | 2,308 |
| Czechoslovakia | 2,527 | 1,627 | 1,348 | — | 500 | — |
| Germany (D.R.) | 2,368 | 2,640 | 1,667 | 1,667 | — | — |
| Austria | 710 | 1,205 | 4,050 | 6,071 | 3,335 | 3,800 |
| Denmark | 482 | 320 | 3,686 | 9,605 | 3,581 | 4,695 |
| Spain | — | 416 | 27,553 | 39,574 | 10,841 | 21,047 |
| Poland | — | 4,133 | — | 5,000 | — | 23,500 |
| Gibraltar | — | — | 6,170 | 8,327 | 1,668 | — |
| Greece | — | — | 4,229 | 1,502 | 251 | — |
| Sweden | — | — | 1,824 | 9,180 | 8,357 | 11,037 |
| Hungary | — | — | 933 | 1,745 | — | 6,338 |
| Ireland | — | — | 107 | 134 | — | — |
| **TOTAL EUROPE** | 665,013 | 829,190 | 1,129,234 | 1,228,215 | 1,082,189 | 1,335,997 |
| **AFRICA** | | | | | | |
| Portuguese Possessions | 8,598 | 10,475 | — | — | — | — |
| Morocco | 3,957 | — | 27,782 | 4,672 | — | — |
| Algeria | 1,646 | 93 | — | — | — | — |
| South Africa | 334 | 5,655 | 57,431 | 38,254 | 5,758 | 19,116 |
| Rhodesia & Nyasaland | 134 | 84 | 134 | 100 | 193 | 91 |
| Canary Islands | 34 | — | — | — | — | — |
| Tunisia | — | — | 11,676 | 15,012 | — | — |
| Southwest Africa | — | — | — | — | 29 | 7 |
| Guinea | — | — | — | — | — | 50 |
| **TOTAL AFRICA** | 14,703 | 16,307 | 97,023 | 58,038 | 5,980 | 19,264 |
| **ASIA & OCEANIA** | | | | | | |
| Iraq | 2,251 | 2,598 | — | 1,667 | — | — |
| Australia | 2,007 | — | — | 334 | — | — |
| New Zealand | 167 | — | — | — | — | — |
| Japan | 50 | 1,634 | 10,919 | 8,789 | — | 1,900 |
| Jordan | — | 417 | 585 | 1,919 | — | — |
| Kuwait | — | — | 5,838 | — | — | 8,334 |
| Israel | — | — | — | 167 | — | — |
| Lebanon | — | — | — | — | 167 | — |
| **TOTAL ASIA & OCEANIA** | 4,475 | 4,649 | 17,342 | 12,876 | 167 | 10,234 |
| **OTHERS*** | — | 34,125 | — | — | — | — |
| **TOTAL EXPORTS** | 1,454,342 | 1,975,963 | 2,619,683 | 2,396,775 | 2,309,379 | 2,715,016 |

Source: Instituto do Café de Angola.
(*) Destination unknown.

## EQ-22. KENYA: EXPORTS OF GREEN COFFEE, 1965-1966

(Bags of 60 kilograms or 132.276 pounds each)

| COUNTRIES OF DESTINATION | 1966 | 1965 | Percentage of Total 1966 | Percentage of Total 1965 | Increase or Decrease 1966 over 1965 VOLUME | Increase or Decrease 1966 over 1965 PERCENT |
|---|---|---|---|---|---|---|
| UNITED STATES | 162,284 | 41,805 | 17.9 | 6.6 | +120,479 | +288.2 |
| CANADA | 55,234 | 49,559 | 6.1 | 7.9 | + 5,675 | + 11.5 |
| EUROPE | | | | | | |
|   Germany (F.R.) | 302,851 | 259,080 | 33.3 | 41.1 | + 43,771 | + 16.9 |
|   Netherlands | 87,690 | 29,308 | 9.7 | 4.6 | + 58,382 | +199.2 |
|   Sweden | 79,046 | 65,083 | 8.7 | 10.3 | + 13,963 | + 21.5 |
|   United Kingdom | 75,799 | 62,938 | 8.4 | 10.0 | + 12,861 | + 20.4 |
|   Finland | 27,802 | 25,722 | 3.1 | 4.1 | + 2,080 | + 8.1 |
|   Italy | 12,710 | 7,789 | 1.4 | 1.2 | + 4,921 | + 63.2 |
|   Poland | 12,054 | 250 | 1.3 | — | + 11,804 | + (o) |
|   Czechoslovakia | 11,879 | 10,538 | 1.3 | 1.7 | + 1,341 | + 12.7 |
|   Norway | 8,747 | 7,664 | 1.0 | 1.2 | + 1,083 | + 14.1 |
|   U.S.S.R. | 5,082 | 6,788 | 0.6 | 1.1 | − 1,706 | − 25.1 |
|   Belgium | 3,590 | 1,172 | 0.4 | 0.2 | + 2,418 | +206.3 |
|   France | 3,326 | 2,360 | 0.4 | 0.4 | + 966 | + 40.9 |
|   Hungary | 3,275 | 7,381 | 0.4 | 1.2 | − 4,106 | − 55.6 |
|   Austria | 3,201 | 1,972 | 0.3 | 0.3 | + 1,229 | + 62.3 |
|   Switzerland | 596 | 1,568 | 0.1 | 0.2 | − 972 | − 62.0 |
|   Germany (D.R.) | 350 | — | — | — | + 350 | + --- |
|   Denmark | 134 | 315 | — | 0.1 | − 181 | − 57.5 |
|   Eire | 121 | 176 | — | — | − 55 | − 31.3 |
| TOTAL EUROPE | 638,253 | 490,104 | 70.4 | 77.7 | +148,149 | + 30.2 |
| AFRICA | | | | | | |
|   Somalia | 1,666 | 23 | 0.2 | — | + 1,643 | + (o) |
|   United Arab Republic | 146 | — | — | — | + 146 | + --- |
|   Seychelles | 15 | — | — | — | + 15 | + --- |
|   Rhodesia | — | 286 | — | — | − 286 | − --- |
|   Mozambique | — | 50 | — | — | − 50 | − --- |
| TOTAL AFRICA | 1,827 | 359 | 0.2 | — | + 1,468 | +408.9 |
| ASIA & OCEANIA | | | | | | |
|   Iraq | 10,214 | 4,584 | 1.1 | 0.7 | + 5,630 | +122.8 |
|   China | 8,489 | — | 0.9 | — | + 8,489 | + --- |
|   Saudi Arabia | 6,811 | 4,139 | 0.9 | 0.7 | + 2,672 | + 64.6 |
|   New Zealand | 4,699 | 3,020 | 0.5 | 0.5 | + 1,679 | + 55.6 |
|   Aden | 3,447 | 722 | 0.4 | 0.1 | + 2,725 | +377.4 |
|   Japan | 3,134 | 3,336 | 0.3 | 0.5 | − 202 | − 6.1 |
|   Australia | 2,886 | 5,439 | 0.3 | 0.9 | − 2,553 | − 46.9 |
|   Bahrein | 2,534 | 4,746 | 0.3 | 0.8 | − 2,212 | − 46.6 |
|   Kuwait | 2,507 | 2,622 | 0.3 | 0.4 | − 115 | − 4.4 |
|   Israel | 2,186 | 1,024 | 0.2 | 0.2 | + 1,162 | +113.5 |
|   Trucial States | 1,044 | 799 | 0.1 | 0.1 | + 245 | + 30.7 |
|   Muscat & Oman | 851 | — | 0.1 | — | + 851 | + --- |
|   Qatar | 510 | 430 | 0.1 | 0.1 | + 80 | + 18.6 |
|   Jordan | 200 | 17,636 | — | 2.8 | − 17,436 | − 98.9 |
|   Singapore | 25 | — | — | — | + 25 | + --- |
|   Lebanon | — | 85 | — | — | − 85 | − --- |
| TOTAL ASIA & OCEANIA | 49,537 | 48,582 | 5.4 | 7.8 | + 955 | + 2.0 |
| TOTAL EXPORTS | 907,135 | 630,409 | 100.0 | 100.0 | +276,726 | + 43.9 |

Source: Coffee Board of Kenya.

(o) Increase over 1,000 percent.

## EQ-22A. KENYA: EXPORTS OF GREEN COFFEE, 1960-1965

(Bags of 60 kilograms or 132.276 pounds each)

| COUNTRIES OF DESTINATION | 1960 | 1961 | 1962 | 1963 | 1964 | 1965 |
|---|---|---|---|---|---|---|
| UNITED STATES | 75,182 | 127,503 | 58,355 | 36,636 | 130,504 | 41,805 |
| CANADA | 25,939 | 42,614 | 28,436 | 25,700 | 30,363 | 49,559 |
| **EUROPE** | | | | | | |
| Germany (F.R.) | 219,947 | 189,594 | 242,591 | 242,918 | 240,165 | 259,080 |
| United Kingdom | 45,261 | 68,437 | 66,031 | 70,200 | 64,770 | 62,938 |
| Netherlands | 17,017 | 31,228 | 24,244 | 36,454 | 40,043 | 29,308 |
| Sweden | 15,583 | 23,905 | 21,804 | 41,354 | 57,533 | 65,083 |
| Italy | 11,162 | 12,212 | 11,483 | 12,199 | 7,534 | 7,789 |
| Finland | 3,582 | 3,919 | 4,829 | 11,489 | 18,422 | 25,722 |
| Belgium — Luxembourg | 1,544 | 1,261 | 309 | 2,889 | 1,754 | 1,172 |
| Ireland | 619 | 180 | 191 | 128 | 31 | 176 |
| U.S.S.R. | — | — | — | — | — | 6,788 |
| France | 180 | — | 802 | 1,645 | 1,839 | 2,360 |
| Norway | 108 | 189 | 853 | 3,218 | 4,163 | 7,664 |
| Greece | 40 | — | 173 | — | — | — |
| Denmark | — | 3 | — | 25 | — | 315 |
| Switzerland | — | 1,100 | 750 | 1,950 | 1,049 | 1,568 |
| Austria | 614 | 87 | 218 | 2,337 | 1,167 | 1,972 |
| Gibraltar | — | 85 | 2 | — | — | — |
| Hungary | — | — | — | 16,357 | 21,475 | 7,381 |
| Yugoslavia | — | — | — | 8,335 | 6,700 | — |
| Czechoslovakia | — | — | — | — | 10,963 | 10,538 |
| Poland | — | — | — | — | 13,501 | 250 |
| Others | 11,884 | — | — | — | — | — |
| **TOTAL EUROPE** | 327,541 | 332,200 | 374,280 | 451,498 | 491,109 | 490,104 |
| **AFRICA** | | | | | | |
| South Africa | 9,858 | 7,754 | 9,691 | 26,919 | — | — |
| Somaliland | 7,125 | 328 | 138 | 296 | 184 | 23 |
| Rhodesia & Nyasaland | 249 | 371 | 235 | 447 | 397 | 286 |
| Libya | 80 | — | — | — | 69 | — |
| Mozambique | 68 | — | 73 | 25 | 8,144 | 50 |
| Zanzibar | 25 | — | — | — | — | — |
| Sudan | — | — | 684 | 362 | — | — |
| South West Africa | — | — | 113 | 40 | — | — |
| Seychelles | — | — | — | 23 | — | — |
| **TOTAL AFRICA** | 17,405 | 8,453 | 10,934 | 28,112 | 8,794 | 359 |
| **ASIA & OCEANIA** | | | | | | |
| Australia | 14,911 | 11,536 | 3,247 | 3,516 | 1,683 | 5,439 |
| Saudi Arabia | 4,052 | 680 | 3,083 | 8,556 | 9,339 | 4,139 |
| New Zealand | 2,757 | 3,520 | 3,398 | 2,449 | 3,328 | 3,020 |
| Jordan | 223 | 300 | 2,305 | 9,118 | 7,284 | 17,636 |
| Israel | 129 | 1,720 | 2,626 | 742 | 1,662 | 1,024 |
| Japan | 50 | — | 100 | 3,500 | 5,942 | 3,336 |
| Lebanon | — | 211 | 100 | 40 | — | 85 |
| Aden | — | — | 1,508 | 273 | 100 | 722 |
| Kuwait | — | — | 749 | 1,698 | 1,667 | 2,622 |
| Bahrein | — | — | 836 | 2,880 | 5,781 | 4,746 |
| Muscat & Oman | — | — | 858 | 446 | — | — |
| Qatar | — | — | 267 | 1,094 | 911 | 430 |
| Philippine Republic | — | — | 1,150 | 1,400 | — | — |
| Iraq | — | — | 34 | 1,778 | 3,923 | 4,584 |
| Trucial Oman | — | — | 144 | 57 | 282 | 799 |
| Iran | — | — | — | 87 | — | — |
| Syria | — | — | — | 600 | — | — |
| Others | 8,774 | 6,870 | — | — | — | — |
| **TOTAL ASIA & OCEANIA** | 30,896 | 24,837 | 20,405 | 38,234 | 41,902 | 48,582 |
| **TOTAL EXPORTS** | 476,963 | 535,607 | 492,410 | 580,180 | 702,672 | 630,409 |

Source: Coffee Board of Kenya.

## EQ-23. TANZANIA: EXPORTS OF GREEN COFFEE, 1965-1966

(Bags of 60 kilograms or 132.276 pounds each)

| COUNTRIES OF DESTINATION | 1966 | 1965 | Percentage of Total 1966 | 1965 | Increase or Decrease 1966 over 1965 VOLUME | PERCENT |
|---|---|---|---|---|---|---|
| UNITED STATES | 246,410 | 133,690 | 29.0 | 28.2 | + 112,720 | + 84.3 |
| CANADA | 86,129 | 54,727 | 10.2 | 11.5 | + 31,402 | + 57.4 |
| EUROPE | | | | | | |
| Germany (F.R.) | 100,440 | 68,438 | 11.8 | 14.4 | + 32,002 | + 46.8 |
| United Kingdom | 66,603 | 26,683 | 7.8 | 5.6 | + 39,920 | +149.6 |
| Netherlands | 36,213 | 26,410 | 4.3 | 5.6 | + 9,803 | + 37.1 |
| Poland | 35,262 | 1,200 | 4.2 | 0.2 | + 34,062 | + (o) |
| Sweden | 32,790 | 22,649 | 3.9 | 4.8 | + 10,141 | + 44.8 |
| Spain | 22,496 | — | 2.6 | — | + 22,496 | --- |
| Italy | 14,026 | 9,317 | 1.7 | 2.0 | + 4,709 | + 50.5 |
| Germany (D.R.) | 12,101 | — | 1.4 | — | + 12,101 | --- |
| Belgium | 10,062 | 8,527 | 1.2 | 1.8 | + 1,535 | + 18.0 |
| Switzerland | 6,503 | 1,258 | 0.8 | 0.3 | + 5,245 | +416.9 |
| Rumania | 5,100 | — | 0.6 | — | + 5,100 | --- |
| U.S.S.R. | 3,409 | 3,400 | 0.4 | 0.7 | + 9 | + 0.3 |
| Hungary | 1,697 | — | 0.2 | — | + 1,697 | --- |
| Czechoslovakia | 1,695 | — | 0.2 | — | + 1,695 | --- |
| Austria | 1,684 | 786 | 0.2 | 0.2 | + 898 | +114.2 |
| Finland | 1,073 | 1,856 | 0.1 | 0.4 | − 783 | − 42.2 |
| Yugoslavia | 967 | — | 0.1 | — | + 967 | --- |
| Norway | 571 | 857 | 0.1 | 0.2 | − 286 | − 33.4 |
| France | 482 | 2,203 | 0.1 | 0.5 | − 1,721 | − 78.1 |
| Eire | 391 | 448 | — | 0.1 | − 57 | − 12.7 |
| Denmark | 250 | — | — | — | + 250 | --- |
| TOTAL EUROPE | 353,815 | 174,032 | 41.7 | 36.8 | +179,783 | +103.3 |
| AFRICA | | | | | | |
| Somalia | 989 | 240 | 0.1 | — | + 749 | +312.1 |
| Libya | 255 | 34 | — | — | + 221 | +650.0 |
| TOTAL AFRICA | 1,244 | 274 | 0.1 | — | + 970 | +354.0 |
| ASIA & OCEANIA | | | | | | |
| Saudi Arabia | 31,381 | 7,448 | 3.7 | 1.6 | + 23,933 | +321.3 |
| Jordan | 25,678 | 48,380 | 3.0 | 10.2 | − 22,702 | − 46.9 |
| Japan | 21,184 | 8,479 | 2.5 | 1.8 | + 12,705 | +149.8 |
| Bahrein | 17,391 | 8,586 | 2.0 | 1.8 | + 8,805 | +102.6 |
| China | 12,140 | 5,079 | 1.4 | 1.1 | + 7,061 | +139.0 |
| New Zealand | 11,818 | 5,946 | 1.4 | 1.2 | + 5,872 | + 98.8 |
| Kuwait | 8,700 | 4,550 | 1.0 | 1.0 | + 4,150 | + 91.2 |
| Iraq | 5,967 | 3,675 | 0.7 | 0.8 | + 2,292 | + 62.4 |
| Aden | 5,710 | 1,324 | 0.7 | 0.3 | + 4,386 | +331.3 |
| Australia | 5,215 | 4,597 | 0.6 | 1.0 | + 618 | + 13.4 |
| Syria | 5,113 | 696 | 0.6 | 0.1 | + 4,417 | +634.6 |
| Israel | 3,310 | 2,066 | 0.4 | 0.4 | + 1,244 | + 60.2 |
| Trucial States | 2,456 | 6,111 | 0.3 | 1.3 | − 3,655 | − 59.8 |
| Muscat & Oman | 2,281 | 2,394 | 0.3 | 0.5 | − 113 | − 4.7 |
| Qatar | 2,193 | 1,353 | 0.3 | 0.3 | + 840 | + 62.1 |
| Thailand | 850 | — | 0.1 | — | + 850 | --- |
| Lebanon | 158 | 445 | — | 0.1 | − 287 | − 64.5 |
| Hong Kong | 1 | — | — | — | + 1 | --- |
| TOTAL ASIA & OCEANIA | 161,546 | 111,129 | 19.0 | 23.5 | + 50,417 | + 45.4 |
| TOTAL EXPORTS | 849,144 | 473,852 | 100.0 | 100.0 | +375,292 | + 79.2 |

Source: Coffee Board of Kenya.
(o) Increase over 1,000 percent.

## EQ-23A. TANZANIA: EXPORTS OF GREEN COFFEE, 1960-1965

(Bags of 60 kilograms or 132.276 pounds each)

| COUNTRIES OF DESTINATION | 1960 | 1961 | 1962 | 1963 | 1964 | 1965 |
|---|---|---|---|---|---|---|
| UNITED STATES | 172,532 | 220,817 | 163,334 | 136,191 | 192,353 | 133,690 |
| CANADA | 22,016 | 23,418 | 19,718 | 33,523 | 40,472 | 54,727 |
| **EUROPE** | | | | | | |
| Germany (F.R.) | 75,726 | 64,419 | 83,706 | 82,256 | 87,898 | 68,438 |
| Netherlands | 45,163 | 35,229 | 46,839 | 35,442 | 44,052 | 26,410 |
| United Kingdom | 37,817 | 20,926 | 52,340 | 64,706 | 49,684 | 26,683 |
| Italy | 9,524 | 5,554 | 7,771 | 7,402 | 9,555 | 9,317 |
| Belgium — Luxembourg | 6,098 | 5,144 | 12,396 | 6,797 | 10,937 | 8,527 |
| Finland | 2,110 | 1,500 | 638 | 1,014 | 6,023 | 1,856 |
| Austria | 2,076 | 255 | 2,048 | 541 | 150 | 786 |
| Ireland | 1,649 | 976 | 1,227 | 1,122 | 355 | 448 |
| Switzerland | 213 | 150 | 1,100 | 1,040 | 2,333 | 1,258 |
| France | — | 926 | 2,205 | 621 | 613 | 2,203 |
| Sweden | 1,105 | 1,264 | 2,800 | 2,563 | 21,614 | 22,649 |
| Norway | — | — | 1,680 | 2,069 | 2,307 | 857 |
| Denmark | — | — | 65 | — | — | — |
| Poland | — | — | — | 4,590 | 20,710 | 1,200 |
| Yugoslavia | — | — | — | 6,729 | 3,339 | — |
| U.S.S.R. | — | — | — | — | 8,524 | 3,400 |
| Others | 7,699 | — | — | — | — | — |
| **TOTAL EUROPE** | 189,180 | 136,343 | 214,865 | 216,892 | 268,094 | 174,032 |
| **AFRICA** | | | | | | |
| South Africa | 3,623 | 3,340 | 2,862 | 2,845 | — | — |
| Sudan | 1,744 | — | 5,408 | 10,561 | — | — |
| Zanzibar | 16 | — | — | — | — | — |
| Rhodesia & Nyasaland | — | 136 | — | — | 50 | — |
| Somalia | — | 58 | 82 | 24 | — | 240 |
| Mozambique | — | — | 45 | — | 104 | — |
| South West Africa | — | — | 31 | 22 | — | — |
| Mauritius | — | — | — | 153 | — | — |
| Libya | — | — | — | — | — | 34 |
| **TOTAL AFRICA** | 5,383 | 3,534 | 8,428 | 13,605 | 154 | 274 |
| **ASIA & OCEANIA** | | | | | | |
| Australia | 12,822 | 9,819 | 7,530 | 9,552 | 2,482 | 4,597 |
| Israel | 4,619 | 3,763 | 1,111 | 995 | 4,875 | 2,066 |
| Jordan | 2,390 | 1,100 | 330 | 185 | 5,496 | 48,380 |
| New Zealand | 2,231 | 3,814 | 4,755 | 8,336 | 4,160 | 5,946 |
| Japan | 1,487 | 1,638 | 1,517 | 1,525 | 9,383 | 8,479 |
| Syria | 725 | 279 | 1,246 | 50 | — | 696 |
| Iraq | 637 | 386 | 493 | 68 | 872 | 3,675 |
| Arabia | 284 | — | — | — | — | — |
| Lebanon | 105 | 197 | 84 | 295 | 494 | 445 |
| Aden | — | — | 1,557 | 458 | 804 | 1,324 |
| Kuwait | — | — | 371 | 667 | 2,393 | 4,550 |
| Bahrein | — | — | 353 | 1,118 | 4,623 | 8,586 |
| Saudi Arabia | — | — | 316 | 509 | 9,220 | 7,448 |
| Hong Kong | — | — | 279 | 168 | — | 2,394 |
| Muscat & Oman | — | — | 170 | 971 | 3,759 | — |
| Trucial Oman | — | — | 8 | 221 | 3,469 | 6,111 |
| Malaysia | — | — | — | 51 | 34 | — |
| Iran | — | — | — | 68 | — | — |
| Qatar | — | — | — | — | 423 | 1,353 |
| China | — | — | — | — | — | 5,079 |
| Others | 5,339 | 14,084 | — | — | — | — |
| **TOTAL ASIA & OCEANIA** | 30,639 | 35,080 | 20,120 | 25,237 | 52,487 | 111,129 |
| **TOTAL EXPORTS** | 419,750 | 419,192 | 426,465 | 425,448 | 553,560 | 473,852 |

Source: Coffee Board of Kenya.

## EQ-24. UGANDA: EXPORTS OF GREEN COFFEE, 1965-1966
### (Bags of 60 kilograms or 132.276 pounds each)

| COUNTRIES OF DESTINATION | 1966 | 1965 | Percentage of Total 1966 | Percentage of Total 1965 | Increase or Decrease 1966 over 1965 VOLUME | PERCENT |
|---|---|---|---|---|---|---|
| UNITED STATES | 960,273 | 1,033,987 | 32.3 | 41.6 | − 73,714 | − 7.1 |
| CANADA | 108,119 | 89,433 | 3.6 | 3.6 | + 18,686 | + 20.9 |
| OTHER AMERICAS | | | | | | |
| Uruguay | 850 | 3,410 | --- | 0.1 | − 2,560 | − 75.1 |
| Jamaica | 850 | 255 | --- | --- | + 595 | +233.3 |
| Argentina | --- | 6,000 | --- | 0.2 | − 6,000 | --- |
| TOTAL OTHER AMERICAS | 1,700 | 9,665 | --- | 0.3 | − 7,965 | − 82.4 |
| EUROPE | | | | | | |
| United Kingdom | 542,445 | 594,069 | 18.2 | 23.9 | − 51,624 | − 8.7 |
| Poland | 188,655 | 34,680 | 6.3 | 1.4 | +153,975 | +444.0 |
| Rumania | 147,845 | --- | 5.0 | --- | +147,845 | --- |
| Hungary | 40,780 | 63,585 | 1.4 | 2.6 | − 22,805 | − 35.9 |
| Germany (F.R.) | 33,895 | 28,481 | 1.1 | 1.1 | + 5,414 | + 19.0 |
| Sweden | 31,702 | 19,584 | 1.1 | 0.8 | + 12,118 | + 61.9 |
| Netherlands | 19,586 | 13,268 | 0.7 | 0.5 | + 6,318 | + 47.6 |
| Spain | 16,700 | --- | 0.6 | --- | + 16,700 | --- |
| Germany (D.R.) | 10,676 | --- | 0.4 | --- | + 10,676 | --- |
| Finland | 7,458 | 4,544 | 0.3 | 0.2 | + 2,914 | + 64.1 |
| Belgium | 3,019 | 4,873 | 0.1 | 0.2 | − 1,854 | − 38.0 |
| Italy | 2,987 | 7,497 | 0.1 | 0.3 | − 4,510 | − 60.2 |
| Norway | 2,914 | 1,321 | 0.1 | 0.1 | + 1,593 | +120.6 |
| Greece | 1,854 | 5,299 | 0.1 | 0.2 | − 3,445 | − 65.0 |
| Eire | 1,278 | 1,358 | --- | 0.1 | − 80 | − 5.9 |
| France | 1,049 | 42,255 | --- | 1.7 | − 41,206 | − 97.5 |
| Denmark | 248 | 1,340 | --- | 0.1 | − 1,092 | − 81.5 |
| Switzerland | 200 | 255 | --- | --- | − 55 | − 21.6 |
| Cyprus | 170 | --- | --- | --- | + 170 | --- |
| Austria | 100 | --- | --- | --- | + 100 | --- |
| Czechoslovakia | --- | 1,816 | --- | 0.1 | − 1,816 | --- |
| Gibraltar | --- | 425 | --- | --- | − 425 | --- |
| Malta | --- | 211 | --- | --- | − 211 | --- |
| TOTAL EUROPE | 1,053,561 | 824,861 | 35.5 | 33.3 | +228,700 | + 27.7 |

A-62

EQ-24. UGANDA: EXPORTS OF GREEN COFFEE, 1965-1966 (Continued)

| COUNTRIES OF DESTINATION | 1966 | 1965 | Percentage of Total 1966 | Percentage of Total 1965 | Increase or Decrease 1966 over 1965 VOLUME | PERCENT |
|---|---|---|---|---|---|---|
| AFRICA |  |  |  |  |  |  |
| Sudan | 40,800 | 136,000 | 1.4 | 5.5 | − 95,200 | − 70.0 |
| United Arab Republic | 12,601 | 10,260 | 0.4 | 0.4 | + 2,341 | + 22.8 |
| Libya | 7,097 | 5,240 | 0.2 | 0.2 | + 1,857 | + 35.4 |
| Tunisia | — | 6,730 | — | 0.3 | − 6,730 | --- |
| Mozambique | — | 289 | — | — | − 289 | --- |
| Somalia | — | 137 | — | — | − 137 | --- |
| Seychelles | — | 44 | — | — | − 44 | --- |
| TOTAL AFRICA | 60,498 | 158,700 | 2.0 | 6.4 | − 98,202 | − 61.9 |
| ASIA & OCEANIA |  |  |  |  |  |  |
| Saudi Arabia | 120,728 | 5,165 | 4.1 | 0.2 | +115,563 | + (o) |
| Thailand | 101,941 | 10,200 | 3.4 | 0.4 | + 91,741 | +899.4 |
| Iraq | 101,573 | 1,165 | 3.4 | — | +100,408 | + (o) |
| Australia | 96,847 | 72,698 | 3.3 | 2.9 | + 24,149 | + 33.2 |
| Bahrein | 94,050 | 5,012 | 3.2 | 0.2 | + 89,038 | + (o) |
| Jordan | 92,476 | 115,160 | 3.1 | 4.6 | − 22,684 | − 19.7 |
| Japan | 67,375 | 68,086 | 2.3 | 2.7 | − 711 | − 1.0 |
| New Zealand | 33,777 | 28,853 | 1.1 | 1.2 | + 4,924 | + 17.1 |
| Kuwait | 25,236 | 1,435 | 0.8 | 0.1 | + 23,801 | + (o) |
| Israel | 25,186 | 32,777 | 0.8 | 1.3 | − 7,591 | − 23.2 |
| Trucial States | 17,823 | 8,435 | 0.6 | 0.3 | + 9,388 | +111.3 |
| Qatar | 8,500 | — | 0.3 | — | + 8,500 | --- |
| Muscat & Oman | 3,496 | 11,597 | 0.1 | 0.5 | − 8,101 | − 69.9 |
| Aden | 3,232 | 6,623 | 0.1 | 0.3 | − 3,391 | − 51.2 |
| Lebanon | 35 | 538 | — | — | − 503 | − 93.5 |
| Hong Kong | — | 3,289 | — | 0.1 | − 3,289 | --- |
| Formosa | — | 136 | — | — | − 136 | --- |
| Malaysia | — | 76 | — | — | − 76 | --- |
| TOTAL ASIA & OCEANIA | 792,275 | 371,245 | 26.6 | 14.8 | +421,030 | +113.4 |
| TOTAL EXPORTS | 2,976,426 | 2,487,891 | 100.0 | 100.0 | +488,535 | + 19.6 |

Source: Coffee Board of Kenya.
(o) Increase over 1,000 percent.

## EQ-24A. UGANDA: EXPORTS OF GREEN COFFEE, 1960-1965

(Bags of 60 kilograms or 132.276 pounds each)

| COUNTRIES OF DESTINATION | 1960 | 1961 | 1962 | 1963 | 1964 | 1965 |
|---|---|---|---|---|---|---|
| **UNITED STATES** | 693,772 | 686,509 | 1,189,704 | 1,208,673 | 993,421 | 1,033,987 |
| **CANADA** | 43,950 | 60,610 | 57,848 | 53,854 | 60,789 | 89,433 |
| **OTHER AMERICAS** | | | | | | |
| Argentina | 3,130 | 48,879 | 16,688 | 5,050 | 8,000 | 6,000 |
| Uruguay | 935 | 900 | 1,183 | — | 2,340 | 3,410 |
| Chile | 500 | — | — | — | — | — |
| Jamaica | — | — | — | — | — | 255 |
| Others | 600 | — | — | — | — | — |
| **TOTAL OTHER AMERICAS** | 5,165 | 49,779 | 17,871 | 5,050 | 10,340 | 9,665 |
| **EUROPE** | | | | | | |
| United Kingdom | 372,589 | 449,464 | 526,336 | 624,154 | 303,763 | 594,069 |
| Bulgaria | 76,254 | — | — | — | — | — |
| Germany (F.R.) | 60,988 | 45,569 | 48,930 | 28,117 | 104,550 | 28,481 |
| Finland | 27,915 | 38,283 | 24,172 | 6,909 | 5,765 | 4,544 |
| Italy | 26,346 | 7,210 | 6,357 | 8,678 | 29,328 | 7,497 |
| Netherlands | 22,253 | 20,195 | 20,694 | 5,470 | 113,599 | 13,268 |
| Sweden | 15,873 | 16,628 | 18,749 | 10,778 | 10,460 | 19,584 |
| Gibraltar | 12,194 | 5,380 | 1,142 | — | — | 425 |
| Greece | 4,983 | 2,193 | 2,042 | 1,497 | 1,352 | 5,299 |
| France | 3,839 | 136 | 18,013 | — | 14,228 | 42,255 |
| Belgium — Luxembourg | 3,544 | 2,874 | 4,788 | 3,882 | 91,369 | 4,873 |
| Malta | 2,318 | 782 | 245 | 136 | 65 | 211 |
| Austria | 2,100 | 840 | 215 | — | — | — |
| Norway | 1,766 | 310 | 518 | 2,168 | 1,519 | 1,321 |
| Denmark | 1,250 | 357 | 187 | 50 | 1,230 | 1,340 |
| Ireland | 1,047 | 979 | 1,637 | 996 | 781 | 1,358 |
| Cyprus | 938 | 1,100 | 600 | — | 51 | — |
| Switzerland | 665 | 262 | 264 | 250 | 17 | 255 |
| Spain | 450 | — | — | — | — | — |
| Yugoslavia | — | 250 | — | 170 | 3,366 | — |
| Hungary | — | — | — | 17,000 | 18,700 | 63,585 |
| Poland | — | — | — | — | 17,000 | 34,680 |
| Germany (D.R.) | — | — | — | — | 19,410 | — |
| Czechoslovakia | — | — | — | — | — | 1,816 |
| Others | 45,399 | — | — | — | — | — |
| **TOTAL EUROPE** | 682,711 | 592,812 | 674,889 | 710,255 | 736,553 | 824,861 |
| **AFRICA** | | | | | | |
| Sudan | 103,203 | 92,116 | 83,818 | 107,875 | 98,600 | 136,000 |
| South Africa | 81,772 | 64,607 | 58,350 | 108,143 | — | — |
| United Arab Republic | 74,813 | 14,718 | 9,005 | 386 | 150 | 10,260 |
| Morocco | 6,193 | — | — | — | — | — |
| Zanzibar | 2,211 | — | — | — | — | — |
| Mozambique | 1,365 | 459 | 729 | 85 | 159 | 289 |
| Algeria | 1,214 | 833 | — | — | — | — |
| Rhodesia & Nyasaland | 136 | — | 187 | 220 | — | — |
| Libya | — | 6,622 | 7,655 | 3,883 | 6,262 | 5,240 |
| Somalia | — | 2,531 | 3,299 | 318 | 425 | 137 |
| Southwest Africa | — | — | 30 | — | — | — |
| Seychelles | — | — | 1 | — | 17 | 44 |
| Mauritius | — | — | — | 83 | — | — |
| Tunisia | — | — | — | — | — | 6,730 |
| **TOTAL AFRICA** | 270,907 | 181,886 | 163,074 | 220,993 | 105,613 | 158,700 |

**EQ-24A.  UGANDA: EXPORTS OF GREEN COFFEE, 1960-1965 (Continued)**

(Bags of 60 kilograms or 132.276 pounds each)

| COUNTRIES OF DESTINATION | 1960 | 1961 | 1962 | 1963 | 1964 | 1965 |
|---|---|---|---|---|---|---|
| **ASIA & OCEANIA** | | | | | | |
| Australia | 93,166 | 76,403 | 62,952 | 64,315 | 80,619 | 72,698 |
| Israel | 43,975 | 67,396 | 68,595 | 67,856 | 51,381 | 32,777 |
| Ceylon | 17,544 | 1,478 | — | — | — | — |
| New Zealand | 16,806 | 18,704 | 23,081 | 15,099 | 16,451 | 28,853 |
| Japan | 14,394 | 20,216 | 16,745 | 25,510 | 85,732 | 68,086 |
| Iraq | 7,863 | 3,703 | 7,113 | 10,630 | 31,184 | 1,165 |
| Syria | 5,211 | 1,940 | 444 | 187 | 425 | — |
| Jordan | 3,918 | 6,977 | 6,019 | 12,595 | 55,960 | 115,160 |
| Malaysia | 1,700 | — | — | — | 10,106 | 76 |
| Lebanon | 1,666 | 2,182 | — | 50 | — | 538 |
| Saudi Arabia | 1,476 | — | 2,160 | 6,880 | 18,907 | 5,165 |
| Singapore | 850 | — | — | — | — | — |
| Iran | 381 | 322 | 85 | — | — | — |
| Hong Kong | 210 | — | — | — | 51,000 | 3,289 |
| Philippine Republic | — | 154 | 66 | 2,198 | — | — |
| Muscat & Oman | — | — | 10,498 | 6,572 | 8,379 | 11,597 |
| Trucial Oman | — | — | 4,655 | 5,586 | 12,242 | 8,435 |
| Kuwait | — | — | 3,788 | 10,111 | 8,670 | 1,435 |
| Aden | — | — | 1,768 | 1,112 | 984 | 6,623 |
| Bahrein | — | — | 1,272 | 5,479 | 6,510 | 5,012 |
| Qatar | — | — | 904 | — | 85 | — |
| Thailand | — | — | — | 5,094 | 8,539 | 10,200 |
| Formosa | — | — | — | — | — | 136 |
| Others | 8,785 | 8,540 | — | — | — | — |
| **TOTAL ASIA & OCEANIA** | 217,945 | 208,015 | 210,145 | 239,274 | 447,174 | 371,245 |
| **OTHERS** | 34,336 | 26,639 | — | — | 85 | — |
| **TOTAL EXPORTS** | 1,948,786 | 1,806,250 | 2,313,531 | 2,438,099 | 2,353,975 | 2,487,891 |

Source:   Coffee Board of Kenya.

## EQ-25. IVORY COAST: EXPORTS OF GREEN COFFEE, 1965-1966

(Bags of 60 kilograms or 132.276 pounds each)

| COUNTRIES OF DESTINATION | 1966° | 1965* | Percent of Total 1966 | Percent of Total 1965 | Increase or Decrease 1966 over 1965 VOLUME | Increase or Decrease 1966 over 1965 PERCENT |
|---|---|---|---|---|---|---|
| UNITED STATES | 808,084 | 806,700 | 26.8 | 26.0 | + 1,384 | + 0.2 |
| **EUROPE** | | | | | | |
| France | 1,214,568 | 1,253,117 | 40.3 | 40.4 | − 38,549 | − 3.1 |
| Italy | 115,733 | 241,284 | 3.8 | 7.8 | − 125,551 | − 52.0 |
| Poland | 33,600 | 71,917 | 1.1 | 2.3 | − 38,317 | − 53.3 |
| Hungary | 33,583 | 18,467 | 1.1 | 0.6 | + 15,116 | + 81.9 |
| United Kingdom | 8,400 | — | 0.3 | — | + 8,400 | + --- |
| Spain | 8,400 | 17,200 | 0.3 | 0.6 | − 8,800 | − 51.2 |
| Netherlands | 6,117 | 3,433 | 0.2 | 0.1 | + 2,684 | + 78.2 |
| Germany (F.R.) | 3,017 | 55,433 | 0.1 | 1.8 | − 52,416 | − 94.6 |
| Austria | 2,200 | — | 0.1 | — | + 2,200 | + --- |
| Belgium | 1,283 | — | 0.1 | — | + 1,283 | + --- |
| Norway | 217 | — | — | — | + 217 | + --- |
| Various | — | 1,000 | — | — | − 1,000 | − --- |
| **TOTAL EUROPE** | 1,427,118 | 1,661,851 | 47.4 | 53.6 | − 234,733 | − 14.1 |
| **AFRICA** | | | | | | |
| Algeria | 104,967 | 130,250 | 3.5 | 4.2 | − 25,283 | − 19.4 |
| Morocco | 92,300 | 81,517 | 3.1 | 2.6 | + 10,783 | + 13.2 |
| Sudan | 84,700 | — | 2.8 | — | + 84,700 | + --- |
| Senegal | 31,367 | 26,633 | 1.0 | 0.9 | + 4,734 | + 17.8 |
| Bechuanaland | 26,234 | — | 0.9 | — | + 26,234 | + --- |
| South Africa | 11,850 | — | 0.4 | — | + 11,850 | + --- |
| Tunisia | 1,667 | — | 0.1 | — | + 1,667 | + --- |
| Various | — | 1,767 | — | 0.1 | − 1,767 | − --- |
| **TOTAL AFRICA** | 353,085 | 240,167 | 11.8 | 7.8 | +112,918 | + 47.0 |
| **ASIA & OCEANIA** | | | | | | |
| Japan | 277,983 | 46,650 | 9.2 | 1.5 | +231,333 | +495.9 |
| Thailand | 31,349 | 8,717 | 1.1 | 0.3 | + 22,632 | +259.6 |
| Kuwait | 25,067 | — | 0.8 | — | + 25,067 | + --- |
| Jordan | 24,350 | 78,583 | 0.8 | 2.5 | − 54,233 | − 69.0 |
| Bahrein | 18,467 | 16,700 | 0.6 | 0.6 | + 1,767 | + 10.6 |
| Israel | 10,001 | 6,700 | 0.3 | 0.2 | + 3,301 | + 49.3 |
| Australia | 417 | — | — | — | + 417 | + --- |
| Saudi Arabia | — | 53,650 | — | 1.7 | − 53,650 | − --- |
| Muscat | — | 27,300 | — | 0.9 | − 27,300 | − --- |
| Lebanon | — | 20,983 | — | 0.7 | − 20,983 | − --- |
| Iraq | — | 13,333 | — | 0.4 | − 13,333 | − --- |
| Iran | — | 4,150 | — | 0.1 | − 4,150 | − --- |
| Oman | — | 1,967 | — | 0.1 | − 1,967 | − --- |
| **TOTAL ASIA & OCEANIA** | 387,634 | 278,733 | 12.8 | 9.0 | +108,901 | + 39.1 |
| OTHERS † | 36,815 | 111,297 | 1.2 | 3.6 | − 74,482 | − 66.9 |
| **TOTAL EXPORTS** | 3,012,736 | 3,098,748 | 100.0 | 100.0 | − 86,012 | − 2.8 |

Source: Ivory Coast Stabilization Fund.
(o) Preliminary.
(*) Revised.
(†) Destination unknown.

## EQ-25A. IVORY COAST: EXPORTS OF GREEN COFFEE, 1960-1965

(Bags of 60 kilograms or 132.276 pounds each)

| COUNTRIES OF DESTINATION | 1960 | 1961 | 1962 | 1963 | 1964 | 1965 |
|---|---|---|---|---|---|---|
| UNITED STATES | 729,932 | 599,079 | 480,383 | 652,983 | 1,172,650 | 806,700 |
| CANADA | — | 19,266 | — | 12,983 | 1,683 | — |
| **OTHER AMERICAS** | | | | | | |
| Chile | 999 | 2,017 | — | — | — | — |
| Martinique | — | 750 | — | — | — | — |
| Others | — | — | — | — | — | 2,383 |
| TOTAL OTHER AMERICAS | 999 | 2,767 | — | — | — | 2,383 |
| **EUROPE** | | | | | | |
| France | 1,243,080 | 1,289,446 | 1,307,884 | 1,718,717 | 1,195,967 | 1,253,117 |
| Italy | 136,185 | 74,816 | 101,717 | 95,967 | 118,067 | 241,284 |
| Belgium — Luxembourg | 23,366 | 1,467 | 4,550 | 3,850 | 34,133 | — |
| Germany (F.R.) | 21,082 | 24,000 | 10,333 | 4,050 | 46,750 | 55,433 |
| Netherlands | 12,949 | 8,518 | 11,417 | 17,550 | 52,117 | 3,433 |
| Greece | 6,317 | 3,918 | 933 | 466 | 3,583 | — |
| Switzerland | 6,149 | 4,999 | 10,433 | 13,283 | 4,983 | — |
| United Kingdom | 2,834 | 15,350 | 9,283 | 550 | 46,783 | — |
| Spain | 1,866 | 467 | — | 26,450 | 18,517 | 17,200 |
| Norway | 1,650 | 782 | — | 216 | 717 | — |
| Gibraltar | 1,250 | 500 | — | — | — | — |
| Denmark | 833 | — | — | — | — | — |
| Yugoslavia | 667 | — | — | — | — | — |
| Austria | 617 | 233 | — | 11,667 | 7,317 | — |
| Sweden | 150 | 250 | — | 767 | 2,300 | — |
| Malta | 67 | — | — | — | — | — |
| Ireland | 50 | — | — | — | — | — |
| Poland | — | — | — | — | 21,800 | 71,917 |
| Hungary | — | — | — | 3,367 | 26,917 | 18,467 |
| Finland | — | — | — | — | 10,100 | — |
| Czechoslovakia | — | — | — | — | 5,033 | — |
| Rumania | — | — | — | 1,683 | 8,817 | — |
| Others | 8,300 | — | — | — | 833 | 1,000 |
| TOTAL EUROPE | 1,471,312 | 1,424,746 | 1,456,550 | 1,898,583 | 1,604,734 | 1,661,851 |
| **AFRICA** | | | | | | |
| Algeria | 381,281 | 398,398 | 304,900 | 268,167 | 330,133 | 130,250 |
| Morocco | 85,650 | 84,451 | 56,533 | 70,517 | 66,567 | 81,517 |
| South Africa | 26,367 | 31,349 | 20,550 | 67,067 | — | — |
| Tunisia | 7,252 | 14,115 | 983 | 1,133 | 15,117 | — |
| Liberia | 767 | 834 | — | — | 3,367 | — |
| Senegal | — | — | — | 8,983 | 21,400 | 26,633 |
| Gambia | — | — | — | — | 5,000 | — |
| Nigeria | — | — | — | — | 1,700 | — |
| Rhodesia | — | — | — | — | 200 | — |
| Others | 167 | 50 | — | 1,683 | 10,917 | 1,767 |
| TOTAL AFRICA | 501,484 | 529,197 | 382,966 | 417,550 | 454,401 | 240,167 |
| **ASIA & OCEANIA** | | | | | | |
| Japan | 1,200 | 2,185 | 2,268 | 28,867 | 69,200 | 46,650 |
| Australia | 1,099 | 999 | 5,635 | 250 | 333 | — |
| Cambodia | 600 | — | 1,196 | — | — | — |
| China | — | 833 | — | — | — | — |
| Israel | — | — | 927 | 12,067 | 22,700 | 6,700 |
| Oman | — | — | — | 334 | 3,817 | 1,967 |
| Jordan | — | — | — | 1,683 | 3,333 | 78,583 |
| Muscat | — | — | — | 1,683 | 2,783 | 25,333 |
| Iran | — | — | — | — | 167 | 4,150 |
| Bahrein | — | — | — | — | — | 16,700 |
| Saudi Arabia | — | — | — | — | — | 53,650 |
| Lebanon | — | — | — | — | — | 20,983 |
| Iraq | — | — | — | — | — | 13,333 |
| Thailand | — | — | — | — | — | 8,717 |
| Others | — | — | 22,124 | — | — | — |
| TOTAL ASIA & OCEANIA | 2,899 | 4,017 | 32,150 | 44,884 | 102,333 | 276,766 |
| OTHERS | 367 | 301 | — | 17,584 | 76,999 | 110,881 |
| TOTAL EXPORTS | 2,706,993 | 2,579,373 | 2,352,049 | 3,044,567 | 3,412,800 | 3,098,748 |

Source: Caisse de Stabilisation des Prix du Café, Ivory Coast.

## EQ-26A. CONGO (KINSHASA): EXPORTS OF GREEN COFFEE, 1960-1965

(Bags of 60 kilograms or 132.276 pounds each)

| COUNTRIES OF DESTINATION | 1960 | 1961 | 1962 | 1963 | 1964 | 1965 |
|---|---|---|---|---|---|---|
| UNITED STATES | 183,166 | 107,207 | 16,088 | 34,715 | 133,325 | 143,242 |
| CANADA | — | — | — | — | 567 | 652 |
| **OTHER AMERICAS** | | | | | | |
| Argentina | — | 700 | — | — | — | — |
| **EUROPE** | | | | | | |
| Belgium | 349,258 | 127,686 | 134,628 | 216,759 | 48,526 | 43,406 |
| Italy | 208,865 | 230,814 | 182,044 | 257,401 | 203,176 | 181,935 |
| France | 14,987 | 7,738 | 10,161 | — | 148,300 | 132,711 |
| Finland | 7,607 | 7,655 | — | — | 2,700 | — |
| United Kingdom | 5,353 | 2,199 | 5,080 | 5,927 | 12,790 | 10,852 |
| Switzerland | 1,902 | 3,542 | — | — | 1,843 | 2,436 |
| Germany (F.R.) | 1,622 | — | 5,080 | 5,927 | 42,631 | 37,997 |
| Greece | 1,000 | — | — | — | — | — |
| Gibraltar | 906 | 3,013 | — | — | — | — |
| Cyprus | 500 | — | — | — | — | — |
| Norway | 300 | — | — | — | — | — |
| Czechoslovakia | — | 870 | — | — | — | — |
| Spain | — | — | 15,241 | 38,102 | 18,999 | 24,411 |
| Netherlands | — | — | 847 | 847 | 10,884 | 9,877 |
| Denmark | — | — | — | — | — | 3 |
| **TOTAL EUROPE** | 592,300 | 383,517 | 353,081 | 524,963 | 489,849 | 443,628 |
| **AFRICA** | | | | | | |
| Sudan | 17,692 | 3,087 | — | — | — | — |
| Morocco | 17,093 | 417 | — | — | — | — |
| Tunisia | 11,875 | 4,350 | — | — | — | — |
| Algeria | 10,036 | — | — | — | — | — |
| Congo (Brazza) | 59 | — | — | — | — | — |
| Kenya | 47 | — | — | — | — | — |
| East Africa | — | — | 114,306 | 169,343 | — | — |
| Mozambique | — | — | — | — | — | 56 |
| **TOTAL AFRICA** | 56,802 | 7,854 | 114,306 | 169,343 | — | 56 |
| **ASIA & OCEANIA** | | | | | | |
| Japan | 4,423 | — | — | — | — | — |
| United Arab Republic | 83 | — | — | — | — | — |
| China | 68 | — | — | — | — | — |
| New Zealand | — | — | — | — | 426 | 570 |
| **TOTAL ASIA & OCEANIA** | 4,574 | — | — | — | 426 | 570 |
| **OTHERS** | 41,174 | — | 63,503 | 44,029 | — | — |
| **TOTAL EXPORTS** | 878,016 | 499,278 | 546,978 | 773,050 | 624,167 | 588,148 |

Source: International Coffee Organization: George Gordon Paton & Co.

## EQ-28A. ETHIOPIA: EXPORTS OF GREEN COFFEE, 1960-1965

(Bags of 60 kilograms or 132.276 pounds each)

| COUNTRIES OF DESTINATION | 1960 | 1961 | 1962 | 1963 | 1964 | 1965 |
|---|---|---|---|---|---|---|
| UNITED STATES | 566,310 | 679,190 | 713,833 | 764,533 | 928,571 | 1,043,460 |
| CANADA | 858 | — | — | — | 117 | 67 |
| **EUROPE** | | | | | | |
| Italy | 67,314 | 51,147 | 65,250 | 54,583 | 51,828 | 38,018 |
| Norway | 25,983 | 20,581 | 21,150 | 24,267 | 14,215 | 17,109 |
| France | 21,125 | 17,082 | 12,533 | 14,817 | 17,247 | 16,765 |
| Sweden | 19,481 | 16,103 | 11,550 | 15,433 | 10,528 | 14,247 |
| Switzerland | 7,489 | 6,824 | 11,800 | 5,567 | 3,759 | 1,867 |
| Germany (F.R.) | 7,095 | 9,295 | 13,533 | 11,850 | 28,682 | 34,538 |
| United Kingdom | 5,713 | 7,773 | 17,917 | 10,817 | 12,010 | 7,095 |
| Greece | 3,950 | 2,217 | — | 5,333 | 1,903 | 2,333 |
| Netherlands | 3,376 | 885 | — | 617 | 7,536 | 2,084 |
| Finland | 1,421 | 1,266 | — | — | 500 | 2,247 |
| Austria | 797 | 622 | — | — | — | — |
| Denmark | 731 | 725 | — | — | 200 | 449 |
| Belgium — Luxembourg | 152 | 375 | — | — | 199 | 1,673 |
| Yugoslavia | — | — | 8,167 | 8,333 | 15,849 | — |
| U.S.S.R. | — | — | 17,483 | 18,767 | 4,167 | 26,300 |
| Hungary | — | — | — | — | 478 | 11,617 |
| Spain | — | — | — | — | — | 14,667 |
| Cyprus | — | — | — | — | — | 100 |
| Various | 7,913 | 485 | 5,183 | 5,300 | — | — |
| **TOTAL EUROPE** | 172,540 | 135,380 | 184,566 | 175,684 | 169,101 | 191,109 |
| **AFRICA** | | | | | | |
| South Africa | 193 | 251 | — | — | — | — |
| Sudan | — | — | 13,033 | 6,267 | 28,458 | 29,184 |
| French Somaliland | — | — | 9,250 | 18,067 | 29,744 | 7,784 |
| Libya | — | — | — | — | — | 83 |
| **TOTAL AFRICA** | 193 | 251 | 22,283 | 24,334 | 58,202 | 37,051 |
| **ASIA & OCEANIA** | | | | | | |
| Japan | 24,092 | 27,237 | 8,583 | 16,733 | 11,657 | 16,023 |
| Australia | 1,603 | 2,055 | — | — | 498 | 659 |
| Aden | — | — | 48,800 | 37,417 | 34,312 | 5,157 |
| Saudi Arabia | — | — | 47,500 | 52,633 | 21,325 | 35,074 |
| Israel | — | — | 4,633 | 2,766 | 6,212 | 5,537 |
| Iraq | — | — | — | — | 2,434 | 6,017 |
| Jordan | — | — | — | — | 137 | 4,883 |
| Lebanon | — | — | — | — | 839 | 546 |
| New Zealand | — | — | — | — | 84 | 250 |
| Taiwan | — | — | 4,000 | — | — | 11,666 |
| Kuwait | — | — | — | — | — | 1,350 |
| Iran | — | — | — | — | — | 1,034 |
| **TOTAL ASIA & OCEANIA** | 25,695 | 29,292 | 113,516 | 109,549 | 77,498 | 88,196 |
| OTHERS | 83,404 | 105,887 | 6,950 | 6,100 | — | — |
| **TOTAL EXPORTS** | 849,000 | 950,000 | 1,041,148 | 1,080,200 | 1,233,489 | 1,359,883 |

Source: International Coffee Organization: George Gordon Paton & Co.

## EQ-29. INDIA: EXPORTS OF GREEN COFFEE, 1965-1966

(Bags of 60 kilograms or 132.276 pounds each)

| COUNTRIES OF DESTINATION | 1966 | 1965 | Percent of Total 1966 | Percent of Total 1965 | Increase or Decrease 1966 over 1965 VOLUME | Increase or Decrease 1966 over 1965 PERCENT |
|---|---|---|---|---|---|---|
| UNITED STATES | 47,994 | 70,664 | 11.5 | 17.1 | − 22,670 | − 32.1 |
| CANADA | 1,335 | 2,290 | 0.3 | 0.6 | − 955 | − 41.7 |
| EUROPE | | | | | | |
| U.S.S.R. | 113,359 | 117,075 | 27.2 | 28.4 | − 3,716 | − 3.2 |
| Yugoslavia | 73,807 | 44,488 | 17.7 | 10.8 | +29,319 | + 65.9 |
| Germany (D.R.) | 53,862 | 67,860 | 12.9 | 16.4 | − 13,998 | − 20.6 |
| Czechoslovakia | 16,012 | 8,140 | 3.8 | 2.0 | + 7,872 | + 96.7 |
| Germany (F.R.) | 15,354 | 8,939 | 3.7 | 2.2 | + 6,415 | + 71.8 |
| Italy | 14,599 | 14,879 | 3.5 | 3.6 | − 280 | − 1.9 |
| Bulgaria | 11,239 | 2,150 | 2.7 | 0.5 | + 9,089 | +422.7 |
| Greece | 11,049 | 1,934 | 2.7 | 0.5 | + 9,115 | +471.3 |
| Netherlands | 10,173 | 13,012 | 2.4 | 3.1 | − 2,839 | − 21.8 |
| France | 9,520 | 9,789 | 2.3 | 2.4 | − 269 | − 2.7 |
| Norway | 8,511 | 9,147 | 2.0 | 2.2 | − 636 | − 7.0 |
| United Kingdom | 6,773 | 6,067 | 1.6 | 1.5 | + 706 | + 11.6 |
| Hungary | 6,268 | 11,778 | 1.5 | 2.9 | − 5,510 | − 46.8 |
| Poland | 5,033 | − | 1.2 | − | + 5,033 | + --- |
| Belgium | 4,939 | 11,194 | 1.2 | 2.7 | − 6,255 | − 55.9 |
| Switzerland | 1,531 | 1,601 | 0.4 | 0.4 | − 70 | − 4.4 |
| Sweden | 1,042 | 3,939 | 0.3 | 1.0 | − 2,897 | − 73.5 |
| Austria | 692 | 1,206 | 0.2 | 0.3 | − 514 | − 42.6 |
| Denmark | 83 | − | − | − | + 83 | + --- |
| Rumania | − | 2,550 | − | 0.6 | − 2,550 | − --- |
| Finland | − | 198 | − | − | − 198 | − --- |
| TOTAL EUROPE | 363,846 | 335,946 | 87.3 | 81.5 | +27,900 | + 8.3 |
| OTHERS | | | | | | |
| Kuwait | 1,151 | 1,937 | 0.3 | 0.5 | − 786 | − 40.6 |
| New Zealand | 461 | 240 | 0.1 | 0.1 | + 221 | + 92.1 |
| Hong Kong | 365 | 310 | 0.1 | 0.1 | + 55 | + 17.7 |
| Iraq | 259 | 99 | 0.1 | − | + 160 | +161.6 |
| Singapore | 202 | − | 0.1 | − | + 202 | + --- |
| Australia | 192 | 86 | 0.1 | − | + 106 | +123.3 |
| Nepal | 153 | − | 0.1 | − | + 153 | + --- |
| Bahrein | 124 | 578 | − | 0.1 | − 454 | − 78.5 |
| Saudi Arabia | 72 | − | − | − | + 72 | + --- |
| Japan | 44 | − | − | − | + 44 | + --- |
| Sudan | − | 190 | − | − | − 190 | − --- |
| West Pakistan | − | 82 | − | − | − 82 | − --- |
| Muscat | − | 6 | − | − | − 6 | − --- |
| Various | 477 | − | − | − | + 477 | + --- |
| TOTAL OTHERS | 3,500 | 3,528 | 0.9 | 0.8 | − 28 | − 0.8 |
| TOTAL EXPORTS | 416,675 | 412,428 | 100.0 | 100.0 | + 4,247 | + 1.0 |

Source: Indian Coffee Board & International Coffee Organization.

## EQ-29A. INDIA: EXPORTS OF GREEN COFFEE, 1960-1965

(Bags of 60 kilograms or 132.276 pounds each)

| COUNTRIES OF DESTINATION | 1960 | 1961 | 1962 | 1963 | 1964 | 1965 |
|---|---|---|---|---|---|---|
| UNITED STATES | 12,633 | 37,433 | 9,494 | 33,298 | 67,333 | 70,664 |
| CANADA | — | 3,750 | — | 150 | 1,856 | 2,290 |
| **EUROPE** | | | | | | |
| Germany (F.R.) | 51,767 | 103,633 | 23,022 | 28,506 | 56,355 | 8,939 |
| Yugoslavia | 37,167 | 32,750 | 92,562 | 56,728 | 37,834 | 44,488 |
| U.S.S.R. | 37,583 | 33,450 | 37,691 | 33,366 | 138,731 | 117,075 |
| Netherlands | 26,317 | 44,417 | 8,448 | 12,590 | 29,473 | 13,012 |
| Italy | 23,983 | 66,000 | 19,845 | 47,419 | 10,472 | 14,879 |
| Germany (D.R.) | 16,533 | 40,050 | 61,524 | 60,041 | 45,769 | 67,860 |
| Belgium — Luxembourg | 15,000 | 22,717 | 8,983 | 12,825 | 15,087 | 11,194 |
| France | 11,750 | 20,150 | 2,887 | 19,707 | 20,634 | 9,789 |
| Norway | 10,517 | 8,600 | 1,682 | 5,887 | 10,360 | 9,147 |
| United Kingdom | 6,117 | 32,117 | 5,111 | 7,923 | 32,316 | 6,067 |
| Sweden | 2,783 | 12,583 | 92 | 5,604 | 3,060 | 3,939 |
| Czechoslovakia | 1,933 | 11,067 | 5,156 | 9,321 | 9,681 | 8,140 |
| Finland | 950 | 3,733 | — | 420 | 1,440 | 198 |
| Switzerland | 567 | 1,367 | — | 220 | 1,298 | 1,601 |
| Austria | 533 | — | 94 | 1,616 | 406 | 1,206 |
| Ireland | 100 | 166 | — | — | 145 | — |
| Bulgaria | — | 3,183 | — | 9,526 | 1,847 | 2,150 |
| Hungary | — | 3,250 | 9,477 | 2,342 | 10,367 | 11,778 |
| Denmark | 50 | 50 | 25 | — | — | — |
| Spain | — | — | 3,183 | — | — | — |
| Poland | — | 5,317 | 31,199 | 14,421 | 6,273 | — |
| Greece | — | — | — | 660 | 8,284 | 1,934 |
| Rumania | — | — | — | — | 5,833 | 2,550 |
| Malta | — | — | — | — | 25 | — |
| TOTAL EUROPE | 243,650 | 444,600 | 310,981 | 329,122 | 445,690 | 335,946 |
| **AFRICA** | | | | | | |
| Algeria | 100 | 166 | — | — | — | — |
| United Arab Republic | — | 11,967 | 370 | — | — | — |
| Sudan | — | — | — | — | — | 190 |
| TOTAL AFRICA | 100 | 12,133 | 370 | — | — | 190 |
| **ASIA & OCEANIA** | | | | | | |
| Bahrein | 4,567 | 11,567 | 1,241 | 855 | 1,993 | 578 |
| Kuwait | 4,417 | 5,583 | 544 | 2,952 | 2,095 | 1,937 |
| Saudi Arabia | 1,667 | 4,117 | 314 | 220 | 1,093 | — |
| Iraq | 1,017 | 867 | 482 | 358 | 134 | 99 |
| Trucial Oman & Qatar | 466 | 717 | 59 | 178 | 1,195 | — |
| Iran | 300 | 283 | 75 | — | — | — |
| Ceylon | 150 | 16 | 2 | 2 | — | — |
| Cambodia | 100 | — | — | — | — | — |
| West Pakistan | 50 | 100 | 106 | 102 | 132 | 82 |
| Japan | 50 | 250 | — | — | — | — |
| East Pakistan | 16 | — | — | — | — | — |
| Aden | — | 83 | 63 | — | — | — |
| Hong Kong | — | 417 | — | — | 692 | 310 |
| Muscat | — | 117 | 17 | — | — | 6 |
| Australia | 850 | 1,200 | 373 | 497 | 2,021 | 86 |
| New Zealand | 400 | 2,383 | 151 | 368 | 266 | 240 |
| Israel | — | — | — | 100 | — | — |
| Malaysia | — | — | — | — | 1,325 | — |
| Afghanistan | — | — | — | — | 67 | — |
| TOTAL ASIA & OCEANIA | 14,050 | 27,700 | 3,427 | 5,632 | 11,013 | 3,338 |
| VARIOUS | — | 50 | 135 | 5,994 | 500 | — |
| TOTAL EXPORTS | 270,433 | 525,666 | 324,407 | 374,196 | 526,392 | 412,428 |

Source: International Coffee Organization: India Coffee Board: George Gordon Paton & Co.

EQ-30. "OAMCAF" COUNTRIES:
(in bags of 60 kilograms or

| COUNTRIES OF DESTINATION | Ivory Coast* | Cameroon | Madagascar | Togo Republic |
|---|---|---|---|---|
| UNITED STATES | 808,084 | 239,050 | 265,934 | 833 |
| **EUROPE** | | | | |
| France | 1,214,568 | 388,767 | 402,251 | 192,549 |
| Italy | 115,733 | 81,734 | 10,450 | 21,768 |
| Poland | 33,600 | 13,467 | — | — |
| Hungary | 33,583 | 25,200 | — | — |
| United Kingdom | 8,400 | 3,084 | — | 800 |
| Spain | 8,400 | 8,417 | 20,117 | — |
| Netherlands | 6,117 | 6,883 | 416 | 1,300 |
| Germany (F.R.) | 3,017 | 44,598 | 14,099 | — |
| Austria | 2,200 | — | — | — |
| Belgium | 1,283 | 11,383 | 417 | 11,017 |
| Norway | 217 | — | — | — |
| Rumania | — | 25,200 | — | — |
| Russia | — | 5,033 | — | — |
| Switzerland | — | — | — | — |
| **TOTAL EUROPE** | 1,427,118 | 613,766 | 447,750 | 227,434 |
| **AFRICA** | | | | |
| Algeria | 104,967 | — | — | — |
| Morocco | 92,300 | 11,599 | 18,484 | — |
| Sudan | 84,700 | — | — | — |
| Senegal | 31,367 | — | — | — |
| Bechuanaland | 26,234 | — | — | — |
| South Africa | 11,850 | — | — | — |
| Tunisia | 1,667 | — | — | — |
| Others | — | — | 24,400 | 2,850 |
| **TOTAL AFRICA** | 353,085 | 11,599 | 42,884 | 2,850 |
| **ASIA & OCEANIA** | | | | |
| Japan | 277,983 | 5,450 | — | — |
| Thailand | 31,349 | — | — | — |
| Kuwait | 25,067 | 30,233 | — | — |
| Jordan | 24,350 | 96,867 | — | — |
| Bahrein | 18,467 | 28,249 | — | — |
| Israel | 10,001 | — | — | — |
| Australia | 417 | — | — | — |
| Iran | — | 86,867 | — | — |
| Iraq | — | 10,000 | — | — |
| Saudi Arabia | — | 1,250 | — | — |
| Oman | — | 21,167 | — | — |
| **TOTAL ASIA & OCEANIA** | 387,634 | 280,083 | — | — |
| **OTHERS** | 36,815 | 66,600 | 4,367 | — |
| **TOTAL EXPORTS** | 3,012,736 | 1,211,098 | 760,935 | 231,117 |

SOURCE: Organization Africaine et Malgache du Cafe.

\* Data from Ivory Coast Stabilization Fund.

**EXPORTS OF GREEN COFFEE, 1966**
132.276 pounds each)

| Central African Republic | Congo (Brazzaville) | Gabon | Dahomey | Total |
|---|---|---|---|---|
| — | — | — | — | 1,313,901 |
| | | | | |
| 143,751 | 13,333 | 1,400 | 12,699 | 2,369,318 |
| 40,201 | 4,901 | — | — | 274,787 |
| | | | | 47,067 |
| — | — | — | — | 58,783 |
| — | — | — | — | 12,284 |
| — | — | — | — | 36,934 |
| — | — | — | — | 14,716 |
| 367 | — | — | — | 62,081 |
| — | — | — | — | 2,200 |
| 3,983 | 1,116 | — | — | 29,199 |
| — | — | — | — | 217 |
| — | — | — | — | 25,200 |
| — | — | — | — | 5,033 |
| 350 | — | — | — | 350 |
| **188,652** | **19,350** | **1,400** | **12,699** | **2,938,169** |
| | | | | |
| — | — | — | — | 104,967 |
| 349 | — | — | — | 122,732 |
| — | — | — | — | 84,700 |
| — | — | — | — | 31,367 |
| — | — | — | — | 26,234 |
| — | — | — | — | 11,850 |
| — | — | — | — | 1,667 |
| — | — | 14,367 | — | 41,617 |
| **349** | — | **14,367** | — | **425,134** |
| | | | | |
| 499 | — | — | — | 283,932 |
| — | — | — | — | 31,349 |
| — | — | — | — | 55,300 |
| — | — | — | — | 121,217 |
| — | — | — | — | 46,716 |
| — | — | — | — | 10,001 |
| — | — | — | — | 417 |
| — | — | — | — | 86,867 |
| — | — | — | — | 10,000 |
| — | — | — | — | 1,250 |
| — | — | — | — | 21,167 |
| **499** | — | — | — | **668,216** |
| — | — | — | — | 107,782 |
| **189,500** | **19,350** | **15,767** | **12,699** | **5,453,202** |

## EQ-19A. CUBA: EXPORTS OF GREEN COFFEE, 1960-1965

(Bags of 60 kilograms or 132.276 pounds each)

| COUNTRIES OF DESTINATION | 1960 | 1961 | 1962 | 1963 | 1964 | 1965 |
|---|---|---|---|---|---|---|
| **EUROPE** | | | | | | |
| Spain | 50,364 | — | — | — | — | — |
| Hungary | 3,331 | — | 19,863 | 150 | — | — |
| Czechoslovakia | 1,339 | 17,658 | 5,198 | 333 | — | — |
| Rumania | 480 | 2,167 | 3,884 | 6,393 | — | — |
| Switzerland | 467 | 2,784 | 6,719 | — | — | — |
| Germany (D.R.) | — | 16,651 | 38,466 | — | — | — |
| Italy | — | 11,379 | — | — | — | — |
| Netherlands | — | 2,297 | — | 1,617 | — | — |
| Bulgaria | — | 1,915 | — | — | — | — |
| Poland | — | — | 8,003 | — | — | — |
| Albania | — | — | 4,833 | 1,668 | — | — |
| United Kingdom | — | — | — | 137 | — | — |
| **TOTAL EUROPE** | 55,981 | 54,851 | 86,966 | 10,298 | — | — |
| **OTHERS** | | | | | | |
| United Arab Republic | 33,573 | 29,857 | — | — | — | — |
| Others(°) | — | — | 51,666 | — | — | — |
| **TOTAL OTHERS** | 33,573 | 29,857 | 51,666 | — | — | — |
| **TOTAL EXPORTS** | 89,554 | 84,708 | 138,632 | 10,298 | — | — |

Source: Empresa Cubana Exportadora y Importadora de Alimentos.
(°) Destination unknown

REV-4. WORLD: RELATIVE IMPORTANCE OF COFFEE IN VALUE OF TOTAL TRADE, 1966*

(Millions of U. S. Dollars)

| COUNTRIES OF ORIGIN | Exports all Commodities | Exports of Coffee | Coffee Percent of all Exports |
|---|---|---|---|
| **WESTERN HEMISPHERE** | | | |
| Pan-American Coffee Bureau | | | |
| Brazil | 1730.0 | 773.5 | 44.7 |
| Colombia | 506.5 | 339.2 | 67.0 |
| El Salvador | 192.0 | 90.6 | 47.2 |
| Guatemala | 223.0 | 102.3 | 45.9 |
| Mexico | 1223.9 | 82.3 | 6.7 |
| Costa Rica | 124.1 | 52.2 | 42.1 |
| Ecuador | 190.5 | 32.1 | 16.9 |
| Peru | 764.0 | 29.4 | 3.8 |
| Nicaragua | 147.0 | 23.7 | 16.1 |
| Honduras | 136.4 | 18.9 | 13.9 |
| Haiti | 32.8 | 17.8 | 54.3 |
| Dominican Republic | 137.4 | 21.0 | 15.3 |
| Venezuela | 2926.4 | 17.1 | 0.6 |
| Panama | 87.2 | 2.2 | 2.5 |
| Cuba | — | — | — |
| **TOTAL PAN-AMERICAN COFFEE BUREAU** | 8421.2 | 1602.3 | 19.0 |
| **OTHER WESTERN HEMISPHERE (1)** | 860.0 | 9.8 | 1.1 |
| **TOTAL WESTERN HEMISPHERE** | 9281.2 | 1612.1 | 17.4 |
| **AFRICA** | | | |
| Uganda | 184.5 | 103.3 | 56.0 |
| Kenya | 173.0 | 52.6 | 30.4 |
| Tanzania | 231.0 | 42.3 | 18.3 |
| Ivory Coast | 304.0 | 111.4 | 36.6 |
| Angola | 221.3 | 107.4 | 48.5 |
| Ethiopia | 112.0 | 98.0 | 87.5 |
| Cameroun | 216.4 | 41.7 | 19.3 |
| Madagascar | 97.8 | 30.8 | 31.5 |
| Congo (D.R.) | 475.9 | 25.3 | 5.3 |
| Burundi | 26.5 | 18.7 | 70.6 |
| Rwanda | 8.9 | 7.1 | 80.0 |
| Togo | 38.0 | 12.2 | 32.1 |
| Central African Republic | 31.2 | 9.0 | 28.8 |
| Guinea | 53.0 | 8.3 | 15.7 |
| Spanish Africa | 24.6 | 4.1 | 16.7 |
| Nigeria | 778.0 | 5.3 | 0.7 |
| Various (2) | 392.0 | 19.6 | 5.0 |
| **TOTAL AFRICA** | 3368.1 | 697.1 | 20.7 |
| **ASIA & OCEANIA** | | | |
| Indonesia | 1536.1 | 33.8 | 2.2 |
| India | 1575.6 | 22.5 | 1.4 |
| Yemen | 5.5 | 4.1 | 74.5 |
| Various (3) | 1728.6 | 12.1 | 0.7 |
| **TOTAL ASIA & OCEANIA** | 4845.8 | 72.5 | 1.5 |
| **TOTAL EXPORTS** | 17495.1 | 2381.7 | 13.6 |

Source: Statistical offices and official trade entities of exporting countries.
International Financial Statistics and Direction of International Trade.

(*) Preliminary.

(1) Includes: Bolivia, Guadeloupe, Hawaii, Jamaica, Paraguay, Trinidad & Tobago, Surinam and Puerto Rico.

(2) Includes: Cape Verde, Congo (Brazzaville), Dahomey, Gabon, Ghana, Liberia, Nigeria, São Thomé and Principe and Sierra Leone.

(3) Includes: New Caledonia, New Guinea, New Hebrides, Singapore and Timor.

## IQ-11. UNITED STATES: VOLUME OF COFFEE IMPORTS

|  | 1960 Value | 1960 Percent of World | 1961 Value | 1961 Percent of World | 1962 Value | 1962 Percent of World |
|---|---|---|---|---|---|---|
| **WESTERN HEMISPHERE** | | | | | | |
| **Pan-American Coffee Bureau** | | | | | | |
| Brazil | 713 | 37.5 | 710 | 38.6 | 643 | 34.2 |
| Colombia | 332 | 17.5 | 308 | 16.7 | 325 | 17.3 |
| El Salvador | 77 | 4.1 | 70 | 3.8 | 76 | 4.0 |
| Guatemala | 75 | 3.9 | 67 | 3.6 | 67 | 3.6 |
| Mexico | 62 | 3.3 | 63 | 3.4 | 64 | 3.4 |
| Costa Rica | 44 | 2.3 | 43 | 2.3 | 48 | 2.5 |
| Ecuador | 22 | 1.2 | 14 | 0.8 | 21 | 1.1 |
| Peru | 19 | 1.0 | 23 | 1.3 | 24 | 1.3 |
| Nicaragua | 19 | 1.0 | 17 | 0.9 | 15 | 0.8 |
| Honduras | 12 | 0.6 | 9 | 0.5 | 11 | 0.6 |
| Haiti | 16 | 0.8 | 13 | 0.7 | 24 | 1.3 |
| Dominican Republic | 23 | 1.2 | 14 | 0.8 | 20 | 1.1 |
| Venezuela | 22 | 1.2 | 23 | 1.3 | 19 | 1.0 |
| Panama | 1 | 0.1 | — | — | 1 | 0.1 |
| Cuba | 4 | 0.2 | 3 | 0.2 | 6 | 0.3 |
| **TOTAL P.A.C.B.** | 1,441 | 75.9 | 1,377 | 74.9 | 1,364 | 72.6 |
| **OTHER WESTERN HEMISPHERE (1)** | 45 | 2.4 | 50 | 2.7 | 64 | 3.4 |
| **TOTAL WESTERN HEMISPHERE** | 1,486 | 78.3 | 1,427 | 77.6 | 1,428 | 76.0 |
| **AFRICA** | | | | | | |
| Uganda | 42 | 2.2 | 39 | 2.1 | 56 | 3.0 |
| Kenya | 29 | 1.5 | 30 | 1.6 | 30 | 1.6 |
| Tanzania | 21 | 1.1 | 19 | 1.0 | 18 | 1.0 |
| Ivory Coast | 76 | 4.0 | 82 | 4.5 | 78 | 4.1 |
| Angola | 44 | 2.3 | 49 | 2.7 | 65 | 3.4 |
| Ethiopia | 46 | 2.4 | 38 | 2.1 | 43 | 2.3 |
| Cameroun | 19 | 1.0 | 21 | 1.1 | 21 | 1.1 |
| Madagascar | 27 | 1.4 | 22 | 1.2 | 30 | 1.6 |
| Congo (Kinshasa) | 30 | 1.6 | 6 | 0.3 | 14 | 0.7 |
| Burundi | * | * | 17 | 0.9 | 15 | 0.8 |
| Rwanda | * | * | * | * | * | * |
| Togo | 3 | 0.2 | 5 | 0.3 | 6 | 0.3 |
| Central African Republic | 3 | 0.2 | 4 | 0.2 | 3 | 0.2 |
| Guinea | 9 | 0.5 | 6 | 0.3 | 3 | 0.2 |
| Spanish Africa | 3 | 0.2 | 3 | 0.2 | 2 | 0.1 |
| Various (2) | 13 | 0.7 | 9 | 0.5 | 10 | 0.5 |
| **TOTAL AFRICA** | 365 | 19.3 | 350 | 19.0 | 394 | 20.9 |
| **ASIA & OCEANIA** | | | | | | |
| Indonesia | 14 | 0.7 | 14 | 0.8 | 13 | 0.7 |
| India | 14 | 0.7 | 20 | 1.1 | 16 | 0.8 |
| Yemen | 4 | 0.2 | 4 | 0.2 | 4 | 0.2 |
| Various (3) | 16 | 0.8 | 24 | 1.3 | 26 | 1.4 |
| **TOTAL ASIA & OCEANIA** | 48 | 2.4 | 62 | 3.4 | 59 | 3.1 |
| **TOTAL** | 1,899 | 100.0 | 1,839 | 100.0 | 1,881 | 100.0 |

Source: Statistical Agencies of Governments, International Financial Statistics, Direction of International Trade, Commodity Trade Statistics, Series D. (United Nations) and Trade Yearbook (FAO).

(*) Included in Congo (Kinshasa).

(1) Includes: Bolivia, Guadeloupe, Hawaii, Jamaica, Paraguay, Trinidad & Tobago, Surinam and Puerto Rico.

**BY COUNTRY OF ORIGIN, 1953-1966 (continued)**

| 1963 | | 1964 | | 1965 | | 1966 | |
|---|---|---|---|---|---|---|---|
| Value | Percent of World | Value | Percent of World | Value | Percent of World | Value | Percent of World |
| 748 | 38.1 | 760 | 32.0 | 707 | 32.7 | 774 | 32.5 |
| 303 | 15.4 | 394 | 16.6 | 344 | 15.9 | 339 | 14.2 |
| 75 | 3.5 | 91 | 3.8 | 96 | 4.4 | 91 | 3.8 |
| 78 | 4.0 | 72 | 3.0 | 86 | 4.0 | 102 | 4.3 |
| 44 | 2.2 | 102 | 4.3 | 76 | 3.5 | 82 | 3.4 |
| 46 | 2.3 | 48 | 2.0 | 46 | 2.1 | 52 | 2.2 |
| 18 | 0.9 | 22 | 0.9 | 37 | 1.7 | 32 | 1.3 |
| 26 | 1.3 | 37 | 1.6 | 29 | 1.3 | 29 | 1.2 |
| 18 | 0.9 | 24 | 1.0 | 28 | 1.3 | 24 | 1.0 |
| 14 | 0.7 | 17 | 0.7 | 23 | 1.1 | 19 | 0.8 |
| 16 | 0.8 | 19 | 0.8 | 20 | 0.9 | 18 | 0.8 |
| 19 | 1.0 | 30 | 1.3 | 22 | 1.0 | 21 | 0.9 |
| 23 | 1.2 | 18 | 0.8 | 17 | 0.8 | 17 | 0.7 |
| — | — | 2 | 0.1 | 1 | — | 2 | 0.1 |
| 1 | — | — | — | — | — | — | — |
| 1,429 | 72.6 | 1,636 | 68.9 | 1,532 | 70.7 | 1,602 | 67.2 |
| 34 | 1.7 | 38 | 1.6 | 13 | 0.6 | 10 | 0.4 |
| 1,463 | 74.3 | 1,674 | 70.5 | 1,545 | 71.3 | 1,612 | 67.6 |
| 76 | 3.9 | 99 | 4.2 | 79 | 3.6 | 103 | 4.3 |
| 31 | 1.6 | 43 | 1.8 | 39 | 1.8 | 53 | 2.2 |
| 19 | 1.0 | 31 | 1.3 | 24 | 1.1 | 42 | 1.8 |
| 99 | 5.0 | 129 | 5.4 | 112 | 5.2 | 111 | 4.7 |
| 65 | 3.3 | 100 | 4.2 | 103 | 4.8 | 108 | 4.5 |
| 44 | 2.2 | 64 | 2.7 | 70 | 3.2 | 98 | 4.1 |
| 24 | 1.2 | 26 | 1.1 | 29 | 1.3 | 42 | 1.8 |
| 24 | 1.2 | 25 | 1.1 | 29 | 1.3 | 31 | 1.3 |
| 22 | 1.1 | 33 | 1.4 | 25 | 1.2 | 25 | 1.1 |
| 7 | 0.4 | 17 | 0.7 | 12 | 0.6 | 19 | 0.8 |
| * | * | 7 | 0.3 | 8 | 0.4 | 7 | 0.3 |
| 3 | 0.2 | 10 | 0.4 | 8 | 0.4 | 12 | 0.5 |
| 3 | 0.2 | 9 | 0.4 | 5 | 0.2 | 9 | 0.4 |
| N.A. | — | 7 | 0.3 | 3 | 0.1 | 8 | 0.3 |
| 3 | 0.2 | 4 | 0.2 | 4 | 0.2 | 4 | 0.2 |
| 3 | 0.2 | 1 | — | 7 | 0.3 | 25 | 1.0 |
| 423 | 21.7 | 605 | 25.4 | 557 | 25.7 | 697 | 29.3 |
| 30 | 1.5 | 32 | 1.3 | 21 | 1.0 | 34 | 1.4 |
| 16 | 0.8 | 26 | 1.1 | 24 | 1.1 | 23 | 1.0 |
| 5 | 0.3 | 6 | 0.3 | 6 | 0.3 | 4 | 0.2 |
| 27 | 1.4 | 34 | 1.4 | 13 | 0.6 | 12 | 0.5 |
| 78 | 4.0 | 98 | 4.1 | 64 | 3.0 | 73 | 3.1 |
| 1,964 | 100.0 | 2,377 | 100.0 | 2,166 | 100.0 | 2,382 | 100.0 |

(2) Includes: Cape Verde, Congo (Brazzaville), Dahomey, Gabon, Ghana, Liberia, Nigeria, São Thomé and Principe and Sierra Leone.

(3) Includes: New Caledonia, New Guinea, New Hebrides, Singapore and Timor.

REV-6. WORLD: SHARE OF COFFEE IN FOREIGN

(in U. S.

| COUNTRIES | 1960 Coffee | 1960 Percent | 1961 Coffee | 1961 Percent | 1962 Coffee | 1962 Percent |
|---|---|---|---|---|---|---|
| **WESTERN HEMISPHERE** | | | | | | |
| *Pan-American Coffee Bureau* | | | | | | |
| Brazil | 712,710 | 56.2 | 710,436 | 50.6 | 642,629 | 52.9 |
| Colombia | 351,223 | 75.6 | 307,827 | 70.9 | 343,065 | 71.6 |
| El Salvador | 72,578 | 67.3 | 70,222 | 57.2 | 74,227 | 61.1 |
| Guatemala | 78,564 | 67.7 | 69,161 | 62.6 | 68,227 | 57.6 |
| Mexico | 71,568 | 9.7 | 70,454 | 8.8 | 71,286 | 7.9 |
| Costa Rica | 43,920 | 53.0 | 43,300 | 53.3 | 47,204 | 52.0 |
| Ecuador | 21,946 | 20.7 | 14,254 | 18.1 | 20,901 | 16.5 |
| Peru | 18,542 | 4.3 | 22,770 | 4.6 | 24,191 | 4.5 |
| Nicaragua | 19,221 | 30.6 | 17,612 | 25.4 | 15,430 | 17.1 |
| Honduras | 11,823 | 18.9 | 9,030 | 12.5 | 11,450 | 14.3 |
| Haiti | 17,306 | 53.0 | 13,451 | 39.9 | 20,627 | 50.6 |
| Dominican Republic | 22,570 | 14.5 | 14,353 | 8.4 | 19,849 | 11.7 |
| Venezuela | 21,830 | 0.9 | 22,654 | 1.0 | 18,687 | 0.8 |
| Panama | 1,111 | 5.6 | 258 | 1.2 | 1,392 | 3.8 |
| Cuba | 3,700 | 0.7 | 4,094 | 0.7 | 5,545 | 1.3 |
| Other Western Hemisphere (1) | N.A. | N.A. | N.A. | N.A. | N.A. | N.A. |
| **AFRICA** | | | | | | |
| Uganda | 42,240 | 40.8 | 39,141 | 35.7 | 56,487 | 53.6 |
| Kenya | 28,770 | 29.2 | 29,705 | 30.0 | 29,666 | 27.9 |
| Tanzania | 20,540 | 13.4 | 18,934 | 13.9 | 18,410 | 12.8 |
| Ivory Coast | 75,720 | 50.0 | 82,426 | 46.7 | 76,649 | 39.7 |
| Angola | 43,960 | 35.4 | 48,639 | 36.2 | 63,085 | 42.7 |
| Ethiopia | 45,580 | 55.4 | 37,721 | 50.1 | 44,444 | 45.5 |
| Cameroun | 18,670 | 16.0 | 19,425 | 18.8 | 21,008 | 21.2 |
| Madagascar | 26,560 | 31.5 | 22,472 | 29.0 | 30,055 | 31.9 |
| Congo (Kinshasa) | 30,040 | 8.7 | 23,320 | N.A. | 13,580 | 3.7 |
| Burundi | N.A. | N.A. | 160 | 62.8 | 126 | 63.9 |
| Rwanda | * | * | * | * | * | * |
| Togo | 2,570 | 17.7 | 5,043 | 27.0 | 5,793 | 33.7 |
| Central African Republic | 3,450 | 24.9 | 3,925 | 28.6 | 4,116 | 28.9 |
| Guinea | N.A. | N.A. | N.A. | N.A. | N.A. | N.A. |
| Spanish Africa | N.A. | N.A. | N.A. | N.A. | N.A. | N.A. |
| Nigeria | N.A. | N.A. | 190 | 0.1 | 260 | 0.1 |
| Various (2) | | | | | | |
| **ASIA & OCEANIA** | | | | | | |
| Indonesia | 13,680 | 1.6 | 13,742 | 1.7 | 12,508 | 1.8 |
| India | 14,010 | 1.0 | 15,171 | 1.1 | 18,939 | 1.4 |
| Yemen | N.A. | N.A. | N.A. | N.A. | N.A. | N.A. |
| Various (3) | N.A. | N.A. | N.A. | N.A. | N.A. | N.A. |

Source: Statistical offices and official trade entities of exporting countries, International Financial Statistics and Direction of International Trade.

(*) Included in Burundi

(1) Includes: Bolivia, Guadeloupe, Hawaii, Jamaica, Paraguay, Trinidad and Tobago, Surinam and Puerto Rico.

**EXCHANGE REVENUES, 1960-1966**

dollars)

| 1963 Coffee | Percent | 1964 Coffee | Percent | 1965 Coffee | Percent | 1966 Coffee | Percent |
|---|---|---|---|---|---|---|---|
| 746,952 | 53.1 | 759,708 | 53.2 | 707,000 | 44.3 | 773,500 | 44.7 |
| 303,006 | 67.8 | 393,577 | 71.9 | 344,000 | 62.4 | 339,200 | 67.0 |
| 74,520 | 46.2 | 90,809 | 50.3 | 96,000 | 50.8 | 90,600 | 47.2 |
| 78,100 | 50.7 | 72,293 | 46.5 | 86,000 | 46.0 | 102,300 | 45.9 |
| 52,240 | 5.6 | 101,791 | 9.9 | 76,000 | 6.7 | 82,300 | 6.7 |
| 45,816 | 48.5 | 47,940 | 42.3 | 46,000 | 41.1 | 52,200 | 42.1 |
| 18,400 | 14.3 | 21,682 | 15.3 | 37,000 | 24.5 | 32,100 | 16.9 |
| 25,563 | 4.7 | 37,451 | 5.6 | 29,000 | 4.5 | 29,400 | 3.8 |
| 17,481 | 16.4 | 24,308 | 20.8 | 28,000 | 18.2 | 23,700 | 16.1 |
| 13,983 | 17.3 | 16,700 | 17.7 | 23,000 | 18.3 | 18,900 | 13.9 |
| 16,187 | 38.9 | 19,393 | 45.9 | 20,000 | 55.6 | 17,800 | 54.3 |
| 18,541 | 9.8 | 30,200 | 13.6 | 22,000 | 17.9 | 21,000 | 15.3 |
| 23,155 | 1.0 | 17,033 | 0.7 | 17,000 | 0.6 | 17,100 | 0.6 |
| 392 | 0.8 | 1,528 | 2.4 | 1,000 | 1.3 | 2,200 | 2.5 |
| 461 | 0.1 | — | — | — | — | — | — |
| N.A. | N.A. | N.A. | N.A. | 13,000 | 1.5 | 9,800 | 1.1 |
| | | | | | | | |
| 76,107 | 52.8 | 99,058 | 54.9 | 79,000 | 48.5 | 103,300 | 56.0 |
| 30,642 | 25.1 | 43,109 | 32.7 | 39,000 | 26.9 | 52,600 | 30.4 |
| 19,152 | 10.8 | 30,940 | 15.8 | 24,000 | 13.6 | 42,300 | 18.3 |
| 98,326 | 43.1 | 99,136 | 43.4 | 112,000 | 42.6 | 111,400 | 36.6 |
| 67,947 | 41.5 | 99,758 | N.A. | 103,000 | 50.7 | 107,400 | 48.5 |
| 45,120 | 53.3 | 64,680 | 64.6 | 70,000 | 58.8 | 98,000 | 87.5 |
| 22,940 | 21.9 | 30,793 | 24.3 | 29,000 | 23.2 | 41,700 | 19.3 |
| 23,761 | 29.0 | 24,560 | 26.8 | 29,000 | 31.5 | 30,800 | 31.5 |
| 28,860 | 6.9 | 33,114 | N.A. | 25,000 | 8.1 | 25,300 | 5.3 |
| 56 | 40.7 | 163 | 93.9 | 12,000 | 70.6 | 18,700 | 70.6 |
| * | * | 69 | 65.6 | 8,000 | 80.0 | 7,100 | 80.0 |
| 3,245 | 17.8 | 10,229 | 33.9 | 8,000 | 26.7 | 12,200 | 32.1 |
| 3,171 | 14.4 | 8,009 | 27.7 | 5,000 | 18.5 | 9,000 | 28.8 |
| N.A. | N.A. | N.A. | N.A. | 3,000 | 6.3 | 8,300 | 15.7 |
| N.A. | N.A. | N.A. | N.A. | 4,000 | 16.7 | 4,100 | 16.7 |
| 652 | 0.1 | 2,251 | 0.5 | N.A. | N.A. | 5,300 | 0.7 |
| N.A. | N.A. | N.A. | N.A. | 7,000 | 0.5 | 19,600 | 5.0 |
| | | | | | | | |
| 19,636 | 2.8 | N.A. | N.A. | 21,000 | 2.2 | 33,800 | 2.2 |
| 15,986 | 1.1 | 17,434 | 1.1 | 24,000 | 1.4 | 22,500 | 1.4 |
| N.A. | N.A. | N.A. | N.A. | 6,000 | 75.0 | 4,100 | 74.5 |
| N.A. | N.A. | N.A. | N.A. | 13,000 | 0.7 | 12,100 | 0.7 |

(2) Includes: Cape Verde, Congo (Brazzaville), Dahomey, Gabon, Ghana, Liberia, Nigeria, São Thomé and Principe and Sierra Leone.

(3) Includes: New Caledonia, New Guinea, New Hebrides, Singapore and Timor.

T-1. UNITED STATES: BALANCE OF TRADE WITH

(U. S.

|  | 1966 | | | 1965 | | |
|---|---|---|---|---|---|---|
| U. S. MERCHANDISE* TRADE WITH | Exports | Imports | Balance of Trade | Exports | Imports | Balance of Trade |
| **PAN-AMERICAN COFFEE BUREAU** | | | | | | |
| Brazil | 565.3 | 602.6 | − 37.3 | 328.6 | 511.9 | − 183.3 |
| Colombia | 282.4 | 245.7 | + 36.7 | 196.4 | 276.7 | − 80.3 |
| Mexico | 1131.1 | 705.1 | +426.0 | 1105.2 | 637.9 | +467.3 |
| Guatemala | 88.9 | 82.0 | + 6.9 | 95.1 | 66.7 | + 28.4 |
| El Salvador | 68.9 | 44.3 | + 24.6 | 60.6 | 48.2 | + 12.4 |
| Venezuela | 591.7 | 1024.7 | − 433.0 | 623.7 | 1020.6 | − 396.9 |
| Peru | 303.3 | 297.1 | + 6.2 | 280.7 | 241.1 | + 39.6 |
| Dominican Republic | 86.6 | 130.6 | − 44.0 | 75.6 | 110.6 | − 35.0 |
| Costa Rica | 61.8 | 59.9 | + 1.9 | 60.9 | 57.0 | + 3.9 |
| Ecuador | 80.0 | 94.3 | − 14.3 | 77.7 | 105.9 | − 28.2 |
| Honduras | 67.1 | 82.4 | − 15.3 | 53.5 | 71.6 | − 18.1 |
| Nicaragua | 70.4 | 31.2 | + 39.2 | 68.6 | 36.0 | + 32.6 |
| Haiti | 21.5 | 18.6 | + 2.9 | 21.4 | 20.5 | + 0.9 |
| Panama | 136.7 | 67.8 | + 68.9 | 124.6 | 59.6 | + 65.0 |
| Cuba | — | 1.6 | − 1.6 | — | — | — |
| **TOTAL P.A.C.B.** | 3,555.7 | 3,487.9 | + 67.8 | 3,172.6 | 3,264.3 | − 91.7 |
| **VALUE OF ALL U. S. TRADE WITH WORLD** | 29,899.0 | 25,366.6 | | 27,003.0 | 21,366.0 | |
| **PERCENT SHARE OF 15 COFFEE-PRODUCING COUNTRIES** | 11.9 | 13.7 | | 11.7 | 15.3 | |

Source: United States Department of Commerce.

(*) Merchandise only. Military and "Special Category" items excluded.

# FIFTEEN LATIN AMERICAN COFFEE-PRODUCING COUNTRIES, 1962-1966

$ millions)

|  | 1964 |  |  | 1963 |  |  | 1962 |  |
|---|---|---|---|---|---|---|---|---|
| Exports | Imports | Balance of Trade | Exports | Imports | Balance of Trade | Exports | Imports | Balance of Trade |
| 387.8 | 534.7 | − 146.9 | 382.0 | 561.8 | − 179.8 | 424.8 | 540.9 | − 116.1 |
| 246.2 | 280.4 | − 34.2 | 240.2 | 248.5 | − 8.3 | 226.6 | 275.2 | − 48.6 |
| 1092.4 | 643.1 | + 449.3 | 861.4 | 594.4 | + 267.0 | 805.2 | 578.2 | + 227.0 |
| 83.3 | 62.7 | + 20.6 | 73.6 | 69.9 | + 3.7 | 61.1 | 62.6 | − 1.5 |
| 66.3 | 43.2 | + 23.1 | 49.6 | 40.5 | + 9.1 | 40.6 | 44.1 | − 3.5 |
| 606.3 | 956.4 | − 350.1 | 509.1 | 935.8 | − 426.7 | 470.6 | 975.8 | − 505.2 |
| 219.0 | 212.9 | + 6.1 | 193.8 | 215.3 | − 21.5 | 183.9 | 190.7 | − 6.8 |
| 114.3 | 127.8 | − 13.5 | 91.4 | 140.2 | − 48.8 | 71.0 | 153.4 | − 82.4 |
| 60.3 | 54.0 | + 6.3 | 53.4 | 41.6 | + 11.8 | 49.5 | 40.0 | + 9.5 |
| 83.3 | 87.3 | − 4.0 | 56.6 | 76.0 | − 19.4 | 45.0 | 71.7 | − 26.7 |
| 49.1 | 41.6 | + 7.5 | 43.8 | 31.5 | + 12.3 | 43.0 | 32.5 | + 10.5 |
| 57.2 | 33.6 | + 23.6 | 45.1 | 35.1 | + 10.0 | 46.1 | 27.6 | + 18.5 |
| 23.6 | 24.1 | − 0.5 | 21.2 | 25.5 | − 4.3 | 24.3 | 24.4 | − 0.1 |
| 110.5 | 40.1 | + 70.4 | 109.2 | 31.9 | + 77.3 | 104.5 | 22.9 | + 81.6 |
| — | — | — | 36.5 | — | + 36.5 | 13.4 | 6.8 | + 6.6 |
| 3,199.6 | 3,141.9 | + 57.7 | 2,766.9 | 3,048.0 | − 281.1 | 2,609.6 | 3,046.8 | − 437.2 |
| 26,136.0 | 18,684.0 |  | 23,062.0 | 17,138.0 |  | 21,431.0 | 16,380.0 |  |
| 12.2 | 16.8 |  | 12.0 | 17.8 |  | 12.2 | 18.6 |  |

EV-2. LATIN AMERICA: VALUE OF GREEN COFFEE EXPORTS, 1965-1966

(Thousands of U. S. Dollars)

| COUNTRIES OF ORIGIN | 1966* | 1965 | Percent of Total 1966 | Percent of Total 1965 | Increase or Decrease 1966 over 1965 AMOUNT | PERCENT | 1966 Average Prices Per Bag | Per Lb. |
|---|---|---|---|---|---|---|---|---|
| PAN-AMERICAN COFFEE BUREAU | | | | | | | | |
| Brazil | 773,522 | 707,366 | 48.3 | 46.2 | + 66,156 | + 9.4 | 45.42 | 34.34 |
| Colombia | 339,257 | 343,584 | 21.2 | 22.4 | − 4,327 | − 1.3 | 60.96 | 46.09 |
| El Salvador | 90,566 | 96,156 | 5.6 | 6.3 | − 5,590 | − 5.8 | 55.93 | 42.28 |
| Guatemala | 102,344 | 86,088 | 6.4 | 5.6 | + 16,256 | + 18.9 | 54.91 | 41.51 |
| Mexico | 82,319 | 75,654 | 5.1 | 4.9 | + 6,665 | + 8.8 | 53.58 | 40.51 |
| Costa Rica | 52,179 | 46,443 | 3.3 | 3.0 | + 5,736 | + 12.4 | 57.94 | 43.80 |
| Ecuador | 32,100 | 37,200 | 2.0 | 2.4 | − 5,100 | − 13.7 | 44.09 | 33.33 |
| Peru | 29,440 | 28,852 | 1.8 | 1.9 | + 588 | + 2.0 | 50.20 | 37.95 |
| Nicaragua | 23,663 | 28,345 | 1.5 | 1.9 | − 4,682 | − 16.5 | 56.12 | 42.43 |
| Honduras | 18,880 | 22,150 | 1.2 | 1.5 | − 3,270 | − 14.8 | 50.21 | 37.96 |
| Haiti | 17,816 | 19,790 | 1.1 | 1.3 | − 1,974 | − 10.0 | 50.87 | 38.46 |
| Dominican Republic | 21,000 | 21,100 | 1.3 | 1.4 | − 100 | − 0.5 | 50.28 | 38.01 |
| Venezuela | 17,083 | 17,421 | 1.1 | 1.1 | − 338 | − 1.9 | 56.33 | 42.58 |
| Panama | 2,174 | 1,070 | 0.1 | 0.1 | + 1,104 | + 103.2 | 48.08 | 36.35 |
| Cuba | − | − | − | − | − | − | − | − |
| TOTAL PAN-AMERICAN COFFEE BUREAU | 1,602,343 | 1,531,219 | 100.0 | 100.0 | + 71,124 | + 4.6 | 50.48 | 38.16 |
| SUMMARY BY PRINCIPAL SOURCES | | | | | | | | |
| Brazil | 773,522 | 707,366 | 48.3 | 46.2 | + 66,156 | + 9.4 | 45.42 | 34.34 |
| Colombia | 339,257 | 343,584 | 21.2 | 22.4 | − 4,327 | − 1.3 | 60.96 | 46.09 |
| Fedecame | 489,564 | 480,269 | 30.5 | 31.4 | + 9,295 | + 1.9 | 53.51 | 40.45 |
| TOTAL PAN-AMERICAN COFFEE BUREAU | 1,602,343 | 1,531,219 | 100.0 | 100.0 | + 71,124 | + 4.6 | 50.48 | 38.16 |

Source: Statistical offices and official trade entities of exporting countries.

(*) Estimated.

## IQ-1. WORLD: IMPORTS OF GREEN COFFEE, 1965-1966
(Thousands of bags of 60 kilograms or 132.276 pounds each)

| COUNTRIES OF DESTINATION | 1966* | 1965+ | Percentage of Total 1966 | Percentage of Total 1965 | Increase or Decrease 1966 over 1965 VOLUME | Increase or Decrease 1966 over 1965 PERCENT |
|---|---|---|---|---|---|---|
| **UNITED STATES** | 22,092 | 21,347 | 44.2 | 45.2 | + 745 | + 3.5 |
| **CANADA** | 1,164 | 1,258 | 2.3 | 2.7 | − 94 | − 7.5 |
| **OTHER AMERICAS** | | | | | | |
| Argentina | 673 | 505 | 1.4 | 1.1 | + 168 | + 33.3 |
| Chile | 153 | 151 | 0.3 | 0.3 | + 2 | + 1.3 |
| Uruguay | 24 | 8 | — | — | + 16 | +200.0 |
| Various (1) | 1 | 1 | — | — | — | — |
| **TOTAL OTHER AMERICAS** | 851 | 665 | 1.7 | 1.4 | + 186 | + 28.0 |
| **EUROPE** | | | | | | |
| Germany (F.R.) | 4,663 | 4,597 | 9.3 | 9.7 | + 66 | + 1.4 |
| France | 3,794 | 3,617 | 7.6 | 7.7 | + 177 | + 4.9 |
| Italy | 2,058 | 2,006 | 4.1 | 4.3 | + 52 | + 2.6 |
| Netherlands | 1,417 | 1,378 | 2.9 | 2.9 | + 39 | + 2.8 |
| Belgium−Luxembourg | 905 | 1,129 | 1.8 | 2.4 | − 224 | − 19.8 |
| Total European Economic Community | 12,837 | 12,727 | 25.7 | 27.0 | + 110 | + 0.9 |
| Sweden | 1,615 | 1,532 | 3.2 | 3.2 | + 83 | + 5.4 |
| United Kingdom | 1,360 | 973 | 2.7 | 2.1 | + 387 | + 39.8 |
| Denmark | 886 | 824 | 1.8 | 1.7 | + 62 | + 7.5 |
| Spain | 911 | 810 | 1.8 | 1.7 | + 101 | + 12.5 |
| Switzerland | 671 | 736 | 1.4 | 1.6 | − 65 | − 8.8 |
| Finland | 767 | 673 | 1.5 | 1.4 | + 94 | + 14.0 |
| Norway | 576 | 482 | 1.2 | 1.0 | + 94 | + 19.5 |
| Yugoslavia | 459 | 293 | 0.9 | 0.6 | + 166 | + 56.7 |
| Austria | 292 | 282 | 0.6 | 0.6 | + 10 | + 3.5 |
| Portugal | 220 | 215 | 0.4 | 0.5 | + 5 | + 2.3 |
| Greece | 172 | 166 | 0.4 | 0.4 | + 6 | + 3.6 |
| Various (2) | 111 | 111 | 0.2 | 0.2 | — | — |
| Total Other Western Europe | 8,040 | 7,097 | 16.1 | 15.0 | + 943 | + 13.3 |
| USSR | 504 | 503 | 1.0 | 1.1 | + 1 | + 0.2 |
| Germany (D.R.) | 605 | 597 | 1.2 | 1.3 | + 8 | + 1.3 |
| Poland | 412 | 257 | 0.8 | 0.5 | + 155 | +60.3 |
| Hungary | 300 | 211 | 0.6 | 0.4 | + 89 | +42.2 |
| Czechoslovakia | 177 | 172 | 0.4 | 0.4 | + 5 | + 2.9 |
| Various (3) | 50 | 40 | 0.1 | 0.1 | + 10 | +25.0 |
| Total East Europe | 2,048 | 1,780 | 4.1 | 3.8 | + 268 | +15.1 |
| **TOTAL EUROPE** | 22,925 | 21,604 | 45.9 | 45.8 | +1,321 | + 6.1 |
| **AFRICA** | | | | | | |
| Algeria | 259 | 269 | 0.5 | 0.6 | − 10 | − 3.7 |
| South Africa | 213 | 168 | 0.4 | 0.4 | + 45 | +26.8 |
| Morocco | 140 | 160 | 0.3 | 0.3 | − 20 | − 12.5 |
| Sudan | 233 | 158 | 0.5 | 0.3 | + 75 | +47.5 |
| United Arab Republic | 98 | 50 | 0.2 | 0.1 | + 48 | +96.0 |
| Tunisia | 23 | 35 | 0.1 | 0.1 | − 12 | − 34.3 |
| Various (4) | 13 | 13 | — | — | — | — |
| **TOTAL AFRICA** | 979 | 853 | 2.0 | 1.8 | + 126 | + 14.8 |
| **ASIA & OCEANIA** | | | | | | |
| Japan | 769 | 365 | 1.5 | 0.8 | + 404 | +110.7 |
| Australia | 269 | 245 | 0.5 | 0.5 | + 24 | + 9.8 |
| Lebanon | 75 | 76 | 0.2 | 0.1 | − 1 | − 1.3 |
| Israel | 100 | 83 | 0.2 | 0.2 | + 17 | + 20.5 |
| Thailand | 102 | 76 | 0.2 | 0.1 | + 26 | + 34.2 |
| Syria | 41 | 41 | 0.1 | 0.1 | — | — |
| Various (5) | 576 | 600 | 1.2 | 1.3 | − 24 | − 4.0 |
| **TOTAL ASIA & OCEANIA** | 1,932 | 1,486 | 3.9 | 3.1 | + 446 | + 30.0 |
| **TOTAL IMPORTS** | 49,943 | 47,213 | 100.0 | 100.0 | +2,730 | + 5.8 |

Source: Central statistical offices and trade sources in importing countries.
(*) Preliminary.
(+) Revised.
(1) Includes: Netherlands West Indies and other Caribbean Islands.
(2) Includes: Andorra, Gibraltar, Iceland, Ireland, Malta, Monaco and Turkey.
(3) Includes: Albania, Bulgaria, Roumania.
(4) Includes: Libya, Malawi, Mozambique and Rhodesia.
(5) Includes: Bahrein, China, Cyprus, Formosa, Hong Kong, Iran, Iraq, Jordan, Kuwait, Macao, Muscat, New Zealand, Oman, Qatar, Saudi Arabia and Trucial Oman.

## IQ-2. WORLD: IMPORTS
(Thousands of bags of 60 Kilograms)

| COUNTRIES OF DESTINATION | 1947 | 1948 | 1949 | 1950 | 1951 | 1952 | 1953 | 1954 | 1955 |
|---|---|---|---|---|---|---|---|---|---|
| **UNITED STATES** | 18,911 | 20,969 | 22,105 | 18,440 | 20,357 | 20,274 | 21,065 | 17,092 | 19,651 |
| **CANADA** | 388 | 662 | 742 | 626 | 669 | 738 | 813 | 721 | 785 |
| **OTHER AMERICAS** | | | | | | | | | |
| Argentina | 580 | 705 | 308 | 504 | 476 | 518 | 494 | 566 | 469 |
| Chile | 162 | 40 | 177 | 110 | 68 | 67 | 99 | 91 | 112 |
| Uruguay | 48 | 64 | 64 | 54 | 42 | 40 | 61 | 55 | 67 |
| Various (1) | 8 | 7 | 7 | 2 | 147 | 12 | 51 | 13 | 5 |
| **TOTAL OTHER AMERICAS** | 798 | 816 | 556 | 670 | 733 | 637 | 705 | 725 | 653 |
| **EUROPE** | | | | | | | | | |
| Germany (F.R.) | — | 233 | 359 | 443 | 677 | 942 | 1,311 | 1,727 | 1,997 |
| France | 1,271 | 1,185 | 1,459 | 2,493 | 2,522 | 2,771 | 2,842 | 2,811 | 3,042 |
| Italy | 470 | 678 | 743 | 636 | 889 | 1,188 | 1,189 | 1,158 | 1,206 |
| Netherlands | 354 | 352 | 401 | 373 | 283 | 327 | 472 | 461 | 524 |
| Belgium-Luxembourg | 1,520 | 1,425 | 1,505 | 996 | 912 | 867 | 876 | 714 | 782 |
| **Total European Economic Community** | 3,615 | 3,873 | 4,467 | 4,941 | 5,283 | 6,095 | 6,690 | 6,871 | 7,551 |
| Sweden | 781 | 576 | 576 | 576 | 699 | 793 | 854 | 803 | 885 |
| United Kingdom | 751 | 887 | 745 | 675 | 721 | 720 | 507 | 568 | 574 |
| Denmark | 214 | 205 | 269 | 293 | 272 | 338 | 426 | 405 | 469 |
| Finland | 87 | 153 | 189 | 249 | 246 | 363 | 384 | 466 | 496 |
| Norway | 188 | 292 | 277 | 245 | 257 | 366 | 308 | 290 | 354 |
| Switzerland | 248 | 422 | 305 | 421 | 331 | 304 | 319 | 319 | 299 |
| Spain | 502 | 238 | 225 | 131 | 102 | 121 | 102 | 123 | 147 |
| Austria | — | — | 62 | 80 | 85 | 74 | 74 | 80 | 95 |
| Portugal | 105 | 177 | 164 | 112 | 140 | 175 | 158 | 145 | 166 |
| Yugoslavia | — | 25 | 16 | 8 | — | — | — | 25 | 60 |
| Greece | 27 | 129 | 118 | 85 | 101 | 100 | 88 | 83 | 94 |
| Various (2) | 97 | 339 | 508 | 447 | 195 | 118 | 112 | 110 | 196 |
| **Total Other West Europe** | 3,000 | 3,443 | 3,454 | 3,322 | 3,149 | 3,472 | 3,332 | 3,417 | 3,835 |
| USSR | — | — | — | — | — | — | — | — | — |
| Germany (D.R.) | — | — | — | — | — | — | — | — | — |
| Czechoslovakia | 71 | 27 | 25 | 33 | — | — | — | 45 | 84 |
| Poland | — | — | — | 7 | — | — | — | — | — |
| Hungary | — | — | — | — | — | — | — | — | — |
| Various (3) | — | — | — | — | 104 | 125 | 159 | 180 | 152 |
| **Total East Europe** | 71 | 27 | 25 | 40 | 104 | 125 | 159 | 225 | 236 |
| **TOTAL EUROPE** | 6,686 | 7,343 | 7,946 | 8,303 | 8,536 | 9,692 | 10,181 | 10,513 | 11,622 |
| **AFRICA** | | | | | | | | | |
| Algeria | 251 | 234 | 131 | 333 | 353 | 319 | 333 | 349 | 370 |
| South Africa | — | 401 | 371 | 280 | 198 | 201 | 196 | 174 | 180 |
| Sudan | — | — | — | — | — | — | — | — | — |
| Morocco | — | — | — | — | 60 | 60 | 75 | 68 | 97 |
| U.A.R. | 167 | 366 | 283 | 194 | 185 | 195 | 233 | 184 | 202 |
| Tunisia | 80 | 27 | 34 | 10 | 60 | 22 | 12 | 27 | 28 |
| Various (4) | 11 | 27 | 53 | 47 | 14 | 13 | 22 | 20 | 20 |
| **TOTAL AFRICA** | 509 | 1,055 | 872 | 864 | 870 | 810 | 871 | 822 | 897 |
| **ASIA & OCEANIA** | | | | | | | | | |
| Japan | — | — | — | — | 22 | 40 | 56 | 44 | 69 |
| Lebanon | 60 | 46 | 43 | 35 | 43 | — | — | — | — |
| Australia | 69 | 61 | 55 | 63 | 58 | 59 | 70 | 80 | 77 |
| Thailand | — | — | — | — | — | — | — | — | 39 |
| Israel | — | — | 6 | 17 | — | — | 20 | 16 | 19 |
| Syria | — | — | — | — | — | — | — | — | — |
| Various (5) | 221 | 672 | 489 | 404 | 272 | 346 | 264 | 94 | 174 |
| **TOTAL ASIA & OCEANIA** | 350 | 779 | 593 | 519 | 395 | 445 | 410 | 234 | 378 |
| **TOTAL IMPORTS** | 27,642 | 31,624 | 32,814 | 29,422 | 31,560 | 32,596 | 34,045 | 30,107 | 33,986 |

Source: Central statistical offices and official trade entities in importing countries. See note to table IQ-1.

## OF GREEN COFFEE, 1947-1966

or 132.276 pounds each)

| 1956 | 1957 | 1958 | 1959 | 1960 | 1961 | 1962 | 1963 | 1964 | 1965 | 1966 |
|---|---|---|---|---|---|---|---|---|---|---|
| **21,252** | **20,858** | **20,169** | **23,270** | **22,091** | **22,464** | **24,549** | **23,893** | **22,892** | **21,347** | **22,092** |
| **829** | **836** | **895** | **1,015** | **995** | **1,119** | **1,230** | **1,288** | **1,247** | **1,258** | **1,164** |
| 460 | 584 | 672 | 315 | 460 | 582 | 486 | 485 | 482 | 505 | 673 |
| 127 | 99 | 91 | 107 | 92 | 88 | 69 | 69 | 101 | 151 | 153 |
| 55 | 54 | 52 | 79 | 50 | 45 | 40 | 36 | 17 | 8 | 24 |
| 5 | 5 | 5 | 5 | 5 | 5 | 5 | 5 | — | 1 | 1 |
| **647** | **742** | **820** | **506** | **607** | **720** | **600** | **595** | **600** | **665** | **851** |
| 2,251 | 2,567 | 2,661 | 3,110 | 3,323 | 3,540 | 3,899 | 3,958 | 4,276 | 4,597 | 4,663 |
| 3,240 | 3,026 | 3,151 | 3,398 | 3,477 | 3,454 | 3,472 | 3,645 | 3,842 | 3,617 | 3,794 |
| 1,262 | 1,295 | 1,348 | 1,400 | 1,653 | 1,753 | 1,865 | 1,935 | 1,993 | 2,006 | 2,058 |
| 689 | 653 | 721 | 853 | 917 | 1,147 | 1,063 | 1,257 | 1,380 | 1,378 | 1,417 |
| 1,015 | 847 | 875 | 983 | 1,109 | 1,036 | 923 | 922 | 1,049 | 1,129 | 905 |
| **8,457** | **8,388** | **8,756** | **9,744** | **10,479** | **10,930** | **11,222** | **11,717** | **12,540** | **12,727** | **12,837** |
| 966 | 956 | 1,067 | 1,132 | 1,222 | 1,295 | 1,397 | 1,467 | 1,522 | 1,532 | 1,615 |
| 746 | 762 | 735 | 883 | 920 | 978 | 1,155 | 1,275 | 1,303 | 973 | 1,360 |
| 522 | 549 | 621 | 640 | 698 | 727 | 761 | 883 | 805 | 824 | 886 |
| 544 | 505 | 523 | 572 | 568 | 638 | 654 | 703 | 796 | 673 | 767 |
| 369 | 395 | 441 | 419 | 483 | 450 | 516 | 560 | 554 | 482 | 576 |
| 374 | 367 | 384 | 446 | 498 | 541 | 507 | 576 | 601 | 736 | 671 |
| 154 | 204 | 208 | 298 | 262 | 418 | 481 | 577 | 697 | 810 | 911 |
| 122 | 138 | 149 | 164 | 203 | 218 | 224 | 252 | 285 | 282 | 292 |
| 138 | 144 | 179 | 175 | 350 | 210 | 204 | 223 | 179 | 215 | 220 |
| 74 | 47 | 64 | 99 | 153 | 143 | 171 | 296 | 262 | 293 | 459 |
| 91 | 100 | 116 | 124 | 127 | 132 | 146 | 158 | 163 | 166 | 172 |
| 65 | 100 | — | 38 | 19 | 145 | — | 97 | 103 | 111 | 111 |
| **4,165** | **4,267** | **4,487** | **4,990** | **5,503** | **5,895** | **6,216** | **7,067** | **7,270** | **7,097** | **8,040** |
| — | — | 68 | 125 | 317 | 371 | 376 | 415 | 487 | 503 | 504 |
| — | — | 136 | 142 | 289 | 298 | 425 | 425 | 474 | 597 | 605 |
| 117 | 86 | 90 | 160 | 85 | 175 | 147 | 71 | 201 | 172 | 177 |
| — | 26 | 27 | 130 | 65 | 89 | 120 | 167 | 186 | 257 | 412 |
| — | — | 26 | 97 | 55 | 39 | 57 | 94 | 149 | 211 | 300 |
| 224 | 171 | — | 125 | 225 | 10 | — | 38 | 40 | 40 | 50 |
| **341** | **283** | **347** | **779** | **1,036** | **982** | **1,125** | **1,210** | **1,537** | **1,780** | **2,048** |
| **12,963** | **12,938** | **13,590** | **15,513** | **17,018** | **17,807** | **18,563** | **19,994** | **21,347** | **21,604** | **22,925** |
| 454 | 460 | 455 | 498 | 491 | 428 | 456 | 408 | 616 | 269 | 259 |
| 183 | 185 | 185 | 187 | 194 | 185 | 206 | 313 | 168 | 168 | 213 |
| — | 132 | 73 | 133 | 106 | 154 | 128 | 200 | 186 | 158 | 233 |
| 113 | 108 | 111 | 88 | 140 | 129 | 143 | 178 | 152 | 160 | 140 |
| 259 | 82 | 143 | 102 | 127 | 71 | 58 | 65 | 46 | 50 | 98 |
| 33 | 34 | 33 | 41 | 38 | 48 | 43 | 48 | 34 | 35 | 23 |
| 20 | 20 | 20 | 20 | 50 | 50 | 50 | 1 | 9 | 13 | 13 |
| **1,062** | **1,021** | **1,020** | **1,069** | **1,146** | **1,065** | **1,084** | **1,213** | **1,211** | **853** | **979** |
| 84 | 93 | 108 | 135 | 179 | 252 | 256 | 337 | 364 | 365 | 769 |
| — | — | — | — | 43 | 49 | 58 | 53 | 41 | 76 | 75 |
| 117 | 107 | 124 | 168 | 186 | 156 | 185 | 185 | 231 | 245 | 269 |
| 50 | 49 | 35 | 35 | 91 | 83 | 79 | 31 | 82 | 76 | 102 |
| 27 | 32 | 37 | 56 | 62 | 74 | 83 | 91 | 110 | 83 | 100 |
| — | — | — | — | 35 | 31 | 28 | 70 | 51 | 41 | 41 |
| 212 | 182 | 155 | 164 | 140 | 97 | 200 | 251 | 457 | 600 | 576 |
| **490** | **463** | **459** | **558** | **736** | **742** | **889** | **1,018** | **1,336** | **1,486** | **1,932** |
| **37,243** | **36,858** | **36,953** | **41,931** | **42,593** | **43,917** | **46,915** | **48,001** | **48,633** | **47,213** | **49,943** |

## IQ-3. WORLD: IMPORTS OF GREEN COFFEE BY COUNTRY OR REGION AND BY GENERIC TYPE, 1953-1966

(Thousands of 60-Kilo bags)

|  | 1953 | 1954 | 1955 | 1956 | 1957 | 1958 | 1959 | 1960 | 1961 | 1962 | 1963 | 1964 | 1965 | 1966 |
|---|---|---|---|---|---|---|---|---|---|---|---|---|---|---|
| **UNITED STATES** | | | | | | | | | | | | | | |
| Arabica | 20,207 | 16,048 | 18,330 | 19,499 | 18,606 | 18,115 | 21,245 | 19,451 | 19,204 | 20,468 | 19,841 | 18,033 | 16,217 | 16,128 |
| Robusta | 858 | 1,044 | 1,321 | 1,753 | 2,252 | 2,054 | 2,025 | 2,640 | 3,200 | 4,106 | 4,052 | 4,859 | 5,130 | 5,964 |
| TOTAL | 21,065 | 17,092 | 19,651 | 21,252 | 20,858 | 20,169 | 23,270 | 22,091 | 22,404 | 24,574 | 23,893 | 22,892 | 21,347 | 22,092 |
| **CANADA** | | | | | | | | | | | | | | |
| Arabica | 798 | 689 | 743 | 768 | 796 | 854 | 960 | 935 | 1,045 | 1,170 | 1,178 | 1,124 | 1,106 | 954 |
| Robusta | 15 | 32 | 42 | 61 | 40 | 41 | 55 | 60 | 74 | 60 | 110 | 123 | 152 | 210 |
| TOTAL | 813 | 721 | 785 | 829 | 836 | 895 | 1,015 | 995 | 1,119 | 1,230 | 1,288 | 1,247 | 1,258 | 1,164 |
| **OTHER WESTERN HEMISPHERE** | | | | | | | | | | | | | | |
| Arabica | 705 | 725 | 653 | 647 | 742 | 820 | 500 | 592 | 695 | 651 | 585 | 590 | 652 | 849 |
| Robusta | — | — | — | — | — | — | 6 | 15 | 25 | 18 | 10 | 10 | 13 | 2 |
| TOTAL | 705 | 725 | 653 | 647 | 742 | 820 | 506 | 607 | 720 | 669 | 595 | 600 | 665 | 851 |
| **TOTAL WESTERN HEMISPHERE** | | | | | | | | | | | | | | |
| Arabica | 21,710 | 17,462 | 19,726 | 20,914 | 20,144 | 19,789 | 22,705 | 20,978 | 20,944 | 22,289 | 21,604 | 19,747 | 17,975 | 17,931 |
| Robusta | 873 | 1,076 | 1,363 | 1,814 | 2,292 | 2,095 | 2,086 | 2,715 | 3,299 | 4,184 | 4,172 | 4,992 | 5,295 | 6,176 |
| TOTAL | 22,583 | 18,538 | 21,089 | 22,728 | 22,436 | 21,884 | 24,791 | 23,693 | 24,243 | 26,473 | 25,776 | 24,739 | 23,270 | 24,107 |
| **EUROPE** | | | | | | | | | | | | | | |
| Arabica | 6,576 | 6,931 | 7,681 | 8,765 | 8,267 | 9,120 | 10,761 | 11,752 | 12,291 | 13,196 | 13,954 | 14,274 | 14,820 | 15,383 |
| Robusta | 3,602 | 3,582 | 3,790 | 4,191 | 4,550 | 4,662 | 4,714 | 5,256 | 5,548 | 5,295 | 6,050 | 7,073 | 6,784 | 7,542 |
| TOTAL | 10,178 | 10,513 | 11,471 | 12,956 | 12,817 | 13,782 | 15,475 | 17,008 | 17,839 | 18,491 | 20,004 | 21,347 | 21,604 | 22,925 |
| **AFRICA** | | | | | | | | | | | | | | |
| Arabica | 266 | 215 | 237 | 265 | 242 | 379 | 294 | 379 | 352 | 293 | 423 | 409 | 150 | 383 |
| Robusta | 555 | 572 | 611 | 742 | 779 | 641 | 775 | 767 | 744 | 808 | 790 | 802 | 703 | 596 |
| TOTAL | 821 | 787 | 848 | 1,007 | 1,021 | 1,020 | 1,069 | 1,146 | 1,096 | 1,101 | 1,213 | 1,211 | 853 | 979 |
| **ASIA & OCEANIA** | | | | | | | | | | | | | | |
| Arabica | 202 | 111 | 191 | 247 | 209 | 225 | 273 | 372 | 407 | 461 | 695 | 820 | 536 | 865 |
| Robusta | 238 | 153 | 217 | 282 | 252 | 233 | 286 | 363 | 404 | 364 | 323 | 516 | 950 | 1,067 |
| TOTAL | 440 | 264 | 408 | 529 | 461 | 458 | 559 | 735 | 811 | 825 | 1,018 | 1,336 | 1,486 | 1,932 |
| **TOTAL EASTERN HEMISPHERE** | | | | | | | | | | | | | | |
| Arabica | 7,044 | 7,257 | 8,109 | 9,277 | 8,718 | 9,724 | 11,328 | 12,503 | 13,050 | 13,950 | 15,072 | 15,503 | 15,506 | 16,631 |
| Robusta | 4,395 | 4,307 | 4,618 | 5,215 | 5,581 | 5,536 | 5,775 | 6,386 | 6,696 | 6,467 | 7,163 | 8,391 | 8,437 | 9,205 |
| TOTAL | 11,439 | 11,564 | 12,727 | 14,492 | 14,299 | 15,260 | 17,103 | 18,889 | 19,746 | 20,417 | 22,235 | 23,894 | 23,943 | 25,836 |
| **WORLD** | | | | | | | | | | | | | | |
| Arabica | 28,754 | 24,719 | 27,835 | 30,191 | 28,862 | 29,513 | 34,033 | 33,481 | 33,994 | 36,239 | 36,676 | 35,250 | 33,481 | 34,562 |
| Robusta | 5,268 | 5,383 | 5,981 | 7,029 | 7,873 | 7,631 | 7,861 | 9,101 | 9,995 | 10,651 | 11,335 | 13,383 | 13,732 | 15,381 |
| TOTAL | 34,022 | 30,102 | 33,816 | 37,220 | 36,735 | 37,144 | 41,894 | 42,582 | 43,989 | 46,890 | 48,011 | 48,633 | 47,213 | 49,943 |

Source: U. S., Canada, Other Western Hemisphere, Africa, Asia & Oceania—PACB estimates: Europe — Jacques Louis-Delamare et Cie.

**IQ-3a. WORLD: IMPORTS OF GREEN COFFEE BY COUNTRY OR REGION AND BY GENERIC TYPE, 1953-1966**

(Percent of Regional Totals)

| | 1953 | 1954 | 1955 | 1956 | 1957 | 1958 | 1959 | 1960 | 1961 | 1962 | 1963 | 1964 | 1965 | 1966 |
|---|---|---|---|---|---|---|---|---|---|---|---|---|---|---|
| **UNITED STATES** | | | | | | | | | | | | | | |
| Arabica | 95.9 | 93.9 | 93.3 | 91.8 | 89.2 | 89.8 | 91.3 | 88.0 | 85.7 | 83.3 | 83.0 | 78.8 | 76.0 | 73.0 |
| Robusta | 4.1 | 6.1 | 6.7 | 8.2 | 10.8 | 10.2 | 8.7 | 12.0 | 14.3 | 16.7 | 17.0 | 21.2 | 24.0 | 27.0 |
| TOTAL | 100.0 | 100.0 | 100.0 | 100.0 | 100.0 | 100.0 | 100.0 | 100.0 | 100.0 | 100.0 | 100.0 | 100.0 | 100.0 | 100.0 |
| **CANADA** | | | | | | | | | | | | | | |
| Arabica | 98.2 | 95.6 | 94.6 | 92.6 | 95.2 | 95.4 | 94.6 | 94.0 | 93.4 | 95.1 | 91.5 | 90.1 | 87.9 | 82.0 |
| Robusta | 1.8 | 4.4 | 5.4 | 7.4 | 4.8 | 4.1 | 5.4 | 6.0 | 6.6 | 4.9 | 8.5 | 9.9 | 12.1 | 18.0 |
| TOTAL | 100.0 | 100.0 | 100.0 | 100.0 | 100.0 | 100.0 | 100.0 | 100.0 | 100.0 | 100.0 | 100.0 | 100.0 | 100.0 | 100.0 |
| **OTHER WESTERN HEMISPHERE** | | | | | | | | | | | | | | |
| Arabica | 100.0 | 100.0 | 100.0 | 100.0 | 100.0 | 100.0 | 98.8 | 97.5 | 96.5 | 97.3 | 98.3 | 98.3 | 97.9 | 99.8 |
| Robusta | — | — | — | — | — | — | 1.2 | 2.5 | 3.5 | 2.7 | 1.7 | 1.7 | 2.1 | 0.2 |
| TOTAL | 100.0 | 100.0 | 100.0 | 100.0 | 100.0 | 100.0 | 100.0 | 100.0 | 100.0 | 100.0 | 100.0 | 100.0 | 100.0 | 100.0 |
| **TOTAL WESTERN HEMISPHERE** | | | | | | | | | | | | | | |
| Arabica | 96.1 | 94.2 | 93.5 | 92.0 | 89.8 | 90.4 | 91.6 | 88.6 | 86.5 | 84.3 | 83.9 | 79.9 | 77.3 | 74.4 |
| Robusta | 3.9 | 5.8 | 6.5 | 8.0 | 10.2 | 9.6 | 8.4 | 11.4 | 13.5 | 15.7 | 16.1 | 20.1 | 22.7 | 25.6 |
| TOTAL | 100.0 | 100.0 | 100.0 | 100.0 | 100.0 | 100.0 | 100.0 | 100.0 | 100.0 | 100.0 | 100.0 | 100.0 | 100.0 | 100.0 |
| **EUROPE** | | | | | | | | | | | | | | |
| Arabica | 64.6 | 65.9 | 67.0 | 67.7 | 64.5 | 66.2 | 69.5 | 69.1 | 68.9 | 71.4 | 69.8 | 66.9 | 68.6 | 67.1 |
| Robusta | 35.4 | 34.1 | 33.0 | 32.3 | 35.5 | 33.8 | 30.5 | 30.9 | 31.1 | 28.6 | 30.2 | 33.1 | 31.4 | 32.9 |
| TOTAL | 100.0 | 100.0 | 100.0 | 100.0 | 100.0 | 100.0 | 100.0 | 100.0 | 100.0 | 100.0 | 100.0 | 100.0 | 100.0 | 100.0 |
| **AFRICA** | | | | | | | | | | | | | | |
| Arabica | 32.4 | 27.3 | 27.9 | 26.3 | 23.7 | 37.2 | 27.5 | 33.1 | 32.1 | 26.6 | 34.9 | 33.8 | 17.6 | 39.1 |
| Robusta | 67.6 | 72.7 | 72.1 | 73.7 | 76.3 | 62.8 | 72.5 | 66.9 | 67.9 | 73.4 | 65.1 | 66.2 | 82.4 | 60.9 |
| TOTAL | 100.0 | 100.0 | 100.0 | 100.0 | 100.0 | 100.0 | 100.0 | 100.0 | 100.0 | 100.0 | 100.0 | 100.0 | 100.0 | 100.0 |
| **ASIA & OCEANIA** | | | | | | | | | | | | | | |
| Arabica | 45.9 | 42.0 | 46.8 | 46.7 | 45.3 | 49.1 | 48.8 | 50.6 | 50.2 | 55.9 | 68.3 | 61.4 | 36.1 | 44.8 |
| Robusta | 54.1 | 58.0 | 53.2 | 53.3 | 54.7 | 50.9 | 51.2 | 49.4 | 49.8 | 44.1 | 31.7 | 38.6 | 63.9 | 55.2 |
| TOTAL | 100.0 | 100.0 | 100.0 | 100.0 | 100.0 | 100.0 | 100.0 | 100.0 | 100.0 | 100.0 | 100.0 | 100.0 | 100.0 | 100.0 |
| **TOTAL EASTERN HEMISPHERE** | | | | | | | | | | | | | | |
| Arabica | 61.6 | 62.8 | 63.7 | 64.0 | 61.0 | 63.7 | 66.2 | 66.2 | 66.1 | 68.3 | 67.8 | 64.9 | 64.8 | 64.4 |
| Robusta | 38.4 | 37.2 | 36.3 | 36.0 | 39.0 | 36.3 | 33.8 | 33.8 | 33.9 | 31.7 | 32.2 | 35.1 | 35.2 | 35.6 |
| TOTAL | 100.0 | 100.0 | 100.0 | 100.0 | 100.0 | 100.0 | 100.0 | 100.0 | 100.0 | 100.0 | 100.0 | 100.0 | 100.0 | 100.0 |
| **WORLD** | | | | | | | | | | | | | | |
| Arabica | 84.5 | 82.1 | 82.3 | 81.1 | 78.6 | 79.5 | 81.3 | 78.7 | 77.3 | 77.3 | 76.4 | 72.5 | 70.9 | 69.2 |
| Robusta | 15.5 | 17.9 | 17.7 | 18.9 | 21.4 | 20.5 | 18.7 | 21.3 | 22.7 | 22.7 | 23.6 | 27.5 | 29.1 | 30.8 |
| TOTAL | 100.0 | 100.0 | 100.0 | 100.0 | 100.0 | 100.0 | 100.0 | 100.0 | 100.0 | 100.0 | 100.0 | 100.0 | 100.0 | 100.0 |

Source: U. S., Canada, Other Western Hemisphere, Africa, Asia & Oceania — PACB estimates: Europe — Jacques Louis-Delamare et Cie.

## IQ-3b. WORLD: IMPORTS OF GREEN COFFEE BY COUNTRY OR REGION AND BY GENERIC TYPE, 1953-1966

(Percent of World Total)

| | 1953 | 1954 | 1955 | 1956 | 1957 | 1958 | 1959 | 1960 | 1961 | 1962 | 1963 | 1964 | 1965 | 1966 |
|---|---|---|---|---|---|---|---|---|---|---|---|---|---|---|
| **UNITED STATES** | | | | | | | | | | | | | | |
| Arabica | 59.40 | 53.31 | 54.20 | 52.39 | 50.65 | 48.77 | 50.71 | 45.68 | 43.66 | 43.65 | 41.33 | 37.08 | 34.35 | 32.29 |
| Robusta | 2.52 | 3.47 | 3.91 | 4.71 | 6.13 | 5.53 | 4.84 | 6.20 | 7.27 | 8.76 | 8.44 | 9.99 | 10.86 | 11.94 |
| TOTAL | 61.92 | 56.78 | 58.11 | 57.10 | 56.78 | 54.30 | 55.55 | 51.88 | 50.93 | 52.41 | 49.77 | 47.07 | 45.21 | 44.23 |
| **CANADA** | | | | | | | | | | | | | | |
| Arabica | 2.35 | 2.29 | 2.20 | 2.06 | 2.17 | 2.30 | 2.29 | 2.20 | 2.37 | 2.49 | 2.45 | 2.31 | 2.34 | 1.91 |
| Robusta | 0.04 | 0.10 | 0.12 | 0.16 | 0.11 | 0.11 | 0.13 | 0.14 | 0.17 | 0.13 | 0.23 | 0.26 | 0.32 | 0.42 |
| TOTAL | 2.39 | 2.39 | 2.32 | 2.22 | 2.28 | 2.41 | 2.42 | 2.34 | 2.54 | 2.62 | 2.68 | 2.57 | 2.66 | 2.33 |
| **OTHER WESTERN HEMISPHERE** | | | | | | | | | | | | | | |
| Arabica | 2.07 | 2.41 | 1.93 | 1.74 | 2.02 | 2.21 | 1.19 | 1.39 | 1.58 | 1.39 | 1.22 | 1.21 | 1.38 | 1.70 |
| Robusta | – | – | – | – | – | – | .01 | .04 | .06 | .04 | .02 | .02 | .03 | – |
| TOTAL | 2.07 | 2.41 | 1.93 | 1.74 | 2.02 | 2.21 | 1.20 | 1.42 | 1.64 | 1.43 | 1.24 | 1.23 | 1.41 | 1.70 |
| **TOTAL WESTERN HEMISPHERE** | | | | | | | | | | | | | | |
| Arabica | 63.82 | 58.01 | 58.33 | 56.19 | 54.84 | 53.28 | 54.20 | 49.26 | 47.61 | 47.53 | 45.00 | 40.60 | 38.07 | 35.90 |
| Robusta | 2.56 | 3.57 | 4.03 | 4.87 | 6.24 | 5.64 | 4.98 | 6.38 | 7.50 | 8.92 | 8.69 | 10.27 | 11.22 | 12.37 |
| TOTAL | 66.38 | 61.58 | 62.36 | 61.06 | 61.08 | 58.92 | 59.18 | 55.64 | 55.11 | 56.45 | 53.69 | 50.87 | 49.29 | 48.27 |
| **EUROPE** | | | | | | | | | | | | | | |
| Arabica | 19.33 | 23.03 | 22.71 | 23.55 | 22.50 | 24.55 | 25.69 | 27.60 | 27.94 | 28.14 | 29.06 | 29.35 | 31.39 | 30.80 |
| Robusta | 10.59 | 11.90 | 11.21 | 11.26 | 12.39 | 12.55 | 11.25 | 12.34 | 12.61 | 11.29 | 12.60 | 14.54 | 14.37 | 15.10 |
| TOTAL | 29.92 | 34.93 | 33.92 | 34.81 | 34.89 | 37.10 | 36.94 | 39.94 | 40.55 | 39.43 | 41.66 | 43.89 | 45.76 | 45.90 |
| **AFRICA** | | | | | | | | | | | | | | |
| Arabica | 0.78 | 0.71 | 0.70 | 0.71 | 0.66 | 1.02 | 0.70 | 0.89 | 0.80 | 0.63 | 0.88 | 0.84 | 0.32 | 0.77 |
| Robusta | 1.63 | 1.90 | 1.81 | 2.00 | 2.12 | 1.72 | 1.85 | 1.80 | 1.69 | 1.72 | 1.65 | 1.65 | 1.49 | 1.19 |
| TOTAL | 2.41 | 2.61 | 2.51 | 2.71 | 2.78 | 2.74 | 2.55 | 2.69 | 2.49 | 2.35 | 2.53 | 2.49 | 1.81 | 1.96 |
| **ASIA & OCEANIA** | | | | | | | | | | | | | | |
| Arabica | 0.59 | 0.37 | 0.57 | 0.66 | 0.57 | 0.61 | 0.65 | 0.87 | 0.93 | 0.98 | 1.45 | 1.69 | 1.14 | 1.73 |
| Robusta | 0.70 | 0.51 | 0.64 | 0.76 | 0.68 | 0.63 | 0.68 | 0.86 | 0.92 | 0.78 | 0.67 | 1.06 | 2.01 | 2.14 |
| TOTAL | 1.29 | 0.88 | 1.21 | 1.42 | 1.25 | 1.24 | 1.33 | 1.73 | 1.85 | 1.76 | 2.12 | 2.75 | 3.15 | 3.87 |
| **TOTAL EASTERN HEMISPHERE** | | | | | | | | | | | | | | |
| Arabica | 20.70 | 24.11 | 23.98 | 24.92 | 23.73 | 26.18 | 27.04 | 29.36 | 29.67 | 29.75 | 31.39 | 31.88 | 32.84 | 33.30 |
| Robusta | 12.92 | 14.31 | 13.66 | 14.02 | 15.19 | 14.90 | 13.78 | 15.00 | 15.22 | 13.79 | 14.92 | 17.25 | 17.87 | 18.43 |
| TOTAL | 33.62 | 38.42 | 37.64 | 38.94 | 38.92 | 41.08 | 40.82 | 44.36 | 44.89 | 43.54 | 46.31 | 49.13 | 50.71 | 51.73 |
| **WORLD** | | | | | | | | | | | | | | |
| Arabica | 84.52 | 82.12 | 82.31 | 81.11 | 78.57 | 79.46 | 81.24 | 78.63 | 77.28 | 77.28 | 76.39 | 72.48 | 70.31 | 69.20 |
| Robusta | 15.48 | 17.88 | 17.69 | 18.89 | 21.43 | 20.54 | 18.76 | 21.37 | 22.72 | 22.72 | 23.61 | 27.52 | 29.09 | 30.80 |
| TOTAL | 100.00 | 100.00 | 100.00 | 100.00 | 100.00 | 100.00 | 100.00 | 100.00 | 100.00 | 100.00 | 100.00 | 100.00 | 100.00 | 100.00 |

Source: U. S., Canada, Other Western Hemisphere, Africa, Asia & Oceania – PACB estimates: Europe – Jacques Louis Delamare et Cie.

## IQ-4. UNITED STATES: VOLUME OF IMPORTS OF COFFEE, 1965-1966
### By Coastal Zones and Customs Districts

(Thousands of bags of 60 kilograms or 132.276 pounds each)

| COASTAL ZONES AND CUSTOMS DISTRICTS | 1966 | 1965 | Percentage of Total 1966 | Percentage of Total 1965 | Increase or Decrease 1966 over 1965 VOLUME | PERCENT |
|---|---|---|---|---|---|---|
| **ATLANTIC COASTAL ZONE** | | | | | | |
| New York | 458,615 | 475,353 | 42.9 | 44.8 | − 16,738 | − 3.5 |
| Tampa | 70,983 | 46,813 | 6.6 | 4.4 | + 24,170 | + 51.6 |
| Maryland | 12,620 | 15,881 | 1.2 | 1.5 | − 3,261 | − 20.5 |
| Massachusetts | 5,735 | 7,770 | 0.5 | 0.7 | − 2,035 | − 26.2 |
| Philadelphia | 4,813 | 3,493 | 0.5 | 0.3 | + 1,320 | + 37.8 |
| Virginia | 1,594 | 1,021 | 0.2 | 0.1 | + 573 | + 56.1 |
| South Carolina | 357 | 501 | — | 0.1 | − 144 | − 28.7 |
| TOTAL ATLANTIC COASTAL ZONE | 554,717 | 550,832 | 51.9 | 51.9 | + 3,885 | + 0.7 |
| **GULF COASTAL ZONE** | | | | | | |
| New Orleans | 194,786 | 207,397 | 18.2 | 19.6 | − 12,611 | − 6.1 |
| Houston | 149,887 | 122,589 | 14.0 | 11.6 | + 27,298 | + 22.3 |
| Port Arthur | 1,562 | 1,219 | 0.1 | 0.1 | + 343 | + 28.1 |
| TOTAL GULF COASTAL ZONE | 346,235 | 331,205 | 32.3 | 31.3 | + 15,030 | + 4.5 |
| **PACIFIC COASTAL ZONE** | | | | | | |
| San Francisco | 128,125 | 139,200 | 12.0 | 13.1 | − 11,075 | − 8.0 |
| Los Angeles | 22,890 | 22,804 | 2.1 | 2.2 | + 86 | + 0.4 |
| Oregon | 8,268 | 8,896 | 0.8 | 0.8 | − 628 | − 7.1 |
| Washington | 2,201 | 2,091 | 0.2 | 0.2 | + 110 | + 5.3 |
| San Diego | 2,769 | 2,341 | 0.3 | 0.2 | + 428 | + 18.3 |
| El Paso | 1,611 | 1,589 | 0.2 | 0.2 | + 22 | + 1.4 |
| TOTAL PACIFIC COASTAL ZONE | 165,864 | 176,921 | 15.6 | 16.7 | − 11,057 | − 6.2 |
| All Others | 1,764 | 1,573 | 0.2 | 0.1 | + 191 | + 12.1 |
| TOTAL IMPORTS | 1,068,580 | 1,060,531 | 100.0 | 100.0 | + 8,049 | + 0.8 |

Source: United States Department of Commerce. See note to Table IQV-3.

IQV-3. UNITED STATES: VOLUME AND

(Volume in bags of 60 kilograms or 132.276

| COUNTRIES OF ORIGIN WESTERN HEMISPHERE | VOLUME | | VALUE | |
|---|---|---|---|---|
| Pan-American Coffee Bureau | 1966 | 1965 | 1966 | 1965 |
| Brazil | 6,730,398 | 5,744,024 | 327,430 | 303,385 |
| Colombia | 2,716,078 | 3,323,724 | 163,784 | 199,593 |
| Guatemala | 1,110,122 | 903,830 | 59,333 | 50,962 |
| Mexico | 1,044,722 | 1,159,929 | 57,427 | 65,329 |
| El Salvador | 592,682 | 713,785 | 31,253 | 40,207 |
| Peru | 447,307 | 454,235 | 22,439 | 23,635 |
| Ecuador | 432,279 | 502,483 | 19,380 | 24,712 |
| Dominican Republic | 353,710 | 309,715 | 17,739 | 16,312 |
| Venezuela | 266,251 | 236,744 | 14,559 | 13,452 |
| Honduras | 248,555 | 290,139 | 12,840 | 15,422 |
| Costa Rica | 231,384 | 305,405 | 12,678 | 17,214 |
| Nicaragua | 135,377 | 250,949 | 7,623 | 13,937 |
| Haiti | 89,479 | 100,383 | 4,527 | 4,960 |
| Panama | 24,297 | 9,990 | 1,154 | 446 |
| Cuba | — | — | — | — |
| Total Pan-American Coffee Bureau | 14,422,641 | 14,305,335 | 752,166 | 789,566 |
| OTHER WESTERN HEMISPHERE | | | | |
| Bolivia | 44,574 | 15,321 | 2,143 | 740 |
| Paraguay | 23,087 | 45,295 | 879 | 1,721 |
| Trinidad & Tobago | 11,152 | 25,506 | 439 | 791 |
| Surinam | 8,669 | 3,749 | 353 | 174 |
| Guyana | 1,954 | 928 | 75 | 41 |
| British Honduras | 643 | — | 29 | — |
| Canada | 65 | 272 | 7 | 27 |
| Jamaica | 60 | 178 | 7 | 10 |
| Netherlands West Indies | — | 834 | — | 38 |
| Total Other Western Hemisphere | 90,204 | 92,083 | 3,932 | 3,542 |
| TOTAL WESTERN HEMISPHERE | 14,512,845 | 14,397,418 | 756,098 | 793,108 |
| AFRICA | | | | |
| Uganda | 1,218,029 | 1,108,480 | 50,428 | 39,146 |
| Tanzania | 237,153 | 122,264 | 11,479 | 5,843 |
| Kenya | 173,808 | 118,172 | 9,602 | 5,160 |
| Portuguese Africa | 1,211,525 | 1,285,167 | 50,166 | 46,116 |
| Franc Zone | | | | |
| Ivory Coast | 787,362 | 840,669 | 31,529 | 30,532 |
| Cameroun | 331,550 | 147,083 | 13,681 | 4,726 |
| Madagascar | 230,452 | 404,926 | 9,164 | 14,003 |
| Togo | 8,871 | 16,834 | 269 | 693 |
| Gabon | 4,830 | 4,313 | 206 | 201 |
| Central African Republic | — | 441 | — | 17 |
| Others (1) | 5,096 | 5,339 | 260 | 234 |
| Ethiopia | 792,100 | 1,158,256 | 40,666 | 59,752 |
| Liberia | 709,095 | 188,170 | 29,521 | 6,706 |
| Rwanda & Burundi | 333,372 | 340,080 | 16,443 | 17,239 |
| Guinea | 164,268 | 208,321 | 6,548 | 7,418 |
| Sierra Leone | 128,641 | 19,774 | 4,349 | 685 |
| Congo (D.R.) | 35,839 | 145,746 | 1,833 | 6,082 |
| Ghana | 35,326 | 20,214 | 1,269 | 782 |
| South Africa | 27,265 | 18,615 | 1,268 | 843 |
| Nigeria | 20,723 | 9,591 | 838 | 291 |
| Mauritius | — | 420 | — | 13 |
| TOTAL AFRICA | 6,455,305 | 6,162,875 | 279,519 | 246,482 |
| ASIA & OCEANIA | | | | |
| Indonesia | 974,349 | 643,291 | 26,214 | 14,293 |
| India | 45,282 | 73,397 | 2,116 | 3,745 |
| Arabia (2) | 16,728 | 27,859 | 725 | 1,181 |
| Others (3) | 85,089 | 39,068 | 3,771 | 1,527 |
| TOTAL ASIA & OCEANIA | 1,121,448 | 783,615 | 32,826 | 20,746 |
| VARIOUS (4) | 2,181 | 2,875 | 137 | 195 |
| TOTAL IMPORTS | 22,091,779 | 21,346,783 | 1,068,580 | 1,060,531 |

Source: United States Department of Commerce.
(1) Includes: Mali, Niger, Upper Volta, Dahomey, Congo (Brazzaville) and French Somaliland.
(2) Includes: Yemen, Sultanate of Oman, Trucial Sheikhdoms and Qatar.
(3) Includes: Aden, Australia, Malaysia, New Guinea, Laos, Bhutan, Brunei and Portuguese Timor, Singapore and South Viet Nam.

**VALUE OF IMPORTS OF COFFEE\*, 1965-1966**

pounds each and Value in thousands of U. S. Dollars)

| Percentage of Total | | | | Increase or Decrease 1966 over 1965 | | | |
|---|---|---|---|---|---|---|---|
| VOLUME | | VALUE | | VOLUME | | VALUE | |
| 1966 | 1965 | 1966 | 1965 | BAGS | PERCENT | AMOUNT | PERCENT |
| 30.5 | 26.9 | 30.6 | 28.6 | + 986,374 | + 17.2 | + 24,045 | + 7.9 |
| 12.3 | 15.6 | 15.3 | 18.8 | − 607,646 | − 18.3 | − 35,809 | − 17.9 |
| 5.0 | 4.2 | 5.6 | 4.8 | + 206,292 | + 22.8 | + 8,371 | + 16.4 |
| 4.7 | 5.4 | 5.4 | 6.2 | − 115,207 | − 9.9 | − 7,902 | − 12.1 |
| 2.7 | 3.3 | 2.9 | 3.8 | − 121,103 | − 17.0 | − 8,954 | − 22.3 |
| 2.0 | 2.1 | 2.1 | 2.2 | − 6,928 | − 1.5 | − 1,196 | − 5.1 |
| 2.0 | 2.4 | 1.8 | 2.3 | − 70,204 | − 14.0 | − 5,332 | − 21.6 |
| 1.6 | 1.5 | 1.7 | 1.5 | + 43,995 | + 14.2 | + 1,427 | + 8.7 |
| 1.2 | 1.1 | 1.4 | 1.3 | + 29,507 | + 12.5 | + 1,107 | + 8.2 |
| 1.1 | 1.4 | 1.2 | 1.5 | − 41,584 | − 14.3 | − 2,582 | − 16.7 |
| 1.1 | 1.4 | 1.2 | 1.6 | − 74,021 | − 24.2 | − 4,536 | − 26.4 |
| 0.6 | 1.2 | 0.7 | 1.3 | − 115,572 | − 46.1 | − 6,314 | − 45.3 |
| 0.4 | 0.5 | 0.4 | 0.5 | − 10,904 | − 10.9 | − 433 | − 8.7 |
| 0.1 | − | 0.1 | − | + 14,307 | + 143.2 | + 708 | + 158.7 |
| − | − | − | − | | | | |
| 65.3 | 67.0 | 70.4 | 74.4 | + 117,306 | + 0.8 | − 37,400 | − 4.7 |
| | | | | | | | |
| 0.2 | 0.1 | 0.2 | 0.1 | + 29,253 | + 190.9 | + 1,403 | + 189.6 |
| 0.1 | 0.2 | 0.1 | 0.2 | − 22,208 | − 49.0 | − 842 | − 48.9 |
| 0.1 | 0.1 | 0.1 | 0.1 | − 14,354 | − 56.3 | − 352 | − 44.5 |
| − | − | − | − | + 4,920 | + 131.2 | + 179 | + 102.9 |
| − | − | − | − | + 1,026 | + 110.6 | + 34 | + 82.9 |
| − | − | − | − | + 643 | + --- | + 29 | + --- |
| − | − | − | − | − 207 | − 76.1 | − 20 | − 74.1 |
| − | − | − | − | − 118 | − 66.3 | − 3 | − 30.0 |
| − | − | − | − | − 834 | − --- | − 38 | − --- |
| 0.4 | 0.4 | 0.4 | 0.4 | − 1,879 | − 2.0 | + 390 | + 11.0 |
| 65.7 | 67.4 | 70.8 | 74.8 | + 115,427 | + 0.8 | − 37,010 | − 4.7 |
| | | | | | | | |
| 5.5 | 5.2 | 4.7 | 3.7 | + 109,549 | + 9.9 | + 11,282 | + 28.8 |
| 1.1 | 0.6 | 1.1 | 0.6 | + 114,889 | + 94.0 | + 5,636 | + 96.5 |
| 0.8 | 0.6 | 0.9 | 0.5 | + 55,636 | + 47.1 | + 4,442 | + 86.1 |
| 5.5 | 6.0 | 4.7 | 4.4 | − 73,642 | − 5.7 | + 4,050 | + 8.8 |
| | | | | | | | |
| 3.6 | 3.9 | 2.9 | 2.9 | − 53,307 | − 6.3 | + 997 | + 3.3 |
| 1.5 | 0.7 | 1.3 | 0.4 | + 184,467 | + 125.4 | + 8,955 | + 189.5 |
| 1.0 | 1.9 | 0.9 | 1.3 | − 174,474 | − 43.1 | − 4,839 | − 34.6 |
| − | 0.1 | − | 0.1 | − 7,963 | − 47.3 | − 424 | − 61.2 |
| − | − | − | − | + 517 | + 12.0 | + 5 | + 2.5 |
| − | − | − | − | − 441 | − --- | − 17 | − --- |
| − | − | − | − | − 243 | − 4.6 | + 26 | + 11.1 |
| 3.6 | 5.4 | 3.8 | 5.6 | − 366,156 | − 31.6 | − 19,086 | − 31.9 |
| 3.2 | 0.9 | 2.8 | 0.6 | + 520,925 | + 276.8 | + 22,815 | + 340.2 |
| 1.5 | 1.6 | 1.5 | 1.6 | − 6,708 | − 2.0 | − 796 | − 4.6 |
| 0.7 | 1.0 | 0.6 | 0.7 | − 44,053 | − 21.1 | − 870 | − 11.7 |
| 0.6 | 0.1 | 0.4 | 0.1 | + 108,867 | + 550.6 | + 3,664 | + 534.9 |
| 0.2 | 0.7 | 0.2 | 0.6 | − 109,907 | − 75.4 | − 4,249 | − 69.9 |
| 0.2 | 0.1 | 0.1 | 0.1 | + 15,112 | + 74.8 | + 487 | + 62.3 |
| 0.1 | 0.1 | 0.1 | 0.1 | + 8,650 | + 46.5 | + 425 | + 50.4 |
| 0.1 | − | 0.1 | − | + 11,132 | + 116.1 | + 547 | + 188.0 |
| − | − | − | − | − 420 | − --- | − 13 | − --- |
| 29.2 | 28.9 | 26.1 | 23.3 | + 292,430 | + 4.7 | + 33,037 | + 13.4 |
| | | | | | | | |
| 4.4 | 3.0 | 2.5 | 1.3 | + 331,058 | + 51.5 | + 11,921 | + 83.4 |
| 0.2 | 0.4 | 0.2 | 0.4 | − 28,115 | − 38.3 | − 1,629 | − 43.5 |
| 0.1 | 0.1 | 0.1 | 0.1 | − 11,131 | − 40.0 | − 456 | − 38.6 |
| 0.4 | 0.2 | 0.3 | 0.1 | + 46,021 | + 117.8 | + 2,244 | + 147.0 |
| 5.1 | 3.7 | 3.1 | 1.9 | + 337,833 | + 43.1 | + 12,080 | + 58.2 |
| − | − | − | − | − 694 | − 24.1 | − 58 | − 29.7 |
| | | | | | | | |
| 100.0 | 100.0 | 100.0 | 100.0 | + 744,996 | + 3.5 | + 8,049 | + 0.8 |

(4) Includes: Italy, Sweden, Switzerland, Germany (F.R.), France, Portugal, United Kingdom and Netherlands.

(\*) Includes green equivalent of roasted coffee 36,487 bags (56,357); green coffee imports totaled 22,055,292 bags (21,290,426).

IV-5. UNITED STATES: VALUE OF IMPORTS OF COFFEE, 1965-1966
By Coastal Zones and Customs Districts

(Thousands of U. S. Dollars)

| COASTAL ZONES AND CUSTOMS DISTRICTS | 1966 | 1965 | Percentage of Total 1966 | Percentage of Total 1965 | Increase or Decrease 1966 over 1965 VOLUME | Increase or Decrease 1966 over 1965 PERCENT |
|---|---|---|---|---|---|---|
| ATLANTIC COASTAL ZONE | | | | | | |
| New York | 9,545 | 9,699 | 43.2 | 45.4 | − 154 | − 1.6 |
| Tampa | 1,424 | 943 | 6.5 | 4.4 | + 481 | + 51.0 |
| Maryland | 254 | 306 | 1.2 | 1.4 | − 52 | − 17.0 |
| Massachusetts | 114 | 145 | 0.5 | 0.7 | − 31 | − 21.4 |
| Philadelphia | 95 | 63 | 0.4 | 0.3 | + 32 | + 50.8 |
| Virginia | 32 | 21 | 0.1 | 0.1 | + 11 | + 52.4 |
| South Carolina | 9 | 11 | — | 0.1 | − 2 | − 18.2 |
| TOTAL ATLANTIC COASTAL ZONE | 11,473 | 11,188 | 51.9 | 52.4 | + 285 | + 2.5 |
| GULF COASTAL ZONE | | | | | | |
| New Orleans | 4,004 | 4,085 | 18.1 | 19.2 | − 81 | − 2.0 |
| Houston | 3,129 | 2,540 | 14.2 | 11.9 | + 589 | + 23.2 |
| Port Arthur | 38 | 27 | 0.2 | 0.1 | + 11 | + 40.7 |
| TOTAL GULF COASTAL ZONE | 7,171 | 6,652 | 32.5 | 31.2 | + 519 | + 7.8 |
| PACIFIC COASTAL ZONE | | | | | | |
| San Francisco | 2,591 | 2,688 | 11.7 | 12.6 | − 97 | − 3.6 |
| Los Angeles | 529 | 509 | 2.4 | 2.4 | + 20 | + 3.9 |
| Oregon | 161 | 163 | 0.7 | 0.8 | − 2 | − 1.2 |
| Washington | 42 | 41 | 0.2 | 0.2 | + 1 | + 2.4 |
| San Diego | 51 | 45 | 0.2 | 0.2 | + 6 | + 13.3 |
| El Paso | 39 | 29 | 0.2 | 0.1 | + 10 | + 34.5 |
| TOTAL PACIFIC COASTAL ZONE | 3,413 | 3,475 | 15.4 | 16.3 | − 62 | − 1.8 |
| All Others | 35 | 32 | 0.2 | 0.1 | + 3 | + 9.4 |
| TOTAL IMPORTS | 22,092 | 21,347 | 100.0 | 100.0 | + 745 | + 3.5 |

Source: United States Department of Commerce. See note to Table IQV-3.

IQV-10. UNITED STATES: STATISTICAL SUMMARY OF IMPORTS OF COFFEE, 1966

| COUNTRIES OF ORIGIN | VOLUME Bags* | VOLUME Pounds | VALUE U.S. $ | Unit Value Per Bag U.S. $ | Unit Value Per Pound U.S. ¢ | Unit Value Index Per Pound 1955 = 100 |
|---|---|---|---|---|---|---|
| WESTERN HEMISPHERE | | Thousands | | | | |
| Pan-American Coffee Bureau | | | | | | |
| Brazil | 6,731 | 890,270 | 327,430 | 48.65 | 36.78 | 77 |
| Colombia | 2,716 | 359,272 | 163,784 | 60.30 | 45.59 | 73 |
| Guatemala | 1,110 | 146,842 | 59,333 | 53.45 | 40.41 | 74 |
| Mexico | 1,045 | 138,192 | 57,427 | 54.95 | 41.54 | 76 |
| El Salvador | 593 | 78,398 | 31,253 | 52.70 | 39.84 | 74 |
| Peru | 447 | 59,168 | 22,439 | 50.20 | 37.95 | 71 |
| Ecuador | 432 | 57,180 | 19,380 | 44.86 | 33.91 | 73 |
| Dominican Republic | 354 | 46,787 | 17,739 | 50.11 | 37.88 | 69 |
| Venezuela | 266 | 35,219 | 14,559 | 54.73 | 41.38 | 74 |
| Honduras | 249 | 32,878 | 12,840 | 51.57 | 38.99 | 81 |
| Costa Rica | 231 | 30,606 | 12,678 | 54.88 | 41.49 | 71 |
| Nicaragua | 135 | 17,907 | 7,623 | 56.47 | 42.69 | 76 |
| Haiti | 90 | 11,836 | 4,527 | 50.30 | 38.03 | 78 |
| Panama | 24 | 3,214 | 1,154 | 48.08 | 36.35 | 66 |
| Cuba | — | — | — | — | — | — |
| Total Pan-American Coffee Bureau | 14,423 | 1,907,769 | 752,166 | 52.15 | 39.42 | 72 |
| Total Other Western Hemisphere (1) | 90 | 11,932 | 3,932 | 43.69 | 33.03 | 79 |
| TOTAL WESTERN HEMISPHERE | 14,513 | 1,919,701 | 756,098 | 52.10 | 39.39 | 73 |
| AFRICA | | | | | | |
| Uganda | 1,218 | 161,116 | 50,428 | 41.40 | 31.30 | N.A. |
| Tanzania | 237 | 31,370 | 11,479 | 48.43 | 36.61 | N.A. |
| Kenya | 174 | 22,991 | 9,602 | 55.18 | 41.72 | N.A. |
| Portuguese Africa | 1,212 | 160,256 | 50,166 | 41.39 | 31.29 | 80 |
| Franc Zone | | | | | | |
| Ivory Coast | 787 | 104,149 | 31,529 | 40.06 | 30.28 | N.A. |
| Cameroun | 332 | 43,856 | 13,681 | 41.21 | 31.15 | 91 |
| Madagascar | 230 | 30,483 | 9,164 | 39.84 | 30.12 | 90 |
| Togo | 9 | 1,173 | 269 | 29.89 | 22.60 | N.A. |
| Gabon | 5 | 639 | 206 | 41.20 | 31.15 | N.A. |
| Others (2) | 5 | 674 | 260 | 52.00 | 39.31 | N.A. |
| Ethiopia | 792 | 104,776 | 40,666 | 51.35 | 38.82 | 88 |
| Liberia | 709 | 93,796 | 29,521 | 41.64 | 31.48 | 92 |
| Rwanda & Burundi | 333 | 44,097 | 16,443 | 49.38 | 37.33 | N.A. |
| Guinea | 164 | 21,729 | 6,548 | 39.93 | 30.19 | N.A. |
| Sierra Leone | 129 | 17,016 | 4,349 | 33.71 | 25.48 | N.A. |
| Congo (D.R.) | 36 | 4,741 | 1,833 | 50.92 | 38.50 | N.A. |
| Various (3) | 83 | 11,020 | 3,375 | 40.66 | 30.74 | N.A. |
| TOTAL AFRICA | 6,455 | 853,882 | 279,519 | 43.30 | 32.73 | 80 |
| ASIA & OCEANIA | | | | | | |
| Indonesia | 975 | 128,883 | 26,214 | 26.89 | 20.33 | 37 |
| India | 45 | 5,990 | 2,116 | 47.02 | 35.55 | 69 |
| Various (4) | 102 | 13,468 | 4,496 | 44.08 | 33.32 | N.A. |
| TOTAL ASIA & OCEANIA | 1,122 | 148,341 | 32,826 | 29.26 | 22.12 | N.A. |
| OTHERS (5) | 2 | 288 | 137 | 68.50 | 51.79 | N.A. |
| TOTAL IMPORTS | 22,092 | 2,922,212 | 1,068,580 | 48.37 | 36.57 | 70 |

Source: United States Department of Commerce.
(*) Bags of 60 Kilograms or 132.276 pounds each.
(1) Includes: Bolivia, Canada, Guyana, British Honduras, Jamaica, Surinam, Paraguay, Trinidad & Tobago.
(2) Includes: Chad, Congo (Brazzaville), Dahomey, French Somaliland, Mali, Niger and Upper Volta.
(3) Includes: Ghana, Nigeria and South Africa.
(4) Includes: Aden, Australia, Laos, Malaysia, New Guinea, Bhutan, Brunei and Portuguese Timor, Singapore, South Viet Nam, Yemen, Sultanate of Oman, Trucial Sheikhdoms and Qatar.
(5) Includes: France, Italy, Netherlands, Portugal, Switzerland, United Kingdom and Germany (F.R.).

## IQ-6. UNITED STATES: ORIGIN AND

By Customs

(Bags of 60 kilograms or

| COUNTRIES OF ORIGIN WESTERN HEMISPHERE Pan-American Coffee Bureau | Massachusetts | New York | Philadelphia | Maryland | Virginia | Tampa |
|---|---|---|---|---|---|---|
| Brazil | 77,712 | 2,771,661 | 67,853 | 209,052 | 27,811 | 537,603 |
| Colombia | 12 | 1,389,647 | 8,602 | 33,452 | — | 394,269 |
| Guatemala | — | 540,384 | 6,425 | 1,150 | — | — |
| Mexico | — | 292,687 | 5,978 | 575 | 1,437 | 24,728 |
| El Salvador | — | 248,473 | — | 1,134 | — | 144 |
| Peru | — | 129,357 | 2,712 | 287 | — | 2,261 |
| Ecuador | — | 232,245 | — | 835 | — | 2,262 |
| Dominican Republic | — | 216,085 | — | — | — | 312 |
| Venezuela | — | 186,417 | — | 494 | — | — |
| Honduras | — | 103,650 | — | — | — | — |
| Costa Rica | 11 | 67,612 | — | — | — | 627 |
| Nicaragua | — | 7,499 | — | — | — | — |
| Haiti | — | 61,813 | — | — | — | — |
| Panama | 1,540 | 19,472 | — | — | — | — |
| Cuba | — | — | — | — | — | — |
| Total Pan-American Coffee Bureau | 79,275 | 6,267,002 | 91,570 | 246,979 | 29,248 | 962,206 |
| **OTHER WESTERN HEMISPHERE** | | | | | | |
| Bolivia | — | 27,103 | — | — | — | — |
| Paraguay | — | 20,612 | — | — | — | — |
| Trinidad & Tobago | — | 3,269 | — | — | — | — |
| Surinam | 433 | — | — | — | — | — |
| Guyana | 1,954 | — | — | — | — | — |
| British Honduras | — | 643 | — | — | — | — |
| Canada | — | — | — | — | — | — |
| Jamaica | — | 36 | — | — | — | — |
| Total Other Western Hemisphere | 2,387 | 51,663 | — | — | — | — |
| **TOTAL WESTERN HEMISPHERE** | 81,662 | 6,318,665 | 91,570 | 246,979 | 29,248 | 962,206 |
| **AFRICA** | | | | | | |
| Uganda | 3,414 | 462,972 | — | 997 | — | 112,042 |
| Tanzania | 2,857 | 69,765 | — | — | — | 1,013 |
| Kenya | 2,707 | 34,137 | — | 356 | — | 1,914 |
| Portuguese Africa | 1,251 | 515,984 | — | 417 | 1,752 | 23,486 |
| **Franc Zone** | | | | | | |
| Ivory Coast | — | 226,934 | — | — | — | 123,637 |
| Cameroun | 420 | 169,806 | — | — | 500 | 40,114 |
| Madagascar | — | 38,360 | — | — | — | 127,633 |
| Togo | — | 8,047 | 824 | — | — | — |
| Gabon | — | 4,830 | — | — | — | — |
| Others (1) | — | 1,409 | — | — | — | — |
| Ethiopia | 9,852 | 210,217 | — | 250 | — | — |
| Liberia | — | 574,048 | — | 933 | 252 | — |
| Rwanda & Burundi | — | 132,330 | — | — | 250 | — |
| Guinea | — | 103,783 | — | — | — | — |
| Sierra Leone | — | 77,484 | — | — | — | — |
| Congo (D.R.) | 8,075 | 15,795 | 228 | 210 | — | — |
| Ghana | — | 24,712 | — | — | — | — |
| South Africa | — | 3,413 | — | — | — | 23,852 |
| Nigeria | — | 12,353 | — | — | — | — |
| **TOTAL AFRICA** | 28,576 | 2,686,379 | 1,052 | 3,163 | 2,754 | 453,691 |
| **ASIA & OCEANIA** | | | | | | |
| Indonesia | 507 | 512,206 | 2,520 | 2,952 | 417 | — |
| India | 1,334 | 16,230 | — | — | — | — |
| Arabia (2) | 702 | 2,174 | — | — | — | — |
| Others (3) | 839 | 8,008 | — | 416 | — | 8,355 |
| **TOTAL ASIA & OCEANIA** | 3,382 | 538,618 | 2,520 | 3,368 | 417 | 8,355 |
| **VARIOUS (4)** | 52 | 893 | — | — | — | — |
| **TOTAL IMPORTS** | 113,672 | 9,544,555 | 95,142 | 253,510 | 32,419 | 1,424,252 |

Source: United States Department of Commerce.
(1) Includes: Chad, Congo (Brazzaville), Dahomey, French Somaliland, Mali, Niger and Upper Volta.
(2) Includes: Yemen, Sultanate of Oman, Trucial Sheikhdoms and Qatar.

**VOLUME OF IMPORTS OF COFFEE\*, 1966**

Districts

(32.276 pounds each)

| New Orleans | Los Angeles | San Francisco | Oregon | Wash-ington | Houston | Others | TOTAL |
|---|---|---|---|---|---|---|---|
| 1,359,836 | 114,415 | 723,624 | 46,475 | 16,307 | 715,519 | 62,530 | 6,730,398 |
| 201,558 | 5,769 | 356,083 | 5,533 | 1,155 | 319,700 | 298 | 2,716,078 |
| 282,273 | 17,525 | 143,180 | 9,120 | 4,764 | 105,301 | – | 1,110,122 |
| 305,137 | 8,908 | 92,539 | 11,996 | 1,185 | 248,239 | 51,313 | 1,044,722 |
| 128,816 | 7,182 | 138,645 | 8,327 | 411 | 59,550 | – | 592,682 |
| 43,518 | 91,069 | 105,044 | 20,714 | 1,322 | 51,023 | – | 447,307 |
| 55,167 | 38,110 | 46,845 | 1,369 | 1,838 | 53,608 | – | 432,279 |
| 82,240 | 10,712 | 27,845 | 935 | – | 15,510 | 71 | 353,710 |
| 31,221 | – | 1,744 | – | – | 46,375 | – | 266,251 |
| 88,945 | – | – | – | – | 55,102 | 858 | 248,555 |
| 75,385 | 10,865 | 52,479 | 10,631 | 2,360 | 11,414 | – | 231,384 |
| 35,589 | 1,293 | 62,860 | 2,016 | 1,445 | 24,675 | – | 135,377 |
| 5,442 | – | 799 | – | – | 21,425 | – | 89,479 |
| – | – | – | – | – | 2,384 | 901 | 24,297 |
| – | – | – | – | – | – | – | |
| 2,695,127 | 305,848 | 1,751,687 | 117,116 | 30,787 | 1,729,825 | 115,971 | 14,422,641 |
| | | | | | | | |
| 3,297 | 7,526 | 5,589 | – | – | 1,059 | – | 44,574 |
| – | 1,000 | – | – | 595 | 880 | – | 23,087 |
| < | 4,330 | 2,797 | 756 | – | – | – | 11,152 |
| 8,236 | – | – | – | – | – | – | 8,669 |
| – | – | – | – | – | – | – | 1,954 |
| – | – | – | – | – | – | – | 643 |
| – | – | – | – | 32 | – | 33 | 65 |
| – | 3 | 11 | – | – | – | 10 | 60 |
| 11,533 | 12,859 | 8,397 | 756 | 627 | 1,939 | 43 | 90,204 |
| 2,706,660 | 318,707 | 1,760,084 | 117,872 | 31,414 | 1,731,764 | 116,014 | 14,512,845 |
| | | | | | | | |
| 108,924 | 34,408 | 186,826 | 16,605 | 499 | 291,342 | – | 1,218,029 |
| 78,767 | 7,098 | 43,839 | 1,083 | – | 32,731 | – | 237,153 |
| 46,112 | 9,001 | 53,068 | 10,969 | 762 | 14,382 | 400 | 173,808 |
| 446,022 | 8,000 | 62,707 | – | – | 151,489 | 417 | 1,211,525 |
| 56,742 | 40,744 | 25,959 | – | 5,040 | 308,306 | – | 787,362 |
| 32,833 | 3,533 | 30,173 | 840 | – | 53,331 | – | 331,550 |
| 838 | – | – | – | – | 63,621 | – | 230,452 |
| – | – | – | – | – | – | – | 8,871 |
| – | – | – | – | – | – | – | 4,830 |
| 339 | – | 3,330 | – | – | 18 | – | 5,096 |
| 212,877 | 20,908 | 122,383 | 2,757 | 333 | 199,913 | 12,610 | 792,100 |
| 61,396 | 3,404 | 1,254 | – | 1,250 | 27,048 | 39,510 | 709,095 |
| 79,496 | 11,076 | 48,862 | 997 | – | 60,361 | – | 333,372 |
| 844 | – | 10,710 | – | – | 48,931 | – | 164,268 |
| 17,075 | – | – | – | – | 34,082 | – | 128,641 |
| 4,195 | 776 | 1,271 | 884 | – | 4,405 | – | 35,839 |
| 7,620 | – | – | – | – | 2,994 | – | 35,326 |
| – | – | – | – | – | – | – | 27,265 |
| – | 4,370 | – | – | – | 4,000 | – | 20,723 |
| 1,154,080 | 143,318 | 590,382 | 34,135 | 7,884 | 1,296,954 | 52,937 | 6,455,305 |
| | | | | | | | |
| 114,871 | 53,424 | 194,060 | 4,003 | 1,753 | 85,294 | 2,342 | 974,349 |
| 10,840 | 4,000 | 11,211 | – | – | 1,667 | – | 45,282 |
| 10,793 | 250 | 694 | – | – | 2,115 | – | 16,728 |
| 6,002 | 8,708 | 34,310 | 5,437 | 1,322 | 11,022 | 670 | 85,089 |
| 142,506 | 66,382 | 240,275 | 9,440 | 3,075 | 100,098 | 3,012 | 1,121,448 |
| 748 | 46 | | 3 | – | 4 | 435 | 2,181 |
| 4,003,994 | 528,453 | 2,590,744 | 161,447 | 42,373 | 3,128,820 | 172,398 | 22,091,779 |

(3)  Includes: Aden, Australia, Laos, Malaysia, New Guinea, Bhutan, Brunei and Portuguese Timor, Singapore and South Viet Nam.

(4)  Includes: France, Italy, Netherlands, Portugal, Switzerland, United Kingdom and Germany (F.R.).

\*   See footnote to Table IQV-3

## IV-7. UNITED STATES: ORIGIN AND
By Customs
(In U.S.

| COUNTRIES OF ORIGIN WESTERN HEMISPHERE Pan-American Coffee Bureau | Massachusetts | New York | Philadelphia | Maryland | Virginia | Tampa |
|---|---|---|---|---|---|---|
| Brazil | 3,959,104 | 135,495,882 | 3,393,809 | 10,165,586 | 1,383,255 | 26,290,479 |
| Colombia | 725 | 83,424,087 | 526,077 | 1,956,460 | — | 24,016,719 |
| Guatemala | — | 28,735,863 | 357,973 | 59,593 | — | — |
| Mexico | — | 15,732,417 | 319,639 | 32,705 | 77,437 | 1,368,510 |
| El Salvador | — | 13,026,993 | — | 61,500 | — | 8,391 |
| Peru | — | 6,736,636 | 136,992 | 15,060 | — | 116,805 |
| Ecuador | — | 10,409,009 | — | 41,129 | — | 108,384 |
| Dominican Republic | — | 10,667,969 | — | — | — | 14,984 |
| Venezuela | — | 10,095,755 | — | 25,342 | — | — |
| Honduras | — | 5,266,588 | — | — | — | — |
| Costa Rica | 674 | 3,716,137 | — | — | — | 35,534 |
| Nicaragua | — | 378,232 | — | — | — | — |
| Haiti | — | 3,035,283 | — | — | — | — |
| Panama | — | 974,432 | — | — | — | — |
| Cuba | — | — | — | — | — | — |
| TOTAL P.A.C.B. | 3,960,503 | 327,695,283 | 4,734,490 | 12,357,375 | 1,460,692 | 51,959,806 |
| **OTHER WESTERN HEMISPHERE** | | | | | | |
| Bolivia | — | 1,313,853 | — | — | — | — |
| Paraguay | — | 782,292 | — | — | — | — |
| Trinidad & Tobago | — | 137,234 | — | — | — | — |
| Surinam | 15,057 | — | — | — | — | — |
| Guyana | 75,235 | — | — | — | — | — |
| British Honduras | — | 28,561 | — | — | — | — |
| Canada | — | — | — | — | — | — |
| Jamaica | — | 4,740 | — | — | — | — |
| Total Other Western Hemisphere | 90,292 | 2,266,680 | — | — | — | — |
| TOTAL WESTERN HEMISPHERE | 4,050,795 | 329,961,963 | 4,734,490 | 12,357,375 | 1,460,692 | 51,959,806 |
| **AFRICA** | | | | | | |
| Uganda | 173,530 | 19,026,915 | — | 45,915 | — | 4,530,938 |
| Tanzania | 144,820 | 3,267,411 | — | — | — | 42,719 |
| Kenya | 146,011 | 2,302,028 | — | 18,725 | — | 76,676 |
| Portuguese Africa | 56,119 | 21,326,066 | — | 11,033 | 75,015 | 961,871 |
| **Franc Zone** | | | | | | |
| Ivory Coast | — | 9,001,894 | — | — | — | 5,058,965 |
| Cameroun | 17,639 | 6,765,265 | — | — | 24,172 | 1,724,699 |
| Madagascar | — | 1,514,393 | — | — | — | 5,202,159 |
| Togo | — | 242,919 | 25,955 | — | — | — |
| Gabon | — | 206,043 | — | — | — | — |
| Others (1) | — | 65,227 | — | — | — | — |
| Ethiopia | 512,633 | 10,771,330 | — | 12,758 | — | — |
| Liberia | — | 24,119,791 | — | 35,875 | 9,945 | — |
| Rwanda & Burundi | — | 6,579,150 | — | — | 9,590 | — |
| Guinea | — | 4,314,060 | — | — | — | — |
| Sierra Leone | — | 2,701,022 | — | — | — | — |
| Congo (D.R.) | 440,362 | 800,838 | 13,977 | 10,955 | — | — |
| Ghana | — | 893,506 | — | — | — | — |
| South Africa | — | 163,288 | — | — | — | 1,104,307 |
| Nigeria | — | 475,235 | — | — | — | — |
| TOTAL AFRICA | 1,491,114 | 114,536,381 | 39,932 | 135,261 | 118,722 | 18,702,334 |
| **ASIA & OCEANIA** | | | | | | |
| Indonesia | 30,797 | 12,876,098 | 38,934 | 111,038 | 15,166 | — |
| India | 64,683 | 726,157 | — | — | — | — |
| Arabia (2) | 43,876 | 131,214 | — | — | — | — |
| Others (3) | 48,644 | 330,827 | — | 15,959 | — | 320,514 |
| TOTAL ASIA & OCEANIA | 188,000 | 14,064,296 | 38,934 | 126,997 | 15,166 | 320,514 |
| VARIOUS (4) | 5,277 | 52,855 | — | — | — | — |
| TOTAL IMPORTS | 5,735,186 | 458,615,495 | 4,813,356 | 12,619,633 | 1,594,580 | 70,982,654 |

Source: United States Department of Commerce.
(1) Includes: Chad, Congo (Brazzaville), Dahomey, French Somaliland, Mali, Niger and Upper Volta.
(2) Includes: Yemen, Sultanate of Oman, Trucial Sheikhdoms and Qatar.

## VALUE OF IMPORTS OF COFFEE, 1966
Districts
Dollars)

| New Orleans | Los Angeles | San Francisco | Oregon | Washington | Houston | Others | TOTAL |
|---|---|---|---|---|---|---|---|
| 65,975,588 | 5,452,985 | 35,584,601 | 2,364,066 | 815,854 | 33,815,283 | 2,733,494 | 327,429,986 |
| 12,036,914 | 355,243 | 21,638,488 | 338,486 | 69,176 | 19,403,186 | 18,097 | 163,783,658 |
| 15,023,547 | 891,293 | 7,638,319 | 464,764 | 291,183 | 5,870,467 | — | 59,333,002 |
| 16,623,097 | 489,613 | 5,158,019 | 680,211 | 153,692 | 13,992,812 | 2,798,490 | 57,426,642 |
| 6,776,476 | 382,046 | 7,401,979 | 433,477 | 20,710 | 3,141,225 | — | 31,252,797 |
| 2,269,241 | 4,061,695 | 5,363,593 | 1,088,941 | 79,113 | 2,571,392 | — | 22,439,468 |
| 2,482,625 | 1,490,530 | 2,170,602 | 64,393 | 82,458 | 2,531,383 | — | 19,380,513 |
| 4,264,113 | 530,159 | 1,375,439 | 43,932 | — | 838,789 | 3,591 | 17,738,976 |
| 1,774,650 | — | 99,001 | — | — | 2,564,184 | — | 14,558,932 |
| 4,577,729 | — | — | — | — | 2,946,495 | 48,806 | 12,839,618 |
| 4,173,513 | 548,348 | 2,862,482 | 577,229 | 128,374 | 635,324 | — | 12,677,615 |
| 1,976,450 | 72,894 | 3,632,369 | 114,392 | 80,504 | 1,367,994 | — | 7,622,835 |
| 273,737 | — | 42,174 | — | — | 1,176,015 | — | 4,527,209 |
| — | — | — | — | — | 138,740 | 40,675 | 1,153,847 |
| — | — | — | — | — | — | — | — |
| 138,227,680 | 14,274,806 | 92,967,066 | 6,169,891 | 1,721,064 | 90,993,289 | 5,643,153 | 752,165,098 |
| | | | | | | | |
| 166,111 | 348,889 | 254,161 | — | — | 60,258 | — | 2,143,272 |
| — | 39,000 | — | — | 23,205 | 34,320 | — | 878,817 |
| — | 165,571 | 107,163 | 29,375 | — | — | — | 439,343 |
| 338,251 | — | — | — | — | — | — | 353,308 |
| — | — | — | — | — | — | — | 75,235 |
| — | — | — | — | — | — | — | 28,561 |
| — | — | — | — | 3,239 | — | 3,377 | 6,616 |
| — | 279 | 1,314 | — | — | — | 976 | 7,309 |
| 504,362 | 553,739 | 362,638 | 29,375 | 26,444 | 94,578 | 4,353 | 3,932,461 |
| 138,732,042 | 14,828,545 | 93,329,704 | 6,199,266 | 1,747,508 | 91,087,867 | 5,647,506 | 756,097,559 |
| | | | | | | | |
| 4,496,114 | 1,450,431 | 7,778,305 | 721,080 | 25,245 | 12,179,303 | — | 50,427,776 |
| 3,927,847 | 299,716 | 2,169,949 | 48,342 | — | 1,577,996 | — | 11,478,800 |
| 2,437,691 | 415,047 | 2,783,429 | 585,840 | 43,828 | 775,874 | 16,726 | 9,601,875 |
| 18,417,972 | 322,446 | 2,628,223 | — | — | 6,350,394 | 17,065 | 50,166,204 |
| 2,227,926 | 1,623,069 | 1,024,949 | — | 190,496 | 12,401,394 | — | 31,528,693 |
| 1,395,013 | 131,134 | 1,407,324 | 41,745 | — | 2,173,581 | — | 13,680,572 |
| 35,132 | — | — | — | — | 2,412,074 | — | 9,163,758 |
| — | — | — | — | — | — | — | 268,874 |
| — | — | — | — | — | — | — | 206,043 |
| 18,177 | — | 176,192 | — | — | 850 | — | 260,446 |
| 10,856,440 | 1,075,418 | 6,316,321 | 144,340 | 16,993 | 10,318,059 | 641,373 | 40,665,665 |
| 2,448,005 | 126,234 | 50,911 | — | 49,349 | 1,069,786 | 1,611,416 | 29,521,312 |
| 3,918,246 | 448,147 | 2,381,751 | 50,075 | — | 3,056,277 | — | 16,443,236 |
| 30,900 | — | 342,444 | — | — | 1,860,815 | — | 6,548,219 |
| 549,292 | — | — | — | — | 1,098,897 | — | 4,349,211 |
| 183,691 | 36,411 | 60,214 | 44,432 | — | 242,447 | — | 1,833,327 |
| 270,087 | — | — | — | — | 105,990 | — | 1,269,583 |
| — | — | — | — | — | — | — | 1,267,595 |
| — | 172,859 | — | — | — | 189,650 | — | 837,744 |
| 51,212,533 | 6,100,912 | 27,120,012 | 1,635,854 | 325,911 | 55,813,387 | 2,286,580 | 279,518,933 |
| | | | | | | | |
| 3,617,458 | 1,377,048 | 5,452,242 | 147,318 | 74,812 | 2,392,310 | 80,909 | 26,214,130 |
| 538,122 | 184,871 | 527,547 | — | — | 74,957 | — | 2,116,337 |
| 397,308 | 15,397 | 42,732 | — | — | 94,810 | — | 725,337 |
| 232,702 | 378,463 | 1,652,064 | 285,470 | 52,798 | 423,663 | 29,475 | 3,770,579 |
| 4,785,590 | 1,955,779 | 7,674,585 | 432,788 | 127,610 | 2,985,740 | 110,384 | 32,826,383 |
| 55,671 | 4,510 | 441 | — | — | 500 | 18,234 | 137,488 |
| 194,785,836 | 22,889,746 | 128,124,742 | 8,267,908 | 2,201,029 | 149,887,494 | 8,062,704 | 1,068,580,363 |

(3) Includes: Aden, Australia, Laos, Malaysia, New Guinea, Bhutan, Brunei and Portuguese Timor, Singapore and South Viet Nam.
(4) Includes: France, Italy, Netherlands, Portugal, Switzerland, United Kingdom and Germany (F.R.)

## IQ-8. UNITED STATES: VOLUME OF
(Bags of 60 kilograms

| COUNTRIES OF ORIGIN<br>WESTERN HEMISPHERE | January | February | March | April | May |
|---|---|---|---|---|---|
| **Pan American Coffee Bureau** | | | | | |
| Brazil | 488,944 | 545,212 | 530,758 | 596,538 | 570,180 |
| Colombia | 258,343 | 342,422 | 242,737 | 254,721 | 335,734 |
| Guatemala | 113,791 | 128,682 | 201,438 | 126,935 | 89,007 |
| Mexico | 145,402 | 97,047 | 108,880 | 74,718 | 75,643 |
| El Salvador | 33,804 | 40,751 | 23,594 | 27,007 | 23,401 |
| Peru | 39,667 | 68,296 | 18,555 | 9,609 | 37,702 |
| Ecuador | 51,152 | 17,993 | 25,926 | 15,211 | 16,917 |
| Dominican Republic | 84,094 | 26,426 | 6,768 | 46,690 | 5,732 |
| Venezuela | 29,578 | 47,049 | 38,299 | 18,645 | 22,754 |
| Honduras | 7,782 | 24,586 | 56,102 | 38,690 | 64,235 |
| Costa Rica | 39,254 | 20,911 | 14,574 | 28,002 | 30,082 |
| Nicaragua | 12,961 | 15,910 | 48,515 | 11,122 | 10,353 |
| Haiti | 22,482 | 14,766 | 1,401 | 5,300 | 7,662 |
| Panama | 4,157 | 995 | 4,484 | 1,981 | 3,578 |
| Cuba | — | — | — | — | — |
| Total Pan-American Coffee Bureau | 1,331,411 | 1,391,046 | 1,322,031 | 1,255,169 | 1,292,980 |
| **OTHER WESTERN HEMISPHERE** | | | | | |
| Bolivia | 292 | — | 46 | — | 850 |
| Paraguay | 5,954 | 5,951 | 3,802 | 1,815 | 880 |
| Trinidad & Tobago | — | — | 1,228 | 1,436 | 5,443 |
| Surinam | — | — | — | 101 | 81 |
| Guyana | — | — | 705 | — | 599 |
| British Honduras | — | — | — | — | — |
| Canada | 35 | — | 6 | 2 | 3 |
| Jamaica | 6 | 7 | — | — | 3 |
| Total Other Western Hemisphere | 6,287 | 5,958 | 5,787 | 3,354 | 7,859 |
| **TOTAL WESTERN HEMISPHERE** | 1,337,698 | 1,397,004 | 1,327,818 | 1,258,523 | 1,300,839 |
| **AFRICA** | | | | | |
| Uganda | 134,439 | 55,783 | 110,778 | 106,838 | 152,198 |
| Tanzania | 1,730 | 4,709 | 11,906 | 7,311 | 6,045 |
| Kenya | 1,328 | 5,948 | 3,557 | 16,430 | 16,640 |
| Portuguese Africa | 71,873 | 175,786 | 116,226 | 103,959 | 75,816 |
| **Franc Zone** | | | | | |
| Ivory Coast | 60,592 | 27,282 | 93,204 | 69,556 | 55,481 |
| Cameroun | 4,875 | 5,536 | 30,743 | 83,641 | 3,966 |
| Madagascar | 17,414 | 51,218 | 18,725 | — | 17,845 |
| Togo | — | — | — | — | 834 |
| Gabon | — | — | 4,830 | — | — |
| Others (1) | — | 3,330 | 999 | — | — |
| Ethiopia | 18,653 | 53,791 | 180,280 | 120,541 | 76,111 |
| Liberia | 39,510 | 124,000 | 390,546 | 88,194 | 15,933 |
| Rwanda & Burundi | 21,142 | 3,941 | 5,056 | 1,205 | — |
| Guinea | 24,220 | 31,432 | 6,074 | 17,697 | 4,221 |
| Sierra Leone | — | — | 5,088 | 1,696 | 8,897 |
| Congo (D.R.) | 3,474 | 2,360 | 3,872 | 3,520 | 944 |
| Ghana | — | — | — | — | 8,483 |
| South Africa | — | — | 23,852 | — | — |
| Nigeria | 257 | — | 2,118 | 4,969 | 6,655 |
| **TOTAL AFRICA** | 399,507 | 545,116 | 1,007,854 | 625,557 | 450,069 |
| **ASIA & OCEANIA** | | | | | |
| Indonesia | 81,083 | 70,063 | 34,234 | 79,182 | 65,631 |
| India | 1,364 | — | — | — | 2,127 |
| Arabia (2) | 1,387 | 385 | 12,081 | — | 402 |
| Others (3) | 11,855 | 4,152 | 4,702 | 2,953 | 1,592 |
| **TOTAL ASIA & OCEANIA** | 95,689 | 74,600 | 51,017 | 82,135 | 69,752 |
| **VARIOUS (4)** | 432 | — | — | 416 | 16 |
| **TOTAL IMPORTS** | 1,833,326 | 2,016,720 | 2,386,689 | 1,966,631 | 1,820,676 |

Source: United States Department of Commerce.
(1) Includes: Chad, Congo (Brazzaville), Dahomey, French Somaliland, Mali, Niger and Upper Volta.
(2) Includes: Yemen, Sultanate of Oman, Trucial Sheikhdoms and Qatar.

## IMPORTS OF COFFEE* BY MONTH, 1966
or 132.276 pounds each)

| June | July | August | September | October | November | December | TOTAL |
|---|---|---|---|---|---|---|---|
| 559,635 | 450,620 | 153,015 | 960,083 | 946,743 | 455,589 | 473,081 | 6,730,398 |
| 175,417 | 151,632 | 265,694 | 219,415 | 116,943 | 151,522 | 201,498 | 2,716,078 |
| 88,033 | 56,499 | 36,908 | 16,823 | 34,875 | 78,752 | 138,379 | 1,110,122 |
| 64,911 | 119,072 | 118,864 | 52,776 | 29,201 | 87,187 | 71,021 | 1,044,722 |
| 2,926 | 88,319 | 46,834 | 39,443 | 171,272 | 65,775 | 29,556 | 592,682 |
| 46,053 | 34,231 | 46,537 | 28,405 | 45,499 | 39,850 | 32,903 | 447,307 |
| 18,742 | 44,499 | 36,008 | 24,100 | 109,460 | 55,777 | 16,494 | 432,279 |
| 633 | 22,768 | 11,035 | 7,248 | 43,830 | 66,737 | 31,749 | 353,710 |
| 21,350 | 6,682 | 11,014 | 5,858 | 7,638 | 22,719 | 34,665 | 266,251 |
| 27,979 | 13,498 | 6,977 | 5,986 | 1,485 | 660 | 575 | 248,555 |
| 16,266 | 15,702 | 9,360 | 4,575 | 11,840 | 16,545 | 24,273 | 231,384 |
| 589 | 14,364 | 7,210 | 10,040 | 707 | 1,730 | 1,876 | 135,377 |
| 4,923 | 2,944 | 10,406 | 4,626 | 2,297 | 4,040 | 8,632 | 89,479 |
| 1,585 | 2,039 | 1,468 | 2,009 | 1,016 | 985 | – | 24,297 |
| – | – | – | – | – | – | – | – |
| 1,029,042 | 1,022,869 | 761,330 | 1,381,387 | 1,522,806 | 1,047,868 | 1,064,702 | 14,422,641 |
| | | | | | | | |
| 4,429 | 2,980 | 4,705 | 2,594 | 15,744 | 7,211 | 5,723 | 44,574 |
| 3,090 | 1,160 | – | – | – | 435 | – | 23,087 |
| 2,365 | 378 | – | 302 | – | – | – | 11,152 |
| – | – | 135 | 8,236 | – | 116 | – | 8,669 |
| 650 | – | – | – | – | – | – | 1,954 |
| – | – | – | – | – | 356 | 287 | 643 |
| 3 | – | 3 | 2 | – | – | 11 | 65 |
| – | – | – | – | 26 | 5 | 13 | 60 |
| 10,537 | 4,518 | 4,843 | 11,134 | 15,770 | 8,123 | 6,034 | 90,204 |
| | | | | | | | |
| 1,039,579 | 1,027,387 | 766,173 | 1,392,521 | 1,538,576 | 1,055,991 | 1,070,736 | 14,512,845 |
| | | | | | | | |
| 178,610 | 108,268 | 63,315 | 80,808 | 54,900 | 106,332 | 65,760 | 1,218,029 |
| 10,951 | 17,186 | 26,375 | 48,153 | 49,871 | 40,759 | 12,157 | 237,153 |
| 17,103 | 10,780 | 22,313 | 25,426 | 18,437 | 29,518 | 6,328 | 173,808 |
| 63,481 | 80,248 | 81,943 | 76,051 | 88,226 | 123,624 | 154,292 | 1,211,525 |
| | | | | | | | |
| 59,218 | 97,945 | 54,300 | 88,515 | 72,241 | 41,159 | 67,869 | 787,362 |
| 19,610 | 20,783 | 37,468 | 36,792 | 15,122 | 33,907 | 39,107 | 331,550 |
| 25,267 | 4,200 | 1,255 | 5,431 | 36,210 | 11,495 | 41,392 | 230,452 |
| – | 3,923 | 815 | 3,299 | – | – | – | 8,871 |
| – | – | – | – | – | – | – | 4,830 |
| – | 416 | 351 | – | – | – | – | 5,096 |
| 101,783 | 31,760 | 58,325 | 30,990 | 35,420 | 20,161 | 64,285 | 792,100 |
| 12,130 | 9,939 | 10,796 | 4,985 | 7,875 | 3,910 | 1,277 | 709,095 |
| 591 | – | 55,149 | 103,563 | 83,041 | 28,788 | 30,896 | 333,372 |
| 7,190 | 15,384 | – | 17,112 | 21,236 | 3,733 | 15,969 | 164,268 |
| 51,157 | 60,106 | 1,697 | – | – | – | – | 128,641 |
| 3,041 | 4,243 | 5,103 | 1,504 | 2,713 | 2,335 | 2,730 | 35,839 |
| 8,467 | 5,670 | 6,774 | – | 458 | 823 | 4,651 | 35,326 |
| – | – | – | – | – | 500 | 2,913 | 27,265 |
| 2,457 | – | 267 | – | – | – | 4,000 | 20,723 |
| 561,056 | 470,851 | 426,246 | 522,629 | 485,750 | 447,044 | 513,626 | 6,455,305 |
| | | | | | | | |
| 53,938 | 62,376 | 107,766 | 156,249 | 129,090 | 61,290 | 73,447 | 974,349 |
| 5,217 | 2,192 | 3,883 | 8,949 | 6,883 | 4,841 | 9,826 | 45,282 |
| 710 | 335 | 125 | 583 | 670 | 50 | – | 16,728 |
| 20,711 | 8,579 | 6,808 | 10,247 | 8,111 | 3,937 | 1,442 | 85,089 |
| 80,576 | 73,482 | 118,582 | 176,028 | 144,754 | 70,118 | 84,715 | 1,121,448 |
| 22 | 12 | 71 | 10 | 45 | 1,098 | 59 | 2,181 |
| | | | | | | | |
| 1,681,233 | 1,571,732 | 1,311,072 | 2,091,188 | 2,169,125 | 1,574,251 | 1,669,136 | 22,091,779 |

(3) Includes: Aden, Australia, Laos, Malaysia, New Guinea, Bhutan, Brunei and Portuguese Timor, Singapore and South Viet Nam.
(4) Includes: France, Italy, Netherlands, Portugal, Switzerland, United Kingdom and Germany (F.R.).
(*) See Footnote to Table IQV-3.

## IV-9. UNITED STATES: VALUE OF

(In U.S.

| COUNTRIES OF ORIGIN | January | February | March | April | May |
|---|---|---|---|---|---|
| **WESTERN HEMISPHERE** | | | | | |
| *Pan-American Coffee Bureau* | | | | | |
| Brazil | 24,968,205 | 27,843,786 | 26,906,144 | 29,830,549 | 28,039,227 |
| Colombia | 15,640,247 | 20,823,125 | 14,702,390 | 15,229,206 | 20,590,219 |
| Guatemala | 6,514,517 | 7,043,335 | 10,783,788 | 6,974,225 | 4,823,961 |
| Mexico | 8,527,476 | 5,642,646 | 6,110,100 | 4,185,236 | 4,172,548 |
| El Salvador | 1,950,194 | 2,363,090 | 1,358,027 | 1,494,142 | 1,306,925 |
| Peru | 2,037,366 | 3,564,441 | 921,540 | 460,528 | 1,909,293 |
| Ecuador | 2,215,005 | 756,259 | 1,080,337 | 682,875 | 719,408 |
| Dominican Republic | 4,476,939 | 1,423,577 | 363,119 | 2,414,142 | 292,119 |
| Venezuela | 1,734,479 | 2,716,004 | 2,140,523 | 1,021,394 | 1,238,352 |
| Honduras | 426,423 | 1,389,580 | 3,058,516 | 1,994,220 | 3,243,957 |
| Costa Rica | 2,294,389 | 1,234,950 | 845,873 | 1,513,366 | 1,609,671 |
| Nicaragua | 741,534 | 909,241 | 2,788,207 | 620,056 | 563,261 |
| Haiti | 1,158,834 | 793,473 | 74,666 | 264,708 | 383,714 |
| Panama | 242,388 | 46,373 | 210,397 | 91,399 | 160,942 |
| Cuba | — | — | — | — | — |
| TOTAL P.A.C.B. | 72,927,996 | 76,549,880 | 71,343,627 | 66,776,046 | 69,053,597 |
| **OTHER WESTERN HEMISPHERE** | | | | | |
| Bolivia | 14,000 | — | 1,620 | — | 42,749 |
| Paraguay | 225,060 | 226,847 | 145,590 | 68,970 | 34,320 |
| Trinidad & Tobago | — | — | 53,784 | 60,550 | 208,738 |
| Surinam | — | — | — | 3,201 | 3,832 |
| Guyana | — | — | 25,435 | — | 24,000 |
| British Honduras | — | — | — | — | — |
| Canada | 3,546 | — | 608 | 330 | 330 |
| Jamaica | 498 | 883 | — | — | 279 |
| TOTAL OTHER WESTERN HEMISPHERE | 243,104 | 227,730 | 227,037 | 133,051 | 314,248 |
| TOTAL WESTERN HEMISPHERE | 73,171,100 | 76,777,610 | 71,570,664 | 66,909,097 | 69,367,845 |
| **AFRICA** | | | | | |
| Uganda | 5,519,663 | 2,407,656 | 4,571,830 | 4,431,476 | 6,343,603 |
| Tanzania | 78,901 | 251,504 | 680,544 | 365,927 | 311,032 |
| Kenya | 73,327 | 248,205 | 183,282 | 915,138 | 926,397 |
| Portuguese Africa | 3,053,295 | 7,429,317 | 4,912,749 | 4,393,463 | 3,169,517 |
| *Franc Zone* | | | | | |
| Ivory Coast | 2,566,382 | 1,071,804 | 3,975,393 | 2,844,716 | 2,189,715 |
| Cameroun | 249,133 | 211,588 | 1,268,624 | 3,268,589 | 164,664 |
| Madagascar | 751,345 | 2,121,846 | 765,851 | — | 764,425 |
| Togo | — | — | — | — | 34,254 |
| Gabon | — | — | 206,043 | — | — |
| Others (1) | — | 176,192 | 52,874 | — | — |
| Ethiopia | 989,187 | 2,878,560 | 9,550,675 | 6,322,017 | 3,864,746 |
| Liberia | 1,611,416 | 5,158,003 | 16,588,892 | 3,632,348 | 608,152 |
| Rwanda & Burundi | 1,087,751 | 212,683 | 241,415 | 54,226 | — |
| Guinea | 922,356 | 1,311,047 | 265,659 | 705,472 | 165,285 |
| Sierra Leone | — | — | 210,339 | 72,708 | 357,127 |
| Congo (D.R.) | 184,648 | 126,352 | 202,798 | 193,853 | 49,231 |
| Ghana | — | — | — | — | 303,345 |
| South Africa | — | — | 1,104,307 | — | — |
| Nigeria | 9,900 | — | 89,839 | 181,842 | 262,165 |
| TOTAL AFRICA | 17,097,304 | 23,604,757 | 44,871,114 | 27,381,775 | 19,513,658 |
| **ASIA & OCEANIA** | | | | | |
| Indonesia | 1,954,283 | 1,881,382 | 1,097,268 | 2,656,158 | 2,168,337 |
| India | 70,248 | — | — | — | 107,942 |
| Arabia (2) | 86,203 | 23,824 | 451,500 | — | 24,314 |
| Others (3) | 613,860 | 183,451 | 237,039 | 129,534 | 65,614 |
| TOTAL ASIA & OCEANIA | 2,724,594 | 2,088,657 | 1,785,807 | 2,785,692 | 2,366,207 |
| VARIOUS (4) | 23,636 | — | — | 25,015 | 1,600 |
| TOTAL IMPORTS | 93,016,634 | 102,471,024 | 118,227,585 | 97,101,579 | 91,249,310 |

Source: United States Department of Commerce.
(1) Includes: Chad, Congo (Brazzaville), Dahomey, French Somaliland, Mali, Niger and Upper Volta.
(2) Includes: Yemen, Sultanate of Oman, Trucial Sheikhdoms and Qatar.

A-100

## IMPORTS OF COFFEE BY MONTH, 1966
Dollars)

| June | July | August | September | October | November | December | TOTAL |
|---|---|---|---|---|---|---|---|
| 27,282,801 | 21,669,128 | 7,263,473 | 45,884,780 | 45,060,600 | 21,665,693 | 21,015,600 | 327,429,986 |
| 10,693,860 | 9,244,559 | 16,190,836 | 13,305,596 | 7,125,858 | 8,776,301 | 11,461,461 | 163,783,658 |
| 4,713,330 | 2,956,197 | 1,897,906 | 843,050 | 1,777,039 | 4,005,670 | 6,999,984 | 59,333,002 |
| 3,516,399 | 6,304,112 | 6,328,799 | 2,864,447 | 1,615,020 | 4,460,947 | 3,698,912 | 57,426,642 |
| 158,574 | 4,705,258 | 2,485,901 | 2,067,006 | 8,611,984 | 3,257,443 | 1,494,253 | 31,252,797 |
| 2,397,835 | 1,739,407 | 2,410,154 | 1,430,061 | 2,153,031 | 1,857,704 | 1,558,108 | 22,439,468 |
| 874,160 | 2,130,206 | 1,724,175 | 1,157,297 | 5,004,849 | 2,364,458 | 671,484 | 19,380,513 |
| 31,958 | 1,134,658 | 535,810 | 347,064 | 2,053,007 | 3,158,581 | 1,508,002 | 17,738,976 |
| 1,145,098 | 353,126 | 584,187 | 305,989 | 389,826 | 1,150,739 | 1,779,215 | 14,558,932 |
| 1,302,987 | 687,320 | 319,626 | 297,374 | 60,200 | 31,196 | 28,219 | 12,839,618 |
| 866,749 | 857,231 | 487,079 | 250,783 | 617,282 | 825,375 | 1,274,867 | 12,677,615 |
| 31,243 | 759,448 | 370,977 | 637,311 | 34,140 | 80,063 | 87,354 | 7,622,835 |
| 273,343 | 135,472 | 512,373 | 213,394 | 108,066 | 196,315 | 412,851 | 4,527,209 |
| 72,311 | 88,946 | 72,489 | 84,296 | 43,221 | 41,085 | — | 1,153,847 |
| — | — | — | — | — | — | — | — |
| 53,360,648 | 52,765,068 | 41,183,785 | 69,688,448 | 74,654,123 | 51,871,570 | 51,990,310 | 752,165,098 |
|  |  |  |  |  |  |  |  |
| 218,195 | 135,815 | 235,599 | 118,136 | 765,036 | 342,951 | 269,171 | 2,143,272 |
| 117,420 | 44,080 | — | — | — | 16,530 | — | 878,817 |
| 90,571 | 14,500 | — | 11,200 | — | — | — | 439,343 |
| — | — | 4,282 | 338,251 | — | 3,742 | — | 353,308 |
| 25,800 | — | — | — | — | — | — | 75,235 |
| — | — | — | — | — | 14,123 | 14,438 | 28,561 |
| 330 | — | 330 | 307 | — | — | 835 | 6,616 |
| — | — | — | — | 2,393 | 1,456 | 1,800 | 7,309 |
| 452,316 | 194,395 | 240,211 | 467,894 | 767,429 | 378,802 | 286,244 | 3,932,461 |
|  |  |  |  |  |  |  |  |
| 53,812,964 | 52,959,463 | 41,423,996 | 70,156,342 | 75,421,552 | 52,250,372 | 52,276,554 | 756,097,559 |
|  |  |  |  |  |  |  |  |
| 7,303,852 | 4,662,062 | 2,851,811 | 3,417,792 | 2,205,989 | 4,153,874 | 2,558,168 | 50,427,776 |
| 545,618 | 897,630 | 1,352,625 | 2,405,519 | 2,290,711 | 1,758,051 | 540,738 | 11,478,800 |
| 930,460 | 553,414 | 1,184,209 | 1,933,007 | 935,611 | 1,449,367 | 269,458 | 9,601,875 |
| 2,689,162 | 3,364,800 | 3,442,701 | 3,185,543 | 3,570,134 | 4,868,543 | 6,086,980 | 50,166,204 |
| 2,349,744 | 3,872,852 | 2,099,162 | 3,606,366 | 2,718,866 | 1,570,355 | 2,663,338 | 31,528,693 |
| 751,415 | 830,038 | 1,598,933 | 1,604,240 | 618,778 | 1,488,492 | 1,626,078 | 13,680,572 |
| 980,729 | 167,637 | 51,770 | 209,705 | 1,442,826 | 422,611 | 1,485,013 | 9,163,758 |
| — | 103,443 | 26,539 | 104,638 | — | — | — | 268,874 |
| — | — | — | — | — | — | — | 206,043 |
| — | 13,537 | 17,843 | — | — | — | — | 260,446 |
| 5,208,000 | 1,577,399 | 2,905,820 | 1,540,392 | 1,736,513 | 985,006 | 3,107,350 | 40,665,665 |
| 457,587 | 377,456 | 409,058 | 186,555 | 299,356 | 145,283 | 47,206 | 29,521,312 |
| 29,210 | — | 2,742,926 | 5,192,544 | 4,119,580 | 1,377,507 | 1,385,394 | 16,443,236 |
| 297,217 | 614,120 | — | 681,820 | 757,468 | 116,480 | 711,295 | 6,548,219 |
| 1,648,189 | 1,989,923 | 70,925 | — | — | — | — | 4,349,211 |
| 162,381 | 212,940 | 251,223 | 74,733 | 133,028 | 114,643 | 127,497 | 1,833,327 |
| 299,215 | 224,101 | 234,233 | — | 14,451 | 25,885 | 168,353 | 1,269,583 |
| — | — | — | — | — | 19,807 | 143,481 | 1,267,595 |
| 94,570 | — | 9,778 | — | — | — | 189,650 | 837,744 |
| 23,747,349 | 19,461,352 | 19,249,556 | 24,142,854 | 20,843,311 | 18,495,904 | 21,109,999 | 279,518,933 |
|  |  |  |  |  |  |  |  |
| 1,517,955 | 1,737,329 | 2,671,241 | 3,945,647 | 2,906,110 | 1,510,022 | 2,168,398 | 26,214,130 |
| 269,130 | 117,179 | 186,557 | 446,270 | 325,635 | 206,639 | 386,737 | 2,116,337 |
| 35,324 | 18,929 | 7,807 | 34,994 | 39,286 | 3,156 | — | 725,337 |
| 804,617 | 333,336 | 291,636 | 478,030 | 379,221 | 186,590 | 67,651 | 3,770,579 |
| 2,627,026 | 2,206,773 | 3,157,241 | 4,904,941 | 3,650,252 | 1,906,407 | 2,622,786 | 32,826,383 |
|  |  |  |  |  |  |  |  |
| 2,373 | 1,162 | 4,886 | 963 | 4,427 | 67,558 | 5,868 | 137,488 |
|  |  |  |  |  |  |  |  |
| 80,189,712 | 74,628,750 | 63,835,679 | 99,205,100 | 99,919,542 | 72,720,241 | 76,015,207 | 1,068,580,363 |

(3) Includes: Aden, Australia, Laos, Malaysia, New Guinea, Bhutan, Brunei and Portuguese Timor, Singapore and South Viet Nam.
(4) Includes: France, Italy, Netherlands, Portugal, Switzerland, United Kingdom and Germany (F.R.).

## IQ-10. UNITED STATES: IMPORTS OF COFFEE*
### Coffee Year (October 1 to September 30) 1962-1963 to 1965-1966.
(Bags of 60 kilograms or 132.276 pounds each)

| COUNTRIES OF ORIGIN | 1965-66 | 1964-65 | 1963-64 | 1962-63 | 1965-66 | 1964-65 | 1963-64 | 1962-63 |
|---|---|---|---|---|---|---|---|---|
| | | | | | | PERCENTAGE OF TOTAL | | |
| **WESTERN HEMISPHERE** | | | | | | | | |
| *Pan-American Coffee Bureau* | | | | | | | | |
| Brazil | 7,239,735 | 5,379,930 | 8,161,343 | 8,959,052 | 30.0 | 26.6 | 35.0 | 37.4 |
| Colombia | 3,335,138 | 3,505,270 | 3,447,767 | 4,104,886 | 13.8 | 17.3 | 14.8 | 17.1 |
| Guatemala | 1,113,210 | 866,097 | 946,014 | 1,122,048 | 4.6 | 4.3 | 4.0 | 4.7 |
| Mexico | 1,115,765 | 1,263,881 | 1,320,357 | 856,410 | 4.6 | 6.2 | 5.7 | 3.6 |
| El Salvador | 574,914 | 591,866 | 713,025 | 704,753 | 2.4 | 2.9 | 3.1 | 2.9 |
| Peru | 460,566 | 483,446 | 526,624 | 550,705 | 1.9 | 2.4 | 2.3 | 2.3 |
| Ecuador | 462,610 | 356,390 | 275,247 | 294,593 | 1.9 | 1.8 | 1.2 | 1.2 |
| Dominican Republic | 303,195 | 520,809 | 447,825 | 359,205 | 1.2 | 2.6 | 1.9 | 1.5 |
| Venezuela | 281,368 | 198,446 | 315,805 | 299,083 | 1.2 | 1.0 | 1.3 | 1.3 |
| Honduras | 262,097 | 276,934 | 207,661 | 214,601 | 1.1 | 1.4 | 0.9 | 0.9 |
| Costa Rica | 250,332 | 272,587 | 314,542 | 286,150 | 1.0 | 1.3 | 1.3 | 1.2 |
| Nicaragua | 193,558 | 203,075 | 157,380 | 222,678 | 0.8 | 1.0 | 0.7 | 0.9 |
| Haiti | 120,918 | 87,723 | 123,435 | 130,234 | 0.5 | 0.4 | 0.5 | 0.5 |
| Panama | 27,633 | 4,656 | 4,235 | 27,520 | 0.1 | — | — | 0.1 |
| Cuba | — | — | — | — | — | — | — | — |
| **Total Pan-American Coffee Bureau** | 15,741,039 | 14,011,110 | 16,961,260 | 18,131,918 | 65.1 | 69.2 | 72.7 | 75.6 |
| *OTHER WESTERN HEMISPHERE* | | | | | | | | |
| Bolivia | 21,604 | 14,589 | 19,878 | 12,329 | 0.1 | 0.1 | 0.1 | 0.1 |
| Paraguay | 57,197 | 20,601 | 12,988 | 19,611 | 0.2 | 0.1 | 0.1 | 0.1 |
| Trinidad & Tobago | 15,347 | 21,463 | 32,756 | 37,145 | 0.1 | 0.1 | 0.1 | 0.2 |
| Surinam | 10,176 | 2,210 | 2,750 | 2,025 | — | — | — | — |
| Guyana | 1,954 | 928 | 459 | — | — | — | — | — |
| British Honduras | — | 1,173 | 5,064 | — | — | — | — | — |
| Canada | 63 | 329 | 97 | 210 | — | — | — | — |
| Jamaica | 172 | 27 | 990 | 19 | — | — | — | — |
| Netherlands West Indies | 698 | 135 | — | — | — | — | — | — |
| Argentina | — | — | 500 | — | — | — | — | — |
| Chile | — | — | 400 | — | — | — | — | — |
| Uruguay | — | — | — | 2,471 | — | — | — | — |
| **Total Other Western Hemisphere** | 107,211 | 61,455 | 75,882 | 73,810 | 0.4 | 0.3 | 0.3 | 0.4 |
| **TOTAL WESTERN HEMISPHERE** | 15,848,250 | 14,072,565 | 17,037,142 | 18,205,728 | 65.5 | 69.5 | 73.0 | 76.0 |

Source: United States Department of Commerce.
(1) Includes: Ivory Coast, Togo, Guinea, Mali, Dahomey, Upper Volta, Mauritania and Niger.
(2) Includes: French Somaliland, Gabon, Congo (Brazzaville), Ubangi-Shari and Chad.
(3) Includes: Yemen, Sultanate of Oman, Trucial Sheikhdoms and Qatar.

## IQ-10. UNITED STATES: IMPORTS OF COFFEE* (Continued)
### Coffee Year (October 1 to September 30) 1962-1963 to 1965-1966.

(Bags of 60 kilograms or 132.276 pounds each)

| COUNTRIES OF ORIGIN | 1965-66 | 1964-65 | 1963-64 | 1962-63 | 1965-66 | 1964-65 | 1963-64 | 1962-63 |
|---|---|---|---|---|---|---|---|---|
| | | | | | \multicolumn{4}{c}{PERCENTAGE OF TOTAL} |
| **AFRICA** | | | | | | | | |
| East Africa | 1,637,455 | 1,293,662 | 1,460,982 | 1,690,446 | 6.7 | 6.4 | 6.3 | 7.1 |
| Uganda | 1,350,342 | 992,351 | N.A. | N.A. | 5.6 | 4.9 | N.A. | N.A. |
| Kenya | 133,704 | 162,262 | N.A. | N.A. | 0.5 | 0.8 | N.A. | N.A. |
| Tanzania | 153,409 | 139,049 | N.A. | N.A. | 0.6 | 0.7 | N.A. | N.A. |
| Portuguese Africa | 1,248,621 | 1,428,017 | 1,036,777 | 1,370,388 | 5.2 | 7.1 | 4.4 | 5.7 |
| Franc Zone (1) | 879,384 | 811,466 | 1,281,737 | 535,232 | 3.6 | 4.0 | 5.5 | 2.2 |
| Ivory Coast | 854,427 | 796,896 | N.A. | N.A. | 3.5 | 4.0 | N.A. | N.A. |
| Madagascar | 281,030 | 319,929 | 180,220 | 199,413 | 1.2 | 1.6 | 0.8 | 0.8 |
| Cameroun | 262,902 | 139,184 | 147,120 | 120,453 | 1.1 | 0.7 | 0.6 | 0.5 |
| Togo | 20,127 | 5,578 | N.A. | N.A. | 0.1 | — | N.A. | N.A. |
| Gabon | 4,830 | 8,051 | N.A. | N.A. | — | — | N.A. | N.A. |
| Central African Republic | — | 941 | N.A. | N.A. | — | — | N.A. | N.A. |
| Others (2) | 9,562 | 1,539 | 23,787 | 32,970 | — | — | 0.1 | 0.1 |
| Ethiopia | 814,061 | 1,121,194 | 916,022 | 775,316 | 3.4 | 5.5 | 3.9 | 3.2 |
| Congo (D.R. & Rawanda & Burundi) | 582,736 | 454,012 | 490,494 | 448,328 | 2.4 | 2.2 | 2.1 | 1.9 |
| Congo (D.R.) | 138,579 | 64,897 | N.A. | N.A. | 0.6 | 0.3 | N.A. | N.A. |
| Rwanda & Burundi | 444,157 | 389,115 | N.A. | N.A. | 1.8 | 1.9 | N.A. | N.A. |
| Liberia | 836,188 | 53,520 | 159,981 | 44,901 | 3.5 | 0.3 | 0.7 | 0.2 |
| Guinea | 259,515 | 79,075 | N.A. | N.A. | 1.1 | 0.4 | N.A. | N.A. |
| Ghana | 39,080 | 15,616 | 20,174 | 17,919 | 0.2 | 0.1 | 0.1 | 0.1 |
| Sierra Leone | 134,942 | 15,167 | 41,081 | 40,263 | 0.6 | 0.1 | 0.2 | 0.2 |
| South Africa | 40,199 | 3,378 | 5,467 | 3,199 | 0.2 | — | — | — |
| Nigeria | 25,299 | 2,075 | 4,603 | — | 0.1 | — | — | — |
| Mauritius | 420 | — | — | — | — | — | — | — |
| **TOTAL AFRICA** | 7,051,394 | 5,737,834 | 5,768,445 | 5,278,828 | 29.3 | 28.4 | 24.7 | 22.0 |
| **ASIA & OCEANIA** | | | | | | | | |
| Indonesia | 1,080,247 | 324,305 | 436,474 | 446,085 | 4.5 | 1.6 | 1.9 | 1.9 |
| India | 57,996 | 64,332 | 67,981 | 11,455 | 0.2 | 0.3 | 0.3 | — |
| Arabia (3) | 26,145 | 24,750 | 17,033 | 10,029 | 0.1 | 0.1 | 0.1 | — |
| Others (4) | 96,939 | 16,669 | 10,025 | 12,345 | 0.4 | 0.1 | — | 0.1 |
| **TOTAL ASIA & OCEANIA** | 1,261,327 | 430,056 | 531,513 | 479,914 | 5.2 | 2.1 | 2.3 | 2.0 |
| **VARIOUS (5)** | 2,979 | 2,456 | 1,303 | 2,421 | — | — | — | — |
| **TOTAL IMPORTS** | 24,163,950 | 20,242,911 | 23,338,403 | 23,966,891 | 100.0 | 100.0 | 100.0 | 100.0 |

(4) Includes: Thailand, Laos, Aden, Malaysia, Australia, Bhutan, Brunei and Portuguese Timor, New Guinea, New Zealand, Viet Nam, Philippine Republic, Saudi Arabia and Singapore.
(5) Includes: Belgium, Italy, Netherlands, Sweden, Switzerland, Germany (F.R.), Portugal, United Kingdom and France.
(*) See footnote to Table IQV-3.

## IQV-II. CANADA: VOLUME AND VALUE OF GREEN COFFEE IMPORTS 1965-1966

(Volume in bags of 60 kilograms or 132.276 pounds each and Value in thousands of Canadian Dollars)

| COUNTRIES OF ORIGIN | VOLUME 1966* | VOLUME 1965 | VALUE 1966* | VALUE 1965 | Percentage of Total VOLUME 1966 | Percentage of Total VOLUME 1965 | Percentage of Total VALUE 1966 | Percentage of Total VALUE 1965 | Increase or Decrease 1966 over 1965 VOLUME BAGS | VOLUME PERCENT | VALUE AMOUNT | VALUE PERCENT |
|---|---|---|---|---|---|---|---|---|---|---|---|---|
| **WESTERN HEMISPHERE** | | | | | | | | | | | | |
| **Pan-American Coffee Bureau** | | | | | | | | | | | | |
| Brazil | 364,213 | 385,333 | 19,985 | 22,950 | 31.2 | 30.6 | 30.7 | 31.8 | − 21,120 | − 5.5 | − 2,965 | − 12.9 |
| Colombia | 137,482 | 200,362 | 9,180 | 13,382 | 11.8 | 15.9 | 14.1 | 18.6 | − 62,880 | − 31.4 | − 4,202 | − 31.4 |
| Guatemala | 37,341 | 36,200 | 2,303 | 2,354 | 3.2 | 2.9 | 3.5 | 3.3 | + 1,141 | + 3.2 | − 51 | − 2.2 |
| Mexico | 35,783 | 50,599 | 2,221 | 3,208 | 3.1 | 4.0 | 3.4 | 4.5 | − 14,816 | − 29.3 | − 987 | − 30.8 |
| El Salvador | 34,203 | 41,091 | 2,020 | 2,553 | 2.9 | 3.3 | 3.1 | 3.5 | − 6,888 | − 16.8 | − 533 | − 20.9 |
| Costa Rica | 24,775 | 27,372 | 1,542 | 1,758 | 2.1 | 2.2 | 2.4 | 2.4 | − 2,597 | − 9.5 | − 216 | − 12.3 |
| Peru | 8,489 | 7,083 | 504 | 455 | 0.7 | 0.6 | 0.8 | 0.6 | + 1,406 | + 19.9 | + 49 | + 10.8 |
| Dominican Republic | 5,891 | 10,525 | 346 | 671 | 0.5 | 0.8 | 0.5 | 0.9 | − 4,634 | − 44.0 | − 325 | − 48.4 |
| Ecuador | 3,059 | 8,171 | 151 | 487 | 0.3 | 0.6 | 0.2 | 0.7 | − 5,112 | − 62.6 | − 336 | − 69.0 |
| Honduras | 2,074 | 3,921 | 122 | 237 | 0.2 | 0.3 | 0.2 | 0.3 | − 1,847 | − 47.1 | − 115 | − 48.5 |
| Venezuela | 1,812 | 3,314 | 116 | 220 | 0.1 | 0.3 | 0.2 | 0.3 | − 1,502 | − 45.3 | − 104 | − 47.3 |
| Haiti | 1,073 | 2,366 | 64 | 140 | 0.1 | 0.2 | 0.1 | 0.2 | − 1,293 | − 54.6 | − 76 | − 54.3 |
| Nicaragua | 721 | 1,714 | 47 | 105 | 0.1 | 0.1 | 0.1 | 0.2 | − 993 | − 57.9 | − 58 | − 55.2 |
| Panama | — | — | — | — | — | — | — | — | — | — | — | — |
| Cuba | — | — | — | — | — | — | — | — | — | — | — | — |
| Total Pan-American Coffee Bureau | 656,916 | 778,051 | 38,601 | 48,520 | 56.3 | 61.8 | 59.3 | 67.3 | − 121,135 | − 15.6 | − 9,919 | − 20.4 |
| **OTHER WESTERN HEMISPHERE** | | | | | | | | | | | | |
| United States | 169,527 | 209,039 | 8,703 | 9,666 | 14.5 | 16.6 | 13.4 | 13.4 | − 39,512 | − 18.9 | − 963 | − 10.0 |
| Trinidad & Tobago | 9,035 | 9,521 | 378 | 382 | 0.8 | 0.8 | 0.6 | 0.5 | − 486 | − 5.1 | − 4 | − 1.0 |
| Jamaica | 319 | 250 | 18 | 16 | — | — | — | — | + 69 | + 27.6 | + 2 | + 12.5 |
| Paraguay | — | 1,090 | — | 65 | — | 0.1 | — | 0.1 | − 1,090 | ... | − 65 | ... |
| Netherlands West Indies | — | 291 | — | 19 | — | — | — | — | − 291 | ... | − 19 | ... |
| Bolivia | — | 250 | — | 15 | — | — | — | — | − 250 | ... | − 15 | ... |
| Puerto Rico | — | 226 | — | 13 | — | — | — | — | − 226 | ... | − 13 | ... |
| Total Other Western Hemisphere | 178,881 | 220,667 | 9,099 | 10,176 | 15.3 | 17.5 | 14.0 | 14.0 | − 41,786 | − 18.9 | − 1,077 | − 10.6 |
| Total Western Hemisphere | 835,797 | 998,718 | 47,700 | 58,696 | 71.6 | 79.3 | 73.3 | 81.3 | − 162,921 | − 16.3 | − 10,996 | − 18.7 |

*Preliminary

A-104

## IQV-II. CANADA: VOLUME AND VALUE OF GREEN COFFEE IMPORTS 1965-1966 (Continued)

| COUNTRIES OF ORIGIN | VOLUME 1966* | VOLUME 1965 | VALUE 1966* | VALUE 1965 | Percentage of Total VOLUME 1966 | VOLUME 1965 | VALUE 1966 | VALUE 1965 | Increase or Decrease 1966 over 1965 VOLUME BAGS | VOLUME PERCENT | VALUE AMOUNT | VALUE PERCENT |
|---|---|---|---|---|---|---|---|---|---|---|---|---|
| **AFRICA** | | | | | | | | | | | | |
| Uganda | 100,753 | 92,469 | 5,033 | 4,092 | 8.6 | 7.4 | 7.7 | 5.7 | + 8,284 | + 9.0 | + 941 | + 23.0 |
| Tanzania | 66,623 | 50,942 | 3,744 | 2,892 | 5.7 | 4.1 | 5.8 | 4.0 | + 15,681 | + 30.8 | + 852 | + 29.5 |
| Kenya | 66,166 | 57,941 | 4,002 | 3,682 | 5.7 | 4.6 | 6.2 | 5.1 | + 8,225 | + 14.2 | + 320 | + 8.7 |
| Portuguese Africa | 66,099 | 31,156 | 2,991 | 1,372 | 5.7 | 2.5 | 4.6 | 1.9 | + 34,943 | +112.2 | +1,619 | +118.0 |
| Congo (D.R.) | 2,194 | 2,882 | 162 | 196 | 0.2 | 0.2 | 0.2 | 0.3 | − 688 | − 23.9 | − 34 | − 17.3 |
| Ghana | 2,117 | — | 94 | — | 0.2 | — | 0.1 | — | + 2,117 | + --- | + 94 | + --- |
| Ethiopia | 616 | 1,090 | 38 | 65 | 0.1 | 0.1 | 0.1 | 0.1 | − 474 | − 43.5 | − 27 | − 41.5 |
| Madagascar | 416 | 453 | 21 | 17 | — | — | — | — | − 37 | − 8.2 | + 4 | + 23.5 |
| French Africa N.E.S. | 50 | 3 | 3 | — | — | — | — | — | — | — | — | — |
| Cameroun | — | 833 | — | 38 | — | 0.1 | — | 0.1 | − 833 | − --- | − 38 | − --- |
| Total Africa | 305,034 | 237,816 | 16,088 | 12,357 | 26.2 | 19.0 | 24.7 | 17.2 | + 67,218 | + 28.3 | +3,731 | + 30.2 |
| **ASIA & OCEANIA** | | | | | | | | | | | | |
| Australia | 5,069 | — | 323 | — | 0.4 | — | 0.5 | — | + 5,069 | + --- | + 323 | + --- |
| Malaysia | 4,229 | 1,443 | 180 | 61 | 0.4 | 0.1 | 0.3 | 0.1 | + 2,786 | +193.1 | + 119 | +195.1 |
| Indonesia | 3,676 | — | 176 | — | 0.3 | — | 0.3 | — | + 3,676 | + --- | + 176 | + --- |
| Aden | 1,141 | — | 77 | — | 0.1 | — | 0.1 | — | + 1,141 | + --- | + 77 | + --- |
| India | 363 | 3,436 | 22 | 211 | — | 0.3 | — | 0.3 | − 3,073 | − 89.4 | − 189 | − 89.6 |
| Total Asia & Oceania | 14,478 | 4,879 | 778 | 272 | 1.2 | 0.4 | 1.2 | 0.4 | + 9,599 | +196.7 | + 506 | +186.0 |
| VARIOUS | 11,763 | 16,235 | 528 | 804 | 1.0 | 1.3 | 0.8 | 1.1 | − 4,472 | − 27.5 | − 276 | − 34.3 |
| TOTAL IMPORTS | 1,167,072 | 1,257,648 | 65,094 | 72,129 | 100.0 | 100.0 | 100.0 | 100.0 | − 90,576 | − 7.2 | −7,035 | − 9.8 |

Source: Dominion Bureau of Statistics.

*Preliminary

A-105

## IQ-11. UNITED STATES: VOLUME OF COFFEE

(Bags of 60 Kilograms or

|  | 1953 | 1954 | 1955 | 1956 | 1957 | 1958 |
|---|---|---|---|---|---|---|
| **WESTERN HEMISPHERE** | | | | | | |
| **Pan-American Coffee Bureau** | | | | | | |
| Brazil | 8,970,439 | 6,351,764 | 7,682,768 | 9,908,645 | 8,889,280 | 7,477,701 |
| Colombia | 5,605,561 | 4,911,067 | 4,937,174 | 4,560,318 | 4,130,125 | 4,245,533 |
| Mexico | 1,031,752 | 997,728 | 1,203,111 | 1,041,548 | 1,240,974 | 1,201,739 |
| Guatemala | 808,664 | 697,991 | 817,070 | 814,712 | 829,780 | 882,080 |
| El Salvador | 1,018,638 | 767,106 | 854,627 | 605,506 | 676,025 | 724,135 |
| Ecuador | 241,256 | 235,735 | 275,774 | 221,891 | 315,226 | 361,515 |
| Peru | 45,073 | 60,239 | 54,850 | 72,419 | 93,601 | 244,891 |
| Honduras | 158,664 | 148,531 | 161,673 | 139,727 | 118,200 | 147,847 |
| Costa Rica | 267,364 | 145,299 | 144,606 | 80,163 | 165,513 | 302,330 |
| Dominican Republic | 283,177 | 350,746 | 316,279 | 382,855 | 296,315 | 381,164 |
| Nicaragua | 298,564 | 232,561 | 277,582 | 208,346 | 239,035 | 247,276 |
| Venezuela | 685,119 | 381,095 | 420,861 | 313,838 | 368,619 | 533,772 |
| Haiti | 106,446 | 183,038 | 93,593 | 85,218 | 80,793 | 210,744 |
| Panama | 6,725 | 1,582 | 8,014 | 1,852 | 100 | 14,286 |
| Cuba | — | — | 59,794 | 200,012 | 124,249 | 91,464 |
| **Total Pan-American Coffee Bureau** | **19,527,442** | **15,464,482** | **17,307,776** | **18,637,050** | **17,567,835** | **17,066,477** |
| **OTHER WESTERN HEMISPHERE** | | | | | | |
| Paraguay | — | — | — | — | — | — |
| Trinidad & Tobago | 3,991 | 4,011 | 8,955 | 6,969 | 14,087 | 20,001 |
| Bolivia | 2,040 | 2,261 | 1,585 | 414 | 1,304 | 2,157 |
| Surinam | — | — | — | 448 | — | 10,243 |
| Guyana | — | — | — | — | 541 | 500 |
| Netherlands West Indies | 748 | 187 | 2,502 | 2,049 | 4,744 | 3,728 |
| Canada | 4 | 26 | 3 | 9 | 6 | 35 |
| Jamaica | 6,173 | 4,883 | 7,320 | 4,646 | 4,417 | 1,807 |
| British Honduras | — | — | — | 283 | 340 | 648 |
| Chile | 584 | — | 739 | — | 7 | 1,532 |
| Argentina | — | — | — | — | — | — |
| Uruguay | — | — | — | — | — | — |
| British West Indies | — | 23 | 409 | — | — | — |
| French Guiana | — | — | — | — | — | 6,692 |
| **Total Other Western Hemisphere** | **13,530** | **11,391** | **21,513** | **14,818** | **25,446** | **47,343** |
| **TOTAL WESTERN HEMISPHERE** | **19,540,982** | **15,475,873** | **17,329,289** | **18,651,868** | **17,593,281** | **17,113,820** |

**IMPORTS BY COUNTRY OF ORIGIN, 1953-1966**

132.276 pounds each)

| 1959 | 1960 | 1961 | 1962 | 1963 | 1964 | 1965 | 1966 |
|---|---|---|---|---|---|---|---|
| 10,653,122 | 9,250,950 | 8,575,894 | 9,093,982 | 9,278,261 | 7,213,233 | 5,744,024 | 6,730,398 |
| 4,905,861 | 4,258,668 | 4,086,503 | 4,332,184 | 3,951,980 | 3,711,610 | 3,323,724 | 2,716,078 |
| 1,083,497 | 1,101,720 | 1,315,988 | 1,407,799 | 840,769 | 1,479,593 | 1,159,929 | 1,044,722 |
| 989,657 | 796,355 | 949,532 | 966,535 | 1,079,816 | 788,843 | 903,830 | 1,110,122 |
| 620,650 | 445,552 | 582,725 | 847,177 | 762,544 | 682,966 | 713,785 | 592,682 |
| 241,802 | 316,888 | 202,221 | 369,208 | 293,613 | 230,382 | 502,483 | 432,279 |
| 232,475 | 346,907 | 382,484 | 474,369 | 490,737 | 541,256 | 454,235 | 447,307 |
| 146,378 | 332,043 | 144,974 | 159,647 | 218,376 | 200,613 | 290,139 | 248,555 |
| 246,694 | 271,274 | 369,204 | 384,594 | 287,043 | 292,940 | 305,405 | 231,384 |
| 307,564 | 403,309 | 262,709 | 417,734 | 367,506 | 531,792 | 309,715 | 353,710 |
| 153,917 | 175,136 | 224,944 | 190,492 | 224,292 | 170,106 | 250,949 | 135,377 |
| 401,629 | 344,643 | 344,042 | 271,597 | 312,687 | 261,700 | 236,744 | 266,251 |
| 85,067 | 63,877 | 75,532 | 154,105 | 122,270 | 122,260 | 100,383 | 89,479 |
| 21,598 | 16,170 | 5,942 | 765 | 27,503 | 4,235 | 9,990 | 24,297 |
| 34,742 | 1,427 | 411 | — | — | — | — | — |
| **20,124,653** | **18,124,919** | **17,523,105** | **19,070,188** | **18,257,397** | **16,231,529** | **14,305,335** | **14,422,641** |
| 2,654 | 34,838 | 17,292 | 7,882 | 18,899 | 20,171 | 45,295 | 23,087 |
| 31,517 | 25,619 | 42,197 | 17,762 | 37,379 | 32,295 | 25,506 | 11,152 |
| 4,531 | 14,268 | 14,206 | 12,303 | 10,855 | 23,172 | 15,321 | 44,574 |
| 9,037 | 25,061 | 6,835 | 8,073 | 2,223 | 1,238 | 3,749 | 8,669 |
| — | 30 | 3,154 | 3,278 | 107 | 352 | 928 | 1,954 |
| 4,219 | 1,714 | 2,797 | 438 | — | — | 834 | — |
| 19 | 15 | — | 223 | 3 | 160 | 272 | 65 |
| 3,667 | 2,632 | 362 | 407 | 15 | 996 | 178 | 60 |
| 1,597 | 398 | 1,739 | 1,715 | — | 6,237 | — | 643 |
| 258 | 200 | 125 | 175 | 200 | 200 | — | — |
| — | 662 | 1,497 | 2,097 | 500 | — | — | — |
| — | — | — | — | 2,471 | — | — | — |
| — | — | — | — | — | — | — | — |
| 11,668 | — | — | 2,004 | — | — | — | — |
| **69,167** | **105,437** | **90,204** | **56,357** | **72,652** | **84,821** | **92,083** | **90,204** |
| 20,193,820 | 18,230,356 | 17,613,309 | 19,126,545 | 18,330,049 | 16,316,350 | 14,397,418 | 14,512,845 |

## IQ-11. UNITED STATES: VOLUME OF COFFEE IMPORTS

|  | 1953 | 1954 | 1955 | 1956 | 1957 | 1958 |
|---|---:|---:|---:|---:|---:|---:|
| **AFRICA** | | | | | | |
| East Africa (1) | 147,508 | 208,500 | 537,173 | 455,750 | 766,510 | 766,258 |
|   Uganda | N.A. | N.A. | N.A. | N.A. | N.A. | N.A. |
|   Kenya | N.A. | N.A. | N.A. | N.A. | N.A. | N.A. |
|   Tanzania | N.A. | N.A. | N.A. | N.A. | N.A. | N.A. |
| Portuguese Africa | 627,758 | 509,638 | 562,963 | 797,194 | 818,028 | 714,097 |
| **Franc Zone** | | | | | | |
|   Western Africa (1) | 1,294 | 230,699 | 169,141 | 378,832 | 252,941 | 304,869 |
|     Ivory Coast | N.A. | N.A. | N.A. | N.A. | N.A. | N.A. |
|     Guinea | N.A. | N.A. | N.A. | N.A. | N.A. | N.A. |
|     Togo | N.A. | N.A. | N.A. | N.A. | N.A. | N.A. |
|     Central African Republic | N.A. | N.A. | N.A. | N.A. | N.A. | N.A. |
|     Gabon | N.A. | N.A. | N.A. | N.A. | N.A. | N.A. |
| Madagascar | N.A. | 44,581 | 103,258 | 130,007 | 255,024 | 154,318 |
| Cameroun | 917 | 9,004 | 3,423 | 12,726 | 2,272 | 6,629 |
| Others (2) | 676 | 204 | — | 541 | 2,513 | 2,738 |
| Ethiopia | 455,586 | 357,639 | 472,212 | 309,019 | 465,954 | 457,912 |
| **Congo (D.R.) & Rwanda-Burundi (1)** | 206,562 | 170,712 | 389,516 | 389,839 | 510,013 | 512,666 |
|   Rwanda-Burundi | N.A. | N.A. | N.A. | N.A. | N.A. | N.A. |
|   Congo (D.R.) | N.A. | N.A. | N.A. | N.A. | N.A. | N.A. |
| Liberia | — | 1,956 | 384 | 2,184 | 793 | 3,007 |
| Sierra Leone | 21,244 | 4,775 | 7,868 | 16,101 | 38,093 | 46,206 |
| Ghana | — | — | — | — | 339 | — |
| Nigeria | — | — | — | — | — | — |
| South Africa | 2,077 | — | 17 | — | 1,530 | 1,129 |
| Mauritius | — | — | — | — | — | — |
| Italian East Africa | 1,432 | — | — | — | 4 | — |
| Anglo-Egyptian Sudan | 425 | 417 | — | — | — | — |
| **TOTAL AFRICA** | 1,465,479 | 1,538,125 | 2,245,955 | 2,492,193 | 3,114,014 | 2,969,829 |
| **ASIA & OCEANIA** | | | | | | |
| Indonesia | 33,909 | 36,418 | 9,301 | 47,693 | 92,280 | 20,531 |
| India | — | 7,712 | 869 | — | 6,864 | 7,359 |
| Arabia (3) | 22,792 | 32,647 | 53,947 | 54,143 | 45,011 | 46,333 |
| Others (4) | 1,709 | 1,464 | 1,066 | 7,763 | 7,948 | 8,551 |
| **TOTAL ASIA & OCEANIA** | 58,410 | 78,241 | 65,183 | 109,599 | 152,103 | 82,774 |
| **VARIOUS (5)** | 8 | 197 | 1,268 | — | 198 | 2,101 |
| **TOTAL IMPORTS** | 21,064,879 | 17,092,436 | 19,641,695 | 21,253,660 | 20,859,596 | 20,168,524 |

Source: United States Department of Commerce.
(1) Prior to January 1964 import figures for individual countries were not available.
(2) Includes: Chad, Congo (Brazzaville), Dahomey, French Somaliland, Mali, Niger and Upper Volta.
(3) Includes: Ghana, Mauritius, Nigeria, Sierra Leone and South Africa.

A-108

## BY COUNTRY OF ORIGIN, 1953-1966 (continued)

**COUNTRIES OF ORIGIN**

| 1959 | 1960 | 1961 | 1962 | 1963 | 1964 | 1965 | 1966 |
|---|---|---|---|---|---|---|---|
| 729,801 | 934,052 | 1,246,393 | 1,388,104 | 1,497,122 | — | — | — |
| N.A. | N.A. | N.A. | N.A. | N.A. | 960,435 | 1,108,480 | 1,218,029 |
| N.A. | N.A. | N.A. | N.A. | N.A. | 289,990 | 118,172 | 173,808 |
| N.A. | N.A. | N.A. | N.A. | N.A. | 131,867 | 122,264 | 237,153 |
| 752,434 | 803,913 | 1,031,067 | 1,479,713 | 1,123,939 | 1,246,417 | 1,285,167 | 1,211,525 |
| | | | | | | | |
| 337,501 | 657,534 | 735,857 | 606,848 | 705,638 | — | — | — |
| N.A. | N.A. | N.A. | N.A. | N.A. | 1,191,660 | 840,669 | 787,362 |
| N.A. | N.A. | N.A. | N.A. | N.A. | 58,177 | 208,321 | 164,268 |
| N.A. | N.A. | N.A. | N.A. | N.A. | 29,486 | 16,834 | 8,871 |
| N.A. | N.A. | N.A. | N.A. | N.A. | 15,868 | 441 | — |
| N.A. | N.A. | N.A. | N.A. | N.A. | 11,960 | 4,313 | 4,830 |
| 33,233 | 83,021 | 113,959 | 164,723 | 207,078 | 169,604 | 404,926 | 230,452 |
| 8,418 | 35,560 | 70,994 | 123,634 | 120,640 | 151,420 | 147,083 | 331,550 |
| 9,076 | 15,395 | 15,444 | 48,863 | 35,859 | 20,869 | 5,339 | 5,096 |
| 267,276 | 566,310 | 679,190 | 660,981 | 816,293 | 924,257 | 1,158,256 | 792,100 |
| 812,826 | 644,567 | 592,533 | 497,323 | 447,985 | — | — | — |
| N.A. | N.A. | N.A. | N.A. | N.A. | 436,703 | 340,080 | 333,372 |
| N.A. | N.A. | N.A. | N.A. | N.A. | 196,191 | 145,746 | 35,839 |
| 11,982 | 12,199 | 16,416 | 29,511 | 50,232 | 155,448 | 188,170 | 709,095 |
| 58,876 | 50,095 | 58,668 | 34,024 | 40,263 | 42,777 | 19,774 | 128,641 |
| 5,580 | 1,672 | 5,431 | 35,962 | 13,785 | 23,570 | 20,214 | 35,326 |
| — | — | 2,417 | 5,296 | 37 | 5,626 | 9,591 | 20,723 |
| 3,216 | 4,979 | 10,885 | 5,756 | 3,085 | 4,997 | 18,615 | 27,265 |
| — | — | — | — | — | 3,746 | 420 | |
| — | — | — | — | — | — | — | — |
| — | — | — | — | — | — | — | — |
| 3,030,219 | 3,809,297 | 4,579,254 | 5,080,738 | 5,061,956 | 6,071,068 | 6,162,875 | 6,455,305 |
| | | | | | | | |
| 12,962 | 19,114 | 138,002 | 301,436 | 453,939 | 391,760 | 643,291 | 974,349 |
| 6,006 | 7,860 | 47,357 | 11,779 | 23,893 | 76,458 | 73,397 | 45,282 |
| 15,160 | 12,945 | 10,094 | 11,989 | 10,377 | 21,954 | 27,859 | 16,728 |
| 8,218 | 9,569 | 13,248 | 8,724 | 10,983 | 12,411 | 39,068 | 85,089 |
| | | | | | | | |
| 42,346 | 49,488 | 208,701 | 333,928 | 499,192 | 502,583 | 783,615 | 1,121,448 |
| | | | | | | | |
| 3,449 | 1,859 | 2,429 | 7,728 | 1,940 | 2,388 | 2,875 | 2,181 |
| | | | | | | | |
| 23,269,834 | 22,091,000 | 22,403,693 | 24,548,939 | 23,893,137 | 22,892,389 | 21,346,783 | 22,091,779 |

4) Includes: Aden, Australia, Ceylon, Iraq, Laos, Malaysia, New Guinea, New Zealand, Philippine Rep., Saudi Arabia, Singapore, Southern Asia (Bhutan, Brunei and Portuguese Timor), Thailand and Viet Nam.

(5) Includes: Azores, Belgium, Italy, Netherlands, Portugal, Sweden, Switzerland, Germany and United Kingdom.

## IV-11. UNITED STATES: AVERAGE UNIT

(In U. S. Cents)

| COUNTRIES OF ORIGIN | 1947 | 1948 | 1949 | 1950 | 1951 | 1952 |
|---|---|---|---|---|---|---|
| **WESTERN HEMISPHERE** | | | | | | |
| Pan American Coffee Bureau | | | | | | |
| Brazil | 22.54 | 23.03 | 25.39 | 44.98 | 49.44 | 50.12 |
| Colombia | 27.16 | 29.33 | 31.09 | 49.59 | 55.49 | 56.93 |
| Mexico | 25.36 | 27.46 | 31.00 | 44.45 | 50.80 | 51.10 |
| Guatemala | 24.65 | 27.21 | 28.70 | 39.31 | 49.06 | 48.61 |
| El Salvador | 22.67 | 25.61 | 27.22 | 36.67 | 47.02 | 48.08 |
| Ecuador | 17.25 | 17.46 | 24.70 | 42.71 | 43.39 | 46.80 |
| Peru | 26.85 | 27.04 | 28.47 | 46.12 | 51.10 | 46.87 |
| Dominican Republic | 25.37 | 25.89 | 29.56 | 43.70 | 49.97 | 48.46 |
| Costa Rica | 27.00 | 27.89 | 30.07 | 41.43 | 54.51 | 54.28 |
| Honduras | 25.88 | 21.75 | 25.65 | 40.60 | 47.78 | 47.85 |
| Nicaragua | 24.68 | 25.99 | 27.29 | 35.91 | 49.06 | 49.90 |
| Venezuela | 26.37 | 27.39 | 28.98 | 48.69 | 55.34 | 53.61 |
| Haiti | 22.39 | 21.58 | 24.74 | 39.16 | 46.72 | 48.15 |
| Panama | 18.54 | 23.35 | 25.93 | 43.92 | 52.71 | 49.17 |
| Cuba | — | 12.72 | — | — | — | — |
| Total Pan American Coffee Bureau | 24.13 | 25.23 | 27.26 | 45.01 | 50.75 | 51.60 |
| **TOTAL OTHER WESTERN HEMISPHERE** | 15.95 | 18.92 | 28.57 | 33.29 | 45.87 | 50.67 |
| **TOTAL WESTERN HEMISPHERE** | 24.13 | 25.22 | 27.26 | 44.98 | 50.73 | 51.56 |
| **AFRICA** | | | | | | |
| East Africa | 26.27 | 27.34 | 30.10 | 38.40 | 44.75 | 45.74 |
| Uganda | N.A. | N.A. | N.A. | N.A. | N.A. | N.A. |
| Kenya | N.A. | N.A. | N.A. | N.A. | N.A. | N.A. |
| Tanzania | N.A. | N.A. | N.A. | N.A. | N.A. | N.A. |
| Portuguese Africa | 14.95 | 15.60 | 20.68 | 35.53 | 44.07 | 44.38 |
| Franc Zone | — | — | — | 37.19 | 42.20 | 42.22 |
| Ivory Coast | — | — | — | N.A. | N.A. | N.A. |
| Madagascar | — | — | — | N.A. | 46.10 | — |
| Cameroun | — | — | — | N.A. | N.A. | 44.32 |
| Togo | — | — | — | N.A. | N.A. | N.A. |
| Central African Republic | — | — | — | N.A. | N.A. | N.A. |
| Gabon | — | — | — | N.A. | N.A. | N.A. |
| Others | — | — | — | N.A. | N.A. | 46.47 |
| Ethiopia | 25.06 | 24.99 | 27.22 | 42.86 | 47.63 | 47.32 |
| Rep. of Congo & Rwanda-Burundi | 21.89 | 26.25 | 27.66 | 41.28 | 49.90 | 50.73 |
| Congo (D.R.) | N.A. | N.A. | N.A. | N.A. | N.A. | N.A. |
| Rwanda & Burundi | N.A. | N.A. | N.A. | N.A. | N.A. | N.A. |
| Liberia | — | 16.50 | 17.20 | 47.60 | 37.96 | 34.98 |
| Guinea | — | — | — | — | — | — |
| Ghana | — | — | — | — | — | — |
| South Africa | 21.31 | 15.88 | 16.33 | 34.33 | 44.09 | 52.16 |
| Nigeria | — | — | — | — | 38.41 | — |
| Various | — | 18.26 | 25.50 | 37.01 | — | 43.94 |
| **TOTAL AFRICA** | 17.58 | 20.39 | 24.17 | 38.86 | 46.12 | 46.49 |
| **ASIA & OCEANIA** | | | | | | |
| Indonesia | 35.74 | 33.84 | 30.75 | 42.80 | 46.48 | 45.58 |
| India | 32.75 | 50.95 | — | 34.09 | — | — |
| Arabia | 25.78 | 27.96 | 30.82 | 49.23 | 52.33 | 53.22 |
| Various | 29.79 | 27.18 | 32.90 | 36.51 | 48.07 | 47.11 |
| **TOTAL ASIA & OCEANIA** | 28.10 | 28.12 | 30.83 | 44.15 | 49.82 | 49.83 |
| **OTHERS** | — | — | 21.20 | 27.59 | 52.92 | 43.19 |
| **ALL IMPORTS** | 24.00 | 25.14 | 27.20 | 44.68 | 50.50 | 51.26 |

Source: U. S. Department of Commerce.

**VALUE OF GREEN COFFEE IMPORTS, 1947-1966**

Per Pound)

| 1953 | 1954 | 1955 | 1956 | 1957 | 1958 | 1959 | 1960 | 1961 | 1962 | 1963 | 1964 | 1965 | 1966 |
|---|---|---|---|---|---|---|---|---|---|---|---|---|---|
| 52.92 | 64.79 | 47.70 | 46.12 | 44.94 | 41.23 | 32.14 | 32.59 | 32.24 | 30.14 | 29.65 | 39.58 | 39.93 | 36.78 |
| 55.94 | 70.99 | 62.60 | 61.84 | 63.59 | 51.81 | 45.01 | 43.39 | 41.92 | 39.49 | 37.76 | 45.53 | 45.40 | 45.59 |
| 50.35 | 66.60 | 54.43 | 62.14 | 56.70 | 46.27 | 38.79 | 39.58 | 37.26 | 35.16 | 33.59 | 43.02 | 42.58 | 41.54 |
| 49.44 | 59.87 | 54.58 | 60.63 | 55.59 | 45.71 | 38.09 | 38.73 | 34.79 | 33.26 | 32.98 | 41.95 | 42.62 | 40.41 |
| 47.78 | 59.27 | 53.90 | 54.58 | 53.28 | 42.49 | 36.87 | 37.90 | 34.72 | 32.16 | 32.21 | 38.99 | 42.57 | 39.84 |
| 46.57 | 59.87 | 46.34 | 57.91 | 47.24 | 39.91 | 35.43 | 33.58 | 29.73 | 30.97 | 29.03 | 40.50 | 37.22 | 33.91 |
| 52.31 | 69.78 | 53.37 | 62.60 | 53.34 | 43.73 | 36.98 | 33.66 | 31.40 | 30.18 | 29.73 | 42.40 | 39.36 | 37.95 |
| 50.73 | 59.87 | 54.96 | 56.62 | 54.14 | 43.49 | 37.07 | 35.80 | 32.36 | 31.00 | 31.02 | 40.23 | 39.78 | 37.88 |
| 54.88 | 68.04 | 58.29 | 67.89 | 61.21 | 48.17 | 40.30 | 39.43 | 35.55 | 33.61 | 33.63 | 41.48 | 42.67 | 41.49 |
| 49.37 | 69.32 | 48.38 | 52.92 | 52.70 | 44.79 | 36.35 | 35.23 | 33.72 | 32.92 | 31.65 | 40.71 | 40.20 | 38.99 |
| 49.97 | 65.85 | 56.47 | 57.76 | 53.94 | 46.52 | 36.51 | 36.36 | 34.36 | 33.27 | 32.25 | 40.21 | 41.98 | 42.69 |
| 53.37 | 69.40 | 55.57 | 66.07 | 59.20 | 48.32 | 38.71 | 39.46 | 35.36 | 33.89 | 32.72 | 42.21 | 42.91 | 41.38 |
| 51.56 | 63.05 | 48.53 | 44.91 | 42.09 | 37.45 | 31.11 | 31.17 | 28.03 | 27.83 | 28.45 | 38.08 | 37.50 | 38.03 |
| 51.20 | 56.65 | 55.00 | 63.90 | 65.40 | 47.62 | 40.11 | 38.58 | 33.89 | 31.00 | 29.93 | 32.70 | 33.72 | 36.35 |
| — | — | 44.98 | 45.13 | 50.58 | 44.96 | 34.86 | 42.88 | — | — | — | — | — | — |
| 53.10 | 66.40 | 54.96 | 52.74 | 51.93 | 44.97 | 36.55 | 36.35 | 35.32 | 33.07 | 32.08 | 41.56 | 41.73 | 39.42 |
| 48.35 | 60.04 | 38.64 | 41.21 | 34.93 | 34.48 | 28.42 | 26.57 | 25.23 | 23.80 | 24.28 | 31.52 | 29.11 | 33.03 |
| 53.09 | 66.38 | 53.60 | 52.77 | 51.85 | 44.95 | 36.52 | 36.33 | 35.14 | 33.05 | 32.05 | 41.50 | 41.65 | 39.39 |
| 45.81 | 57.83 | 37.35 | 45.21 | 36.79 | 37.25 | 28.69 | 24.01 | 22.38 | 21.04 | 24.52 | — | — | — |
| N.A. | N.A. | N.A. | N.A. | N.A. | N.A. | N.A. | N.A. | N.A. | N.A. | N.A. | 35.47 | 26.69 | 31.30 |
| N.A. | N.A. | N.A. | N.A. | N.A. | N.A. | N.A. | N.A. | N.A. | N.A. | N.A. | 39.73 | 33.06 | 41.72 |
| N.A. | N.A. | N.A. | N.A. | N.A. | N.A. | N.A. | N.A. | N.A. | N.A. | N.A. | 40.60 | 36.20 | 36.61 |
| 46.34 | 55.11 | 39.01 | 31.83 | 34.20 | 35.24 | 27.00 | 22.35 | 18.05 | 18.82 | 22.94 | 32.52 | 27.13 | 31.29 |
| 41.77 | 55.35 | 36.95 | 29.24 | 31.86 | 35.75 | 26.13 | 18.28 | 17.37 | 17.76 | 23.53 | — | — | — |
| N.A. | N.A. | N.A. | N.A. | N.A. | N.A. | N.A. | N.A. | N.A. | N.A. | N.A. | 32.67 | 27.44 | 30.28 |
| — | 51.54 | 33.39 | 29.73 | 30.60 | 32.36 | 26.62 | 18.79 | 16.62 | 16.98 | 20.40 | 28.54 | 26.14 | 30.12 |
| 47.90 | N.A. | 34.28 | 29.29 | 31.43 | 35.56 | 28.16 | 18.51 | 17.18 | 18.17 | 21.98 | 35.55 | 24.31 | 31.15 |
| N.A. | N.A. | N.A. | N.A. | N.A. | N.A. | N.A. | N.A. | N.A. | N.A. | N.A. | 33.89 | 30.81 | 22.60 |
| N.A. | N.A. | N.A. | N.A. | N.A. | N.A. | N.A. | N.A. | N.A. | N.A. | N.A. | 36.20 | 29.82 | — |
| N.A. | N.A. | N.A. | N.A. | N.A. | N.A. | N.A. | N.A. | N.A. | N.A. | N.A. | 32.64 | 37.99 | 31.15 |
| 48.54 | 68.13 | — | 31.14 | 28.51 | 41.65 | 32.19 | 32.13 | 20.77 | 22.54 | 25.81 | 32.90 | 35.38 | 39.31 |
| 48.99 | 65.02 | 44.30 | 50.73 | 48.26 | 42.01 | 33.04 | 32.93 | 32.80 | 30.40 | 29.60 | 40.45 | 39.01 | 38.82 |
| 50.20 | 62.75 | 49.74 | 51.10 | 47.87 | 40.55 | 33.78 | 30.06 | 27.99 | 27.19 | 26.85 | — | — | — |
| N.A. | N.A. | N.A. | N.A. | N.A. | N.A. | N.A. | N.A. | N.A. | N.A. | N.A. | 35.26 | 31.49 | 38.50 |
| N.A. | N.A. | N.A. | N.A. | N.A. | N.A. | N.A. | N.A. | N.A. | N.A. | N.A. | 41.53 | 38.33 | 37.33 |
| — | 52.43 | 34.06 | 28.17 | 29.21 | 34.83 | 27.08 | 18.65 | 16.95 | 17.69 | 23.95 | 34.22 | 26.97 | 31.48 |
| — | — | — | — | — | — | — | — | — | — | — | 32.09 | 26.96 | 30.19 |
| 34.50 | 56.10 | 34.83 | 30.31 | 32.85 | — | 29.38 | 19.52 | 16.79 | 17.99 | 21.56 | 32.94 | 29.23 | 27.17 |
| 55.14 | — | 59.98 | — | 30.32 | 29.90 | 28.56 | 24.89 | 18.68 | 19.73 | 25.86 | 35.29 | 34.25 | 35.15 |
| — | 47.00 | — | 32.54 | 31.50 | 37.87 | 25.63 | 31.51 | 15.88 | 17.28 | 27.01 | 32.00 | 22.96 | 30.56 |
| 53.60 | 57.05 | 33.28 | 29.76 | — | — | — | 18.19 | — | — | — | 29.70 | 26.14 | — |
| 47.55 | 58.59 | 41.13 | 39.08 | 38.65 | 37.64 | 29.68 | 24.79 | 22.52 | 21.56 | 24.77 | 35.49 | 30.23 | 32.73 |
| 40.91 | 49.19 | 54.82 | 37.28 | 31.90 | 42.76 | 43.54 | 36.26 | 16.86 | 16.35 | 20.52 | 26.38 | 16.81 | 20.33 |
| — | 69.40 | 51.57 | — | 47.18 | 45.33 | 38.34 | 37.85 | 32.32 | 24.56 | 26.68 | 38.66 | 38.26 | 35.55 |
| 57.22 | 73.53 | 58.13 | 61.30 | 61.70 | 49.42 | 42.44 | 39.91 | 36.39 | 33.23 | 33.33 | 42.52 | 32.04 | 32.78 |
| 53.96 | 63.87 | 59.00 | 55.74 | 39.57 | 45.98 | 41.55 | 34.59 | 21.93 | 19.97 | 29.79 | 35.48 | 29.56 | 33.50 |
| 47.66 | 61.52 | 57.58 | 50.37 | 41.76 | 47.03 | 42.02 | 37.09 | 21.64 | 17.34 | 21.28 | 29.23 | 20.00 | 22.12 |
| 63.31 | 72.57 | 101.89 | — | 51.85 | 50.30 | 41.46 | 42.43 | 34.03 | 22.31 | 34.53 | 39.66 | 49.14 | 51.79 |
| 52.69 | 65.70 | 52.16 | 51.18 | 49.81 | 43.89 | 35.65 | 34.34 | 32.44 | 30.44 | 30.28 | 39.63 | 37.56 | 36.57 |

A-111

## IQ-12. CANADA: VOLUME OF GREEN

(Bags of 60 kilograms or

| COUNTRIES OF DESTINATION | 1953 | 1954 | 1955 | 1956 | 1957 | 1958 |
|---|---|---|---|---|---|---|
| **WESTERN HEMISPHERE** | | | | | | |
| **Pan-American Coffee Bureau** | | | | | | |
| Brazil | 325,314 | 230,207 | 301,315 | 359,040 | 358,841 | 339,250 |
| Colombia | 279,063 | 246,688 | 239,316 | 214,274 | 219,589 | 242,946 |
| El Salvador | 23,125 | 12,052 | 33,813 | 11,729 | 15,830 | 12,753 |
| Mexico | 39,806 | 35,591 | 36,366 | 37,958 | 46,645 | 45,562 |
| Guatemala | 15,109 | 16,486 | 26,675 | 26,151 | 29,287 | 27,461 |
| Costa Rica | 9,858 | 3,711 | 12,566 | 5,965 | 8,401 | 16,957 |
| Peru | 5,483 | 5,024 | 2,316 | 2,907 | 3,279 | 9,583 |
| Dominican Republic | 5,299 | 16,060 | 6,804 | 14,476 | 10,660 | 26,360 |
| Venezuela | 20,401 | 6,787 | 3,413 | 4,907 | 3,221 | 8,778 |
| Honduras | — | — | 627 | — | 875 | 1,375 |
| Ecuador | 6,692 | 6,136 | 7,019 | 6,730 | 9,440 | 11,437 |
| Nicaragua | 5,529 | 1,969 | 4,442 | 1,737 | 6,638 | 5,254 |
| Haiti | 1,907 | 7,203 | 5,062 | 4,228 | 1,784 | 5,851 |
| Panama | — | — | — | — | — | 942 |
| Cuba | — | — | — | 813 | 2,151 | 5,500 |
| **Total Pan-American Coffee Bureau** | **737,586** | **587,914** | **679,734** | **690,915** | **716,641** | **760,009** |
| **OTHER WESTERN HEMISPHERE** | | | | | | |
| United States | 18,529 | 9,547 | 27,797 | 28,627 | 36,752 | 50,829 |
| Trinidad & Tobago | 5,298 | 7,358 | 2,675 | 3,682 | 2,869 | 3,638 |
| Jamaica | 701 | 1,509 | 2,464 | 1,343 | 1,152 | 706 |
| Paraguay | — | — | — | — | — | — |
| Puerto Rico | 2,310 | 7,971 | — | 844 | — | 398 |
| Bolivia | — | — | — | — | — | — |
| **Total Other Western Hemisphere** | **26,838** | **26,385** | **32,936** | **34,496** | **40,773** | **55,571** |
| **TOTAL WESTERN HEMISPHERE** | **764,424** | **614,299** | **712,670** | **725,411** | **757,414** | **815,580** |
| **AFRICA** | | | | | | |
| East Africa | 34,299 | 71,091 | 59,077 | 84,595 | 63,468 | 60,048 |
| Uganda | N.A. | N.A. | N.A. | N.A. | N.A. | N.A. |
| Kenya | N.A. | N.A. | N.A. | N.A. | N.A. | N.A. |
| Tanzania | N.A. | N.A. | N.A. | N.A. | N.A. | N.A. |
| Congo (D.R.) | 2,229 | 1,745 | 6,871 | 10,555 | 8,905 | 13,223 |
| Portuguese Africa | 497 | 1,908 | 332 | 780 | 416 | — |
| Ethiopia | 570 | 1,030 | 1,214 | 1,431 | 922 | 117 |
| Ivory Coast | — | — | — | — | — | — |
| French Africa N.E.S. | — | — | 845 | — | 415 | — |
| Others (1) | — | 4,399 | — | 482 | 100 | 653 |
| **TOTAL AFRICA** | **37,595** | **80,173** | **68,339** | **97,843** | **74,226** | **74,041** |
| **OTHERS** | | | | | | |
| Malaysia | — | 238 | — | — | — | — |
| India | — | — | — | — | — | — |
| Various | 10,642 | 26,373 | 3,607 | 5,500 | 4,096 | 5,048 |
| **TOTAL OTHERS** | **10,642** | **26,611** | **3,607** | **5,500** | **4,096** | **5,048** |
| **TOTAL IMPORTS** | **812,661** | **721,083** | **784,616** | **828,754** | **835,736** | **894,669** |

SOURCE: Dominion Bureau of Statistics
 * Preliminary
 (1) Includes: Nyassaland, Madagascar, South Africa, Sierra Leone, Nigeria, Cameroun, and Ghana.

**COFFEE IMPORTS, 1953-1966**

132.276 pounds each)

| 1959 | 1960 | 1961 | 1962 | 1963 | 1964 | 1965 | 1966 |
|---|---|---|---|---|---|---|---|
| 441,536 | 410,378 | 456,665 | 485,954 | 488,977 | 450,666 | 385,333 | 364,213 |
| 269,986 | 216,964 | 217,150 | 245,453 | 220,710 | 209,408 | 200,362 | 137,482 |
| 18,034 | 15,051 | 23,974 | 33,220 | 36,765 | 50,421 | 41,091 | 34,203 |
| 47,294 | 58,478 | 51,857 | 65,062 | 60,250 | 48,178 | 50,599 | 35,783 |
| 25,910 | 25,123 | 24,455 | 30,396 | 36,259 | 21,264 | 36,200 | 37,341 |
| 13,716 | 13,642 | 14,448 | 22,038 | 22,255 | 15,909 | 27,372 | 24,775 |
| 7,513 | 3,542 | 3,884 | 7,148 | 12,685 | 14,647 | 7,083 | 8,489 |
| 12,560 | 16,331 | 10,234 | 9,314 | 5,417 | 10,844 | 10,525 | 5,891 |
| 6,200 | 4,675 | 8,437 | 6,561 | 9,213 | 6,831 | 3,314 | 1,812 |
| 735 | 6,837 | 3,528 | 3,361 | 5,525 | 3,437 | 3,921 | 2,074 |
| 4,742 | 5,908 | 3,779 | 9,145 | 5,613 | 2,828 | 8,171 | 3,059 |
| 3,523 | 1,906 | 1,952 | 1,119 | 1,387 | 1,719 | 1,799 | 721 |
| 4,016 | 944 | 2,081 | 2,567 | 2,521 | 2,280 | 2,366 | 1,073 |
| 302 | 943 | — | — | — | — | — | — |
| 339 | — | — | 594 | — | — | — | — |
| **856,406** | **780,722** | **822,444** | **921,932** | **907,577** | **838,432** | **778,051** | **656,916** |
| 69,020 | 86,231 | 126,962 | 178,865 | 204,931 | 206,859 | 209,039 | 169,527 |
| 3,094 | 2,318 | 5,355 | 549 | 5,900 | 6,589 | 9,521 | 9,035 |
| 2,030 | 2,226 | 624 | 1,750 | 1,746 | 2,495 | 250 | 319 |
| — | 287 | 100 | — | 3,428 | 842 | 1,090 | — |
| — | 1,327 | — | — | — | 567 | 226 | — |
| — | 199 | 101 | 642 | — | 307 | 250 | — |
| **74,144** | **92,588** | **133,142** | **181,806** | **216,005** | **217,659** | **220,376** | **178,881** |
| **930,550** | **873,310** | **955,586** | **1,103,738** | **1,123,582** | **1,056,091** | **998,427** | **835,797** |
| 55,325 | — | — | — | — | — | — | — |
| N.A. | 37,813 | 64,626 | 56,901 | 59,236 | 72,505 | 92,469 | 100,753 |
| N.A. | 32,945 | 49,642 | 35,646 | 38,584 | 48,135 | 57,941 | 66,166 |
| N.A. | 27,238 | 21,501 | 15,721 | 32,247 | 32,950 | 50,942 | 66,623 |
| 23,754 | 14,425 | 9,974 | 9,655 | 7,370 | 15,203 | 2,882 | 2,194 |
| — | 5,062 | 5,004 | 3,469 | 16,147 | 4,789 | 31,156 | 66,099 |
| 556 | 858 | — | — | 413 | 2,227 | 1,090 | 616 |
| — | — | 4,994 | 2,502 | 2,520 | 1,680 | — | — |
| — | — | — | 67 | 67 | 299 | 50 | 50 |
| 294 | 735 | 976 | — | — | 249 | 1,286 | 2,533 |
| **79,929** | **119,076** | **156,717** | **123,961** | **156,584** | **178,037** | **237,816** | **305,034** |
| — | — | 186 | 438 | 6,007 | 4,583 | 1,443 | 4,229 |
| — | — | 4,012 | — | 150 | 3,850 | 3,436 | 363 |
| 4,662 | 2,660 | 2,494 | 1,667 | 1,215 | 3,606 | 16,526 | 21,649 |
| **4,662** | **2,660** | **6,692** | **2,105** | **7,372** | **12,039** | **21,405** | **26,241** |
| **1,015,141** | **995,046** | **1,118,995** | **1,229,804** | **1,287,538** | **1,246,167** | **1,257,648** | **1,167,072** |

## IQ-15. EUROPE: IMPORTS
(Bags of 60 kilograms)

| COUNTRIES OF ORIGIN WESTERN HEMISPHERE | Germany (F.R.) | France | Italy | Sweden | Netherlands | United Kingdom |
|---|---|---|---|---|---|---|
| **Pan-American Coffee Bureau** | | | | | | |
| Brazil | 898,857 | 617,201 | 1,037,912 | 1,024,102 | 363,834 | 85,986 |
| Colombia | 776,550 | 36,799 | 48,317 | 278,268 | 177,217 | 52,153 |
| El Salvador | 775,678 | 816 | 3,595 | 6,350 | 25,500 | – |
| Guatemala | 377,994 | 4,900 | 11,876 | 24,250 | 38,617 | 2,944 |
| Mexico | 146,070 | 20,449 | 2,343 | 850 | 14,950 | 5,341 |
| Costa Rica | 246,635 | 29,200 | 27,603 | 73,817 | 50,284 | 11,981 |
| Ecuador | 101,418 | 75,250 | 29,359 | 10,783 | 4,567 | 288 |
| Peru | 12,963 | 8,183 | 16,586 | 9,000 | 15,900 | 1,781 |
| Nicaragua | 128,512 | 2,516 | 12,213 | 183 | 32,917 | 2,302 |
| Honduras | 132,365 | 14,026 | 3,740 | 417 | 3,533 | 2,152 |
| Haiti | 3,938 | 64,117 | 77,114 | 2,033 | 1,733 | – |
| Dominican Republic | 1,342 | 26,184 | 27,571 | – | 2,033 | 2,619 |
| Venezuela | 9,327 | 16,216 | 1,873 | 516 | 4,817 | – |
| Panama | 15,037 | – | – | – | – | – |
| Cuba | – | – | – | – | – | – |
| **TOTAL P.A.C.B.** | 3,626,686 | 915,857 | 1,300,102 | 1,430,569 | 735,902 | 167,547 |
| Other Western Hemisphere (3) | 1,076 | 7,573 | 2,701 | 1,700 | 3,933 | 14,084 |
| **TOTAL WESTERN HEMISPHERE** | 3,627,762 | 923,430 | 1,302,803 | 1,432,269 | 739,835 | 181,631 |
| **AFRICA** | | | | | | |
| Franc Zone (4) | 124,932 | 1,892,685 | 352,509 | 200 | 18,016 | 14,123 |
| Uganda | 147,502 | 27,250 | 1,902 | 29,650 | 10,300 | 539,984 |
| Kenya | 319,192 | 3,285 | 6,984 | 83,233 | 48,133 | 113,344 |
| Tanzania | 111,805 | 1,350 | 8,597 | 32,883 | 9,300 | 46,213 |
| Angola | 112,678 | 26,201 | 587 | 1,667 | 469,168 | 19,471 |
| Ethiopia | 38,227 | 21,032 | 38,561 | 11,233 | – | 5,246 |
| Congo (Kinshasa) | 72,627 | 164,984 | 159,350 | – | 850 | 2,676 |
| Madagascar | 24,953 | 348,967 | 6,586 | – | 417 | – |
| Rwanda-Burundi | 12,790 | 9,412 | 595 | 250 | 150 | 4,181 |
| Various (5) | 288 | 37,768 | 1,400 | 5,551 | 2,316 | 221,829 |
| **TOTAL AFRICA** | 964,994 | 2,532,934 | 577,071 | 164,667 | 558,650 | 967,067 |
| **ASIA & OCEANIA** | | | | | | |
| Indonesia | 13,662 | 213,450 | 119,066 | 14,733 | 67,966 | 8,934 |
| India | 20,978 | 11,917 | 14,949 | 2,700 | 4,633 | 6,384 |
| Yemen | – | 8,268 | – | – | – | – |
| Various (6) | 29,766 | 97,747 | 25,906 | 633 | 17,882 | 38,485 |
| **TOTAL ASIA & OCEANIA** | 64,406 | 331,382 | 159,921 | 18,066 | 90,481 | 53,803 |
| **OTHERS (7)** | 5,958 | 6,138 | 18,091 | 501 | 28,537 | 157,042 |
| **TOTAL IMPORTS** | 4,663,120 | 3,793,884 | 2,057,886 | 1,615,503 | 1,417,503 | 1,359,543 |

Source: Statistical Publications of governments and unofficial estimates.
(†) Preliminary.
(1) Albania, Bulgaria, Czechoslovakia, East Germany, Hungary, Poland, Rumania, USSR, etc.
(2) Cyprus, Gibraltar, Greece, Iceland, Ireland, Malta, Trieste, Turkey, Yugoslavia, etc.
(3) Argentina, Bolivia, British & French Guiana, Guadeloupe, Jamaica, Martinique, Paraguay, Puerto Rico, Surinam, United States.
(4) Cameroun, Central Africa Republic, Comores Is., Dahomey, Gabon, Ivory Coast, Republic of Congo, Senegal, Somalia, Togo.

**OF GREEN COFFEE, 1966**
or 132.276 pounds each)

| Belgium | Denmark | Switzerland | Spain | Finland | Norway | Austria | Portugal | Eastern Europe (1) | Others (2) | TOTAL |
|---|---|---|---|---|---|---|---|---|---|---|
| 244,861 | 656,150 | 121,221 | 83,300 | 371,011 | 419,090 | 116,590 | — | 891,085 | 619,792 | 7,550,992 |
| 122,230 | 52,467 | 30,779 | 299,957 | 179,993 | 45,532 | 23,352 | — | 300,568 | 8,225 | 2,432,407 |
| 1,989 | — | 19,543 | 6,660 | 21,414 | 6,485 | 11,399 | — | 2,500 | 114 | 882,043 |
| 28,964 | 5,686 | 61,816 | 16,666 | 49,525 | 14,543 | 20,604 | — | 11,200 | 58 | 669,643 |
| 8,160 | 4,666 | 40,822 | 99,593 | 3,877 | 2,758 | 7,783 | — | 62,108 | 122 | 419,892 |
| 24,734 | 5,990 | 50,423 | 6,660 | 42,867 | 709 | 21,287 | — | 11,861 | 317 | 604,368 |
| 247 | 86 | 12,073 | 8,334 | 34 | 67 | 2,445 | — | 23,000 | — | 267,951 |
| 5,387 | — | 6,976 | — | 10,553 | 113 | 2,277 | — | 9,601 | — | 99,320 |
| 22,047 | — | 6,926 | — | 1,275 | 1,974 | 12,894 | — | — | — | 223,759 |
| 140 | — | 8,812 | — | 3,817 | 1 | 5,615 | — | — | — | 174,618 |
| 51,141 | 11,123 | 28,771 | — | 48 | 7,351 | 418 | — | — | 100 | 247,887 |
| 5,913 | 1,699 | 3,676 | 4,997 | 762 | 250 | 2,085 | — | 3,125 | — | 82,256 |
| 4,208 | 5,123 | — | — | 37 | — | 693 | — | 2,334 | — | 45,144 |
| — | — | — | — | 3,914 | — | 1,870 | — | — | — | 20,821 |
| — | — | — | — | 11 | — | 643 | — | — | — | 654 |
| 520,021 | 742,990 | 391,838 | 526,167 | 689,138 | 498,873 | 229,955 | — | 1,317,382 | 628,728 | 13,721,755 |
| 34,100 | 1,110 | 1,259 | 13,130 | 1,033 | 3,501 | 372 | — | — | 50 | 85,622 |
| 554,121 | 744,100 | 393,097 | 539,297 | 690,171 | 502,374 | 230,327 | — | 1,317,382 | 628,778 | 13,807,377 |
| 15,828 | 363 | 10,985 | 36,935 | — | 347 | 6,368 | — | 67,183 | 2,908 | 2,543,382 |
| 38 | — | 7,889 | 23,872 | 4,790 | 2,375 | 6,098 | — | 240,956 | 3,302 | 1,045,908 |
| 3,570 | 490 | 10,531 | — | 36,774 | 11,422 | 7,760 | — | 32,640 | 121 | 677,479 |
| 4,690 | 251 | 41,223 | 32,166 | 1,359 | 2,218 | 6,048 | — | 59,264 | 1,358 | 358,725 |
| 56,102 | 8,197 | 48,209 | 41,677 | 14,239 | 9,796 | 11,160 | 212,850 | 44,175 | 75 | 1,076,252 |
| 374 | 1,390 | 6,863 | 16,651 | 5,464 | 19,843 | 2,013 | — | 28,287 | 13,133 | 208,317 |
| 32,015 | — | 9,631 | 77,006 | 172 | — | 1,998 | — | 1,205 | 676 | 523,190 |
| 842 | — | 97 | — | 664 | — | 1,682 | — | — | — | 384,208 |
| 1,717 | — | — | — | — | — | 30 | — | — | — | 29,125 |
| 9,584 | 1,159 | 1,431 | 139,382 | 1,747 | 4,658 | 1,924 | 6,532 | — | — | 435,569 |
| 124,760 | 11,850 | 136,859 | 367,689 | 65,209 | 50,659 | 45,081 | 219,382 | 473,710 | 21,573 | 7,282,155 |
| 89,239 | 117,805 | 131,008 | — | 357 | 7,360 | 4,735 | — | 51,464 | 2,454 | 842,233 |
| 3,017 | — | 6,648 | — | — | 9,797 | 4,013 | — | 205,773 | 84,856 | 375,665 |
| 172 | 782 | 1,821 | — | — | — | 8 | — | — | — | 11,051 |
| 26,334 | 10,315 | 1,194 | 4,167 | 5,729 | 3,982 | 3,984 | — | — | 4,150 | 270,274 |
| 118,762 | 128,902 | 140,671 | 4,167 | 6,086 | 21,139 | 12,740 | — | 257,237 | 91,460 | 1,499,223 |
| 107,129 | 804 | — | — | 6,036 | 1,812 | 3,433 | 665 | — | — | 336,146 |
| 904,772 | 885,656 | 670,627 | 911,153 | 767,502 | 575,984 | 291,581 | 220,047 | 2,048,329 | 741,811 | 22,924,901 |

(5) British West Africa, Cape Verde, Guinea, Liberia, Nigeria, Portuguese Guinea, Rhodesia & Nyasaland, Sao Tome & Principe, Sierre Leone, Spanish Africa.
(6) Aden, Australia, French Polynesia, Malaya, New Guinea, New Caldeonia, New Hebrides, Portuguese Timor, Singapore.
(7) Origins Unknown

## IQ-16 EUROPE: IMPORTS OF

(Bags of 60 Kilograms or

| COUNTRIES OF ORIGIN | 1955 | 1956 | 1957 | 1958 |
|---|---|---|---|---|
| **WESTERN HEMISPHERE** | | | | |
| **Pan-American Coffee Bureau** | | | | |
| Brazil | 4,609,555 | 5,064,342 | 4,518,984 | 4,375,503 |
| Colombia | 842,807 | 656,678 | 639,967 | 911,702 |
| El Salvador | 287,478 | 343,279 | 548,416 | 606,973 |
| Costa Rica | 320,887 | 267,636 | 319,151 | 393,231 |
| Guatemala | 158,536 | 140,341 | 240,382 | 293,649 |
| Mexico | 155,948 | 209,805 | 201,072 | 176,185 |
| Ecuador | 74,726 | 65,024 | 148,875 | 135,449 |
| Nicaragua | 82,476 | 73,044 | 106,874 | 127,535 |
| Honduras | 13,688 | 33,500 | 43,748 | 40,174 |
| Venezuela | 82,597 | 88,800 | 59,642 | 75,392 |
| Dominican Republic | 34,936 | 85,101 | 29,360 | 39,310 |
| Panama | 2,357 | — | — | 4,941 |
| Cuba | 8,444 | 64,664 | 67,345 | 49,199 |
| Peru | 35,751 | 152,958 | 46,214 | 60,286 |
| Haiti | 229,378 | 310,225 | 262,892 | 319,380 |
| **Total Pan-American Coffee Bureau** | **6,939,564** | **7,555,397** | **7,232,922** | **7,608,909** |
| Other Western Hemisphere (1) | 28,072 | 53,737 | 26,597 | 36,903 |
| **AFRICA** | | | | |
| OAMCAF (2) | 1,334,829 | 1,703,007 | 1,658,702 | 1,857,565 |
| Kenya, Uganda and Tanzania | 794,838 | 854,851 | 892,204 | 963,221 |
| Angola | 320,520 | 398,165 | 526,897 | 591,153 |
| Ethiopia | 119,582 | 41,749 | 146,775 | 163,758 |
| Congo (D.R.) | 357,970 | 378,028 | 474,282 | 536,064 |
| Madagascar | 620,836 | 853,568 | 621,552 | 692,152 |
| Rwanda & Burundi | * | * | * | * |
| Various (3) | 138,506 | 155,223 | 128,531 | 164,790 |
| **TOTAL AFRICA** | **3,687,081** | **4,384,591** | **4,448,943** | **4,968,703** |
| **ASIA & OCEANIA** | | | | |
| Indonesia | 221,833 | 301,541 | 420,447 | 265,088 |
| India | 120,622 | 72,820 | 163,396 | 189,250 |
| Yemen | * | * | 10,678 | 41,991 |
| Various (4) | 104,446 | 316,298 | 375,273 | 238,114 |
| **TOTAL ASIA & OCEANIA** | **446,901** | **690,659** | **969,794** | **734,443** |
| **OTHERS (5)** | **520,453** | **278,301** | **260,089** | **241,499** |
| **TOTAL IMPORTS** | **11,622,071** | **12,962,685** | **12,938,345** | **13,590,457** |

Source: Statistical publications of Governments and *Coffee Report*. Jacques-Louis Delamare, Paris, and G.G. Paton.

† Preliminary

(1) Argentina, Bolivia, British & French Guiana, Guadeloupe, Jamaica, Martinique, Paraguay, Puerto Rico, Surinam, United States.

(2) Cameroun, Central African Republic, Dahomey, Gabon, Ivory Coast, Republic of Congo (Brazzaville), Togo. Does not include Madagascar. Includes Comores Islands, Senegal, and Somalia.

A-116

**GREEN COFFEE, 1955-1966**
132.276 Pounds Each)

| 1959 | 1960 | 1961 | 1962 | 1963 | 1964 | 1965 | 1966† |
|---|---|---|---|---|---|---|---|
| 5,781,560 | 6,219,555 | 6,401,872 | 6,691,063 | 7,321,953 | 6,846,148 | 6,804,650 | 7,550,992 |
| 1,274,720 | 1,421,528 | 1,551,408 | 1,816,626 | 2,069,057 | 2,522,565 | 2,628,423 | 2,432,407 |
| 634,058 | 727,485 | 735,930 | 810,928 | 747,390 | 908,450 | 1,038,458 | 882,043 |
| 455,231 | 451,528 | 504,228 | 543,501 | 526,343 | 555,814 | 503,438 | 604,368 |
| 402,593 | 457,354 | 456,069 | 487,247 | 513,580 | 552,223 | 600,155 | 669,643 |
| 160,667 | 213,430 | 150,817 | 198,098 | 209,305 | 249,983 | 221,406 | 419,892 |
| 97,950 | 167,814 | 208,580 | 144,778 | 157,953 | 172,373 | 233,607 | 267,951 |
| 114,094 | 123,049 | 140,020 | 130,480 | 150,989 | 180,805 | 229,719 | 223,759 |
| 70,496 | 74,490 | 63,486 | 77,219 | 84,849 | 106,022 | 110,919 | 174,618 |
| 80,389 | 53,878 | 52,539 | 56,271 | 61,732 | 69,889 | 34,866 | 45,144 |
| 47,221 | 54,854 | 55,296 | 57,658 | 54,728 | 54,126 | 64,398 | 82,256 |
| 22 | 2,869 | 2,238 | 9,198 | 4,987 | 15,717 | 13,156 | 20,821 |
| 20,586 | 75,418 | 2,565 | 4,920 | 3,030 | 160 | 1,043 | 654 |
| 64,792 | 84,670 | 129,415 | 117,538 | 142,948 | 123,610 | 125,572 | 99,320 |
| 204,447 | 329,289 | 230,898 | 346,611 | 282,542 | 264,674 | 304,092 | 247,887 |
| **9,408,826** | **10,457,211** | **10,685,361** | **11,492,136** | **12,331,386** | **12,622,559** | **12,913,902** | **13,721,755** |
| 316,582 | 159,393 | 122,206 | 87,593 | 121,666 | 187,902 | 77,544 | 85,622 |
| 1,739,079 | 2,176,737 | 2,193,863 | 2,215,000 | 2,484,875 | 2,664,712 | 2,403,926 | 2,543,382 |
| 1,043,454 | 1,004,280 | 1,080,252 | 1,178,848 | 1,440,897 | 1,331,794 | 1,705,876 | 2,082,112 |
| 565,185 | 689,176 | 836,534 | 1,016,859 | 1,061,505 | 1,179,591 | 1,346,654 | 1,076,252 |
| 182,921 | 171,103 | 134,060 | 184,472 | 185,776 | 165,400 | 191,900 | 208,317 |
| 575,650 | 568,385 | 552,880 | 452,820 | 430,790 | 491,973 | 553,978 | 523,190 |
| 650,454 | 601,905 | 528,739 | 528,088 | 518,871 | 506,972 | 414,961 | 384,208 |
| * | * | * | * | 319 | 10,378 | 30,108 | 29,125 |
| 233,254 | 343,113 | 322,927 | 232,996 | 291,376 | 572,185 | 344,833 | 435,569 |
| **4,989,997** | **5,554,699** | **5,649,255** | **5,809,083** | **6,414,409** | **6,923,005** | **6,992,236** | **7,282,155** |
| 177,462 | 176,280 | 398,900 | 336,240 | 419,390 | 622,473 | 708,589 | 842,233 |
| 239,033 | 177,629 | 400,932 | 345,234 | 263,795 | 455,986 | 359,255 | 375,665 |
| 27,375 | 21,420 | 25,313 | 26,292 | 23,515 | 30,913 | 15,476 | 11,051 |
| 176,392 | 198,501 | 165,818 | 202,360 | 222,391 | 174,649 | 103,215 | 270,274 |
| **620,262** | **573,830** | **990,963** | **910,126** | **929,091** | **1,283,721** | **1,186,535** | **1,499,223** |
| 177,604 | 272,981 | 359,745 | 264,219 | 197,374 | 329,900 | 433,600 | 336,146 |
| 15,513,271 | 17,018,114 | 17,807,530 | 18,563,157 | 19,993,926 | 21,347,087 | 21,603,817 | 22,924,901 |

(3) British West Africa, Cape Verde, Guinea, Liberia, Nigeria, Portuguese Guinea, Rhodesia, Malawi, São Tomé & Principe, Sierra Leone, Spanish Africa.

(4) Aden, Australia, French Polynesia, Malaya, New Guinea, New Caledonia, New Hebrides, Portuguese Timor, Singapore.

(*) Included in regional various figure.

## C-6. UNITED STATES: NET CIVILIAN

(thousands of 60-kilo

|  | 1951 | 1952 | 1953 | 1954 | 1955 | 1956 |
|---|---|---|---|---|---|---|
| **TOTAL IMPORTS*** | 20,414 | 20,341 | 21,212 | 17,239 | 19,723 | 21,392 |
| Less: Exports & Reexports | 166 | 189 | 222 | 274 | 317 | 407 |
| **TOTAL NEW SUPPLY** | 20,248 | 20,152 | 20,990 | 16,965 | 19,406 | 20,985 |
| Less: Armed Forces | 1,264 | 509 | 545 | 335 | 376 | 424 |
| **NEW SUPPLY FOR CIVILIAN CONSUMPTION** | 18,984 | 19,643 | 20,445 | 16,630 | 19,030 | 20,561 |
| Plus: Previous December Stocks | 2,936 | 2,759 | 2,905 | 3,169 | 2,032 | 2,187 |
| **TOTAL CIVILIAN AVAILABLE SUPPLY** | 21,920 | 22,402 | 23,350 | 19,799 | 21,062 | 22,748 |
| Less: Latter December Stocks | 2,759 | 2,905 | 3,169 | 2,032 | 2,187 | 2,806 |
| **NET CIVILIAN AVAILABLE SUPPLY** | 19,161 | 19,497 | 20,181 | 17,767 | 18,875 | 19,942 |
| Less: Estimated Additions to Retail & Wholesale Inventories | N.A. | N.A. | N.A. | N.A. | N.A. | N.A. |
| **NET CIVILIAN VISIBLE DISAPPEARANCE** | 19,161 | 19,497 | 20,181 | 17,767 | 18,875 | 19,942 |
| Regular | 18,195 | 18,316 | 18,702 | 15,729 | 16,592 | 17,152 |
| Soluble | 966 | 1,181 | 1,479 | 2,038 | 2,283 | 2,790 |
| **HOUSEHOLD PURCHASES** | 14,083 | 14,974 | 15,145 | 14,160 | 15,043 | 15,196 |
| Regular | 13,308 | 14,016 | 13,903 | 12,348 | 12,997 | 12,765 |
| Soluble | 775 | 958 | 1,242 | 1,812 | 2,046 | 2,431 |
| **NON-HOUSEHOLD PURCHASES** | 5,078 | 4,523 | 5,036 | 3,607 | 3,832 | 4,746 |
| Regular | 4,887 | 4,300 | 4,799 | 3,381 | 3,595 | 4,387 |
| Soluble | 191 | 223 | 237 | 226 | 237 | 359 |
| **CIVILIAN POPULATION** (as of July 1st) in thousands | 151,599 | 153,892 | 156,595 | 159,695 | 162,967 | 166,055 |
| **GREEN-COFFEE EQUIVALENT PER CAPITA** (lbs.) | | | | | | |
| All Coffee | 16.7 | 16.8 | 17.0 | 14.7 | 15.3 | 15.9 |
| Regular | 15.9 | 15.7 | 15.8 | 13.0 | 13.5 | 13.7 |
| Soluble | 0.8 | 1.1 | 1.2 | 1.7 | 1.8 | 2.2 |

Source:  U.S. Department of Commerce & Market Research Corp. of America.

*Includes net supply from Hawaii and Puerto Rico.

N.B.:  See Chapter on *Trends in Soluble Coffee* for explanation of rates of conversion from soluble to green-coffee equivalent.

**VISIBLE DISAPPEARANCE, 1951-1966**

bags of green coffee)

| 1957 | 1958 | 1959 | 1960 | 1961 | 1962 | 1963 | 1964 | 1965 | 1966 |
|---|---|---|---|---|---|---|---|---|---|
| 21,010 | 20,356 | 23,184 | 22,331 | 22,619 | 24,695 | 24,077 | 23,072 | 21,512 | 22,330 |
| 547 | 674 | 756 | 749 | 713 | 944 | 845 | 982 | 773 | 653 |
| 20,463 | 19,682 | 22,428 | 21,582 | 21,906 | 23,751 | 23,232 | 22,090 | 20,739 | 21,677 |
| 389 | 254 | 417 | 392 | 460 | 436 | 436 | 420 | 516 | 440 |
| 20,074 | 19,428 | 22,011 | 21,190 | 21,446 | 23,315 | 22,796 | 21,670 | 20,223 | 21,237 |
| 2,806 | 2,959 | 2,114 | 3,370 | 3,204 | 2,815 | 3,964 | 4,726 | 4,470 | 3,143 |
| 22,880 | 22,387 | 24,125 | 24,560 | 24,650 | 26,130 | 26,760 | 26,396 | 24,693 | 24,380 |
| 2,959 | 2,114 | 3,370 | 3,204 | 2,815 | 3,964 | 4,726 | 4,470 | 3,143 | 3,141 |
| 19,921 | 20,273 | 20,755 | 21,356 | 21,835 | 22,166 | 22,034 | 21,926 | 21,550 | 21,239 |
| N.A. | N.A. | N.A. | 167 | 61 | 83 | 126 | 53 | (100) | (130) |
| 19,921 | 20,273 | 20,755 | 21,189 | 21,774 | 22,083 | 21,908 | 21,873 | 21,650 | 21,369 |
| 16,702 | 16,898 | 17,182 | 17,441 | 17,899 | 18,179 | 18,106 | 18,176 | 18,092 | 17,756 |
| 3,219 | 3,375 | 3,573 | 3,748 | 3,875 | 3,904 | 3,802 | 3,697 | 3,558 | 3,613 |
| 15,399 | 15,640 | 15,504 | 15,765 | 16,091 | 16,030 | 15,612 | 15,117 | 14,764 | 14,423 |
| 12,566 | 12,621 | 12,419 | 12,517 | 12,760 | 12,661 | 12,425 | 12,077 | 11,816 | 11,556 |
| 2,833 | 3,019 | 3,085 | 3,248 | 3,331 | 3,369 | 3,187 | 3,040 | 2,948 | 2,867 |
| 4,522 | 4,633 | 5,251 | 5,424 | 5,681 | 6,053 | 6,296 | 6,756 | 6,886 | 6,946 |
| 4,136 | 4,277 | 4,763 | 4,924 | 5,139 | 5,518 | 5,681 | 6,099 | 6,276 | 6,200 |
| 386 | 356 | 488 | 500 | 544 | 535 | 615 | 657 | 610 | 746 |
| 169,110 | 172,226 | 175,277 | 178,153 | 181,207 | 183,796 | 186,667 | 189,372 | 191,874 | 193,707 |
| 15.6 | 15.6 | 15.7 | 15.7 | 15.9 | 15.9 | 15.5 | 15.3 | 14.9 | 14.6 |
| 13.1 | 13.0 | 13.0 | 12.9 | 13.1 | 13.1 | 12.8 | 12.7 | 12.5 | 12.1 |
| 2.5 | 2.6 | 2.7 | 2.8 | 2.8 | 2.8 | 2.7 | 2.6 | 2.4 | 2.5 |

## C-5. UNITED STATES: CONSUMPTION OF COFFEE
## NET CIVILIAN VISIBLE DISAPPEARANCE, 1965-1966
(Thousands)

|  | 1966 Green Equivalent Bags of 60 kilos | 1966 Pounds | 1966 Roasted Equivalent Pounds | 1965* Green Equivalent Bags of 60 kilos | 1965* Pounds | 1965* Roasted Equivalent Pounds |
|---|---|---|---|---|---|---|
| TOTAL IMPORTS° | 22,330 | 2,953,723 | 2,482,120 | 21,512 | 2,845,521 | 2,391,194 |
| Less: Exports and Re-exports | 653 | 93,255 | 78,334 | 773 | 102,249 | 85,924 |
| TOTAL NEW SUPPLY | 21,677 | 2,867,347 | 2,409,535 | 20,739 | 2,743,272 | 2,305,271 |
| Less: Armed Forces | 440 | 58,201 | 48,889 | 516 | 68,254 | 57,333 |
| NEW SUPPLY FOR CIVILIAN CONSUMPTION | 21,237 | 2,809,145 | 2,360,626 | 20,223 | 2,675,018 | 2,247,914 |
| Plus: Previous December Stocks | 3,143 | 415,743 | 349,224 | 4,470 | 591,274 | 496,670 |
| TOTAL CIVILIAN AVAILABLE SUPPLY | 24,380 | 3,224,889 | 2,709,991 | 24,693 | 3,266,291 | 2,744,783 |
| Less: Latter December Stocks | 3,141 | 415,479 | 349,002 | 3,143 | 415,743 | 349,224 |
| NET CIVILIAN AVAILABLE SUPPLY | 21,239 | 2,809,410 | 2,360,849 | 21,550 | 2,850,548 | 2,395,418 |
| Less: Estimated Additions to Retail & Wholesale Inventories | (130) | (17,196) | (14,445) | (100) | (13,228) | (11,112) |
| NET CIVILIAN VISIBLE DISAPPEARANCE | 21,369 | 2,826,606 | 2,375,299 | 21,650 | 2,863,775 | 2,406,534 |
| CIVILIAN POPULATION, JULY 1st |  | 193,707 |  |  | 191,874 |  |
| POUNDS PER CAPITA |  | 14.6 |  |  | 14.9 |  |

Source: United States Department of Commerce.
*Revised
°Includes net supply from Puerto Rico and Hawaii.

A-120

## C-15. UNITED STATES: PER CAPITA CONSUMPTION
(Based on Net Civilian Visible Disappearance), 1946-1966

(Green Coffee)

| Year | N.C.V.D. (In Millions of Pounds) | Civilian Population (In Millions) | Per Capita (Pounds) | Civilian Population 10 Yrs. & over (In Millions) | Per Capita (Pounds) |
|---|---|---|---|---|---|
| 1935-39 | 1,814 | 130.7 | 13.9 | 109.5 | 16.6 |
| 1946 | 2,776 | 138.4 | 20.1 | 113.3 | 24.5 |
| 1947 | 2,487 | 142.6 | 17.4 | 115.9 | 21.5 |
| 1948 | 2,676 | 145.2 | 18.4 | 117.2 | 22.8 |
| 1949 | 2,761 | 147.6 | 18.7 | 118.3 | 23.3 |
| 1950 | 2,434 | 150.8 | 16.1 | 121.2 | 20.0 |
| 1951 | 2,535 | 151.6 | 16.7 | 120.5 | 21.0 |
| 1952 | 2,579 | 153.9 | 16.8 | 121.6 | 21.3 |
| 1953 | 2,669 | 156.6 | 17.0 | 123.4 | 21.6 |
| 1954 | 2,350 | 159.7 | 14.7 | 125.4 | 18.6 |
| 1955 | 2,497 | 163.0 | 15.3 | 127.5 | 19.5 |
| 1956 | 2,638 | 166.1 | 15.9 | 129.6 | 20.4 |
| 1957 | 2,635 | 169.1 | 15.6 | 131.7 | 20.0 |
| 1958 | 2,682 | 172.2 | 15.6 | 134.1 | 20.0 |
| 1959 | 2,745 | 175.3 | 15.7 | 136.6 | 20.2 |
| 1960 | 2,803 | 178.2 | 15.7 | 139.1 | 20.1 |
| 1961 | 2,880 | 181.2 | 15.9 | 141.3 | 20.4 |
| 1962 | 2,921 | 183.8 | 15.9 | 143.4 | 20.3 |
| 1963 | 2,898 | 186.7 | 15.5 | 145.9 | 19.8 |
| 1964 | 2,893 | 189.4 | 15.3 | 148.3 | 19.4 |
| 1965 | 2,864 | 191.9 | 14.9 | 150.9 | 18.9 |
| 1966 | 2,827 | 193.7 | 14.6 | 153.1 | 18.4 |

Source: Per capita figures calculated by Department of Statistics and Economic Research; population data from the Bureau of the Census.
N.B.: Data for 1951-1965 revised.

## C-7. UNITED STATES: TRENDS OF COFFEE DRINKING, WINTERS OF 1960-1967 BY PLACE OF CONSUMPTION AND PERIOD OF DAY
(Cups Per Person Per Day)

|  |  | \multicolumn{3}{c}{At Meal Time} | \multicolumn{3}{c}{PERIOD OF DAY Between Meals} | \multicolumn{3}{c}{Total} |  |
|---|---|---|---|---|---|---|---|---|---|---|
|  |  | Regular | Instant | All Coffee | Regular | Instant | All Coffee | Regular | Instant | All Coffee |
| 1960: | Home | 1.38 | 0.41 | 1.79 | 0.40 | 0.11 | 0.51 | 1.78 | 0.52 | 2.30 |
|  | Eating Places | 0.13 | * | 0.13 | 0.12 | 0.01 | 0.13 | 0.25 | * | 0.25 |
|  | At Work | 0.06 | 0.02 | 0.08 | 0.12 | 0.02 | 0.14 | 0.18 | 0.04 | 0.22 |
|  | Total | 1.57 | 0.43 | 2.00 | 0.64 | 0.13 | 0.77 | 2.21 | 0.56 | 2.77 |
| 1961: | Home | 1.45 | 0.44 | 1.89 | 0.45 | 0.15 | 0.60 | 1.90 | 0.59 | 2.49 |
|  | Eating Places | 0.12 | 0.01 | 0.13 | 0.14 | * | 0.14 | 0.26 | 0.01 | 0.27 |
|  | At Work | 0.07 | 0.01 | 0.08 | 0.10 | 0.03 | 0.13 | 0.17 | 0.04 | 0.21 |
|  | Total | 1.64 | 0.46 | 2.10 | 0.69 | 0.18 | 0.87 | 2.33 | 0.64 | 2.97 |
| 1962: | Home | 1.46 | 0.47 | 1.93 | 0.49 | 0.15 | 0.64 | 1.95 | 0.62 | 2.57 |
|  | Eating Places | 0.13 | * | 0.13 | 0.15 | 0.01 | 0.16 | 0.28 | 0.01 | 0.29 |
|  | At Work | 0.07 | 0.01 | 0.08 | 0.15 | 0.03 | 0.18 | 0.22 | 0.04 | 0.26 |
|  | Total | 1.66 | 0.48 | 2.14 | 0.79 | 0.19 | 0.98 | 2.45 | 0.67 | 3.12 |
| 1963: | Home | 1.44 | 0.46 | 1.90 | 0.49 | 0.14 | 0.63 | 1.93 | 0.60 | 2.53 |
|  | Eating Places | 0.11 | * | 0.11 | 0.11 | * | 0.11 | 0.22 | * | 0.22 |
|  | At Work | 0.06 | 0.01 | 0.07 | 0.15 | 0.04 | 0.19 | 0.21 | 0.05 | 0.26 |
|  | Total | 1.61 | 0.47 | 2.08 | 0.75 | 0.18 | 0.93 | 2.36 | 0.65 | 3.01 |
| 1964: | Home | 1.37 | 0.42 | 1.79 | 0.49 | 0.14 | 0.63 | 1.86 | 0.56 | 2.42 |
|  | Eating Places | 0.12 | * | 0.12 | 0.12 | * | 0.12 | 0.24 | * | 0.24 |
|  | At Work | 0.06 | 0.02 | 0.08 | 0.13 | 0.03 | 0.16 | 0.19 | 0.05 | 0.24 |
|  | Total | 1.55 | 0.44 | 1.99 | 0.74 | 0.17 | 0.91 | 2.29 | 0.61 | 2.90 |
| 1965: | Home | 1.30 | 0.41 | 1.71 | 0.46 | 0.12 | 0.58 | 1.76 | 0.53 | 2.29 |
|  | Eating Places | 0.12 | * | 0.12 | 0.12 | * | 0.13 | 0.24 | 0.01 | 0.25 |
|  | At Work | 0.07 | 0.01 | 0.08 | 0.14 | 0.03 | 0.17 | 0.21 | 0.04 | 0.25 |
|  | Total | 1.49 | 0.42 | 1.91 | 0.72 | 0.15 | 0.88 | 2.21 | 0.58 | 2.79 |
| 1966: | Home | 1.29 | 0.43 | 1.72 | 0.46 | 0.13 | 0.59 | 1.75 | 0.56 | 2.31 |
|  | Eating Places | 0.13 | 0.01 | 0.14 | 0.12 | * | 0.12 | 0.25 | 0.01 | 0.26 |
|  | At Work | 0.08 | 0.02 | 0.10 | 0.15 | 0.04 | 0.19 | 0.23 | 0.06 | 0.29 |
|  | Total | 1.50 | 0.46 | 1.96 | 0.73 | 0.17 | 0.90 | 2.23 | 0.63 | 2.86 |
| 1967: | Home | 1.26 | 0.43 | 1.69 | 0.46 | 0.14 | 0.60 | 1.72 | 0.57 | 2.29 |
|  | Eating Places | 0.12 | * | 0.13 | 0.11 | * | 0.12 | 0.23 | 0.02 | 0.25 |
|  | At Work | 0.07 | 0.01 | 0.08 | 0.17 | 0.04 | 0.22 | 0.24 | 0.06 | 0.30 |
|  | Total | 1.45 | 0.45 | 1.90 | 0.74 | 0.20 | 0.94 | 2.19 | 0.65 | 2.84 |

Source: Beverage studies made by Corby Research Service, 1960-1964, and Professional Research Associates Inc., 1965-1966.
(*) Less than .005 cups per person per day.

## C-8. UNITED STATES: REVIEW OF COFFEE CONSUMPTION, 1950-1967.
(Cups Per Person Per Day)

| | 1950 | 1951 | 1952 | 1953 | 1954 | 1955 | 1956 | 1957 | 1958 | 1959 | 1960 | 1961 | 1962 | 1963 | 1964 | 1965 | 1966 | 1967 |
|---|---|---|---|---|---|---|---|---|---|---|---|---|---|---|---|---|---|---|
| **All Coffee** | 2.38 | 2.44 | N.A. | 2.57 | 2.60 | 2.67 | 2.68 | 2.82 | 2.87 | 2.94 | 2.77 | 2.97 | 3.12 | 3.01 | 2.90 | 2.79 | 2.86 | 2.84 |
| **Type:** | | | | | | | | | | | | | | | | | | |
| Regular | N.A. | N.A. | N.A. | 2.31 | 2.30 | 2.30 | 2.22 | 2.32 | 2.32 | 2.34 | 2.21 | 2.33 | 2.45 | 2.36 | 2.29 | 2.21 | 2.23 | 2.19 |
| Instant | N.A. | N.A. | N.A. | .26 | .30 | .37 | .46 | .50 | .55 | .60 | .56 | .64 | .67 | .65 | .61 | .58 | .63 | .65 |
| Decaffeinated* | N.A. | N.A. | N.A. | N.A. | N.A. | N.A. | N.A. | N.A. | .04 | .05 | .08 | .08 | .10 | .09 | .12 | .10 | .13 | .16 |
| **Region:** | | | | | | | | | | | | | | | | | | |
| East | 2.27 | 2.40 | N.A. | 2.34 | 2.40 | 2.56 | 2.52 | 2.72 | 2.62 | 2.76 | 2.54 | 2.64 | 2.91 | 2.76 | 2.54 | 2.50 | 2.66 | 2.39 |
| Midwest | 2.72 | 2.64 | N.A. | 2.86 | 2.92 | 2.94 | 2.88 | 2.99 | 3.13 | 3.22 | 3.15 | 3.37 | 3.34 | 3.30 | 3.20 | 3.14 | 3.23 | 3.18 |
| South | 1.91 | 2.14 | N.A. | 2.26 | 2.35 | 2.57 | 2.37 | 2.48 | 2.56 | 2.54 | 2.27 | 2.56 | 2.78 | 2.54 | 2.61 | 2.48 | 2.53 | 2.63 |
| West | 2.79 | 2.56 | N.A. | 3.01 | 2.86 | 3.16 | 3.11 | 3.25 | 3.41 | 3.31 | 3.23 | 3.51 | 3.52 | 3.56 | 3.38 | 3.09 | 3.00 | 3.19 |
| **Age Group:** | | | | | | | | | | | | | | | | | | |
| 10-14 | .21 | N.A. | N.A. | .20 | .21 | .22 | .18 | .19 | .20 | .16 | .21 | .15 | .18 | .18 | .18 | .12 | .13 | .19 |
| 15-19 | 1.13 | N.A. | N.A. | 1.07 | 1.12 | 1.01 | 1.11 | 1.11 | 1.09 | 1.14 | 1.01 | .96 | 1.09 | .89 | .71 | .77 | .97 | .82 |
| 20-24 | 2.34 | 2.35 | N.A. | 2.47 | 2.52 | 2.62 | 2.70 | 2.60 | 2.98 | 2.80 | 2.71 | 2.93 | 2.99 | 2.70 | 2.30 | 2.42 | 2.25 | 2.22 |
| 25-29 | 2.78 | 2.96 | N.A. | 3.05 | 3.02 | 3.38 | 3.12 | 3.65 | 3.50 | 3.67 | 3.65 | 3.46 | 3.88 | 3.76 | 3.64 | 3.35 | 3.45 | 3.21 |
| 30-39 | 3.02 | 3.22 | N.A. | 3.23 | 3.40 | 3.47 | 3.52 | 3.67 | 4.08 | 4.12 | 3.76 | 4.21 | 4.50 | 4.38 | 4.14 | 4.01 | 4.21 | 3.99 |
| 40-49 | 2.98 | 3.08 | N.A. | 3.33 | 3.29 | 3.39 | 3.50 | 3.74 | 3.83 | 3.99 | 3.74 | 4.13 | 4.44 | 4.27 | 4.33 | 4.16 | 4.05 | 4.48 |
| 50-59 | 2.85 | 2.75 | N.A. | 2.99 | 2.95 | 3.02 | 3.04 | 3.16 | 3.33 | 3.53 | 3.30 | 3.64 | 3.83 | 3.75 | 3.68 | 3.54 | 3.81 | 3.70 |
| 60-69 | 2.22+ | 2.33+ | N.A. | 2.38+ | 2.46+ | 2.65 | 2.69 | 2.75 | 2.78 | 2.78 | 2.84 | 3.03 | 3.01 | 3.17 | 3.06 | 2.96 | 3.09 | 3.16 |
| 70 and over | N.A. | N.A. | N.A. | N.A. | N.A. | 2.21 | 2.06 | 2.29 | 2.28 | 2.28 | 2.32 | 2.41 | 2.39 | 2.40 | 2.47 | 2.47 | 2.66 | 2.50 |
| **Sex:** | | | | | | | | | | | | | | | | | | |
| Male | 2.49 | 2.51 | N.A. | 2.67 | 2.69 | 2.75 | 2.73 | 2.91 | 2.97 | 3.08 | 2.88 | 3.00 | 3.28 | 3.02 | 2.99 | 2.91 | 2.98 | 2.93 |
| Female | 2.28 | 2.35 | N.A. | 2.48 | 2.54 | 2.60 | 2.63 | 2.73 | 2.77 | 2.81 | 2.66 | 2.96 | 2.98 | 3.00 | 2.83 | 2.68 | 2.76 | 2.77 |
| **Location:** | | | | | | | | | | | | | | | | | | |
| Home | 1.98 | 2.00 | N.A. | 2.11 | 2.10 | 2.23 | 2.20 | 2.35 | 2.40 | 2.45 | 2.30 | 2.49 | 2.57 | 2.53 | 2.42 | 2.29 | 2.31 | 2.29 |
| Work | .09 | .14 | N.A. | .18 | .18 | .19 | .20 | .21 | .19 | .22 | .22 | .21 | .26 | .26 | .24 | .25 | .29 | .30 |
| Eating Places | .31 | .30 | N.A. | .28 | .32 | .25 | .28 | .26 | .28 | .27 | .25 | .27 | .29 | .22 | .24 | .25 | .26 | .25 |
| **Time of Day:** | | | | | | | | | | | | | | | | | | |
| Breakfast | 1.03 | 1.04 | N.A. | 1.06 | 1.07 | 1.09 | 1.07 | 1.14 | 1.14 | 1.15 | 1.11 | 1.18 | 1.17 | 1.18 | 1.14 | 1.12 | 1.13 | 1.13 |
| Other Meals | .91 | .92 | N.A. | .94 | .94 | .96 | .96 | .96 | .98 | .96 | .89 | .92 | .98 | .90 | .85 | .79 | .82 | .77 |
| Between Meals | .44 | .48 | N.A. | .57 | .59 | .62 | .65 | .72 | .75 | .83 | .77 | .87 | .97 | .93 | .91 | .88 | .91 | .94 |

*Decaffeinated is not separate from regular and instant coffee but is included in both of the latter types.
+Includes all persons 60 years of age and older.

N.B.: Based on population 10 years of age and over.

## C-20. CANADA: NET IMPORTS OF COFFEE, 1950-1966
(in 60-kilo bags of green-coffee equivalent)

|  | 1950 | 1951 | 1952 | 1953 | 1954 | 1955 | 1956 | 1957 |
|---|---|---|---|---|---|---|---|---|
| Green Coffee Imports | 625,849 | 670,097 | 737,838 | 812,661 | 721,083 | 784,616 | 828,754 | 835,736 |
| Roasted Coffee Imports | 5,586 | 5,473 | 9,137 | 12,625 | 18,868 | 19,312 | 17,501 | 22,011 |
| Soluble Coffee Imports | 9,589 | 11,320 | 20,370 | 24,685 | 22,190 | 41,438 | 87,800 | 119,220 |
| Total Imports | 641,024 | 686,890 | 767,349 | 849,971 | 762,141 | 845,366 | 934,055 | 976,967 |
| Less: Exports | 1,040 | 1,600 | 1,540 | 12,699 | 14,380 | 8,420 | 18,792 | 3,142 |
| Net Imports | 639,984 | 685,290 | 765,809 | 837,272 | 747,761 | 836,946 | 915,263 | 973,825 |
| Population | (13,709,000) | (14,009,000) | (14,459,000) | (14,845,000) | (15,287,000) | (15,698,000) | (16,081,000) | (16,610,000) |
| Net Imports per Capita (Green lbs.) | 6.18 | 6.46 | 7.00 | 7.52 | 6.53 | 7.05 | 7.55 | 7.66 |

Source: Dominion Bureau of Statistics.

N.B.: Negligible quantities of coffee substitutes are included in the Soluble Import-Export data.

## C-20. CANADA: NET IMPORTS OF COFFEE, 1950-1966 (Continued)

(in 60-kilo bags of green coffee equivalent)

|  | 1958 | 1959 | 1960 | 1961 | 1962 | 1963 | 1964 | 1965 | 1966 |
|---|---|---|---|---|---|---|---|---|---|
| Green Coffee Imports | 894,669 | 1,015,141 | 995,046 | 1,118,995 | 1,229,804 | 1,287,538 | 1,246,167 | 1,257,648 | 1,163,602 |
| Roasted Coffee Imports | 21,566 | 18,860 | 16,612 | 17,224 | 17,695 | 20,107 | 19,682 | 23,770 | 31,272 |
| Soluble Coffee Imports | 127,897 | 124,058 | 128,122 | 94,935 | 76,527 | 64,619 | 57,515 | 45,801 | 53,088 |
| Total Imports | 1,044,132 | 1,158,059 | 1,139,780 | 1,231,154 | 1,324,026 | 1,372,264 | 1,323,364 | 1,327,219 | 1,247,962 |
| Less: Exports | 1,311 | 1,476 | 1,994 | 34,576 | 41,740 | 81,290 | 43,728 | 33,810 | 21,525 |
| Net Imports | 1,042,821 | 1,156,583 | 1,137,786 | 1,196,578 | 1,282,286 | 1,290,974 | 1,279,636 | 1,293,409 | 1,226,437 |
| Population | (17,080,000) | (17,483,000) | (17,870,000) | (18,238,000) | (18,570,000) | (18,896,000) | (19,235,000) | (19,571,000) | (19,960,000) |
| Net Imports per Capita (Green lbs.) | 7.99 | 8.67 | 8.34 | 8.59 | 9.09 | 9.02 | 8.80 | 8.74 | 8.13 |

Source: Dominion Bureau of Statistics.

N.B.: Negligible quantities of coffee substitutes are included in the Soluble Import-Export data.

C-25. WORLD: PER CAPITA IMPORTS OF GREEN COFFEE IN PRINCIPAL COUNTRIES, 1956-1966.

(in pounds)

| | 1956 | 1957 | 1958 | 1959 | 1960 | 1961 | 1962 | 1963 | 1964 | 1965 | 1966 |
|---|---|---|---|---|---|---|---|---|---|---|---|
| **WESTERN EUROPE** | | | | | | | | | | | |
| **EEC** | | | | | | | | | | | |
| Belgium – Luxembourg | 14.6 | 12.1 | 12.4 | 13.9 | 15.6 | 14.4 | 12.8 | 12.8 | 14.7 | 15.2 | 12.1 |
| France | 9.8 | 9.5 | 9.5 | 9.6 | 10.1 | 9.7 | 9.8 | 10.1 | 10.5 | 9.8 | 10.1 |
| Germany (F.R.) | 5.8 | 6.3 | 6.5 | 7.8 | 8.2 | 8.3 | 9.1 | 9.4 | 9.8 | 10.7 | 10.7 |
| Italy | 3.5 | 3.5 | 3.7 | 3.8 | 4.4 | 4.6 | 5.0 | 5.1 | 5.2 | 5.1 | 5.2 |
| Netherlands | 8.4 | 7.9 | 8.5 | 9.9 | 10.6 | 13.2 | 11.9 | 13.9 | 15.1 | 14.8 | 15.1 |
| **OTHER WESTERN EUROPE** | | | | | | | | | | | |
| Austria | 2.3 | 2.6 | 2.8 | 3.1 | 3.8 | 3.8 | 4.2 | 4.6 | 5.3 | 5.1 | 5.3 |
| Denmark | 15.6 | 16.2 | 18.1 | 18.8 | 20.3 | 20.8 | 21.7 | 24.9 | 22.6 | 22.9 | 24.5 |
| Finland | 16.8 | 15.4 | 15.8 | 17.1 | 16.9 | 17.4 | 19.0 | 20.2 | 22.9 | 19.3 | 21.9 |
| Greece | 1.5 | 1.5 | 1.8 | 1.6 | 2.0 | 2.0 | 2.3 | 2.4 | 2.5 | 2.1 | 2.6 |
| Norway | 14.1 | 15.0 | 16.5 | 15.6 | 17.8 | 16.5 | 18.6 | 20.2 | 19.8 | 17.1 | 20.3 |
| Portugal | 2.1 | 2.1 | 2.7 | 2.6 | 0.8 | 3.0 | 3.0 | 3.2 | 2.6 | 3.1 | 3.2 |
| Spain | 0.7 | 0.8 | 0.9 | 1.4 | 1.2 | 1.9 | 1.7 | 2.7 | 2.9 | 3.4 | 3.8 |
| Sweden | 17.5 | 17.2 | 18.7 | 20.1 | 21.6 | 22.9 | 24.4 | 25.1 | 26.3 | 26.2 | 27.4 |
| Switzerland | 9.9 | 9.5 | 9.8 | 11.3 | 12.4 | 13.2 | 12.6 | 13.1 | 13.9 | 16.3 | 14.8 |
| Turkey | 0.3 | 0.1 | – | 0.1 | 0.9 | 1.7 | 0.1 | 0.3 | 0.1 | 0.2 | 0.2 |
| United Kingdom | 1.9 | 2.0 | 1.9 | 2.3 | 2.3 | 2.3 | 2.7 | 3.1 | 3.2 | 2.4 | 3.3 |
| Yugoslavia | – | – | – | – | – | – | – | 1.6 | 1.8 | 2.0 | 3.1 |
| **OTHERS** | | | | | | | | | | | |
| Argentina | – | – | – | – | – | – | – | 3.0 | 3.1 | 3.0 | 3.9 |
| Australia | – | – | – | 2.2 | 2.4 | 2.4 | 2.5 | 2.4 | 2.4 | 2.8 | 3.1 |
| Canada | – | – | – | – | – | – | – | 9.0 | 8.5 | 8.5 | 7.7 |
| Chile | – | – | – | 1.9 | 2.7 | 1.8 | 1.1 | 3.0 | 1.9 | 2.3 | 2.3 |
| Israel | – | – | – | 3.6 | 3.9 | 3.4 | 4.7 | 5.1 | 6.3 | 4.3 | 5.0 |
| Japan | – | – | – | – | – | – | – | – | 0.5 | 0.5 | 1.0 |
| Jordan | – | – | – | – | – | – | – | – | 2.1 | 2.0 | 2.0 |
| Morocco | – | – | – | 1.1 | 1.6 | 1.4 | 1.5 | 1.9 | 2.4 | 1.5 | 1.4 |
| New Zealand | – | – | – | – | – | – | – | – | 2.6 | 2.8 | 3.3 |
| Tunisia | – | – | – | 1.4 | 1.3 | 1.3 | 1.2 | 1.2 | 1.0 | 1.0 | 0.7 |
| South Africa | – | – | – | 1.7 | 1.7 | 1.5 | 1.6 | 1.7 | 1.3 | 1.3 | 1.5 |
| United Arab Republic | – | – | – | 0.3 | 0.6 | 0.3 | 0.2 | 0.4 | 0.2 | 0.2 | 0.2 |
| United States | 16.0 | 15.7 | 15.6 | 15.9 | 15.7 | 15.9 | 15.9 | 15.5 | 15.2 | 14.5 | 14.8 |

Source: Department of Statistics and Economic Research

## CP-17. UNITED STATES: AVERAGE ANNUAL SPOT PRICES OF SELECTED GROWTHS AND TYPES OF COFFEES IN THE NEW YORK MARKET, 1953-1966

(U.S. Cents Per Pound)

| | 1953 | 1954 | 1955 | 1956 | 1957 | 1958 | 1959 | 1960 | 1961 | 1962 | 1963 | 1964 | 1965 | 1966 |
|---|---|---|---|---|---|---|---|---|---|---|---|---|---|---|
| **Brazil** Santos 4 | 57.93 | 78.71 | 57.09 | 58.10 | 56.92 | 48.41 | 36.97 | 36.60 | 36.01 | 33.96 | 34.11 | 46.66 | 44.71 | 40.83 |
| **Columbia** MAMS[a] | 59.93 | 80.09 | 64.63 | 73.99 | 63.94 | 52.34 | 45.22 | 44.89 | 43.62 | 40.77 | 39.55 | 48.80 | 48.49 | 47.43 |
| **El Salvador** Central Standard[b] | 55.67 | N.A. | 59.46 | 67.27 | 62.15 | 50.17 | 42.47 | 41.54 | 37.93 | 35.86 | 35.44 | 47.20 | 45.55 | 42.54 |
| **Guatamala** Prime Washed[c] | 56.85 | N.A. | 60.28 | 68.48 | 62.94 | 49.81 | 42.62 | 41.33 | 37.55 | 35.83 | 35.40 | 47.16 | 45.51 | 42.25 |
| **Mexico** Prime Washed[d] | 57.74 | 78.37 | 60.12 | 70.88 | 60.87 | 49.93 | 42.89 | 41.61 | 37.53 | 35.87 | 35.56 | 47.16 | 45.54 | 42.41 |
| **Ethiopia** Djimmas UGQ[e] | 52.66 | 72.48 | 50.48 | 55.73 | 49.94 | 44.88 | 36.59 | 34.85 | 34.75 | 32.68 | 32.75 | 43.75 | 42.76 | 40.44 |
| **Port. West Africa** Ambriz No. 2AA[f] | 49.22 | 63.02 | 45.23 | 38.35 | 40.22 | 40.25 | 30.60 | 25.27 | 19.93 | 21.55 | 28.73 | 36.38 | 31.59 | 33.98 |
| **Uganda** W & C No. 10[g] | 47.59 | 57.86 | 38.41 | 33.59 | 34.65 | 38.10 | 29.29 | 20.65 | 18.92 | 21.07 | 28.14 | 35.82 | 31.33 | 33.88 |

Source: Department of Statics and Economic Research, PACB

[a] Medellin prior to 1958.
[b] Good Washed prior to 1958.
[c] Straight Hard Bean prior to 1958.
[d] Coatepec prior to 1958.
[e] Abyssinia prior to 1956.
[f] Ambriz prior to 1958.
[g] Native Uganda prior to 1958.

## CP-1. UNITED STATES: SPOT
Monthly Average,
In U. S. cents

|  |  | Jan. | Feb. | Mar. | Apr. | May |
|---|---|---|---|---|---|---|
| BRAZIL | Santos type 2/3 | 43.45 | 42.48 | 42.03 | 41.83 | 41.23 |
|  | Santos type 4 | 43.13 | 42.18 | 41.73 | 41.55 | 40.93 |
|  | Parana type 4 | 41.40 | 41.15 | 40.78 | 40.63 | 40.05 |
| COLOMBIA | MAMS | 49.45 | 49.68 | 49.53 | 48.93 | 48.30 |
| COSTA RICA | Hard bean | 47.33 | 46.13 | N.A. | 44.83 | 43.92 |
|  | Good Atlantic | 46.63 | N.A. | N.A. | N.A. | 43.21 |
| DOMINICAN REPUBLIC | Bani | 45.28 | 43.68 | 42.55 | 42.35 | 41.75 |
|  | Cibao | 44.30 | 42.88 | 42.10 | 41.83 | 41.05 |
| ECUADOR | Washed | N.A. | N.A. | N.A. | N.A. | N.A. |
|  | Extra Sup. Nat. | N.A. | N.A. | N.A. | N.A. | 35.50 |
| EL SALVADOR | High grown | 46.94 | N.A. | 43.91 | N.A. | 43.42 |
|  | Central Standard | 46.40 | 44.75 | 43.63 | 43.88 | 43.18 |
| GUATEMALA | Prime washed | 46.30 | 44.35 | 43.23 | 43.25 | 42.55 |
|  | Good washed | 46.07 | N.A. | 43.00 | 42.93 | 42.23 |
| HAITI | Washed | N.A. | N.A. | 42.75 | N.A. | N.A. |
|  | XX T.A.L.M. | 41.79 | 41.25 | 40.38 | 40.94 | 40.54 |
| MEXICO | High grown | 47.13 | N.A. | 44.35 | 44.13 | 43.66 |
|  | Prime washed | 46.40 | 44.45 | 43.38 | 43.40 | 43.00 |
| NICARAGUA | Washed | N.A. | 44.00 | N.A. | N.A. | 42.00 |
| PERU | Hard bean hand picked | 46.88 | 44.98 | N.A. | N.A. | 43.94 |
|  | Hard bean machine cleaned | 46.57 | 44.63 | 43.35 | 43.73 | 43.25 |
| VENEZUELA | Tachira fine washed | 46.98 | 45.05 | 43.83 | 43.78 | 43.75 |
|  | Tachira good washed | 46.65 | 44.80 | 43.48 | 43.20 | 43.33 |
| ETHIOPIA | Djimmas, UGQ | 43.33 | 42.18 | 41.40 | 41.15 | 40.45 |
| RWANDA & BURUNDI | Ociru #2 | N.A. | N.A. | N.A. | N.A. | N.A. |
| CONGO | Robusta N2B | N.A. | N.A. | N.A. | N.A. | N.A. |
| INDONESIA | EK 20/25 | 34.13 | N.A. | N.A. | N.A. | N.A. |
| IVORY COAST | Superior | N.A. | 33.83 | 33.79 | N.A. | N.A. |
| MADAGASCAR | Superior | N.A. | 33.94 | 33.04 | N.A. | N.A. |
| PORT. W. AFRICA | Ambriz No. 2 AA | 36.95 | 35.05 | 34.60 | 35.08 | 35.30 |
| UGANDA | Washed Cleaned | 36.85 | 34.93 | 34.43 | 34.83 | 34.95 |
|  | Native standard | 36.68 | 34.70 | 34.20 | 34.60 | 34.78 |

NOTE: P.A.C.B. weekly survey of the New York market, ordinarily made on Thursday. Prices quoted include all marketing charges such as freight, insurance, weighing, financing, etc.

**COFFEE PRICES, 1966**
High & Low
per pound

| June | July | Aug. | Sept. | Oct. | Nov. | Dec. | Average | High | Low |
|------|------|------|-------|------|------|------|---------|------|-----|
| 40.98 | 40.90 | 40.73 | 40.48 | 40.08 | 39.83 | 39.55 | 41.13 | 43.75 | 39.38 |
| 40.63 | 40.50 | 40.45 | 40.23 | 39.80 | 39.55 | 39.33 | 40.83 | 43.50 | 39.25 |
| 39.38 | 39.38 | 39.43 | 39.03 | 38.18 | 37.93 | 37.78 | 39.59 | 41.75 | 37.63 |
| 48.48 | 48.08 | 46.80 | 45.40 | 45.20 | 45.10 | 44.18 | 47.43 | 49.88 | 44.00 |
| N.A. | 43.10 | 42.88 | N.A. | 42.17 | N.A. | 41.38 | 43.97 | 47.50 | 41.25 |
| 43.06 | 42.21 | 41.94 | N.A. | 41.50 | N.A. | 40.88 | 42.78 | 46.75 | 40.50 |
| 41.22 | 40.68 | 40.50 | 40.00 | 39.13 | 38.95 | 38.78 | 41.24 | 45.50 | 38.15 |
| 40.63 | 39.98 | 39.80 | 39.08 | 38.43 | 38.40 | 38.28 | 40.56 | 44.50 | 38.00 |
| 40.78 | 40.18 | 40.28 | 39.55 | 38.45 | 38.68 | 38.43 | 39.48 | 41.38 | 38.25 |
| 35.50 | N.A. | N.A. | 34.71 | N.A. | N.A. | N.A. | N.A. | N.A. | N.A. |
| 43.17 | 42.29 | 42.23 | 42.30 | 41.28 | 40.75 | 40.03 | 42.63 | 47.50 | 39.63 |
| 42.50 | 41.98 | 41.78 | 41.78 | 40.85 | 40.10 | 39.68 | 42.54 | 46.88 | 39.50 |
| 41.80 | 41.55 | 41.73 | 41.68 | 40.85 | 40.08 | 39.60 | 42.25 | 46.88 | 39.25 |
| 41.71 | 41.21 | N.A. | 41.56 | N.A. | N.A. | 39.21 | 42.24 | 46.38 | 38.88 |
| N.A. | N.A. | N.A. | N.A. | N.A. | N.A. | N.A. | N.A. | N.A. | N.A. |
| 40.04 | N.A. | N.A. | N.A. | N.A. | N.A. | N.A. | N.A. | N.A. | N.A. |
| 43.10 | 42.64 | 42.25 | 42.33 | N.A. | N.A. | 40.25 | 43.32 | 47.38 | 40.00 |
| 42.43 | 41.83 | 41.80 | 41.65 | 40.73 | 40.15 | 39.75 | 42.41 | 46.88 | 39.50 |
| 41.50 | 41.00 | N.A. | N.A. | N.A. | N.A. | N.A. | N.A. | N.A. | N.A. |
| 42.92 | 42.44 | 42.34 | 42.10 | N.A. | 41.00 | 40.35 | 42.99 | 47.25 | 39.75 |
| 42.65 | 42.05 | 42.05 | 41.80 | 41.03 | 40.85 | 39.84 | 42.65 | 47.00 | 39.63 |
| 42.88 | 42.33 | 42.00 | N.A. | 41.69 | 41.68 | 40.90 | 43.17 | 47.50 | 40.38 |
| 42.50 | 41.85 | N.A. | N.A. | 41.46 | 41.54 | 40.33 | 42.91 | 47.13 | 40.00 |
| 39.70 | 40.23 | 40.85 | 40.05 | 39.23 | 38.78 | 37.90 | 40.44 | 43.50 | 37.50 |
| N.A. | N.A. | 41.50 | 41.33 | 40.73 | 40.10 | 39.88 | N.A. | N.A. | 39.63 |
| N.A. | N.A. | N.A. | N.A. | N.A. | N.A. | N.A. | N.A. | N.A. | N.A. |
| N.A. | 28.75 | 25.73 | 23.40 | 24.23 | 25.88 | 27.00 | 27.02 | 34.63 | 22.50 |
| N.A. | N.A. | N.A. | N.A. | N.A. | N.A. | N.A. | N.A. | N.A. | N.A. |
| N.A. | N.A. | N.A. | 30.25 | 31.33 | N.A. | N.A. | N.A. | N.A. | N.A. |
| 33.88 | 33.62 | 33.13 | 32.28 | 32.83 | 32.80 | 32.18 | 33.98 | 37.25 | 31.75 |
| 33.70 | 33.33 | 32.95 | 32.23 | 32.73 | 33.08 | 32.53 | 33.88 | 37.13 | 31.88 |
| 33.45 | 33.13 | 32.70 | 31.98 | 32.38 | 32.75 | 31.97 | 33.61 | 37.00 | 31.38 |

## CP-2. UNITED STATES SPOT COFFEE PRICES ANNUAL
(in U.S. Cents)

| | | 1947 | 1948 | 1949 | 1950 | 1951 | 1952 |
|---|---|---|---|---|---|---|---|
| BRAZIL | Santos type 2/3 (a) | 27.85 | 28.51 | 33.81 | 52.51 | 55.10 | 54.73 |
| | Santos type 4 | 26.72 | 27.06 | 31.76 | 50.52 | 54.20 | 54.04 |
| | Parana type 4 (b) | N.A. | N.A. | N.A. | N.A. | 53.14 | 53.19 |
| COLOMBIA | MAMS (c) | 30.11 | 32.54 | 37.41 | 53.25 | 58.74 | 57.01 |
| COSTA RICA | Hard bean (d) | 30.37 | 32.46 | 37.49 | 53.67 | 58.82 | 57.25 |
| | Good Atlantic (e) | 25.51 | 28.78 | 34.74 | 51.05 | 57.48 | 56.22 |
| DOMINICAN REPUBLIC | Bani (f) | 26.85 | 28.12 | 32.18 | 49.85 | 54.23 | 53.19 |
| | Cibao (g) | 22.98 | 22.55 | 28.56 | 44.49 | N.A. | N.A. |
| ECUADOR | Washed | N.A. | N.A. | N.A. | N.A. | N.A. | 54.04 |
| | Extra Sup. Nat. (h) | 20.91 | 18.06 | 25.56 | 43.84 | 47.73 | 47.31 |
| EL SALVADOR | High grown (i) | 29.86 | 32.17 | 36.76 | 52.98 | 57.71 | 56.42 |
| | Central Standard (j) | 25.78 | 26.05 | 30.68 | 46.47 | 48.40 | 44.66 |
| GUATEMALA | Prime washed (k) | N.A. | N.A. | N.A. | N.A. | 58.58 | 57.05 |
| | Good washed (l) | 28.59 | 30.58 | 34.88 | 51.37 | 55.35 | 54.83 |
| HAITI | Washed | 26.70 | 28.25 | 32.42 | 50.13 | 54.70 | 53.99 |
| | XX T.A.L.M. | 23.88 | 23.85 | 28.00 | 46.15 | 51.68 | 50.89 |
| MEXICO | High grown (m) | 30.37 | 32.28 | 36.94 | 52.60 | 57.34 | 56.15 |
| | Prime washed (n) | 28.67 | 30.69 | 35.68 | 51.55 | 56.43 | 54.94 |
| NICARAGUA | Washed | 26.97 | 28.40 | 33.11 | 50.82 | 55.76 | 54.90 |
| PERU | Hard bean hand picked | N.A. | N.A. | N.A. | N.A. | N.A. | N.A. |
| | Hard bean machine cleaned | N.A. | N.A. | N.A. | N.A. | N.A. | N.A. |
| VENEZUELA | Tachira fine washed (o) | 29.56 | 31.42 | 36.76 | 52.73 | 58.02 | 56.13 |
| | Tachira good washed (p) | 25.01 | 25.81 | 31.14 | 48.03 | 54.93 | 53.79 |
| ETHIOPIA | Djimmas, UGQ (q) | N.A. | N.A. | N.A. | N.A. | N.A. | 50.66 |
| RWANDA-BURUNDI | Ociru No. 2 | N.A. | N.A. | N.A. | N.A. | N.A. | N.A. |
| CONGO | Robusta N2B | N.A. | N.A. | N.A. | N.A. | N.A. | N.A. |
| INDONESIA | EK 20/25 (r) | N.A. | N.A. | N.A. | N.A. | N.A. | N.A. |
| IVORY COAST | Superior | N.A. | N.A. | N.A. | N.A. | N.A. | N.A. |
| MADAGASCAR | Superior | N.A. | N.A. | N.A. | N.A. | N.A. | N.A. |
| PORT. W. AFRICA | Ambriz No. 2 AA (s) | 18.88 | 18.67 | 25.43 | 41.53 | 47.56 | 46.17 |
| UGANDA | Washed Cleaned (t) | 19.00 | 18.76 | 19.62 | N.A. | N.A. | N.A. |
| | Native Standard (u) | 17.99 | 17.79 | 18.94 | 40.14 | 46.85 | 44.03 |

Source: Department of Statistics and Economic Research, Pan American Coffee Bureau.

(a) Santos 2 from 1947 to 1963. (b) Type 4 1951 to 1958. Type 4/5 1959 to 1963. (c) Marrizales 1947 to 1957. (d) High grown 1947 to 1950. Strictly Hard 1951 to 1960. (e) Washed low grade 1947 to 1951. (f) Washed 1947 to 1950. Good washed 1951 to 1958. (g) Natural 1947 to 1950. (h) Natural 1947 to 1950. (i) Washed high grown 1947 to 1952. (j) Natural 1947 to 1952. Good washed 1953 to 1957. (k)

**FOR THE NEW YORK MARKET, 1947-1966**
**AVERAGES**
Per Pound)

| 1953 | 1954 | 1955 | 1956 | 1957 | 1958 | 1959 | 1960 | 1961 | 1962 | 1963 | 1964 | 1965 | 1966 |
|------|------|------|------|------|------|------|------|------|------|------|------|------|------|
| 58.75 | 79.65 | 58.13 | 59.49 | 58.50 | 49.23 | 37.47 | 36.97 | 36.40 | 34.31 | 34.37 | 46.96 | 44.99 | 41.13 |
| 57.93 | 78.71 | 57.09 | 58.10 | 56.92 | 48.41 | 36.97 | 36.60 | 36.01 | 33.96 | 34.11 | 46.66 | 44.71 | 40.83 |
| 57.19 | 77.70 | 54.99 | 53.52 | 53.43 | 47.29 | 36.09 | 35.67 | 34.78 | 32.68 | 32.94 | 45.32[4] | 43.19 | 39.59 |
| 59.82 | 80.02 | 64.57 | 73.97 | 63.94 | 52.34 | 45.22 | 44.89 | 43.62 | 40.77 | 39.55 | 48.80 | 48.49 | 47.43 |
| 57.09 | N.A. | 60.42 | N.A. | N.A. | 51.33 | N.A. | 42.40 | 39.44 | N.A. | 37.61 | 48.46 | 46.19 | 43.97 |
| 56.06 | N.A. | 58.95 | N.A. | 63.31 | N.A. | N.A. | N.A. | 38.69 | 36.93 | N.A. | N.A. | 45.34 | 42.78 |
| 56.53 | 76.92 | 58.85 | 62.73 | 58.89 | 47.91 | 40.89 | 39.52 | 37.18 | 34.96 | 34.84 | 46.34 | 44.33 | 41.24 |
| N.A. | N.A. | N.A. | N.A. | N.A. | 46.24 | 39.62 | 37.97 | 36.11 | 33.89 | 33.84 | 45.44 | 43.57 | 40.56 |
| 56.78 | 76.58 | 59.74 | 64.39 | 58.89 | 47.80 | 40.90 | 38.11 | 36.27 | N.A. | 33.88 | 46.51 | 43.79 | 39.48 |
| 51.23 | 62.96 | 47.76 | 47.79 | 48.41 | N.A. | N.A. | N.A. | N.A. | N.A. | N.A. | N.A. | 38.08 | N.A. |
| 56.41 | N.A. | 61.25 | 68.84 | 62.82 | 50.85 | N.A. | 42.20 | 38.58 | 36.54 | 36.11 | 47.48 | 45.68 | 42.63 |
| 55.67 | N.A. | 59.46 | 67.27 | 62.15 | 50.17 | 42.47 | 41.54 | 37.93 | 35.86 | 35.44 | 47.20 | 45.55 | 42.54 |
| 56.85 | N.A. | 60.28 | 68.48 | 62.94 | 49.81 | 42.62 | 41.33 | 37.55 | 35.83 | 35.40 | 47.16 | 45.51 | 42.25 |
| 55.21 | N.A. | 58.38 | 67.56 | 61.70 | 49.11 | 41.98 | 40.94 | 37.38 | N.A. | 35.40 | 46.36 | 44.79 | 42.24 |
| 52.41 | 75.87 | 59.23 | 64.87 | 60.53 | 48.02 | 40.20 | 40.12 | 36.45 | 35.19 | N.A. | N.A. | N.A. | N.A. |
| 50.29 | 72.22 | 52.75 | 52.65 | 52.01 | 42.68 | 35.23 | 33.59 | 32.63 | 30.01 | 31.03 | 43.05 | N.A. | N.A. |
| 57.74 | 78.37 | 60.12 | 70.88 | 60.87 | 50.76 | 43.20 | 42.43 | 39.27 | 36.90 | 36.51 | 47.80 | 45.69 | 43.32 |
| 56.89 | 77.24 | 59.31 | 69.75 | 60.29 | 49.93 | 42.89 | 41.61 | 37.53 | 35.87 | 35.56 | 47.16 | 45.54 | 42.41 |
| 56.24 | N.A. | 55.23 | 66.62 | N.A. | N.A. | N.A. | N.A. | N.A. | N.A. | 34.87 | N.A. | N.A. | N.A. |
| N.A. | N.A. | N.A. | N.A. | N.A. | N.A. | N.A. | N.A. | N.A. | N.A. | N.A. | 48.15 | 45.15 | 42.99 |
| N.A. | N.A. | N.A. | N.A. | N.A. | N.A. | N.A. | N.A. | N.A. | N.A. | N.A. | 47.72 | 45.24 | 42.65 |
| 58.48 | 78.60 | 61.84 | 70.87 | 60.98 | 49.94 | 42.93 | 41.45 | 37.87 | 36.32 | 35.76 | 47.52 | 45.80 | 43.17 |
| 54.08 | 73.82 | 53.30 | 70.99 | 61.07 | 49.98 | 42.94 | 41.56 | 37.40 | 35.90 | 35.48 | 47.15 | 45.32 | 42.91 |
| 52.66 | 72.48 | 50.48 | 55.73 | 49.94 | 44.88 | 36.59 | 34.85 ugq | 34.75 | 32.68 | 32.75 | 43.75 | 42.76 | 40.44 |
| N.A. | N.A. | N.A. | N.A. | N.A. | N.A. | 41.40 | N.A. | 36.46 | N.A. | 33.90 | 47.96 | N.A. | N.A. |
| N.A. | N.A. | N.A. | N.A. | 39.67 | 30.34 | 23.80 | 19.30 | N.A. | 29.37 | 35.82 | 29.86 | N.A. | |
| N.A. | N.A. | N.A. | N.A. | N.A. | N.A. | N.A. | N.A. | N.A. | N.A. | N.A. | 36.01 | N.A. | 27.02 |
| N.A. | N.A. | N.A. | N.A. | N.A. | N.A. | N.A. | N.A. | N.A. | N.A. | N.A. | 35.78 | 29.40 | N.A. |
| N.A. | N.A. | N.A. | 31.64 | 33.86 | 36.39 | 27.19 | 19.28 | N.A. | N.A. | 28.21 | 35.54 | 28.73 | N.A. |
| 49.22 | 63.02 | 45.23 | 38.35 | 40.22 | 40.25 | 30.60 | 25.27 | 19.93 | 21.55 | 28.73 | 36.38 | 31.59 | 33.98 |
| N.A. | N.A. | N.A. | N.A. | N.A. | 38.10 | 29.29 | 20.65 | 18.92 | 21.07 | 28.14 | 35.82 | 31.33 | 33.88 |
| 47.59 | 57.86 | 38.41 | 33.59 | 34.65 | 37.57 | 28.72 | 20.18 | 18.48 | 20.63 | 27.86 | 35.56 | 31.12 | 33.61 |

Good washed 1947 to 1950. Str. hard bean 1951 to 1957. (l) Bourbon 1947 to 1950. (m) Coatepec 1947 to 1957. (n) Tapachula 1947 to 1957. (o) Tachira washed 1947 to 1950. Maracaibo washed 1951 to 1960. (p) Tachira natural 1947 to 1955. Tachira washed 1956 to 1960. (q) Abyssinia 1952 to 1955. (r) AP-1 1964-65. (s) Amboim 1947 to 1950. Ambriz 1950 to 1957. (t) Washed 1947 to 1950. Natural 1951 to 1957. W&C No. 10 1958 to 1963. (u) Natural 1947 to 1950. Native Uganda 1951 to 1957. Native No. 10 1958 to 1963.

A-131

**CP-3. SPOT COFFEE**

(Basis MAMS)

(U. S. cents

| 1953 | JAN. | FEB. | MAR. | APR. | MAY |
|---|---|---|---|---|---|
| MAMS | 55.80 | 56.42 | 59.15 | 55.95 | 55.67 |
| Santos 4 | − 1.85 | − 1.67 | − 1.82 | + 0.10 | − 0.54 |
| C.R. Strictly hard | + 0.70 | + 0.71 | − 0.73 | + 0.22 | + 0.13 |
| Cuba Wsh. | − | − | − | − | − |
| D. R. Bani | − 3.20 | − 2.77 | − 2.90 | − 1.65 | − 1.68 |
| Ecuador Wsh. | − 2.25 | − 2.37 | − 3.65 | − 2.30 | − 2.02 |
| El Sal. Wsh. Hi Grown | − 0.67 | − 0.85 | − 0.98 | − 0.25 | − 0.37 |
| Guat. Prime Wsh. | + 0.20 | + 0.39 | − 0.73 | − 0.05 | − 0.17 |
| Haiti Wsh. | − 2.00 | − 1.97 | − 2.07 | − 1.13 | − 1.23 |
| Mexican High Grown | − 1.20 | − 1.47 | − 1.23 | − 0.65 | − 0.56 |
| Nic. Good Wsh. | − 2.30 | − 2.52 | − 2.15 | − 1.15 | − 1.06 |
| Venez. Maracaibo Wsh. | − 1.60 | − 1.97 | − 1.48 | − 0.75 | − 1.02 |
| Bel. Congo Ociru #2 | − 0.55 | − 0.42 | − 0.25 | − 0.50 | − 0.95 |
| Yemen Mocha | + 3.00 | + 2.23 | + 0.75 | + 1.02 | − 0.03 |
| Ethiopia Djimmas UGQ | − 6.61 | − 7.09 | − 5.55 | − 5.20 | − 6.30 |
| Ambriz No. 2 AA | −12.45 | −10.97 | − 8.60 | − 7.05 | − 8.05 |
| Uganda W&C #10 | −13.83 | −12.40 | − 9.75 | − 8.27 | − 9.07 |
| Ivory Coast Courant | − | − | − | − | − |

| 1954 | | | | | |
|---|---|---|---|---|---|
| MAMS | 71.85 | 77.82 | 91.50 | 91.15 | 85.20 |
| Santos 4 | − 2.10 | − 1.82 | − 3.70 | − 1.40 | + 0.75 |
| C. R. Strictly hard | − | − | − | − | − |
| Cuba Wsh. | − | − | − | − | − |
| D. R. Bani | − 3.80 | − 3.42 | − 4.85 | − 3.00 | − 1.60 |
| Ecuador Wsh. | − 3.90 | − 3.27 | − 5.67 | − 4.02 | − 2.90 |
| El Sal. Wsh. Hi Grown | − | − | − | − | − |
| Guat. Prime Wsh. | − | − | − | − | − |
| Haiti Wsh. | − 3.00 | − 3.52 | − 5.87 | − | − 1.57 |
| Mexico High Grown | − 1.85 | − 2.02 | − 2.00 | − 1.50 | − 1.15 |
| Nic. Good Wsh. | − | − | − | − | − |
| Venez. Maracaibo Wsh. | − 1.65 | − 1.77 | − 3.10 | − 1.80 | − 0.70 |
| Bel. Congo Ociru #2 | − 3.60 | − | − | − 2.35 | − 1.30 |
| Yemen Mocha | − 1.20 | − 1.82 | − 3.25 | − 1.80 | + 1.00 |
| Ethiopia Djimmas UGQ | − 7.75 | − 7.37 | −10.25 | − 7.65 | − 5.20 |
| Ambriz No. 2 AA | −15.20 | −16.72 | −19.10 | −16.30 | −12.90 |
| Uganda W&C #10 | −16.95 | −19.37 | −25.65 | −22.90 | −20.95 |
| Ivory Coast Courant | − | − | − | − | − |

| 1955 | | | | | |
|---|---|---|---|---|---|
| MAMS | 70.90 | 60.55 | 59.38 | 61.50 | 59.03 |
| Santos 4 | − 4.05 | − 2.32 | − 1.43 | − 3.68 | − 4.83 |
| C.R. Strictly Hard | − | − 0.42 | − 0.19 | − 0.10 | + 0.35 |
| Cuba Wsh. | − | − | − | − | − |
| D. R. Bani | − 4.65 | − 4.20 | − 4.38 | − 5.15 | − 4.41 |
| Ecuador Wsh. | − 3.65 | − 4.05 | − 4.03 | − 5.15 | − 4.28 |
| El Sal. Wsh. Hi Grown | − 2.15 | − 2.65 | − 1.75 | − 3.53 | − 3.18 |
| Guat. Prime Wsh. | − | − 0.99 | − 0.66 | − 1.10 | − 0.27 |
| Haiti Wsh. | − 4.00 | − 4.15 | − 4.03 | − 5.25 | − 6.03 |
| Mexico High Grown | − 3.35 | − 3.22 | − 2.38 | − 3.88 | − 4.16 |
| Nic. Good Wsh. | − | − 4.55 | − 4.03 | − 5.20 | − 4.78 |
| Venez. Maracaibo Wsh. | − 2.10 | − 3.30 | − 3.43 | − 4.22 | − 3.21 |
| Bel. Congo Ociru #2 | − 2.67 | − 2.75 | − 2.33 | − 3.75 | − 3.53 |
| Yemen Mocha | − 1.35 | − 1.10 | − 3.03 | − 4.80 | − 2.43 |
| Ethiopia Djimmas UGQ | − 7.80 | − 6.45 | − 8.63 | −12.65 | −16.73 |
| Ambriz No. 2 AA | −18.90 | − 8.00 | − 7.13 | − 9.95 | −14.18 |
| Uganda W&C #10 | −23.25 | −13.70 | −16.73 | −23.85 | −26.63 |
| Ivory Coast Courant | − | − | − | − | − |

**PRICE DIFFERENTIALS**
1953-1966

per pound)

| JUNE | JULY | AUG. | SEPT. | OCT. | NOV. | DEC. | AVERAGE | HIGH | LOW |
|---|---|---|---|---|---|---|---|---|---|
| 56.53 | 58.88 | 61.28 | 63.95 | 63.40 | 65.50 | 66.60 | 59.93 | 67.25 | 55.00 |
| − 0.35 | + 0.17 | + 0.02 | − 2.40 | − 4.10 | − 7.30 | − 4.25 | − 2.00 | − 1.75 | − 1.25 |
| + 0.10 | + 0.12 | − | − | − | − | − | − 2.84 | − 6.75 | + 0.15 |
| − | − | − | − | − | − | − | − | − | − |
| − 2.00 | − 3.23 | − 3.28 | − 4.15 | − 4.15 | − 6.60 | − 5.20 | − 3.40 | − 4.00 | − 2.50 |
| − 2.23 | − 2.63 | − 3.03 | − 3.70 | − 3.60 | − 5.45 | − 4.55 | − 3.15 | − 4.00 | − 2.00 |
| − 0.48 | − 0.03 | − | − | − | − | − | − 3.52 | − 6.75 | − 0.35 |
| + 0.02 | − 0.13 | − | − | − | − | − | − 3.08 | − 6.25 | − 0.35 |
| − 1.69 | − 2.38 | − | − 2.95 | − 4.07 | − 5.65 | − 3.80 | − 7.52 | − 3.25 | − 1.50 |
| − 0.87 | − 0.88 | − | − | − | − 2.45 | − 1.55 | − 2.19 | − 1.75 | − 0.75 |
| − 1.45 | − 1.88 | − | − | − | − | − 2.60 | − 3.69 | − 3.25 | − 1.75 |
| − 1.20 | − 1.60 | − 1.20 | − 1.50 | − 1.70 | − 2.10 | − 1.27 | − 1.45 | − 1.60 | − 1.25 |
| − 1.11 | − 0.54 | − 0.78 | − 1.90 | − 0.90 | − 1.87 | − 1.85 | − 0.97 | − 2.00 | − 0.75 |
| + 0.37 | + 0.37 | − 0.08 | − 0.95 | − 0.80 | − 1.65 | − 1.10 | + 0.26 | − 1.00 | + 0.25 |
| − 6.73 | − 6.42 | − 6.41 | − 8.00 | − 8.85 | −10.75 | − 9.35 | − 7.27 | − 9.00 | − 6.00 |
| − 8.09 | − 8.24 | − 8.81 | −10.75 | −13.40 | −16.60 | −15.45 | −10.71 | −13.75 | −12.25 |
| −10.21 | −10.28 | −11.13 | −12.80 | −15.20 | −17.75 | −17.35 | −12.34 | −15.75 | −13.25 |
| − | − | − | − | − | − | − | − | − | − |

| 84.78 | 84.14 | 80.05 | 74.38 | 71.55 | 75.95 | 72.70 | 80.09 | 98.50 | 67.25 |
|---|---|---|---|---|---|---|---|---|---|
| + 3.37 | + 3.50 | + 1.53 | − 3.73 | − 3.30 | − 5.20 | − 4.45 | − 1.38 | − 5.00 | − 1.75 |
| − | − | − | − | − | − | + 0.80 | − | − | − |
| − | − | − | − | − | − | − | − | − | − |
| − 1.58 | − 2.14 | + 0.20 | − 5.05 | − 3.60 | − 4.95 | − 4.25 | − 3.17 | − 7.00 | − 4.00 |
| − 2.03 | − 2.39 | − 2.30 | − 3.83 | − 3.50 | − 4.75 | − 3.60 | − 3.51 | − 6.50 | − 4.00 |
| − | − | − | − | − | − | − 0.70 | − | − | − |
| − | − | − | − | − | − | + 1.30 | − | − | − |
| − 1.43 | − 1.47 | − 2.02 | − 3.83 | − 4.00 | − 4.90 | − 3.75 | − 4.22 | − 8.25 | − 3.25 |
| − 0.63 | − 0.74 | − 1.47 | − 2.19 | − 1.60 | − 2.65 | − 2.88 | − 1.72 | − 2.25 | − 1.75 |
| − | − | − 2.64 | − | − | − | − 4.70 | − | − | − |
| − 0.63 | − 0.74 | − 0.97 | − 0.83 | − 1.65 | − 2.10 | − 1.95 | − 1.49 | − 4.50 | − 1.75 |
| − 1.78 | − 0.69 | − 1.05 | − 1.88 | − 1.85 | − 3.60 | − 3.10 | − 3.03 | − 5.50 | − 2.00 |
| + 1.82 | + 0.41 | + 0.78 | + 0.12 | + 0.35 | − 2.65 | − 1.65 | − 0.66 | − 5.25 | − 1.00 |
| − 5.43 | − 5.79 | − 7.13 | − 8.98 | − 7.45 | −10.80 | − 7.45 | − 7.61 | −11.75 | − 9.00 |
| −11.53 | −12.79 | −15.38 | −17.63 | −20.30 | −25.20 | −21.80 | −17.07 | −19.25 | −18.00 |
| −20.03 | −20.04 | −21.80 | −23.78 | −23.55 | −26.57 | −25.22 | −22.23 | −28.50 | −21.25 |
| − | − | − | − | − | − | − | − | − | − |

| 62.53 | 61.74 | 64.27 | 72.08 | 71.02 | 68.21 | 64.30 | 64.63 | 75.00 | 56.50 |
|---|---|---|---|---|---|---|---|---|---|
| − 5.48 | − 7.41 | − 7.72 | −13.35 | −14.69 | −14.04 | −1.1.38 | − 7.54 | − 7.00 | − 4.00 |
| − 0.53 | − | − | − | − | − | − | − 4.21 | −11.50 | + 0.50 |
| − 6.46 | − 4.63 | − 5.42 | − 8.53 | − 6.59 | − 7.01 | − 7.92 | − 5.78 | − 6.75 | − 3.50 |
| − 6.28 | − 4.64 | − 4.22 | − 7.38 | − 5.47 | − 4.11 | − 5.40 | − 4.89 | − 6.00 | − 2.00 |
| − | − | − | − | − | − 1.96 | + 0.12 | − 3.38 | − 3.00 | − 3.15 |
| − 0.28 | − | − | − | − | − | − 2.30 | − 4.35 | −11.00 | + 0.50 |
| − 6.40 | − 3.99 | − 4.67 | − 8.28 | − 6.17 | − 5.52 | − 6.32 | − 5.40 | − 6.50 | − 6.50 |
| − 4.68 | − 1.89 | − 3.27 | − | − | − 2.54 | − 1.80 | − 4.51 | − 5.00 | − 3.85 |
| − 8.28 | − | − | − | − | − | − | − 9.40 | −17.00 | − 4.00 |
| − 3.96 | − 1.84 | − 1.92 | − 4.33 | − 4.42 | − 1.61 | − 1.17 | − 2.79 | − 4.00 | − 2.00 |
| − 4.53 | − 3.61 | − 3.07 | − 4.53 | − 2.77 | − 3.56 | − 3.35 | − 3.37 | − 3.50 | − 3.00 |
| − 3.91 | − 1.62 | − 3.17 | − 9.08 | − 7.57 | − 6.61 | − 4.00 | − 4.06 | − 3.75 | − 1.00 |
| −18.21 | −16.69 | −15.98 | −19.18 | −17.42 | −15.21 | −14.80 | −14.15 | −10.00 | −15.75 |
| −19.89 | −18.46 | −20.17 | −28.63 | −28.74 | −29.36 | −29.37 | −19.40 | −20.50 | −23.25 |
| −28.13 | −26.93 | −28.12 | −33.23 | −31.27 | −31.39 | −31.31 | −26.22 | −26.00 | −26.50 |
| − | − | − | − | − | − | − | − | − | − |

A-133

## CP-3. UNITED STATES: SPOT COFFEE

(Basis MAMS)

(U.S. cents

|  | JAN. | FEB. | MAR. | APR. | MAY |
|---|---|---|---|---|---|
| **1956** | | | | | |
| MAMS | 66.00 | 73.05 | 70.75 | 67.50 | 70.88 |
| Santos 4 | −12.57 | −16.25 | −15.30 | −12.50 | −14.08 |
| C. R. Strictly hard | − | − | − | − | − |
| Cuba Wsh. | −12.07 | −17.27 | −13.37 | −10.83 | −13.91 |
| D. R. Bani | −10.01 | −13.00 | −10.40 | − 8.02 | − 8.98 |
| Ecuador | − 8.87 | −11.02 | − 8.25 | − 7.50 | − 7.38 |
| El Sal. Wsh. Hi Grown | − 2.30 | − 1.00 | + 1.25 | − | − 4.38 |
| Guat. Prime Wsh. | − 0.59 | − 0.45 | + 1.25 | − | − 3.88 |
| Haiti Wsh. | − 7.77 | −10.50 | − 8.90 | − 6.15 | − 6.78 |
| Mexico High Grown | − 2.95 | − 1.90 | − 1.60 | − 1.75 | − 2.28 |
| Nic. Good Wsh. | − 3.50 | − 1.80 | − 1.00 | − 3.00 | − 9.88 |
| Venez. Maracaibo Wsh. | − 2.73 | − 2.75 | − 1.60 | − 1.88 | − 2.78 |
| Bel. Congo Ociru #2 | − 4.15 | − 4.25 | − 4.15 | − 5.00 | − 5.46 |
| Yemen Mocha | − 5.45 | − 9.25 | − 6.98 | − 5.02 | − 6.65 |
| Ethiopia Djimmas UGQ | −16.97 | −18.26 | −16.88 | −15.25 | −15.35 |
| Ambriz No. 2 AA | −31.55 | −34.84 | −32.62 | −30.82 | −33.43 |
| Uganda W&C #10 | −33.47 | −38.50 | −37.15 | −35.12 | −38.62 |
| Ivory Coast Courant | −37.75 | −42.15 | −40.50 | −37.80 | −39.66 |
| **1957** | | | | | |
| MAMS | 72.40 | 70.68 | 68.18 | 65.45 | 66.33 |
| Santos 4 | −11.77 | −10.23 | − 8.53 | − 6.07 | − 7.55 |
| C. R. Strictly hard | − 1.20 | − 0.21 | + 0.32 | − 0.95 | − 1.45 |
| Cuba Wsh. | −11.65 | − 9.18 | − 6.35 | − | − 7.01 |
| D. R. Bani | − 7.75 | − 6.25 | − 4.90 | − 3.97 | − 4.88 |
| Ecuador Wsh. | − 8.47 | − 6.90 | − 5.49 | − 2.95 | − 4.16 |
| El Sal. Wsh. Hi Grown | − 4.82 | − 4.15 | − 3.60 | − 2.60 | − 2.93 |
| Guat. Prime Wsh. | − 4.85 | − 3.85 | − 3.64 | − 2.60 | − 2.14 |
| Haiti Wsh. | − 7.84 | − 6.80 | − 4.53 | − 3.70 | − 5.23 |
| Mexico High Grown | − 6.00 | − 5.18 | − 4.43 | − 3.85 | − 3.93 |
| Nic. Good Wsh. | − 6.80 | − 5.87 | − 5.68 | − 4.47 | − 4.28 |
| Venez. Maracaibo Wsh. | − 5.72 | − 5.83 | − 4.15 | − 3.15 | − 3.78 |
| Bel. Congo Ociru #2 | − 6.12 | − 5.08 | − 4.35 | − 2.55 | − 3.10 |
| Yemen Mocha | − 2.25 | − 2.43 | − 1.48 | − 0.30 | − 2.33 |
| Ethiopia Djimmas UGQ | −14.35 | −13.75 | −13.73 | −13.87 | −16.83 |
| Ambriz No. 2 AA | −33.87 | −30.93 | −28.35 | −24.35 | −25.13 |
| Uganda W&C #10 | −37.60 | −35.48 | −33.58 | −30.92 | −32.08 |
| Ivory Coast Courant | −39.85 | −36.80 | −34.43 | −30.75 | −32.13 |
| **1958** | | | | | |
| MAMS | 56.80 | 53.65 | 54.18 | 54.70 | 54.38 |
| Santos 4 | − 1.92 | + 0.60 | − 0.18 | − 2.45 | − 3.90 |
| C. R. Strictly hard | − 0.86 | − | − 0.90 | − 1.40 | − 1.53 |
| Cuba Wsh. | − 4.67 | − 3.05 | − 3.90 | − 5.17 | − 5.75 |
| D. R. Bani | − 3.51 | − 2.02 | − 2.90 | − 3.77 | − 5.05 |
| Ecuador Wsh. | − 3.97 | − 2.32 | − | − | − |
| El Sal. Wsh. Hi Grown | − 1.67 | − 1.34 | − 1.58 | − 2.32 | − 2.53 |
| Guat. Prime Wsh. | − 1.23 | − 1.87 | − 2.05 | − 2.72 | − 3.47 |
| Haiti Wsh. | − 3.72 | − 2.46 | − 4.10 | − 4.53 | − 4.71 |
| Mexico High Grown | − 2.42 | − 1.15 | − 1.63 | − 2.42 | − 3.33 |
| Nic. Good Wsh. | − | − | − | − | − |
| Venez. Maracaibo Wsh. | − 2.72 | − 2.02 | − 2.25 | − 2.37 | − 3.85 |
| Bel. Congo Ociru #2 | − | − | − | − | − |
| Yemen Mocha | − 1.80 | − 0.15 | − 0.49 | − 2.48 | − |
| Ethiopia Djimmas UGQ | − 9.75 | − 8.20 | − 9.80 | −11.27 | −10.88 |
| Ambriz No. 2 AA | −16.80 | −11.92 | −10.98 | −11.45 | −11.40 |
| Uganda W&C #10 | −20.17 | −14.34 | −13.70 | −15.20 | −15.03 |
| Ivory Coast Courant | −21.80 | −15.87 | −15.83 | −18.07 | −17.65 |

**PRICE DIFFERENTIALS (Continued)**

1953-1966

per pound)

| JUNE | JULY | AUG. | SEPT. | OCT. | NOV. | DEC. | AVERAGE | HIGH | LOW |
|---|---|---|---|---|---|---|---|---|---|
| 76.75 | 78.15 | 80.45 | 81.08 | 78.28 | 74.70 | 70.30 | 73.99 | 82.25 | 64.25 |
| −18.04 | −19.05 | −20.45 | −20.18 | −17.98 | −14.35 | −10.00 | −15.89 | −21.00 | −11.50 |
| − | − | − | − | − | − | − 0.30 | − | − | − |
| −16.25 | −17.15 | − | − | −15.28 | −13.45 | − 7.63 | −15.07 | −16.25 | −10.75 |
| −14.05 | −11.90 | −14.32 | −14.70 | −12.43 | −10.05 | − 7.32 | −11.26 | −15.25 | − 9.50 |
| − 7.17 | − 8.57 | −10.82 | −13.00 | −13.98 | −11.25 | − 7.45 | − 9.60 | −10.25 | − 9.50 |
| − | − | − | − | − | − 2.16 | − 3.92 | − 5.15 | − 7.50 | − 2.75 |
| − | − | − | − | − | − | − 4.45 | − 5.51 | − 7.25 | − 0.12 |
| − 8.85 | − 8.27 | −12.45 | −12.98 | −11.70 | − 8.75 | − 6.35 | − 9.12 | −11.25 | − 8.00 |
| − 2.80 | − 2.75 | − 4.03 | − 3.75 | − 5.00 | − 3.62 | − 4.85 | − 3.11 | − 3.75 | − 3.50 |
| − 7.00 | − | − | − | − | − 4.70 | − 6.13 | − 7.37 | −10.00 | − 4.25 |
| − 3.85 | − 3.40 | − 4.52 | − 4.23 | − 3.63 | − 2.70 | − 3.40 | − 3.12 | − 5.00 | − 2.25 |
| − | − 4.32 | − 3.27 | − 3.75 | − 4.33 | − 3.27 | − 4.67 | − 4.49 | − 4.25 | − 4.25 |
| −10.40 | −10.05 | −11.85 | −12.43 | −10.30 | − 4.87 | − 0.70 | − 7.83 | −11.75 | − 4.00 |
| −19.00 | −21.22 | −23.22 | −23.30 | −20.63 | −16.65 | −12.25 | −18.26 | −23.25 | −16.25 |
| −37.20 | −37.35 | −38.23 | −38.20 | −40.55 | −38.10 | −34.75 | −35.64 | −38.25 | −31.25 |
| −43.23 | −44.04 | −46.15 | −46.55 | −43.98 | −41.15 | −36.90 | −40.40 | −46.75 | −33.25 |
| −44.40 | −46.42 | −48.69 | −48.63 | −36.70 | −43.47 | −39.32 | −42.96 | −49.50 | −36.25 |

| 67.13 | 63.50 | 63.20 | 58.85 | 56.00 | 57.40 | 58.20 | 63.94 | 73.50 | 54.25 |
|---|---|---|---|---|---|---|---|---|---|
| − 9.78 | − 7.97 | − 9.51 | − 5.76 | − 2.07 | − 2.25 | − 2.85 | − 7.02 | −12.62 | − 1.75 |
| − 2.13 | − | − | − | − | − | − | − | − | − |
| − 8.13 | − | − | − 6.78 | − | − 4.90 | − 5.67 | − 6.51 | −11.50 | − 2.75 |
| − 5.05 | − 3.20 | − 4.20 | − 7.10 | − 4.45 | − 3.82 | − 5.10 | − 5.05 | − 8.25 | − 5.25 |
| − 5.21 | − 3.58 | − 6.78 | − 5.65 | − 3.52 | − 3.42 | − 4.55 | − 5.05 | − 8.75 | − 2.75 |
| − 1.78 | + 0.25 | − | − | − | − 1.96 | − 2.28 | − 1.12 | − 5.25 | + 1.00 |
| − 1.19 | − | − | − | − | − 1.65 | − 2.32 | − 1.00 | − 4.50 | + 1.25 |
| − 5.13 | − | − | − | − | − 3.47 | − 4.85 | − 3.41 | − 8.35 | − 1.25 |
| − 2.55 | − 0.93 | − 1.55 | − 2.35 | − 1.92 | − 1.32 | − 2.87 | − 3.07 | − 6.37 | − 1.75 |
| − 3.38 | − | − | − | − | − | − | − | − | − |
| − 2.98 | − 0.95 | − 1.67 | − 2.42 | − 1.40 | − 1.10 | − 2.35 | − 2.96 | − 6.00 | − 1.12 |
| − 2.85 | − 1.30 | − 3.62 | − 4.17 | − 2.42 | − 2.44 | − 3.14 | − 3.42 | − 6.75 | − 1.75 |
| − 2.93 | − 0.90 | − 1.29 | + 0.07 | − 0.19 | − 1.45 | − 2.15 | − 1.47 | − 2.75 | + 1.00 |
| −18.30 | −16.60 | −17.27 | −13.72 | −10.47 | − 9.00 | −10.20 | −14.00 | −15.00 | − 9.50 |
| −26.18 | −21.17 | −20.52 | −18.92 | −17.10 | −18.62 | −19.57 | −23.72 | −30.50 | −17.62 |
| −32.98 | −29.00 | −28.60 | −23.97 | −21.15 | −22.65 | −23.55 | −29.29 | −38.00 | −20.62 |
| −32.98 | −29.05 | −28.57 | −23.97 | −21.55 | −23.10 | −24.00 | −29.77 | −38.25 | −23.12 |

| 53.85 | 52.93 | 51.65 | 50.25 | 50.88 | 48.73 | 46.08 | 52.34 | 58.25 | 45.00 |
|---|---|---|---|---|---|---|---|---|---|
| − 5.30 | − 6.00 | − 5.86 | − 6.05 | − 6.60 | − 4.98 | − 4.58 | − 3.94 | − 3.00 | − 4.12 |
| − | − | − | − | − | − 0.98 | − 1.25 | − 1.01 | − 2.25 | − 0.50 |
| − 5.85 | − | − | − | − | − | − 6.39 | − | − 5.62 | − 6.62 |
| − 6.00 | − 5.83 | − 4.82 | − 4.25 | − 5.50 | − 3.73 | − 5.80 | − 4.43 | − 4.25 | − 5.62 |
| − 4.85 | − 4.68 | − 3.97 | − 3.22 | − 3.78 | − 1.95 | − 5.87 | − 4.54 | − 4.75 | − 5.62 |
| − 1.85 | − 1.30 | − | − | − | − 0.85 | − 4.25 | − 1.49 | − 2.25 | − 3.87 |
| − | − | − | − | − 2.83 | − 2.05 | − 4.70 | − 2.53 | − 2.12 | − 4.50 |
| − 5.54 | − 4.43 | − 4.77 | − | − 5.38 | − 4.00 | − 6.01 | − 4.32 | − 4.62 | − 6.25 |
| − 2.30 | − 1.58 | − 0.87 | − 1.04 | − | − | − 4.14 | − 1.58 | − 2.87 | − 3.12 |
| − | − | − | − | − | − | − | − | − | − |
| − 2.82 | − 2.00 | − 1.06 | − 1.05 | − 1.63 | − 1.50 | − 5.48 | − 2.40 | − 2.37 | − 5.50 |
| − | − 4.27 | − 3.42 | − 2.72 | − 2.98 | − 1.29 | − | − | − | − |
| − 2.64 | − 2.99 | − 2.90 | − 1.75 | − 1.88 | − | − | − 1.03 | − 2.25 | + 3.50 |
| − 8.00 | − 6.78 | − 5.35 | − 4.31 | − 4.95 | − 3.80 | − 6.48 | − 7.46 | −10.75 | − 6.00 |
| −11.45 | −10.83 | − 9.48 | − 8.80 | −13.78 | −13.93 | −13.90 | −12.09 | −14.87 | −13.62 |
| −14.30 | −13.03 | −11.51 | −10.85 | −13.73 | −14.15 | −14.88 | −14.24 | −17.25 | −14.12 |
| −16.17 | −14.43 | −13.02 | −12.30 | −14.28 | −15.15 | −15.64 | −15.85 | −19.00 | −15.25 |

## CP-3. SPOT COFFEE PRICE
(Basis MAMS)

(U. S. cents)

|  | JAN. | FEB. | MAR. | APR. | MAY |
|---|---|---|---|---|---|
| **1959** |  |  |  |  |  |
| **MAMS** | 46.68 | 46.23 | 45.08 | 45.55 | 44.83 |
| Santos 4 | − 5.53 | − 6.73 | − 7.80 | − 8.20 | − 7.90 |
| C. R. Strictly Hard | − 3.92 | − | − | − | − |
| Cuba Wsh. | − 7.68 | − | − | − 5.17 | − |
| D. R. Bani | − 6.73 | − 6.38 | − 5.50 | − 3.59 | − 2.35 |
| Ecuador Wsh. | − 6.74 | − 6.31 | − 5.83 | − | − |
| El Sal. Cent'l St'd. | − 5.45 | − 4.25 | − 2.78 | − 1.73 | − 0.83 |
| Guat. Prime Wsh. | − 5.55 | − 4.45 | − 2.88 | − 1.95 | − 0.90 |
| Haiti Wsh. | − 7.63 | − 6.35 | − 5.14 | − 4.92 | − 3.83 |
| Mexico Prime Wsh. | − 5.40 | − 4.40 | − 2.93 | − 1.77 | − 0.80 |
| Nic. Good Wsh. | − | − 4.98 | − | − | − |
| Venez. Maracaibo Wsh. | − 5.93 | − 4.70 | − 3.98 | − 2.45 | − 1.05 |
| Belgian Congo Ociru #2 | − 6.55 | − | − | − | − |
| Yemen Mocha | − | − | − | − 0.05 | − 0.33 |
| Ethiopia Djimmas UGQ | − 8.33 | − 8.45 | − 8.30 | − 9.37 | − 8.48 |
| Ambriz No. 2 AA | −15.28 | −13.92 | −11.58 | −12.65 | −12.38 |
| Uganda W&C #10 | −15.90 | −15.03 | −13.68 | −14.00 | −13.55 |
| Ivory Coast Courant | −17.02 | −18.03 | −16.60 | −16.97 | −16.28 |
| **1960** |  |  |  |  |  |
| **MAMS** | 45.68 | 45.95 | 45.10 | 45.20 | 44.73 |
| Santos 4 | − 9.35 | − 8.90 | − 8.15 | − 8.25 | − 7.48 |
| C. R. Strictly Hard | − | − | − | − 2.32 | − |
| Cuba Wsh. | − | − | − | − | − |
| D. R. Bani | − 5.03 | − 5.25 | − 4.47 | − 4.87 | − 4.63 |
| Ecuador Wsh. | − 5.18 | − | − | − | − |
| El Sal. Cent'l St'd. | − 4.43 | − 4.40 | − 3.15 | − 3.65 | − 2.80 |
| Guatemala Prime Wsh. | − 4.55 | − 4.47 | − 3.82 | − 3.77 | − 2.95 |
| Haiti Wsh. | − 5.08 | − 5.24 | − 4.41 | − 4.51 | − 4.44 |
| Mexico Prime Wsh. | − 4.18 | − 4.32 | − 3.60 | − 3.67 | − 2.98 |
| Nic. Good Wsh. | − | − | − | − 4.63 | − |
| Venez. Maracaibo Wsh. | − 2.73 | − 2.97 | − 3.15 | − 3.67 | − 4.05 |
| Belgian Congo Ociru #2 | − | − | − | − | − |
| Yemen Mocha | − 1.62 | − 1.98 | − 0.14 | − 0.60 | − 0.16 |
| Ethiopia Djimmas UGQ | −10.08 | −10.37 | −10.60 | −11.27 | −11.33 |
| Ambriz No. 2 AA | −21.03 | −19.17 | −17.70 | −18.45 | −18.10 |
| Uganda W&C #10 | −21.50 | −22.60 | −23.87 | −24.47 | −23.80 |
| Ivory Coast Superior | −23.73 | −24.42 | −25.12 | −24.92 | −24.65 |
| **1961** |  |  |  |  |  |
| **MAMS** | 44.80 | 44.58 | 44.30 | 43.90 | 43.50 |
| Santos 4 | − 8.27 | − 7.33 | − 6.85 | − 6.90 | − 6.32 |
| C. R. Hard Bean | − 3.30 | − 4.13 | − 4.64 | − 4.42 | − 4.05 |
| Cuba Wsh. | − | − | − | − | − |
| D. R. Bani | − 6.22 | − 5.98 | − 5.87 | − 5.77 | − 5.30 |
| Ecuador Wsh. | − | − | − | − | − 6.58 |
| El Sal. Cent'l St'd. | − 4.82 | − 5.25 | − 5.17 | − 5.57 | − 5.60 |
| Guat. Prime Wsh. | − 5.47 | − 5.63 | − 5.77 | − 6.22 | − 5.60 |
| Haiti Wsh. | − | − | − | − 6.48 | − |
| Mexico Prime Wsh. | − 4.65 | − 5.40 | − 5.47 | − 6.17 | − 5.57 |
| Nic. Good Wsh. | − | − | − 6.34 | − 6.40 | − 6.12 |
| Venez. Tach. Fine Wsh. | − 4.87 | − 5.50 | − 6.07 | − 6.10 | − 5.77 |
| Belgian Congo Ociru #2 | − | − | − | − | − |
| Ethiopia Djimmas UGQ | − 9.67 | − 9.78 | − 9.35 | − 9.80 | − 9.95 |
| Ambriz No. 2 AA | −23.90 | −23.83 | −24.25 | −24.15 | −24.07 |
| Uganda W&C | −25.82 | −25.98 | −25.52 | −25.17 | −24.80 |
| Ivory Coast Superior | −25.82 | −25.90 | −25.52 | −25.30 | −24.97 |

**DIFFERENTIALS (Continued)**
1953-1966

per pound)

| | JUNE | JULY | AUG. | SEPT. | OCT. | NOV. | DEC. | AVERAGE | HIGH | LOW |
|---|---|---|---|---|---|---|---|---|---|---|
| | 44.30 | 44.80 | 45.13 | 45.83 | 45.03 | 45.18 | 43.95 | 45.22 | 47.00 | 43.63 |
| | − 8.00 | − 8.12 | − 9.10 | −11.05 | − 9.75 | − 8.58 | − 8.17 | − 8.25 | − 5.12 | − 9.13 |
| | − | − | − | − | − | − | − | − | − | − |
| | − 2.88 | − 3.11 | − | − | − 4.43 | − 4.18 | − 3.57 | − 4.33 | − 3.37 | − 4.75 |
| | − | − 2.17 | − 2.78 | − 4.23 | − 3.80 | − 4.25 | − 3.70 | − 4.32 | − 4.25 | − 4.63 |
| | − | − | − | − | − | − 2.49 | − 2.65 | − 2.75 | − 2.62 | − 3.38 |
| | − 1.01 | − 1.30 | − | − 2.39 | − 2.53 | − 2.88 | − 2.77 | − 2.60 | − 2.62 | − 3.25 |
| | − | − | − | − | − 4.59 | − 4.38 | − 4.16 | − 5.02 | − 5.75 | − 4.88 |
| | − 1.07 | − 1.30 | − 1.25 | − 1.89 | − 2.62 | − 2.38 | − 2.17 | − 2.33 | − 2.62 | − 3.00 |
| | − | − | − | − | − | − | − | − | − | − |
| | − 1.06 | − 1.00 | − 1.18 | − 1.88 | − 1.53 | − 1.95 | − 0.70 | − 2.29 | − 2.75 | − 3.38 |
| | − | − 1.61 | − 2.73 | − 4.50 | − 4.05 | − 3.64 | − 3.70 | − 3.82 | − 3.62 | − 3.63 |
| | − | − | − | − 1.64 | − 0.90 | − 0.93 | + 0.05 | − 0.79 | − | − 0.13 |
| | − 7.83 | − 7.67 | − 8.21 | − 9.55 | − 9.56 | − 9.10 | − 8.66 | − 8.63 | − 8.00 | − 8.63 |
| | −12.10 | −13.35 | −14.20 | −15.13 | −16.70 | −18.70 | −19.45 | −14.62 | −13.37 | −20.00 |
| | −13.97 | −15.62 | −15.98 | −17.55 | −18.03 | −18.78 | −19.00 | −15.93 | −15.25 | −19.50 |
| | −16.52 | −17.32 | −17.85 | −19.28 | −20.03 | −21.28 | −21.30 | −18.21 | −16.87 | −21.63 |
| | 44.38 | 44.55 | 45.15 | 44.85 | 44.90 | 44.35 | 43.85 | 44.89 | 47.25 | 43.50 |
| | − 7.38 | − 8.07 | − 9.17 | − 8.62 | − 8.65 | − 8.00 | − 7.60 | − 8.29 | − 9.75 | − 7.75 |
| | − | − | − 3.21 | − 2.93 | − 2.47 | − 1.47 | − 1.52 | − 2.49 | − 5.25 | − 1.75 |
| | − | − | − | − | − | − | − | − | − | − |
| | − 4.45 | − 5.40 | − 6.37 | − 6.91 | − 6.46 | − 5.50 | − 5.17 | − 5.37 | − 6.37 | − 6.62 |
| | − 4.04 | − 5.60 | − 8.07 | − 8.40 | − 8.57 | − 7.22 | − | − 6.78 | − 6.50 | − 7.50 |
| | − 2.58 | − 2.77 | − 3.46 | − 3.37 | − 3.00 | − 2.75 | − 3.37 | − 3.35 | − 5.00 | − 3.25 |
| | − 2.68 | − 2.84 | − 3.48 | − 3.22 | − 2.92 | − 3.52 | − 4.52 | − 3.56 | − 5.12 | − 4.50 |
| | − 4.34 | − 5.36 | − | − | − 5.52 | − 4.85 | − | − 4.77 | − 6.25 | − 4.50 |
| | − 2.50 | − 2.80 | − 3.47 | − 3.27 | − 3.07 | − 2.52 | − 2.97 | − 3.28 | − 5.12 | − 2.87 |
| | − | − | − | − 4.85 | − 4.80 | − | − | − | − 6.37 | − 3.50 |
| | − 4.05 | − 3.97 | − 3.92 | − 3.52 | − 3.32 | − 2.70 | − 3.26 | − 3.44 | − 3.87 | − 3.50 |
| | − | − 4.17 | − 4.45 | − 3.72 | − 3.65 | − 3.47 | − | − | − 5.87 | − 3.37 |
| | + 0.20 | − 0.42 | − 2.02 | − 1.77 | − 1.65 | − 1.05 | − 0.60 | − 0.98 | − 2.00 | − 1.00 |
| | −10.48 | −10.02 | −10.20 | − 9.60 | − 9.35 | − 8.80 | − 8.37 | −10.04 | −11.12 | −10.50 |
| | −18.45 | −20.72 | −20.77 | −19.32 | −19.40 | −20.47 | −21.90 | −19.62 | −19.62 | −22.50 |
| | −24.05 | −25.90 | −25.97 | −25.85 | −24.67 | −24.02 | −24.25 | −24.24 | −23.00 | −25.50 |
| | −25.40 | −27.92 | −28.02 | −27.10 | −25.40 | −24.32 | −24.32 | −25.44 | −25.25 | −27.50 |
| | 43.33 | 43.50 | 43.53 | 43.33 | 43.15 | 43.05 | 42.80 | 43.62 | 44.75 | 42.50 |
| | − 5.98 | − 6.67 | − 7.60 | − 8.48 | − 9.42 | − 9.12 | − 8.77 | − 7.61 | − 7.12 | − 9.00 |
| | − 3.88 | − 4.56 | − 4.38 | − | − | − 4.76 | − 4.77 | − 4.18 | − 2.75 | − 4.75 |
| | − | − | − | − | − | − | − | − | − | − |
| | − 5.30 | − 5.57 | − 6.65 | − 7.50 | − 8.60 | − 7.35 | − 7.05 | − 6.44 | − 6.00 | − 8.12 |
| | − 6.45 | − 6.54 | − 7.03 | − 7.23 | − 7.82 | − | − 7.63 | − 7.35 | − 7.62 | − 7.50 |
| | − 5.25 | − 5.60 | − 6.38 | − 6.79 | − | − 6.50 | − 6.52 | − 5.69 | − 4.25 | − 7.12 |
| | − 5.25 | − 5.60 | − 6.45 | − | − 8.1 | − 6.57 | − 6.60 | − 6.07 | − 5.25 | − 7.75 |
| | − 6.26 | − | − 6.90 | − | − | − 7.67 | − 7.05 | − 7.17 | − 7.12 | − 8.00 |
| | − 5.33 | − 5.67 | − 6.48 | − 7.28 | − 8.22 | − 6.55 | − 6.62 | − 6.09 | − 4.12 | − 7.87 |
| | − 6.20 | − | − | − | − | − | − | − | − 6.62 | − 5.37 |
| | − 5.45 | − 5.52 | − 6.15 | − 6.24 | − | − 6.01 | − 5.92 | − 5.75 | − 4.12 | − 6.00 |
| | − 5.40 | − 5.72 | − 7.05 | − 8.15 | − 8.12 | − 6.72 | − | − 7.16 | − 6.75 | − 8.12 |
| | − 8.80 | − 8.17 | − 8.08 | − 8.18 | − 8.22 | − 8.27 | − 8.47 | − 8.87 | − 9.25 | − 9.12 |
| | −24.13 | −24.00 | −23.95 | −23.80 | −23.92 | −23.05 | −21.57 | −23.69 | −23.25 | −23.50 |
| | −24.68 | −24.70 | −24.70 | −24.58 | −24.40 | −23.80 | −22.57 | −24.70 | −24.25 | −24.37 |
| | −24.88 | −25.10 | −25.08 | −24.90 | −24.62 | −24.22 | −23.47 | −24.95 | −24.25 | −24.12 |

A-137

## CP-3. UNITED STATES: SPOT COFFEE

(Basis MAMS)

(U.S. cents

|  | JAN. | FEB. | MAR. | APR. | MAY |
|---|---|---|---|---|---|
| **1962** | | | | | |
| MAMS | 42.80 | 42.78 | 42.05 | 41.40 | 40.45 |
| Santos 4 | − 8.60 | − 8.73 | − 7.97 | − 7.32 | − 6.02 |
| C. R. Hard Bean | − 4.80 | − | − 2.67 | − 2.15 | − 2.45 |
| Cuba Wsh. | − | − | − | − | − |
| D. R. Bani | − 7.55 | − 7.48 | − 6.42 | − 6.02 | − 5.12 |
| Ecuador Wsh. | − | − | − | − | − |
| El Sal. Cent'l St'd. | − 6.27 | − 5.60 | − 4.50 | − 4.67 | − 3.95 |
| Guat. Prime Wsh. | − 6.35 | − 5.73 | − 4.60 | − 4.75 | − 3.97 |
| Haiti Wsh. | − 7.42 | − 7.15 | − 6.05 | − 5.71 | − |
| Mexico Prime Wsh. | − 6.30 | − 5.70 | − 4.55 | − 4.70 | − 3.92 |
| Nic. Good Wsh. | − 7.36 | − 7.00 | − 5.84 | − | − 4.23 |
| Venez. Tach. Fine Wsh. | − 6.12 | − 5.88 | − 5.12 | − 4.80 | − 3.95 |
| Belgian Congo Ociru #2 | − | − | − | − | − |
| Ethiopia Djimmas UGQ | − 9.27 | − 9.43 | − 9.12 | − 9.00 | − 7.87 |
| Ambriz No. 2 AA | −21.72 | −22.30 | −21.55 | −20.47 | −18.85 |
| Uganda W&C | −22.67 | −22.68 | −21.67 | −20.82 | −19.40 |
| Ivory Coast Superior | −23.35 | −23.30 | −22.20 | −21.27 | −19.80 |
| **1963** | | | | | |
| MAMS | 40.50 | 39.43 | 39.78 | 39.65 | 39.15 |
| Santos 4 | − 6.65 | − 6.10 | − 5.33 | − 6.65 | − 5.82 |
| C. R. Hard Bean | − 2.42 | − 1.43 | − 1.93 | − 2.12 | − 1.80 |
| Cuba Wsh. | − | − | − | − | − |
| D. R. Bani | − 5.55 | − 4.93 | − 5.45 | − 5.52 | − 5.15 |
| Ecuador Wsh. | − | − | − | − | − |
| El Sal. Cent'l St'd. | − 4.65 | − 3.95 | − 4.03 | − 3.82 | − 3.52 |
| Guat. Prime Wsh. | − 4.47 | − 3.98 | − 4.20 | − 3.87 | − 3.55 |
| Haiti Wsh. | − | − | − 4.99 | − | − 4.82 |
| Mexico Prime Wsh. | − 4.12 | − 3.53 | − 3.95 | − 3.75 | − 3.52 |
| Nic. Good Wsh. | − 5.83 | − 4.50 | − 4.80 | − 4.52 | − 4.07 |
| Venez. Tach. Fine Wsh. | − 4.30 | − 3.75 | − 4.15 | − 3.92 | − 3.47 |
| Belgian Congo Ociru #2 | − | − | − | − | − |
| Ethiopia Djimmas UGQ | − 7.87 | − 7.13 | − 7.73 | − 8.07 | − 7.80 |
| Ambriz No. 2 AA | −15.62 | −13.83 | −12.40 | −12.07 | −11.50 |
| Uganda W&C | −16.30 | −14.18 | −12.60 | −12.52 | −12.20 |
| Ivory Coast Superior | − | − | −13.78 | −13.05 | −12.20 |
| **1964** | | | | | |
| MAMS | 45.00 | 45.70 | 49.95 | 48.55 | 49.28 |
| Santos 4 | − 0.17 | + 0.60 | − 0.10 | + 0.05 | − 1.93 |
| C. R. Hard Bean | − | − | − | − 0.51 | − 1.28 |
| D. R. Bani | − 1.40 | − 1.37 | − 1.76 | − 1.86 | − 2.03 |
| Ecuador Wsh. | − | − | − | − | − |
| El Sal. Cent'l St'd. | − 0.80 | − 0.67 | − 0.62 | − 1.02 | − 2.15 |
| Guat. Prime Wsh. | − 0.80 | − 0.70 | − 0.77 | − 1.05 | − 2.18 |
| Haiti Wsh. | − 2.62 | − | − | − | − 3.53 |
| Mexico Prime Wsh. | − 0.77 | − 0.67 | − 0.72 | − 1.00 | − 2.06 |
| Nicaragua Wsh. | − 0.90 | − | − | − | − |
| Venez. Tach. Fine Wsh. | − 0.70 | − 0.70 | − 0.75 | − 0.57 | − 1.87 |
| Rwanda-Burundi Ociru #2 | − | − | − | − | − |
| Ethiopia Djimmas UGQ | − 1.75 | − 1.82 | − 2.62 | − 3.47 | − 4.87 |
| Ambriz No. 2 AA | − 4.57 | − 5.42 | − 8.40 | − 8.25 | − 9.28 |
| Uganda W&C | − 4.75 | − 5.80 | − 9.17 | − 9.07 | −11.15 |
| Ivory Coast Superior | − 8.00 | − 6.70 | −10.00 | − 9.30 | −10.65 |

A-138

**PRICE DIFFERENTIALS (Continued)**

1953-1966

per pound)

| JUNE | JULY | AUG. | SEPT. | OCT. | NOV. | DEC. | AVERAGE | HIGH | LOW |
|---|---|---|---|---|---|---|---|---|---|
| 39.50 | 39.88 | 40.15 | 40.45 | 39.78 | 39.85 | 40.10 | 40.77 | 43.00 | 38.88 |
| − 4.77 | − 5.33 | − 6.07 | − 7.05 | − 6.60 | − 6.52 | − 6.70 | − 6.81 | − 8.12 | − 5.75 |
| − | − | − | − | − | − | − 2.47 | − | − 3.50 | − 1.63 |
| − | − | − | − | − | − | − | − | − | − |
| − | − | − | − | − 6.34 | − 5.22 | − 5.37 | − 5.81 | − 7.25 | − 6.50 |
| − 4.16 | − 5.45 | − 6.97 | − 8.20 | − 7.40 | − | − | − | − 7.25 | − 6.75 |
| − 3.55 | − 4.75 | − 5.42 | − 6.20 | − 5.18 | − 4.52 | − | − 4.91 | − 5.37 | − 4.75 |
| − 3.52 | − 4.70 | − 5.34 | − 6.17 | − 5.38 | − 4.52 | − 4.17 | − 4.94 | − 5.50 | − 5.13 |
| − 4.58 | − | − | − | − 5.61 | − | − 5.51 | − 5.58 | − 6.87 | − 4.88 |
| − 3.60 | − 4.75 | − 5.30 | − 6.17 | − 5.20 | − 4.45 | − 4.10 | − 4.90 | − 5.37 | − 4.75 |
| − | − | − | − | − | − | − | − | − 6.25 | − 3.63 |
| − 3.27 | − 3.92 | − | − | − 4.50 | − 3.97 | − 3.87 | − 4.45 | − 6.00 | − 3.88 |
| − 6.67 | − | − 5.75 | − 6.97 | − 6.15 | − 5.56 | − | − | − 8.25 | − 5.63 |
| − | − 7.10 | − 7.75 | − 8.27 | − 7.53 | − 7.40 | − 7.57 | − 8.09 | − 9.37 | − 6.75 |
| −18.20 | −18.41 | −18.75 | −18.77 | −18.25 | −17.37 | −15.90 | −19.22 | −18.00 | −18.63 |
| −18.45 | −18.80 | −19.17 | −19.32 | −18.73 | −18.02 | −16.67 | −19.70 | −19.00 | −18.88 |
| −18.55 | −19.09 | −19.65 | − | − | − | − | − | −22.00 | −19.50 |
|  |  |  |  |  |  |  |  |  |  |
| 39.25 | 39.58 | 39.50 | 39.38 | 39.48 | 39.60 | 39.28 | 39.55 | 41.00 | 38.75 |
| − 4.92 | − 6.00 | − 6.77 | − 6.43 | − 4.50 | − 3.05 | − 1.83 | − 5.44 | − 2.25 | − 6.25 |
| − 1.97 | − 2.75 | − | − | − 2.48 | − 1.85 | − 0.90 | − 1.94 | − 1.25 | − 2.50 |
| − | − | − | − | − | − | − | − | − | − |
| − 5.25 | − 5.60 | − | − | − 4.06 | − 3.30 | − 2.53 | − 4.71 | − 3.75 | − 5.12 |
| − | − 5.85 | − 6.90 | − 6.78 | − 4.73 | − 3.90 | − | − 5.67 | − 5.00 | − 6.50 |
| − 3.87 | − 5.13 | − 6.31 | − 5.73 | − 3.43 | − 2.60 | − 1.78 | − 4.11 | − 3.00 | − 6.00 |
| − 3.92 | − 5.15 | − 6.25 | − 5.75 | − 3.55 | − 3.02 | − 2.13 | − 4.15 | − 3.00 | − 5.75 |
| − | − | − | − | − | − | − 3.15 | − | − 4.75 | − 4.75 |
| − 3.85 | − 5.08 | − 6.22 | − 5.90 | − 3.40 | − 2.75 | − 1.75 | − 3.99 | − 2.87 | − 5.75 |
| − 4.25 | − 5.27 | − | − | − | − | − | − 4.68 | − 5.75 | − 5.00 |
| − 3.70 | − 4.68 | − 5.37 | − 4.90 | − 3.38 | − 2.40 | − 1.45 | − 3.79 | − 2.75 | − 4.75 |
| − | − | − 6.31 | − 6.08 | − 4.20 | − | − | − 5.65 | − 5.50 | − 5.75 |
| − 7.67 | − 7.80 | − 7.77 | − 7.48 | − 5.10 | − 3.97 | − 3.18 | − 6.80 | − 4.62 | − 7.50 |
| −11.60 | −11.85 | −12.35 | −11.28 | − 8.33 | − 4.77 | − 4.28 | −10.82 | − 5.50 | −14.25 |
| −12.60 | −12.90 | −13.12 | −11.95 | − 8.95 | − 5.05 | − 4.53 | −11.41 | − 5.50 | −15.25 |
| −12.15 | −12.73 | −12.50 | −12.18 | −10.63 | − 7.30 | − 6.08 | −11.34 | − 7.50 | −13.75 |
|  |  |  |  |  |  |  |  |  |  |
| 48.60 | 49.33 | 50.58 | 50.05 | 50.08 | 49.90 | 48.60 | 48.80 | 50.88 | 42.25 |
| − 1.70 | − 2.68 | − 4.75 | − 5.05 | − 3.50 | − 3.02 | − 3.42 | − 2.14 | − 0.38 | − 1.12 |
| − | − | − | − | − 0.89 | − 0.77 | − 0.66 | − 0.34 | − 1.38 | + 4.13 |
| − | − | − | − 3.95 | − 2.98 | − 2.10 | − 2.60 | − 2.46 | − 2.38 | − 3.25 |
| − 2.77 | − 3.60 | − 4.43 | − 3.60 | − 2.98 | − 2.10 | − | − 2.29 | − 2.88 | + 2.75 |
| − 2.15 | − 2.78 | − 2.60 | − 1.82 | − 1.60 | − 1.33 | − 1.67 | − 1.60 | − 1.13 | − 1.00 |
| − 2.17 | − 2.78 | − 2.65 | − 2.00 | − 1.65 | − 1.27 | − 1.70 | − 1.64 | − 1.38 | − 1.00 |
| − | − | − | − | − | − | − | − | − | − |
| − 2.10 | − 2.73 | − 2.50 | − 1.95 | − 1.98 | − 1.57 | − 1.67 | − 1.64 | − 1.38 | − 1.00 |
| − | − | − | − | − | − | − 2.18 | − | − | − |
| − 1.37 | − 2.00 | − 2.18 | − 1.52 | − 1.55 | − 1.02 | − 1.15 | − 1.28 | − 1.13 | − 1.00 |
| − | − 2.70 | − 2.50 | − 1.77 | − 1.73 | − 1.46 | − | − 0.84 | − 1.88 | + 4.25 |
| − 5.15 | − 6.80 | − 8.25 | − 7.70 | − 7.28 | − 6.02 | − 4.92 | − 5.05 | − 2.63 | − 2.25 |
| −10.62 | −14.40 | −16.93 | −18.20 | −17.25 | −17.32 | −18.37 | −12.42 | − 8.88 | −13.87 |
| −12.22 | −14.75 | −17.08 | −18.25 | −17.48 | −17.55 | −18.55 | −12.98 | − 9.13 | −14.12 |
| −11.70 | − | −16.58 | −17.55 | −18.02 | −17.07 | −17.10 | −13.02 | −10.88 | −13.25 |

## CP-3. SPOT COFFEE PRICE
(Basis MAMS)

(U. S. cents)

|  | JAN. | FEB. | MAR. | APR. | MAY |
|---|---|---|---|---|---|
| **1965** | | | | | |
| **MAMS** | 48.88 | 49.68 | 47.20 | 47.45 | 47.53 |
| Santos 4 | − 3.63 | − 3.73 | − 2.07 | − 2.50 | − 2.28 |
| C. R. Hard Bean | − 2.38 | − 2.33 | − 1.40 | − 2.20 | − 2.83 |
| D. R. Bani | − 3.83 | − 4.20 | − 3.55 | − 3.65 | − 3.90 |
| Ecuador Wsh. | − 4.46 | — | — | — | — |
| El Sal. Cent'l St'd. | − 3.00 | − 2.55 | − 2.32 | − 3.00 | − 3.48 |
| Guat. Prime Wsh. | − 3.03 | − 2.58 | − 2.30 | − 3.10 | − 3.53 |
| Haiti Wsh. | — | — | — | — | — |
| Mexico Prime Wsh. | − 3.03 | − 2.55 | − 2.30 | − 2.95 | − 3.48 |
| Nic. Good Wsh. | — | — | — | — | — |
| Venez. Tach. Fine Wsh. | − 2.30 | − 2.33 | − 1.75 | − 3.12 | − 3.43 |
| Rwanda-Burundi Ociru #2 | — | — | — | — | — |
| Ethiopia Djimmas UGQ | − 5.95 | − 5.88 | − 5.25 | − 6.27 | − 7.83 |
| Ambriz No. 2 AA | −20.35 | −20.18 | −20.82 | −21.92 | −24.06 |
| Uganda W&C | −21.58 | −20.88 | −21.22 | −22.05 | −24.28 |
| Ivory Coast Superior | −20.00 | −20.30 | −20.25 | −21.25 | −23.33 |
| **1966** | | | | | |
| **MAMS** | 49.45 | 49.68 | 49.53 | 48.93 | 48.30 |
| Santos 4 | − 6.32 | − 7.50 | − 7.80 | − 7.38 | − 7.37 |
| C. R. Hard Bean | − 2.12 | − 3.55 | — | − 4.10 | − 4.38 |
| D. R. Bani | − 4.17 | − 6.00 | − 6.98 | − 6.58 | − 6.55 |
| Ecuador Wsh. | — | — | — | — | — |
| El Sal. Cent'l St'd. | − 3.05 | − 4.93 | − 5.90 | − 5.05 | − 5.12 |
| Guat. Prime Wsh. | − 3.15 | − 5.33 | − 6.30 | − 5.68 | − 5.75 |
| Haiti Wsh. | — | — | − 6.78 | — | — |
| Mexico Prime Wsh. | − 3.05 | − 5.23 | − 6.15 | − 5.53 | − 5.30 |
| Nic. Good Wsh. | — | − 5.68 | — | — | − 6.30 |
| Venez. Tach. Fine Wsh. | − 2.47 | − 4.63 | − 5.70 | − 5.15 | − 4.55 |
| Rwanda-Burundi Ociru #2 | — | — | — | — | — |
| Ethiopia Djimmas UGQ | − 6.12 | − 7.50 | − 8.13 | − 7.78 | − 7.85 |
| Ambriz No. 2 AA | −12.50 | −14.63 | −14.93 | −13.85 | −13.00 |
| Uganda W&C | −12.60 | −14.75 | −15.10 | −14.10 | −13.35 |
| Ivory Coast Superior | — | −15.85 | −15.74 | — | — |

Source: Pan-American Coffee Bureau

**DIFFERENTIALS (Continued)**

1953-1966

per pound)

| JUNE | JULY | AUG. | SEPT. | OCT. | NOV. | DEC. | AVERAGE | HIGH | LOW |
|---|---|---|---|---|---|---|---|---|---|
| 47.50 | 47.35 | 48.23 | 49.40 | 48.78 | 49.95 | 49.93 | 48.49 | 50.63 | 46.75 |
| − 2.30 | − 2.30 | − 3.00 | − 5.32 | − 5.50 | − 6.57 | − 6.48 | − 3.78 | − 4.50 | − 3.75 |
| − 2.00 | − 2.06 | − 2.60 | − 2.77 | − 2.03 | − 2.63 | − 2.38 | − 2.30 | − 2.88 | − 3.00 |
| − 3.52 | − 3.80 | − 4.76 | − | − | − 4.67 | − 4.50 | − 4.16 | − 4.63 | − 4.12 |
| − 3.47 | − 3.90 | − 4.75 | − 6.00 | − 5.28 | − 5.73 | − | − 4.70 | − 5.63 | − 3.75 |
| − 2.70 | − 2.82 | − 3.29 | − 2.20 | − 2.63 | − 3.27 | − 3.03 | − 2.94 | − 3.13 | − 3.75 |
| − 2.70 | − 2.85 | − 3.32 | − 3.27 | − 2.65 | − 3.32 | − 3.10 | − 2.98 | − 3.13 | − 3.62 |
| − | − | − | − | − | − | − | − | − | − |
| − 2.75 | − 2.85 | − 3.26 | − 3.32 | − 2.65 | − 3.27 | − 3.00 | − 2.95 | − 3.13 | − 3.50 |
| − 3.28 | − 3.29 | − 3.31 | − | − 2.90 | − | − | − | − | − |
| − 2.55 | − 2.60 | − 3.15 | − 3.25 | − 2.48 | − 2.87 | − 2.43 | − 2.69 | − 2.63 | − 3.25 |
| − | − | − 3.27 | − 3.22 | − 2.75 | − 3.70 | − 3.71 | − | − | − |
| − 5.67 | − 4.62 | − 3.80 | − 5.65 | − 5.12 | − 6.27 | − 6.50 | − 5.73 | − 6.13 | − 8.25 |
| −18.95 | −14.45 | −11.03 | −12.17 | −10.75 | −14.65 | −13.43 | −16.90 | −12.13 | −24.00 |
| −19.05 | −14.60 | −11.25 | −12.62 | −11.08 | −14.77 | −13.51 | −17.16 | −12.38 | −24.62 |
| −19.62 | −16.72 | − | − | − | −15.22 | −14.18 | −19.09 | −14.50 | −23.25 |
| | | | | | | | | | |
| 48.48 | 48.08 | 46.80 | 45.40 | 45.20 | 45.10 | 44.18 | 47.43 | 49.88 | 44.00 |
| − 7.85 | − 7.58 | − 6.35 | − 5.17 | − 5.40 | − 5.55 | − 4.85 | − 6.60 | − 6.38 | − 4.75 |
| − | − 4.98 | − 3.92 | − | − 3.03 | − | − 2.80 | − 3.46 | − 2.38 | − 2.75 |
| − 7.26 | − 7.40 | − 5.50 | − 5.40 | − 6.07 | − 6.15 | − 5.40 | − 6.19 | − 4.38 | − 5.25 |
| − 7.70 | − 7.90 | − 6.52 | − | − 6.75 | − 6.42 | − 5.75 | − 7.95 | − 8.50 | − 5.75 |
| − 5.98 | − 6.10 | − 5.02 | − 3.62 | − 4.35 | − 5.00 | − 4.50 | − 4.89 | − 3.00 | − 4.50 |
| − 6.68 | − 6.53 | − 5.07 | − 3.72 | − 4.35 | − 5.02 | − 4.58 | − 5.18 | − 3.00 | − 4.75 |
| − | − | − | − | − | − | − | − | − | − |
| − 6.05 | − 6.25 | − 5.00 | − 3.75 | − 4.47 | − 4.95 | − 4.43 | − 5.02 | − 3.00 | − 4.50 |
| − 6.98 | − 7.08 | − | − | − | − | − | − | − | − |
| − 5.60 | − 5.75 | − 4.80 | − | − 3.51 | − 3.42 | − 3.28 | − 4.26 | − 2.38 | − 3.62 |
| − | − | − 5.30 | − 4.07 | − 4.47 | − 5.00 | − 4.30 | − | − | − 4.37 |
| − 8.78 | − 7.85 | − 5.95 | − 5.35 | − 5.97 | − 6.32 | − 6.28 | − 6.99 | − 6.38 | − 6.50 |
| −14.60 | −22.31 | −13.67 | −13.12 | −12.37 | −12.30 | −12.00 | −13.45 | −12.63 | −12.25 |
| −14.78 | −14.75 | −13.85 | −13.17 | −12.47 | −12.02 | −11.65 | −13.55 | −12.75 | −12.12 |
| − | − | − | − | − | − | − | − | − | − |

## CP-9. UNITED STATES: AVERAGE MONTHLY WHOLESALE PRICES OF COFFEE* 1954-1966
### Roasted Coffee in One-Pound Vacuum Can; Instant Coffee in Six-Ounce Jars

(In U.S. Cents)

| Year | | Jan. | Feb. | Mar. | April | May | June | July | Aug. | Sept. | Oct. | Nov. | Dec. | Annual Average |
|---|---|---|---|---|---|---|---|---|---|---|---|---|---|---|
| 1954 | Regular | — | — | 108.9 | 119.7 | 119.7 | 119.7 | 119.7 | 116.5 | 105.0 | 105.0 | 100.1 | 103.1 | 111.8 |
| 1955 | Regular | 103.1 | 93.6 | 90.3 | 90.3 | 90.3 | 86.4 | 86.4 | 87.4 | 89.3 | 93.2 | 89.3 | 89.3 | 90.7 |
| 1956 | Regular | 89.3 | 93.2 | 98.1 | 95.1 | 95.1 | 97.1 | 100.0 | 100.0 | 103.0 | 103.0 | 103.0 | 100.0 | 98.1 |
| 1957 | Regular | 100.0 | 99.1 | 97.1 | 93.2 | 93.2 | 93.2 | 93.2 | 93.2 | 90.2 | 87.3 | 87.3 | 87.3 | 92.9 |
| 1958 | Regular | 87.3 | 87.3 | 84.4 | 84.4 | 84.4 | 84.4 | 82.4 | 79.5 | 79.5 | 79.5 | 79.5 | 77.5 | 82.5 |
| 1959 | Regular | 75.5 | 72.6 | 72.6 | 70.6 | 70.6 | 70.6 | 70.6 | 70.6 | 70.6 | 70.6 | 70.6 | 70.6 | 71.3 |
| | Instant | 103.9 | 103.9 | 94.8 | 94.8 | 94.8 | 94.8 | 94.8 | 94.8 | 94.8 | 94.8 | 94.8 | 94.8 | 96.3 |
| 1960 | Regular | 70.6 | 70.6 | 70.6 | 70.6 | 70.6 | 70.6 | 70.6 | 68.9 | 68.9 | 68.9 | 68.9 | 68.9 | 69.9 |
| | Instant | 94.8 | 94.8 | 94.8 | 94.8 | 94.8 | 94.8 | 94.8 | 94.8 | 94.8 | 94.8 | 94.8 | 94.8 | 94.8 |
| 1961 | Regular | 68.9 | 68.9 | 68.9 | 68.9 | 68.9 | 68.9 | 68.9 | 68.9 | 68.9 | 66.9 | 66.9 | 66.9 | 68.4 |
| | Instant | 88.5 | 88.5 | 88.5 | 88.5 | 88.5 | 88.5 | 88.5 | 88.5 | 88.5 | 88.5 | 88.5 | 88.5 | 88.5 |
| 1962 | Regular | 66.9 | 66.9 | 66.9 | 66.9 | 66.9 | 66.9 | 66.9 | 66.9 | 66.9 | 64.3 | 64.3 | 64.3 | 66.3 |
| | Instant | 88.5 | 88.5 | 88.5 | 88.5 | 88.5 | 88.5 | 88.5 | 88.5 | 88.5 | 88.5 | 88.5 | 88.5 | 88.5 |
| 1963 | Regular | 63.8 | 63.8 | 62.5 | 64.6 | 64.6 | 64.6 | 64.6 | 64.6 | 64.6 | 65.2 | 66.6 | 68.5 | 64.8 |
| | Instant | 88.5 | 88.5 | 88.5 | 88.5 | 88.5 | 88.5 | 88.5 | 88.5 | 88.5 | 90.7 | 97.3 | 97.3 | 90.2 |
| 1964 | Regular | 72.4 | 76.4 | 80.3 | 80.3 | 80.3 | 80.3 | 80.3 | 80.3 | 80.3 | 80.3 | 80.3 | 80.3 | 79.3 |
| | Instant | 106.0 | 110.2 | 111.6 | 111.6 | 111.6 | 111.6 | 111.6 | 111.6 | 111.6 | 111.6 | 111.6 | 111.6 | 111.0 |
| 1965 | Regular | 80.3 | 80.3 | 80.3 | 80.3 | 80.3 | 80.3 | 80.3 | 80.3 | 80.3 | 80.3 | 80.3 | 80.3 | 80.3 |
| | Instant | 106.1 | 103.7 | 88.1 | 88.1 | 88.1 | 88.1 | 84.0 | 84.0 | 84.0 | 84.0 | 84.0 | 84.0 | 88.9 |
| 1966 | Regular | 80.3 | 80.3 | 80.3 | 80.3 | 80.3 | 80.3 | 80.3 | 80.3 | 76.7 | 76.7 | 76.7 | 76.6 | 79.1 |
| | Instant | 84.1 | 84.0 | 84.0 | 84.0 | 84.0 | 84.0 | 84.0 | 84.0 | 84.0 | 84.0 | 84.0 | 84.0 | 84.0 |

Source: Bureau of Labor Statistics.
*Producer to wholesaler or jobber, delivered destination Eastern United States.

A-142

## CP-14. UNITED STATES: AVERAGE MONTHLY RETAIL PRICES OF COFFEE* 1939–1966
(U. S. Cents per Pound Regular or 6 oz. Instant)

| Year | | Jan. | Feb. | Mar. | April | May | June | July | Aug. | Sept. | Oct. | Nov. | Dec. | Annual Average |
|---|---|---|---|---|---|---|---|---|---|---|---|---|---|---|
| 1939 | Regular | 22.9 | 22.8 | 22.8 | 22.6 | 22.4 | 22.3 | 22.3 | 22.3 | 22.3 | 22.2 | 22.1 | 22.1 | 22.4 |
| 1946 | Regular | 30.4 | 30.4 | 30.5 | 30.4 | 30.7 | 30.7 | 30.9 | 31.0 | 40.4 | 41.6 | 41.9 | 44.1 | 34.4 |
| 1947 | Regular | 44.7 | 45.9 | 47.0 | 47.6 | 47.5 | 45.5 | 45.3 | 45.6 | 46.9 | 47.9 | 48.8 | 49.8 | 46.9 |
| 1948 | Regular | 50.6 | 51.2 | 51.3 | 51.3 | 51.4 | 51.4 | 51.5 | 51.5 | 51.6 | 51.6 | 51.8 | 52.1 | 51.4 |
| 1949 | Regular | 52.3 | 52.4 | 52.3 | 52.2 | 52.0 | 52.1 | 52.2 | 52.4 | 52.9 | 53.6 | 66.6 | 73.4 | 55.4 |
| 1950 | Regular | 75.1 | 76.4 | 78.1 | 77.1 | 75.0 | 74.2 | 76.4 | 82.5 | 84.5 | 86.3 | 83.6 | 83.4 | 79.4 |
| 1951 | Regular | 85.7 | 86.4 | 86.3 | 86.6 | 87.2 | 87.2 | 87.1 | 87.1 | 86.9 | 86.8 | 86.9 | 86.9 | 86.8 |
| 1952 | Regular | 86.8 | 87.0 | 87.0 | 87.0 | 86.8 | 86.8 | 86.7 | 86.7 | 86.7 | 86.6 | 86.5 | 86.6 | 86.8 |
| 1953 | Regular | 86.4 | 86.3 | 86.7 | 89.3 | 88.9 | 88.0 | 88.6 | 90.0 | 91.1 | 91.6 | 91.4 | 91.5 | 89.2 |
| 1954 | Regular | 94.5 | 99.4 | 105.2 | 113.6 | 118.0 | 120.9 | 123.0 | 123.3 | 111.6 | 110.0 | 105.1 | 105.3 | 110.8 |
| 1955 | Regular | 105.8 | 97.0 | 94.2 | 92.5 | 92.2 | 89.0 | 89.1 | 89.0 | 90.5 | 92.3 | 93.0 | 91.6 | 93.0 |
| 1956 | Regular Vacuum | 96.2 | 96.2 | 99.4 | 110.1 | 100.3 | 101.8 | 105.0 | 105.9 | 108.0 | 109.0 | 109.3 | 108.9 | 103.4 |
| | Regular Bag | 79.1 | 79.9 | 83.2 | 83.2 | 83.6 | 85.3 | 89.1 | 89.2 | 92.6 | 93.0 | 92.6 | 90.9 | 86.8 |
| 1957 | Regular Vacuum | 108.2 | 107.7 | 106.3 | 104.4 | 102.5 | 102.4 | 101.7 | 101.5 | 99.3 | 96.2 | 95.1 | 95.0 | 101.7 |
| | Regular Bag | 90.8 | 89.9 | 89.6 | 86.9 | 86.1 | 86.1 | 83.1 | 83.0 | 78.2 | 76.9 | 76.9 | 76.8 | 83.7 |
| 1958 | Regular Vacuum | 95.3 | 95.2 | 92.3 | 92.8 | 92.2 | 91.8 | 90.6 | 89.3 | 87.7 | 87.2 | 86.8 | 85.3 | 90.5 |
| | Regular Bag | 77.9 | 77.9 | 77.9 | 77.2 | 75.9 | 75.4 | 75.0 | 73.0 | 69.4 | 69.1 | 68.9 | 66.3 | 73.7 |
| 1959 | Regular Vacuum | 83.7 | 80.5 | 79.5 | 78.1 | 77.2 | 76.9 | 77.0 | 76.8 | 76.6 | 76.7 | 76.3 | 76.4 | 77.9 |
| | Regular Bag | 64.0 | 62.3 | 61.9 | 61.5 | 57.9 | 57.1 | 57.1 | 57.0 | 56.9 | 58.0 | 58.2 | 58.1 | 59.2 |
| 1960 | Regular Vacuum | 76.1 | 75.4 | 75.4 | 75.6 | 75.8 | 75.7 | 76.2 | 74.9 | 74.7 | 74.5 | 74.6 | 74.4 | 75.3 |
| | Regular Bag | 59.6 | 59.6 | 59.6 | 59.6 | 59.5 | 59.8 | 60.0 | 58.1 | 57.4 | 59.0 | 59.2 | 59.0 | 59.2 |
| 1961 | Regular Vacuum | 74.3 | 74.6 | 74.4 | 74.7 | 74.4 | 74.5 | 73.5 | 73.5 | 73.1 | 72.7 | 71.8 | 71.4 | 73.6 |
| | Regular Bag | 59.0 | 59.3 | 58.8 | 59.2 | 58.8 | 59.1 | 58.8 | 58.6 | 58.7 | 57.8 | 57.5 | 57.4 | 58.6 |
| | Instant | | | | | | | | | 92.9 | 93.1 | 92.7 | 91.6 | |
| 1962 | Regular Vacuum | 71.2 | 71.0 | 71.0 | 71.1 | 71.0 | 70.9 | 71.2 | 71.3 | 71.4 | 71.1 | 69.5 | 69.2 | 70.8 |
| | Regular Bag | 57.4 | 57.4 | 57.2 | 56.9 | 57.3 | 57.1 | 57.3 | 57.4 | 57.5 | 56.5 | 56.7 | 56.7 | 57.1 |
| | Instant | 91.6 | 91.6 | 90.4 | 90.7 | 90.0 | 89.3 | 89.0 | 90.3 | 91.9 | 91.8 | 91.7 | 91.2 | 90.8 |
| 1963 | Regular Vacuum | 69.2 | 69.1 | 68.7 | 68.7 | 69.0 | 69.5 | 69.6 | 69.3 | 69.6 | 69.7 | 69.8 | 70.1 | 69.4 |
| | Regular Bag | 56.6 | 57.0 | 56.8 | 56.9 | 56.4 | 57.0 | 57.1 | 56.5 | 56.7 | 56.6 | 56.7 | 56.8 | 56.8 |
| | Instant | 91.7 | 92.6 | 93.1 | 92.7 | 92.6 | 92.5 | 92.4 | 92.6 | 91.9 | 90.7 | 91.4 | 91.9 | 92.2 |
| 1964 | Regular Vacuum | 71.1 | 74.1 | 78.3 | 80.9 | 82.4 | 83.9 | 84.4 | 84.9 | 84.9 | 84.6 | 84.9 | 84.8 | 81.6 |
| | Regular Bag | 58.1 | 60.6 | 65.1 | 70.0 | 72.2 | 72.7 | 72.9 | 73.3 | 72.2 | 72.9 | 72.2 | 71.6 | 69.5 |
| | Instant | 94.4 | 99.1 | 104.3 | 107.9 | 109.9 | 110.7 | 110.3 | 110.2 | 109.9 | 108.1 | 107.9 | 108.1 | 106.7 |
| 1965 | Regular Vacuum | 84.5 | 84.3 | 83.9 | 83.8 | 83.3 | 83.2 | 83.4 | 83.5 | 82.9 | 82.7 | 82.1 | 82.1 | 83.3 |
| | Regular Bag | 72.4 | 72.3 | 72.2 | 71.7 | 71.7 | 71.4 | 70.7 | 71.8 | 70.9 | 70.1 | 69.3 | 69.9 | 71.1 |
| | Instant | 107.2 | 106.4 | 98.5 | 91.8 | 90.3 | 92.1 | 92.8 | 93.4 | 93.7 | 92.9 | 92.5 | 91.3 | 95.2 |
| 1966 | Regular Vacuum | 82.2 | 82.3 | 82.5 | 82.8 | 83.0 | 83.2 | 83.2 | 83.5 | 82.5 | 81.1 | 80.6 | 80.7 | 82.3 |
| | Regular Bag | 69.8 | 69.8 | 69.5 | 69.7 | 69.6 | 69.9 | 69.9 | 69.2 | 69.7 | 68.4 | 68.2 | 67.9 | 69.3 |
| | Instant | 90.4 | 89.2 | 89.7 | 91.0 | 91.7 | 92.5 | 92.5 | 93.0 | 91.7 | 90.1 | 89.2 | 89.8 | 90.9 |

Source: Bureau of Labor Statistics.

*Prices represent averages of mid-month quotations in the leading cities of the United States. The BLS changed the price basis as of January, 1956 from a combined average of vacuum and bag packed coffee to the vacuum type only. In 1957 the BLS again revised its reporting to both vacuum and bag packed prices and provided as well the back information for 1956. A new series was started in January, 1964 in which prices represent special benchmark averages computed annually and adjusted for price changes to the current month as shown by data collected for the new series, Consumer Price Index.

## CP-15. UNITED STATES: AVERAGE MONTHLY PRICES PAID BY CONSUMERS FOR REGULAR AND INSTANT COFFEE*, 1952-1966
### Regular coffee per pound; Instant coffee per 2 ounce equivalent

(U.S. Cents)

| Year | | Jan. | Feb. | Mar. | April | May | June | July | Aug. | Sept. | Oct. | Nov. | Dec. | Annual Average |
|---|---|---|---|---|---|---|---|---|---|---|---|---|---|---|
| 1952 | Regular | 84.6 | 84.6 | 84.9 | 84.6 | 84.7 | 84.6 | 84.7 | 84.7 | 84.8 | 84.5 | 84.5 | 84.6 | 84.5 |
| | Instant | 52.5 | 51.6 | 52.3 | 52.0 | 51.1 | 50.6 | 50.7 | 51.6 | 50.6 | 49.2 | 49.7 | 51.0 | 51.0 |
| 1953 | Regular | 84.8 | 84.5 | 84.7 | 86.8 | 86.7 | 86.1 | 86.0 | 87.2 | 88.3 | 88.8 | 89.2 | 89.4 | 86.9 |
| | Instant | 51.6 | 51.2 | 51.3 | 51.9 | 51.1 | 51.5 | 51.5 | 52.0 | 50.7 | 51.1 | 52.7 | 54.0 | 51.7 |
| 1954 | Regular | 92.3 | 95.5 | 102.0 | 108.7 | 112.8 | 115.5 | 117.5 | 116.2 | 107.6 | 105.2 | 102.2 | 102.3 | 105.6 |
| | Instant | 54.2 | 53.7 | 57.9 | 61.0 | 64.2 | 64.8 | 65.5 | 65.5 | 62.7 | 60.9 | 60.0 | 60.0 | 60.6 |
| 1955 | Regular | 101.9 | 95.9 | 91.1 | 89.8 | 88.7 | 86.6 | 86.6 | 86.4 | 87.5 | 89.0 | 89.3 | 88.3 | 90.1 |
| | Instant | 59.8 | 58.2 | 55.6 | 55.0 | 54.4 | 53.3 | 52.9 | 52.2 | 52.4 | 51.9 | 51.9 | 49.2 | 53.6 |
| 1956 | Regular | 88.1 | 87.7 | 90.5 | 90.8 | 91.3 | 93.0 | 95.3 | 95.6 | 97.9 | 93.4 | 98.3 | 98.0 | 93.7 |
| | Instant | 48.2 | 47.8 | 50.0 | 50.5 | 50.7 | 50.7 | 50.4 | 50.4 | 50.0 | 48.6 | 48.7 | 48.6 | 49.5 |
| 1957 | Regular | 97.4 | 96.9 | 96.0 | 94.9 | 93.2 | 93.3 | 92.7 | 92.1 | 90.2 | 87.3 | 86.1 | 86.5 | 92.2 |
| | Instant | 48.2 | 47.7 | 46.5 | 47.0 | 46.0 | 45.2 | 45.7 | 45.2 | 44.7 | 43.4 | 42.0 | 42.0 | 45.3 |
| 1958 | Regular | 86.8 | 86.2 | 84.7 | 83.7 | 84.0 | 83.2 | 83.0 | 81.6 | 79.4 | 78.6 | 77.5 | 76.2 | 82.1 |
| | Instant | 42.3 | 41.6 | 41.6 | 41.6 | 40.8 | 41.1 | 41.2 | 40.2 | 39.7 | 39.4 | 39.2 | 38.7 | 40.6 |
| 1959 | Regular | 74.4 | 71.9 | 71.0 | 68.6 | 68.1 | 67.4 | 68.1 | 67.6 | 67.4 | 67.1 | 67.0 | 66.8 | 68.8 |
| | Instant | 37.7 | 37.0 | 35.1 | 34.6 | 34.4 | 34.4 | 34.1 | 33.6 | 33.7 | 33.8 | 33.5 | 33.3 | 34.6 |
| 1960 | Regular | 67.2 | 66.6 | 66.8 | 66.7 | 66.6 | 66.9 | 66.2 | 66.1 | 65.3 | 65.4 | 65.5 | 65.2 | 66.2 |
| | Instant | 33.3 | 33.2 | 32.6 | 32.7 | 32.8 | 32.6 | 32.9 | 32.5 | 32.5 | 32.7 | 32.4 | 32.4 | 32.7 |
| 1961 | Regular | 64.7 | 64.4 | 64.0 | 64.1 | 63.8 | 64.0 | 64.6 | 64.4 | 63.9 | 63.4 | 62.4 | 62.5 | 63.8 |
| | Instant | 31.7 | 31.2 | 30.7 | 30.7 | 30.8 | 30.5 | 30.4 | 30.5 | 30.5 | 30.3 | 30.2 | 30.3 | 30.6 |
| 1962 | Regular | 62.4 | 61.4 | 62.2 | 62.1 | 62.1 | 62.3 | 62.4 | 62.2 | 62.2 | 61.0 | 60.1 | 60.1 | 61.7 |
| | Instant | 30.0 | 29.8 | 29.9 | 30.0 | 29.6 | 29.2 | 28.1 | 28.4 | 28.6 | 28.3 | 28.7 | 28.8 | 29.1 |
| 1963 | Regular | 60.9 | 60.7 | 60.5 | 60.3 | 60.5 | 61.0 | 61.0 | 60.8 | 60.9 | 60.1 | 60.5 | 61.8 | 60.8 |
| | Instant | 28.6 | 28.5 | 28.9 | 28.6 | 28.5 | 28.7 | 28.6 | 28.7 | 28.6 | 28.2 | 28.1 | 28.8 | 28.6 |
| 1964 | Regular | 63.4 | 66.5 | 69.3 | 72.7 | 74.1 | 75.1 | 75.2 | 75.3 | 75.0 | 74.7 | 74.6 | 74.7 | 72.5 |
| | Instant | 30.2 | 31.3 | 32.3 | 33.5 | 34.0 | 33.8 | 33.8 | 33.7 | 33.1 | 33.3 | 33.0 | 33.8 | 33.0 |
| 1965 | Regular | 74.8 | 74.1 | 73.9 | 74.4 | 74.0 | 74.1 | 73.7 | 73.5 | 73.2 | 72.8 | 72.2 | 72.3 | 73.6 |
| | Instant | 32.9 | 32.7 | 30.0 | 28.9 | 28.5 | 28.8 | 29.0 | 29.1 | 29.2 | 29.3 | 29.5 | 28.8 | 29.7 |
| 1966 | Regular | 72.8 | 72.2 | 72.4 | 72.3 | 72.5 | 72.9 | 72.8 | 72.8 | 71.2 | 70.3 | 69.8 | 70.4 | 71.9 |
| | Instant | 28.2 | 28.4 | 29.0 | 29.6 | 29.6 | 29.9 | 30.0 | 30.0 | 29.4 | 29.4 | 29.4 | 29.9 | 29.4 |

Source: Market Research Corporation of America.
*N.B.: The above prices are those actually paid and include special promotions and deals.

## CP-16. UNITED STATES: AVERAGE MONTHLY IMPORT PRICES OF GREEN COFFEE, 1953-1966

(U.S. Cents Per Pound)

| | 1953 | 1954 | 1955 | 1956 | 1957 | 1958 | 1959 | 1960 | 1961 | 1962 | 1963 | 1964 | 1965 | 1966 |
|---|---|---|---|---|---|---|---|---|---|---|---|---|---|---|
| January | 50.84 | 54.09 | 62.68 | 49.06 | 53.19 | 48.03 | 37.91 | 35.01 | 33.49 | 30.47 | 29.54 | 33.38 | 40.75 | 38.36 |
| February | 50.73 | 55.75 | 61.07 | 49.21 | 51.46 | 48.51 | 35.89 | 35.82 | 33.66 | 30.74 | 29.84 | 36.05 | 40.19 | 38.42 |
| March | 50.67 | 61.82 | 54.21 | 50.52 | 49.52 | 46.96 | 35.55 | 35.62 | 32.86 | 30.81 | 29.01 | 38.29 | 38.93 | 37.46 |
| April | 52.31 | 69.23 | 50.89 | 50.37 | 52.10 | 45.68 | 35.76 | 34.41 | 32.24 | 30.51 | 29.26 | 40.45 | 38.15 | 37.33 |
| May | 53.04 | 73.46 | 51.24 | 50.58 | 49.48 | 44.48 | 37.21 | 34.28 | 32.71 | 30.78 | 29.76 | 39.82 | 37.57 | 37.90 |
| June | 52.49 | 76.92 | 50.04 | 52.81 | 49.68 | 44.18 | 36.56 | 33.28 | 33.74 | 30.96 | 29.14 | 40.90 | 37.02 | 36.06 |
| July | 52.85 | 78.64 | 50.13 | 51.40 | 52.48 | 45.60 | 36.99 | 33.01 | 33.22 | 31.59 | 30.23 | 41.02 | 37.17 | 35.90 |
| August | 53.32 | 77.73 | 50.40 | 52.26 | 51.04 | 44.32 | 34.73 | 34.13 | 33.01 | 31.55 | 30.70 | 41.05 | 37.58 | 36.81 |
| September | 55.46 | 74.17 | 49.17 | 52.94 | 49.36 | 42.72 | 33.95 | 33.69 | 31.99 | 31.65 | 31.03 | 41.19 | 34.85 | 35.87 |
| October | 54.27 | 66.12 | 50.21 | 51.13 | 46.42 | 40.15 | 33.73 | 34.10 | 30.69 | 30.25 | 30.62 | 40.96 | 36.43 | 34.83 |
| November | 53.71 | 64.71 | 48.83 | 51.65 | 46.90 | 40.33 | 34.75 | 34.34 | 31.14 | 27.70 | 30.63 | 41.16 | 37.31 | 34.92 |
| December | 53.25 | 63.40 | 49.45 | 52.76 | 46.97 | 38.53 | 36.15 | 34.19 | 30.72 | 29.29 | 31.73 | 42.49 | 37.96 | 34.44 |
| Year | 52.70 | 65.68 | 52.18 | 51.17 | 49.82 | 43.89 | 35.65 | 34.34 | 32.44 | 30.44 | 30.28 | 39.63 | 37.56 | 36.53 |

Source: Department of Research, PACB, from data collected by the U.S. Department of Commerce.

## CP-18A. INTERNATIONAL COFFEE ORGANIZATION
(In U.S. Cents)

| | ARABICAS Washed | Unwashed | Robusta | Daily Price | | ARABICAS Washed | Unwashed | Robusta | Daily Price |
|---|---|---|---|---|---|---|---|---|---|
| MARCH | | | | | JUNE | | | | |
| 22 | 45.54 | 45.00 | 24.42 | 38.32 | 1 | 46.00 | 44.50 | 25.22 | 38.57 |
| 23 | 45.19 | 45.00 | 23.83 | 38.01 | 2 | 46.13 | 44.50 | 26.17 | 38.93 |
| 24 | 45.32 | 45.00 | 23.64 | 37.99 | 3 | 46.13 | 44.50 | 27.68 | 39.44 |
| 25 | 45.50 | 45.00 | 24.00 | 38.17 | 4 | 46.13 | 44.50 | 28.18 | 39.60 |
| 26 | 45.50 | 45.00 | 24.00 | 38.17 | 7 | 46.19 | 44.50 | 27.68 | 39.46 |
| 29 | 45.63 | 45.25 | 24.08 | 38.32 | 8 | 46.07 | 44.25 | 27.42 | 39.25 |
| 30 | 45.38 | 45.00 | 24.43 | 38.27 | 9 | 46.00 | 44.25 | 27.00 | 39.08 |
| 31 | 45.38 | 45.00 | 24.68 | 38.35 | 10 | 46.00 | 44.25 | 27.25 | 39.17 |
| | | | | | 11 | 46.03 | 44.25 | 27.68 | 39.32 |
| APRIL | | | | | 14 | 46.09 | 44.15 | 28.25 | 39.50 |
| 1 | 45.25 | 45.00 | 24.18 | 38.14 | 15 | 46.01 | 44.25 | 28.33 | 39.53 |
| 2 | 45.25 | 45.00 | 24.18 | 38.14 | 16 | 45.82 | 44.00 | 28.33 | 39.38 |
| 5 | 45.82 | 45.00 | 25.00 | 38.61 | 17 | 45.88 | 44.00 | 28.35 | 39.41 |
| 6 | 46.06 | 45.00 | 25.39 | 38.82 | 18 | 45.63 | 44.00 | 28.17 | 39.27 |
| 7 | 46.06 | 45.00 | 25.52 | 38.86 | 21 | 45.63 | 44.00 | 28.00 | 39.21 |
| 8 | 46.13 | 45.00 | 25.43 | 38.85 | 22 | 45.50 | 44.00 | 28.00 | 39.17 |
| 9 | 46.04 | 45.00 | 25.18 | 38.74 | 23 | 45.51 | 44.00 | 27.92 | 39.14 |
| 12 | 46.00 | 45.00 | 25.43 | 38.81 | 24 | 45.44 | 43.70 | 28.09 | 39.08 |
| 13 | 45.88 | 45.00 | 25.43 | 38.77 | 25 | 45.82 | 43.70 | 28.17 | 39.23 |
| 14 | 45.91 | 45.00 | 25.35 | 38.75 | 28 | 45.78 | 43.70 | 28.50 | 39.33 |
| 15 | 45.94 | 45.00 | 25.31 | 38.75 | 29 | 45.94 | 43.70 | 28.75 | 39.46 |
| 19 | 45.88 | 45.00 | 25.31 | 38.73 | 30 | 45.88 | 43.50 | 28.68 | 39.35 |
| 20 | 45.90 | 45.00 | 25.10 | 38.67 | | | | | |
| 21 | 45.84 | 45.00 | 25.00 | 38.61 | JULY | | | | |
| 22 | 45.88 | 45.00 | 25.00 | 38.63 | 1 | 45.82 | 43.50 | 29.50 | 39.61 |
| 23 | 45.53 | 44.25 | 24.75 | 38.18 | 2 | 45.82 | 43.50 | 29.68 | 39.67 |
| 26 | 45.63 | 44.25 | 24.75 | 38.21 | 6 | 45.82 | 43.50 | 30.13 | 39.82 |
| 27 | 45.53 | 44.00 | 24.50 | 38.01 | 7 | 45.82 | 43.50 | 30.52 | 39.95 |
| 28 | 45.42 | 44.00 | 24.00 | 37.81 | 8 | 45.82 | 43.50 | 30.69 | 40.00 |
| 29 | 45.09 | 43.75 | 23.28 | 37.37 | 9 | 45.94 | 43.50 | 30.94 | 40.13 |
| 30 | 44.92 | 43.75 | 23.93 | 37.20 | 12 | 45.94 | 43.75 | 31.02 | 40.24 |
| | | | | | 13 | 45.94 | 43.50 | 31.08 | 40.17 |
| MAY | | | | | 14 | 45.96 | 43.50 | 31.18 | 40.21 |
| 3 | 44.92 | 43.50 | 22.67 | 37.03 | 15 | 46.01 | 43.75 | 31.52 | 40.43 |
| 4 | 44.88 | 43.50 | 21.92 | 36.77 | 16 | 45.94 | 43.75 | 32.35 | 40.68 |
| 5 | 44.75 | 43.50 | 21.92 | 36.72 | 19 | 46.07 | 43.60 | 33.92 | 41.20 |
| 6 | 44.61 | 43.65 | 22.10 | 36.79 | 20 | 46.01 | 43.60 | 34.58 | 41.40 |
| 7 | 44.65 | 43.65 | 21.65 | 36.65 | 21 | 45.98 | 43.50 | 34.42 | 41.30 |
| 10 | 44.61 | 43.65 | 21.57 | 36.61 | 22 | 45.91 | 43.50 | 34.17 | 41.19 |
| 11 | 44.82 | 43.65 | 21.10 | 36.52 | 23 | 45.94 | 43.50 | 34.17 | 41.20 |
| 12 | 44.94 | 43.75 | 21.10 | 36.60 | 26 | 46.00 | 43.50 | 33.92 | 41.14 |
| 13 | 45.10 | 43.65 | 20.77 | 36.51 | 27 | 45.91 | 43.50 | 34.18 | 41.20 |
| 14 | 44.94 | 43.75 | 20.68 | 36.46 | 28 | 45.97 | 43.75 | 34.42 | 41.38 |
| 17 | 45.07 | 44.00 | 21.08 | 36.72 | 29 | 45.97 | 43.75 | 34.93 | 41.55 |
| 18 | 45.13 | 44.00 | 21.25 | 36.79 | 30 | 46.00 | 43.75 | 35.02 | 41.59 |
| 19 | 45.25 | 44.00 | 21.67 | 36.97 | | | | | |
| 20 | 45.38 | 44.00 | 22.33 | 37.24 | AUGUST | | | | |
| 21 | 45.50 | 44.13 | 22.50 | 37.38 | 2 | 45.97 | 43.75 | 35.08 | 41.60 |
| 24 | 45.50 | 44.25 | 22.80 | 37.52 | 3 | 45.94 | 43.75 | 35.68 | 41.79 |
| 25 | 45.56 | 44.25 | 22.93 | 37.58 | 4 | 46.04 | 43.63 | 35.08 | 41.58 |
| 26 | 45.88 | 44.25 | 23.34 | 37.82 | 5 | 46.04 | 43.63 | 34.42 | 41.36 |
| 27 | 45.94 | 44.25 | 24.08 | 38.09 | 6 | 45.94 | 43.63 | 36.27 | 41.95 |
| 28 | 45.94 | 44.25 | 24.58 | 38.26 | 9 | 46.13 | 43.63 | 35.75 | 41.84 |

**DAILY INDICATOR PRICE, MARCH-DECEMBER 1965**
Per Pound)

|  | ARABICAS Washed | Unwashed | Robusta | Daily Price |  | ARABICAS Washed | Unwashed | Robusta | Daily Price |
|---|---|---|---|---|---|---|---|---|---|
| **AUGUST** (Continued) |  |  |  |  | **OCTOBER** (Continued) |  |  |  |  |
| 10 | 46.19 | 43.63 | 35.17 | 41.66 | 20 | 46.88 | 42.75 | 36.50 | 42.04 |
| 11 | 46.19 | 43.63 | 36.00 | 41.94 | 21 | 46.94 | 42.60 | 36.50 | 42.01 |
| 12 | 46.44 | 43.63 | 36.22 | 42.10 | 22 | 47.13 | 42.60 | 36.50 | 42.08 |
| 13 | 46.50 | 43.75 | 35.33 | 41.86 | 25 | 47.23 | 42.65 | 36.50 | 42.13 |
| 16 | 46.44 | 43.75 | 36.47 | 42.22 | 26 | 47.32 | 42.60 | 36.33 | 42.08 |
| 17 | 46.88 | 43.75 | 36.85 | 42.49 | 27 | 47.34 | 42.60 | 36.08 | 42.01 |
| 18 | 47.00 | 43.75 | 36.77 | 42.51 | 28 | 47.38 | 42.60 | 36.00 | 41.99 |
| 19 | 47.07 | 43.75 | 36.50 | 42.44 | 29 | 47.32 | 42.60 | 35.91 | 41.94 |
| 20 | 47.13 | 43.75 | 36.50 | 42.46 |  |  |  |  |  |
| 23 | 47.25 | 43.65 | 36.93 | 42.61 | **NOVEMBER** |  |  |  |  |
| 24 | 47.69 | 43.65 | 37.02 | 42.79 | 1 | 47.63 | 42.60 | 35.46 | 41.90 |
| 25 | 47.50 | 43.60 | 37.02 | 42.71 | 3 | 47.69 | 42.60 | 35.50 | 41.93 |
| 26 | 47.75 | 43.60 | 35.17 | 42.17 | 4 | 47.75 | 42.60 | 35.41 | 41.92 |
| 27 | 48.00 | 43.60 | 36.50 | 42.70 | 5 | 47.75 | 42.60 | 34.67 | 41.67 |
| 30 | 48.25 | 43.60 | 36.58 | 42.81 | 8 | 47.63 | 42.60 | 34.83 | 41.69 |
| 31 | 48.50 | 43.60 | 36.08 | 42.73 | 9 | 47.69 | 42.60 | 34.25 | 41.51 |
|  |  |  |  |  | 10 | 47.63 | 42.60 | 33.83 | 41.35 |
| **SEPTEMBER** |  |  |  |  | 12 | 47.63 | 42.65 | 33.83 | 41.37 |
| 1 | 48.50 | 43.40 | 36.23 | 42.71 | 15 | 48.13 | 42.65 | 33.00 | 41.29 |
| 2 | 47.88 | 43.00 | 36.07 | 42.32 | 16 | 48.38 | 42.65 | 33.42 | 41.48 |
| 3 | 47.75 | 43.00 | 36.05 | 42.27 | 17 | 48.38 | 42.65 | 33.83 | 41.62 |
| 7 | 47.50 | 42.50 | 35.50 | 41.83 | 18 | 48.32 | 42.65 | 34.33 | 41.77 |
| 8 | 47.50 | 42.50 | 34.58 | 41.53 | 19 | 48.44 | 42.65 | 34.08 | 41.72 |
| 9 | 47.38 | 42.50 | 34.25 | 41.38 | 22 | 48.50 | 42.75 | 33.75 | 41.67 |
| 10 | 47.38 | 42.50 | 34.43 | 41.44 | 23 | 48.63 | 42.75 | 33.58 | 41.65 |
| 13 | 47.38 | 42.50 | 34.43 | 41.44 | 24 | 48.57 | 42.75 | 34.58 | 41.97 |
| 14 | 47.00 | 42.50 | 34.43 | 41.31 | 26 | 48.63 | 42.75 | 34.92 | 42.10 |
| 15 | 46.82 | 42.50 | 34.43 | 41.25 | 29 | 48.69 | 42.75 | 34.75 | 42.06 |
| 16 | 46.82 | 42.50 | 34.17 | 41.16 | 30 | 48.84 | 42.75 | 35.17 | 42.25 |
| 17 | 46.79 | 42.50 | 35.08 | 41.46 |  |  |  |  |  |
| 20 | 46.88 | 42.50 | 35.60 | 41.66 | **DECEMBER** |  |  |  |  |
| 21 | 46.81 | 42.50 | 35.58 | 41.63 | 1 | 48.75 | 42.75 | 35.17 | 42.22 |
| 22 | 46.69 | 42.50 | 35.68 | 41.62 | 2 | 48.69 | 42.80 | 35.25 | 42.25 |
| 23 | 46.66 | 42.50 | 35.37 | 41.51 | 3 | 48.65 | 42.80 | 35.67 | 42.37 |
| 24 | 46.60 | 42.50 | 35.10 | 41.40 | 6 | 47.96 | 42.80 | 35.42 | 42.06 |
| 27 | 46.63 | 42.50 | 35.63 | 41.59 | 7 | 47.96 | 42.80 | 35.67 | 42.14 |
| 28 | 46.61 | 42.50 | 35.67 | 41.59 | 8 | 48.09 | 42.80 | 35.67 | 42.19 |
| 29 | 46.44 | 42.50 | 36.08 | 41.67 | 9 | 48.09 | 42.80 | 35.75 | 42.21 |
| 30 | 46.50 | 42.50 | 36.42 | 41.81 | 10 | 48.15 | 42.80 | 35.42 | 42.12 |
|  |  |  |  |  | 13 | 48.04 | 42.80 | 35.58 | 42.14 |
| **OCTOBER** |  |  |  |  | 14 | 47.94 | 42.80 | 35.92 | 42.22 |
| 1 | 46.50 | 42.50 | 36.42 | 41.81 | 15 | 48.19 | 42.80 | 36.00 | 42.33 |
| 4 | 46.84 | 42.75 | 36.67 | 42.09 | 16 | 48.00 | 42.80 | 36.33 | 42.38 |
| 5 | 46.87 | 43.00 | 36.67 | 42.18 | 17 | 48.00 | 42.80 | 36.33 | 42.38 |
| 6 | 47.03 | 43.00 | 36.92 | 42.32 | 20 | 47.75 | 42.80 | 36.33 | 42.29 |
| 7 | 47.01 | 43.00 | 36.92 | 42.31 | 21 | 47.94 | 42.80 | 36.33 | 42.36 |
| 8 | 47.01 | 43.00 | 37.08 | 42.36 | 22 | 48.00 | 42.80 | 36.33 | 42.38 |
| 11 | 47.19 | 43.00 | 37.00 | 42.40 | 23 | 48.04 | 42.80 | 36.58 | 42.47 |
| 13 | 47.15 | 42.75 | 37.42 | 42.44 | 27 | 48.00 | 43.00 | 36.83 | 42.61 |
| 14 | 47.07 | 42.75 | 37.17 | 42.33 | 28 | 47.88 | 43.00 | 36.58 | 42.49 |
| 15 | 47.07 | 42.75 | 36.75 | 42.19 | 29 | 47.96 | 43.15 | 36.54 | 42.55 |
| 18 | 47.19 | 42.75 | 36.50 | 42.15 | 30 | 47.86 | 43.15 | 36.38 | 42.46 |
| 19 | 46.97 | 42.75 | 36.50 | 42.07 |  |  |  |  |  |

## CP-18B. INTERNATIONAL COFFEE

(In U. S. Cents

| | ARABICAS Washed | Unwashed | Robusta | Daily Price | | ARABICAS Washed | Unwashed | Robusta | Daily Price |
|---|---|---|---|---|---|---|---|---|---|
| **JANUARY** | | | | | **APRIL** | | | | |
| 3 | 47.82 | 43.15 | 36.58 | 42.52 | 1 | 45.90 | 40.40 | 33.71 | 40.00 |
| 4 | 48.00 | 43.25 | 36.46 | 42.57 | 4 | 46.01 | 40.40 | 33.96 | 40.12 |
| 5 | 48.00 | 43.00 | 36.54 | 42.51 | 5 | 46.03 | 40.40 | 34.08 | 40.17 |
| 6 | 47.90 | 43.00 | 36.58 | 42.49 | 6 | 45.88 | 40.40 | 34.46 | 40.25 |
| 7 | 47.67 | 42.75 | 36.75 | 42.39 | 7 | 45.88 | 40.50 | 34.33 | 40.24 |
| 10 | 47.65 | 42.75 | 36.75 | 42.38 | 11 | 45.92 | 40.50 | 34.33 | 40.25 |
| 11 | 47.65 | 42.75 | 36.75 | 42.38 | 12 | 45.88 | 40.50 | 34.58 | 40.32 |
| 12 | 47.57 | 42.50 | 36.75 | 42.27 | 13 | 45.96 | 40.50 | 34.58 | 40.35 |
| 13 | 47.57 | 42.50 | 36.75 | 42.27 | 14 | 46.00 | 40.50 | 35.08 | 40.53 |
| 14 | 47.52 | 42.50 | 36.84 | 42.29 | 15 | 45.82 | 40.50 | 35.08 | 40.47 |
| 17 | 47.61 | 42.50 | 36.92 | 42.34 | 18 | 45.63 | 40.50 | 34.83 | 40.32 |
| 18 | 47.57 | 42.50 | 36.67 | 42.25 | 19 | 45.69 | 40.60 | 34.33 | 40.21 |
| 19 | 47.50 | 42.50 | 36.00 | 42.00 | 20 | 45.57 | 40.60 | 34.58 | 40.25 |
| 20 | 47.38 | 42.50 | 36.08 | 41.99 | 21 | 45.50 | 40.60 | 34.58 | 40.23 |
| 21 | 47.25 | 42.50 | 36.00 | 41.92 | 22 | 45.69 | 40.60 | 34.58 | 40.29 |
| 24 | 47.32 | 42.50 | 36.00 | 41.94 | 25 | 45.64 | 40.65 | 34.58 | 40.29 |
| 25 | 47.07 | 42.50 | 36.00 | 41.86 | 26 | 45.79 | 40.65 | 34.58 | 40.34 |
| 26 | 47.15 | 42.50 | 36.04 | 41.90 | 27 | 46.02 | 40.75 | 34.58 | 40.45 |
| 27 | 47.07 | 42.50 | 35.92 | 41.83 | 28 | 45.98 | 40.75 | 34.58 | 40.44 |
| 28 | 47.00 | 42.50 | 35.79 | 41.76 | 29 | 46.07 | 40.75 | 34.71 | 40.51 |
| 31 | 46.84 | 41.50 | 35.42 | 41.25 | **MAY** | | | | |
| **FEBRUARY** | | | | | 2 | 46.00 | 40.85 | 34.83 | 40.56 |
| 1 | 46.98 | 41.25 | 35.42 | 41.22 | 3 | 46.00 | 40.85 | 34.83 | 40.56 |
| 2 | 47.00 | 41.25 | 35.17 | 41.14 | 4 | 46.29 | 41.00 | 34.83 | 40.71 |
| 3 | 47.07 | 41.50 | 34.92 | 41.16 | 5 | 46.19 | 40.85 | 34.75 | 40.60 |
| 4 | 46.94 | 41.50 | 34.92 | 41.12 | 6 | 46.29 | 40.90 | 34.83 | 40.67 |
| 7 | 47.07 | 41.50 | 34.92 | 41.16 | 9 | 46.34 | 40.90 | 35.08 | 40.77 |
| 8 | 47.13 | 41.50 | 34.42 | 41.02 | 10 | 46.25 | 41.00 | 35.08 | 40.78 |
| 9 | 47.00 | 41.50 | 34.42 | 40.97 | 11 | 46.07 | 41.00 | 34.67 | 40.58 |
| 10 | 46.88 | 41.50 | 34.17 | 40.85 | 12 | 45.82 | 40.85 | 34.67 | 40.45 |
| 11 | 46.96 | 41.50 | 33.92 | 40.79 | 13 | 45.69 | 40.75 | 34.50 | 40.31 |
| 14 | 47.00 | 41.50 | 33.92 | 40.81 | 16 | 45.75 | 40.75 | 34.33 | 40.28 |
| 15 | 47.03 | 41.50 | 33.67 | 40.73 | 17 | 45.63 | 40.75 | 34.58 | 40.32 |
| 16 | 46.88 | 41.50 | 34.04 | 40.81 | 18 | 45.63 | 40.75 | 34.83 | 40.40 |
| 17 | 46.65 | 41.50 | 34.17 | 40.77 | 19 | 45.75 | 40.75 | 34.59 | 40.36 |
| 18 | 46.67 | 41.50 | 34.17 | 40.78 | 20 | 45.82 | 40.75 | 34.55 | 40.37 |
| 21 | 46.63 | 41.50 | 34.17 | 40.77 | 23 | 45.63 | 40.75 | 34.46 | 40.28 |
| 23 | 46.69 | 41.50 | 34.17 | 40.79 | 24 | 45.78 | 40.75 | 34.75 | 40.43 |
| 24 | 46.51 | 41.50 | 34.33 | 40.78 | 25 | 45.50 | 40.75 | 34.67 | 40.31 |
| 25 | 46.66 | 41.50 | 34.17 | 40.78 | 26 | 45.59 | 40.75 | 34.67 | 40.34 |
| 28 | 46.75 | 41.55 | 34.08 | 40.79 | 27 | 45.54 | 40.75 | 34.67 | 40.32 |
| **MARCH** | | | | | 31 | 45.71 | 40.75 | 34.46 | 40.31 |
| 1 | 46.50 | 41.50 | 34.33 | 40.78 | **JUNE** | | | | |
| 2 | 46.50 | 41.50 | 34.33 | 40.78 | 1 | 45.38 | 40.75 | 34.50 | 40.21 |
| 3 | 46.48 | 41.50 | 34.33 | 40.77 | 2 | 45.25 | 40.75 | 34.50 | 40.17 |
| 4 | 46.19 | 41.50 | 34.33 | 40.67 | 3 | 45.25 | 40.75 | 34.17 | 40.06 |
| 7 | 46.23 | 41.55 | 34.33 | 40.70 | 6 | 45.25 | 40.75 | 34.00 | 40.00 |
| 8 | 46.13 | 40.50 | 33.58 | 40.07 | 7 | 45.38 | 40.75 | 33.75 | 39.96 |
| 9 | 45.84 | 40.50 | 33.71 | 40.02 | 8 | 45.50 | 40.75 | 33.50 | 39.92 |
| 10 | 45.84 | 40.50 | 33.83 | 40.06 | 9 | 45.27 | 40.75 | 33.67 | 39.90 |
| 11 | 45.80 | 40.50 | 34.08 | 40.13 | 10 | 45.32 | 40.75 | 33.42 | 39.83 |
| 14 | 45.84 | 40.50 | 34.33 | 40.22 | 13 | 45.25 | 40.75 | 33.25 | 39.75 |
| 15 | 45.67 | 40.40 | 33.83 | 39.97 | 14 | 45.25 | 40.75 | 33.42 | 39.81 |
| 16 | 45.67 | 40.40 | 33.92 | 40.00 | 15 | 45.15 | 40.75 | 33.21 | 39.70 |
| 17 | 45.67 | 40.40 | 33.92 | 40.00 | 16 | 45.09 | 40.75 | 33.17 | 39.67 |
| 18 | 45.67 | 40.40 | 33.42 | 39.83 | 17 | 45.11 | 40.75 | 33.33 | 39.73 |
| 21 | 45.67 | 40.40 | 33.42 | 39.83 | 20 | 45.07 | 40.75 | 33.33 | 39.72 |
| 22 | 45.67 | 40.40 | 33.58 | 39.88 | 21 | 45.04 | 40.75 | 33.58 | 39.79 |
| 23 | 45.84 | 40.40 | 33.58 | 39.94 | 22 | 45.00 | 40.75 | 33.58 | 39.78 |
| 24 | 46.13 | 40.40 | 33.33 | 39.95 | 23 | 44.96 | 40.75 | 33.75 | 39.82 |
| 25 | 46.23 | 40.40 | 33.33 | 39.99 | 24 | 44.75 | 40.75 | 33.57 | 39.69 |
| 28 | 46.36 | 40.40 | 32.83 | 39.86 | 27 | 44.92 | 40.75 | 33.58 | 39.75 |
| 29 | 46.21 | 40.40 | 33.08 | 39.90 | 28 | 44.84 | 40.75 | 33.33 | 39.64 |
| 30 | 46.05 | 40.40 | 33.33 | 39.93 | 29 | 44.79 | 40.75 | 33.33 | 39.62 |
| 31 | 45.96 | 40.40 | 33.33 | 39.90 | 30 | 44.67 | 40.75 | 33.58 | 39.67 |

A-148

## ORGANIZATION DAILY INDICATOR PRICE, 1966

(Per Pound)

|  | ARABICAS Washed | Unwashed | Robusta | Daily Price |  | Colombian Mild Arabicas | Other Mild Arabicas | Unwashed Arabicas | Robusta |
|---|---|---|---|---|---|---|---|---|---|
| **JULY** |  |  |  |  | **OCTOBER** |  |  |  |  |
| 1 | 44.84 | 40.75 | 33.58 | 39.72 | 3 | 44.88 | 39.79 | 40.00 | 31.38 |
| 5 | 44.84 | 40.75 | 33.58 | 39.72 | 4 | 44.75 | 39.79 | 40.00 | 31.33 |
| 6 | 44.79 | 40.75 | 33.33 | 39.62 | 5 | 44.75 | 39.79 | 40.00 | 31.42 |
| 7 | 44.88 | 40.75 | 33.33 | 39.65 | 6 | 44.88 | 39.92 | 40.00 | 31.83 |
| 8 | 44.75 | 40.75 | 33.25 | 39.58 | 7 | 45.00 | 39.92 | 40.00 | 31.83 |
| 11 | 44.88 | 40.75 | 33.25 | 39.63 | 10 | 45.25 | 39.92 | 40.00 | 31.92 |
| 12 | 44.88 | 40.75 | 33.42 | 39.68 | 11 | 45.25 | 39.92 | 40.00 | 31.92 |
| 13 | 44.79 | 40.75 | 33.25 | 39.60 | 13 | 45.50 | 40.17 | 40.00 | 32.67 |
| 14 | 44.79 | 40.75 | 33.00 | 39.51 | 14 | 45.75 | 40.46 | 40.00 | 32.92 |
| 15 | 44.84 | 40.75 | 33.00 | 39.53 | 17 | 45.75 | 40.50 | 40.00 | 32.84 |
| 18 | 44.79 | 40.50 | 33.25 | 39.51 | 18 | 45.75 | 40.63 | 40.00 | 32.96 |
| 19 | 44.75 | 40.50 | 33.00 | 39.42 | 19 | 46.25 | 40.63 | 40.00 | 33.21 |
| 20 | 44.79 | 40.50 | 33.00 | 39.43 | 20 | 46.00 | 40.63 | 40.00 | 33.09 |
| 21 | 44.75 | 40.50 | 33.00 | 39.42 | 21 | 45.75 | 40.50 | 40.00 | 32.84 |
| 22 | 44.79 | 40.50 | 32.75 | 39.35 | 24 | 45.75 | 40.50 | 40.00 | 32.83 |
| 25 | 44.79 | 40.50 | 32.75 | 39.35 | 25 | 45.75 | 40.50 | 40.00 | 32.83 |
| 26 | 44.75 | 40.50 | 32.75 | 39.33 | 26 | 45.75 | 40.50 | 40.00 | 32.83 |
| 27 | 44.75 | 40.25 | 32.75 | 39.25 | 27 | 45.75 | 40.50 | 40.00 | 32.83 |
| 28 | 44.75 | 40.25 | 32.75 | 39.25 | 28 | 45.75 | 40.38 | 40.00 | 32.83 |
| 29 | 44.75 | 40.25 | 32.75 | 39.25 | 31 | 45.50 | 40.50 | 39.75 | 32.92 |
| **AUGUST** |  |  |  |  |  |  |  |  |  |
| 1 | 44.75 | 40.00 | 32.75 | 39.17 |  |  |  |  |  |
| 2 | 44.75 | 40.00 | 32.75 | 39.17 | **NOVEMBER** |  |  |  |  |
| 3 | 44.63 | 40.00 | 32.75 | 39.13 | 1 | 45.50 | 40.44 | 39.75 | 32.92 |
| 4 | 44.38 | 40.00 | 32.75 | 39.04 | 2 | 45.50 | 40.42 | 39.75 | 32.92 |
| 5 | 44.38 | 40.00 | 32.75 | 39.04 | 3 | 45.50 | 40.33 | 39.75 | 32.67 |
| 8 | 44.69 | 40.50 | 33.00 | 39.40 | 4 | 45.50 | 40.38 | 39.75 | 32.67 |
| 9 | 44.71 | 40.50 | 33.25 | 39.49 | 7 | 45.50 | 40.33 | 39.75 | 32.67 |
| 10 | 44.63 | 40.50 | 33.00 | 39.38 | 9 | 45.50 | 40.25 | 39.50 | 32.67 |
| 11 | 44.50 | 40.50 | 33.00 | 39.33 | 10 | 45.00 | 40.17 | 39.30 | 32.67 |
| 12 | 44.50 | 40.50 | 33.00 | 39.33 | 14 | 45.00 | 40.25 | 39.30 | 32.67 |
| 15 | 44.46 | 40.50 | 33.00 | 39.32 | 15 | 45.00 | 40.25 | 39.30 | 32.67 |
| 16 | 44.46 | 40.50 | 32.75 | 39.24 | 16 | 44.75 | 40.17 | 39.30 | 32.67 |
| 17 | 44.46 | 40.50 | 32.75 | 39.24 | 17 | 44.75 | 40.17 | 39.30 | 32.67 |
| 18 | 44.50 | 40.50 | 32.75 | 39.25 | 18 | 44.75 | 40.17 | 39.30 | 32.71 |
| 19 | 44.38 | 40.50 | 32.50 | 39.13 | 22 | 44.50 | 40.17 | 39.30 | 32.58 |
| 22 | 44.38 | 40.50 | 32.25 | 39.04 | 23 | 44.38 | 40.33 | 39.30 | 32.58 |
| 23 | 44.50 | 40.25 | 32.00 | 38.92 | 25 | 44.50 | 40.21 | 39.30 | 32.58 |
| 24 | 44.38 | 40.25 | 31.88 | 38.84 | 29 | 44.50 | 40.13 | 39.50 | 32.58 |
| 25 | 44.32 | 40.25 | 32.00 | 38.86 | 30 | 44.50 | 39.96 | 39.50 | 32.67 |
| 26 | 44.38 | 40.25 | 32.00 | 38.88 |  |  |  |  |  |
| 29 | 44.25 | 40.25 | 32.50 | 39.00 |  |  |  |  |  |
| 30 | 44.25 | 40.25 | 32.50 | 39.00 |  |  |  |  |  |
| 31 | 44.25 | 40.25 | 32.25 | 38.92 | **DECEMBER** |  |  |  |  |
| **SEPTEMBER** |  |  |  |  | 1 | 44.25 | 39.92 | 39.50 | 32.67 |
| 1 | 44.13 | 40.25 | 32.25 | 38.88 | 2 | 44.00 | 39.92 | 39.50 | 32.67 |
| 2 | 44.13 | 40.25 | 32.25 | 38.88 | 5 | 44.00 | 39.71 | 39.50 | 32.67 |
| 6 | 44.13 | 40.25 | 32.50 | 38.96 | 6 | 44.00 | 39.75 | 39.50 | 32.67 |
| 7 | 43.63 | 40.00 | 32.50 | 38.71 | 7 | 44.00 | 39.75 | 39.50 | 32.58 |
| 8 | 43.50 | 40.00 | 32.25 | 38.58 | 8 | 44.00 | 39.75 | 39.50 | 32.58 |
| 9 | 43.50 | 40.00 | 32.00 | 38.50 | 9 | 44.00 | 39.75 | 39.50 | 32.58 |
| 12 | 43.50 | 40.00 | 32.25 | 38.58 | 12 | 44.25 | 39.83 | 39.50 | 32.58 |
| 13 | 43.46 | 40.00 | 31.92 | 38.46 | 13 | 44.25 | 39.83 | 39.50 | 32.58 |
| 14 | 43.46 | 40.00 | 31.67 | 38.38 | 14 | 44.25 | 39.67 | 39.50 | 32.50 |
| 15 | 43.46 | 40.00 | 31.67 | 38.38 | 15 | 44.25 | 39.58 | 39.50 | 32.29 |
| 16 | 43.46 | 40.00 | 31.50 | 38.32 | 16 | 44.00 | 39.67 | 39.50 | 32.29 |
| 19 | 43.00 | 40.00 | 31.25 | 38.08 | 19 | 44.00 | 39.67 | 39.50 | 32.29 |
| 20 | 42.94 | 40.00 | 31.25 | 38.06 | 20 | 43.88 | 39.58 | 39.50 | 32.29 |
| 21 | 42.82 | 40.00 | 31.25 | 38.02 | 21 | 43.88 | 39.42 | 39.50 | 32.29 |
| 22 | 42.76 | 40.00 | 31.25 | 38.00 | 22 | 43.88 | 39.42 | 39.50 | 32.29 |
| 23 | 42.44 | 40.00 | 31.50 | 37.98 | 23 | 43.88 | 39.42 | 39.50 | 32.29 |
| 26 | 42.51 | 40.00 | 31.25 | 37.92 | 27 | 43.88 | 39.42 | 39.50 | 32.29 |
| 27 | 42.44 | 40.00 | 31.50 | 37.98 | 28 | 43.50 | 39.17 | 39.50 | 32.29 |
| 28 | 42.44 | 40.00 | 31.42 | 37.95 | 29 | 43.50 | 39.08 | 39.50 | 32.29 |
| 29 | 42.38 | 40.00 | 31.42 | 37.93 | 30 | 43.50 | 39.08 | 39.50 | 32.29 |
| 30 | 42.32 | 40.00 | 31.42 | 37.92 |  |  |  |  |  |

## CP-18C. INTERNATIONAL COFFEE ORGANIZATION DAILY INDICATOR PRICE, JANUARY-APRIL, 1967

(In U. S. Cents Per Pound)

| | Colombian Mild Arabicas | Other Mild Arabicas | Unwashed Arabicas | Robusta | | Colombian Mild Arabicas | Other Mild Arabicas | Unwashed Arabicas | Robusta |
|---|---|---|---|---|---|---|---|---|---|
| JANUARY | | | | | MARCH | | | | |
| 3 | 43.50 | 39.08 | 39.50 | 32.13 | 1 | 42.00 | 37.50 | 38.00 | 33.00 |
| 4 | 43.63 | 38.92 | 39.50 | 32.13 | 2 | 41.75 | 37.42 | 38.00 | 32.92 |
| 5 | 43.88 | 38.92 | 39.50 | 31.92 | 3 | 41.50 | 37.42 | 38.00 | 32.92 |
| 6 | 44.00 | 39.00 | 39.50 | 31.83 | 6 | 41.50 | 37.42 | 38.00 | 32.96 |
| 9 | 44.00 | 39.00 | 39.50 | 31.03 | 7 | 41.25 | 37.33 | 38.00 | 32.96 |
| 10 | 43.75 | 38.92 | 39.50 | 31.79 | 8 | 41.25 | 37.21 | 38.00 | 32.96 |
| 11 | 43.50 | 38.83 | 38.50 | 31.83 | 9 | 41.25 | 37.21 | 38.00 | 33.00 |
| 12 | 43.50 | 38.67 | 38.50 | 31.75 | 10 | 41.00 | 37.25 | 38.00 | 32.92 |
| 13 | 43.50 | 38.58 | 38.50 | 31.75 | 13 | 41.00 | 37.25 | 38.00 | 32.92 |
| 16 | 43.50 | 38.58 | 38.50 | 31.75 | 14 | 40.75 | 37.25 | 38.00 | 32.88 |
| 17 | 43.50 | 38.33 | 38.50 | 31.75 | 15 | 40.75 | 36.25 | 38.00 | 32.88 |
| 18 | 43.25 | 38.17 | 38.50 | 31.83 | 16 | 40.50 | 37.25 | 38.00 | 32.83 |
| 19 | 43.38 | 38.25 | 38.50 | 31.92 | 17 | 40.25 | 37.25 | 38.00 | 32.83 |
| 20 | 43.13 | 38.25 | 38.50 | 31.92 | 20 | 40.50 | 37.25 | 38.00 | 32.88 |
| 23 | 43.13 | 38.33 | 38.50 | 32.17 | 21 | 40.25 | 37.25 | 38.00 | 32.88 |
| 24 | 42.50 | 38.33 | 38.50 | 32.21 | 22 | 40.25 | 37.33 | 38.00 | 32.88 |
| 25 | 42.50 | 38.33 | 38.50 | 32.25 | 23 | 40.25 | 37.33 | 38.00 | 32.88 |
| 26 | 42.50 | 38.25 | 38.50 | 32.33 | 27 | 40.50 | 37.42 | 38.00 | 32.88 |
| 27 | 42.25 | 38.25 | 38.25 | 32.33 | 28 | 40.50 | 37.53 | 38.00 | 32.96 |
| 30 | 42.50 | 38.25 | 38.25 | 32.33 | 29 | 40.75 | 37.67 | 38.00 | 32.92 |
| 31 | 42.25 | 38.42 | 38.25 | 32.50 | 30 | 40.75 | 37.67 | 38.00 | 32.92 |
| FEBRUARY | | | | | 31 | 41.00 | 37.67 | 38.00 | 32.92 |
| 1 | 42.25 | 38.42 | 38.25 | 32.75 | APRIL | | | | |
| 2 | 42.25 | 38.67 | 38.00 | 33.25 | 3 | 41.00 | 37.71 | 38.00 | 32.92 |
| 3 | 42.25 | 38.67 | 38.00 | 33.25 | 4 | 41.00 | 37.75 | 38.00 | 33.08 |
| 6 | 42.38 | 38.67 | 38.00 | 33.50 | 5 | 41.38 | 37.75 | 38.00 | 33.17 |
| 7 | 42.38 | 38.67 | 38.00 | 33.25 | 6 | 41.50 | 37.96 | 38.00 | 33.25 |
| 8 | 42.38 | 38.75 | 38.00 | 33.25 | 7 | 41.50 | 37.96 | 38.00 | 33.50 |
| 9 | 42.63 | 38.75 | 38.00 | 33.25 | 10 | 41.63 | 37.96 | 38.25 | 33.50 |
| 10 | 42.50 | 38.54 | 38.00 | 33.00 | 11 | 41.25 | 38.07 | 38.25 | 33.50 |
| 13 | | | | | 12 | 41.25 | 38.17 | 38.25 | 33.75 |
| 14 | 42.50 | 38.42 | 38.00 | 33.00 | 13 | 41.25 | 38.42 | 38.25 | 33.88 |
| 15 | 42.50 | 38.25 | 38.00 | 32.92 | 14 | 41.25 | 38.84 | 38.50 | 34.33 |
| 16 | 42.50 | 38.17 | 38.00 | 32.83 | 17 | 41.25 | 38.96 | 38.50 | 34.46 |
| 17 | 42.50 | 38.08 | 38.00 | 32.75 | 18 | 41.63 | 39.09 | 38.63 | 34.33 |
| 20 | 42.50 | 38.08 | 38.00 | 32.75 | 19 | 41.38 | 38.96 | 38.63 | 34.33 |
| 21 | 42.25 | 38.00 | 38.00 | 32.88 | 20 | 41.38 | 38.96 | 38.75 | 34.33 |
| 22 | | | | | 21 | 41.50 | 38.96 | 38.75 | 34.33 |
| 23 | 42.25 | 37.88 | 38.00 | 32.96 | 24 | 41.50 | 39.09 | 38.75 | 34.21 |
| 24 | 42.25 | 37.83 | 38.00 | 33.09 | 25 | 41.50 | 39.09 | 38.75 | 34.05 |
| 27 | 42.25 | 37.83 | 38.00 | 33.25 | 26 | 41.50 | 39.21 | 38.75 | 34.17 |
| 38 | 42.00 | 37.58 | 38.00 | 33.00 | 27 | 41.50 | 39.33 | 38.75 | 34.33 |
| | | | | | 28 | | | | |

## CP-18D. INTERNATIONAL COFFEE ORGANIZATION: UNOFFICIAL CALCULATION OF COMPOSITE AVERAGE I.C.O. INDICATOR PRICES, OCTOBER 1966—MARCH 1967

(In U.S. cents per pound)

### 1966

| Month | Day | Price |
|---|---|---|
| October | 3 | 37.91 |
|  | 4 | 37.87 |
|  | 5 | 37.90 |
|  | 6 | 38.08 |
|  | 7 | 38.10 |
|  | 10 | 38.17 |
|  | 11 | 38.17 |
|  | 13 | 38.50 |
|  | 14 | 38.68 |
|  | 17 | 38.66 |
|  | 18 | 38.72 |
|  | 19 | 38.88 |
|  | 20 | 38.80 |
|  | 21 | 38.66 |
|  | 24 | 38.70 |
|  | 25 | 38.65 |
|  | 26 | 38.65 |
|  | 27 | 38.65 |
|  | 28 | 38.63 |
|  | 31 | 38.56 |
| November | 1 | 38.55 |
|  | 2 | 38.54 |
|  | 3 | 38.45 |
|  | 4 | 38.45 |
|  | 7 | 38.45 |
|  | 9 | 38.35 |
|  | 10 | 38.19 |
|  | 14 | 38.20 |
|  | 15 | 38.20 |
|  | 16 | 38.14 |
|  | 17 | 38.14 |
|  | 18 | 38.11 |
|  | 21 | 38.16 |
|  | 22 | 38.07 |
|  | 23 | 38.08 |
|  | 25 | 38.08 |
|  | 28 | 38.09 |
|  | 29 | 38.13 |
|  | 30 | 38.13 |
| December | 1 | 38.09 |
|  | 2 | 38.04 |
|  | 5 | 38.01 |
|  | 6 | 38.02 |
|  | 7 | 37.99 |
|  | 8 | 37.99 |
|  | 9 | 37.99 |
|  | 12 | 38.04 |
|  | 13 | 38.04 |
|  | 14 | 37.99 |
|  | 15 | 37.90 |
|  | 16 | 37.88 |
|  | 19 | 37.88 |
|  | 20 | 37.84 |
|  | 21 | 37.81 |
|  | 22 | 37.81 |
|  | 23 | 37.81 |
|  | 27 | 37.81 |
|  | 28 | 37.71 |
|  | 29 | 37.69 |
|  | 30 | 37.69 |

### 1967

| Month | Day | Price |
|---|---|---|
| January | 3 | 37.64 |
|  | 4 | 37.64 |
|  | 5 | 37.61 |
|  | 6 | 37.61 |
|  | 9 | 37.61 |
|  | 10 | 37.54 |
|  | 11 | 37.17 |
|  | 12 | 37.11 |
|  | 13 | 37.10 |
|  | 16 | 37.10 |
|  | 17 | 37.06 |
|  | 18 | 37.01 |
|  | 19 | 37.08 |
|  | 20 | 37.04 |
|  | 23 | 37.13 |
|  | 24 | 37.04 |
|  | 25 | 37.06 |
|  | 26 | 37.07 |
|  | 27 | 36.94 |
|  | 30 | 36.99 |
|  | 31 | 37.03 |
| February | 1 | 37.11 |
|  | 2 | 37.24 |
|  | 3 | 37.24 |
|  | 6 | 37.34 |
|  | 7 | 37.26 |
|  | 8 | 37.27 |
|  | 9 | 37.31 |
|  | 10 | 37.17 |
|  | 14 | 37.15 |
|  | 15 | 37.10 |
|  | 16 | 37.06 |
|  | 17 | 37.01 |
|  | 20 | 37.01 |
|  | 21 | 37.00 |
|  | 23 | 37.01 |
|  | 24 | 37.04 |
|  | 27 | 37.10 |
|  | 28 | 36.93 |
| March | 1 | 36.92 |
|  | 2 | 36.84 |
|  | 3 | 36.79 |
|  | 6 | 36.81 |
|  | 7 | 36.75 |
|  | 8 | 36.73 |
|  | 9 | 36.74 |
|  | 10 | 36.68 |
|  | 13 | 36.68 |
|  | 14 | 36.63 |
|  | 15 | 36.63 |
|  | 16 | 36.57 |
|  | 17 | 36.53 |
|  | 20 | 36.59 |
|  | 21 | 36.54 |
|  | 22 | 36.56 |
|  | 23 | 36.56 |
|  | 27 | 36.61 |
|  | 28 | 36.66 |
|  | 29 | 36.72 |
|  | 30 | 36.71 |
|  | 31 | 36.75 |

## CP-19. UNITED STATES: AVERAGE IMPORT PRICES OF GREEN COFFEE, 1953-66
(U. S. Cents Per Pound)

| COUNTRIES OF ORIGIN | 1953 | 1954 | 1955 | 1956 | 1957 | 1958 | 1959 | 1960 | 1961 | 1962 | 1963 | 1964 | 1965 | 1966 |
|---|---|---|---|---|---|---|---|---|---|---|---|---|---|---|
| **WESTERN HEMISPHERE** | | | | | | | | | | | | | | |
| Pan-American Coffee Bureau | | | | | | | | | | | | | | |
| Brazil | 52.9 | 64.8 | 47.7 | 46.1 | 44.9 | 41.2 | 32.1 | 32.6 | 32.2 | 30.1 | 29.7 | 39.6 | 39.9 | 36.8 |
| Colombia | 55.9 | 71.0 | 62.6 | 61.8 | 63.6 | 51.8 | 45.0 | 43.4 | 41.9 | 39.5 | 37.8 | 45.5 | 45.4 | 45.6 |
| Mexico | 50.3 | 66.6 | 54.4 | 62.1 | 46.7 | 46.3 | 38.8 | 39.6 | 37.3 | 35.2 | 33.6 | 43.0 | 42.6 | 41.5 |
| Guatemala | 49.4 | 59.3 | 54.6 | 60.6 | 55.6 | 45.7 | 38.1 | 38.7 | 34.8 | 33.3 | 33.0 | 42.0 | 42.6 | 40.4 |
| El Salvador | 47.8 | 59.3 | 53.9 | 54.6 | 55.3 | 42.5 | 36.1 | 37.9 | 34.7 | 32.2 | 32.2 | 39.0 | 42.6 | 39.8 |
| Peru | 52.3 | 69.8 | 53.4 | 62.6 | 53.3 | 43.7 | 37.0 | 33.7 | 31.4 | 30.2 | 29.7 | 42.4 | 39.4 | 38.0 |
| Dominican Republic | 50.7 | 59.9 | 55.0 | 56.6 | 54.1 | 43.5 | 37.1 | 35.8 | 32.4 | 31.0 | 31.0 | 40.2 | 39.8 | 37.9 |
| Costa Rica | 54.9 | 68.0 | 58.3 | 67.9 | 61.2 | 48.2 | 40.3 | 39.4 | 35.6 | 33.6 | 33.6 | 41.5 | 42.7 | 41.5 |
| Venezuela | 53.4 | 69.4 | 55.6 | 66.1 | 59.2 | 48.3 | 38.7 | 39.5 | 35.4 | 33.9 | 32.7 | 42.2 | 42.9 | 41.4 |
| Ecuador | 46.6 | 59.9 | 46.3 | 57.9 | 47.2 | 39.9 | 35.4 | 33.6 | 29.7 | 31.0 | 29.0 | 40.5 | 37.2 | 33.9 |
| Honduras | 49.4 | 69.3 | 48.4 | 52.9 | 52.7 | 44.8 | 36.4 | 35.2 | 33.7 | 32.9 | 31.7 | 40.7 | 40.2 | 39.0 |
| Nicaragua | 50.0 | 65.8 | 56.5 | 57.8 | 53.9 | 46.5 | 36.5 | 36.4 | 34.4 | 33.3 | 32.3 | 40.2 | 42.0 | 42.7 |
| Haiti | 51.6 | 63.0 | 48.5 | 44.9 | 42.1 | 37.5 | 31.1 | 31.2 | 28.0 | 27.8 | 28.5 | 38.1 | 37.5 | 38.0 |
| Panama | 51.2 | 56.7 | 55.0 | 63.9 | 65.4 | 53.3 | 40.1 | 38.6 | 33.9 | 31.0 | 29.9 | 32.7 | 33.7 | 36.4 |
| Cuba | — | — | 45.0 | 45.1 | 50.6 | 45.0 | 34.9 | 42.9 | — | — | — | — | — | — |
| OTHER WESTERN HEMISPHERE (2) | 47.9 | 60.4 | 39.0 | 40.0 | 35.3 | 34.6 | 28.4 | 26.6 | 25.2 | 23.8 | 24.3 | 31.5 | 29.1 | 33.0 |
| **AFRICA** | | | | | | | | | | | | | | |
| East Africa (1) | 45.8 | 57.8 | 37.3 | 45.2 | 36.8 | 37.3 | 28.7 | 24.0 | 22.4 | 21.0 | 24.5 | — | — | — |
| Uganda | N.A. | N.A. | N.A. | N.A. | N.A. | N.A. | N.A. | N.A. | N.A. | N.A. | N.A. | 35.5 | 26.7 | 31.3 |
| Kenya | N.A. | N.A. | N.A. | N.A. | N.A. | N.A. | N.A. | N.A. | N.A. | N.A. | N.A. | 39.7 | 33.1 | 41.7 |
| Tanzania | N.A. | N.A. | N.A. | N.A. | N.A. | N.A. | N.A. | N.A. | N.A. | N.A. | N.A. | 40.6 | 36.2 | 36.6 |
| Portuguese Africa | 46.3 | 55.1 | 39.0 | 31.8 | 34.2 | 35.2 | 27.0 | 22.4 | 18.1 | 18.8 | 22.9 | 32.5 | 27.1 | 31.3 |
| Franc Zone | | | | | | | | | | | | | | |
| Western Africa (1) | 44.5 | 55.4 | 37.0 | 29.2 | 31.8 | 35.8 | 26.3 | 18.3 | 17.4 | 17.8 | 23.5 | — | — | — |
| Ivory Coast | N.A. | N.A. | N.A. | N.A. | N.A. | N.A. | N.A. | N.A. | N.A. | N.A. | N.A. | 32.7 | 27.4 | 30.3 |
| Guinea | N.A. | N.A. | N.A. | N.A. | N.A. | N.A. | N.A. | N.A. | N.A. | N.A. | N.A. | 32.1 | 27.0 | 30.2 |
| Togo | N.A. | N.A. | N.A. | N.A. | N.A. | N.A. | N.A. | N.A. | N.A. | N.A. | N.A. | 33.9 | 30.8 | 22.6 |
| Central African Rep. | N.A. | N.A. | N.A. | N.A. | N.A. | N.A. | N.A. | N.A. | N.A. | N.A. | N.A. | 36.2 | 29.8 | N.A. |
| Gabon | N.A. | N.A. | N.A. | N.A. | N.A. | N.A. | N.A. | N.A. | N.A. | N.A. | N.A. | 32.6 | 38.0 | 31.2 |
| Others (3) | N.A. | N.A. | N.A. | N.A. | N.A. | N.A. | N.A. | 29.3 | 20.8 | 22.5 | 25.8 | 32.9 | 35.3 | 39.3 |
| Madagascar | — | 51.5 | 33.4 | 29.7 | 30.6 | 32.4 | 26.6 | 18.8 | 16.6 | 17.0 | 20.4 | 28.5 | 26.1 | 30.1 |
| Cameroun | 47.9 | 62.8 | 34.3 | 29.3 | 31.4 | 35.6 | 28.2 | 18.5 | 17.2 | 18.2 | 22.0 | 35.6 | 24.3 | 31.2 |
| Ethiopia | 49.0 | 65.0 | 44.3 | 50.7 | 48.3 | 42.0 | 33.0 | 32.9 | 32.8 | 30.4 | 29.6 | 40.5 | 39.0 | 38.8 |

## CP-19. UNITED STATES: AVERAGE IMPORT PRICES OF GREEN COFFEE, 1953-66 (Continued)
(U. S. Cents Per Pound)

| COUNTRIES OF ORIGIN | 1953 | 1954 | 1955 | 1956 | 1957 | 1958 | 1959 | 1960 | 1961 | 1962 | 1963 | 1964 | 1965 | 1966 |
|---|---|---|---|---|---|---|---|---|---|---|---|---|---|---|
| AFRICA (Continued) | | | | | | | | | | | | | | |
| Rep. of Congo & Rwanda-Burundi (1) | 50.2 | 62.7 | 49.7 | 51.1 | 47.9 | 40.6 | 33.8 | 30.1 | 28.0 | 27.2 | 26.9 | — | — | — |
| Rwanda-Burundi | N.A. | N.A. | N.A. | N.A. | N.A. | N.A. | N.A. | N.A. | N.A. | N.A. | N.A. | 41.5 | 38.3 | 37.3 |
| Congo (D.R.) | N.A. | N.A. | N.A. | N.A. | N.A. | N.A. | N.A. | N.A. | N.A. | N.A. | N.A. | 35.3 | 31.5 | 38.5 |
| Liberia | — | 52.4 | 34.1 | 28.2 | 29.2 | 34.8 | 27.1 | 18.6 | 16.9 | 17.7 | 21.8 | 34.2 | 27.0 | 31.5 |
| Various (4) | 41.0 | 55.3 | 33.6 | 30.3 | 31.6 | 27.4 | 27.4 | 19.6 | 16.6 | 18.0 | 21.3 | 31.3 | 28.6 | 30.7 |
| ASIA & OCEANIA | | | | | | | | | | | | | | |
| Indonesia | 40.9 | 49.2 | 54.8 | 37.3 | 31.9 | 42.8 | 43.5 | 36.3 | 16.9 | 16.4 | 20.5 | 26.4 | 16.8 | 20.3 |
| India | — | 69.4 | 51.6 | — | 47.2 | 45.3 | 38.3 | 37.8 | 32.3 | 24.6 | 26.8 | 38.7 | 38.3 | 35.6 |
| Various (5) | 57.0 | 72.9 | 58.1 | 60.5 | 51.7 | 48.8 | 42.1 | 37.5 | 28.2 | 27.6 | 27.6 | 40.4 | 30.6 | 33.3 |
| OTHERS (6) | 77.4 | 72.6 | 101.9 | — | 43.6 | 50.3 | 49.4 | 35.7 | 33.6 | 19.3 | 34.5 | 47.3 | 49.1 | 51.8 |
| TOTAL IMPORTS | 52.7 | 65.7 | 52.2 | 51.2 | 49.3 | 43.9 | 35.7 | 34.3 | 32.4 | 30.4 | 30.3 | 39.6 | 37.3 | 36.6 |

Source: United States Department of Commerce.
  Prior to January 1964 import figures for individual countries were not available.
 (1) Includes: Argentina, Guyana, British Honduras, Bolivia, Canada, Chile, Jamaica, Netherlands Guiana, Paraguay, Trinidad & Tobago and Uruguay.
 (2) 
 (3) Includes: Chad, Congo (Brazzaville), Dahomey, French Somaliland, Mali, Niger and Upper Volta.
 (4) Includes: Ghana, Mauritius, Nigeria, Sierra Leone and South Africa.
 (5) Includes: Aden, Australia, Ceylon, Iraq, Laos, Malaysia, New Guinea, New Zealand, Philippine Republic, Saudi Arabia, Singapore, Southern Asia (Bhutan, Brunei and Portuguese Timor), Thailand and Viet Nam.
 (6) Includes: Azores, Belgium, Italy, Netherlands, Portugal, Sweden, Switzerland, West Germany and United Kingdom.

## ES-1. UNITED STATES: EXPORTS OF

(60 kilo bags of

| COUNTRIES OF DESTINATION | 1956 | 1957 | 1958 | 1959 | 1960 |
|---|---|---|---|---|---|
| CANADA | 70,504 | 98,031 | 103,537 | 115,329 | 125,784 |
| **OTHER WESTERN HEMISPHERE** | | | | | |
| Bahamas | 87 | 74 | 144 | 401 | 840 |
| Netherlands West Indies | 2,430 | 2,568 | 2,812 | 3,343 | 2,891 |
| Mexico | 11 | 22 | 55 | 36 | 71 |
| Bermuda | 524 | 595 | 660 | 990 | 1,214 |
| Trinidad & Tobago | — | 21 | 45 | 139 | 482 |
| Barbados | — | — | 19 | 84 | 84 |
| Guyana | — | — | — | — | 258 |
| Leeward-Windward Islands | — | 44 | — | 37 | 64 |
| Surinam | — | — | 83 | — | 138 |
| Jamaica | — | — | 72 | 387 | 385 |
| British Honduras | — | — | — | 87 | 23 |
| Peru | 36 | 263 | 45 | 42 | 47 |
| Dominican Republic | 76 | 146 | 84 | 79 | 127 |
| TOTAL OTHER WESTERN HEMISPHERE | 3,164 | 3,733 | 4,019 | 5,625 | 6,624 |
| **EUROPE** | | | | | |
| United Kingdom | 16 | — | 14 | 19,395 | 10,542 |
| Finland | — | — | — | 952 | 2,963 |
| Netherlands | 2,045 | 3,087 | 2,973 | 16,134 | 4,014 |
| Sweden | 175 | 113 | 749 | 648 | 1,378 |
| Norway | 8 | — | — | — | 54 |
| Denmark | 16 | 41 | 38 | 65 | 157 |
| Germany (F.R.) | 1,562 | 12,242 | 2,561 | 3,979 | 4,426 |
| Belgium | 56 | 93 | 91 | 47 | 629 |
| Italy | 16 | — | — | 25 | 91 |
| Greece | 29 | 60 | 91 | 5 | 5 |
| TOTAL EUROPE | 3,923 | 15,636 | 6,517 | 41,250 | 24,259 |
| **AFRICA** | | | | | |
| Liberia | 36 | 63 | 118 | 147 | 335 |
| Libya | — | 75 | 107 | 114 | 194 |
| Nigeria | — | — | — | — | 16 |
| United Arab Republic | — | 15 | 12 | 9 | 70 |
| TOTAL AFRICA | 36 | 153 | 237 | 270 | 615 |
| **ASIA & OCEANIA** | | | | | |
| Japan | 793 | 311 | 1,055 | 1,022 | 1,790 |
| Australia | — | 20 | — | 20 | 11,982 |
| Nampo Islands | 1,428 | 2,345 | 2,632 | 4,612 | 7,750 |
| Thailand | 153 | 586 | 646 | 810 | 878 |
| Singapore | — | — | 46 | 70 | 233 |
| Hong Kong | 69 | 68 | 86 | 232 | 529 |
| Lebanon | 54 | 58 | 115 | 325 | 433 |
| Taiwan | — | 12 | — | — | — |
| Syria | 324 | 396 | 766 | 97 | 505 |
| Saudi Arabia | — | 69 | 65 | 162 | 300 |
| South Korea | — | — | — | 41 | — |
| Trust Pacific Islands | — | 6 | 109 | 56 | 140 |
| Malaysia | 30 | 194 | — | — | 44 |
| Jordan | 7 | — | 13 | 52 | 88 |
| Kuwait | — | 23 | — | 50 | 7 |
| Pakistan | 30 | 133 | 99 | 106 | 158 |
| New Guinea | — | — | — | 12 | 56 |
| India | — | 7 | 29 | 36 | 73 |
| Iran | 51 | 110 | 158 | 107 | 112 |
| Philippine Republic | 798 | 4,761 | 311 | 90 | 155 |
| TOTAL ASIA & OCEANIA | 3,737 | 9,099 | 6,130 | 7,900 | 25,233 |
| OTHERS | 2,096 | 3,980 | 1,468 | 2,096 | 2,445 |
| TOTAL EXPORTS | 83,460 | 130,632 | 121,908 | 172,470 | 184,960 |

Source: U.S. Department of Commerce.
   * Conversion rate = 33.3 percent; the standard factor in international trade adopted by the ICO.

**SOLUBLE COFFEE, 1956-1966**

Green Coffee Equivalent)*

| 1961 | 1962 | 1963 | 1964 | 1965 | 1966 |
|---|---|---|---|---|---|
| 89,835 | 68,438 | 57,786 | 60,282 | 43,326 | 49,739 |
| | | | | | |
| 820 | 692 | 774 | 1,035 | 1,117 | 1,951 |
| 2,968 | 3,317 | 2,768 | 2,750 | 2,388 | 1,823 |
| 91 | — | 7 | 63 | 207 | 3,421 |
| 1,221 | 1,043 | 1,359 | 856 | 1,201 | 1,287 |
| 631 | 722 | 603 | 497 | 557 | 610 |
| 107 | 173 | 390 | 270 | 299 | 381 |
| 45 | — | 94 | 280 | 680 | 509 |
| 68 | 117 | 144 | 142 | 235 | 277 |
| 138 | 155 | 245 | 286 | 400 | 359 |
| 979 | 631 | 85 | 69 | 187 | 249 |
| 15 | 46 | 20 | 83 | 166 | 89 |
| 63 | 180 | 85 | 99 | 108 | 101 |
| 38 | 61 | 95 | 66 | 159 | 40 |
| 7,184 | 7,137 | 6,669 | 6,496 | 7,704 | 11,097 |
| | | | | | |
| 24,624 | 37,182 | 66,804 | 63,271 | 20,983 | 38,289 |
| 5,869 | 4,751 | 4,740 | 5,227 | 3,585 | 2,468 |
| 4,079 | 1,973 | 2,132 | 1,202 | 1,039 | 2,270 |
| 1,692 | 3,048 | 2,006 | 5,152 | 3,927 | 2,507 |
| 51 | 79 | 42 | 71 | 1,860 | 1,811 |
| 159 | 220 | 294 | 814 | 1,653 | 1,136 |
| 9,546 | 8,494 | 9,637 | 2,093 | 3,363 | 284 |
| 902 | 1,663 | 1,110 | 808 | 409 | 252 |
| 102 | 44 | 48 | — | — | 229 |
| 2 | — | 41 | — | — | 54 |
| 47,026 | 57,454 | 86,854 | 78,638 | 36,819 | 49,300 |
| | | | | | |
| 332 | 208 | 451 | 319 | 496 | 522 |
| 173 | 146 | 223 | 336 | 405 | 294 |
| 13 | 12 | — | 491 | 144 | 184 |
| 95 | 94 | 103 | 53 | — | 69 |
| 613 | 460 | 777 | 1,199 | 1,045 | 1,069 |
| | | | | | |
| 89,413 | 126,930 | 142,736 | 163,912 | 163,121 | 43,070 |
| 14,886 | 22,768 | 17,593 | 15,184 | 7,397 | 5,526 |
| 4,196 | 2,200 | 2,067 | 2,299 | 2,590 | 2,332 |
| 1,237 | 1,165 | 2,067 | 1,430 | 2,442 | 1,996 |
| 406 | 2,213 | 337 | — | — | 1,214 |
| 710 | 443 | 443 | 609 | 981 | 587 |
| 427 | 566 | 354 | 595 | 348 | 850 |
| 8 | — | — | 233 | — | 527 |
| 105 | 1,102 | 641 | 2,010 | 551 | 334 |
| 344 | 104 | 493 | 241 | 374 | 1,011 |
| — | 22 | 60 | 147 | 515 | 615 |
| 132 | 82 | 218 | 437 | 485 | 484 |
| 81 | 446 | 163 | 824 | 2,076 | 433 |
| 92 | 183 | 158 | 133 | 84 | 150 |
| 68 | 334 | 246 | 94 | 452 | 238 |
| 255 | 213 | 221 | 61 | 48 | 122 |
| 81 | 69 | 200 | 72 | 136 | 122 |
| 83 | 58 | 106 | 41 | — | 105 |
| 243 | 12 | 151 | 246 | 170 | 120 |
| 919 | 563 | 721 | 287 | 1,103 | — |
| 113,686 | 159,473 | 168,975 | 188,855 | 182,873 | 59,836 |
| | | | | | |
| 1,355 | 1,420 | 7,620 | 2,106 | 2,941 | 1,261 |
| | | | | | |
| 259,699 | 294,382 | 328,681 | 337,576 | 274,708 | 172,302 |

A-155

ESV-1. UNITED STATES: VALUE OF

(U. S.

| COUNTRIES OF DESTINATION | 1956 | 1957 | 1958 | 1959 |
|---|---|---|---|---|
| CANADA | 7,050,297 | 8,930,722 | 8,061,781 | 7,505,293 |
| **OTHER WESTERN HEMISPHERE** | | | | |
| Bahamas | 12,393 | 8,044 | 14,307 | 34,106 |
| Netherlands West Indies | 309,934 | 292,890 | 319,538 | 388,103 |
| Mexico | 1,124 | 1,080 | 4,040 | 1,666 |
| Bermuda | 53,474 | 61,024 | 71,295 | 98,682 |
| Trinidad & Tobago | — | 1,170 | 5,204 | 12,003 |
| Barbados | — | — | 2,174 | 7,654 |
| Guyana | — | — | — | — |
| Leeward, Windward Islands | — | 2,781 | — | 2,562 |
| Surinam | — | — | 4,569 | — |
| Jamaica | — | — | 3,612 | 24,815 |
| British Honduras | — | — | — | 10,984 |
| Peru | 5,556 | 21,795 | 8,197 | 7,488 |
| Dominican Republic | 10,040 | 15,954 | 11,566 | 11,900 |
| TOTAL OTHER WESTERN HEMISPHERE | 392,521 | 404,738 | 444,502 | 599,963 |
| **EUROPE** | | | | |
| United Kingdom | 1,368 | — | 600 | 1,182,258 |
| Finland | — | — | — | 91,412 |
| Netherlands | 170,046 | 238,515 | 200,561 | 906,320 |
| Sweden | 21,752 | 11,576 | 77,960 | 59,653 |
| Norway | 1,220 | — | — | — |
| Denmark | 630 | 5,550 | 4,654 | 6,437 |
| Germany (F.R.) | 162,615 | 1,120,390 | 215,906 | 238,103 |
| Belgium | 6,758 | 8,581 | ⁻12,144 | 4,671 |
| Italy | 2,410 | — | — | 2,377 |
| Greece | 4,120 | 7,780 | 9,105 | 511 |
| TOTAL EUROPE | 370,919 | 1,392,392 | 520,930 | 2,491,742 |
| **AFRICA** | | | | |
| Liberia | 4,675 | 8,223 | 11,899 | 14,573 |
| Libya | — | 2,130 | 8,728 | 9,852 |
| Nigeria | — | — | — | — |
| United Arab Republic | — | 2,127 | 1,385 | 891 |
| TOTAL AFRICA | 4,675 | 12,480 | 22,012 | 25,316 |
| **ASIA & OCEANIA** | | | | |
| Japan | 107,634 | 41,565 | 117,401 | 110,305 |
| Australia | — | 1,290 | — | 1,880 |
| Nampo Islands | 201,975 | 308,369 | 320,105 | 494,736 |
| Thailand | 17,567 | 37,831 | 52,017 | 78,320 |
| Singapore | — | — | 3,481 | 4,419 |
| Hong Kong | 9,173 | 7,357 | 7,937 | 18,085 |
| Lebanon | 7,447 | 5,817 | 13,623 | 19,546 |
| Taiwan | — | 1,038 | — | — |
| Syria | 45,308 | 51,254 | 87,322 | 7,650 |
| Saudi Arabia | — | 9,406 | 9,235 | 13,075 |
| South Korea | — | — | — | 2,600 |
| Trust Pacific Islands | — | 713 | 10,110 | 3,019 |
| Malaysia | 4,180 | 11,634 | — | — |
| Jordan | 1,050 | — | 1,330 | 5,478 |
| Kuwait | — | 875 | — | 4,200 |
| Pakistan | 4,141 | 8,045 | 6,241 | 4,626 |
| New Guinea | — | — | — | 1,231 |
| India | — | 580 | 1,888 | 3,614 |
| Iran | 6,018 | 11,041 | 18,548 | 11,038 |
| Philippine Republic | 96,917 | 588,191 | 12,961 | 13,200 |
| TOTAL ASIA & OCEANIA | 501,410 | 1,085,006 | 662,199 | 797,022 |
| **OTHERS** | 223,759 | 403,041 | 155,125 | 170,142 |
| **TOTAL EXPORTS** | 8,543,581 | 12,228,379 | 9,866,549 | 11,589,478 |

Source:  U. S. Department of Commerce.

**SOLUBLE COFFEE EXPORTS, 1956-1966**

Dollars)

| 1960 | 1961 | 1962 | 1963 | 1964 | 1965 | 1966 |
|---|---|---|---|---|---|---|
| 7,134,461 | 4,920,683 | 3,917,810 | 3,453,646 | 4,513,301 | 3,099,524 | 3,271,501 |
| | | | | | | |
| 58,368 | 61,082 | 64,647 | 69,307 | 110,556 | 113,907 | 182,697 |
| 284,711 | 267,843 | 338,292 | 300,229 | 336,340 | 284,955 | 208,039 |
| 4,072 | 7,354 | — | 1,034 | 5,818 | 19,956 | 209,820 |
| 103,505 | 112,747 | 114,386 | 134,758 | 102,108 | 132,742 | 136,053 |
| 47,168 | 60,951 | 77,796 | 63,873 | 58,135 | 52,273 | 56,113 |
| 7,260 | 9,353 | 18,009 | 35,457 | 26,800 | 31,615 | 36,260 |
| 22,260 | 3,592 | — | 4,316 | 17,937 | 40,468 | 33,065 |
| 4,994 | 6,422 | 11,246 | 11,628 | 16,432 | 24,714 | 28,699 |
| 9,790 | 8,850 | 10,145 | 15,078 | 25,172 | 35,961 | 21,191 |
| 28,326 | 67,223 | 46,099 | 9,142 | 6,117 | 16,643 | 17,159 |
| 2,104 | 1,516 | 5,028 | 1,675 | 9,272 | 17,780 | 13,411 |
| 5,730 | 7,296 | 13,379 | 10,925 | 15,073 | 16,738 | 13,028 |
| 10,968 | 3,562 | 5,786 | 10,771 | 7,412 | 14,927 | 3,111 |
| 589,256 | 617,791 | 704,813 | 668,193 | 737,172 | 802,679 | 958,646 |
| | | | | | | |
| 440,322 | 1,062,088 | 1,829,423 | 3,261,039 | 3,110,716 | 1,115,145 | 1,890,540 |
| 282,118 | 531,795 | 463,359 | 455,577 | 581,418 | 424,544 | 280,047 |
| 217,658 | 220,826 | 159,533 | 135,388 | 86,465 | 78,937 | 159,296 |
| 109,071 | 133,262 | 222,163 | 135,182 | 343,577 | 273,389 | 174,973 |
| 5,147 | 4,253 | 9,438 | 3,609 | 7,225 | 153,166 | 143,703 |
| 14,597 | 14,109 | 22,235 | 29,997 | 92,602 | 146,241 | 102,743 |
| 243,578 | 510,041 | 442,393 | 487,876 | 136,167 | 255,303 | 17,444 |
| 28,585 | 48,344 | 88,791 | 67,551 | 46,191 | 27,789 | 14,312 |
| 11,600 | 6,574 | 4,194 | 5,679 | — | — | 10,858 |
| 484 | 230 | — | 2,365 | — | — | 2,906 |
| 1,353,160 | 2,531,522 | 3,241,529 | 4,584,263 | 4,404,361 | 2,474,514 | 2,796,822 |
| | | | | | | |
| 24,038 | 25,344 | 22,187 | 39,608 | 34,466 | 55,462 | 55,755 |
| 19,118 | 16,064 | 15,826 | 23,627 | 39,077 | 43,121 | 29,232 |
| 1,582 | 1,328 | 1,354 | — | 60,263 | 16,836 | 19,788 |
| 4,609 | 9,049 | 10,315 | 10,011 | 7,198 | — | 6,835 |
| 49,347 | 51,785 | 49,682 | 73,246 | 141,004 | 115,419 | 111,610 |
| | | | | | | |
| 173,308 | 7,330,935 | 12,569,361 | 13,086,668 | 15,436,343 | 15,119,832 | 3,887,704 |
| 729,055 | 877,646 | 1,600,608 | 1,035,272 | 1,149,812 | 504,282 | 408,999 |
| 810,082 | 420,332 | 244,857 | 217,345 | 244,672 | 227,216 | 207,478 |
| 79,707 | 105,037 | 112,407 | 208,776 | 156,099 | 217,469 | 158,682 |
| 14,879 | 32,579 | 212,274 | 37,337 | — | — | 93,912 |
| 39,310 | 55,297 | 47,947 | 51,714 | 73,289 | 100,313 | 53,511 |
| 23,487 | 37,619 | 57,624 | 29,047 | 56,453 | 36,066 | 66,002 |
| — | 892 | — | — | 19,561 | — | 52,378 |
| 40,922 | 8,370 | 93,178 | 49,804 | 171,462 | 42,097 | 29,540 |
| 24,620 | 34,656 | 11,493 | 47,199 | 29,654 | 46,299 | 73,552 |
| — | — | 1,909 | 4,500 | 15,445 | 46,511 | 46,130 |
| 6,626 | 11,451 | 8,425 | 17,785 | 42,444 | 42,496 | 32,956 |
| 3,606 | 7,348 | 41,131 | 17,885 | 83,465 | 193,463 | 46,618 |
| 8,186 | 8,903 | 19,377 | 12,792 | 15,330 | 8,582 | 16,185 |
| 682 | 6,212 | 26,344 | 19,866 | 10,250 | 41,500 | 17,894 |
| 8,721 | 23,940 | 17,492 | 16,214 | 5,871 | 4,114 | 10,145 |
| 5,241 | 7,520 | 7,447 | 17,521 | 7,390 | 12,756 | 11,609 |
| 7,041 | 7,388 | 6,224 | 9,886 | 5,113 | — | 7,851 |
| 7,218 | 15,397 | 1,175 | 12,925 | 20,766 | 18,709 | 10,639 |
| 17,786 | 97,054 | 66,015 | 78,478 | 22,169 | 146,497 | — |
| 2,000,477 | 9,088,576 | 15,145,288 | 14,971,014 | 17,565,588 | 16,808,202 | 5,231,785 |
| | | | | | | |
| 169,008 | 114,276 | 137,582 | 428,638 | 205,565 | 211,956 | 101,794 |
| | | | | | | |
| 11,295,709 | 17,324,633 | 23,196,704 | 24,179,000 | 27,566,991 | 23,512,294 | 12,472,158 |

## ES-5. UNITED STATES: EXPORTS

(Soluble

| COUNTRIES OF DESTINATION | January | February | March | April | May |
|---|---|---|---|---|---|
| CANADA | 149,398 | 54,924 | 249,695 | 86,388 | 121,025 |
| **OTHER WESTERN HEMISPHERE** | | | | | |
| Bahamas | 9,514 | 15,045 | 8,503 | 6,299 | 14,439 |
| Netherlands West Indies | 5,343 | 4,922 | 9,892 | 10,415 | 6,544 |
| Mexico | 1,212 | 1,300 | 600 | 900 | 782 |
| Bermuda | 8,045 | 3,713 | 3,299 | 6,469 | 10,232 |
| Trinidad & Tobago | 2,241 | 1,100 | 923 | 5,251 | 2,212 |
| Barbados | 460 | 1,725 | 1,425 | 2,320 | 1,320 |
| Guyana | — | — | — | 13,112 | — |
| Leeward, Windward Islands | — | 714 | 1,053 | 314 | 230 |
| Surinam | 4,310 | — | — | 3,713 | — |
| Jamaica | 539 | 83 | 1,704 | 375 | 1,724 |
| British Honduras | — | — | — | — | — |
| Peru | — | — | — | 958 | 842 |
| Dominican Republic | — | 730 | 1,035 | — | — |
| TOTAL OTHER WESTERN HEMISPHERE | 31,664 | 29,332 | 28,434 | 50,126 | 38,325 |
| **EUROPE** | | | | | |
| United Kingdom | 223,684 | 179,800 | 239,875 | 214,525 | 59,063 |
| Finland | 3,992 | 10,074 | 10,941 | 3,632 | 3,205 |
| Netherlands | 1,716 | 22,470 | 38,024 | 22,020 | — |
| Sweden | — | — | 2,642 | 37,793 | 5,214 |
| Norway | 338 | 20,481 | 333 | 2,000 | — |
| Denmark | 833 | — | 4,519 | 3,237 | 1,761 |
| Germany (F.R.) | — | 1,644 | 6,203 | 560 | 754 |
| Belgium | 2,745 | 2,640 | 1,100 | — | 450 |
| Italy | 750 | 1,450 | 1,191 | 2,221 | 1,155 |
| Greece | — | 2,060 | — | — | — |
| TOTAL EUROPE | 234,058 | 240,619 | 304,828 | 285,988 | 71,602 |
| **AFRICA** | | | | | |
| Liberia | 2,310 | 660 | 1,899 | 1,050 | 660 |
| Libya | 731 | 1,019 | 1,431 | 724 | 709 |
| Nigeria | 2,625 | — | 944 | — | 1,125 |
| United Arab Republic | — | — | — | 348 | 2,700 |
| TOTAL AFRICA | 5,666 | 1,679 | 4,274 | 2,122 | 5,194 |
| **ASIA & OCEANIA** | | | | | |
| Japan | 463,923 | 734,956 | 421,187 | 20,780 | 13,319 |
| Australia | 24,135 | 17,100 | 30,607 | 15,283 | 20,040 |
| Nampo Islands | 5,973 | 12,774 | 8,496 | 13,024 | 9,409 |
| Thailand | 2,880 | 7,663 | 11,339 | 2,198 | 11,885 |
| Singapore | 2,902 | 5,030 | 9,270 | 3,660 | 15,830 |
| Hong Kong | 2,220 | 1,055 | 1,525 | 3,532 | 4,655 |
| Lebanon | 1,078 | 4,475 | — | 4,717 | — |
| Taiwan | 1,480 | 2,648 | — | 3,007 | — |
| Syria | — | — | — | — | — |
| Saudi Arabia | — | — | 1,425 | 8,958 | 720 |
| South Korea | — | 1,200 | 5,550 | — | 225 |
| Trust Pacific Islands | — | 214 | 3,248 | 2,180 | 1,863 |
| Malaysia | — | — | — | 1,041 | 2,468 |
| Jordan | 1,009 | — | — | — | — |
| Kuwait | — | 788 | 4,232 | 405 | 292 |
| Pakistan | — | 1,081 | 587 | 352 | 1,789 |
| New Guinea | — | — | — | — | 2,401 |
| India | — | 1,500 | — | — | — |
| Iran | — | — | — | 840 | 1,725 |
| TOTAL ASIA & OCEANIA | 505,600 | 790,484 | 497,466 | 79,977 | 86,621 |
| OTHERS | 4,152 | 4,019 | 6,109 | 3,009 | 4,975 |
| TOTAL | 930,538 | 1,121,057 | 1,090,806 | 507,610 | 327,742 |

Source: U. S. Department of Commerce.

## OF SOLUBLE COFFEE, 1966

Pounds)

| June | July | August | September | October | November | December | Total | Bags (Green Equiv.) |
|---|---|---|---|---|---|---|---|---|
| 294,988 | 273,101 | 216,228 | 257,280 | 115,725 | 220,509 | 153,808 | 2,193,069 | 49,739 |
| | | | | | | | | |
| 4,078 | 5,040 | 6,736 | 7,839 | 2,182 | 2,599 | 3,772 | 86,046 | 1,951 |
| 7,401 | 5,896 | 480 | 10,302 | 5,608 | 7,284 | 6,277 | 80,364 | 1,823 |
| 1,470 | 40,300 | 1,280 | 70,280 | — | 32,125 | 600 | 150,849 | 3,421 |
| 3,101 | 2,862 | 4,737 | 5,285 | 3,588 | 873 | 4,530 | 56,734 | 1,287 |
| 2,996 | 1,140 | 3,091 | 1,279 | 3,294 | 1,196 | 2,167 | 26,890 | 610 |
| 4,096 | 432 | 542 | 971 | 979 | 1,059 | 1,461 | 16,790 | 381 |
| — | 4,350 | 3,612 | 90 | — | 1,293 | — | 22,457 | 509 |
| 1,153 | 2,263 | 1,080 | 190 | 2,648 | 1,478 | 1,084 | 12,207 | 277 |
| 993 | — | — | 5,267 | — | 1,547 | — | 15,830 | 359 |
| 981 | 390 | 1,506 | 263 | 1,400 | 1,476 | 533 | 10,974 | 249 |
| 1,080 | 1,005 | 843 | — | 90 | 915 | — | 3,933 | 89 |
| 466 | 830 | 540 | — | 698 | 106 | — | 4,440 | 101 |
| — | — | — | — | — | — | — | 1,765 | 40 |
| 27,815 | 64,508 | 24,447 | 101,766 | 20,487 | 51,951 | 20,424 | 489,279 | 11,097 |
| | | | | | | | | |
| 53,040 | 132,687 | 181,890 | 139,321 | 150,521 | 25,020 | 88,812 | 1,688,238 | 38,289 |
| 34,771 | 2,284 | 504 | 2,616 | 4,431 | 31,209 | 1,178 | 108,837 | 2,468 |
| 2,271 | 1,048 | 11,534 | 563 | 450 | — | — | 100,096 | 2,270 |
| 176 | 3,514 | 5,486 | 39,486 | 8,565 | 6,050 | 1,620 | 110,546 | 2,507 |
| — | — | — | 13,348 | 5,934 | 7,828 | 29,569 | 79,831 | 1,811 |
| 4,394 | 1,192 | 6,473 | 697 | 7,089 | 3,153 | 16,758 | 50,106 | 1,136 |
| — | — | 227 | 2,254 | — | — | 886 | 12,528 | 284 |
| 200 | 2,010 | 900 | — | — | 200 | 847 | 11,092 | 252 |
| 1,440 | — | 200 | 759 | — | 502 | 428 | 10,096 | 229 |
| — | — | — | — | — | 338 | — | 2,398 | 54 |
| 96,292 | 142,735 | 207,214 | 199,044 | 176,990 | 74,300 | 140,098 | 2,173,768 | 49,300 |
| | | | | | | | | |
| 3,361 | 541 | 1,508 | 3,898 | 2,310 | 3,335 | 1,457 | 22,989 | 522 |
| 1,741 | 1,654 | — | 1,615 | 1,474 | 777 | 1,088 | 12,963 | 294 |
| — | — | — | 3,420 | — | — | — | 8,114 | 184 |
| — | — | — | — | — | — | — | 3,048 | 69 |
| 5,102 | 2,195 | 1,508 | 8,933 | 3,784 | 4,112 | 2,545 | 47,114 | 1,069 |
| | | | | | | | | |
| 30,344 | 6,022 | 24,031 | 32,729 | 100,258 | 37,765 | 13,735 | 1,899,049 | 43,070 |
| 33,283 | 5,145 | 24,300 | 10,522 | 21,087 | 14,534 | 27,610 | 243,646 | 5,526 |
| 11,705 | 7,531 | 5,798 | 6,727 | 972 | 12,348 | 8,075 | 102,832 | 2,332 |
| 18,066 | 10,132 | 4,141 | 6,035 | 5,274 | 5,853 | 2,531 | 87,997 | 1,996 |
| 2,548 | 2,910 | 787 | — | 1,320 | 5,748 | 3,522 | 53,527 | 1,214 |
| 1,114 | 575 | 4,437 | 2,236 | 225 | 1,282 | 3,021 | 25,877 | 587 |
| 750 | 2,250 | — | 1,801 | 6,338 | 8,094 | 7,995 | 37,498 | 850 |
| — | — | 3,060 | 5,625 | 600 | 3,600 | 3,195 | 23,215 | 527 |
| 2,650 | 2,910 | 9,177 | — | — | — | — | 14,737 | 334 |
| 1,099 | 1,704 | 1,811 | 2,320 | 7,897 | 10,917 | 7,712 | 44,563 | 1,011 |
| — | 720 | 7,230 | 3,900 | — | 5,505 | 2,791 | 27,121 | 615 |
| 1,514 | 2,065 | 1,065 | 2,756 | 3,625 | 1,053 | 1,763 | 21,346 | 484 |
| 960 | — | 285 | 1,924 | 10,640 | 1,012 | 750 | 19,080 | 433 |
| 889 | 4,050 | — | — | — | 675 | — | 6,623 | 150 |
| 1,418 | 292 | 292 | 825 | 563 | 563 | 825 | 10,495 | 238 |
| 210 | 541 | 300 | 248 | 277 | — | — | 5,385 | 122 |
| 1,050 | — | 749 | 340 | 413 | 440 | — | 5,393 | 122 |
| 1,560 | 1,388 | — | — | — | — | 200 | 4,648 | 105 |
| 474 | — | 945 | — | 1,020 | — | 270 | 5,274 | 120 |
| 109,634 | 48,235 | 88,408 | 77,988 | 160,509 | 109,389 | 83,995 | 2,638,306 | 59,836 |
| | | | | | | | | |
| 2,383 | 7,296 | 1,853 | 6,178 | 6,333 | 5,876 | 3,418 | 55,601 | 1,261 |
| | | | | | | | | |
| 536,214 | 538,070 | 539,658 | 651,189 | 483,828 | 466,137 | 404,288 | 7,597,137 | 172,302 |

A-159

ESV-5. UNITED STATES: VALUE OF

(U. S.

| COUNTRIES OF DESTINATION | January | February | March | April | May |
|---|---|---|---|---|---|
| CANADA | 259,192 | 102,731 | 360,997 | 116,027 | 209,573 |
| OTHER WESTERN HEMISPHERE | | | | | |
| Bahamas | 23,346 | 29,519 | 17,897 | 17,749 | 33,451 |
| Netherlands West Indies | 14,861 | 11,924 | 26,329 | 27,325 | 16,016 |
| Mexico | 2,902 | 3,308 | 1,244 | 1,866 | 1,506 |
| Bermuda | 19,623 | 7,584 | 8,239 | 16,706 | 21,611 |
| Trinidad & Tobago | 5,033 | 2,413 | 2,380 | 10,187 | 5,154 |
| Barbados | 1,105 | 4,093 | 3,470 | 3,842 | 3,933 |
| Guyana | — | — | — | 14,738 | — |
| Leeward, Windward Islands | — | 1,628 | 2,782 | 834 | 539 |
| Surinam | 4,500 | — | — | 3,749 | — |
| Jamaica | 1,048 | 272 | 3,207 | 787 | 1,858 |
| British Honduras | — | — | — | — | 3,294 |
| Peru | — | — | — | 3,048 | 2,512 |
| Dominican Republic | — | 1,644 | 1,467 | — | — |
| TOTAL OTHER WESTERN HEMISPHERE | 72,418 | 62,385 | 67,015 | 100,831 | 89,874 |
| EUROPE | | | | | |
| United Kingdom | 242,892 | 199,776 | 260,049 | 236,425 | 64,538 |
| Finland | 11,866 | 24,860 | 26,399 | 12,058 | 8,511 |
| Netherlands | 4,736 | 34,936 | 59,738 | 33,220 | — |
| Sweden | — | — | 4,779 | 59,856 | 10,975 |
| Norway | 767 | 37,139 | 798 | 1,940 | — |
| Denmark | 1,948 | — | 12,199 | 9,972 | 4,290 |
| Germany (F.R.) | — | 2,863 | 6,047 | 952 | 1,235 |
| Belgium | 3,408 | 2,441 | 1,416 | — | 1,072 |
| Italy | 1,640 | 1,355 | — | 1,993 | 927 |
| Greece | — | 2,530 | — | — | — |
| TOTAL EUROPE | 267,257 | 305,900 | 371,425 | 356,416 | 91,548 |
| AFRICA | | | | | |
| Liberia | 6,093 | 1,686 | 4,515 | 2,315 | 1,972 |
| Libya | 2,013 | 2,723 | 3,775 | 1,902 | 1,148 |
| Nigeria | 6,409 | — | 2,299 | — | 2,747 |
| United Arab Republic | — | — | — | 1,097 | 5,738 |
| TOTAL AFRICA | 14,515 | 4,409 | 10,589 | 5,314 | 11,605 |
| ASIA & OCEANIA | | | | | |
| Japan | 959,364 | 1,574,174 | 877,405 | 41,598 | 19,850 |
| Australia | 37,470 | 27,826 | 40,120 | 24,125 | 28,723 |
| Nampo Islands | 11,635 | 18,544 | 18,261 | 18,670 | 21,619 |
| Thailand | 5,732 | 16,032 | 27,354 | 3,740 | 22,283 |
| Singapore | 5,935 | 8,336 | 16,096 | 6,308 | 26,972 |
| Hong Kong | 5,251 | 2,303 | 1,854 | 5,692 | 7,732 |
| Lebanon | 1,680 | 9,006 | — | 10,374 | — |
| Taiwan | 2,923 | 6,132 | — | 2,876 | — |
| Syria | — | — | — | — | — |
| Saudi Arabia | — | — | 2,532 | 10,090 | 1,775 |
| South Korea | — | 2,251 | 12,817 | — | 629 |
| Trust Pacific Islands | — | 352 | 3,284 | 3,072 | 2,688 |
| Malaysia | — | — | — | 2,329 | 6,637 |
| Jordan | 2,121 | — | — | — | — |
| Kuwait | — | 1,889 | 6,982 | 1,044 | 706 |
| Pakistan | — | 1,418 | 1,158 | 833 | 3,492 |
| New Guinea | — | — | — | — | 4,805 |
| India | — | 3,146 | — | — | — |
| Iran | — | — | — | 1,486 | 4,663 |
| TOTAL ASIA & OCEANIA | 1,032,111 | 1,671,409 | 1,007,863 | 132,237 | 152,574 |
| OTHERS | 7,396 | 8,930 | 13,090 | 3,757 | 6,747 |
| TOTAL | 1,652,889 | 2,155,764 | 1,830,979 | 714,582 | 561,921 |

Source: U. S. Department of Commerce.

## SOLUBLE COFFEE EXPORTS, 1966

(Dollars)

| June | July | August | September | October | November | December | Total |
|---|---|---|---|---|---|---|---|
| 466,960 | 367,397 | 329,204 | 403,702 | 184,915 | 278,327 | 192,476 | 3,271,501 |
| | | | | | | | |
| 8,759 | 8,573 | 13,473 | 15,025 | 3,789 | 4,669 | 6,447 | 182,697 |
| 18,154 | 16,348 | 952 | 22,283 | 15,912 | 20,426 | 17,509 | 208,039 |
| 2,436 | 42,622 | 2,002 | 74,060 | — | 76,630 | 1,244 | 209,820 |
| 7,723 | 7,026 | 11,573 | 12,287 | 10,031 | 1,326 | 12,324 | 136,053 |
| 4,959 | 2,722 | 6,800 | 2,864 | 6,534 | 2,525 | 4,542 | 56,113 |
| 8,379 | 1,144 | 1,488 | 2,397 | 1,466 | 1,433 | 3,510 | 36,260 |
| — | 6,191 | 7,500 | 216 | — | 4,420 | — | 33,065 |
| 2,238 | 5,418 | 2,526 | 504 | 5,820 | 3,855 | 2,555 | 28,699 |
| 3,100 | — | — | 4,950 | — | 4,892 | — | 21,191 |
| 2,193 | 756 | 2,356 | 659 | 1,185 | 1,558 | 1,280 | 17,159 |
| 2,861 | 2,585 | 2,111 | — | 214 | 2,346 | — | 13,411 |
| 1,669 | 1,542 | 1,982 | — | 1,925 | 350 | — | 13,028 |
| — | — | — | — | — | — | — | 3,111 |
| 62,471 | 94,927 | 52,763 | 135,245 | 46,876 | 124,430 | 49,411 | 958,646 |
| | | | | | | | |
| 57,872 | 146,482 | 200,783 | 193,952 | 166,381 | 22,768 | 98,622 | 1,890,540 |
| 97,026 | 5,561 | 939 | 6,574 | 10,501 | 72,112 | 3,640 | 280,047 |
| 3,900 | 1,985 | 18,444 | 1,283 | 1,054 | — | — | 159,296 |
| 398 | 7,340 | 11,597 | 51,809 | 13,189 | 11,885 | 3,145 | 174,973 |
| — | — | — | 24,740 | 11,533 | 20,867 | 45,919 | 143,703 |
| 11,907 | 2,301 | 9,890 | 1,629 | 13,695 | 6,263 | 28,649 | 102,743 |
| — | — | 645 | 4,195 | — | — | 1,507 | 17,444 |
| 503 | 2,080 | 891 | — | — | 502 | 1,999 | 14,312 |
| 1,952 | — | 548 | 1,147 | — | 844 | 452 | 10,858 |
| — | — | — | — | — | 376 | — | 2,906 |
| 173,558 | 165,749 | 243,737 | 285,329 | 216,353 | 135,617 | 183,933 | 2,796,822 |
| | | | | | | | |
| 7,430 | 1,388 | 3,821 | 9,060 | 5,960 | 7,924 | 3,591 | 55,755 |
| 4,379 | 3,603 | — | 1,384 | 3,572 | 1,863 | 2,870 | 29,232 |
| — | — | — | 8,333 | — | — | — | 19,788 |
| — | — | — | — | — | — | — | 6,835 |
| 11,809 | 4,991 | 3,821 | 18,777 | 9,532 | 9,787 | 6,461 | 111,610 |
| | | | | | | | |
| 50,877 | 7,812 | 39,055 | 58,199 | 166,059 | 67,442 | 25,869 | 3,887,704 |
| 62,358 | 7,299 | 47,019 | 21,138 | 38,484 | 19,914 | 54,523 | 408,999 |
| 25,180 | 16,394 | 12,958 | 15,406 | 2,181 | 29,625 | 17,005 | 207,478 |
| 26,600 | 17,017 | 6,001 | 10,675 | 5,285 | 12,121 | 5,842 | 158,682 |
| 4,096 | 5,036 | 1,322 | — | 2,010 | 9,971 | 7,830 | 93,912 |
| 2,902 | 1,247 | 9,717 | 5,265 | 1,025 | 3,207 | 7,316 | 53,511 |
| 1,726 | 5,556 | — | 4,449 | 13,046 | 11,675 | 8,490 | 66,002 |
| — | — | 7,652 | 13,733 | 2,028 | 10,194 | 6,840 | 52,378 |
| 5,250 | 6,615 | 17,675 | — | — | — | — | 29,540 |
| 2,820 | 2,541 | 2,355 | 5,525 | 9,799 | 23,611 | 12,504 | 73,552 |
| — | 948 | 6,298 | 3,334 | — | 13,798 | 6,055 | 46,130 |
| 3,371 | 4,357 | 2,009 | 2,645 | 5,955 | 2,373 | 2,850 | 32,956 |
| 1,891 | — | 573 | 3,871 | 27,381 | 2,280 | 1,656 | 46,618 |
| 2,294 | 10,512 | — | — | — | 1,258 | — | 16,185 |
| 1,496 | 706 | 706 | 700 | 1,482 | 1,483 | 700 | 17,894 |
| 392 | 1,159 | 526 | 575 | 592 | — | — | 10,145 |
| 1,864 | — | 1,642 | 857 | 1,415 | 1,026 | — | 11,609 |
| 1,456 | 2,853 | — | — | — | — | 396 | 7,851 |
| 592 | — | 1,770 | — | 1,894 | — | 234 | 10,639 |
| 195,165 | 90,052 | 157,278 | 146,372 | 278,636 | 209,978 | 158,110 | 5,231,785 |
| | | | | | | | |
| 2,228 | 14,504 | 4,348 | 11,965 | 12,025 | 10,428 | 6,376 | 101,794 |
| | | | | | | | |
| 912,191 | 737,620 | 791,151 | 1,001,390 | 748,337 | 768,567 | 596,767 | 12,472,158 |

## ES-7. UNITED STATES: EXPORTS
(Soluble

| COUNTRIES OF DESTINATION | January | February | March | April | May |
|---|---|---|---|---|---|
| **CANADA** | 50,481 | 114,813 | 153,512 | 169,798 | 176,039 |
| **OTHER AMERICAS** | | | | | |
| Netherlands West Indies | 4,284 | 13,822 | 19,080 | 7,231 | 8,434 |
| Bermuda | 4,701 | 3,074 | 5,876 | 7,787 | 8,243 |
| Bahamas | 1,642 | 2,479 | 5,201 | 11,982 | 5,164 |
| Guyana | — | — | — | — | — |
| Trinidad & Tobago | — | 1,707 | 4,069 | 3,331 | 4,384 |
| Surinam | — | — | — | 5,890 | — |
| Barbados | — | 2,508 | 1,026 | 889 | 1,968 |
| Leeward, Windward Islands | — | 226 | 1,504 | 1,584 | 113 |
| Mexico | 421 | 144 | 492 | 1,180 | 600 |
| Jamaica | 1,060 | 786 | 342 | 1,481 | 628 |
| British Honduras | — | — | 958 | 855 | — |
| Dominican Republic | — | — | — | — | — |
| Peru | — | 196 | 1,090 | — | — |
| **TOTAL OTHER AMERICAS** | 12,108 | 24,942 | 39,638 | 42,210 | 29,534 |
| **EUROPE** | | | | | |
| United Kingdom | 27,800 | 150,098 | 707 | — | 500 |
| Sweden | — | 792 | — | 42,150 | 50,584 |
| Finland | — | 330 | 43,880 | 7,778 | 14,971 |
| Germany (F.R.) | — | 208 | 18,000 | 30,000 | 160 |
| Norway | — | — | — | 1,390 | 15,000 |
| Denmark | 14,437 | — | 2,782 | 1,337 | 20,450 |
| France | — | — | — | — | — |
| Netherlands | 675 | — | — | 10,707 | — |
| Belgium | — | — | 3,532 | 2,350 | 2,800 |
| Gibraltar | — | — | — | — | 414 |
| **TOTAL EUROPE** | 42,912 | 151,428 | 68,901 | 95,712 | 104,879 |
| **AFRICA** | | | | | |
| Liberia | — | — | 2,820 | — | 1,025 |
| Libya | — | — | 1,141 | 1,200 | 1,162 |
| Nigeria | — | — | 3,453 | — | — |
| **TOTAL AFRICA** | — | — | 7,414 | 1,200 | 2,187 |
| **ASIA & OCEANIA** | | | | | |
| Japan | 213,064 | 164,483 | 106,928 | 51,708 | 304,770 |
| Australia | 8,775 | 74,678 | 48,231 | 28,053 | 45,804 |
| Nampo Islands | 5,840 | 6,839 | 3,482 | 6,360 | 4,060 |
| Thailand | 19,887 | 15,495 | 19,784 | 8,595 | 13,725 |
| Malaysia | 10,552 | 8,024 | 7,205 | 31,711 | 3,952 |
| Philippine Republic | 8,640 | — | 22,575 | — | 9,805 |
| Hong Kong | 2,947 | 1,504 | 4,928 | 10,683 | 3,217 |
| Syria | — | — | — | 2,009 | 5,300 |
| South Korea | 1,781 | 5,025 | 132 | — | 462 |
| Trust Pacific Islands | 2,126 | 1,955 | 560 | 4,082 | 1,074 |
| Kuwait | 1,421 | 536 | 956 | 3,182 | 3,150 |
| Saudi Arabia | — | 4,623 | 4,465 | 4,530 | — |
| Lebanon | — | 490 | 2,850 | 914 | 488 |
| Iran | — | — | 2,016 | 1,491 | — |
| New Guinea | — | — | 1,460 | — | — |
| Israel | — | — | — | 1,313 | 1,185 |
| Pakistan | 1,085 | — | 635 | 394 | — |
| Aden | — | — | 520 | 1,568 | — |
| Jordan | — | — | — | — | 1,100 |
| **TOTAL ASIA & OCEANIA** | 276,118 | 283,652 | 226,727 | 621,903 | 398,092 |
| **OTHERS** | 1,420 | 644 | 5,745 | 5,996 | 1,814 |
| **TOTAL POUNDS INSTANT** | 383,039 | 575,479 | 501,937 | 936,819 | 712,545 |
| **TOTAL BAGS (Green Equivalent)** | 8,687 | 13,052 | 11,384 | 21,247 | 16,160 |

Source: U. S. Department of Commerce.

**OF SOLUBLE COFFEE, 1965**

Pounds)

| June | July | August | September | October | November | December | Total | Bags (Green Equiv.) |
|---|---|---|---|---|---|---|---|---|
| 334,298 | 123,201 | 68,988 | 187,258 | 234,618 | 211,720 | 85,606 | 1,910,332 | 43,326 |
| | | | | | | | | |
| 5,664 | 8,431 | 9,855 | 4,200 | 14,269 | 6,575 | 3,451 | 105,296 | 2,388 |
| 6,773 | 1,157 | 4,176 | 3,254 | 2,869 | 2,184 | 2,872 | 52,966 | 1,201 |
| 1,232 | 8,161 | 1,329 | 3,045 | 2,095 | 3,969 | 2,962 | 49,261 | 1,117 |
| 4,214 | 7,322 | – | 8,430 | – | 9,996 | – | 29,962 | 680 |
| 1,653 | 513 | 1,996 | 899 | 2,155 | 2,265 | 1,585 | 24,557 | 557 |
| 3,300 | 650 | 3,381 | – | 1,575 | 2,826 | – | 17,622 | 400 |
| 1,365 | 1,022 | 1,167 | 1,249 | 375 | 400 | 1,230 | 13,199 | 299 |
| 1,048 | 800 | 708 | – | 1,901 | 1,579 | 912 | 10,375 | 235 |
| 300 | 544 | 735 | 2,779 | 600 | 1,020 | 300 | 9,115 | 207 |
| 537 | 706 | 338 | 899 | 274 | – | 1,179 | 8,230 | 187 |
| 1,229 | 140 | – | 1,194 | – | 825 | 2,115 | 7,316 | 166 |
| – | – | – | – | – | 4,453 | 2,559 | 7,012 | 159 |
| – | – | 516 | 1,020 | 956 | 60 | 940 | 4,778 | 108 |
| 27,315 | 29,446 | 24,201 | 26,969 | 27,069 | 36,152 | 20,105 | 339,689 | 7,704 |
| | | | | | | | | |
| 5,647 | 89,094 | 53,072 | 153,659 | 115,616 | 68,479 | 260,498 | 925,170 | 20,983 |
| 250 | 8,526 | 16,248 | 46,475 | – | 7,998 | 122 | 173,145 | 3,927 |
| 9,431 | 17,120 | 6,559 | 14,447 | 9,661 | 1,500 | 32,372 | 158,049 | 3,585 |
| 6,630 | 18,000 | 8,954 | 21,786 | 30,890 | 12,759 | 900 | 148,287 | 3,363 |
| 300 | 613 | 24,957 | 25,172 | – | 588 | 13,988 | 82,008 | 1,860 |
| 990 | 14,917 | 16,379 | 450 | – | 723 | 419 | 72,884 | 1,653 |
| – | – | 952 | 60,724 | – | – | – | 61,676 | 1,399 |
| 932 | – | 8,216 | 1,629 | 2,868 | 1,118 | 19,662 | 45,807 | 1,039 |
| 683 | 928 | 150 | 349 | 761 | 867 | 5,635 | 18,055 | 409 |
| 2,732 | – | – | – | – | – | – | 3,146 | 71 |
| 27,595 | 149,198 | 135,487 | 324,691 | 159,796 | 94,032 | 333,596 | 1,688,227 | 38,289 |
| | | | | | | | | |
| 2,995 | 2,289 | 4,574 | 3,739 | 1,230 | 2,541 | 660 | 21,873 | 496 |
| 6,592 | 1,610 | 1,272 | 1,870 | 1,921 | 870 | 225 | 17,863 | 405 |
| 248 | – | – | 1,875 | 750 | – | – | 6,326 | 144 |
| 9,835 | 3,899 | 5,846 | 7,484 | 3,901 | 3,411 | 885 | 46,062 | 1,045 |
| | | | | | | | | |
| 702,319 | 1,384,482 | 1,053,038 | 519,014 | 920,983 | 754,085 | 552,167 | 7,192,351 | 163,121 |
| 50,970 | 14,278 | 6,569 | 20,998 | 6,430 | 6,521 | 14,819 | 326,126 | 7,397 |
| 8,079 | 6,841 | 8,288 | 23,975 | 1,968 | 19,036 | 19,440 | 114,208 | 2,590 |
| 900 | 4,676 | 2,745 | 3,480 | 2,663 | 3,128 | 12,586 | 107,664 | 2,442 |
| 7,179 | 2,639 | 3,324 | 2,060 | 2,852 | 7,683 | 4,373 | 91,554 | 2,076 |
| – | – | – | 3,780 | 638 | – | 3,175 | 48,613 | 1,103 |
| 4,061 | 1,375 | 5,203 | 3,592 | 1,678 | 2,130 | 1,913 | 43,231 | 981 |
| – | – | – | 10,044 | 1,325 | – | 5,618 | 24,296 | 551 |
| – | 11,175 | 2,126 | – | – | 796 | 1,200 | 22,697 | 515 |
| 1,720 | 270 | 2,499 | 553 | 2,897 | – | 3,660 | 21,396 | 485 |
| 1,446 | 900 | 6,188 | 1,348 | 795 | – | – | 19,922 | 452 |
| 180 | 1,478 | – | 270 | 300 | – | 640 | 16,486 | 374 |
| 789 | 536 | 386 | 2,246 | 1,507 | 2,646 | 2,491 | 15,343 | 348 |
| 720 | – | 518 | 216 | – | 1,635 | 914 | 7,510 | 170 |
| – | – | – | – | 2,626 | 1,740 | 190 | 6,016 | 136 |
| 1,290 | – | – | 1,013 | – | – | 548 | 5,349 | 121 |
| – | – | – | – | – | – | – | 2,114 | 48 |
| – | – | – | – | – | – | – | 2,088 | 47 |
| 2,616 | – | – | – | – | – | – | 3,716 | 84 |
| 782,269 | 1,428,650 | 1,090,884 | 592,589 | 946,662 | 799,400 | 623,734 | 8,070,680 | 183,041 |
| | | | | | | | | |
| 5,676 | 8,518 | 3,620 | 8,414 | 6,152 | 2,431 | 7,039 | 57,469 | 1,303 |
| | | | | | | | | |
| 1,186,988 | 1,742,912 | 1,329,026 | 1,147,405 | 1,378,198 | 1,147,146 | 1,070,965 | 12,112,459 | 274,708 |
| | | | | | | | | |
| 26,921 | 39,529 | 30,142 | 26,023 | 31,257 | 26,017 | 24,289 | 274,708 | |

ESV-7. UNITED STATES: VALUE OF

(U. S.

| COUNTRIES OF DESTINATION | January | February | March | April | May |
|---|---|---|---|---|---|
| CANADA | 50,559 | 194,175 | 265,848 | 280,693 | 299,672 |
| **OTHER AMERICAS** | | | | | |
| Netherlands West Indies | 13,400 | 36,397 | 53,600 | 15,483 | 25,522 |
| Bermuda | 13,722 | 7,787 | 15,033 | 18,270 | 18,365 |
| Bahamas | 4,820 | 4,413 | 10,971 | 28,010 | 13,603 |
| Guyana | — | — | — | — | — |
| Trinidad & Tobago | — | 3,843 | 9,288 | 6,589 | 8,783 |
| Surinam | — | — | — | 12,572 | — |
| Barbados | — | 5,729 | 2,446 | 2,077 | 5,297 |
| Leeward, Windward Islands | — | 619 | 3,933 | 3,930 | 240 |
| Mexico | 1,522 | 598 | 1,226 | 2,984 | 1,244 |
| Jamaica | 2,183 | 1,779 | 844 | 3,070 | 1,074 |
| British Honduras | — | — | 1,880 | 2,218 | — |
| Dominican Republic | — | — | — | — | — |
| Peru | — | 722 | 3,564 | — | — |
| **TOTAL OTHER AMERICAS** | 35,647 | 61,887 | 102,785 | 95,203 | 74,128 |
| **EUROPE** | | | | | |
| United Kingdom | 41,579 | 168,685 | 780 | — | 715 |
| Sweden | — | 2,047 | — | 66,710 | 80,226 |
| Finland | — | 840 | 118,180 | 20,677 | 39,092 |
| Germany (F.R.) | — | 588 | 28,440 | 47,400 | 320 |
| Norway | — | — | — | 2,195 | 28,128 |
| Denmark | 28,323 | — | 7,463 | 3,168 | 35,352 |
| France | — | — | — | — | — |
| Netherlands | 1,245 | — | — | 18,069 | — |
| Belgium | — | — | 4,823 | 2,758 | 3,189 |
| Gibraltar | — | — | — | — | 589 |
| **TOTAL EUROPE** | 71,147 | 172,160 | 159,686 | 160,977 | 187,611 |
| **AFRICA** | | | | | |
| Liberia | — | — | 6,927 | — | 1,856 |
| Libya | — | — | 2,802 | 2,885 | 2,956 |
| Nigeria | — | — | 9,829 | — | — |
| **TOTAL AFRICA** | — | — | 19,558 | 2,885 | 4,812 |
| **ASIA & OCEANIA** | | | | | |
| Japan | 482,631 | 356,980 | 274,581 | 1,133,230 | 790,007 |
| Australia | 18,415 | 79,364 | 72,527 | 51,075 | 80,002 |
| Nampo Islands | 13,474 | 15,464 | 6,545 | 13,571 | 9,150 |
| Thailand | 38,027 | 41,762 | 36,422 | 18,648 | 21,360 |
| Malaysia | 22,168 | 14,496 | 16,007 | 82,061 | 6,493 |
| Philippine Republic | 27,297 | — | 66,509 | — | 29,244 |
| Hong Kong | 6,119 | 3,913 | 14,177 | 24,329 | 7,629 |
| Syria | — | — | — | 2,400 | 8,000 |
| South Korea | 4,027 | 7,046 | 368 | — | 721 |
| Trust Pacific Islands | 3,875 | 4,391 | 695 | 6,324 | 2,595 |
| Kuwait | 3,180 | 1,150 | 2,239 | 7,049 | 8,309 |
| Saudi Arabia | — | 14,536 | 12,652 | 11,503 | — |
| Lebanon | — | 1,180 | 7,157 | 2,433 | 1,297 |
| Iran | — | — | 5,416 | 3,602 | — |
| New Guinea | — | — | 4,105 | — | — |
| Israel | — | — | — | 3,373 | 3,165 |
| Pakistan | 2,113 | — | 1,277 | 724 | — |
| Aden | — | — | 1,158 | 4,079 | — |
| Jordan | — | — | — | — | 2,600 |
| **TOTAL ASIA & OCEANIA** | 621,326 | 540,282 | 521,835 | 1,364,401 | 970,572 |
| **OTHERS** | 3,682 | 994 | 12,564 | 15,398 | 4,377 |
| **TOTAL** | 782,361 | 969,498 | 1,082,276 | 1,919,557 | 1,541,172 |

Source: United States Department of Commerce.

**SOLUBLE COFFEE EXPORTS, 1965**

Dollars)

| June | July | August | September | October | November | December | Total |
|---|---|---|---|---|---|---|---|
| 477,839 | 195,718 | 143,806 | 315,127 | 396,163 | 319,473 | 160,451 | 3,099,524 |
| | | | | | | | |
| 12,195 | 24,788 | 27,252 | 10,777 | 40,658 | 18,342 | 6,541 | 284,955 |
| 17,957 | 2,763 | 11,019 | 8,498 | 7,539 | 5,593 | 6,196 | 132,742 |
| 3,749 | 19,583 | 3,268 | 5,835 | 4,454 | 9,390 | 5,811 | 113,907 |
| 9,100 | 9,100 | — | 9,268 | — | 13,000 | — | 40,468 |
| 3,785 | 1,156 | 4,603 | 1,484 | 4,820 | 4,904 | 3,018 | 52,273 |
| 7,000 | 1,063 | 5,400 | — | 4,026 | 5,900 | — | 35,961 |
| 3,403 | 2,486 | 2,687 | 2,421 | 916 | 961 | 3,192 | 31,615 |
| 2,628 | 1,902 | 1,550 | — | 4,111 | 3,649 | 2,152 | 24,714 |
| 622 | 1,390 | 1,756 | 4,424 | 1,244 | 2,324 | 622 | 19,956 |
| 1,133 | 1,370 | 632 | 1,758 | 440 | — | 2,360 | 16,643 |
| 3,033 | 254 | — | 2,918 | — | 2,108 | 5,369 | 17,780 |
| — | — | — | — | — | 9,699 | 5,228 | 14,927 |
| — | — | 1,887 | 3,743 | 3,327 | 206 | 3,289 | 16,738 |
| 64,605 | 65,855 | 60,054 | 51,126 | 71,535 | 76,076 | 43,778 | 802,679 |
| | | | | | | | |
| 15,642 | 107,006 | 89,401 | 180,984 | 142,945 | 70,268 | 297,140 | 1,115,145 |
| 582 | 16,895 | 32,843 | 57,429 | — | 16,441 | 216 | 273,389 |
| 26,801 | 48,431 | 18,064 | 38,507 | 19,855 | 4,202 | 89,895 | 424,544 |
| 11,546 | 28,260 | 21,986 | 35,285 | 59,905 | 20,108 | 1,465 | 255,303 |
| 850 | 1,556 | 45,765 | 47,633 | — | 1,353 | 25,686 | 153,166 |
| 2,358 | 36,122 | 29,473 | 1,072 | — | 1,735 | 1,175 | 146,241 |
| — | — | 2,289 | 67,148 | — | — | — | 69,437 |
| 1,314 | — | 12,122 | 2,444 | 4,620 | 1,505 | 37,618 | 78,937 |
| 1,711 | 2,237 | 308 | 847 | 1,839 | 2,144 | 7,933 | 27,789 |
| 8,589 | — | — | — | — | — | — | 9,178 |
| 69,393 | 240,507 | 252,251 | 431,349 | 229,164 | 117,756 | 461,128 | 2,553,129 |
| | | | | | | | |
| 8,365 | 5,807 | 11,375 | 8,490 | 3,698 | 6,846 | 2,098 | 55,462 |
| 18,181 | 4,203 | 2,751 | 3,247 | 3,176 | 2,352 | 568 | 43,121 |
| 598 | — | — | 4,578 | 1,831 | — | — | 16,836 |
| 27,144 | 10,010 | 14,126 | 16,315 | 8,705 | 9,198 | 2,666 | 115,419 |
| | | | | | | | |
| 1,549,623 | 2,871,454 | 2,265,252 | 1,032,704 | 1,804,627 | 1,471,801 | 1,086,942 | 15,119,832 |
| 101,787 | 22,205 | 10,055 | 29,075 | 10,088 | 9,977 | 19,712 | 504,282 |
| 18,047 | 13,411 | 16,806 | 37,211 | 4,294 | 41,854 | 37,389 | 227,216 |
| 2,291 | 10,854 | 6,629 | 6,109 | 5,698 | 6,286 | 23,383 | 217,469 |
| 12,405 | 4,517 | 6,938 | 3,267 | 4,644 | 12,445 | 8,022 | 193,463 |
| — | — | — | 10,516 | 2,511 | — | 10,420 | 146,497 |
| 9,789 | 3,491 | 10,491 | 7,311 | 3,643 | 5,247 | 4,174 | 100,313 |
| — | — | — | 18,562 | 2,325 | — | 10,810 | 42,097 |
| — | 26,670 | 4,733 | — | — | 1,664 | 1,282 | 46,511 |
| 3,478 | 510 | 5,408 | 1,038 | 6,110 | — | 8,072 | 42,496 |
| 3,007 | 2,050 | 10,323 | 2,142 | 2,051 | — | — | 41,500 |
| 320 | 4,020 | — | 646 | 1,113 | — | 1,509 | 46,299 |
| 1,813 | 1,290 | 589 | 5,190 | 2,980 | 6,451 | 5,686 | 36,066 |
| 1,902 | — | 1,263 | 590 | — | 3,792 | 2,144 | 18,709 |
| — | — | — | — | 5,214 | 3,057 | 380 | 12,756 |
| 3,072 | — | — | 2,558 | — | — | 590 | 12,758 |
| — | — | — | — | — | — | — | 4,114 |
| — | — | — | — | — | — | — | 5,237 |
| 5,982 | — | — | — | — | — | — | 8,582 |
| 1,713,516 | 2,960,472 | 2,338,487 | 1,156,919 | 1,855,298 | 1,562,574 | 1,220,515 | 16,826,197 |
| | | | | | | | |
| 12,206 | 14,515 | 4,860 | 14,503 | 11,955 | 5,464 | 14,828 | 115,346 |
| | | | | | | | |
| 2,364,703 | 3,487,077 | 2,813,584 | 1,985,339 | 2,572,820 | 2,090,541 | 1,903,366 | 23,512,294 |

## IS-1. UNITED STATES: IMPORTS OF SOLUBLE COFFEE, 1956-1966

(60 kilo bags of Green-Coffee Equivalent)*

| COUNTRIES OF ORIGIN | 1956 | 1957 | 1958 | 1959 | 1960 | 1961 | 1962 | 1963 | 1964 | 1965 | 1966 |
|---|---|---|---|---|---|---|---|---|---|---|---|
| **Pan American Coffee Bureau** | | | | | | | | | | | |
| Brazil | — | 27 | — | — | — | — | — | — | — | — | 135,996 |
| Guatemala | — | — | 7,698 | 32,595 | 55,711 | 13,678 | 3,297 | 7,385 | 749 | 6,251 | 31,859 |
| Nicaragua | — | — | — | — | — | 36,033 | 52,457 | 54,898 | 14,778 | 8,381 | 19,587 |
| El Salvador | 37,423 | 64,386 | 54,293 | 57,416 | 56,120 | 40,646 | 863 | 2,028 | 36,012 | 42,149 | 17,444 |
| Mexico | — | 24,790 | 36,872 | 35,431 | 13,956 | 2,609 | 29,370 | 34,301 | 3,274 | 6,832 | 22,937 |
| Costa Rica | — | 375 | — | — | — | — | — | — | 44,813 | 183 | — |
| Colombia | — | 30 | — | — | 15 | 43 | 21 | 3 | 27 | — | — |
| Venezuela | — | — | — | — | — | 4 | — | — | — | — | — |
| Ecuador | — | — | — | — | — | — | 11 | 122 | 28 | 23 | — |
| Total Pan American Coffee Bureau | 37,423 | 89,608 | 98,863 | 125,442 | 125,802 | 93,013 | 86,019 | 98,737 | 99,681 | 63,819 | 227,823 |
| **OTHER WESTERN HEMISPHERE** | | | | | | | | | | | |
| Jamaica | — | — | — | — | — | — | — | 5 | 1 | — | 68 |
| Canada | 54 | 395 | 54 | — | — | — | 4,909 | 41,633 | 20,154 | 464 | 66 |
| Bahamas | 374 | — | — | — | — | — | — | — | — | — | — |
| Total Other Western Hemisphere | 428 | 395 | 54 | — | — | — | 4,909 | 41,638 | 20,155 | 464 | 134 |
| **TOTAL WESTERN HEMISPHERE** | 37,851 | 90,003 | 98,917 | 125,442 | 125,802 | 93,013 | 90,928 | 140,375 | 119,836 | 64,283 | 227,957 |
| **OTHERS** | | | | | | | | | | | |
| France | — | — | — | — | — | — | — | 64 | — | 7 | 7,270 |
| Switzerland | 17 | 15 | 34 | 112 | 65 | 94 | 122 | 118 | 49 | 6 | 3,000 |
| United Kingdom | — | — | — | 23 | 7 | 85 | 118 | 1 | 19 | 13 | 141 |
| Netherlands | — | — | — | 18 | 30 | 6 | — | 56 | 4 | 5 | 5 |
| Germany (F.R.) | — | — | 3 | — | 6 | 12 | — | 10 | 30 | 29 | 17 |
| Spain | — | — | — | — | — | 1 | — | — | — | — | — |
| Belgium | — | — | — | — | — | — | 2 | 1301 | — | — | — |
| Italy | — | — | — | — | — | — | 1 | 3 | — | — | — |
| Poland | — | — | — | — | — | — | — | — | 5 | 31 | — |
| South Viet Nam | — | — | — | — | — | — | — | — | — | — | 932 |
| Australia | — | — | — | — | — | — | — | — | — | — | 7 |
| Hong Kong | — | — | — | — | — | — | — | — | — | — | 6 |
| Philippine Republic | — | 42 | — | 44 | — | — | 7 | 17 | 27 | 10 | — |
| Israel | — | — | — | — | 11 | 13 | 12 | — | — | — | — |
| TOTAL OTHERS | 17 | 57 | 37 | 197 | 119 | 211 | 262 | 1,570 | 134 | 101 | 11,378 |
| **TOTAL VOLUME** | 37,868 | 90,060 | 98,954 | 125,639 | 125,921 | 93,224 | 91,190 | 141,945 | 119,970 | 64,384 | 239,335 |

Source: U. S. Department of Commerce.

*Conversion rate = 33.3 percent; the standard factor in international trade adopted by the ICO.

A-166

## ISV-1. UNITED STATES: VALUE OF SOLUBLE COFFEE IMPORTS, 1956-1966
(U. S. Dollars)

| COUNTRIES OF ORIGIN | 1956 | 1957 | 1958 | 1959 | 1960 | 1961 | 1962 | 1963 | 1964 | 1965 | 1966 |
|---|---|---|---|---|---|---|---|---|---|---|---|
| **WESTERN HEMISPHERE** | | | | | | | | | | | |
| **Pan American Coffee Bureau** | | | | | | | | | | | |
| Brazil | — | — | — | — | — | — | — | — | 13,893 | 299,878 | 6,471,142 |
| Guatemala | — | 2,957 | 626,657 | 2,463,231 | 3,404,811 | 838,586 | 205,171 | 350,575 | 762,949 | 406,656 | 1,231,245 |
| Nicaragua | — | — | — | — | — | 1,834,293 | 3,136,660 | 3,246,457 | 2,706,175 | 2,359,961 | 1,134,808 |
| El Salvador | 4,024,257 | 6,627,725 | 5,661,590 | 4,792,562 | 4,096,715 | 2,566,464 | 51,311 | 109,006 | 172,991 | 314,780 | 749,541 |
| Mexico | — | 2,505,577 | 3,117,816 | 1,627,055 | 634,856 | 123,278 | 1,137,737 | 1,677,640 | 2,422,046 | 7,269 | 723,820 |
| Costa Rica | — | 39,904 | — | — | — | — | — | 336 | 148 | — | — |
| Colombia | — | 3,129 | — | — | 744 | 2,232 | 1,302 | — | — | — | — |
| Venezuela | — | — | — | — | — | 438 | — | — | — | 1,975 | — |
| Ecuador | — | — | — | — | — | — | 912 | 7,205 | 2,470 | — | — |
| Total Pan American Coffee Bureau | 4,024,257 | 9,179,292 | 9,406,063 | 8,882,848 | 8,137,126 | 5,365,291 | 4,533,093 | 5,391,219 | 6,080,672 | 3,390,519 | 10,310,556 |
| **OTHER WESTERN HEMISPHERE** | | | | | | | | | | | |
| Jamaica | — | — | — | — | — | — | — | 832 | 235 | — | 4,503 |
| Canada | 2,463 | 41,704 | 4,200 | — | — | — | 217,146 | 1,897,375 | 1,112,182 | 16,310 | 4,285 |
| Bahamas | 37,980 | — | — | — | — | — | — | — | — | — | 8,788 |
| Total Other Western Hemisphere | 40,443 | 41,704 | 4,200 | — | — | — | 217,146 | 1,898,207 | 1,112,417 | 16,310 | 8,788 |
| **TOTAL WESTERN HEMISPHERE** | 4,064,700 | 9,220,996 | 9,410,263 | 8,882,848 | 8,137,126 | 5,365,291 | 4,750,239 | 7,289,426 | 7,193,089 | 3,406,829 | 10,319,344 |
| **OTHERS** | | | | | | | | | | | |
| France | — | — | — | 10,447 | 6,285 | 8,367 | 12,917 | 6,883 | — | 1,365 | 507,503 |
| Switzerland | 1,219 | 959 | 2,308 | 1,872 | 996 | 5,751 | 8,740 | 8,821 | 3,656 | 407 | 66,850 |
| United Kingdom | — | — | — | — | — | 240 | — | 150 | 389 | 698 | 7,373 |
| Netherlands | — | — | — | 1,665 | 1,865 | 908 | — | 4,728 | 432 | 550 | 613 |
| Germany (F.R.) | — | — | 277 | — | 424 | — | 527 | 550 | 3,149 | 2,930 | 2,365 |
| Spain | — | — | — | — | — | 120 | — | — | — | — | — |
| Belgium | — | — | — | — | — | — | 155 | 58,756 | — | — | — |
| Italy | — | — | — | — | — | — | — | 165 | — | 1,260 | — |
| Poland | — | — | — | — | — | — | — | — | 455 | — | — |
| South Viet Nam | — | — | — | — | — | — | — | — | — | — | 44,374 |
| Australia | — | — | — | — | — | — | — | — | — | — | 504 |
| Hong Kong | — | — | — | — | — | — | — | — | — | — | 900 |
| Philippine Republic | — | 3,177 | — | 2,845 | — | 967 | 600 | 1,500 | 2,160 | 602 | — |
| Israel | 1,219 | 4,136 | 2,585 | 16,829 | 10,312 | 16,353 | 1,044 23,983 | 81,553 | 10,241 | 7,812 | 630,482 |
| Total Others | 1,219 | 4,136 | 2,585 | 16,829 | 10,312 | 16,353 | 23,983 | 81,553 | 10,241 | 7,812 | 630,482 |
| **TOTAL** | 4,065,919 | 9,225,132 | 9,412,848 | 8,899,677 | 8,147,438 | 5,381,644 | 4,774,222 | 7,370,979 | 7,203,330 | 3,414,641 | 10,949,826 |

Source: U. S. Department of Commerce.

## IS-5. UNITED STATES: IMPORTS OF SOLUBLE COFFEE, 1966
(Soluble Pounds)

| COUNTRIES OF ORIGIN | Jan. | Feb. | March | April | May | June | July | Aug. | Sept. | Oct. | Nov. | Dec. | Total |
|---|---|---|---|---|---|---|---|---|---|---|---|---|---|
| **Pan American Coffee Bureau** | | | | | | | | | | | | | |
| Brazil | 253,590 | 201,030 | 335,651 | 148,926 | 113,438 | 437,219 | 449,222 | 382,748 | 785,336 | 777,290 | 1,453,195 | 658,704 | 5,996,349 |
| Guatemala | 39,880 | 19,738 | 43,000 | 111,000 | 107,880 | 255,840 | 140,000 | 274,240 | 120,000 | 183,080 | — | 110,080 | 1,404,738 |
| Nicaragua | 90,960 | 213,600 | — | 185,999 | 59,520 | — | 120,960 | — | 66,358 | — | 65,880 | 60,360 | 863,637 |
| El Salvador | 3,876 | 55,000 | 50,462 | 33,733 | 45,397 | 9,000 | 143,479 | 143,562 | 174,672 | 38,500 | 42,463 | 29,000 | 769,143 |
| Mexico | 24,000 | — | — | 10,512 | — | — | 19,015 | 165,928 | 207,409 | 86,703 | — | 497,782 | 1,011,349 |
| Total Pan American Coffee Bureau | 412,306 | 489,368 | 429,113 | 490,170 | 326,235 | 702,059 | 872,675 | 966,478 | 1,353,775 | 1,085,573 | 1,561,538 | 1,355,926 | 10,045,216 |
| **OTHER WESTERN HEMISPHERE** | | | | | | | | | | | | | |
| Jamaica | — | — | — | — | — | — | — | — | 1,950 | — | — | 600 | 2,992 |
| Canada | 520 | 442 | — | 550 | 175 | — | — | 100 | — | — | 195 | 1,354 | 2,894 |
| Total Other Western Hemisphere | 520 | 442 | — | 550 | 175 | — | — | 100 | 1,950 | — | 195 | 1,954 | 5,886 |
| TOTAL WESTERN HEMISPHERE | 412,826 | 489,810 | 429,113 | 490,720 | 326,410 | 702,059 | 872,675 | 966,578 | 1,355,725 | 1,085,573 | 1,561,733 | 1,357,880 | 10,051,102 |
| **OTHERS** | | | | | | | | | | | | | |
| France | — | — | — | — | — | — | 1,329 | — | — | 67,555 | 245,660 | 6,000 | 320,544 |
| Switzerland | — | — | 516 | 85 | — | — | — | — | — | 131,676 | — | — | 132,277 |
| United Kingdom | — | — | — | 5,040 | — | — | — | — | — | — | 1,200 | — | 6,240 |
| Netherlands | — | — | — | — | — | — | — | — | — | — | 205 | — | 205 |
| Germany (F.R.) | — | — | — | — | — | — | — | — | — | — | 119 | 635 | 754 |
| South Viet Nam | — | — | — | — | — | — | — | — | — | 41,087 | — | — | 41,087 |
| Australia | — | — | — | 300 | — | — | — | — | — | — | — | — | 300 |
| Hong Kong | — | — | — | — | — | — | — | — | 279 | — | — | — | 279 |
| TOTAL OTHERS | — | — | 516 | 5,425 | — | — | 1,329 | — | 279 | 240,318 | 247,184 | 6,635 | 501,686 |
| TOTAL SOLUBLE POUNDS | 412,826 | 489,810 | 429,629 | 496,145 | 326,410 | 702,059 | 874,004 | 966,578 | 1,356,004 | 1,325,891 | 1,808,917 | 1,364,515 | 10,552,788 |

Source: U. S. Department of Commerce

## ISV-5. UNITED STATES: VALUE OF SOLUBLE COFFEE IMPORTS, 1966

(U. S. Dollars)

| COUNTRIES OF ORIGIN | Jan. | Feb. | March | April | May | June | July | Aug. | Sept. | Oct. | Nov. | Dec. | Total |
|---|---|---|---|---|---|---|---|---|---|---|---|---|---|
| **Pan American Coffee Bureau** | | | | | | | | | | | | | |
| Brazil | 274,934 | 217,943 | 363,982 | 151,840 | 122,513 | 472,198 | 485,875 | 413,367 | 848,164 | 839,473 | 1,569,452 | 711,401 | 6,471,142 |
| Guatemala | 44,354 | 19,764 | 42,058 | 95,970 | 93,269 | 222,414 | 121,200 | 233,962 | 100,800 | 155,376 | — | 102,078 | 1,231,245 |
| Nicaragua | 106,423 | 260,592 | — | 226,920 | 86,304 | — | 175,392 | — | 95,373 | — | 96,282 | 87,522 | 1,134,808 |
| El Salvador | 4,513 | 51,790 | 51,639 | 33,822 | 46,112 | 8,550 | 132,576 | 136,931 | 174,840 | 39,286 | 42,454 | 27,028 | 749,541 |
| Mexico | 29,447 | — | — | 10,767 | — | — | 6,245 | 60,907 | 76,528 | 31,397 | — | 508,529 | 723,820 |
| Total Pan American Coffee Bureau | 459,671 | 550,089 | 457,679 | 519,319 | 348,198 | 703,162 | 921,288 | 845,167 | 1,295,705 | 1,065,532 | 1,708,188 | 1,436,558 | 10,310,556 |
| **OTHER WESTERN HEMISPHERE** | | | | | | | | | | | | | |
| Jamaica | — | 1,663 | — | — | 348 | — | — | — | 2,193 | — | — | 647 | 4,503 |
| Canada | 680 | — | — | 1,100 | — | — | — | 500 | — | — | 786 | 871 | 4,285 |
| Total Other Western Hemisphere | 680 | 1,663 | — | 1,100 | 348 | — | — | 500 | 2,193 | — | 786 | 1,518 | 8,788 |
| **TOTAL WESTERN HEMISPHERE** | 460,351 | 551,752 | 457,679 | 520,419 | 348,546 | 703,162 | 921,288 | 845,667 | 1,297,898 | 1,065,532 | 1,708,974 | 1,438,076 | 10,319,344 |
| **OTHERS** | | | | | | | | | | | | | |
| France | — | — | — | — | — | — | 2,507 | — | — | 108,893 | 379,303 | 16,800 | 507,503 |
| Switzerland | — | — | 574 | 394 | — | — | — | — | — | 65,882 | — | — | 66,850 |
| United Kingdom | — | — | — | 2,520 | — | — | — | — | — | — | 4,853 | — | 7,373 |
| Netherlands | — | — | — | — | — | — | — | — | — | — | 613 | — | 613 |
| Germany (F.R.) | — | — | — | — | — | — | — | — | — | — | 311 | 2,054 | 2,365 |
| South Viet Nam | — | — | — | 504 | — | — | — | — | — | 44,374 | — | — | 44,374 |
| Australia | — | — | — | — | — | — | — | — | — | — | — | — | 504 |
| Hong Kong | — | — | — | — | — | — | — | — | 900 | — | — | — | 900 |
| TOTAL OTHERS | — | — | 574 | 3,418 | — | — | 2,507 | — | 900 | 219,149 | 385,080 | 18,854 | 630,482 |
| TOTAL VALUE | 460,351 | 551,752 | 458,253 | 523,837 | 348,546 | 703,162 | 923,795 | 845,667 | 1,298,798 | 1,284,681 | 2,094,054 | 1,456,930 | 10,949,826 |

Source: U. S. Department of Commerce

## IS-7. UNITED STATES: IMPORTS OF SOLUBLE COFFEE, 1965

(Soluble pounds)

| COUNTRIES OF ORIGIN | Jan. | Feb. | March | April | May | June | July | Aug. | Sept. | Oct. | Nov. | Dec. | Total |
|---|---|---|---|---|---|---|---|---|---|---|---|---|---|
| **Pan American Coffee Bureau** | | | | | | | | | | | | | |
| Nicaragua | 114,000 | 114,000 | 5,040 | 100,800 | 136,800 | 363,240 | 119,040 | 300,000 | 92,400 | 160,560 | 119,520 | 233,040 | 1,858,440 |
| Guatemala | 134,560 | 13,760 | 13,500 | 37,440 | 14,800 | 11,040 | 6,000 | 11,400 | 19,000 | 61,670 | 25,000 | 21,370 | 369,540 |
| El Salvador | 450 | 5,175 | 53,500 | 64,990 | 62,713 | 23,260 | 24,368 | 12,867 | 15,170 | 1,572 | 19,191 | 17,985 | 301,241 |
| Brazil | — | — | — | — | — | — | — | — | — | 49,975 | 49,475 | 176,191 | 275,641 |
| Mexico | — | — | — | — | 4,850 | — | — | — | 3,197 | — | — | — | 8,047 |
| Ecuador | — | — | — | — | — | — | — | — | 1,000 | — | — | — | 1,000 |
| Total Pan American Coffee Bureau | 249,010 | 132,935 | 72,040 | 203,230 | 219,163 | 397,540 | 149,408 | 324,267 | 130,767 | 273,777 | 213,186 | 448,586 | 2,813,909 |
| **OTHER WESTERN HEMISPHERE** | | | | | | | | | | | | | |
| Canada | — | — | — | — | — | — | 200 | — | 530 | — | 19,215 | 520 | 20,465 |
| TOTAL WESTERN HEMISPHERE | 249,010 | 132,935 | 72,040 | 203,230 | 219,163 | 397,540 | 149,608 | 324,267 | 131,297 | 273,777 | 232,401 | 449,106 | 2,834,374 |
| **OTHERS** | | | | | | | | | | | | | |
| Italy | — | — | — | — | — | — | — | 1,350 | — | — | — | — | 1,350 |
| Germany (F.R.) | — | — | — | — | — | 265 | — | 529 | 317 | 179 | — | — | 1,290 |
| United Kingdom | — | — | 560 | — | — | — | — | — | — | — | — | — | 560 |
| France | — | — | — | — | — | — | — | — | 300 | — | — | — | 300 |
| Switzerland | — | — | — | — | — | — | 269 | — | — | — | — | — | 269 |
| Netherlands | — | — | — | — | — | 72 | — | — | — | 163 | — | — | 235 |
| Israel | — | — | — | — | — | — | — | 275 | — | — | — | 150 | 425 |
| TOTAL OTHERS | — | — | 560 | — | — | 337 | 269 | 2,154 | 617 | 342 | — | 150 | 4,429 |
| TOTAL | 249,010 | 132,935 | 72,600 | 203,230 | 219,163 | 397,877 | 149,877 | 326,421 | 131,914 | 274,119 | 232,401 | 449,256 | 2,838,803 |

Source: United States Department of Commerce.

ISV-7. UNITED STATES: VALUE OF SOLUBLE COFFEE IMPORTS, 1965

(U. S. Dollars)

| COUNTRIES OF ORIGIN | Jan. | Feb. | March | April | May | June | July | Aug. | Sept. | Oct. | Nov. | Dec. | Total |
|---|---|---|---|---|---|---|---|---|---|---|---|---|---|
| **Pan American Coffee Bureau** | | | | | | | | | | | | | |
| Nicaragua | 202,603 | 164,969 | 8,064 | 133,920 | 191,520 | 435,888 | 143,007 | 369,365 | 108,108 | 187,855 | 139,838 | 274,824 | 2,359,961 |
| Guatemala | 148,789 | 18,940 | 14,310 | 46,485 | 18,644 | 12,091 | 6,600 | 12,560 | 14,400 | 65,913 | 25,500 | 22,424 | 406,656 |
| El Salvador | 830 | 7,972 | 52,435 | 62,272 | 58,252 | 28,205 | 28,027 | 14,199 | 16,838 | 3,395 | 20,715 | 21,640 | 314,780 |
| Brazil | — | — | — | — | — | — | — | — | 54,168 | 53,615 | 192,095 | 299,878 |
| Mexico | — | — | — | — | 4,951 | — | — | — | 2,318 | — | — | — | 7,269 |
| Ecuador | — | — | — | — | — | — | — | — | 1,975 | — | — | — | 1,975 |
| Total Pan American Coffee Bureau | 352,222 | 191,881 | 74,809 | 242,677 | 273,367 | 476,184 | 177,634 | 396,124 | 143,639 | 311,331 | 239,668 | 510,983 | 3,390,519 |
| **OTHER WESTERN HEMISPHERE** | | | | | | | | | | | | | |
| Canada | — | — | — | — | — | — | 276 | — | 798 | — | 14,556 | 680 | 16,310 |
| TOTAL WESTERN HEMISPHERE | 352,222 | 191,881 | 74,809 | 242,677 | 273,367 | 476,184 | 177,910 | 396,124 | 144,437 | 311,331 | 254,224 | 511,663 | 3,406,829 |
| **OTHERS** | | | | | | | | | | | | | |
| Italy | — | — | — | — | — | — | — | 1,260 | — | — | — | — | 1,260 |
| Germany (F.R.) | — | — | — | — | — | 628 | — | 1,247 | 753 | 302 | — | — | 2,930 |
| United Kingdom | — | — | 698 | — | — | — | — | — | — | — | — | — | 698 |
| France | — | — | — | — | — | — | — | — | 1,365 | — | — | — | 1,365 |
| Switzerland | — | — | — | — | — | — | 407 | — | — | — | — | — | 407 |
| Netherlands | — | — | — | — | — | 196 | — | — | — | 354 | — | — | 550 |
| Israel | — | — | — | — | — | — | — | 348 | — | — | — | 254 | 602 |
| TOTAL OTHERS | — | — | 698 | — | — | 824 | 407 | 2,855 | 2,118 | 656 | — | 254 | 7,812 |
| TOTAL | 352,222 | 191,881 | 75,507 | 242,677 | 273,367 | 477,008 | 178,317 | 398,979 | 146,555 | 311,987 | 254,224 | 511,917 | 3,414,641 |

Source: U. S. Department of Commerce.

ISV-10. UNITED STATES: AVERAGE IMPORT PRICE OF SOLUBLE COFFEE, 1956-1966

(U. S. Dollars per Pound)

| COUNTRIES OF ORIGIN | 1956 | 1957 | 1958 | 1959 | 1960 | 1961 | 1962 | 1963 | 1964 | 1965 | 1966 |
|---|---|---|---|---|---|---|---|---|---|---|---|
| **Pan American Coffee Bureau** | | | | | | | | | | | |
| Brazil | — | 2.94 | — | — | — | — | — | — | 0.42 | 1.09 | 1.08 |
| Guatemala | — | — | 2.22 | 2.06 | 1.66 | 1.67 | 1.41 | 1.08 | 1.17 | 1.10 | 0.88 |
| Nicaragua | — | — | — | — | — | 1.39 | 1.36 | 1.34 | 1.70 | 1.27 | 1.31 |
| El Salvador | 2.93 | 2.80 | 2.84 | 2.27 | 1.99 | 1.72 | 1.35 | 1.22 | 1.20 | 1.04 | 0.97 |
| Mexico | — | 2.75 | 2.30 | 1.25 | 1.24 | 1.29 | 0.88 | 1.11 | 1.23 | 0.90 | 0.72 |
| Costa Rica | — | 2.90 | — | — | — | — | — | — | — | — | — |
| Colombia | — | 2.84 | — | — | 1.41 | 1.41 | 1.41 | 2.24 | 0.12 | — | — |
| Venezuela | — | — | — | — | — | 3.04 | — | — | — | — | — |
| Ecuador | — | — | — | — | — | — | 1.88 | 1.34 | 2.03 | 1.98 | — |
| **OTHER WESTERN HEMISPHERE** | | | | | | | | | | | |
| Jamaica | 1.23 | — | — | — | — | — | — | 3.70 | 3.92 | — | 1.51 |
| Canada | 2.76 | 2.87 | 2.13 | — | — | — | 1.00 | 1.03 | 1.25 | 0.80 | 1.48 |
| Bahamas | — | — | — | — | — | — | — | — | — | — | — |
| **OTHERS** | | | | | | | | | | | |
| France | — | — | — | — | — | — | — | — | — | — | — |
| Switzerland | 1.97 | 1.76 | 1.87 | 2.54 | 2.62 | 2.43 | 2.39 | 2.45 | 1.68 | 4.55 | 1.58 |
| United Kingdom | — | — | — | 2.17 | 3.72 | 1.84 | 1.68 | 1.69 | 0.47 | 1.51 | 0.51 |
| Netherlands | — | — | — | — | — | 1.07 | — | 4.69 | 2.48 | 1.25 | 1.18 |
| Germany (F.R.) | — | — | 2.52 | 2.54 | 1.71 | 2.08 | — | 1.93 | 2.38 | 2.34 | 2.99 |
| Spain | — | — | — | — | 1.93 | 5.45 | 6.67 | 1.22 | — | 2.27 | 3.14 |
| Belgium | — | — | — | — | — | — | — | 1.02 | — | — | — |
| Italy | — | — | — | — | — | — | 7.38 | 1.43 | — | 0.93 | — |
| Poland | — | — | — | — | — | — | — | — | 2.09 | — | — |
| South Viet Nam | — | — | — | — | — | — | — | — | — | — | 1.08 |
| Australia | — | — | — | — | — | — | — | — | — | — | 1.68 |
| Hong Kong | — | 2.04 | — | — | — | — | — | — | — | — | 3.23 |
| Philippine Republic | — | — | — | 1.78 | — | — | 2.00 | 2.00 | 1.80 | 1.42 | — |
| Israel | — | — | — | — | 1.84 | 2.04 | 1.99 | — | — | — | — |
| **TOTAL** | 2.92 | 2.79 | 2.59 | 1.93 | 1.76 | 1.57 | 1.19 | 1.18 | 1.36 | 1.20 | 1.04 |

Source: U. S. Department of Commerce.

A-172

ESV-10. UNITED STATES: AVERAGE EXPORT PRICE OF SOLUBLE COFFEE 1956-1966

(U. S. Dollars Per Pound)

| COUNTRIES OF DESTINATION | 1956 | 1957 | 1958 | 1959 | 1960 | 1961 | 1962 | 1963 | 1964 | 1965 | 1966 |
|---|---|---|---|---|---|---|---|---|---|---|---|
| CANADA | 2.72 | 2.48 | 2.12 | 1.77 | 1.54 | 1.49 | 1.30 | 1.36 | 1.70 | 1.62 | 1.49 |
| **OTHER WESTERN HEMISPHERE** | | | | | | | | | | | |
| Bahamas | 3.90 | 2.96 | 2.70 | 2.31 | 1.89 | 2.03 | 2.12 | 2.03 | 2.42 | 2.31 | 2.12 |
| Netherlands West Indies | 3.47 | 3.10 | 3.09 | 3.16 | 2.68 | 2.46 | 2.31 | 2.46 | 2.77 | 2.71 | 2.59 |
| Mexico | 2.73 | 1.35 | 1.99 | 1.27 | 1.56 | 2.19 | — | 3.30 | 2.10 | 2.19 | 1.39 |
| Bermuda | 2.78 | 2.79 | 2.94 | 2.71 | 2.32 | 2.51 | 2.49 | 2.25 | 2.71 | 2.51 | 2.40 |
| Trinidad & Tobago | — | 1.52 | 3.15 | 2.34 | 2.66 | 2.63 | 2.44 | 2.40 | 2.65 | 2.13 | 2.09 |
| Barbados | — | — | 3.11 | 2.49 | 2.36 | 2.38 | 2.36 | 2.07 | 2.25 | 2.40 | 2.16 |
| Guyana | — | — | — | — | 2.34 | 2.16 | — | 1.04 | 1.45 | 1.35 | 1.47 |
| Leeward, Windward Islands | — | 1.72 | — | 1.89 | 2.13 | 2.55 | 2.19 | 1.83 | 2.62 | 2.38 | 2.35 |
| Surinam | — | — | 1.51 | — | 1.92 | 1.75 | 1.48 | 1.40 | 1.99 | 2.04 | 1.34 |
| Jamaica | — | — | 1.37 | 1.75 | 2.00 | 1.87 | 1.66 | 2.45 | 2.01 | 2.02 | 1.56 |
| British Honduras | — | — | — | 3.43 | 2.53 | 2.70 | 2.47 | 1.88 | 2.54 | 2.43 | 3.41 |
| Peru | 4.21 | 2.26 | 4.96 | 4.86 | 3.32 | 3.18 | 1.69 | 2.91 | 3.45 | 3.50 | 2.93 |
| Dominican Republic | 3.60 | 2.98 | 3.74 | 4.10 | 2.35 | 2.53 | 2.16 | 2.58 | 2.55 | 2.13 | 1.76 |
| **EUROPE** | | | | | | | | | | | |
| United Kingdom | 2.28 | — | 1.20 | 1.66 | 1.14 | 1.17 | 1.12 | 1.11 | 1.12 | 1.21 | 1.12 |
| Finland | — | — | — | 2.61 | 2.59 | 2.47 | 2.21 | 2.18 | 2.52 | 2.69 | 2.57 |
| Netherlands | 2.26 | 2.10 | 1.84 | 1.53 | 1.48 | 1.47 | 1.83 | 1.44 | 1.63 | 1.72 | 1.59 |
| Sweden | 3.38 | 2.80 | 2.83 | 2.50 | 2.15 | 2.14 | 1.65 | 1.53 | 1.51 | 1.58 | 1.58 |
| Norway | 4.07 | — | — | 2.59 | 2.29 | 2.71 | 1.97 | 2.29 | 1.87 | 1.80 | |
| Denmark | 1.05 | 3.70 | 3.37 | 2.68 | 2.53 | 2.42 | 2.29 | 2.32 | 2.58 | 2.01 | 2.05 |
| Germany (F.R.) | 2.83 | 2.49 | 2.29 | — | 1.50 | 1.45 | 1.18 | 1.15 | 1.48 | 1.72 | 1.39 |
| Belgium | 3.30 | 2.52 | 3.62 | 2.68 | 1.24 | 1.46 | 1.21 | 1.38 | 1.30 | 1.54 | 1.29 |
| Italy | 4.02 | — | — | 2.60 | 3.45 | 1.76 | 2.15 | 2.70 | — | — | 1.08 |
| Greece | 3.81 | 3.55 | 2.72 | 2.75 | 2.78 | 2.74 | — | 1.32 | — | — | 1.21 |
| **AFRICA** | | | | | | | | | | | |
| Liberia | 3.56 | 3.56 | 2.74 | 2.70 | 1.95 | 2.08 | 2.42 | 1.99 | 2.45 | 2.54 | 2.43 |
| Libya | — | 0.77 | 2.23 | 2.34 | 2.68 | 2.53 | 2.46 | 2.40 | 2.64 | 2.41 | 2.26 |
| Nigeria | — | — | — | — | 2.66 | 2.70 | 2.48 | — | 2.78 | 2.66 | 2.44 |
| United Arab Republic | — | 3.73 | 3.08 | 2.83 | 1.80 | 2.59 | 2.48 | 2.20 | 3.08 | — | 2.24 |
| **ASIA & OCEANIA** | | | | | | | | | | | |
| Japan | 3.69 | 3.63 | 3.03 | 2.94 | 2.64 | 2.23 | 2.25 | 2.08 | 2.14 | 2.10 | 2.05 |
| Australia | — | 1.76 | — | 2.51 | 1.66 | 1.60 | 1.59 | 1.33 | 1.72 | 1.55 | 1.68 |
| Nampo Islands | 3.85 | 3.58 | 3.31 | 2.92 | 2.84 | 2.73 | 2.52 | 2.38 | 2.41 | 1.99 | 2.02 |
| Thailand | 3.12 | 1.76 | 2.19 | 2.63 | 2.47 | 2.31 | 2.19 | 2.29 | 2.48 | 2.02 | 1.80 |
| Singapore | — | — | 2.06 | 1.71 | 1.73 | 2.19 | 2.18 | 2.51 | — | — | 1.75 |
| Hong Kong | 3.61 | 2.96 | 2.52 | 2.12 | 2.02 | 2.12 | 2.46 | 2.65 | 2.73 | 2.32 | 2.07 |
| Lebanon | 3.79 | 2.72 | 3.22 | 1.64 | 1.48 | 2.40 | 2.31 | 1.86 | 2.15 | 2.35 | 1.76 |
| Taiwan | — | 2.31 | — | — | — | 2.97 | — | — | 1.90 | — | 2.26 |
| Syria | 3.80 | 3.52 | 3.10 | 2.16 | 2.21 | 2.18 | 1.92 | 1.76 | 1.93 | 1.73 | 2.00 |
| Saudi Arabia | — | 3.73 | 3.86 | 2.20 | 2.23 | 2.74 | 2.51 | 2.17 | 2.79 | 2.81 | 1.65 |
| South Korea | — | — | — | 1.73 | — | — | 1.96 | 1.71 | 2.39 | 2.05 | 1.70 |
| Trust Pacific Islands | — | 3.17 | 2.53 | 1.45 | 1.29 | 2.36 | 2.35 | 1.85 | 2.20 | 1.99 | 1.54 |
| Malaysia | 3.76 | 1.63 | — | — | 2.23 | 2.46 | 2.09 | 2.49 | 2.30 | 2.11 | 2.44 |
| Jordan | 3.89 | — | 3.06 | 2.85 | 2.54 | 2.64 | 2.40 | 1.84 | 2.60 | 2.31 | 2.44 |
| Kuwait | — | 1.03 | — | 2.27 | 2.58 | 2.49 | 1.99 | 1.83 | 2.46 | 2.08 | 1.71 |
| Pakistan | 3.73 | 1.65 | 1.72 | 1.19 | 1.50 | 2.56 | 1.86 | 1.67 | 2.19 | 1.95 | 1.88 |
| New Guinea | — | — | — | 2.74 | 2.53 | 2.87 | 2.47 | 1.99 | 2.34 | 2.12 | 2.15 |
| India | — | 2.32 | 1.80 | 2.74 | 2.64 | 2.42 | 2.43 | 2.11 | 2.85 | — | 1.69 |
| Iran | 3.24 | 2.74 | 3.20 | 2.80 | 1.75 | 1.72 | 2.27 | 1.94 | 1.92 | 2.49 | 2.02 |
| Philippine Republic | 3.31 | 3.36 | 1.14 | 4.00 | 3.13 | 2.87 | 2.66 | 2.47 | 1.75 | 3.01 | — |
| OTHERS | 2.91 | 2.75 | 2.67 | 2.21 | 1.88 | 2.30 | 2.20 | 1.28 | 2.21 | 1.63 | 1.83 |
| TOTAL EXPORTS | 2.79 | 2.55 | 2.20 | 1.83 | 1.66 | 1.82 | 1.79 | 1.67 | 1.85 | 1.94 | 1.64 |

## M-1. WORLD: CUSTOM DUTIES AND INTERNAL TAXES ON COFFEE IN SELECTED COUNTRIES
### (EQUIVALENTS IN U.S. CENTS PER POUND), 1966

| | GREEN | ROASTED | SOLUBLE | INTERNAL TAXES |
|---|---|---|---|---|
| **WESTERN EUROPE** | | | | |
| **EEC** | | | | |
| Belgium | 2%l | 7.5%l/9%ln | 23% | 12% |
| Luxembourg | 2%l + 3% | [7.5%l/9%ln] + 3% | [22.4%/6%p] + 3% | 6.75% |
| France | 0.6%l/21%l/n | 37%/40%n/19.25p | 26.4/6%p | 28.1/5.13 |
| Germany (F.R.) | (12%yy free + 4%)nn essentially 1965 | [2p(22.16yy + 4%)] 1965 | 7% p 3%/24%/7% + 6% | (41/41)nn + nnn |
| Italy | [2p (12.6% + 13.7)yy] nnn (exempt/0.01%)nn (0.03/0.15) | nn + nnn (0.03/0.04)nn (0.04/0.06%)nnn | 32.4aa + 13.5aaa | (55/55)nn + nnn 158-1 42/57/n.a.q. $0.40 per pound green $0.52 per pound roasted |
| Netherlands | 5%lm | 15%/18%ln | 22.4% o/4.8%l | 14.4%/0.50% none |
| **OTHER WESTERN EUROPE** | | | | |
| Austria | free | 12.25 c | 24% d | 5.25% |
| Denmark | 12.3 x | 15.1 | 10% + 42.7 x | 9% |
| Finland | 17.7/25.4 e | 40.0 | 40.0 | 11% |
| Greece | 28.0 | 42.2 | 42.2 | none |
| Norway | free | 6.3 | 6.3 | 12.5% |
| Portugal | 4.4i | 15.7i | 15.7i | none |
| Spain | 1% | 36% | 40.5% | 8%/9%/12% w |
| Sweden | 1.7 | 2.2 | 10% | 10% |
| Switzerland | 5.7 | 10.5 | 31.5 k | none |
| Turkey | 50% | z | no imports | (15%/5%/0.20 + 2½%) xx |
| United Kingdom | 1.2/free/1.2 v | 1.6/1.2/1.6 v | 7.0/5.3/free v | none |
| Yugoslavia | 5%/free u | 20%/10% u | 73%/60% u | 3% |
| **OTHERS** | | | | |
| Argentina | 10.2 + 3%/31% s | t | t | 3% |
| Australia | 4.6 | 2.4 | 44.4 | none |
| Canada | 5.0/2.0/free f (5.0/free/free) fg | [5.0/5.0/3.0f(4.0/2.0)n] | 7.0/7.0/5.0 f | none |
| Chile | 3 | 62.7 | 116.4 | 2.6.0 + 8.2%/43.9 + 30.0% |
| Israel | 47 | 47 | 620 | none |
| Japan | 35%/30%/10% | 35% | 35% | 10% |
| Jordan | 5 | 20% | 20% | 12.5% |
| Morocco | 20% | 50% | 80% | 25% + [2-3/3.4(3.1n)/14.5] w |
| New Zealand | 1-2/1.2 free n | 60%/50%/25% f | 50%/25%/25% j | none |
| Tunisia | 20% | n.a. | n.a. | n.a. |
| South Africa | 1.2 | 3.5 | 3.5 | none |
| United Arab Rep. | 15% | 15% | 15% | none |
| United States | free | free | free | none |

## M-1. WORLD: CUSTOM DUTIES AND INTERNAL TAXES ON COFFEE IN SELECTED COUNTRIES (EQUIVALENTS IN U.S. CENTS PER POUND), 1966 (Continued)

a – Converted at official exchange rates.
b – Includes turnover transactions and other excise taxes at wholesale and/or retail.
c – 30% additional duties on containers of 5 kg. or less.
d – Increased by 30% surcharge on packages of 1-kilo or less.
e – On coffee valued at more than 58.9 cents cif.
f – General/MFN/British Preferential.
g – Rates apply to coffee destined for soluble manufacture.
h – GATT (MFN/British Preferential).
i – Coffee from overseas provinces enters duty-free.
j – General/Australia/British Preferential
k – 80% reduction on soluble coffee from Europe.
l – EEC and AOS exempt.
m – 2% on green coffee originating in Greece.
n – Decaffeinated coffee.
o – 24% for coffee with ethyl alcohol added.
p – EEC and AOS countries.
q – Roasted, decaffeinated, soluble.
r – General/GATT/temporary.
s – Brazil/other.
t – Importation prohibited.
u – General/MFN.
v – General/Commonwealth Preference/free.
w – Green/Roasted/Soluble
x – Coffee for use in manufacture of extracts and essences enter duty-free.
y – 60% reduction on soluble coffee from European Free Trade Area.
z – Imported by state monopoly.
xx – Municipal taxes/stamp duties/consumption tax per pound.
aa – Minimum duty – 15.7¢ if liquid; 20.9¢ if solid.
aaa – Minimum duty – 6.5¢ if liquid; 8.7¢ if solid.
nn – Non-decaffeinated.
nnn – Decaffeinated.
yy – General/MFN/Greece.
qq – Green/roasted.
ww – Turnover tax/administrative fee/statistical fee.

A-175

## M-6. OCEAN FREIGHT
(in U. S.

| FROM: | To New York | To New Orleans | To San Francisco |
|---|---|---|---|
| Colombia: Buenaventura | c$28.00N | c$28.00Ng | c$29.00Na |
| Barranquilla | c 26.00N | c 26.00Ng | c 31.00Na |
| Costa Rica: Limon | c 28.60N | c 28.60Ng | c 35.00Na |
| Puntarenas | c 32.00N | c 32.00Ng | 40.00Na |
| Dominican Republic: Santo Domingo | c 36.25N | c 36.25Ng | c 35.00Nae |
| Ecuador: Guayaquil | c 33.00Nf | c 33.00Nfg | c 31.00Naf |
| Manta | c 33.00Nf | c 33.00Nfg | c 31.00Naf |
| El Salvador: Acajutla | c 32.00N | c 32.00Ng | 32.00Na |
| Guatemala: Puerto Barrios | c 25.00N | c 25.00Ng | 40.00Na |
| Champerico | c 32.00N | c 32.00Ng | 32.00Na |
| Haiti: Port-au-Prince | c 33.00Nb | c 33.00Nbg | c 35.00Nab |
| Honduras: Puerto Cortes | c 25.00N | c 25.00Ng | t |
| Amapala | c 32.50Nh | c 32.50Ng | 32.00Na |
| Mexico: Veracruz | 30.00Mh | 26.00Mgh | t |
| Puerto Angel | t | t | t |
| Nicaragua: Corinto | | | |
| Bluefields | c 32.00N | c 32.00Ng | 32.00Na |
| Panama: Cristobal | c 28.50Nd | c 28.50Ndg | c 30.00Na |
| Peru: Callao | c 39.00M | c 39.00Mg | c 39.00Ma |
| Trinidad and Tobago: Port-of-Spain | c 34.00N | c 34.00Ng | 31.00Na |
| Venezuela: Maracaibo | c 24.00Nj | c 24.00Ngj | 31.00Na |
| Brazil: Vitoria | c 45.85Mk | c 45.85Mkg | 50.40Na |
| Rio de Janeiro | c 45.85Mk | c 45.85Mkg | 50.40Na |
| Angra Dos Reis | c 45.85Mk | c 45.85Mkg | 50.40Na |
| Santos | c 45.85Mk | c 45.85Mkg | 50.40Na |
| Parangua | c 45.85Mk | c 45.85Mkg | 50.40Na |
| Cameroon: Douala | 42.25G | 42.25Gg | 48.75Ga |
| Congo DF: Matadi | 42.25G | 42.25Gg | 48.75Ga |
| Dahomey: Cotonou | 42.25G | 42.25Gg | 48.75Ga |
| Ethiopia: Djibuti | 34.00M | 34.00Mg | 44.00Ma |
| Ghana: Tema | 42.25G | 42.25Gg | 48.75Ga |
| Ivory Coast: Abidjan | 42.25G | 42.25Gg | 48.75Ga |
| Kenya: Mombasa | c 41.50G | 41.50Gg | 49.00Ga |
| Madagascar: Tamatave | c 39.00M | c 39.00Mg | t |
| Nigeria: Lagos | 42.25G | 42.25Gg | 48.75Ga |
| Sierra Leone: Freetown | 42.25G | 42.25Gg | 48.75Ga |
| Tanzania: Dar-Es-Salaam | c 41.50G | c 42.25Gg | 49.00Ga |
| Togo: Lome | 42.25G | 42.25Gg | 48.75Ga |
| India: Bombay | 48.50M | 48.50Mrg | 44.50Ma |
| Indonesia: Surabaya | t | t | 47.25Na |
| Amsterdam | 28.00M | 38.00 / 28.00M Hg | 36.50Ma |
| Hamburg | t | t | t |
| Trieste | c 27.50M | 25.00gML | 38.00Ma |
| Beirut | t | t | 48.00M |
| Hong Kong | c 40.50G | c 42.50G | c 42.50Ga |
| Tangier | t | t | 53.00N |

A — Weight or Measurement
M — Metric Ton or 1,000 Kilos
G — Gross Ton = long ton = 2,240 lb.
N — Net Ton = short ton = 2,000 lb.

(a) — U. S. West Coast port charges: wharfage — $1.00; handling $2.75 per 2,000 lb.
(b) — Additional charges Port-au-Prince: $2.00 wharfage; $1.00 port improvement. $0.75 delivery
(all per 2,000 lb.)
(c) — Contract Rate
(d) — Isthmus handling charge: $3.35/2,000 lb.
(dd) — Isthmus handling charge: $3.70/1,000 kilos.
(e) — Surcharge $2.00 per 2,000 lb.
(f) — Surcharge $0.70 per 2,000 lb.
(g) — New Orleans toll: $0.35 per 2,000 lb. (effective 7/15/67).

A-176

**RATES FOR COFFEE**
(Dollars)

| To Amsterdam | To Hamburg | To Trieste | To Beirut | To Hong Kong | To Tangier — ps |
|---|---|---|---|---|---|
| $48.10M$^p$ | $48.10M | $59.10M | t | t | $73.10M |
| 44.80M$^p$ | 44.80M | 44.80M | t | t | 64.50M |
| 46.20M$^p$ | 46.20M | 46.20M | t | t | 66.00M |
| 46.20M$^p$ | 52.20M | 52.20M | t | t | 67.00M |
| 39.90M$^v$ | 39.90 + 4.00M | 53.20M | t | t | 60.00M |
| 49.00M$^p$ | 49.00 + 1.26M | 60.00M | t | t | 74.00M |
| 49.00M$^p$ | 49.00 + 1.26M | 60.00M | t | t | 74.00M |
| 52.20M$^p$ | 52.20M | 52.20M | t | t | 67.00M |
| 44.80M$^p$ | 44.80M | 44.80M | t | t | 64.00M |
| 52.20M$^p$ | 52.20M | 52.20M | t | t | 67.00M |
| 39.90M$^b$ | 39.90 + 2.00M | 53.20M | t | t | 60.00M |
| 44.80M$^p$ | 44.80M | 44.80M | t | t | 64.00M |
| 52.20M$^p$ | 52.20M | 52.20M | t | t | 67.00M |
| 48.30M$^{ph}$ | 48.30M$^h$ | t | t | t | 66.50M |
| t | 52.20M$^h$ | t | t | t | t |
| 52.20M$^p$ | 52.20M | 52.20M | t | t | 67.00M |
| 49.35M$^{dd}$ | 46.20M | 45.50M | t | t | 65.50M |
| 49.00M$^p$ | 49.00M$^v$ | 60.00M | t | t | 74.00M |
| 39.90M$^{pq}$ | 39.90 + .23G | t | t | t | 60.00M |
| 48.30M$^p$ | 48.30G | 46.20M | $47.00M | t | 65.00M |
| 43.30M | 43.30M | 45.00M | 47.00M | t | t |
| 43.30M | 43.30M | 45.00M | 47.00M | t | t |
| 43.30M | 43.30M | 45.00M | 47.00M | t | t |
| 43.30M | 43.30M | 45.00M | 47.00M | t | t |
| 43.30M | 43.30M | 45.00M | 47.00M | t | t |
| 31.99$^d$G | 31.99G | 22.00M | t | $34.30G$^p$ | 58.38G |
| 30.24G | 27.30G | 22.00M | t | 34.30G$^p$ | 57.68G |
| 31.99$^d$G | 31.99G | 22.00M | t | 34.30G$^p$ | 58.38G |
| $^e$A21.00MB | 18.90G | 15.40M | 22.40M | 27.16G$^p$ | 42.70MB |
| 31.99$^d$G | 31.99G | 22.00M | t | 34.30G$^p$ | 58.38G |
| 31.99$^d$G | 31.99G | 22.00M | t | 34.30G$^p$ | 58.38G |
| 42.28G$^{pp}$ | 40.04G | 32.20M | 33.60M | 27.16G$^p$ | 66.50G |
| 46.80M$^{pp}$ | 46.80G | t | t | 27.16G$^p$ | 38.08M |
| 31.99$^d$G | 31.99G | 22.00M | t | 34.30G$^p$ | 58.38G |
| 31.99$^d$G | 31.99G | 22.00M | t | 34.30G$^p$ | 58.38G |
| 42.28G$^{pp}$ | 40.04G | 32.20M | t | 27.16G$^p$ | 66.50G |
| 31.99$^d$G | 31.99G | 22.00M | t | 34.30G$^p$ | 58.38G |
| 46.90M$^x$, 51.80M$^{pp}$ | 46.90M | t | t | 30.94M | 49.00M |
| 49.50M$^{pp}$ | 49.50M | t | t | 41.59M | 64.62M |
| — | t | t | $^c$38.00M / 43.50M J | 49.56M$^{pp}$ | 29.00M |
| t | — | t | t | t | t |
| t | t | — | 14.00MQ, 11.00M | t | 17.00M |
| t | t | t | — | t | t |
| 52.15$^d$G | 52.15$^l$G | 52.15$^d$G | 52.15$^d$G | — | 52.15$^d$G |
| t | t | t | t | t | — |

- (h) — 2.2 percent surcharge on freight amount.
- (j) — Channel toll: $0.10 per 2,000 lb.
- (k) — Rate quoted at $2.75 per 60-kilo bag.
- (kk) — Rate quoted at $3.00 per 60-kilo bag.
- (p) — 10 percent rebate (deferred) to shipper (from Latin American ports).
- (pp) — 10 percent rebate.
- (q) — Wharfage: $0.23 per 1,000 kilos.
- (r) — $4.00 per 1,000 kilos stevedoring surcharge.
- (v) — 3 percent surcharge.
- (s) — All Tangier quotations on basis of 150/300 tons unbagged, all charges included, ship's tackle/ship's tackle (Eastern Hemisphere ports).

- B — Rate quoted actually for Massawa.
- H — Lower rate for cargo in transit from abroad.
- J — 20 percent congestion surcharge.
- K — No special coffee rate; rate listed is for general cargo by weight (2,000 lbs. or net ton)/measurement 40 cubic feet.
- L — Clause 8C applicable: sorting expenses, if any, collected at destination.
- Q — Pallet to pallet.
- x — Lower rate for robusta; higher rate for other types.
- t — Rates subject to negotiation.

## ICO-2: INTERNATIONAL COFFEE ORGANIZATION: EFFECTIVE QUOTAS FOR COFFEE YEAR 1963-64

(bags of 60 kilos)

| Member Countries | October-December | January-March | April-June | July-September | October-September |
|---|---|---|---|---|---|
| Brazil | 4,455,000 | 4,738,500 | 4,749,545 | 4,749,544 | 18,692,589 |
| Burundi | 41,085 | 22,503 | 105,981 | 254,354 | 423,923 |
| Colombia | 1,487,792 | 1,582,470 | 1,586,158 | 1,586,158 | 6,242,578 |
| Congo (D.R.) | 188,100 | 54,506 | 493,277 | 250,670 | 986,553 |
| Costa Rica | 188,100 | 345,634 | 242,606 | 194,085 | 970,425 |
| Cuba | 39,600 | 62,550 | 51,075 | 51,075 | 204,300 |
| Dominican Republic | 176,715 | 161,912 | 108,522 | 82,474 | 529,623 |
| Ecuador | 163,944 | 89,797 | 32,879 | 286,619 | 573,239 |
| El Salvador | 424,562 | 451,578 | 464,182 | 344,181 | 1,684,503 |
| Ethiopia | 131,274 | 460,326 | 232,876 | 212,476 | 1,036,952 |
| Ghana† | – | – | – | 43,925 | 43,925 |
| Guatemala | 399,317 | 473,027 | 319,445 | 319,444 | 1,511,233 |
| Haiti | 149,688 | 159,214 | 102,967 | 102,967 | 514,836 |
| India | 89,100 | 76,383 | 113,378 | 94,991 | 373,852 |
| Indonesia | 291,060 | 309,582 | 310,304 | 310,303 | 1,221,249 |
| Mexico | 268,904 | 578,890 | 398,171 | 321,098 | 1,567,063 |
| Nicaragua | 41,491 | 215,376 | 89,180 | 89,179 | 435,226 |
| Nigeria | 4,500 | 8,000 | 6,458 | 6,458 | 25,416 |
| OAMCAF | 1,064,776 | 1,476,266 | 1,237,474 | 999,143 | 4,777,659 |
| Panama | 6,435 | 6,845 | 6,860 | 6,860 | 27,000 |
| Peru | 172,260 | 103,152 | 69,771 | 297,134 | 642,317 |
| Portugal | 595,860 | 679,377 | 499,320 | 618,304 | 2,392,861 |
| Rwanda | * | * | * | * | * |
| Sierra Leone | 6,435 | 20,124 | 26,559 | 13,280 | 66,398 |
| Tanzania | 129,331 | 137,561 | 92,661 | 92,660 | 452,213 |
| Trinidad & Tobago | 4,356 | 13,528 | 33,673 | 13,389 | 64,946 |
| Uganda | 429,838 | 756,740 | 479,689 | 594,105 | 2,260,372 |
| Venezuela | 117,563 | 173,565 | 97,042 | 97,043 | 485,213 |
| **TOTAL MEMBERS** | 11,067,086 | 13,157,406 | 11,950,053 | 12,031,919 | 48,206,464 |
| **SIGNATORY Non-Members** | | | | | |
| Bolivia | 5,000 | 5,215 | 5,108 | 5,107 | 20,430 |
| Honduras | 28,215 | 119,563 | 118,664 | 67,686 | 334,128 |
| Kenya | 153,500 | 163,268 | 105,590 | 105,589 | 527,947 |
| **TOTAL SIGNATORIES** | 11,253,801 | 13,445,452 | 12,179,415 | 12,210,301 | 49,088,969 |

Source: ED-40/64 Corr.

† Ghana acceded in September 1964.

* Included in Burundi.

## ICO-3: INTERNATIONAL COFFEE ORGANIZATION: EFFECTIVE QUOTAS FOR COFFEE YEAR 1964-65

(bags of 60 kilos)

| Member Countries | October-December | January-March | April-June | July-September | October-September |
|---|---|---|---|---|---|
| Brazil | 4,620,105 | 3,880,888 | 4,560,634 | 3,765,825 | 16,827,452 |
| Burundi | 66,336 | 52,630 | 81,250 | 68,555 | 268,771 |
| Colombia | 1,590,196 | 1,296,061 | 1,499,436 | 1,234,003 | 5,619,696 |
| Congo (D.R.) | 234,085 | 351,128 | 300,545 | 179,981 | 1,065,739 |
| Costa Rica | 195,071 | 302,360 | 240,701 | 149,984 | 888,116 |
| Cuba | 41,068 | 53,387 | 50,674 | 41,842 | 186,971 |
| Dominican Republic | 305,010 | 172,028 | 43,596 | 4,820 | 525,454 |
| Ecuador | 170,020 | 62,341 | 26,513 | 257,168 | 516,042 |
| El Salvador | 440,296 | 416,590 | 428,807 | 275,687 | 1,561,380 |
| Ethiopia | 156,827 | 494,607 | 261,518 | 185,507 | 1,098,459 |
| Ghana | 20,348 | 4,375 | 8,687 | 6,789 | 40,199 |
| Guatemala | 414,116 | 358,900 | 271,635 | 212,267 | 1,256,918 |
| Haiti | 129,363 | 112,115 | 84,854 | 66,309 | 392,641 |
| India | 92,402 | 47,601 | 98,156 | 75,316 | 313,475 |
| Indonesia | 301,847 | 253,551 | 297,960 | 246,034 | 1,099,392 |
| Mexico | 439,214 | 511,242 | 302,160 | 158,066 | 1,410,682 |
| Nicaragua | 43,029 | 197,932 | 84,673 | 129,166 | 454,800 |
| Nigeria | 6,250 | 6,250 | 6,250 | 6,250 | 25,000 |
| OAMCAF | 1,104,237 | 1,147,837 | 1,089,452 | 679,211 | 4,020,737 |
| Panama | 6,674 | 5,605 | 6,588 | 6,133 | 25,000 |
| Peru | 178,644 | 65,503 | 177,632 | 74,504 | 496,283 |
| Portugal | 617,942 | 527,197 | 442,181 | 457,893 | 2,045,213 |
| Rwanda | 65,336 | 55,204 | 43,750 | 34,367 | 198,657 |
| Sierra Leone* | 6,673 | 17,352 | 26,479 | 10,263 | 60,767 |
| Tanzania | 145,857 | 116,241 | 82,112 | 62,882 | 407,092 |
| Trinidad & Tobago | 11,294 | 14,726 | 18,527 | 16,586 | 61,133 |
| Uganda | 445,768 | 542,674 | 381,387 | 394,938 | 1,764,767 |
| Venezuela | 121,920 | 151,180 | 95,967 | 74,991 | 444,058 |
| TOTAL | 11,969,928 | 11,217,505 | 11,012,124 | 8,875,337 | 43,074,894 |
| **Non-Members** | | | | | |
| Bolivia | 6,250 | 6,250 | 6,250 | 6,250 | 25,000 |
| Honduras | 29,261 | 134,599 | 57,579 | 44,997 | 266,436 |
| Kenya | 159,189 | 137,963 | 104,419 | 81,597 | 483,168 |
| TOTAL | 12,164,628 | 11,496,317 | 11,180,372 | 9,008,181 | 43,849,498 |

Source: ED-90/65, ED-104/65 and ED-125/65.

\* Ratified 27 November 1964.

## ICO-4. INTERNATIONAL COFFEE ORGANIZATION: EFFECTIVE QUOTAS FOR COFFEE YEAR 1965-66

(bags of 60 kilos)

| Member Countries | October-December | January-March | April-June | July-September | October-September |
|---|---|---|---|---|---|
| Brazil | 4,243,978 | 4,243,978 | 4,243,978 | 4,243,977 | 16,975,911 |
| Burundi | 67,786 | 67,786 | 67,786 | 67,785 | 271,143 |
| Colombia | 1,587,397 | 1,247,241 | 1,417,319 | 1,417,318 | 5,669,275 |
| Congo (D.R.) | 215,028 | 322,542 | 326,543 | 215,028 | 1,075,141 |
| Costa Rica | 223,988 | 313,583 | 179,190 | 179,190 | 895,951 |
| Cuba | 37,724 | 56,587 | 47,155 | 47,155 | 188,621 |
| Dominican Republic | 149,751 | 129,786 | 79,858 | 59,893 | 419,288 |
| Ecuador | 194,708 | 168,678 | 104,119 | 78,089 | 545,594 |
| El Salvador | 460,701 | 460,701 | 269,634 | 269,634 | 1,460,670 |
| Ethiopia | 351,195 | 351,195 | 240,380 | 221,630 | 1,164,400 |
| Ghana | 13,416 | 13,416 | 9,361 | 9,361 | 45,554 |
| Guatemala | 414,152 | 414,152 | 253,601 | 253,601 | 1,335,506 |
| Haiti | 126,332 | 126,331 | 79,221 | 79,221 | 411,105 |
| India | 97,380 | 80,404 | 101,855 | 84,880 | 364,519 |
| Indonesia | 277,273 | 277,273 | 277,274 | 277,273 | 1,109,093 |
| Mexico | 426,944 | 398,481 | 284,629 | 313,093 | 1,423,147 |
| Nicaragua | 155,311 | 135,624 | 78,749 | 59,061 | 428,745 |
| Nigeria | 10,417 | 10,416 | 10,417 | 10,416 | 41,666 |
| Oamcaf | 1,089,340 | 1,292,208 | 1,089,340 | 886,472 | 4,357,360 |
| Panama | 6,250 | 6,250 | 6,250 | 6,250 | 25,000 |
| Peru | 168,351 | 141,000 | 136,751 | 109,400 | 555,502 |
| Portugal | 656,738 | 615,456 | 450,325 | 491,608 | 2,214,127 |
| Rwanda | 50,102 | 50,103 | 50,102 | 50,103 | 200,410 |
| Sierra Leone | 12,260 | 12,261 | 24,521 | 12,260 | 61,302 |
| Tanzania | 135,705 | 135,705 | 82,137 | 82,137 | 435,684 |
| Trinidad & Tobago | 16,624 | 16,624 | 16,625 | 16,624 | 66,497 |
| Uganda | 478,834 | 478,834 | 478,834 | 478,834 | 1,915,336 |
| Venezuela | 111,994 | 156,791 | 89,595 | 89,595 | 447,975 |
| **TOTAL** | 11,779,679 | 11,723,406 | 10,491,549 | 10,109,888 | 44,104,522 |
| **Non-Members** | | | | | |
| Bolivia | 6,250 | 6,250 | 6,250 | 6,250 | 25,000 |
| Honduras | 26,879 | 134,392 | 53,757 | 53,757 | 268,785 |
| Kenya | 146,229 | 146,229 | 97,486 | 97,486 | 487,430 |
| **TOTAL** | 11,959,037 | 12,010,277 | 10,649,042 | 10,267,381 | 44,885,737 |

Source: ED-164/66 and ED-183/66

## ICO-5. INTERNATIONAL COFFEE ORGANIZATION: EFFECTIVE QUOTAS FOR COFFEE YEAR 1966-67

(bags of 60 kilos)

| EXPORTING COUNTRY | October-December | January-March | April-June | July-September | October-September |
|---|---|---|---|---|---|
| **COLOMBIA MILD ARABICAS** | | | | | |
| Colombia | 1,445,373 | 1,069,065 | 1,411,368 | 1,495,299 | 5,421,105 |
| Kenya | 210,329 | 168,039 | 153,929 | 166,142 | 698,439 |
| Tanzania | 137,651 | 95,978 | 85,917 | 104,748 | 424,294 |
| Sub-Total | 1,793,353 | 1,333,082 | 1,651,214 | 1,766,189 | 6,543,838 |
| **OTHER MILD ARABICAS** | | | | | |
| Burundi | 69,127 | 51,130 | 67,501 | 71,516 | 259,274 |
| Costa Rica | 228,421 | 252,988 | 223,047 | 152,274 | 856,730 |
| Cuba | 38,697 | 44,415 | 46,957 | 50,295 | 180,364 |
| Dominican Republic | 132,145 | 93,801 | 79,827 | 87,501 | 393,274 |
| Ecuador | 173,145 | 121,743 | 103,682 | 113,735 | 512,305 |
| El Salvador | 467,089 | 314,188 | 268,502 | 319,376 | 1,369,155 |
| Guatemala | 420,160 | 296,618 | 252,537 | 276,934 | 1,246,249 |
| Haiti | 128,209 | 92,836 | 78,888 | 86,333 | 386,266 |
| Honduras | 60,874 | 141,600 | 83,304 | 93,057 | 378,835 |
| India | 99,059 | 47,375 | 101,428 | 91,111 | 338,973 |
| Mexico | 433,688 | 308,411 | 283,434 | 335,316 | 1,360,849 |
| Nicaragua | 137,949 | 92,054 | 78,719 | 96,215 | 404,937 |
| Panama | 6,397 | 4,735 | 6,250 | 6,621 | 24,003 |
| Peru | 181,943 | 102,263 | 136,176 | 117,925 | 538,307 |
| Rwanda | 51,094 | 37,791 | 49,892 | 52,860 | 191,637 |
| Venezuela | 114,211 | 126,495 | 89,219 | 98,441 | 428,366 |
| Sub-Total | 2,742,208 | 2,128,443 | 1,949,363 | 2,049,510 | 8,869,524 |
| **UNWASHED ARABICAS** | | | | | |
| Bolivia* | 6,391 | 4,877 | 6,963 | 6,763 | 24,994 |
| Brazil | 4,327,984 | 3,302,998 | 4,714,818 | 4,579,304 | 16,925,104 |
| Ethiopia | 356,445 | 285,245 | 271,348 | 266,795 | 1,179,833 |
| Sub-Total | 4,690,820 | 3,593,120 | 4,993,129 | 4,852,862 | 18,129,931 |
| **ROBUSTA** | | | | | |
| Congo (Kinshasa) | 220,574 | 259,613 | 364,386 | 239,600 | 1,084,173 |
| Ghana | 13,858 | 11,205 | 11,206 | 10,625 | 46,894 |
| Indonesia | 282,761 | 215,796 | 320,670 | 299,182 | 1,118,409 |
| Nigeria | 10,623 | 8,107 | 12,047 | 11,240 | 42,017 |
| Oamcaf | 1,137,918 | 1,077,214 | 1,276,603 | 1,013,710 | 4,505,445 |
| Portugal | 707,770 | 534,399 | 572,777 | 581,522 | 2,396,468 |
| Sierra Leone | 16,826 | 13,056 | 31,131 | 17,804 | 78,817 |
| Trinidad & Tobago | 16,830 | 17,854 | 16,181 | 15,980 | 66,845 |
| Uganda | 503,144 | 392,790 | 563,997 | 532,361 | 1,992,292 |
| Sub-Total | 2,910,304 | 2,530,034 | 3,168,998 | 2,722,024 | 11,331,360 |
| **TOTAL** | 12,136,685 | 9,584,679 | 11,762,704 | 11,390,585 | 44,874,653 |

Source: ED-244/67, 3 May 1967.

(*) Pending Accession.

# I.C.O. INDICATOR PRICE

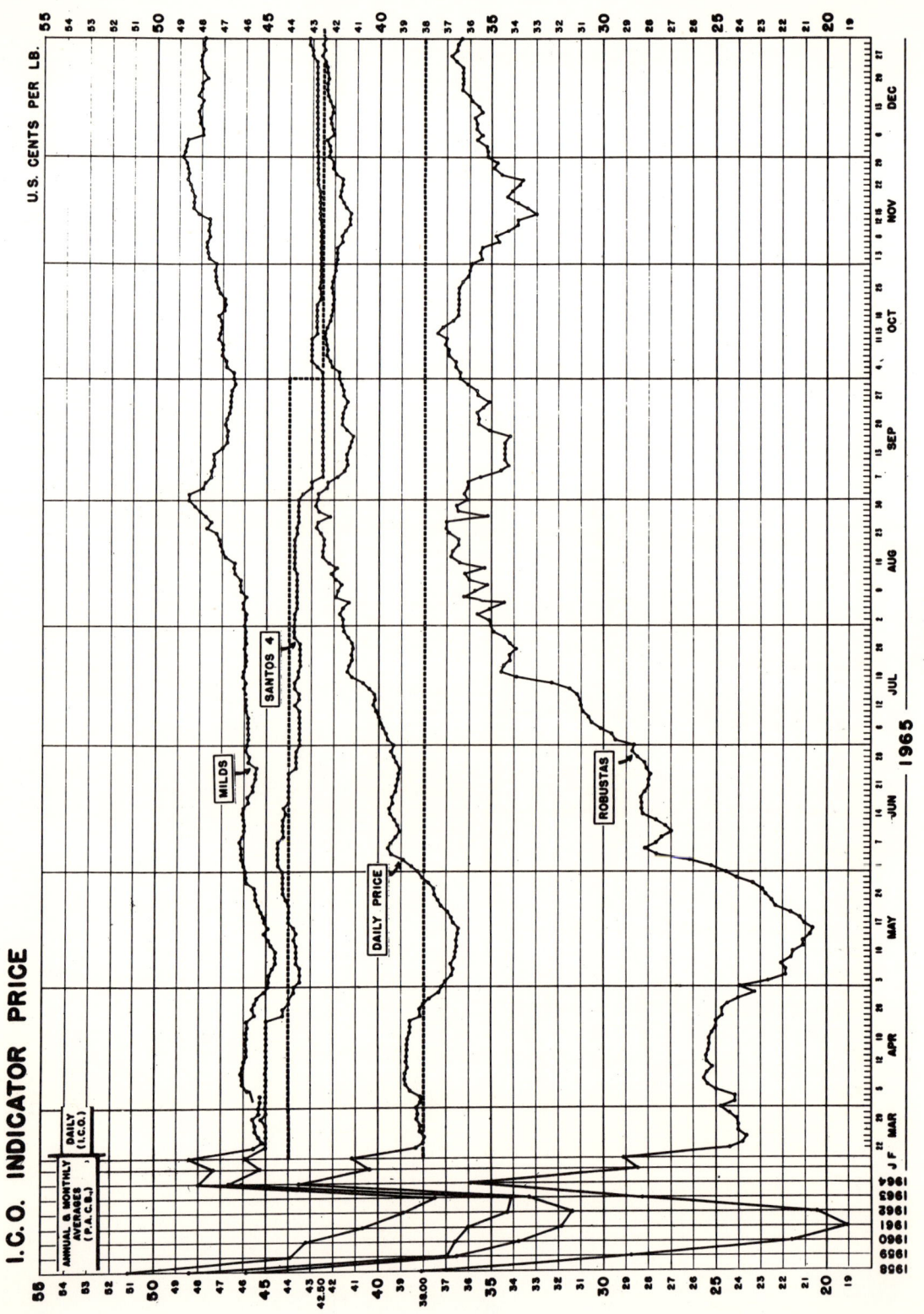

CHART 34

# I.C.O. INDICATOR PRICE

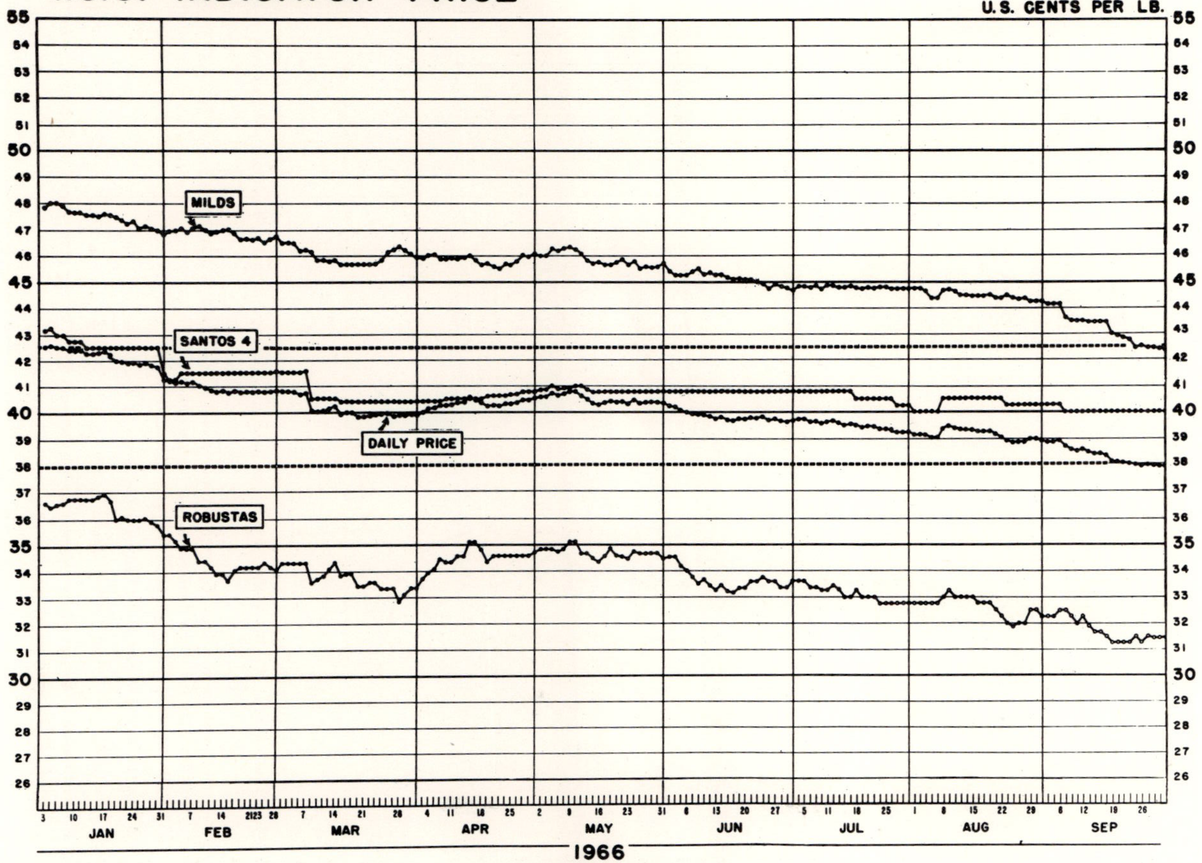

CHART 35
1966

# NOTES TO CHARTS NOS. 36, 37, 38, & 39

## Quota Reductions and Reinstatements

| Type | Date of Action | Quantity (bags) | Explanation |
|---|---|---|---|
| Colombian Mild Arabicas | | | |
| | Feb. 13 | −120,622 | Note 1 |
| | Feb. 21 | −299,305 | Note 2 |
| | March 13 | −16,703 | Note 1 |
| | April 1 | +149,653 | Note 3 |
| | April 27 | −152,014 | Note 1 |
| Other Mild Arabicas | | | |
| | Dec. 26 | −233,628 | Note 1 |
| | Jan. 23 | −164,319 | Note 1 |
| | Feb. 20 | −135,054 | Note 1 |
| | Feb. 21 | −407,281 | Note 2 |
| | March 20 | −100,126 | Note 1 |
| | April 1 | +203,644 | Note 3 |
| | April 27 | −217,908 | Note 1 |
| Unwashed Arabicas | | | |
| | Feb. 21 | −825,315 | Note 2 |
| | April 1 | +412,658 | Note 3 |
| Robustas | | | |
| | Feb. 21 | −468,099 | Note 2 |
| | April 1 | +270,051 | Note 3 |
| | May 3 | +117,021 | Note 4 |
| | May 29 | +117,021 | Note 4 |
| | May 29 | +285,316 | Note 5 |

Note 1. Reduction in annual quota triggered by the indicator price having dropped below the floor level for 15 consecutive days.

Note 2. Pro-rata reduction in annual quotas with the provision of restoring half of the reduction on April 1st, one quarter of the reduction if indicator count remained at 0.75 below the ceiling and further restoration of another quarter if it remained 0.50 below ceiling.

Note 3. Reinstatement of half of the February 21st pro-rata reduction.

Note 4. Restoration of 1/4 of the pro-rata reduction.

Note 5. Restoration of annual quota triggered by the indicator price having gone above the ceiling level for 15 consecutive days.

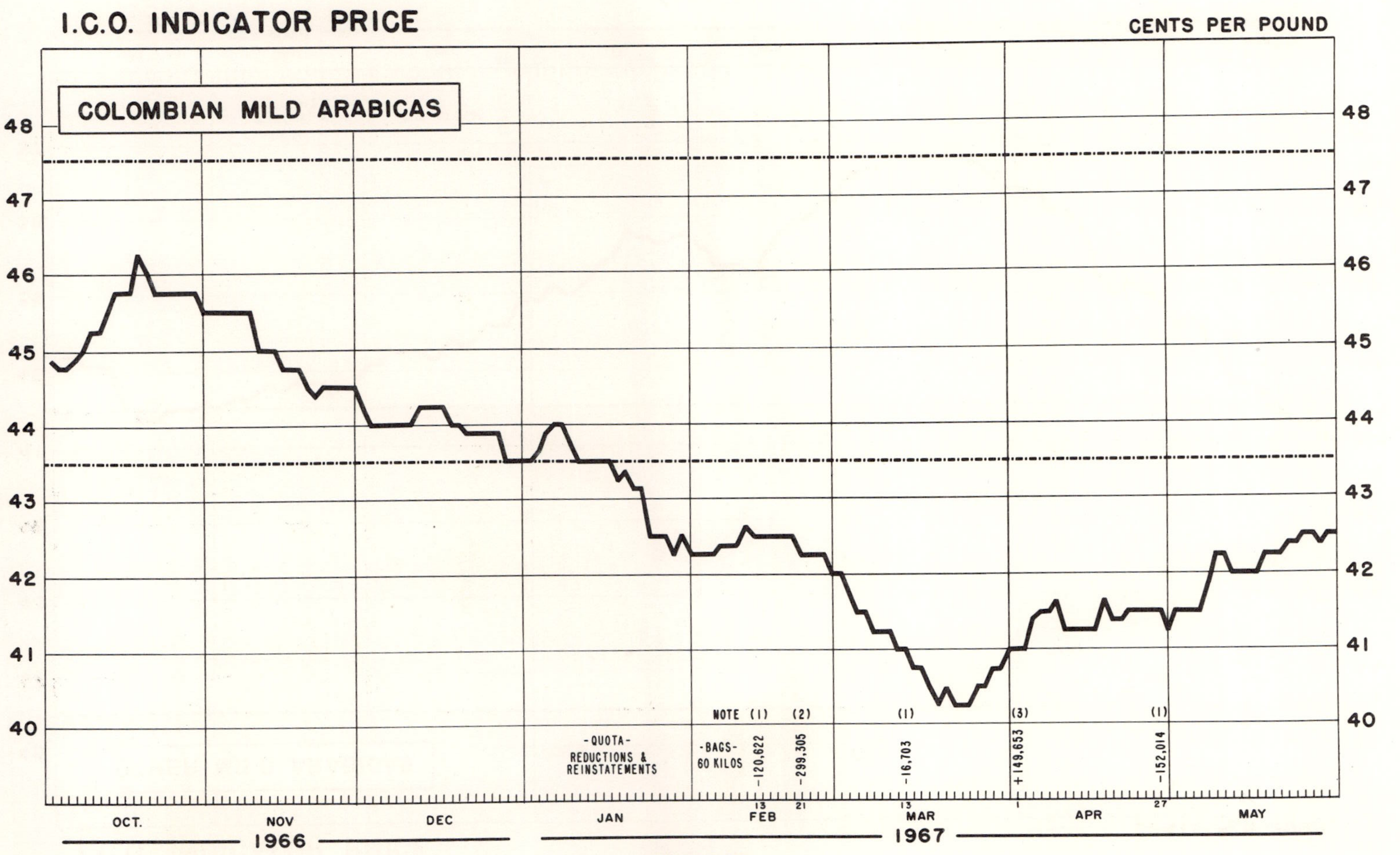

# I.C.O. INDICATOR PRICE

**COLOMBIAN MILD ARABICAS**

CENTS PER POUND

NOTE (1)
-BAGS-
60 KILOS
-120,622
-299,305
-16,703
+149,653
-152,014

-QUOTA-
REDUCTIONS &
REINSTATEMENTS

OCT. | NOV 1966 | DEC | JAN | FEB 13 21 | MAR 13 1967 | APR 27 | MAY

CHART 36

A-185

# I.C.O. INDICATOR PRICE

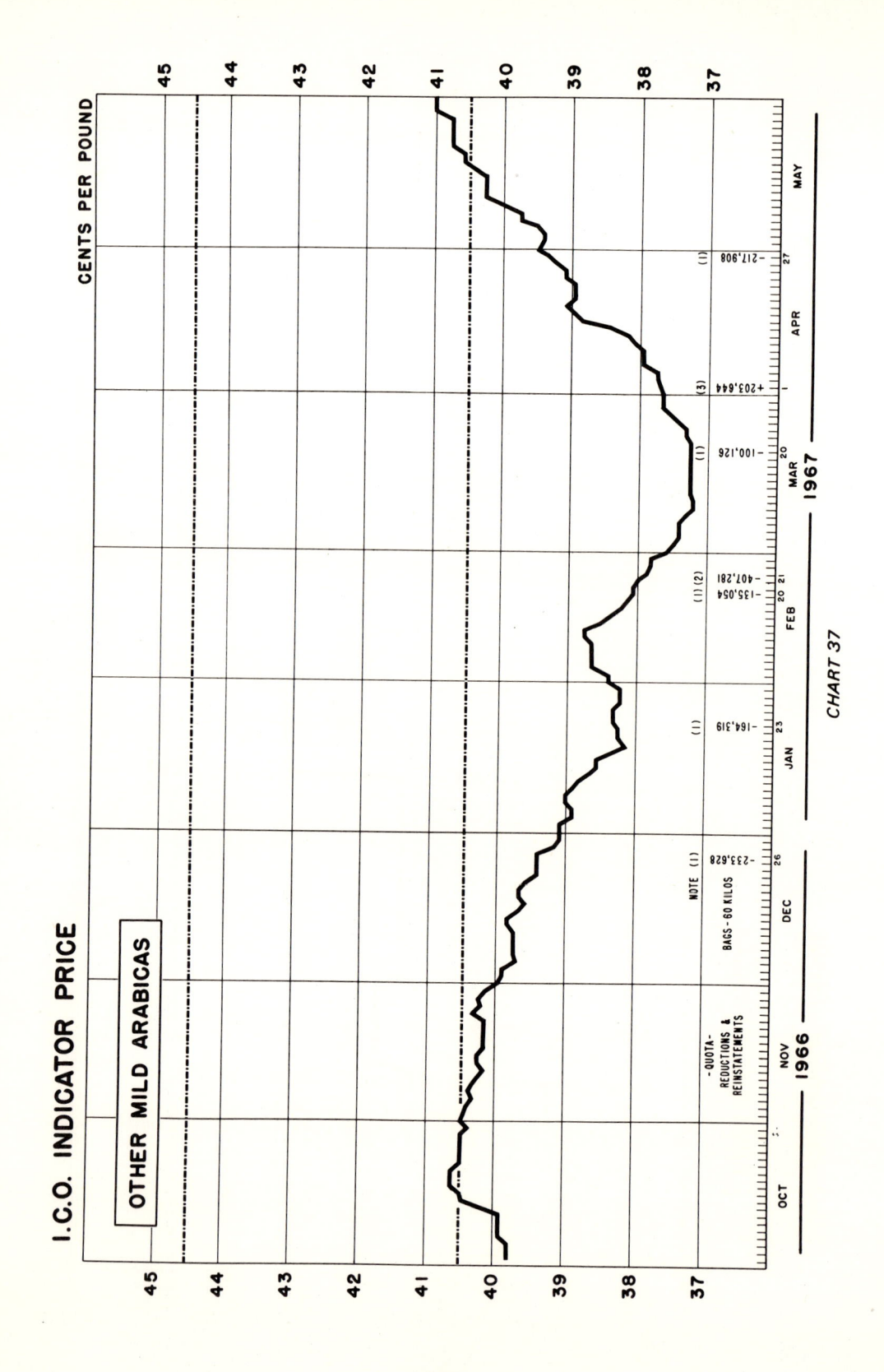

**OTHER MILD ARABICAS**

CHART 37

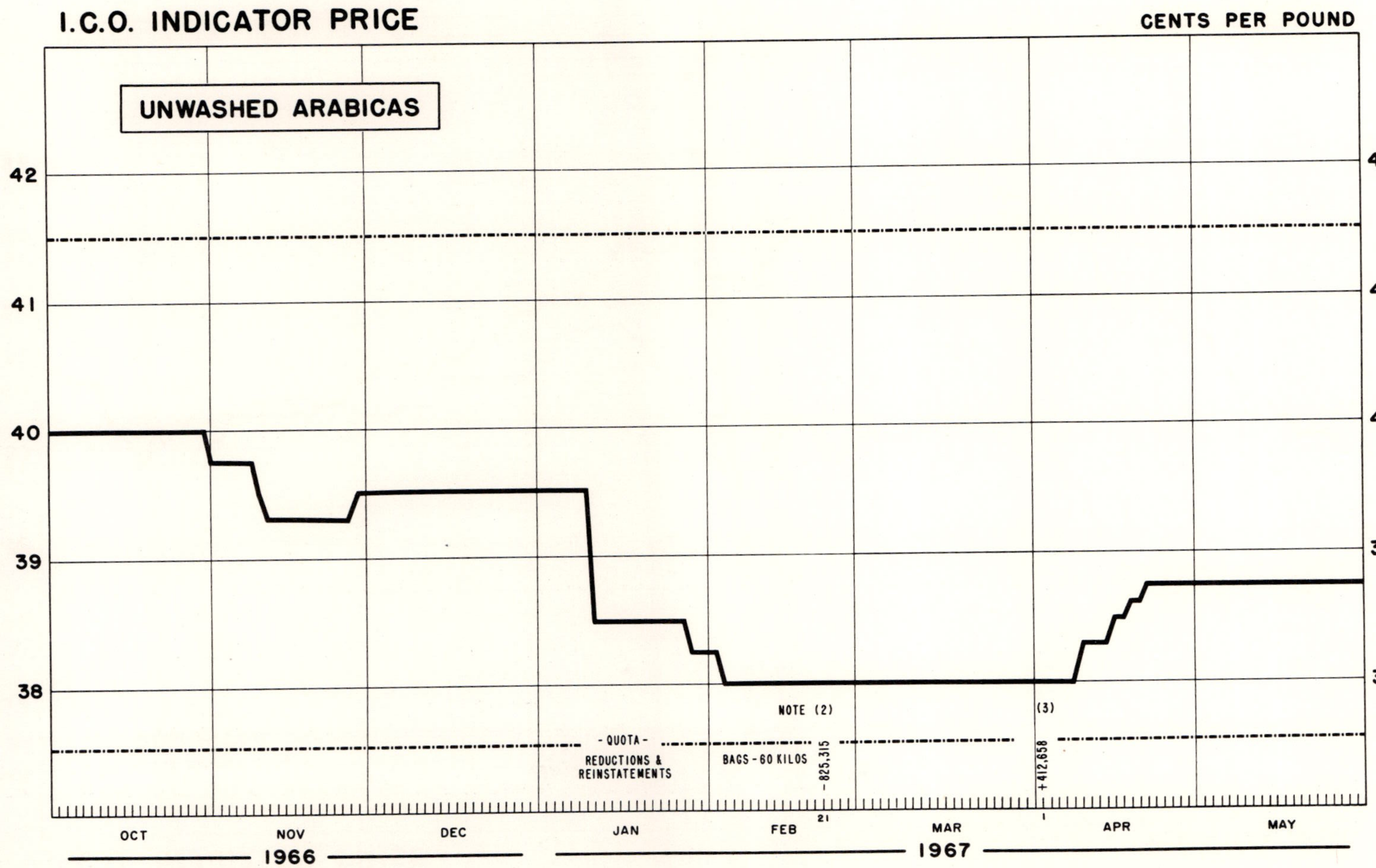

# I.C.O. INDICATOR PRICE

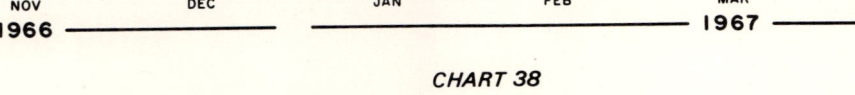

**UNWASHED ARABICAS**

CENTS PER POUND

- QUOTA -
REDUCTIONS &
REINSTATEMENTS

NOTE (2) −825,315
BAGS-60 KILOS

(3) +412,658

1966 | 1967
OCT NOV DEC JAN FEB 21 MAR APR MAY

CHART 38

# I.C.O. INDICATOR PRICE

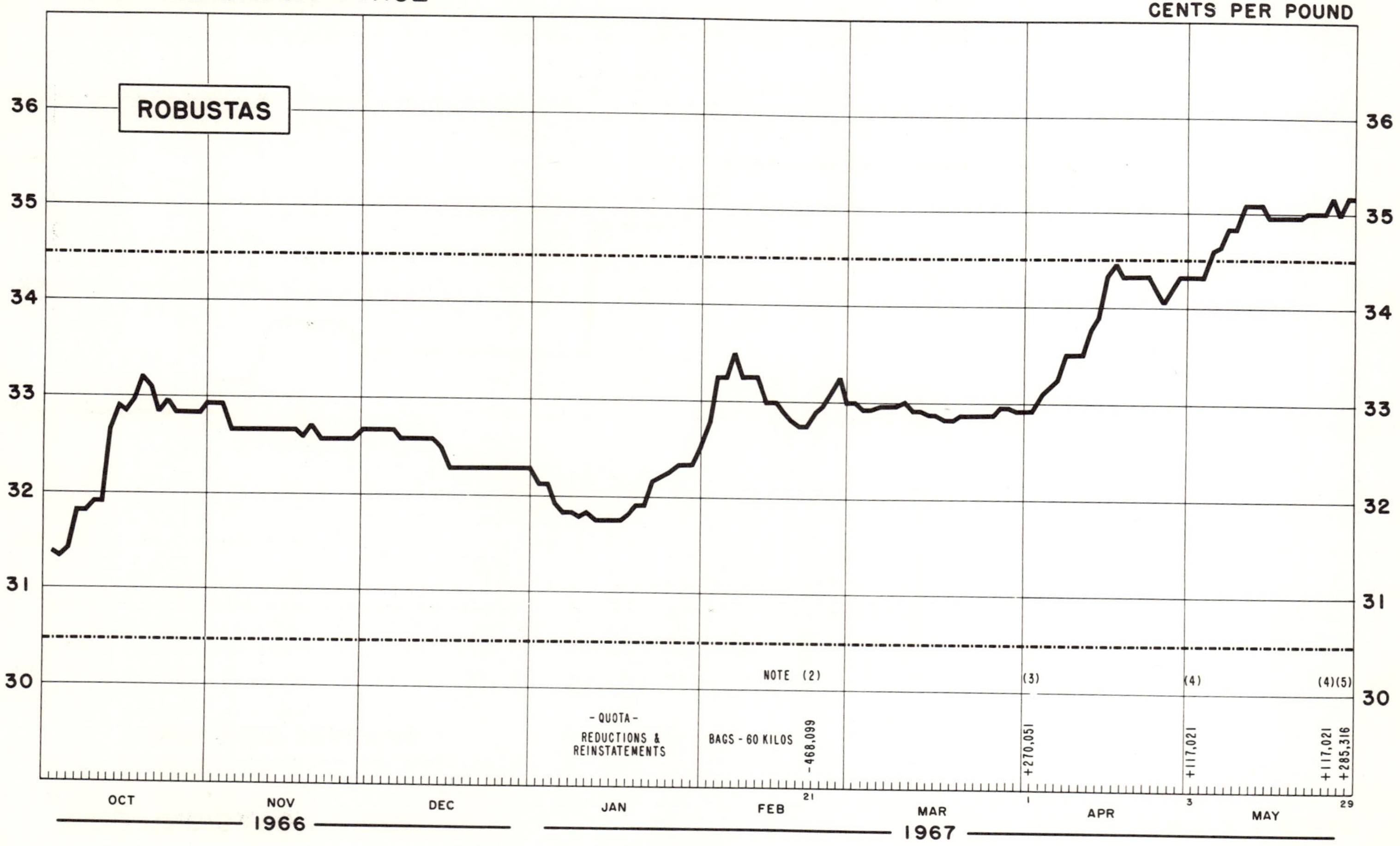

**ROBUSTAS**

CENTS PER POUND

| | 1966 | | | 1967 | | | |
|---|---|---|---|---|---|---|---|
| OCT | NOV | DEC | JAN | FEB 21 | MAR | APR | MAY 3 29 |

- QUOTA -
REDUCTIONS & REINSTATEMENTS

NOTE (2) -468,099
BAGS - 60 KILOS

(3) +270,051
(4) +117,021
(4)(5) +117,021 +285,316

CHART 39

A-188

# Index

# Index

Adulterated coffee: 151

Africa: Exportable production, 71, 72, 81; Exports, total, 105, 106; U.S., 139; Canada, 160; Receipts from coffee, total, 105, 106; U.S., 141, 142; Imports, 104

African growths: Prices, 56

Ahuja, U.K.: 1

Ambriz 2AA: Prices, 57

American Export-Isbrandtsen Lines: Containership terminal, 117

Angola: Exportable production, 81; Receipts from coffee, 106

Annex B List: 18

Annual Quotas: 6

Arabicas: Areas of production, 69; Prices and waivers, 3-7, 21-22, 25-30, 48, 51, 57; Stocks, 13

Argentina: Imports, 104

Armed Forces: U.S. Consumption, 143

Asia & Oceania: Exportable production, 71, 72, 86; Imports, 104; Exports to U.S., 140; Receipts from coffee (total), 105; U.S., 142

Atlantic ports of U.S.: 142

Australia: Imports, 104

Austria: Tariffs, 177


"B" Contract: 44, 67

"B" Option: Monthly average prices, 66

Beale, J.E.M.: 113

Belgium-Luxembourg: Imports, 171; Robusta imports, 174; Per capita, 176; Tariffs, 177

Beltrão, Alexandre Fontana: 2

Brazil: Exports to U.S., 138; Canada, 160; Exportable production, 71; By state, 73; Receipts from coffee (U.S.), 141, 105-106; Coffee receipts share of foreign exchange, 106; Names to ICO Executive Board, 2; Diversification program, 71, 75; Weather Conditions, 71

Brazils: Prices, 51

British Board of Trade: 113

Bulk transportation: 110

Bureau of Labor Statistics: Price series, wholesale, 46; Retail, 58

Burundi: Exportable production, 83; Coffee receipts share of foreign exchange earnings, 106


Cameroun: Exportable production, 86; Exports to U.S., 139

Canada: Imports — Volume, Total, 159, 160; Green, 161; Regular, 160; Soluble, 159, 160, 164; Value — total, 161; Green, 161; Roasted, 161, 163; Soluble, 161; Source of imports, Western Hemisphere, 160; Colombia, 160; U.S., 160; Brazil, 160; Africa, 160; Uganda, 160; Prices — Import, Green, 161; Roasted, 161; Soluble, 161; Prices — Retail, Regular, 164, 165; Soluble, 164, 165; Soluble — Net Imports, 159, 161; Imports, 164; Exports, 164; Production, 162-164; Extraction rate, 163; Processing — Roasted, 163; Soluble, 162-164

Canadian market: Coffee consumption, Coffee Drinking Survey, 165; Cups per person per day, 165; By time of day, 166; At home, 166; By region, 166; By age, 167; Coffee breaks, 167; Vending machines, 167; Price per cup, 167; By type of grind purchased, 167; By container used, 168; By type of coffee pot used, 168; Coffee measure used, 168; Additives (cream and sugar), 168; Attitudes toward coffee, 169, 170

Cargo handling: 111, 113

# INDEX (cont'd)

Cargo protection: 112

Carry over, world: 89, 90

Central African Republic: Coffee receipts share of foreign exchange earnings, 106

Certificates of Origin and Re-Export: 1, 8, 31-36

Chile: Imports, 104

Coffee break: 153

Coffee culture practices: 92

Coffee Drinking Survey: U.S., 151; Canada, 165

Coffee Fund: 11, 12

Coffee, share of total world exports: 105

Colombia: Exportable production, 71; Exports, U.S., 138; Canada, 160; Diversification, 75; Coffee receipts, total, 105, 106; From U.S., 141; Share of foreign exchange earnings, 106; Named to ICO Executive Board, 2

Congo: Exportable production, 86; Named to ICO Executive Board, 2; Exports to U.S., 139

Consumption: Definition, 144

Containerization: Definition, 110; Advantages, 112, 113; Disadvantages, 115, 116; Use by coffee market, 114, 115; Future, 117

Container pools: Explanation, 114

Container services: Types, 111

Container ships: Types, 110, 111

Containers, refrigerated: 116; Technical innovations, 112, 116; Types, 110, 111

Contracts, coffee: Open interest, 65

Conversion rates: Green to soluble, 123

Corby Research: 126

Costa Rica: Exportable production, 71, 78; Coffee receipts, 105; Coffee receipts share of foreign exchange earnings, 106

Crop estimates: U.S. Department of Agriculture, FAS, 69, 72

Cuba: Domestic consumption, 78

Cultivation of coffee: 70

Daily Indicator Price (See Indicator Price)

Deliveries on futures market: 65

Direct selling of coffee: 66, 68

Distribution, U.S. imports: 143

Distribution channels (U.S.): 145

Diversification: General, 11, 12, 37, 38; Brazil, 73; Colombia, 76; Guatemala, 77; Ivory Coast, 81; Uganda, 82

Djimmas UGQ: Prices, 57

Domestic consumption: World, 69; Peru, 80; Ethiopia, 83

Dominican Republic: Exportable production, 78; Named to ICO Executive Board, 2; ICO Working Group, 78; Marketing of coffee, 78, 79

EEC: Imports, 104

Eastern Hemisphere: Exportable production, 71; Estimates of total world exportable production, 72

Eating places: Use of coffee, 145

Ecuador: Exportable production, 79

El Salvador: Exportable production, 71, 77; Exports to U.S., 139; Coffee receipts, 106; Coffee receipts share of foreign exchange earnings, 106; Coffee receipts from U.S., 139

Extraction rate: Green to soluble, 124

Espirito Santo: Exportable production, 73

## INDEX (cont'd)

Ethiopia: Exportable production, 83; Domestic consumption, 83; Coffee receipts, 106; Coffee receipts from U.S., 141; Coffee receipts share of foreign exchange earnings, 106; Exports to U.S., 141

Europe: Imports, 104, 171; By region of export, 173; Robustas, 173; Robustas by country, 173, 174; Per capita, 174; Stocks, 171, 176; Taxation, 177; Tariff regulations, 177

Europe, East: Imports, 172; Per capita imports, 176

Europe, West: Imports, 102

European market: 171; Demand for coffee, 171

Executive Board, ICO: Members, 1

Export authorizations, special: 2-7

Export, net balance: 98

Export quotas: 2, 39, 40

Export Stamp System: 1, 31, 32

Exportable production: Ten-year trend, 71; Aggregate, 71; Eastern Hemisphere, 71; Africa, 72, 81; Asia & Oceania, 71, 72, 86; Brazil, 71; Costa Rica, 71; El Salvador, 71, 77; Nicaragua, 71, 77; Panama, 71, 78; Western Hemisphere, 71, 76; Colombia, 76; Mexico, 76, 77; Guatemala, 77; Honduras, 77; Dominican Republic, 78; Haiti, 79; Ecuador, 79; Peru, 80; Venezuela, 80; Angola, 81; Ivory Coast, 81; Uganda, 82; Burundi, 83; Rwanda, 83; Madagascar, 83; Ethiopia, 83; Guinea, 83; Tanzania, 83; Central African Republic, 84; Togo, 84; Congo, 86; Cameroun, 86; Kenya, 86; Indonesia, 86; India, 87; Yemen, 88; Philippines, 88

Exports, authorized, 1966-1967: 6; World total, 98; By region, 99-101; Soluble, 125

Exports: Excess, 7, 8

Extraction rate: Definition, 124; Official ICO rate, 124

Federation of Provincial Coffee Associations (Dominican Republic): 79

Fertilizer: Use, Indonesia, 87

Finland: Imports, 172

Foreign Agricultural Service: Crop estimates, 69; Fourth estimate, 72

Foreign exchange earnings: 106
(Also see individual exporting countries)

Fourth estimate, Foreign Agriculture Service: 72

France: Named to ICO Executive Board, 2; Imports, 171; Robusta imports, 173; Per capita imports, 175; Tariffs, 177

Frehywot, Ato Lemma: 1

Freight costs: 114, 115

Futures Market: Volume, 63, 65, 66, 68; Deliveries, 65; Prices, 65; Discounts, 65; Effect of ICA, 66; Robustas, 68

GERCA: 73

Germany, F.R.: Named to ICO Executive Board, 2; Imports, 171; Per capita imports, 176; Tariffs, 177

González, Arturo Ramón: 2

Grace Lines: Container shipments, 114

Green coffee: Roastings, 123; Utilization in soluble, 122, 123; Imports into U.S., 137, 140, 142; U.S. imports share of world imports, 137

Growers Associations, National: Brazil, 73; Colombia, 76; Mexico, 76; Guatemala, 77; Dominican Republic, 78

Guatemala: Exportable production, 77; Exports to U.S., 138; Coffee receipts, 106; Coffee receipts from U.S., 141; Coffee receipts as share of foreign exchange

## INDEX (cont'd)

earnings, 106; Diversification, 77; Leaf miner disease, 77, 138

Guinea: Exportable production, 83

Gulf ports: 142

Haiti: Exportable production, 79; Coffee receipts share of foreign exchange earnings, 106

Harvesting: Hand held, 97; Mechanical, 92-94; New techniques, 92

Hawaii: Mechanized harvesting, 92

Honduras: Exportable production, 77

Household consumption (See U.S. market, household consumption)

Houston, port of: 142

Hungary: Imports, 172

Import quotas: 10

Imports, U.S.: (See U.S. Imports); Soluble, 130-132

Imports, world: Total, 98; By region, 99, 102

India: Exportable production, 87; Fourth Development Plan, 87, 88

Indicator Prices: 3, 5, 25-30

Indicator Price System: 44, 46

Indonesia: Exportable production, 86; ICO Mission, 87; Exports to U.S., 139; Use of fertilizers, 87

Input-output ratio: Green to soluble, 123

Institutional market (U.S.): 145

Insurance: 112

International Coffee Agreement: **Art. 2,** 42; **Art. 30,** 26; **Art. 32,** 29; **Art. 33,** 18; **Art. 35,** 29; **Art. 36,** 31; **Art. 40,** 8; **Art. 41,** 25; **Art. 45,** 9, 35, 36; **Art. 48,** 35; **Art. 51,** 41; **Art. 57,** 11; **Art. 58,** 31; **Art. 59,** 13; **Art. 60,** 19; Extension of the Agreement, 15

International Coffee Organization (ICO): Data processing, 69; Membership, 1, 2, 16, 17; New officers elected, 1; Countries named to Executive Board, 2; Working groups, Dominican Republic, 78; Missions, Togo, 84, 85; Indonesia, 87

International Standards Organization: 110

Inventories: World 89; U.S., 137

Italy: Imports, 171; Robusta imports, 173; Tariffs, 177

Ivory Coast: Exportable production, 81; Diversification, 82; Coffee receipts, total, 106; U.S., 141; Share of foreign exchange earnings, 106

Japan: Imports, 104

Kenya: Exportable production, 86; Coffee receipts share of foreign exchange earnings, 106

Kjoelstad, Gunnar: 1

Latin America: Exports, 173

Leaf miner disease: Guatemala, 77, 138

Liberia: Exports to U.S., 139; Coffee receipts from U.S., 141

London Terminal Market: 44, 68

# INDEX (cont'd)

Madagascar: Exportable production, 83; Exports to U.S., 139; Coffee receipts share of foreign exchange earnings, 106

MAMS: Prices, 51, 55, 57

Market Research Corporation of America: 127, 145

Markets, New: 1, 8, 9, 18, 34

Mass harvesting: 94, 97

Matson Lines: Cargo handling, 113

Mechanical shaker: 94-97

Mexican Coffee Institute: 76

Mexican Prime Washed: Prices 54, 57

Mexico: Exportable production, 76; Exports to U.S., 139; Coffee receipts, 106; Coffee receipts from U.S., 141; Trade balance, 107; Coffee promotion, 76

Milds: Prices, 55

Minas Gerais: Exportable production, 73

Monroe, G.E.: 92

Mukasa, Roger Joseph: 1

Myers, A.L.: 92


National Coffee Association of Guatemala: 77

National Federation of Coffee Growers: 76

Net Civilian Visible Disappearance: Definition, 143, 144; U.S. Market, 143, 144

Netherlands: Robusta imports, 173; Per capita imports, 176

New Markets: 1, 8, 9, 18, 34

New Orleans, port of: 142

New York Coffee and Sugar Exchange: 44

New York, port of: 142

New Zealand: Named to ICO Executive Board, 2

Nicaragua: Exportable production, 71, 77; Exports to U.S., 139; Named to ICO Executive Board, 2

Non-Members: 9-11, 18, 36

Norway: Imports, 172; Per capita imports, 175; Tariff, 177


OAMCAF: Named to ICO Executive Board, 2


Pacific ports: 142

Packaging: U.S. market, 148, 149; Prices by type, 63; Sizes, 148, 150

Panama: Exportable production, 78

Paraná: Exportable production, 73

Per capita consumption: U.S., 144; Soluble, 126

Peru: Exportable production, 80; Domestic consumption, 80

Philippines: Exportable production, 88

Piggyback containers: 111

Poland: Imports, 172

Ports: 142

Portuguese Africa: Coffee receipts from U.S., 141

Prices: Canada (See Canada, prices)

Prices: U.S. market: **General movement,** 1966 prices, 47; Arabica-robusta spread, 48; Robusta, 47, 48; Average price per bag, 140; **Import,** definition, 44, 48; 1966 prices, 48; Review 1953-1966, 49; Seasonal factors, 49; **Spot,** definition, 51; 1966 prices, 44, 51; Review 1953-1966, 56; New York market, 44; Arabicas, 51, 57; Brazils, 51; MAMS, 51, 57; Santos 4, 51, 54, 57; Robustas, 56, 57; **Futures,** definition, 44; New York Coffee & Sugar Exchange, 44, 65; "B" contract, 44; "R" contract, 44; London Terminal Market, 44; **Roasted,** wholesale, 46; Level of prices, 46; Real prices, 46; Institutional, 46; **Retail,** 44, 58; 1966 prices, 58; B.L.S. series, 58; M.R.C.A. series, 58-60; Average monthly,

## INDEX (cont'd)

59; Review 1952-1966, 61; Soluble, 60; Seasonal factors, 61; Regular coffee, 62; Price spreads, 62; Vacuum vs. bag, 62, 63

Product cycle: Soluble, 122

Product goals: 12, 13

Production cycle: Green, 71

Production: exportable (see exportable production)

Production: World total, 69; Areas of, 69

Professional Research Associates: 126

Promotional programs: Mexico, 76

Psychological Corporation of America: 126

Quality standards: 13, 14

Quota adjustments, selective: 25-30

Quotas: (See Import quotas, Export quotas)

"R" Contract: 44

Race, consumption by (U.S.): 153

Rainfall, for optimum coffee production: 70

Re-Exports, world: 98

Refrigerated containers: 116

Regional consumption: U.S., 146, 152; Europe, 173

Regular coffee, consumption (U.S.): 146

Research: Coffee harvesting, 93; Storage facilities (Colombia), 76; Coffee technology (Togo), 84

Resolutions: **59,** 11; **67,** 3, 25, 35; **68,** 11; **87,** 26, 30; **93,** 41; **94,** 36; **97,** 11, 12, 37; **98,** 11; **106,** 13; **110,** 12, 39; **111,** 11; **112,** 10; **113,** 10; **114,** 2, 4, 19, 23; **115,** 2, 4, 10, 19-21, 24, 25, 29, 30; **116,** 3, 4, 29; **117,** 9, 35; **118,** 8, 31; **119,** 13, 41; **120,** 12, 21, 38; **121,** 34; **122,** 8, 9; **123,** 7; **125,** 15; **127,** 9, 34; **128,** 5, 29; **130,** 10; **131,** 2, 3, 7, 23; **132,** 7; **134,** 11, **135,** 7; **136,** 7; **138,** 7

Restaurants (See Eating Places)

Retail prices (U.S.): 147, 148

Roasted coffee, imports (U.S.): 137

Robustas: Prices and waivers: 3-7, 22-30, 47, 48, 56, 57; Areas of production, 69, 70; Stocks, 13; Imports (Europe), 173; Imports by country (Europe), 173, 174

San Francisco, Port of: 142

Santos 4: Prices, 51, 54, 57

São Paulo: Exportable production, 73

Scandinavia: Per capita imports, 172, 174

Seasonal consumption (U.S.): 147

Shellenberger, F.A.: 92

Sierra Leone: Exports to U.S., 139

Soils: For optimum coffee production, 70

Soluble: — Production, Brazil, 73-75; U.S., 123; Canada, 162, 164; Technology, 122, 124; Conversion rates, 123, 124; Marketing, Product cycle, 122; U.S. Market, Trends, 122; Net availabilities, 125, 126; Imports, 125, 137; Exports, 125; Per capita consumption, 125

Soviet bloc: Imports, 104

Spain: Imports, 172; Robusta imports, 174; Tariff, 177

Staner, Pierre: 2

Stocks: U.S., 137; Europe, 176; ICO Policy, 12, 13, 39-43

Storage facilities: Colombia, 76

Supply and demand, world: 89

Surplus, world: 90

Sweden: Imports, 172; Robusta imports, 174; Tariff, 177; Per capita imports, 175

## INDEX (cont'd)

Switzerland: Imports, 171; Robusta imports, 173; Tariff, 177; Per capita imports, 176

Tanzania, Exports to U.S., 139; Exportable production, 83

Tariff regulations (Europe): 177; By country, 177

Tariff schedules, freight: 115

Taxation: Europe, 177

Technology: Vending machine, 122

Temperatures: Optimum for coffee production, 70

Thailand: Imports, 104

Time in transit: 112

Togo: Exportable production, 84; ICO Mission, 84; Research in coffee technology, 84; Coffee receipts as share of foreign exchange earnings, 106

Trade balance: U.S., 107; Latin America, 107; Mexico, 107; Venezuela, 107

Trade, coffee (world): Volume, 98; Value, 104

Tree eradication program (Brazil): 71, 73, 75

Uganda: Exportable production, 82; Exports to U.S., 139; Exports to Canada, 160; Named to ICO Executive Board, 2; Diversification, 82; Coffee receipts, 106; Coffee receipts share of foreign exchange earnings, 106

Uganda Native Standards: Prices, 57

United Kingdom: Named to ICO Executive Board, 2; Imports, 172; Robusta imports, 173; Tariff, 177

United States: Imports, value, 140-142; Volume, 104, 137, 140, 142; Source of imports, Western Hemisphere, 138; Brazil, 138; Guatemala, 138; Colombia, 138; Mexico, 139; El Salvador, 139; Nicaragua, 139; Africa, 139; Cameroun, 139; Liberia, 139; Sierra Leone, 139; Tanzania, 139; Uganda, 139; Congo, 139; Ethiopia, 139; Madagascar, 139; Asia & Oceania, 139; Indonesia, 139; Re-Exports, 142; Dollar payments, Western Hemisphere, 141, 142; Brazil, 141; Colombia, 141; Guatemala, 141; Mexico, 141; El Salvador, 141; Africa, 141, 142; Uganda, 141; Portuguese Africa, 141; Ethiopia, 141; Ivory Coast, 141; Liberia, 141; Asia & Oceania, 142; Average price per bag, 140; Named to ICO Executive Board, 2; Prices, (see Prices, U.S.)

U.S. Department of Agriculture: Foreign Agricultural Service, 69; Agricultural Research Service, 92

U.S. Department of Commerce: Green coffee inventories & roastings, 47

U.S. Market: Distribution patterns, 145; Household purchases, consumer, 146; Aggregate, 146; Regular, 146; Soluble, 146; By region 146; Seasonal, 147; Average coffee bill, 147; Retail price, 147, 148; By package type, 148; By size of container, 148, 149; By type of store, 150; By type bought, 150; Adulterated coffee, 151; Coffee Drinking, aggregate, 151; Cups per person per day, 151; By age, 151-153; By time of day, 152; At home, 152; By region, 152; By race, 153; At work, 153

University of Hawaii: Agricultural Experiment Station, 92

Vending machines: Use of soluble, 122; Use of regular, 123; Improvements, 122

Venezuela: Exportable production, 80; Trade balance, 107

## INDEX (cont'd)

Wahl, Jean: 1

Waivers: 3-7, 19-22, 39

Warehousing, automatic: 116

Western Hemisphere: Exportable production, 71, 76; Exports to Canada, 160; Coffee receipts, 105, 106; Coffee receipts (U.S.), 141, 142

Williams, D.G.: 82

Winter Coffee Drinking Survey: U.S., 151; Canada, 165

World Coffee Promotion Committee: 2, 14, 15

Yemen: Exportable production, 88

Yield ratio: Green to soluble, 123